THE
FOOD

OF
ITALY

THE FOOD

<small>With an Introduction by</small>

<small>Samuel Chamberlain</small>

Illustrated by Warren Chappell

WAVERLEY ROOT

OF ITALY

VINTAGE BOOKS
A Division of Random House
New York

FIRST VINTAGE BOOKS EDITION, October 1977
Copyright © 1971 by Waverley Root

All rights reserved under International and Pan-American
Copyright Conventions. Published in the United States
by Random House, Inc., New York, and simultaneously
in Canada by Random House of Canada Limited,
Toronto. Originally published by Atheneum in 1971.

Library of Congress Cataloging in Publication Data

Root, Waverley Lewis, 1903-
    The food of Italy.

    1. Food supply—Italy. 2. Wine and wine
making—Italy. 3. Cookery, Italian. I. Title.
[TX360.18R6 1977]   641'.0945   77-4311
ISBN 0-394-72429-1

Manufactured in the United States of America

Cover photo: Ernst Haas

After reading the voluminous text of this book with care, I have come to an inescapable conclusion: this is destined to become a classic work on the subject of Italian food and wine, and a reference book that will retain its value through decades to come. The enthusiasm that has been lavished on this book can be matched only by the depth and accuracy of the author's research. Its place in gastronomic lore is already assured.

Waverley Root is a dedicated journalist of extensive experience, with an irresistible leaning toward gastronomy. His long years as a foreign correspondent have not been spent in filing dispatches alone. They have been enriched further by joyful and sophisticated explorations of European food. His inquisitive and thoughtful forays into the epicurean scene of France and Italy have brought joy to gourmets of two continents. His recent volume on Paris restaurants is a bible for gastronomes, far more personal and detailed than the famous *Guide Michelin*.

As a by-product of the author's research on food, you are rewarded with more than a smattering of Italy's past. A thread of history winds through every chapter. Another bonus is a revealing glimpse of the Italian language, not to mention local dialects and slang. Imbedded in the text are rare morsels of humor, some subtle, some hilarious.

Mr. Root's epicurean travels in Italy have taken him to all the great regions in the country, including remote areas rarely visited by travelers. If you venture into lonely Basilicata, this book will be your friend just as effectively as in Rome. The single subject of Italian food is so vast that the author has not found space to include recipes or to recommend specific restaurants. Instead, he has hewn to the line, noting the regional cooking, seafood, meat specialties, cheeses, vegetables, pastries, and wines of each region in precise detail, usually with Italian phrases to help the puzzled traveler. The result is as complete as an encyclopedia, though not conforming to the same rigid format. This is an easy-flowing account, rich in history and prodigal in details of the gustatory habits of the Italian race.

Mr. Root's regional explorations begin in Tuscany, the heartland of Italy. Here the people speak the national language in its purest form. Appropriately enough, they grow and grill beef better than anyone else. Florence dominated this center of the Italian Renaissance, and her cooking stood unrivaled. Tuscan beef comes from the famous Chianina steer, and you will see them grazing in the hills. The finest olive oil in Italy cames from Lucca, and Tuscany, according to an old saying, was baptized in wine. The author indulges in a fascinating essay on Tuscan wines to close this chapter. It runs for pages, and tells everything you'll ever need to know about this engrossing subject.

Today's visitors to Rome find dozens of superlative restaurants and hundreds of modest *trattorie* where it is virtually impossible to have a bad meal. Roman gastronomes have several favorite dishes, including suckling pig roasted whole on a spit, and *abbachio*, which is baby lamb that has never tasted a blade of grass. *Saltimbocca* consists of thin slices of veal cooked in butter with a wafer of ham and braised with Marsala. It is so good that it literally "jumps" into the mouth, which is what *saltimbocca* means. Romans are fond of green salads, but with definite restrictions on how the dressing should be made. They say that it takes four people to make a salad properly—a spendthrift for the oil, a miser to pour the vinegar, a wise man to season it, and a madman to mix and toss it. The wines from this region are good, but also poor travelers. Frascati, one of the best, rarely travels beyond Rome, where its friends are many.

The Umbrians were very ancient people, even antedating the Etruscans. Umbria is the only region that has no salt water, that produces black truffles, and that makes a fine art of pawnbroking. Its beautiful hilltop cities of Perugia, Assisi, and Orvieto are cherished by generations of travelers. Its food is hearty mountain food, partly based on the famous Chianina beef cattle. Only one Umbrian wine has the quality to compete with the other regions, and that is the dry, fragrant, pale-yellow Orvieto.

Introduction

The routine traveler rarely visits the Adriatic region known as The Marches, but there is plenty to attract him. Ascoli Piceno and Ancona are beautiful cities, and Pesaro is a thriving seaport and also Rossini's birthplace. Not that you will find *tournedos Rossini* on any restaurant menu. Instead, you will find *brodetto*, a fish chowder invented in Athens and eaten by Achilles beneath the walls of Troy three millennia ago. There is no set formula for the dish, but it contains *scorfano*, the *rascasse* so essential to a good French *bouillabaisse*. Snails are a specialty here, and they are cooked in an exotic sauce of white wine, olive oil, butter, chopped onions, garlic, thyme, and tomato paste. *That* ought to mask the snail taste! The cooking of The Marches is not very distinguished, nor is the wine. The best pasta dish is called *vincisgrassi*, a sort of Adriatic baked lasagna, and the one wine worth noting is called Verdicchio dei Castelli di Jesi, a clean yellow wine that comes in amphora-shaped bottles.

The far-flung region of Emilia-Romagna, stretching from the Adriatic shore to Piacenza on the border of Lombardy, provides enough gastronomic lore for a book in itself. Pigs in profusion make this great ham and sausage country. It produces the famous Parmesan cheese, and even caviar, for fine plump sturgeon are found at the mouth of the River Po from April to June. The rich Adriatic fishing grounds off Ravenna produce a fabulous treasure. Here the author indulges in an extensive portrayal of Adriatic fish that is, in my opinion, a rare accomplishment.

A guided tour of the famous cities along the Via Emilia begins in Ravenna, famed shrine of mosaics. Rimini, a pleasant seaport older than Rome, is known for its Easter cakes called Ciambelli. For good luck the pastry chef breaks the first egg on the head of a small boy.

Bologna, the capital of Emilia-Romagna is also its topmost gastronomic shrine. It is a brick city of endless porticos covering twenty miles of arcaded sidewalks, and its citizens are hearty eaters who drink deep and couple the joys of the table with those of the bed. Its rich and fattening pasta may be a trifle heavy for some restrained visitors. For them, there are lighter pasta dishes such as *tortellini*. These are little pillows stuffed with veal and ham and Parmesan cheese, with a dash of nutmeg. *Lasagna* is a third pasta dish perfected by Bolognese chefs, who also prepare turkey fillets and veal cutlets in great massive sauces.

Along the Via Emilia is Modena, a city of fine churches and open squares. Pigs, however, seem to be the symbol of Modena, and it is known for one picturesque sausage above all. This is *zampone*, and it consists of the lower leg of a pig with the hoof attached, stuffed with fragrant sausage meat. A *bollito* in Modena's Fini restaurant is one of the rare dishes that the author recommends, and it just happens that the present writer has tried it also in the same place. It consists of a steaming cauldron containing a whole tongue, a calf's head, a chicken, cuts of beef and ham, together with a large *zampone*. Who could forget it?

Parmesan cheese is another comestible that leads the author into long and instructive paragraphs. The cheese originated in Reggio in the 14th century and is produced in many cities, but Parma gets the credit. It is sprinkled on dishes the world over. Eggs, spinach, and asparagus wouldn't be the same without it. Famous also is Parma ham, especially when cut paper-thin and served with chilled melon.

Lombardy, the region that contributes Milan, the wealthiest manufacturing city in Italy, also takes enormous pride in its cooking. *Risotto alla milanese* is the classic of rice dishes, and *costoletta alla milanese* is the Italian prototype of *Wiener schnitzel*. Minestrone combines a dozen or more vegetables in its Milanese version. Mr. Root regales us with a most complete compendium of Milanese food, with emphasis on the cheeses.

The author takes you to many famous shrines in Milan, including the huge glass-roofed Galleria, where the ice cream is fabulous and the pastry is so charged with liqueurs that it is almost intoxicating.

It is in Piedmont, the busy northern region, that Italian wine comes into its own. The rich, lustrous Barolo, probably the best red wine in Italy, flourishes on the slopes of Piedmont, as do Barbaresco, Nebbiola, and Barbera, all aristocrats. The most famous of Italian sparkling wines, Asti Spumante, also comes from Piedmont. The author gives an absorbing dissertation on vermouth, a white wine flavored with herbs, roots, and spices in a secret formula that may contain twenty flavors. The world's most famous cocktails lean heavily on vermouth, which is a giant in the Italian economy.

Piedmont is proud of many things—Fiat automobiles and bread sticks, for example. *Grissini*, the slender crusty sticks originated in Turin, and are considered the most digestible form of bread. Their acceptance is now almost world-wide. White truffles are the jewels of Piedmont. They grow near Alba, not only on the roots of oak trees, but on willows, hazelnut trees, and poplars as well. Piedmont is also *polenta* country, and festivals are held to pay tribute to this drab corn cake.

Just north of Piedmont and touching the Alps is the Val d'Aosta, a lovely mountain valley where French is freely spoken. This is the shrine of Fonduta cheese, a superb orange-colored creamy cheese that is excellent for cooking.

In complete contrast is Liguria, a boomerang strip of coastline along the Mediterranean shore. This is the Italian Riviera, radiant with flowers, olive groves, lemons, and oranges. Genoa is its capital and the largest port in the Mediterranean, the best outlet to the sea for land-locked Switzerland.

For two hundred years Venice was the world's greatest maritime power, and spices, especially pepper, were the key to its greatness. You read of many exotic flavors that arrived in the 12th century, including saffron, which became a symbol of cuckoldry, since Venus used it to put her husband to sleep when she expected a visit from Mars.

Present-day Venetian dishes are simple but delicious. *Fegato alla veneziana* might be called just plain liver and onions, but it is far better than that. The secret lies in the freshness of the ingredients and the very rapid cooking. More adventurous diners might try the cuttlefish family, though we don't recommend *seppie*, inkfish stewed in their own black juice with olive oil. Meat plays a scant role in the Venetian diet, and poultry is scarce. We learn of various dubious fowl that can be had, coot and heron, for example, and curlew.

Mr. Root provides a small guided tour of other cities of Veneto, including Padua, where Galileo was a college professor, and where the famous Pedrocchi Café still exists. Verona has the oldest market in Italy, a beautiful square with a sea of colored umbrellas.

There is a saying in Veneto that "God will take water away from him who does not like wine," and there is no dearth of either in this North country. The slopes of Lake Garda produce some of the noblest red wines in Italy, including the fragrant Bardolino. The Valpolicella vineyards are across the River Adige, and are greatly esteemed. Finally, there is Soave, one of Italy's best white wines.

Venetia Tridentina is mountain country, with rugged peasant fare, often stemming from the German tradition. Italian menus mention *crautti* and *gulasch*, obviously derived from German words. There is a charming story about an elephant named Solomon whose keepers tried to bring him across the Brenner Pass in 1551. The pass was snowed in, so the elephant was installed in an old inn at Bressannone for the winter. Solomon brought instant fame to the *auberge*, which promptly changed its name to Elefante.

Venetia Giulia-Friuli is best known for its beautiful capital, the city of Udine. Here again Mr. Root ferrets out the good dishes, mostly dealing with chicken and fish. Grado boasts a fine fish chowder, and Trieste offers an international cuisine ranging from liver dumplings to apple strudel.

The scene jumps to Campania, the busy Naples area and the most densely populated part of Italy. The touristic attractions of Campania are so rich and varied that few travelers ever miss it. Naples is overcrowded, noisy, friendly, and teeming with life, and its museum of Roman treasures has no equal. This is the land of *pizza*, the Italian specialty that has recently conquered America. The author gives plenty of space to this phenomenon and lists a few *pizze*—with mushrooms, chopped ham, cheese, tomatoes, onions, black olives, anchovies—the choice is unlimited. *Mozzarella* cheese, a vital ingredient of *pizza*, comes from water-buffalo milk in Campania. Oysters are another treasure of the region, and the bread is notable. Bread making has always been an art here, perhaps dating back to the days of Pompeii. Meat is rare in this coastal region, but fish is naturally plentiful. Waterfront restaurants in Naples swarm with fish stews and pasta dishes with clams and seafood. There is a pronounced sweet tooth here, and the pastries are fat and luxurious. And there are frozen desserts, including

Introduction

the famous *spumoni*.

Simple wines are grown on the hillsides and on the ashen slopes of Vesuvius. There is the legend of Lacrima Christi (tear of Christ) that comes from the volcanic slopes, but the author refuses to rave about it and deems it quite inferior.

Abruzzi e Molise is a rugged part of Italy with one hundred miles of Adriatic shore, but without a single good harbor. It is mostly mountain country, with a few snow-covered peaks. Wild swine roam the hills eating acorns. Saffron grows here, the only place in Italy. The cuisine follows the contours—along the coast it is dominated by fish. In the hills it is based on pigs, lamb, veal, and poultry.

Apulia is one of the least visited regions in Italy, a vast area given over to producing wheat, olive oil, and a great deal of strong, mediocre wine which is promptly shipped northward to be blended into vermouth. This land is ancient Greece, including Taranto, now famous for its oysters and its Naval Base. Over three million oysters are cultivated yearly in its waters. The land around Foggia now prospers once again as a wheat-growing center.

Calabria, the toe of the Italian boot, is a poor land. Once it was prosperous, we are told, when the city of Sybaris thrived. This was more than 2,500 years ago, and every trace of the city has vanished. Sybaritic is a showy adjective that applies to a splendor long since disappeared. A motley list of settlers have descended upon Calabria, including Byzantines, Saracens, Normans, Poles, and Spanish Bourbons. Calabria is mountainous, with a severe winter climate, and its farmers have a tough time. But the olive groves are plentiful, and citrus fruits thrive, along with figs.

Sicily, the largest region in Italy and the largest island in the Mediterranean, is historically allied to Greece, and Mr. Root produces a fine historical essay. He takes you to its great cities—Palermo and its Byzantine mosaics; Messina, now rebuilt after the earthquake of 1908 that killed 84,000 people; Catania the busy metropolis; Syracuse, Agrigento, and Taormina, of Greek origin. This fertile island produces a tenth of the Italian wheat crop, and most of its olive oil. Mount Etna, its most spectacular feature, is Europe's largest active volcano. Its lower slopes are carpeted with citrus fruits. At the western extremity of the island is Trapani, famed for its sweet Marsala wine. The fishing off the Trapani coast is spectacular. Everything from tuna to flying fishes and sea horses are found there. To the north are the volcanic Lipari islands, including Stromboli, which regularly erupts every two hours. Is it any wonder that tourists flock to Sicily?

The sweet tooth is the key to Sicilian food. Pastry is almost a religious rite, along with exotic ices. *Cassata*, the famous dessert of sponge cake, liqueurs, candied fruit, chocolate, and ice cream, is the constellation of Sicilian sweets, but there are dozens of others. *Zabaglione*, the famous combination of Marsala, egg yolks, and sugar, is a Sicilian creation known the world over.

The Romans appreciated the wines of Sicily, although many of them are too coarse or too sweet for today's palate. Marsala is the most famous wine, and is used widely in cooking, especially in *zabaglione* and a wine sauce for ham.

Sardinia is the only region of Italy that the writer has not visited, and after reading Mr. Root's chapter I can hardly wait. Its history is very ancient, going back to Stone Age man, and very modern, too, since the Aga Khan recently began financing de luxe multistory hotels on its sandy shore. Sardinian shepherds still dress in sheepskins as they did 2,000 years ago, and they are still vitally important citizens. Grazing sheep is a major occupation. Goats provide wool for cloth, not to mention milk for Pecorino cheese. As might be expected, the cuisine is simple, confined to game, meat, and bread. Vegetables are few, but the sweets are as gaudy as they are in Sicily. The author takes two pages to list the various cakes. Finally, the wines are few but acceptable. The best one is Oliena, from the town of the same name, a robust red wine good with game. Some sweet wines are grown here, and serve as apéritifs. Heavy wines they are, leading to drowsiness. With a final show of thoroughness, Mr. Root devotes paragraphs to Sardinian wines.

Such dedication is truly extraordinary, and it marks the author as the most devoted of epicures, and his book the most authoritative volume on the subject of Italian food and wine yet to appear in English.

SAMUEL CHAMBERLAIN

1. From the viewpoint of the English language, it might seem natural to refer to the great divisions of Italy (for instance, Tuscany) as provinces. But the government of Italy calls them regions. It is their subdivisions (for instance, Siena) which are provinces. This nomenclature has been respected in this book. Confusingly, most provinces bear the same names as their capital cities (for instance, Siena may mean a city or a province). If you bear this in mind, the context should enable you to avoid confusion between one and the other.

2. For the benefit of those who do not know Italian and may therefore be disconcerted by an apparent anarchy in the agreement of nouns and verbs, it may be helpful to note that Italian nouns ending in o (masculine) and a (feminine) are normally singular, and those ending in i (masculine) and e (feminine) are normally plural. You must steel yourself to the fact that there are numerous exceptions to these rules.

3. A special case of the singular-plural dilemma is encountered in the case of proper nouns, which change to express number and gender like the others. I have unblushingly maintained Italian plural forms (for instance, Visconti) when it seemed likely that they would be recognized by English-language readers as plurals (in this case because we are accustomed to -us words from Latin forming plurals in -i) but have Anglicized others (for instance, Sforzas).

4. Alas, there is nothing I can do about the Italian habit of packing much of the meaning of a word into suffixes of intensification, diminution, magnification and the like (for instance, *tortellini*, *tortelli*, *tortelloni*, for three different sizes of the same sort of pasta. I trust that these forms will

become self-explanatory as you progress through this book.

5. At the risk of irritating you, I have included the dialect names of local Italian dishes whenever I knew them myself. This is what you are likely to find on menus if you venture into small and, it may even seem at first sight, unappetizing restaurants in out-of-the-way places, which is what I strongly advise you to do if you want to sample genuine regional cooking. In the big well-known restaurants in tourist-frequented cities, you are likely to encounter only generalized "Italian" cooking, an artificial confection without roots in the soil, a patchwork of bits and tatters which echo, usually distantly, a hodgepodge of reminiscences of disparate regional dishes—in short, a sort of gastronomic *lingua franca* which, like the pidgin jargons developed in many parts of the world, possesses a constricted vocabulary and no grammar.

Contents

茶 : 茶 : 茶 : 茶 : 茶 : 茶 : 茶 : 茶 *Maps* 茶 : 茶

Maps prepared by BRUCE KENNEDY *and* ANITA K. KARL
from sketches by the author

THE
FOOD

OF
ITALY

Etruscans, Greeks and Saracens

The food of Italy is a function of the history of Italy.
A major component of that history is the record of
the successive arrivals, over a period of 3,000 years, of wave
after wave of invading peoples. Some of them went away
again, others stayed. Each new race brought with it its own
customs, its own traditions and its own eating habits. Three
of them in particular laid the foundations for the Italian
cooking of today. They were the Etruscans, the Greeks
and the Saracens.

Of the three, the Etruscans and the Greeks exerted a
more profound influence than the Saracens. They were
there earlier. They divided virtually the whole peninsula
between them. Etruscan culture was imposed upon the

older peoples of the North. Greek culture seduced the older peoples of the South. Neither faced in Italy any civilization capable of competing with their own. By the time the Saracens arrived in the South, they could only apply an overlay to the substructure already established solidly by the Greeks. Nevertheless the Saracens' contribution was much greater, quantitatively and qualitatively, than that of any of their successors. They deserve to be classed with the major creators of Italian cooking.

Each of the three left behind a specific trademark. That of the Etruscans was a sort of mush made from grain which at times had the consistency of porridge and at others that of crumbly cake. It does not sound like particularly inspiring food, but on it the Roman Legions conquered the world. When the Romans took it over from the Etruscans, they called it *puls*, and later *pulmentum*. It is polenta today, and it is eaten throughout northern Italy, on the territory once occupied by the Etruscans.

The Greek trademark was fish chowder. Everybody knows that the Greeks bequeathed it to Marseilles, where it is called *bouillabaisse*, when Marseilles was a Greek city; they also implanted it in seaside colonies of the Italian peninsula, particularly, though not exclusively, in the South. It is still relished there, most often under the name of *brodetto*, though there is a limitless number of local aliases also.

The Saracens, when they appeared in the 8th century A.D., left their trademark too. They left it everywhere they passed. You could draw a map of the limits of Moslem invasion by plotting the places where, during the Middle Ages, their fine flaky pastry became established. It is the *pastilla* of Morocco; the rustic *tourtière* and the aristocratic *millefeuille* of France (where they got as far as Poitiers); the *Strudel* of Central Europe (where they reached the Adriatic and threatened Vienna); and in Italy the *mille-*

foglie of Sicily and the *sfogliatelle* of Naples.

The Saracens contributed to the Italian cuisine twice, the second time involuntarily. In the 8th century, it was as the rulers of Sicily and much of southern Italy. In the 11th, their territories of the Holy Land were invaded by the Crusaders, who brought back Oriental foods, including some which the Saracens had carefully hidden from the infidels of Italy when they were on the spot. They planted sugar cane in Spain, where they thought themselves likely to stay forever, but not in Sicily or other parts of Italy, where they were less sure of their staying power. Italy had to wait for sugar cane until the return of the Crusaders.

The Saracens did introduce rice. They were the source also of tarragon; of spinach (*isbānakh* in Arabic); of buckwheat, called "Saracen" to this day in France, Spain and Italy (*sarrasin*, *sarraceno* and *saraceno* respectively); of the true orange (the ancient Romans knew only the bigarade, or bitter orange); of a large number of products the ancient Romans had enjoyed but which disappeared from Italy when the Barbarian invasions cut the communications of the Empire—pomegranates, apricots, lemons; and of a long list of spices. They also imported various techniques: the art of making ice cream and sherbet, which they had learned from the Hindus, who had learned it from the Chinese; new methods for preserving food—fruit by drying; meat by drying or salting; and, above all, distillation, unknown to the ancients. The Arabs invented it, along with its vocabulary—*al cohol* is made by means of an *al embic*. Italian grappa is descended from Saracen fig brandy.

America made no culinary contribution to Italy, but stimulated the native genius by giving it new materials to work with. It is difficult to imagine Italian cooking today without the tomato, which came from Mexico, or the pimento, which came from Peru. Polenta today is usually made from a grain unknown to the ancients, maize (sweet corn). Other American contributions include the turkey; the potato; the peanut; vanilla; chocolate, which Columbus first brought to Spain, which kept its origin secret for a century; the Virginia strawberry (previously the Old World had known only the small wild variety); the string bean; the pumpkin; the Jerusalem artichoke—so called, probably (like the turkey, for that matter), because the early explorers remained ignorant of the existence of America even after they had discovered it, and thought they were in Asia (maize is still called "Turkish wheat" in Italy); and some other foods which had been known in the ancient world but had somehow disappeared from Europe, like the manioc, from which tapioca is made, and certain species of squash.

The other foreign influences to which Italian cooking was exposed were minor, despite the presence at one time or another and in one region or another of Phoenicians, Carthaginians, Illyrians, Vandals, Huns, Ostrogoths, Volces, Celts, Gauls, Byzantines, Longobards, Normans, Spaniards, Catalans, Aragonese, Angevins, Hohenstaufens, Hungarians, Slavs, Austrians and French. Their contributions were meager, even those of the French, despite the existence in Italy of the French-speaking Valle d'Aosta; France, indeed, owes more to Italy in the culinary realm than Italy to France. The echoes of Austrian, Hungarian and Slavic cooking in the northeast do not represent foreign influences applied to Italian cooking; it is a case of foreign peoples doing their own cooking on Italian soil after the territorial annexations which followed World War I. The Spaniards left only a few scattered dishes in the territories they held in Italy from time to time. The Normans did leave a trademark, salt cod, the only one they had to leave, except angelica. The Barbarians had nothing left to offer by the time they reached Italy, for the Romans had already imported and naturalized the products of the north, like the sausages and the beer of Gaul. The Huns raided but did not stay, and even if they had, it is unlikely that Italian cooking would have gained. They showed little interest in eating, though they did in drinking, indulging immoderately in fermented milk or yoghurt, and in *cam*, which was fermented barley. Their chief contribution to gastronomy was raw meat, which they tenderized by placing it under their saddles and riding around on it all day—hence today's term, "Tartar steak."

"What is the basic difference between French and Italian cooking?" Enrico Galozzi, the noted Italian gastronomic expert, echoed my question. "French cooking is formalized, technical and scientific. Order Béarnaise sauce in 200 different French restaurants and you will get exactly the same sauce 200 times. Ask for Bolognese sauce in 200 different Italian restaurants and you will get 200 different versions of *ragù*."

This diversity of Italian cooking is only one facet of the diversity of Italian culture. It is evident even to the foreigner in one of the most fundamental manifestations of any culture, its language. You do not need to speak Italian to realize that the language sounds very different as you move from one part of the country to another. Apart from such phenomena as the speaking of Ladin in Friuli, Catalan in Sardinia, and Albanian in Calabria and Sicily, many local dialects are incomprehensible to other Italians; and local pronunciations of standard Italian differ widely. The accent of Venice echoes the language of the ancient Veneti, whose origin is still in dispute today; and if Florentines tend to substitute the sound of H for the sound of C, it is because they have still not freed themselves from the influence of Etruscan, a language otherwise lost.

When the 500th anniversary of the death of Boccaccio was celebrated in 1875 by the publication of one of his stories in different Italian dialects, the publishers came up with approximately 700 of them. The first word of the story, *dico* (I say) in the classic Tuscan, shifted to *a degh* as nearby as Bologna, and became *diggu* in Sardinia. In the province of Piedmont alone, where the capital, Turin, said *io dio*, there was also *ä dic* (Monferrato), *iv disiis* (Saluzzo) and *mi diva* (Mondovì), while Alba, whose population at the time was only about 10,000, boasted two versions all by itself—*mi dijo* in the center of town, *mi digu* in the outskirts.

The fragmentation of Italian culture began early. Neither of the first two historic races of Italy, who laid its foundations, had any genius for the formation of large-scale political units. There were Greeks, but there was no Greek nation. There were Etruscans, but there was no Etruscan nation. For both, the largest permanent political unit was the city.

But then the ancient Romans came and did construct a vast political unit. For something like half a millennium, they ruled a territory which included most of the then known world. How did it happen that this long period of unity did not erase the particularism fastened on Italy by the Greeks and the Etruscans?

Perhaps it was not a period of unity, but only one of union. The Romans were not so much synthesizers as collectors. Their most indisputable claim to an ability to unify would seem to lie in the construction of the great political conglomerate that was the Roman Empire. Yet outside of the Italian peninsula the colonial areas were never integrated into a unified whole. Each territory was governed, independently of what was happening in the others, by the Roman generals or proconsuls who happened to be on the spot, often with only the scantiest reference to Rome. Each territory retained its own habits, its own customs and its own individuality.

I · *Etruscans, Greeks and Saracens*

Inside the peninsula, unity was blocked by the veneration accorded The City. The unique position granted to Rome, the Urbs, a political unit on a scale no larger than had been achieved by the Greeks and the Etruscans, had as its countereffect the maintenance of the individualism of other cities, whether they were classified legally as Roman colonies, municipalities, communities under Roman law or allied cities. The localism of each remained intact.

The Romans imposed a rule, but not a culture. Indeed Rome had no very profound original culture to share. Romans themselves looked for intellectual inspiration to Greece. The only foreign language significant numbers of Romans acquired was Greek, often, one suspects, out of snobbery—approximately the same impulse which today induces many foreigners to learn French. That the Romans did not study Greek because of natural intellectual curiosity may be deduced from their indifference to another language, so complete that they allowed it to perish. Many thousands of Romans must have spoken Etruscan. For several centuries, Rome was a bilingual city. If Quintus Fabius Rullianus, disguised as an Etruscan peasant, was successful in 310 B.C. in a spying mission inside Etruscan territory which carried him all the way to Clusium (today Chiusi), it was because he spoke perfect Etruscan. Etruscan was still a living language in Perugia in the time of Augustus, at the beginning of our own era. Yet not a single Roman scholar took the trouble to compile a Latin-Etruscan dictionary. Not only did the Romans have little talent for imparting their own culture, borrowed or original, to others; they had little also for assimilating the culture of foreigners.

The Romans were skillful administrators, but their methods were entirely pragmatic. They controlled their territories by using force to check revolt and offering rewards to stimulate self-interested loyalty. The lessons they gave

9

subject peoples were in techniques—engineering, architecture, law. None of this reached the soul. Neither the Empire nor Italy developed spiritual unity. Nevertheless there was an element at hand which might have been expected to develop it. This was the Latin language (inherited in considerable part, it is true, from Greek). But while Latin was the necessary means of communication between the Romans and the peoples they ruled, it was employed for this purpose only by those whose eminent positions, in government or trade, obliged them to deal with Romans—the upper crust. There were no mass educational systems in those days, so the local languages continued to be spoken by subordinate populations. Eventually the regular use of Latin by the elite, and its consequent prestige as the tongue of the powerful, caused it to sift down into the lower layers, where it was altered by the still-existing forms of popular speech. When the Roman power disappeared, Latin remained the language of the upper crust, the international tool for scholars and the Church; but for the common man it split into Portuguese, Spanish, French, Provençal, Ladin, Rumanian, and the many dialects of Italy. In the peninsula, Latin remained the literary language of the learned, but the populace did not speak it; and at last Dante had the courage to write in the vernacular and promote Tuscan into Italian.

When the Empire collapsed, its constituent parts in Italy reverted to the particularism the Greeks and the Etruscans had fastened upon them. The waves of invasion followed. Many of them were on a small scale, affecting only restricted areas. Incursions on a larger scale did not always cover the same territories. Some overlapped, some left gaps. Feudal relationships created exceptional situations, like Benevento's vassalage to the Pope, which gave it a different history from the region which surrounded it. In the end, there were hardly two cities in Italy which had shared the same succession of rulers and consequently the same cultural heritage—of which gastronomic habits were a part.

Historical fragmentation was reinforced by geographical fragmentation. All Italy is mountainous, and mountains tend everywhere to shut each valley into its own tightly closed box, within which local customs develop and harden, uncorrupted by influx from similarly cloistered adjoining valleys. Not only does each province have characteristics of its own for historical reasons, but within a province one valley will cook differently from the valley next to it for geographical reasons. As a result, no other country of comparable size (and possibly no other country regardless of size) possesses a cuisine broken up so minutely into divisions, subdivisions, and sub-subdivisions.

Yet foreigners often express the opinion that all Italian cooking is pretty much alike. That is probably because they have made acquaintance with it in their own countries. The Italian restaurant is an article of export. No large city in the Western world is without Italian restaurants—and Italian restaurants abroad *are* very much alike. Most of them are operated by Neapolitans, who migrate easily, since their part of the country is poor and overcrowded; and they have a talent for cooking.

Thus what is described abroad as "Italian" cooking is really Neapolitan cooking, though the Neapolitan-managed restaurant in a foreign country is not even genuinely Neapolitan. Its bill of fare does not present the Neapolitan repertory. It is composed of a helter-skelter collection of dishes from a dozen different areas which for one reason or another have become familiar to foreigners. Neapolitans abroad have popularized pizza, which *is* Neapolitan, and they are more likely to offer you macaroni or spaghetti from their own South than the soft egg noodles of the North (exception made for *tagliatelle alla bolognese*), but otherwise Naples takes its chances on the menu along with other

Italian cities. Go into almost any Italian restaurant abroad, and you will find already on the table, beside the salt, the pepper and the sugar bowl, a tumbler bristling with what foreigners call "Italian" breadsticks—*grissini*. They are not generically Italian, they are Turinese. The Italian restaurant in foreign parts which offers them will probably also list on its menu *scampi* (Venice), ravioli (Genoa), *ossobuco* (Milan), and *zabaglione* (Sicily).

Curiously enough, you can travel through Italy itself and still come away with the impression that all Italian food is alike—if you eat in the restaurants frequented by tourists, as tourists often do. They give foreigners what they demand because it is what they are accustomed to, and what they are accustomed to is what emigrant Neapolitan restaurant proprietors abroad have put before them. Restaurants of this type, which offer a sort of pidgin-Italian cuisine, rooted in no one school of cooking, but borrowing freely from many, are referred to in Italy as "international restaurants." When I first heard this term, I thought it meant those which serve the stabilized international fare found all over the world, a bastard offspring of the French *haute cuisine* and the Swiss hotel industry. I discovered after a while that for Italians it means those which serve dishes from other parts of Italy than their own. It is highly significant that a native of Bologna refers to a Bolognese restaurant which offers Venetian and Milanese and Roman dishes not as inter-regional but as international. For the Bolognese, a Venetian is in many aspects a foreigner. When Sophia Loren was interviewed on French television after the birth of her baby, she was asked, "What language are you going to teach him first? French? English? Italian?" "Neapolitan," she replied.

In a country so diverse, one might well ask whether there is any such thing as *Italian* cooking, with specific

identifiable characteristics of its own, or if this is not simply
a catchall term bundling together a heterogeneous collection of regional cuisines, each of which is separately identifiable as Venetian, Sicilian, or whatever. Intuition answers
that there is. Venetian cooking may be very different from
Sicilian cooking, but both are immediately recognizable as
belonging to the same category, if only because they are
more like each other than like German or French or any
other foreign cooking.

One unifying factor is geography. Geographically, Italy
is a unit. All of her frontiers are natural. On three sides,
she is surrounded by sea. The fourth is blocked off by the
highest mountain wall in Europe. Within these borders,
climate is as uniform as it could possibly be in any area of
this extent. Italy's long narrow shape, aligned in a north-
south direction, might reasonably be expected to make for
extremes of temperature; but the equalizing effect of the
warm inland sea into which the peninsula extends makes
its effect felt in every part of a territory where only three
out of the 16 regions have no coast and where no point is
more than 150 miles from open water. True, there is a
considerable spread of normal temperatures between extreme north and extreme south, but the whole country
enjoys a long growing season between the last frost of
spring and the first of autumn, permitting in at least part
of every region the lush profusion of fruit and vegetables
which characterizes Italian food resources. This relative
uniformity of raw materials throughout the country is
furthered by its mountainous spine, which penetrates every
region of peninsular Italy, giving each the same combination
of varying heights and pinched plain. You do not have to
move horizontally from one part of the country to another
to change flora and fauna; you can do it by moving verti-
cally up or down wherever you happen to be. The soil of
some regions is of course poorer than that of others, but

this inequality has been minimized by 3,000 years of experience in tilling even the most grudging terrain.

This long experience is in itself a unifying factor, for its lessons and its techniques have been shared throughout Italy. Italians have given longer continuous conscious intensive attention to the growing of food than anyone else in the Western world. Many of the first books on agriculture were written by ancient Romans, and not the least among them—Cato the Elder, Virgil, Ovid, Horace. Not only do Italian farmers benefit from a general experience extending back to ancient times, they also often enjoy specialized experience with specific products, for many areas in Italy have concentrated on single crops for so many centuries that their farmers know more about their chosen specialties than anyone else. *Mollis in aequerea quae crevit spina Ravenna non erit incultis gratior asparagis,* Martial wrote 1,900 years ago, and Ravenna still produces the best asparagus in Italy. An experience only half as long has made Italian spinach as much better than French spinach as French spinach is better than American spinach. After the Italians got rice from the Saracens, they improved the strain so greatly that no less a personage than Thomas Jefferson smuggled some of it illegally out of the country. After they got the tomato from America, they developed from the first crude foreign fruit a plum tomato so superlative that it was re-imported into the United States. The Italian way with vegetables is recognized unconsciously all over the world by the Italian names for them which have passed into foreign languages—broccoli, zucchini, fava beans. Another vegetable referred to by its foreign name throughout the world ought to be in Italian, but isn't—*petits pois* have entered the international lexicon in French, but the French only adopted these tiny tender tasty peas from the Italian *piselli novelli.* They were first imported into France from Genoa in 1660, as a present for Louis XIV, and immediately took the country by storm.

The high quality of Italian vegetables is a unifying factor in Italian cooking technique, for it discourages any but the simplest treatment, which best retains the full natural flavor. Peas, spinach or string beans are apt to be cooked in much the same way everywhere in Italy.

For practically all other food categories too, the different regions of Italy are subject to the unifying influence of a common larder. What has been said about Italian skill with vegetables could be repeated for fruit, copiously consumed throughout the country. Fish are available everywhere, even in the landlocked provinces, which are usually not too far from the sea to receive its products, and when they are, enjoy the compensation of teeming lakes or of Italy's largest river, the Po.

Subject to somewhat more local variation, much the same kind of meat is produced on much the same kind of pasturage throughout the country. Poultry runs everywhere are inhabited by the same birds. The ubiquity of pasta, though its forms are protean, provides another example of unity despite diversity, harking back no doubt to the days when the whole peninsula was under the sway of the Romans, whose fundamental food was grain. It was also the Romans who bequeathed a sweet tooth to the entire nation (reaffirmed later by the Saracens), thus accounting for the rich luscious irresistible Italian desserts. Everywhere in Italy the meal ends with strong black coffee.

Unity despite diversity again: the Italian larder in general, each region's larder in particular, is stocked with those simple basic products which are at once so universal and so different that they are regularly identified everywhere in the world by the names of the places which produce them: wine, sausage, ham, cheese and, to a lesser extent, bread. There is hardly a community in Italy which does not make its own special type of sausage, few which do not boast a local cheese, and not many without a distinctive type of bread. As for wine, whose presence or absence exerts a decisive influence on cooking, Italy is in this respect more unified even than France. A number of French provinces produce no wine. Every Italian region does.

Paradoxically, one of the circumstances which first fastened gastronomic particularism on Italy also inhibits it from developing to an extent which would prevent the different regional cusines from being recognizable as parts of a common whole. This is the competing influences on Italian cooking of the Etruscans, the Greeks and the Saracens. For while these three tendencies may be distinct, they are not incompatible; and if you go far enough back, you may discover that at least two of them, and perhaps all three, share a common origin.

The least important of the three, the Saracen influence, was applied only in the South, superimposed, therefore, upon that of the Greeks. It was accepted there readily for the excellent reason that it was not strikingly different from what the region already knew and liked. The Saracens, like the Greeks, came from the eastern end of the Mediterranean, a region most of whose countries shared the same general type of cooking, which for want of a better word we may call Byzantine. When the Saracens came to Italy in the 8th century, Greek and Saracen food was, except in detail, of much the same type.

The difference between Greek and Etruscan cooking in, say, the 6th century B.C., when the two races shared the peninsula between them, may seem more fundamental; but if we consider their antecedents, we may find reasons to doubt that there can be any basic antagonism between them.

There are three main theories about the origin of the Etruscans. One—that they entered Italy from some unspecified territory to the north—has now been generally abandoned. The second was first stated by Dionysius of Halicarnassus in the 1st century B.C.: "The Etruscan nation emigrated from nowhere; it has always been there." Some modern scholars are inclined to accept this, but more of them plump for the third. This theory originated with Herodotus, who wrote in the 5th century B.C. that the Etruscans had emigrated in the 13th from Lydia. It is indisputable that some Etruscan religious practices resemble those of Asia Minor—for instance, divination, in which the Etruscans were matched only by the Assyrians and the Chaldeans. There seems also to be an affinity between Etruscan and Lydian, neither of them Indo-European languages. This last point gained force with the discovery, on the island of Lemnos, in the northern Aegean, of a stele bearing the only inscription ever found outside of Italy in what, if not definitely the Etruscan of Italian inscriptions, is certainly close to it. Lemnos might easily have been a stop in the course of what Herodotus described as the extensive wanderings of the Lydians on their way to Italy and to their new name of Etruscans; for though archeologists have succeeded only vaguely in delimiting the territory of Asia Minor occupied by Lydia, it seems fairly certain that it possessed a coastline on the Aegean. If the Etruscans came from Lydia, they came like the Greeks from the domain of Byzantine cooking.

But even if the Etruscans did not originate in the same eastern Mediterranean area as the Greeks, they at least were strongly influenced by Greek culture. They admired Greek art, and their own reflected it. "They were the introducers and the imitators of everything which represented Greek civilization in this distant land," wrote a French authority, Jacques Heurgon, "and they lost themselves a little in this mission." The Etruscans may very well have been inspired by the Greeks in their eating habits. The *pulmentum* which they bequeathed to the Romans was essentially the same as the porridge on which the boys of Sparta were raised. If it failed to invade the South also, that was probably because the Greeks who settled in the South, with the single exception of those of Taranto, came from communities which followed the lead of Athens, the antithesis of Sparta. *Pulmentum* was the ration of Spartan youth for reasons deliberately ascetic; the Athenians preferred to regale themselves on fish stew. Thus the Etruscan North and the Greek South were not profoundly antithetical. While Greek and Etruscan particularism fastened fragmentation on Italy at the political level, at another level, the deeper one of cultural affinity, both races endowed Italy with a basic spirit which was Eastern Mediterranean. The two great schools of ancient cooking in Italy were branches of the same family; and as a result, despite strong local divergences, there is a national Italian cuisine today.

Against the background of these profound and ancient influences which link the otherwise very different regional cuisines of Italy, certain other characteristics are shared more or less by all of them. One is that while French cooking has become professional cooking even when it is executed by amateurs, Italian cooking has remained basically amateur cooking even when it is executed by professionals. It is, in short, home cooking, *la cucina casalinga*, human, light-hearted and informal.

A technical similarity is skill in dealing with sauces. Most persons think of the French as the great sauce makers; but it was Italians who first developed this art. The French learned it later from the cooks who came to France in the train of Catherine dei Medici. It is a giveaway that in large French kitchens making the sauces is a job entrusted to a specialist, the *saucier*. In Italy every cook must be able to concoct sauces or he could hardly cook at all. In France, a sauce is an adornment, even a disguise, added to a dish more or less as an afterthought. In Italy, it *is* the dish, its soul, its *raison d'être*, the element which gives it character and flavor. The most widespread Italian foods are bland, neutral; they would produce little impact on the taste buds unassisted. Pasta unadorned could quickly become monotonous. The whole point of *tagliatelle alla bolognese* or *spaghetti con le vongole* is the sauce. Rice, so common in Italy that the Italian word risotto has become naturalized in most countries, is not only a wonderful carrier of sauces, it can hardly get along without them. Even the favorite meat of Italy is the most neutral of all—veal, so popular that Varro thought the very name of Italy was derived from *vitellus*, a theory not shared by modern etymologists.

A superficial shared characteristic of Italian cuisines, a function, no doubt, of the climate, is that their food is admirably adapted to be eaten in the open air. It is probably no accident that an Italian phrase, "*al fresco*," is used all over the world to describe outdoor eating.

The Etruscan North was divided from the Greek South along an ethnic boundary which has now become a gastronomic Mason-Dixon line. You could call it, depending on what concerns you for the moment, the pasta line, the cooking-fats line, the coffee line, the meat line—or the poverty line, which explains some of the others.

All these North-South boundaries coincide. There is one which does not, for it falls where it is for a geographical reason, the quality of pasturage, rather than for the historical reason of the Greek-Etruscan split. This is the veal line, which cuts across the peninsula south of Florence. North of that line, veal is called *vitello* (calf), south of it *vitella* (heifer). Northern cattle are raised primarily for milk. The females are kept and the young males slaughtered. In the South, the cattle are not notable milk producers. They are bred chiefly as draft animals. The stronger males are kept for oxen; the young females often become veal.

The main North-South line is south of the veal line, following the boundaries between Lazio and The Marches to the north, the Campania and Abruzzi to the south. It has held steady since ancient times, despite the long centuries of political shifts and changes which followed the decline of the Roman Empire. It marked successively the northern limit of the Lombard Duchies, of the Norman Kingdom of Sicily, of the Kingdom of the Two Sicilies, and of the Kingdom of Naples, persisting until North and South were finally united late in the 19th century in the newborn Kingdom of Italy.

This is the poverty line today; the regions to the North are distinctly more prosperous than those to the South. That is why it is the meat line. The North can afford more meat than the South, whose typical diet is pasta, fish and vegetables. That is also why it is the coffee line. Italians are great coffee drinkers, and they like the best—which is the most expensive. South of the line they cannot afford the best, so Southerners drink only one-fifth as much coffee as Northerners, and that of poorer quality.

The cooking-fats line is also partly a function of poverty, but for this the factors are more complex. Distinctions among regional cuisines based on cooking fats are more important in France than in Italy, where the olive grows everywhere except in the high Alps, making olive oil the dominant cooking fat for Italy as a whole. Nonetheless, more butter is consumed in the North than in the South. This results primarily from richer northern pasturage, especially in Lombardy, and secondarily from local tastes and habits, formed not only by the greater availability of butter, but also, in Piedmont and Lombardy, by imitation of France. However, the greater use of olive oil in the poorer South depends also on the facts that the olive thrives on unpromising soil, more widespread in the South, and that it costs more to maintain a cow than an olive tree. Pigs can be raised cheaply, so lard it also used often in the South.

The most striking of the North-South divisions is provided by Italy's most universal food, pasta. In the North, the characteristic type is flat and limp, usually with egg, often made at home, and, if bought in a store, carried away still in the form of dough, to be cooked at home (*tagliatelle, lasagne, ravioli*). In the South, it is the stiff brittle factory-made tubular pasta, usually without egg—poverty again (*macaroni, spaghetti*).

The North-South gastronomic boundary, which for 3,000 years was also the political boundary, persisted as long as it did because it was a natural frontier. Starting on the west coast about 220 miles southeast of Rome, it followed the Garigliano River west and north, curved around the barrier of the Gran Sasso, the highest point in the Apennines, and finally followed another river, the Trento, to the Adriatic. This was a line easy to defend, and behind its shelter the ancient Romans built what was probably the first (and for centuries certainly the most important) of the great roads across which they marched to domination—thus stabilizing, fortifying and insuring the longevity of the North-South boundary. The umbilical cord of Empire, in ancient times this road was a great artery along which passed farm carts, chariots, and the marching Legions. Today it is a great artery for automobiles. Drive up the tourist-ridden Via Vittorio Veneto of Rome to the splendid park of the Villa Borghese, turn right along the Corso d'Italia, and in a few blocks you find at your left this ancient Roman road, which you can follow all the way to the Adriatic. It was called the Via Salaria then, and it is called the Via Salaria today. Via Salaria is the Salt Way.

The Via Salaria began when the insignificant tribe of Latin shepherds living miserably at the mouth of the Tiber found they had a surplus of the salt they drew from the sea for their own consumption and for that of their sheep. They trod a way to Rieti, capital of their neighbors, the Sabines, to barter the salt for other goods. With time, the road strengthened and lengthened. It carried other merchandise, became the first great trade route for Rome, and then a highway across which the Legions marched to conquest. You might say that the Roman Empire was sired by salt.

ETRUSCANS,
GREEKS

AND
SARACENS

Tuscany

F orty-two miles east of Florence, pinched between the
wooded mountains of the long narrow Casentino valley,
lies Camaldoli. Somewhat off the main track, it is little visited by tourists. For the few who find it, a favorite excursion is to the summit of La Falterona, at 5,140 feet the highest peak in this part of the Apennines, from which both the
Tyrrhenian and Adriatic seas are visible. A thousand feet
below the summit a clear rivulet escapes from the mountain-
side and sparkles down. It is a tiny stream, but it did not
escape the notice of Dante. *"Un fiumicel che nasce in Falterona,"* he wrote (inappropriately in the *Purgatorio*),
"e cento miglia di corso nol sazia." Thus Italy's greatest

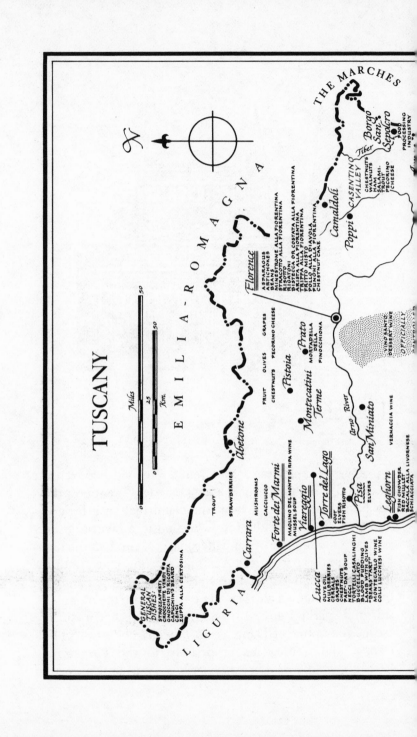

TUSCANY

THE MARCHES

EMILIA-ROMAGNA

LIGURIA

Miles
0   25   50
Km.
0   50

Florence
ASPARAGUS
ARTICHOKES
BEANS
MINESTRONE ALLA FIORENTINA
STRACOTTO ALLA FIORENTINA
RISOTTO
FAGIOLI
BISTECA OR COSTATA ALLA FIORENTINA
TRIPPA ALLA FIORENTINA
FRITTO MISTO
LINGUA DI BUE ALLA CAVOLA
FUNGHI ALLA FIORENTINA
CHESTNUT CAKE

Borgo
San
Sepolcro
FOOD
PROCESSING
INDUSTRY

Tiber

Camaldoli
CHESTNUTS
WALNUTS
SALMI
TROUT
PECORINO
CHEESE

CASENTINO
VALLEY

Poppi

VINO SANTO:
DESSERT WINE

OFFICIALLY

Prato
MORTADELLA
DELLA
FINOCCHIONA

Pistoia
FRUIT   OLIVES   GRAPES
CHESTNUTS
PECORINO CHEESE

Montecatini
Terme

Arno River

San Miniato
VERNACCIA WINE

Abetone

STRAWBERRIES

TROUT

MUSHROOMS

CACCIUCCO

Forte dei Marmi
MAIOLINO DEL MONTE DI RIPA WINE
MUSSEL SOUP

Viareggio

Torre del Lago

Pisa
COOT
ELVERS
FISH RISOTTO

Leghorn
FISH CHOWDER
RED MULLET
TRIGLIE ALLA LIVORNESE
SCHIACCIATA
ELVERS

Carrara

Lucca
OLIVE OIL
MULBERRIES
GRAPES
CHESTNUTS
PETRONI
BOCCELLA CASALINGHI
BLOOD PUDDING
LAMB & OLIVES
"ROAST PIG"
MONTECARLO WINE
COLLI LUCCHESI WINE

GENERAL
TUSCAN
DISHES:
STROZZAPRETI
CROSTINI VERDI
GNOCCHI DI RICOTTA
CAPRUCHIN'S BEARD
CECI
ZUPPA ALLA CERTOSINA

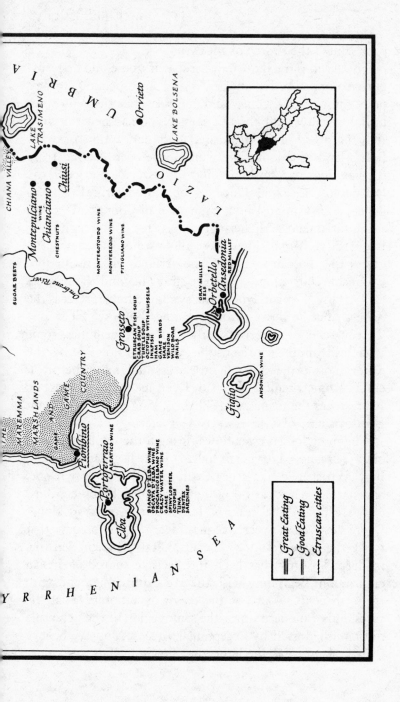

poet saluted the source of the Arno.

The Arno is the most Italian river. If you could be transported miraculously, unwarned and unsuspecting, to any point on its banks, you would know at once that you were in Italy. You would know it even if you had never been in Italy before. For in that case, your conception of what Italy's landscape looks like would have been derived from the paintings of Cimabue, Giotto, Masaccio, Botticelli, the Pollaiuolos, Gozzoli, Duccio, the Lorenzettis, Fra' Angelico, Fra' Filippo Lippi, Francesco di Giorgio, Uccello, the Ghirlandaios, Michelangelo, Sassetta, Luca Signorelli, Leonardo da Vinci. They were all Tuscans, and their scenery is the Tuscan scenery. The Arno is all Tuscan too. From source to mouth, it never strays beyond the borders of Tuscany. For foreigners, the symbolic Italian river is the Tiber, since it flows through Rome. But the Tiber is a Tuscan river too. It rises in the Tuscan Apennines, some 20 miles from the source of the Arno, and flows across the easternmost projection of Tuscany and Umbria before it enters Rome's region of Lazio. Even its name is Etruscan. It preserves the memory of Thebris, king of the important Etruscan city of Caere, today Cerveteri.

The most Italian river flows through the most Italian region. Tuscany (Toscana in Italian) is the heartland of Italy. It is even shaped like a heart, though a badly drawn one. Savonarola, who was not a Tuscan, called Florence, Tuscany's capital, "the heart of Italy." "It is truly striking," wrote the French expert Jacques Heurgon, "to observe that twice the same country of central Italy, ancient Etruria, modern Tuscany, has been the decisive source of Italian civilization. Beginning with the 3rd century B.C. and with the 15th century A.D., at the dawn of antiquity as at the threshold of modern times, the same region of the peninsula distinguished itself by exceptional virtues. Must we believe that the landscape, the light, the climate of Tuscany, more tonic than the heavy air of the Roman plain, have twice produced the same miracle?" Michelangelo, Vasari tells us, attributed "whatever good he might have in his soul to the lively and subtle air one breathes in Arezzo." A gastronomic writer of Arezzo paraphrased this in more material terms. "Does a well-fed race produce more geniuses than others?" he asked. "The list of great men from Arezzo seems to confirm it." He cited, besides Michelangelo, born at Caprese, Piero della Francesca of Borgo San Sepolcro; Luca Signorelli of Cortona; Sansovino of Monte Sansovino; and, from Arezzo itself, Petrarch, Aretino and, of course, Guido d'Arezzo, inventor of the musical scale.

The heartland of a country—that is, the area where its essence has persisted in the strongest and most living fashion—seems usually to be marked by two characteristics, among others. Its people speak the national language in its purest form, and, a particularity rather more difficult to account for, cook the most robust form of food, meat (especially beef), in the simplest manner, without fuss or frills. The purest French is spoken in Touraine, noted for its roasts. The purest Spanish is spoken in Castille, also noted for its roasts. The purest Italian is spoken in Tuscany, noted for its grilled beef.

"*Lingua senese in bocca pistoiese,*" is the Italian description of the purest Italian: "The language of Siena in the mouth of a Pistoian"—both Siena and Pistoia being, of course, in Tuscany. Tuscans *should* speak the best Italian, for modern standard Italian is Tuscan. Dante Alighieri, who converted the formerly despised vernacular into a literary language which displaced Latin, was born in Florence. He had allies in introducing the *dolce stil nuovo*, notably Guido Cavalcanti, but they were Tuscans too. At the time there was no intellectual vigor elsewhere in Italy capable of supplanting Latin. Florence stood head and shoulders above the other Italian capitals, including Rome; she was at the height of her civilization when the rest of Europe could still be described as semi-barbarous; and she emerged from the Middle Ages while the others were still mired down in them. It was no accident that the first academy in the world to compile a dictionary of a modern language was the Tuscan Accademia della Crusca, in 1611.

It is not enough to say that the great period of Florence was that of the Renaissance. Florence *was* the Renaissance. She created it. Rome received it only as an article of import, when Innocent VII called the two Tuscan humanists, Poggio and Bruni, to his capital. The land of the Etruscans served as the midwife at both the birth and the rebirth of the Italian spirit.

Tuscany comes very close to being the heartland of Italy in the simple geographical sense; but it is not quite dead center. Lazio is closer to the middle on the North-South axis, Umbria is centrally placed on both the North-South and East-West lines. Is it pertinent to note that according to Herodotus the first Etruscan settlements were in Umbria? In any case Etruria was in ancient times, and Tuscany is in modern times, the nexus through which the currents of Italy flowed, and flow. In the old days, the South needed the farm products of Lombardy, the North needed the wool of Lazio; they passed each other in Etruria. Today the crack trains from France abandon the coast to cut inland and pass through Florence on their way to Rome; and the main cross-peninsula line from the Adriatic to the Tyrrhenian is Venice-Florence-Rome.

Tuscany, though it is only a little larger than the state of Massachusetts, is a region of tremendous variety. When you move northward from Rome toward Florence via Siena, you encounter a region of bare forbidding mountains, deserts standing on edge, which give way to green wooded hills. Ancient soft-hued towns crown them. As you approach the Arno, the valleys widen and the soil becomes more fertile. It is a foretaste of the lush country you would cross if you turned toward Arezzo. After you have crossed the Arno and left Florence behind, there is another rich area, the Mugello. Farthest north of all, at the limits of the province, the scenery changes abruptly. The mountains lose their soft curves, and stab bare rocks into the sky. Their shapes are characteristic of the Alps, and they are indeed called the Apuan Alps. Some of them are shining in the sun, for their flanks are marble.

The individualism of the Etruscan cities, always resistant to any unification more binding than a temporary confederation against a common enemy, was inherited by Tuscany in the form of independent city-states. Some of them were simple continuations of Etruscan cities—Arezzo, for instance. (Florence was not an Etruscan city, but its suburb, Fiesole, was.) Each of the great Tuscan cities extended its sway over the surrounding countryside, with the smaller towns and villages it contained, until it reached territories where a neighboring city was doing the same. Then, sooner or later, they fought. A series of Florentine victories (interrupted occasionally by a stinging defeat) gradually established the domination of Florence over her rivals, and the Grand Duchy of Tuscany was created.

But the individuality of the different cities remained, and has been transmitted to the nine modern provinces into which Tuscany is now divided, most of them congruent with ancient divisions. They are, along the coast, south to north, Grosseto, Livorno (Leghorn), Pisa, Lucca and Massa-Carrara. Moving inland from Grosseto, you come to Siena, and then to Arezzo, Tuscany's Far East, cradling the province of Florence, just to the north, in their arms. Florence does the same for Pistoia, pinched between herself and Lucca.

*   *   *

The domination of Tuscany by Florence (Firenze) placed the region under the aegis of the city which to this day eats by choice, not necessity, more simply than any other on the mainland. Tuscany as a whole prefers natural food, undisguised by elaborate artifice in the kitchen. Tuscan impatience with complications goes all the way back to what has been called "the sober Etruscan spirit."

It may have been an innate predisposition to sobriety inherited from the Etruscans which influenced Renaissance Florence, but in any case the sort of society which developed there was hostile to excess. Whenever the *populo grasso* (the fat people, meaning the wealthy) showed a tendency to develop extravagant eating and spending habits, the outraged sentiments of the majority applied curbs to them. In 1250 the *primo populo* or *populo vecchio*, the old population, dressed simply and lived on coarse food at little expense. *Firenze dentro della cerchia antica . . . si stava in pace sobria e pudica* was a poet's description of 13th-century Florence: "Florence within her ancient walls stood at peace, sober and modest." As Florentine cloth, eagerly demanded throughout the world, began to make Florence rich, there was a tendency toward higher living. It inspired Dante to consign gluttons and winebibbers to the second circle of hell, where they lay mired in mud, suffering the pangs of hunger and thirst. His countrymen must have agreed with his scarification of excess, for simplicity returned again.

Florence did offer examples of spectacular public festivals, especially under the Medici, but while the Florentines were generous hosts, they were frugal at home. "There was a streak of austerity in Florentine life throughout the Renaissance," wrote Professor Nicolai Rubinstein of the University of London. "The utilitarian outlook of 14th-century merchants, with its caution and frugality, survived in the more pleasure-loving and sumptuous life of the 15th-century patrician, and merged imperceptibly with aristocratic ideals and ambitions."

The Tuscan character was sober, but not dull; we would only need to look at Renaissance art to realize that. But it provided the measure which restrained the artists within reasonable limits, lacking which they might have exploded into the baroque, as indeed they eventually did, but in Rome, not in Florence. Nor was it a narrow soberness, but rather a keenness of mind which can only operate effectively when a certain discipline exists. We recognize that the Florentine was a many-faceted character in the term "Renaissance man," which signifies versatility, and finds its leading prototype in Leonardo da Vinci, painter, sculptor, architect, writer and man of science. If the Tuscan had been simply sober, but without discrimination, he would have adopted a utilitarian attitude toward food, eating because one must eat to live, but without interest in the viands that enabled him to do so. On the contrary he possessed, and possesses, finesse. He wanted quality, and his character saved him from confusing quality with extravagance. When he emerged from the heaviness and gluttony of the Middle Ages, whose cooking was a prolongation of that of the Roman Empire, he did not return to that Empire as an exemplar of the classical world of which he was again becoming conscious, but to the austere Republic, with its simpler healthier food.

Florentines ate only two meals a day (like the Etruscans before them), the first at nine or ten in the morning, the second just before dark. The menus were simple. Not much meat was eaten; pasta had already become the *pièce de résistance* for many meals. A middle-class dinner might begin with fruit, a melon, for instance, and perhaps end with it too, unless the opener was salad and the closer cheese. In between, the main dish, if it were not pasta, might be *fegatelli* (a thin pancake stuffed with chopped liver), or pigeon, or perhaps nothing except bean or squash soup poured over slices of bread—not a cheap dish, since bread was expensive. On gala days, the main course might be kid and there would be a sweet dessert. The wealthy would eat more expensive main dishes (trout, or thrushes, or pheasant, or a stew), but the meal would be no longer.

With the opening of the 15th century, there was another offensive of luxury and another reaction against it. Laws were passed restricting the kinds and quantities of food which might be served at any single meal. Dinners were prohibited for more than 40 guests, who could be served only "three courses or trenchers" (an exception was made for knightings, when 100 guests were permitted, but still no more than three courses). Lorenzo the Magnificent did not consider a mere 40 guests sufficient to celebrate his marriage fittingly, so he managed to entertain 200 by giving five separate banquets from Sunday to Tuesday, each of which strained the legal limits.

Sumptuary legislation has never been very successful in the absence of popular assent (and when there is popular agreement, it is hardly necessary), but in Renaissance Florence majority opinion was in favor of sobriety in eating. Tuscan suspicion of the degenerative effects of luxury may lie at the origin of the common Tuscan saying, *"Si stava meglio quando si stava peggio,"*—"We were better off when we were worse off." Professor Rubinstein suggests that Savonarola's "denunciations of worldliness found a ready response in [the Florentines'] traditional inclinations towards austerity and simplicity of manners."

It may well have been Savonarola, "the gravedigger of Florence" (though the contemporary account does not give the name of the sermonizer), who shouted from his pulpit: "It's not enough for you to eat your pasta fried. No! You think you have to add garlic to it, and when you eat ravioli, it's not enough to boil it in a pot and eat it in its juice, you have to fry it in another pan and cover it with cheese!" It was in any case Savonarola who imposed the severest restrictions of all, toward the end of the 15th century, until the Florentines, wearied of fanaticism, bestowed on him the martyrdom he had so sedulously sought, appropriately by roasting him. There was of course a reaction from his reign of Puritanism, especially in the way of feminine adornment, but the 17th-century Florentine nevertheless did not throw himself into an orgy of eating. Instead, he followed the precepts of Platina, whose new cookbook (1610) counseled moderation.

New foods were reaching Florence. America had been discovered for a century now, and some of its products were being brought back as curiosities. The first to gain favor was the haricot bean, a native of the New World. Some of them were given to Pope Clement VII, who sent a few to a canon of Florence, Pietro Valeriano. Valeriano planted them in pots, tasted the result, and recommended them enthusiastically to Alessandro dei Medici. Two countries became acquainted with the vegetable by this operation, for Alessandro gave a few small bags of beans to his sister Catherine when she left for France to marry the future Henri II. But Tuscany profited most. To this day Tuscans are referred to by other Italians, not necessarily with complimentary intent, as *mangiafagioli*, "bean eaters."

Other New World foods were slower to catch on. The tomato, ubiquitous in Italian cooking today, was not received with any notable enthusiasm. It had reached Italy at least by 1554, when a description of it was published under the name of *pomo d'oro* (it is *pomodoro* today, golden apple). The first tomato the Italians saw was indeed yellow, and not much larger than a cherry. It took two centuries for the Italians to decide to eat tomatoes, and even at that they were the first Europeans to take the risk.

The pimento (introduced to Europe from Peru by the

conquistadores) was equally slow, but the potato, although it was one of the first vegetables to be sent back from the New World, was the slowest of all. Italians grew potatoes in the flower garden as early as 1580, but hesitated to put them on the table. They had dismissed them at first sight as "small truffles," and consequently called them *tartufoli*. They have dropped that name now, but the potato's identification as a truffle persists in the German word for it, *Kartoffel*. Even today the Italians have not really taken the potato to their bosoms.

As for maize (sweet corn in America), there is as far as I know no evidence that Florentines knew it at this time. It got a bad start. Columbus's sailors ate some on board ship on their way home, and didn't like it.

In retrospect, it may seem that Italians were very slow about benefiting by the New World foods, but there are few habits more obdurate to change than eating habits. The new foods the Florentines were accepting fully in the 1600s were the gifts of the Saracens, who had been in certain parts of Italy for eight centuries, while the Crusaders had been bringing back their foods for five.

Florence was eating regularly the most important single contribution of the Saracens—rice, which was being grown on a large scale in Piedmont thanks to cooperatively organized irrigation. Perhaps the Florentines themselves might have thought the most important new food was sugar, obtainable through Venice. They put it in everything, including the rice, which was eaten chiefly sweetened, for dessert. They also showed special appreciation of certain vegetables, like spinach, artichokes (Catherine dei Medici liked artichoke-heart fritters) and cauliflower, which had not yet become naturalized in Italy, but was imported from the Middle East.

Along with new foods, the Florentines had a new cooking utensil—the double boiler. This is called a *bain-marie*

(Mary's bath) in French, a name which baffled the usually well informed Académie des Gastronomes, which in its encyclopedic dictionary notes that "this method of heating being gentler than heating by fire, certain linguists suppose that this gentleness is expressed by 'the gentle name of Mary.' The supposition is all the more probable because the expression goes back to the 14th century, a period of great devotion to Mary." The learned academicians should have looked southward. *Bain-marie* is simply translated from *bagno maria,* and the Mary in question is Maria di Cleofa, who, under the name of Cleopatra the Wise, practiced alchemy and invented the double boiler by chance in the course of her experiments. She described it in her *Trattato della distillazione,* which dealt with the related arts of medicine, magic and cooking.

With a wide variety of foods at their disposition and a knowledge of all the basic techniques of the kitchen, the Florentines of the early 1600s ate well. One popular dish of the times was *sopa*—sliced toasted bread in consommé, with eggs, grated cheese and cinnamon. In the same category were *carabaccia* (also spelled *carabazada*), onion soup; *minestra gialla all'imperiale,* a cream soup with saffron and almonds; *suppa di sparagi in sapor giallo,* asparagus soup with saffron, pine nuts and pistachio nuts; *suppa dorata,* with eggs and saffron; and *suppa di capirotta,* chicken soup.

Fish included all kinds of shellfish, various Mediterranean fish cooked in wine sauce, *anguilla rivestita con camellino* (roast eel with a sauce of bread crumbs and almonds), and *potaccio di pesce all'ongaresca,* something like the modern fish stew of Leghorn.

In the way of poultry, one of the most popular Renaissance dishes was duck with lemon or orange sauce, usually thought of today as a French dish; actually it was not only a Renaissance dish in Italy, but an ancient Roman one. *Pollastri repleni* was simply stuffed chicken, but *pollastri af-*

finocchiati was roast chicken flavored with fennel seeds.

Grilled meat, spitted meat and veal steaks were eaten with pasta. Loin of pork was already known by the name still given it in Tuscany today—*arista*—and had been since the middle of the 15th century. One might be tempted to explain it simply as a deformation of the word *arrosto*, roast, if it were not for the story told about the origin of this term, which is more or less confirmed by the fact that it is applied only to pork. According to this account a Greek archimandrite was served roast loin of pork at a banquet and found it so good that he cried out: *"Aristos!"* (best). The name stuck. *Roso in cisame* was roast veal, served in slices covered with a sauce based on hard-boiled eggs. Liver was sautéed in butter with raisins and cherries, and thickly peppered. Hare was marinated in wine and vinegar and then cooked slowly in the marinating liquid, along with plenty of onions and spices.

The Florentines had almost all the vegetables we know today with the exception of those New World products which had not caught the Renaissance fancy as quickly as the bean. Broccoli had been developed, and so had Savoy cabbage, also known as Milan cabbage, names which underline the Italian origin of this variety; but Brussels sprouts had not yet been born. There was a salad green known as *barba de' Cappuccini*, Capuchins' beard, and *cardone*, edible thistles. Above all there were the *piselli novelli*, the tiny sweet peas which Catherine dei Medici took to France where they were naturalized as *petits pois*. Tuscan fields produced most of these vegetables, but Florence also imported them from other regions, especially Lombardy and Piedmont—and asparagus, of course, from Ravenna.

Other popular Renaissance dishes included *torta manfreda*, a tart of liver and a mixture of different meats; *blasmangeri*, an early variety of risotto, which could be enlivened with different condiments, so long as they did not change its color; *torta di funghi*, a *sformato* of mushrooms with egg, cheese, and bread crumbs soaked in milk; *torta di fagiani e pizzoni*, a pheasant and pigeon pasty; *ova affrittellate alla Medici*, small spinach omelets; and *torta di herbe*, a vegetable tart, like the modern Genoese *torta pasqualina*, Easter tart.

And the Florentine sweet tooth! In their enthusiasm for cane sugar, the Florentines put it even into macaroni, converting it into a dessert; and they did not even wait for the dessert course: there were sweet hors d'oeuvres, such as a cake called *berlingozzo*, which was a popular start for a meal. Dessert pastries proper did not appear in Florence before the 16th century, so when Catherine dei Medici took her pastry cooks with her to France, she was introducing to that country confections which were also still new in hers. *Torta balconata* (cake in tiers) was one favorite—pastry containing almonds and candied fruits. *Malmona* was not pastry; it utilized not only the sugar of the Saracens but also their rice—it was an orange-flavored rice pudding. A very popular sweet, accessible to all since it did not require the still expensive sugar, was *zonclada* or *zanzegha*, made of cottage cheese, honey, candied fruits, pine nuts and pistachio nuts, in pie crust.

Since sugar was so expensive, one form of ostentation was to use it lavishly. Florentines, as we know, were not given to ostentation, but there were exceptions—for instance, Catherine dei Medici and Maria dei Medici, both of whom had inherited the spirit of Lorenzo the Magnificent. Catherine was a glutton; a contemporary chronicler reported that she ate so heavily at the marriage of Mlle. de Martigues that "she just missed kicking the bucket." Maria, on the occasion of her reception at the Palace of the Popes in Avignon in 1601, gave a banquet of which the most admired attraction was the *trionfi di tavola*, the triumphs of the table, in this case statuettes of birds, fish, animals, ancient Emperors, and gods and goddesses, all made of sugar. One of the guests on viewing them exclaimed: "Italy is the mother of all the arts!"—within careful earshot of the Queen of France. At this period, the sugar table ornaments must have represented a small fortune, but of course they could be broken up and put into pastry later.

Though the Florentines knew good cooking, it was not ordinarily extravagant cooking. Some of the heavily spiced dishes of the Middle Ages stayed on the menu, along with rich wine sauces. Elaborate dishes might occasionally appear on the tables of the wealthy. There was a whiff of the Roman Empire about *pavo repleno con la brognata*, peacock stuffed with prunes; but the peacock went out when the turkey came in. Catherine dei Medici left a few notable recipes, hardly representative of everyday cooking. Among them was a dish named for her family, guinea hen Medici, and another which was known as royal carp when she introduced it to the French court, where it was somewhat modified, and rebaptized Carp of the House of France. It became a traditional dish of the French royal family; perhaps it still is.

The use of wine in both of these recipes reminds us that Tuscany had been wine country since Etruscan times and of course still was (and is). You can see today, in some of the Renaissance palaces of Florence, a small ground-floor window near the door. It was the wine window. Through it the concierge sold to all comers the wine of his patrician employer, who was not too proud to profit from a universal demand. Florence drank still wines as a rule, but a contemporary writer reports the serving of a sparkling wine at a banquet, making something of a point of it, from which we may deduce that it was rare.

The Florentines occasionally went overboard when it came to liqueurs, as you can see from these two recipes of the time:

Rossoli: "Soak 250 grams of red rose petals, 125 grams of orange blossoms, eight grams of cinnamon, and 30 grams of cloves for five days in 10 liters of 22-degree alcohol. Distill. Then add five kilograms of sugar and 30 grams of jasmine alcohol."

Elixir of the Popes (so called because it became a papal drink beginning with Leo X, otherwise Giovanni dei Medici): "Crush together in an earthenware vessel thirty grams of cinnamon bark, five grams of cloves, and eight grams of vanilla. Pour over it two liters of a good eau de vie. Let it stand three days, stirring it slowly twice a day. Filter through a fine strainer. Separately, soak ten grams of pulverized cochineal and 250 grams of crystallized alum in fifty grams of distilled rose water, also for three days, then decant and strain as for the first preparation. On the day when the two preparations are to be strained, prepare a syrup from two kilograms of sugar and the requisite amount of water. Let it cool completely. Mix in the first preparation, and after it the second. Add 125 grams of orange-blossom water, and allow the whole to stand for three days in an earthenware vessel, stirring it slowly twice a day. Strain, bottle, and close the bottle hermetically. After three months you can open it. Drink a small glass every morning."

It was in Florence that the first cooking academy since the time of the ancient Romans was formed. Its membership was limited to twelve, and they were all artists, the most celebrated being Andrea del Sarto. It was called the Compagnia del Paiolo, the Company of the Cauldron; each member had to create a new dish for every meeting.

Lorenzo the Magnificent himself composed Carnival songs for the pastry cooks and the olive oil makers. Less illustrious writers also let themselves go on the subject of food. A poet named Mulsa penned a paean of praise for figs, while Benedetto Varchi took time off from his historical works and his political activities to treat the more prosaic subject of boiled eggs. Teofilo Felegno threw Tuscan sobriety to the winds when he described Parnassus as a vast pantry.

"There were rivers full of soup," he dreamed, "which ran together into a lake; and there was a sea of stew, in which, plying to and fro, were thousands of boats made of pastry. The shores were of tender fresh butter; and on them were hundreds of saucepans, smoking to the clouds with ravioli, macaroni and other delights. As for the nymphs, they live on the top of the high mountain, scraping cheese on graters drilled with holes."

Francesco de Barbareino brings us back to Tuscan practicality with the sage advice to wives which he included in his *Costume e Reggimento di Donne:*

"Learn what foods please your husband for dinner and supper, and see that he gets them; and even if you dislike the food that he prefers, you should pretend to like it, for a woman should comply with her husband's pleasure."

Amen.

Florentine cooking begins with careful attention to the selection of raw materials of the highest quality, and continues by cooking them with a minimum of sauces and seasonings. It is spare home cooking, hearty and healthy, subtle in its deliberate eschewing of sophistication, which is perhaps the highest sophistication of all.

Two factors are universally propitious to a good cuisine: the presence of a high-quality cooking fat and the presence of wine. Tuscany produces the finest olive oil in Italy; and while all Italy is wine country, Tuscany is one of the three top regions of the peninsula. It is favored also by being predominantly agricultural country, capable of producing its own food and eating it at its freshest.

The fertility of Tuscan soil has been proverbial since it was Etruscan soil. Besides the vine, the basic crops today are cereals, especially wheat. Rich forage is available for meat-producing animals. The sugar beet is grown extensively in the alluvial lowlands of the principal valleys. Tuscan fruit is of high quality.

If you ask any Italian which dish he associates first of all with Florence, nine times out of ten the answer will be *bistecca alla fiorentina* (or *costata alla fiorentina*, which is another cut treated the same way). Steak may not seem sufficiently exceptional to qualify as a regional specialty, but this one is. You cannot get a Florentine steak anywhere else, not even in Tuscany, except in Siena, unless the restaurant where you order a *fiorentina* has bought its meat already cut from Florence. There is no standard way of cutting up a steer in Italy. It varies from city to city. What Florence gives you is basically a T-bone steak, a rarity in Europe. It is a thick chunk of tender Chianina beef, weighing a trifle over a pound, including the bone, grilled over charcoal, seasoned with olive oil, salt and pepper, and nobody asks you how you want it. You get it rare, very rare—*al sangue*, bloody, is the Italian term for it. If you don't like it that way, ask for it *ben cotta*, well cooked. With luck you may get it that way, though you will be considered perverse. It is usually served with small Tuscan beans (*toscanelli*), and perhaps garnished with lemon wedges.

The one Italian in ten who doesn't name steak as the top Florentine dish will almost certainly vote for *pollo alla diavola*. This is chicken, split open, flattened, and grilled, which you may have heard about as a Roman dish. It is—but not when it is served with a ginger sauce, as in Florence. Florence also fries the breast fillets, dusted lightly with flour, in butter, for once forsaking its cherished olive oil, or marinates cut-up pieces of chicken for two hours in oil, lemon juice, salt, pepper and parsley, then dips them in beaten egg, and deep fries them in olive oil.

You may occasionally run into two other nominees for

43

top place in Florence, *arista* and *trippa alla fiorentina*. When *arista* is *alla fiorentina*, the chief ingredient which distinguishes it from loin of pork cooked elsewhere is rosemary in its seasoning. Garlic and cloves are also used, all three inserted into the meat. It is roasted slowly and basted with water, not oil. *Trippa alla fiorentina* is tripe stewed with tomatoes in a meat sauce rich with herbs, sprinkled with Parmesan cheese.

Besides these headliners, Florentine specialties include the following:

Minestrone alla fiorentina is flavored with *soffritto*, which in this case means a sauce of pork, red peppers, chicken giblets and tomato sauce; in other contexts *soffritto* usually means something else, most often a sauce base made from chopped onions, celery and carrots browned in oil and/or butter. *Uova alla fiorentina* are lightly poached eggs bedded on spinach, which has been first boiled and then sautéed lightly in butter, in a buttered baking dish. Mornay sauce is poured over it, then it is sprinkled with grated cheese and bread crumbs, and baked in the oven. Florence's favorite pasta is *rigatoni*, the large ribbed tubular variety, with veal ragù. *Tagliolini* is Florence's name for the thin ribbon pasta called *trenette* in Genoa and *bonnarelli* in Rome. Risotto comes with chicken giblets.

Stracotto alla fiorentina is an Italian cousin of pot roast, *cazzuola di montone alla fiorentina*, mutton stew containing, besides the mutton, a few samples of minor parts of the pig, white beans or pasta, tomato sauce, an onion with a clove in it, a carrot, garlic, herbs, and a sprinkling of bread crumbs fried in butter on top. *Agnello girato al fuoco di legna* means lamb roasted on a spit over charcoal. Florentines also enjoy calf's leg in sauce, *zampa alla fiorentina*, while a characteristic combination is pigeon with veal. The peculiarity of the Florentine way with beef liver is that after it has been sautéed in olive oil, tomato purée is added to the cooking juices toward the end of the process. Almost every place in Italy has its own variant of *salame* (salami, the form universally used in English, is the plural), and that of Florence is of pure pork and pork fat, both cut into large pieces. When fennel seeds are added, it becomes *finocchiona*.

Game is popular—hare with sweet-and-sour sauce, roast wild boar in rich gravy. You meet *fritto misto* everywhere in Italy, but the Florentine version is particularly luscious. Ingredients vary, but you are likely to find on your plate croquettes, brains, sweetbreads, artichokes, cauliflower, zucchini (summer squash), lamb cutlets and chicken, rolled in egg and bread crumbs and deep-fried in fine Lucca oil.

There is no dearth of fish in Florentine restaurants, but it is rare to find it described as *alla fiorentina*—the province of Florence has no seacoast. The only exception that comes to mind is cod. *Baccalà alla fiorentina* is not much of an exception, for it is made of preserved salt cod. Practically every Italian region has its own salt cod dish, but what distinguishes this one is (a) the cut-up pieces of cod are rolled in flour before cooking; (b) there is plenty of garlic; and (c) the cod is liberally doused in tomato sauce. Other similar dishes duplicate one or two of these characteristics, but so far as I know Florence is the only place where you can get all three together. *Filetti di merluzzo alla fiorentina* is *fresh* cod. Its fillets are simmered in a skillet in red wine and seasoning, and then baked in the oven, bedded on spinach, lapped in Mornay sauce, and sprinkled with grated Parmesan cheese.

Vegetable dishes are numerous. Let us note only *asparagi alla fiorentina*, boiled asparagus tossed in butter with salt, pepper and Parmesan cheese, and served under a blanket of fried eggs; *tortino di carciofi*, quartered artichokes cooked in oil and then doubled into a rich omelet (*frittata*); and *funghi alla fiorentina*. Funghi means, of course, mushrooms, but the local word for the Florentine variety is *faggio*. It seems identical with the French *cèpe*, the flap mushroom which the French prefer to cook in peanut oil, while the Florentines use olive oil.

A favorite Florentine dessert is *castagnaccio*, a cake made from chestnut flour, raisins and pine nuts, cooked in oil. *Stiacciata fiorentina* might be described as pie crust without the pie. It reminds me of the cinnamon sticks my mother used to make from leftover pie-crust dough, which was placed flat in a pie pan like a bottom crust, dusted with sugar and cinnamon, and after cooking, cut into strips, and thus converted into a sort of simple elongated cookie. *Stiacciata* dough, which is leavened, is cooked about the same way, but is a more complicated mixture; among other things, it contains egg, and is flavored with grated orange peel. And perhaps mention should be made here of the hard cookies which in Florence you will see old men dunking in red wine to soften them before biting into them.

Florence dominates its province so completely that there is virtually no local specialty worth mentioning for any other place within it, with the sole exception of Prato's *mortadella della finocchiona*, a boloney-like sausage delicately flavored with fennel. Florence's dominion extends also over the small province of Pistoia, west of the northern half of the province of Florence, which boasts no dishes not found in the Florentine or general Tuscan repertories, though it does make candied almonds for the rest of the country. Besides almonds, Pistoia also makes some pecorino (sheep's milk cheese).

The other two inland provinces, Siena and Arezzo, share with Florence a common asset which shapes the eating of all three—what Titus Livy called the *opulenta arva Etruria*, the rich plains of Etruria. When Livy referred to the *Etrusci campi*, the Etruscan fields, he meant the stretch from Fiesole, in the province of Florence, to Arezzo, which gives its own name to the province of which it is the capital; the westernmost band of this sweep of fertile fields, slopes and valleys lies in the province of Siena.

It is curious that Siena has so little to offer of its own, apart from general Tuscan dishes. On historical grounds, one would expect more independence from the city-state which was the last to yield to Florence, in 1557. Although only 45 miles south of the Tuscan capital, it was old enough, rich enough and stubborn enough so that it might have been expected to possess its own distinct traditions in all fields, including gastronomy. Its device of the she-wolf and the twins recalls the legend that it was founded by Senus, the son of Remus. You can realize Siena's medieval splendor by visiting its old walls, still standing today, and above all a work of art unique in the world, the pavement of its cathedral, covered with mosaics and linear designs. Yet it has had to borrow from Florence and from the rest of Tuscany the food it eats. Its own gastronomic prowess seems to be limited to desserts. "I once talked to a Florentine," Sean O'Faolain wrote in a travel article, "to whom, as far as I could discover, Siena meant nothing except the place from which one got, at Christmas time, a special kind of cake called *panforte*." *Panforte* (which means strong bread) is a rich fruitcake, whose ingredients are flour, butter, eggs, almonds, walnuts, candied fruits (especially melon and lemon) and honey, their contributions dominated by one or another of various natural fruit flavors, such as orange or lemon. It is a direct descendant of a medieval spiced sweetened bread, embodying honey and bits of dried fruit and figs. Other sweets in the same category are *cavallucci*, *copate* and *ricciarelli*. *Copate* are little cakes almost as thin as wafers, *ricciarelli* are almond cookies, and I shall be happy to pay another visit to Siena to track down *cavallucci*, which so far I know only from hearsay.

Arezzo, where Tuscany pushes farthest inland, is another story altogether. One of the twelve major cities of Etruria, the birthplace of Maecenas, its history reaches far back into the past. In 205 B.C., when Scipio was preparing to invade Africa and asked Rome's Etruscan allies for help, Arezzo provided 120,000 bushels of wheat.

Perched on a hilltop, as so many ancient Etruscan cities were, for defense, the city of Arezzo overlooks a fertile basin propitious to cereals, vines and fruit trees—Arezzo's particular specialty is cherries. Its valleys are tremendously fruitful. The Casentino valley produces small juicy hams; its own type of salame; and a local variety of pecorino cheese. The Casentino and its tributaries teem with delicately flavored trout, while the slopes which rise from the valley are covered with walnut and chestnut trees, whose nuts are noted for their tastiness. Pecorino is made in the Tiber valley too, the best chickens in Italy are raised in the Arno valley, giant melons are grown in the Chiana valley. There is much game in the province, which accounts for Arezzo's *pappardelle con la lepre,* flat squares of egg pasta baked in a sauce made from a hare which has hung at least two days. This somewhat heavy pasta is also used in *pappardelle all' aretina,* where it accompanies duck cooked with a considerable variety of vegetables, ham, some of the duck's innards, and nutmeg. Arezzo also has its own special fashion of preparing *porchetta,* roast young pig.

The greatest glory of Arezzo province is the Chianina steer, which provides the beef for Florence's steaks. "There is no good beef in Italy," I have been told again and again; but it is not true. Not only does Italy raise beef cattle, it raises one of the best breeds in the world. The Chianina is so exclusively a meat producer that many Chianina cows give barely enough milk for their calves. Its merits as a beef producer are so great that Chianina bulls have been demanded for crossing by other countries, even including that great beef producer, Argentina.

The merits of the Chianina are these:

1. It produces lean beef, which dresses out at 58 to 60 percent of the animal's dead weight, containing very little fat, none of it in the meat itself.

2. Its growth is rapid. A year-old bull should weigh over 1,000 pounds, a two-year-old often reaches 2,000.

3. This growth is precocious not only in weight, but in kind. The Chianina begins to develop red meat as early as six months. It used to be slaughtered at the age of 20 to 24 months, which has now been reduced to 15 to 17. Other breeds at this age would give only "baby beef," somewhere in between veal and beef, with the merits of neither. The Chianina killed at this age is somewhat similarly named; it is sold not as *manzo*, beef, but as *vitellone*, which, on the analogy of "baby beef" you might translate as "adult veal." The distinction in Italian, however, is not based on the nature of the meat, but on other considerations. *Vitello* (veal) means milk-fed veal. Once the animal begins to graze, it becomes *vitellone*, and may remain that for as long as three years, provided it is not used as a work animal, as many Italian cattle are. If it is, its meat after maturity is *manzo*.

Massively built, pure white, the Chianina in appearance is not unlike the buffaloes you see grazing along the coast below Naples, but they are not related. One important difference is that the buffalo, originally imported from India about 600 A.D., is raised for milk rather than for meat. Nevertheless, the hump on the back of the Chianina and the heavy dewlap which falls from its throat and forelegs, give it a buffalo-like appearance.

The Chianina is the oldest, the heaviest (nearly 4,000 pounds) and the tallest cow in the world. The Chiana valley tends to run to marshland when not properly drained; hence the cattle, like marsh birds, developed long stilt-like legs. It has remained virtually unchanged for at least 3,000 years, the same animal which the ancient Romans sacrificed to the gods. "*Umbria boves progenerat vastos et albos,*" Columella wrote—"Umbria produces tremendous white cattle." His geography seems to have been shaky, for the very name of the breed locates its place of origin, the Chiana valley in the province of Arezzo and the region of Tuscany. Umbria does raise some Chianinas now, an overflow from Tuscany, and even the region next westward, The Marches, has a slightly different breed developed from the Chianina. There are a few Chianinas also in the province of Siena, which is grazed by the Chiana river as it leaves Arezzo.

The coastal provinces of Tuscany look chiefly to the sea for their special dishes, but Grosseto, the southernmost, has another string to its bow. It pushes far inland, and its back country is rich in game. A hunter's and fisherman's paradise, its greatest successes are with fish and game. The fields between the thickets and the sea are productive too, growing cereals and vegetables.

More interesting in many ways than the capital city is Orbetello, a good example of the historical compartmentation characteristic of Italy. Orbetello was Spanish territory from 1557 to 1713, the Spanish Praesidium, to which was added in 1602 the island of Elba, now included in the province of Leghorn. The geography of Orbetello is peculiar too. The city lies at the entrance to what is almost an island, a flipper-shaped peninsula which clings precariously to the mainland by four strips of earth interrupted by two lakes and a lagoon. Archeologists have puzzled over the purpose of ancient tanks found there, but the generally accepted theory now is that they were fish traps into which were lured, and stored for the tables of the Roman Emperors, the delicate gray mullets on which they doted. Orbetello draws from its lagoon not only semi-landlocked fish, but also its great specialty, particularly fat tasty eels called *capitoni.*

Most of them end up in Rome or Naples, where eel is a traditional Christmas Eve dish. Porto Ercole (the port of Hercules), on the other side of the peninsula, was once a quiet fishing village, but it has lately been invaded by money-laden visitors who seem determined to subject it to the horrible fate of St. Tropez. The small fishing fleet is dwindling, despite the presence of a convenient cannery. Porto Ercole is where Caravaggio died; he had taken refuge there from the laws of Tuscany, which could not pursue him into the Spanish-ruled enclave. Porto Ercole still retains two 15th-century Spanish fortresses, and Orbetello also has part of its Spanish fortifications; but there are no traces of Spanish influence in its cooking.

Although Grosseto has lost Elba, the largest island of the Tuscan archipelago, it has retained the second largest, Giglio.

The Romans appreciated Giglio and built vacation villas there. They called it Lily Island, Agilium, but the French novelist Stendhal had another name for it—the Mermaids' Isle. The islanders' comment on this is that Stendhal appreciated not only Giglio in general, but in particular the local red wine, which is full-bodied and authoritative. After taking on a little of it, anyone is likely to see mermaids. The island's *zuppa di pesce alla gigliese* contains no mermaids, but seems to combine every other fish of the area, with the accent on baby octopus. Cold lobster, bathed in olive oil and sprinkled with freshly ground pepper, is another island specialty.

Back on the mainland, the essential feature of Grosseto province, geographically and gastronomically, is the Maremma, a strip of land 15 to 20 miles wide lying along the coast. For some 1,500 years after the Barbarian invasions, the Maremma was marshland, whose rare inhabitants waged a perpetual losing battle against malaria. Yet it had been noted for its fertility in Etruscan and Roman times, and when a railroad was drilled through it, the constructors found out why: their work uncovered the underground canals which in ancient days had carried off surplus water. Leopold II of Tuscany resumed drainage in the first half of the 19th century, and the Maremma has since been freed of malaria and is again habitable. It is good hunting country, providing not only small game, like birds and rabbits, but also deer and wild boar.

The Maremma is the most important single source for food of the province, as you are likely to suspect if you read a local restaurant menu. The dishes it names may include *arselle alla maremmana*, which, if you believe the dictionaries, is a shellfish which has been extinct since prehistoric times; but in this case it is only the local name (used also in Genoa and Sardinia) for the same clams which are called *vongole* in Naples. The game animals of the region offer *coratelle di cinghiala alla maremmana*, the heart, spleen, liver and lungs of wild boar, stewed in a thick sauce; *lepre alla maremmana*, hare in sweet-and-sour sauce; and *uccelletti alla maremmana*, small game birds. *Tortelli alla maremmana* is a variety of stuffed pasta. No translation is needed for *bistecca maremmana*. *Cosciotto di suino alla maremmana* is the local ham. And *chiocciole di Maremma* are snails.

The Maremma is not the only region in Grosseto capable of devising its own dishes. Other provincial specialties include a mixture of octopus and mussels, cooked in oil; stuffed mussels called *telline* in Tuscany, though *cozze* in most other places; smoked marinated eels from the Orbetello lagoon; red mullet from Ansedonia, an Etruscan city near Orbetello which still has its ancient walls of colossal stone blocks; turtle soup; crab soup; *tagliatelle* (ribbon pasta), with a mixture of seafood and spring vegetables in its dressing; risotto with shrimps; black risotto, with inkfish; mussel omelet; a fish soup called "Etruscan," which in this country it might well be; pheasant in a variety of forms:

roasted, used to make consommé, cooked in a paper bag, served cold in aspic, or in a salad; wild boar, roasted, or stewed in sweet-and-sour sauce; and *pappardelle con la lepre all ' uso di Grosseto*, the local change rung on the Arezzo dish described above.

They like picturesque names in Grosseto. Dishes of which I have heard, but of which I have no personal experience, include *misto di Nettuno*, Neptune's mixture, which it is fairly safe to bet is seafood; *pomodori di mare*, sea tomatoes, an hors d'oeuvre, but of what kind?; and *quaglie dei poeti*, poets' quail, which of course might be quail, but which sounds suspiciously like one of those sarcastic names, like Scotch woodcock or prairie oyster.

The province of Leghorn is a narrow strip of coast never wider than 15 miles, for Pisa, which has only a toehold on the sea, cuts around in back of it and deprives it of a hinterland. Leghorn is a comparatively new city for this area, for its development occurred only at the end of the 16th century, under Ferdinand I dei Medici, who may have taken a particularly benevolent interest in the area because for once Florence did not have to fight for it; it was purchased from the Genoese in 1422, a good buy, for the port of Pisa had silted up, and Leghorn thus became the chief harbor of Tuscany. It is perhaps its cool refreshing summer breeze, the *maestrale* (the same word as *mistral*, the French wind considered in that country as maddening rather than refreshing), which since the 18th century has been attracting English expatriates, always good at sniffing out choice spots abroad, preferably inexpensive. Among them were Shelley (a vegetarian), who in 1819 wrote most of *The Cenci* in the Villa Valsovano, and Tobias Smollett, who died in Leghorn.

The situation of Leghorn naturally restricts its specialties to those of the sea, with the exception of several types of pasta; *coniglio alla livornese*, which is rabbit sautéed in oil with tomato sauce, garlic, onion, and minced anchovy fillets; a sort of dry flat bun called a *schiacciata;* and candied lemon. Famed throughout Italy is Leghorn's prime culinary creation, *cacciucco alla livornese.* This is one of the great fish soups of the world, despite the fact that it is made from coarse fish which would be rejected for most other purposes because they bristle with bones, while some are adorned with more or less venomous spines—like the *scorfano,* the Italian equivalent for the French rascasse, the one fish considered essential for the Marseilles *bouillabaisse.* The endearing character of the *scorfano,* which is related to the American sculpin, may be divined from the figurative meaning of its name—monster. Like *bouillabaisse, cacciucco* is made of a mixture of many fish, likely to vary every time it is put together, even by the same cook, but it must contain rock fish. Onions, garlic, parsley and tomato sauce go into it also. Some cooks use other herbs, occasionally a little octopus, and more rarely lobster or crab. It is generally agreed that it should be made with dry white wine, but I have seen an Italian recipe which specified red.

Leghorn's second pride after *cacciucco* is red mullet stewed in a casserole with a thin sauce of tomato, olive oil and herbs (*triglie alla livornese*). A third dish whose reputation has spread beyond the provincial borders is made from salt fish—*baccalà alla livornese,* cod floured and doused with tomato sauce, cooked in a casserole, and served garnished with boiled potatoes, quartered. Less known elsewhere is *tonno alla livornese,* slices from the belly of a tuna, first fried in oil, then stewed in fresh tomato sauce. There is also a Leghorn punch, strong *espresso* coffee with a tablespoon of rum, sugar, and a twist of lemon peel. It is supposed to keep the cold out during the winter, even if the *maestrale,* then biting rather than refreshing, is blowing.

Administratively the island of Elba is part of Leghorn, but it belongs to a different world. It was a source of riches for the Etruscans, who mined copper and iron there. The former had already been exhausted by the 3rd century but the iron is still holding out. The Latin name of Elba was Ilva, from the Etruscan word for iron, but the Greeks called it Athalia, which sounds pretty enough; however, it means Soot Island, referring to the smoke of the smelters. Elba, which is reached by boat at Portoferraio (Iron Harbor), still produces half of all Italy's iron (and Tuscany all of its mercury).

Large-scale commercial fishing from Elba is chiefly for tuna and sardines, but the small fishermen who supply the island itself bring in a little of everything. The time between the catching of these fish and their sale is so brief that they are sold alive. An Elbanese housewife would not think of buying a dead fish; in her eyes it would be no longer fresh. A favorite is the dentex, whose flesh is white and sweet, belying its ferocious expression—it is oversupplied with teeth. Little octopuses (*polipi*) are also prized, and often go into an Elbanese variant on the Leghorn *cacciucco*.

Pisa has a richly charged past and, except for tourism, a somnolent present. When Pisa held not only Corsica and Sardinia, but even the distant Balearic Isles, she was undoubtedly the greatest power in the Mediterranean. It is curious that a state with such a long and brilliant history produced only one great man, Galileo, and only one great dish, in dialect *le cee*, in standard Italian *le cieche*. This means tiny still-blind eels (elvers), fished in the Arno, and cooked in oil seasoned with salt and pepper.

Lucca, politically an independent state from 1369 to 1847, is gastronomically independent today. It lies in the bottom of a plain surrounded by mountains, which caused an 18th-century traveler to remark that it looked as if it were lying on the bottom of a barrel. He was a Burgundian, so no doubt he had a wine barrel in mind. If it had been an oil barrel, he would have been right, for Lucca, figuratively speaking, does lie at the bottom of a barrel. The greatest gastronomic glory of Lucca is its olive oil, the finest in Italy. This influences all its cooking and accounts for some special dishes, like *agnello con le olive*, lamb cooked with the jet-black olives of the region. Besides olives, the province of Lucca grows wheat, maize, grapes, mulberries and clover for pasturage. It makes some good cheeses and of course profits from the innumerable foods of the sea, though it makes rather less of these than might be expected; but after all, its coastline is short and its back-country deep; so it looks inland.

The best eating season in Lucca is the end of summer and the beginning of autumn. This is when the olives are being pressed; fresh oil, essential for certain recipes, is available. One of them is *zuppa di magro*, fast-day soup, and if this represents fasting in Lucca, one wonders what happens when they feast. It contains bacon, a ham bone, black cabbage, squash, kidney beans, carrots, potatoes, celery, parsley, fennel, calamint, sage, borage, garlic cloves, pepper, cinnamon and nutmeg. The soup is poured over slices of bread soaked in newly pressed oil. In the same season the pigs are slaughtered, and there is fresh *biroldo* or *mallegato*, blood pudding flavored with herbs. It is the game season too, and the time when the chestnuts are picked, to be made into a purée to go with the game, or ground into flour for desserts.

But you eat well all the year round in Lucca. In the spring, the province roasts young lambs on the spit; Luccans claim they do spit-roasting better than anybody else. Other favorite meat dishes include *rosticciana di maiale*, roast pork usually served with cornmeal polenta, and *garmugia*, in which diced beef is cooked in olive oil with fresh peas and artichokes. *Trippa alla lucchese* has onion and cinnamon in its seasoning and is sprinkled with grated Parmesan cheese.

For pasta, Lucca has *tortelli casalinghi*, home-made

stuffed rings of dough, while *panzerotti alla Tau* is a dish originally dreamed up by a single restaurant in Altopascio, which has since been copied elsewhere—*cannelloni* stuffed with cooked ham, *mozzarella* cheese, and tomato sauce, baked in the oven.

Lucca seems to have had a sweet tooth for centuries. The record of a trial which took place in 1485 contains a reference to one of the popular desserts of today, *buccellato*, a ring-shaped cake of flour, sugar, vanilla, raisins and anise, of which the center, on serving, is filled with strawberries marinated in sugared wine. Then there is *torto coi becchi*, tart with beaks, so called because of the decorative motif traced on it. It is made of a rather curious mixture of ingredients for a dessert, since there are not only cottage cheese, grapes and raisins, but also vegetables, the whole being combined with a chocolate or egg cream. *Necci* are chestnut flour pancakes, folded diagonally in four to give them a triangular shape, stuffed with cottage cheese, and served piping hot.

As for *local* local specialties, not of the province of Lucca as a whole but of specific places within it, Viareggio, the coastal city renowned for its brilliant Carnival, makes a *zuppa di datteri alla viareggina* from the mussels here called "dates," because that is what their shape suggests to Viareggians, and in France "knife-handle mussels," because that is what the same shape suggests to the French. The soup is highly seasoned with tomatoes, pepper and garlic.

The coast north of Viareggio is the Versilia Riviera, which makes its own type of *cacciucco*, of which the secret is to keep the iron pot in which it cooks well covered so that none of its flavor will escape. You begin by heating fish soup stock, covered. Meanwhile you brown bits of octopus and cuttlefish thoroughly in oil, with garlic and plenty of pepper. Add to this tomato purée and white wine, uncover the pot momentarily while you pour it in, and immediately cover it again. After ten minutes you add your selection of mixed fish—whatever comes to hand. And cover. While it is cooking, rub slices of bread with garlic and place them in the bottom of your soup plates. Now you can uncover, and pour the steaming chowder over the bread.

Another specialty of the Versilia Riviera is the mushrooms of its pine groves, which vie with the reputed funghi of the Serchio valley, which runs straight down the center of the province and by Lucca, and the perhaps even more celebrated variety of the north-central Garfagnana area. The large heads of the Garfagnana mushrooms are cut off, grilled, and served brimming with olive oil, garlic and parsley. The Garfagnana district is also noted for its strawberries and its trout.

Torre del Lago (Tower of the Lake) underestimates itself somewhat, for it not only has Lake Massaciuccoli on one side, but the sea off to the other. This pleasant position may be one of the reasons why Puccini chose to live there while composing *Tosca*, *La Bohême* and *Madame Butterfly*, and may also account for the fact that, small as it is, Torre del Lago has several local specialties. One of these consists of eels even younger than those of Pisa, minute and transparent, hardly out of the larval stage, *cieche alla salvia*, cooked with sage and sometimes folded into an omelet. Another specialty is spitted coots and other birds from the coastal marshes and thickets. Torre del Lago shares with some other places around the lake a risotto with tench and eels, which have either been fried, or cooked in *zemino*, a local word for a combination of tomato juice, olive oil and parsley. Montecarlo prefers to spit-roast thrushes, each with an olive in its beak.

After this richness, Massa-Carrara is a sad comedown. It has little history, gastronomic or otherwise, except that of its marble. So far as I have been able to discover, Massa-

Carrara has never created a single dish of its own. It makes do with the general Tuscan repertory, which is no great hardship. There is plenty of Tuscan food, and we have not yet looked at it. We have considered the individual cooking of the separate provinces, but not the cooking of Tuscany as a whole. We have only once encountered the bean.

Yet the bean is ubiquitous in Tuscany. There are bean *antipasti;* beans in soup (*minestrone di fagioli,* in which they are accompanied by celery and tomato); beans with rice (*riso e fagioli*); beans with fish (*fagioli col tonno,* tuna); and even beans with beans (*lenticchie e fagioli,* lentils and beans). The botanist, of course, would not accept the lentil as a bean, but the untutored eater is apt to regard it as of the same family. Beans often appear as a side dish with Florentine steak, the chief alternative being the tender little peas known as *piselli novelli.* They also serve to heighten the jaded interest of Monday leftovers by adding a new element. This happens in the dish called *ribollita* (reboiled), which is a by-product of the common popular Sunday dish of beef, boiled with carrots and leeks and served with mint sauce and rice. Whatever is left is reheated the following day, and eaten with beans as a refresher. There are also many dishes consisting solely of beans. Besides the minestrone with beans, there is *zuppa di fagioli alla toscana,* where the beans are not just *in* the soup, they *are* the soup, the only other ingredients being seasonings: salt, pepper, garlic, olive oil. After having been soaked overnight, the beans are cooked, half of them are puréed by being forced through a sieve to make the thick soup, into which are put the remaining whole beans—beans in beans. *Fagioli all'uccelletto* means "beans like birds," because their seasoning of sage, garlic and tomato is supposed to make them taste like small game. The most subtle bean dish is probably *fagioli al fiasco,* beans cooked in a bottle so that none of their flavor escapes, after which they are served with a dressing of uncooked oil, salt and pepper, and perhaps, just for a change, a little bean juice.

Tuscany's love affair with the bean does not exclude affection for other vegetables. The chard and the Capuchin's Beard of the Renaissance are still extant. Zucchini is cooked with calves' or lambs' brains. Artichoke slices rolled in flour are doused in beaten eggs and fried (*tortino di carciofi*). There is also an artichoke omelet.

Tuscany, according to an old Italian saying, was baptized in wine. Tuscan wines are not necessarily the best in Italy —Piedmont and Veneto would protest such a judgment— but in any case Siena is the official wine capital of the country. It is there that the Italian Academy of Wine and Grapes and the Italian Wine Institute have their headquarters, and there that a wine museum is housed in the cellars of the Medici castle, which used to harbor a different sort of munition. Siena holds an annual wine fair, in addition to its October grape fair.

The one Italian wine every foreigner knows is Tuscan, Chianti. The pear-shaped straw-covered bottle is familiar all over the world—but the best Chianti does not come in this sort of bottle. Run-of-the-mill Chianti can be drunk soon after it is bottled, and should be, for it goes off fast— hence the shape of the Chianti flask, which, in proportion to the volume of wine it contains, exposes a minimum of surface to the corrupting influence of the air in its neck. Superior Chianti should not be drunk before two years at the very least, is better at five or six, and often remains at top form much longer. Glass holds out indefinitely, but straw would rot in two or three years. Hence, no straw for the longer-lived superior Chiantis.

You are not likely to find the vintage year indicated on Chianti or any Italian wine bottles, though the alcoholic content will be given. Variations from year to year, or from vineyard to vineyard, are much less marked in Italy than in France or Germany. Weather produces fewer changes in the quality of Italian wines than it does in more northern countries, where it is whimsically fickle. The methods of cultivating vines and of treating their wine also tend to give Italian vintages greater uniformity. Italian wines in general are drunk younger than French wines, reducing the importance of the degree of difference from one year to another, since this is apt to intensify with age. Hence, when you find a vintage-year label on an Italian bottle, you may reasonably expect (though there are exceptions) that what it indicates chiefly is snobbish imitation of French practice.

There is really no need for Italian wine makers to feel inferior in the face of the French. True, if you compare the vintages of the two countries without taking into consideration the food they accompany, you will be obliged to admit that French wines, class for class, are superior, but this is a judgment in a vacuum. Wine cannot be divorced from food. Its *raison d'être* is to accompany food. It is hardly iconoclastic to maintain that Italian wines are better than French wines *with Italian food*. Who would think of drinking a fine Médoc with a dish of spaghetti and tomato sauce? Even in France, it would obviously be better to choose a coarser wine, a Beaujolais, say. But the best would be an Italian wine—for instance, Chianti.

The Chianti vineyards produce somewhat under 3,000,-000 gallons of wine per year, of which 50,000,000 gallons are sold: clearly most of the wine sold under the name of Chianti is not Chianti. But what is Chianti? The question is not as easy to answer as you might think.

The simplest case is that of *Chianti classico*. This must be grown in an area whose limits are defined by law, starting a little south of Florence and ending a little north of Siena. Not all wine grown in this area is entitled to call itself *Chianti classico*. The wine which aspires to that name must also meet certain specifications of kind and quality, strictly controlled by the Consorzio per la Difesa del Vino Tipico del Chianti. It is this *consorzio* which decides what wines may be called *Chianti classico*, and issues to their growers small numbered neck labels bearing the insignia of the medieval Chianti League—a black rooster on a gold background in a red frame.

However, some very good wine is produced on the edges of the official *classico* area—just to the east, toward Arezzo; just to the west, near Poggibonsi; or in the right provinces (Florence and Siena) but the wrong areas within them. These are labeled *Chianti tipico*, Chianti-type wines. In general usage, you could call any wine made of the same grapes and by the same processes a Chianti-type wine, wherever it comes from. Some more distant parts of Tuscany have seized the opportunity to cash in on the value of the Chianti name by producing their own Chianti-type wines too far from the Chianti area proper to share its soil and its local weather, the two chief determinants, apart from the grape itself, of the characteristics of a wine.

"*Chianti classico*" is all you need on a label to identify a bottle as belonging to the top Chiantis, but there will of course be another name as well, to give the wine producer credit for his effort and a future for his business—usually that of a family, but occasionally a local place name. Some makers even leave the name "Chianti" out entirely, especially for their finest wines; it is a way of saying that *their* wine transcends the merits possessed by Chianti in general. These merits are nevertheless great. *Chianti classico* tests between 11.5 and 13 degrees of alcoholic content, is easy to digest, and has tonic qualities. In color, it should be a bright ruby-red; in texture, suave; in taste it suggests violets, with a lurking agreeable slight bitterness in the background. Occasionally it delivers a slight sting to the tongue, like a not-quite-gaseous mineral water. It goes best with red meat and game.

Among *Chianti classici*, Brolio holds seniority in setting the standards for Chianti. Its quality in the Middle Ages was due to idleness and its quality today to jealousy. Vines were cultivated on the slopes of the Brolio domain as far back as the year 1000 by the Barons Ricasoli, who held an extensive territory between Florence and Siena, and defended its frontiers. Defense kept them too busy to pay much attention to wine production, but when their ally, Cosimo dei Medici, defeated Siena, they were relieved of military preoccupations, and, having not much else to do, gave full attention to their vineyards. Brolio Chianti became famous in Italy about 1500, and by 1700 it was being exported widely.

In the mid-19th century, the head of the family was the "Iron Baron," Bettino Ricasoli, the Italian statesman who succeeded Cavour as Premier of a freshly united Italy. He married the lovely young Anna Bonaccorsi, and shortly afterward took her to a ball in Florence, where she danced with the same young man too many times for the Baron's liking. "We must leave, my dear," he told her. He led her to their carriage and instructed the driver: "To Brolio." The ride took all night. They arrived shivering, he in his evening clothes, she in her flimsy ball dress. From then on, they lived in the Ricasoli castle in Brolio, which the family had previously abandoned, preferring life in Florence. The Baron restored the castle and busied himself personally with the improvement of Brolio wine. He developed a process of double fermentation (*governo*) still employed today, and established the blend of grapes which is not only the same Brolio uses now, but has been adopted, with slight variations in some other vineyards, by the whole Chianti region. It consists of 70 percent dark Sangiovese grapes, for body; 15 percent dark Canaiolo Nero grapes, sweeter and more velvety, for softness; and 15 percent white Malvasia grapes to give the wine its bright color.

Brolio is not a single wine, but a family of wines, over whose production Baron Bettino Ricasoli continues to preside, though, of course, not the same one. At the bottom of the scale is the ordinary table wine, produced by the *governo* process, which, since it is meant to be drunk young, is offered in the familiar straw-covered *fiasco*. Above it comes Castello di Meleto, from a secondary property of the family, near Brolio proper. Castello di Brolio is richer, fine and dry. The very best Brolio you can get is Brolio Riservato, made only in particularly good years from selected grapes and aged for five years before being released for sale. There is also a dry white, Brolio Bianco, and the straw-colored Arbia, which does not come from the main Brolio vineyards, but from the slopes flanking the Arbia River, which flows through the *classico* area. A superior Arbia called Torricella is deeper colored because it is aged in oak casks. Finally the Ricasoli also make Vino (or Vin) Santo, a heavy rich liqueur-like dessert wine.

To make sure of getting good Chianti, stick to the well-known brands (mostly family names) like Brolio. Another is Antinori. The Ricasoli did not depend for eminence on their wine, but it *was* wine which brought eminence to the Antinori (the two families are now related). The first wine-making Antinori was only an apprentice vintner; but that was in 1385, and he learned his business so well that by 1470 the Antinori palace in Florence was one of the showplaces of a city which did not lack them. As the best wine of the Brolio family is Brolio Riservato, so the best wine of the Antinori family is Villa Antinori, the best of the Ruffino family is Riservato Ducale, and of the Melini family, Stravecchio Melini. The Melini grapes are grown in the *classico* area, but the bottling plant is just outside it, so this wine, with unnecessary severity, is not entitled to use the Chianti

League bottleneck label. The Melini do have the right to use the Florentine *tipico* neck label, which depicts a cherub, but disdain to do so. A simple rule for buying Chianti is to remember the rooster of the *classico* and the cherub of the *tipico* and forget the rest. There are some very good wines in the *tipico* class, the best being perhaps one grown perversely far from the *classico* area, Chianti Rufina, produced northeast of Florence and thus on the other side of the capital from the top Chianti country. A dark ruby-red, nutty and velvety, with a slight tendency to foam when poured, it tests between 11.8 and 12.6 degrees of alcohol, and requires aging to attain its prime. If this is not the best *tipico*, then Nipozzano, which comes from about the same district, is.

Among the better whites of the Chianti area, few of which are called Chianti, a name reserved by purists for reds, are Arbia, 11 to 13 degrees, dry, transparently straw-colored, drunk young, refreshing, with an agreeable veiled sharpness in its aftertaste; Bianco Vergine della Val d'Arbia (a "virgin" wine is one made from the pulp of the grapes alone, not pressed with the stems and stalks, and therefore pleasantly light); and Bianco del Val d'Elsa, 11 to 12 degrees, which, contrary to the rule in Chianti country, is better than the reds of the same area. A pretty name is Lacrima d'Arno, "tear of the Arno," from the upper valley of that river, very much like Arbia. The Ruffino family makes a rosé, Rosatello Ruffino, which, as rosés go, is not bad.

Vino Santo, the equivalent of French Sauternes, is not a Tuscan exclusivity, but is made in many regions of Italy, everywhere in much the same fashion. Its name is attributed to Cardinal Bessarione, who, on being served this wine at a sumptuous banquet in Florence about 1440, exclaimed, "*Ma questo è un vino santo!*" "Now *there* is a holy wine!" This gastronomic equivalent to canonization has determined the title of this wine ever since, though what is reputed to be the second-best Vino Santo of Italy, that of the Casentino valley east of Florence, is sometimes called instead Occhio di Pernice, partridge eye, because of its color, the result of making it from one-third black grapes and two-thirds white grapes. This differentiates the Casentino product from other Vini Santi, including the very best, which is Tuscan also (from the Val di Pesa, south of Florence, in the *zona classica*).

Sauternes grapes derive their high sugar content from being allowed to rot on the vines, but Vino Santo Toscano is made by drying them indoors. The process is a long one—it takes several months to dry the grapes. The raisins, which is what they are by then, are only pressed about Easter, which has given rise to a second explanation of the wine's name. They are then left to ferment for three or four years, the minimum period for maturity. The result is a wine of heavy alcoholic content, 15 to 18 degrees, velvety, extremely sweet, suggesting a liqueur as much as a wine. It is served cool, but not cold. If you want to taste this precious wine, you may have to go to some trouble. It is now on the market, but not much of it; originally it was not made to sell at all. It was the custom in Tuscany for winegrowers to make only a very small amount, which they kept for their own use, and brought out when distinguished guests arrived. That was the case for Cardinal Bessarione, who had come to Florence to attend the synod which was attempting to unite the Greek and Roman churches. The synod was not a success, but the wine was.

Chianti, though it is the most famous, is by no means the be-all and the end-all of Tuscan wines, as the citizens of the hill town of Montepulciano, near Siena, would be the first to point out. They call their "noble wine of Montepulciano" (Vino Nobile di Montepulciano) *"d'ogni vino il re*"—"of all wines the king." They might not have thought of this if the 18th-century poet, Francesco Redi, had not written this line in his *Bacchus in Tuscany*, but once it had been uttered they pounced upon it. Ordinary Montepulciano is an eminently forgettable wine, and its sweet variety is, unfortunately, not even forgettable. So be sure to specify the *vino nobile*, a full-bodied wine, 12 to 13 degrees, a purplish ruby color, with a rich mellow flavor which nevertheless has a flinty edge to it, an excellent accompaniment for roast beef. It is a wine meant for aging, and its qualities become accentuated after about five years in the bottle. A suggestion of violets develops and the aftertaste takes on a slight bitterness which is the delight of connoisseurs. It has been described as "austere," which would make it indeed Tuscan, and a Montepulciano did indeed exist in Etruscan times, but it must have been very different then. It is described as "a small white wine" in an account of 160 B.C. which tells how a traitor gave some to the Gauls to tempt them to attack the region which produced it.

Siena boasts another "big" wine, as the experts like to put it, one of the longest-lived vintages in Italy, since it can stand a half-century in the bottle, and perhaps more. This is Brunello di Montalcino, Brunello being the name of the grape from which it is made. It is prepared for its long life by five or six years' aging in wood, and two more in the bottle before being released for sale, but for best results, wait even longer. Testing 12.5 to 13 degrees of alcohol, a bright garnet, it is dry, tasty, and gives off a delicate perfume of violets, all qualities which become more and more refined as it ages. If you want to taste Brunello, look for it in Italy; it is hardly ever exported, for its high cost would make it non-competitive abroad.

The same town also produces Moscadello di Montalcino, almost unique for the lightness of its alcoholic content, only 8 to 9 degrees—for which reason children are often allowed to drink it. It is an *apéritif* or dessert wine, which tastes much like fresh grape juice, is on the sweet side, and is naturally *frizzante*—that is, it has a slight sparkle but not as much as the champagne-type wines, which are described as *spumanti*. There is also a Moscadello Liquoroso, a heavy dessert wine of 15 to 16 degrees.

Florence too has wines other than Chianti. Pomino, from the Sieve valley, is more or less of the Chianti type, but doesn't claim the name. Colline Sanminiatesi too, a red of 11.5 to 12.5 degrees, might have tried to claim Chianti status, like the Empoli wines grown just across the river from it, but refrained.

As you move farther from the Chianti zone of influence, the wines become more diverse. Grosseto has quite a few, of which the best, it is true, resembles a Chianti—Scanzano, 12 to 13 degrees. The second best, Ansonica, is quite different—and variable, for it is grown not only at Porto Santo Stefano on the Orbetello peninsula but also on the island of Giglio across the way, not to mention Elba; Ansonica is a grape name, not a place name. At its best, Ansonica is a dry, golden yellow, fresh, fruity, and highly alcoholized wine, for a white. If you happen to encounter the semi-sweet version, you may be less enchanted with it.

Lucca's top wine is Montecarlo, an extra-dry 10-to-12-degree red. There is also a white; it seems to be the rule in Lucca that both are produced almost everywhere.

Massa-Carrara, so undistinguished in its cooking, has a few wines of its own, but they are undistinguished too. The red Pollera is all consumed locally without provoking any protest elsewhere. Probably the best, which is not saying much, is Candia, a 12-to-13-degree sweetish spicy white, which is a bright straw color if it does not cloud in the bottle, as it sometimes discouragingly does.

Leghorn produces one quite popular wine, grown on

either side of the capital city itself, Ugolino, also sold as Biserno or Bianco del Littorale Livornese. A very pale straw color, varying from 10 to 12 degrees of alcohol, it has a delicate bouquet and stings a little on the tongue.

Cross seven miles of water, and you reach the Elba wines, said to be tonic because of the iron in the soil, which may well be true. The presence of an unusual amount of tannin is detectable by the eye in the whites, which are apt to be dark yellow. It is not so readily visible in the reds, but they are rich in tannin also. For a territory covering only 94 square miles, Elba shows considerable variety. Its best wine is undoubtedly Procanico Elbano, a dry, straw-colored wine, pale, but clear and bright, 12 to 13 degrees, delicate, fresh, harmonious and slightly astringent. Served chilled, it is admirable with seafood, especially crustaceans. The ordinary Bianco d'Elba, light and also straw-colored, can't touch it, but is drinkable enough. A cut above is the dry white Riminese, so called because the grape from which it is made was originally imported from Rimini. The ordinary red, known variously as Sangiovese, Sangioveto, or Roselba, which should test 13 degrees, can, like the white, be imbibed without pain when it is up to standard; but it is subject to considerable variation.

Elbans like sweet dessert wines, and produce one sweet *red* dessert wine, Aleatico di Portoferraio. Of high alcoholic content, 14 to 15 degrees, it is a deep ruby red and possesses to a mild degree the liqueur taste of white dessert wines. Its white counterpart, Moscato d'Elba, is a heavy (13 to 15 degrees), sweet, bright golden-yellow dessert wine rich in iron and phosphates, and with a strong flavor of the half-dried muscat grapes from which it is produced by a process which makes it akin to a Vino Santo. Sparkling wines are also popular. An ordinary one, dry, light in color, and with a considerable kick, is called Acqua Pazza, "crazy water." *Elba spumante*, dry or semi-sweet, is made by the same process as the most widely known of the Italian imitations of champagne, *Asti spumante*, but falls far short of it. If you don't mind taking it sweet, you can get a better foaming wine without leaving Elba, for there is also a *Moscato spumante*. The easiest on the head is the dry Frizzante di Porto Azzurro, a natural sparkler.

One last word of information—or shall we say warning? You may be offered in Tuscany something called *ponce*. It is a cheap grade of rum. Better not.

Lazio

R oman cooking is Etruscan cooking.

The poor Latin shepherds who lived behind the mud flats at the mouth of the Tiber some 800 years before our era had meager materials on which to found a cuisine—only their sheep. This gave them mutton and cheese (pecorino, which the Etruscans had too, and ricotta, both important in Rome today). The Etruscans were already raising wheat and wine. They were breeding the ancestors of today's Chianina beef cattle, and hogs too. The last were the origin of what many Romans would tell you is their most typical dish today—*porchetta*, spit-roasted whole suckling pig. Tuscany eats *porchetta* too, and it may be

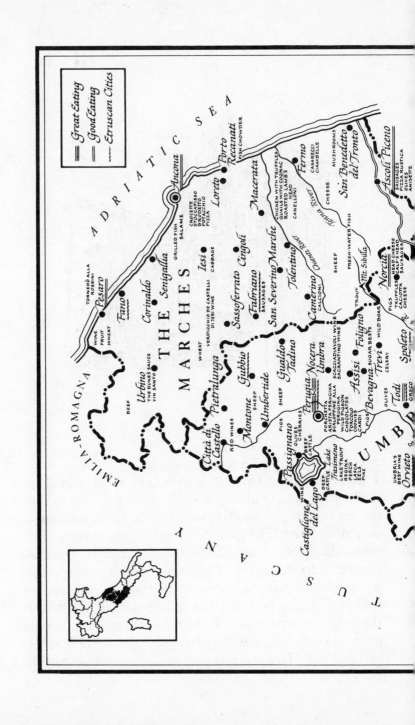

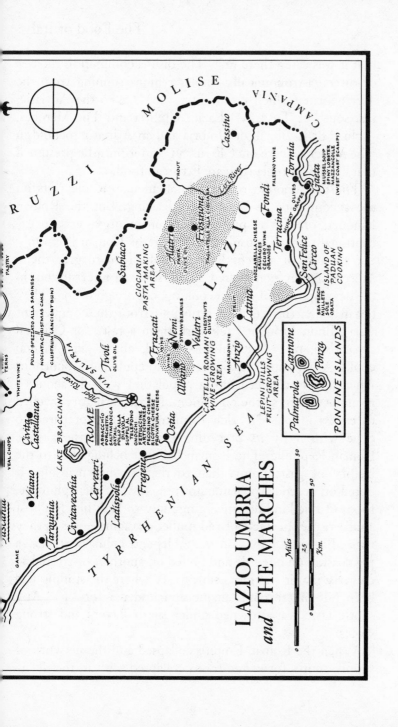

LAZIO, UMBRIA
and THE MARCHES

Miles

Km.

MOLISE

CAMPANIA

ABRUZZI

LAZIO

TROUT

Liri River

Cassito

Formia

GAETA
MUSSEL SOUP
SPINY LOBSTER
MAZZANCOLLE
(WEST COAST SCAMPI)

Gaeta

Formia

Fondi

Terracina

MUSCAT GRAPES

SWEET OLIVES

FALERNO WINE

San Felice
Circeo

SEA PEACH
MUSSELS
SOLE
ORATA

ISLAND OF
PADUAN
COOKING

MOZZARELLA CHEESE
SAUSAGES
CECUBO WINE
ORANGES

Latina

FRUIT

Alatri
PASTA
OLIVE OIL

Frosinone
TAGLIATELLE ALLA CIOCIARA

CIOCIARIA
PASTA-MAKING
AREA

Subiaco

LEPINI HILLS
FRUIT-GROWING
AREA

Arzio

MACARONI PIE

Velletri
WINE

Nemi

STRAWBERRIES

Frascati
WINE

Albano

CASTELLI ROMANI CHESTNUTS
WINE-GROWING OLIVES
AREA

Tivoli
OLIVE OIL

VIA SALARIA

POLLO SPEZZATO ALLA SABINESE
NOCIATA CHRISTMAS CAKE
CIUSTRUM (ANCIENT BUN)

WHITE WINE

TROUT
TERNI

GAME

VEAL CHOPS

Tuscania

Tarquinia

Veiano

Civita
Castellana

Civitavecchia

Cerveteri

LAKE BRACCIANO

Tiber River

ROME
ABBACCHIO
PORCHETTA
SALTIMBOCCA
OXTAIL
POLLO ALLA
DIAVOLA
SUPPLI AL
TELEFONO
GNOCCHI
ARTICHOKES
PECORINO CHEESE
RICOTTA CHEESE
PROVATURA CHEESE

Ladispoli

Fregene

Ostia

TYRRHENIAN SEA

Palmarola

Zannone

Ponza

PONTINE ISLANDS

T Y R R H E N I A N   S E A

that it was eaten there first. The dish is common to the tier of three gastronomically similar regions running from the Tyrrhenian (which means Etruscan) Sea to the Adriatic, just south of Tuscany—Lazio, Umbria and The Marches. A third of Lazio, all of Umbria and an Adriatic toehold in The Marches were once Etruscan, and it must be presumed that in ancient times they ate Etruscan food.

The gastronomic reputation of ancient Rome rests on the accounts of its spectacular feasting. But the Roman banquet, or, if you prefer, the Roman orgy, was an exceptional though conspicuous feature of Roman life. Only 200 families of ancient Rome could afford to give them. Moreover they constituted a diversion, an interruption, in the development of Italian cooking, of foreign origin. They began when the Legions, returning from the conquest of Asia Minor, brought back with them a taste for Oriental sybaritism, new Oriental foods, and, above all, Oriental cooks. As an imported disease rises to epidemic proportions when it is introduced into a population with no acquired immunity to it, so the contagion of Eastern luxury swelled to excess in a newly rich Roman Empire unprepared to cope with it by its preceding experience of the austere Roman Republic. The Roman banquet belongs less to the history of gastronomy than to that of showmanship. It doted on peacocks or flamingos presented in their plumage, foods of one kind designed cunningly to look like foods of another, the spectacle of red mullet changing color as they roasted in glass bowls on the table, and culinary tricks—a pig roasted on one side and boiled on another, or stuffed so cleverly that it was impossible to see where the stuffing had been put in (through an incision under a foreleg). Any subtle taste was drowned under sharp flavors and strong spices.

When the Roman Empire collapsed and the network of supply routes for exotic foods collapsed with it, the diversion was ended. There was a faint flicker of revival in the Renaissance, for the first cookbooks published then leaned heavily on their only predecessors, those of the Roman Empire. Besides, spices had returned, though slowly. The Crusades started in 1096 and returning warriors brought Eastern essences back with them, as the Roman Legions had done 1,000 years earlier. The Saracens, who had always possessed spices, started their Italian conquests in 827 and were ruling all Sicily by 965. But it took nearly a century for the spices of the Crusaders, which entered at Venice, to work their way across the peninsula to Rome, and two to get there from Sicily. The Renaissance reveled briefly in spices, because they were novel and because in the days before refrigeration they preserved food (and masked unpleasant tastes in case it had not been sufficiently well preserved); but the period tired of sensation after a while, and reverted to a soberness that looked back to the period before the gastronomic eruptions of the Empire—that is, to the example of the Etruscans.

The Roman Empire had indeed performed one important service for Etruscan cooking. It distributed it widely. The most conspicuous example is that of the first universal basic dish which Etruria gave Rome, *pulmentum*, which the Legions carried as far as York, England, where it became Yorkshire pudding. Its modern descendant, polenta (now made with corn flour) is not important in the cooking of Lazio today, nor of Tuscany either, but flourishes instead in what was once the northern fringe of Etruscan conquest, Piedmont, Lombardy and the Venetias—because the center of gravity of grain production, which at the beginning was in Etruria, has shifted now to Lombardy, Emilia-Romagna and the Venetias.

Otherwise the basis for the cooking of Lazio today is the cooking of Etruria yesterday. The characteristics of Tuscan cooking are largely reproduced in the characteristics of

Roman cooking, with the addition of exuberance—and often, specifically, of a favorite flavor of ancient and modern Romans alike: mint.

Lazio is a region without geographical unity. Its frontiers are not natural, nor even, in general, historical. It can only be described as the territory which, like iron filings to a magnet, has been attracted to Rome.

The broad sandy beaches of its coastline start at the north with a prolongation of the Tuscan Maremma in the province of Viterbo, once part of Etruria. Next, in the province of Rome itself, comes a stretch of low sandy coast; and last of all, in Latina, the once redoubtable but now tamed Pontine marshes.

Beyond the coast of the province of Rome lies the vegetable-producing Roman *campagna* (countryside), the most fertile area of Lazio; but Lazio is not notably fertile. Mountains cover a third of its territory, and even in the *campagna* the volcanic soil, tufa and pozzolana, while easy to till and not inhospitable to many crops, does not produce large yields for most of them; the sand of the coast and the clay just behind it are refractory to many. North of the Tiber, in the Maccarese region, cereals are grown, but the yield is low. It may have been here that sweet corn was first planted in Italy, for it was once known as "Roman wheat." There are some fruit trees, and many olives, which grow everywhere up to an altitude of 2,000 feet. Vines thrive on volcanic soil; the chief wine-growing centers of Lazio are the area around Lake Bolsena, crater of a vanished volcano, and especially the Alban hills, which produce most of the table wine of Rome. Wine and olive oil are the only two agricultural products for which Lazio is self-sufficient.

Lazio is shaped like a battered shoe, of which the three coastal provinces form the sole, with Latina at the toe. Inland from Latina, Frosinone constitutes the top part of the toe and butts against the province of Rome, center of sole and upper, while Viterbo is the whole heel. Rieti is the oversized tongue, which darts a curiously shaped probe of territory so deeply inland that it passes southward of Umbria and reaches The Marches. This curious strip of land thrust so irrationally far from its region's center of gravity was the corridor through which the Via Salaria passed, the first amoeba-like tendril pushed between the Etruscans to the north and the Greeks to the south by a Rome groping toward Empire.

From the time of the Roman Empire's collapse until the Crusades, the food of Lazio was characterized by an almost complete lack of spices, even of salt; the Romans must have forgotten the methods by which the Latin shepherds had derived it from the sea. The Pontine marshes, which the ancient Romans had drained and cultivated, reverted to quagmire, and the vegetables which had grown there became rare. Those which remained were of the coarser varieties: heavy farinaceous peas (the delicate small *piselli novelli* had not yet appeared), fava beans, squash, leeks, cabbage, beets. Everything was boiled, though for chestnuts there was an option between boiling and roasting. A few varieties of lettuce and herbs, served with vinegar, were still available. This was the menu of the common people, plus various types of polenta, then made from barley, wheat, or other cereals. The well-to-do lived chiefly on meat served on baked pancakes, which were both dishes and food. The drinks were beer, wine, hydromel (a mixture of wine and honey), and fermented honey alone. Hydromel was now called *claré*, a word destined to work its way through three languages and turn up in English as claret, meaning red Bordeaux wine.

As the supremacy of the Popes increased, so did the prosperity of the territory over which they were the temporal as well as the spiritual rulers. By the 13th century, eating had greatly improved. True bread was back, and so were spices. There was a tendency to overuse the latter, as the ancient Romans had done, particularly in the case of pepper, ginger and saffron. Three- and four-course dinners reappeared, and with them the art of presenting foods in decorative patterns and of astonishing guests by making one dish look like another. Somewhere between 1260 and 1290 an anonymous cookbook appeared, in manuscript form—a witness to the progress that had been made in the last century. Boiled meat was still in it—*bollito* is still popular in Italy today—but there was roast meat too, for instance shoulder of mutton. *Bollito* was accompanied either by a *salsa verde* very much like that still served today, or by pepper sauce—the *salsa peperata* of modern Verona. Calf's head was listed as a currently popular dish. Poultry included capons, chickens, ducks, geese—and cranes. Stuffings were recommended for chicken, particularly elaborate ones for goose, and garlic or quince were recommended with smaller birds—a return to ancient Roman practices. There were wine sauces and an almond sauce. There were also recipes for *vermicelli*, *tortelli* and *tortelletti*. This alone would dispose of the fable that Marco Polo brought the art of making pasta from China, for the latest date ascribed to this book is five years before his return. But the ancient Romans knew pasta, and so did the Etruscans; a pasta shaper has been found in an Etruscan tomb.

The Popes spent most of the 14th century in Avignon, fleeing a Rome which had become a battleground for its great and usually unscrupulous families, the Colonnas, Orsini, Savelli, Annibaldi and others. The troubled times may have been one of the reasons why the first work on agriculture to appear in Europe in 1,200 years took more than a century and a half to come out. The *Opus ruralium commodorum* of Pietro de' Crescenti, a native of Bologna, was written in 1305 but was not published until 1471; it may finally have reached the public because movable type had just been invented. It was appropriate that this revival of interest in the art of agriculture should appear in Italy, which had produced the last books on that subject before the Dark Ages set in; and indeed, this one was largely a synthesis of ancient Roman writings, brought up to date, however, by consultations with the only institutions which had continued to study agriculture seriously, the monasteries. A second indication of renewed attention to gastronomy quickly appeared when the first signed cookbook since ancient Roman times was printed in 1475. It was published in Cremona, but it belongs to the history of Roman cooking, for its author was Bartolomeo Sacchi, librarian of the Vatican. His cookbook, which appeared in six different editions over a space of 30 years, was such a success that it changed his name. Its title was *Platine de Honestate Voluptate*, and Sacchi was known thereafter as Platina.

Like the first agricultural work, Platina's book leaned heavily on ancient Roman writers, especially Apicius; but while Apicius was an apostle of complication and extravagance, Platina preached simplicity. The Middle Ages had revived the lavish ancient use of spices, but Platina proposed replacing them with seasonings of lemon juice, orange juice, or wine. He advocated starting meals with fruit, as Romans do today when they combine figs or melon with prosciutto as an hors d'oeuvre. Some 20 years after Platina had resuscitated Apicius, Apicius's own book was reissued, first in Venice and then in Milan—or, rather, an approximation of it, for the original Latin work had been lost and all the Renaissance publisher had to work from were the notes of Apicius's pupils.

Books concerned with eating now began to appear thick and fast, many of them still harking back to the ancients.

Pieranda Mattiolo's *Commentaries on the Six Books of Dioscorides*, published in 1544—1,500 years after the time of Dioscorides, who lived under Nero—was popular throughout Europe, appearing in some 50 editions in many countries. The public may have swooped upon this particular book for medical as much as for gastronomic reasons, for, following the lead of Dioscorides himself, who was, after all, a doctor, it dealt at length with herbs, primarily for their medical value, though their culinary uses were not neglected.

It was evident that interest in cooking was becoming intense in Italy, and the Popes were not the last to be affected by it. One practical result was the evolution of the tiny melon the ancient Romans grew to the one we have today, developed on the Papal property near Rome named Cantelupo—hence, cantaloupe.

Popes entertained, and were entertained, with great lavishness. When, early in the 16th century, Agostino Chigi invited Pope Leo X to dine at his Villa Farnesina, the silver dishes soiled at the table were thrown disdainfully into the Tiber after each course—where a net had been thoughtfully stretched just under the surface of the water to catch them.

Pope Alexander VII gave the second most exclusive banquet ever served, on December 26, 1655, for just two diners, himself and Queen Christina of Sweden. (The most exclusive was the one for which Lucullus exhorted his cook to special efforts because he was alone: "Tonight Lucullus dines with Lucullus!") The occasion raised delicate problems of protocol. It was not considered seemly for a woman to eat in the presence of the Pope. Christina was therefore removed, symbolically, if somewhat fictitiously, from his presence by being served at a separate table, distant the breadth of two palms from the Pope's, which was two-finger widths higher than hers. The question of chairs was more difficult. Only ruling monarchs could occupy armchairs before the Pope, and Christina had abdicated; but it hardly seemed fitting for the Catholic Church to demote her because she had relinquished a Protestant throne to embrace Catholicism; and besides she was a generous benefactor of the Church. No less an artist than Bernini was called in to design a piece of furniture which would be simultaneously an armchair and not an armchair. Proving himself a diplomat as well as an artist, Bernini came up with a chair which could be argued to have no arms since they were not the straight kind ordinarily designated by that name, yet which indubitably did have them, though unorthodoxly twisted; perhaps he was thinking of his great convoluted columns beneath the baldaquin in St. Peter's.

The meal was such a sumptuous one that chroniclers have neglected to give us the menu in their ecstasy about the *trionfi di tavola* which were displayed on the sideboards during the repast and transferred to the tables after it. Made of sugar and marzipan, they depicted deities, monuments, fountains, bouquets of flowers, and so on. The Queen's arms bore a sheaf of wheat, so one of the *trionfi* showed Abundance with her cornucopia, crowned with wheat, and surrounded by cherubs holding sheaves of wheat. Not only at the banquet, but throughout her voyage in Italy, Christina was gratified with *trionfi;* the Pope had sent his specialist in the matter, Luigi Fedele, to meet her at Ferrara and prepare these table decorations wherever she stopped. She was so pleased with the ones he provided at Assisi that after she had retired she asked that they be sent up to her bedroom to examine them again. This sent flunkeys scurrying about town to recover them; they had already been given away. She did not ask that they be delivered to her bedroom at Messina, where they might have proved a trifle messy: Fedele had reproduced the port of Messina in jelly, with live fish swimming in its water.

Christina came to Rome again in 1688 and was feted by another Pope, Clement IX, but this time there was less fuss about chairs. Clement was a Rospiglioso, a family noted for its simplicity, whereas Alexander VII had been a Chigi. The *trionfi* reflected the different spirit; their subjects were religious—one of them was the Last Supper. Once again the *trionfi* overshadowed the food as they did in two other spectacular Roman banquets, one which had occurred before Christina's reception by Alexander, and the other after her visit to Clement. At the first, Alexander had received the Venetian ambassadors with a lavishness, but of course not with a licentiousness, which recalled Imperial Rome. At the second, Lord Castlemaine, His Britannic Majesty's ambassador to Rome by grace of His Britannic Majesty's interest in Lady Castlemaine, invited the entire College of Cardinals to break bread with him at the Palazzo Pamphilii in the Piazza Navona. This may have been the all-time high for *trionfi*. There were 80 of them, all gilded, and the table on which they were displayed stretched the whole length of the palace's long gallery, where the populace was admitted to gape at them.

These gaudy feasts of the 17th century were magnificent, but the same century saw a humbler, at first almost unnoticed, event, which was destined to have a much more important effect on the future of Italian cooking than *trionfi di tavola*. The tomato began to be cultivated in the peninsula.

The violent changeable glittering history of Rome has created a many-faceted human being, inconsistent and unpredictable, volatile and *bon vivant*, and with a dynamic range often restricted to fortissimo.

"A people full of contrasts," wrote Y. and E.-R. Labande in *Rome*. "Well, so was their long history. And the volcanic soil, the changeable climate—do they not contribute in part to explain their diverse and upsetting aspect?

"They have their faults. They're a people extremely noisy and rather negligent of their persons in the cheaper neighborhoods. But they're spontaneous, good-humored, frank, patient in their troubles, simple in the expression of their joy. There is little arrogance among the powerful, little envy among the humble.

"Everyone in Rome loves luxury. Stroll on a summer evening along the Via Barberini or toward the Porta Pia: you will be dazzled by the insolent luxuriousness, the refinement of taste . . . Or, at the other extreme of the social ladder, go in the morning about 11 o'clock to some popular market, best of all to the Campo de' Fiori near the Farnese Palace, where the overabundance of the heavy Mediterranean fruits, overflowing even into the middle of the road, will put you again in the presence of this radiance."

"There is in Rome a zest, an earthiness, a *vivacità*, that surround, excite and thaw the Anglo-Saxon temperament," Doris Muscatine wrote in *A Cook's Tour of Rome*. "The Roman citizen breathes deep, and attacks life with gusto. When he cooks, serves and eats, it is with the same capacity to enjoy that marks his other activities." And she quoted Bruno Rossi, an Italian gastronomic writer: "Romans are robust eaters and hearty drinkers, but they know how, when they are at table, also to capture the mood of festivity, to savor the conversation, to appreciate the company." To which she adds, "One of the ways to know Romans best is to meet them at dinner."

What kind of food appeals to this kind of man? Here is a list of Rome's most typical dishes:

PORCHETTA, suckling pig roasted whole on a spit, is a symbol of Rome, the featured delicacy at the rollicking boisterous noisy week-long outdoor festival of Noantri (Festival of the Rest of Us), held every July in the popular

Trastevere (Across the Tiber) quarter.

ABBACCHIO is another milk-fed animal—baby lamb which has never tasted grass. It is necessarily an Easter dish, since this is the time of year when baby lambs are about. A favorite Easter excursion for Roman families is driving out into the surrounding country to picnic on barbecued lamb, spit-roasted in the open air.

Abbacchio is not necessarily spit-roasted. It can be cooked in the oven in a number of ways; but for it to be genuinely Roman, the essential element is rosemary in the seasoning. One favorite is *abbacchio alla cacciatora* (hunter's style), with olive oil, vinegar, sage, garlic and the indispensable rosemary, to which some cooks add a touch of anchovy. Or cut the lamb into small chunks and cook it in a frying pan with a sauce of olive oil, garlic, white wine, egg yolks and lemon peel, when it becomes *abbacchio brodettato* (if the same method is applied to kid, delicious at the suckling stage, it is *capretto brodettato*). Baby lamb also provides diminutive chops, which are cooked on a flat skillet and turned over with the fingers, fast; hence their name, *braciolette a scottadito*, "burn-your-finger chops."

SALTIMBOCCA is composed of thin slices of veal seasoned with sage, "married" (*maritati*) by means of wooden toothpick skewers to slices of prosciutto ham, the whole sautéd in butter and braised with Marsala wine. The name means "jump into the mouth," the idea being that *saltimbocca* is so delicious that it prompts you almost by its own volition to pop a piece of it in without hesitating for an instant.

Any Roman will tell you that *saltimbocca* is indubitably a purely Roman dish, but I would be inclined to think it is rather a purely Roman name for a dish which appears in modified forms in several parts of Italy and probably originated in Brescia, Lombardy.

CODA ALLA VACCINARA, so far as I know, is unchallenged as a native Roman creation. It is oxtail cut into chunks and simmered lengthily in wine and tomato sauce, with plenty of celery.

POLLO ALLA DIAVOLA has been described as one of the glories of the Roman cuisine. Of the Florentine cuisine too, for it is one of the many dishes which link the cuisines of Lazio and Tuscany. The Roman version is the more austere. The chicken is cut open longitudinally and flattened, and the two halves are grilled on a red-hot plaque. Before serving it is sprinkled with lemon juice and dusted liberally with pepper. Cooks who go easy on the pepper are robbing the dish of its right to its name: *alla diavola,* hot as the devil.

SUPPLÌ AL TELEFONO is a ball of rice with a piece of *provatura* (buffalo-milk cheese) inside. Any croquette is a *supplì,* but these are called "telephone croquettes" because when you bite into them the melted cheese flows out in long tentacles like the wire which dangles about the chin when a telephone receiver is picked up.

GNOCCHI ALLA ROMANA is a subject of hot argument: when is it Roman and when is it not? Gnocchi is made in many regions of Italy of mashed potatoes and flour, which, in the absence of inspiration on the part of the cook, can be pretty insipid. This is why, in several Italian dialects, *gnocco* (the singular) means a stupid person (cf. "pudding-head" in English or *"tête de lard,"* lard-head, in French). For me, *gnocchi alla romana* means the first I ever tasted in Rome, in, I think, 1934—a dream of succulent lightness. The dough was made of semolina flour boiled in milk to which grated Parmesan cheese and beaten eggs had been added. This had been molded into quenelle-like cylinders (most recipes say it should be diced or cut into rounds), and finished in a baking dish in the oven, with plenty of butter and more grated cheese on top. Its rich creaminess melted in the mouth. Alas, I have never tasted *gnocchi* as good since. In its honor, I side against those who describe Roman *gnocchi* as containing potatoes, and consider *gnoc-*

chi alla romana as the kind that does not. You can sidestep this debate by calling the dish *gnocchi di latte* (milk *gnocchi*), which no one can deny is a favorite of Romans. I do not know how old *gnocchi* is, but there is a recipe for it in a 16th-century cookbook—without potatoes, of course, for the potato, as a vegetable, was then unknown. The Renaissance *gnocchi* was made of bread from which the crust had been removed, water, and flour, and was sometimes called macaroni.

FETTUCCINE AL BURRO is associated in every tourist's mind with Rome, possibly because the original Alfredo succeeded in making its serving a spectacle reminiscent of grand opera. *Fettuccine* is not peculiar to Rome. It is the same ribbon-shaped egg pasta that is called *tagliatelle* in Bologna; but the *al burro* preparation is very Roman indeed in its rich simplicity. Nothing is added to the pasta except grated cheese and butter—lots of butter. The recipe calls for *doppio burro*, double butter, which gives it a golden color. Bologna serves its *tagliatelle* with the meat sauce called *ragù*, which you can approximate in Rome by ordering *fettuccine al sugo e burro* (with meat sauce and butter). There is also *fettuccine alla papalina* (Papal style), with butter, bits of ham, and mushrooms.

CARCIOFI (artichokes) come in *two* special forms in Rome—*carciofi alla romana* and *carciofi alla giudia*, artichokes Jewish style. Despite its name, the latter is an authentic Roman dish, introduced to Rome by the Jews of its medieval ghetto; and such is the tenacity of eating habits that the restaurants especially renowned for this specialty are located mostly where the ghetto used to be—between the Via Arenula and the Piazza di Monte Savallo in one direction, and the Synagogue and the Ponte Quattro Capi in the other. *Carciofi alla giudia* are available only at the season when the first tender young artichokes have just ripened but the choke has not yet developed, so that the entire artichoke can be eaten. Deep fried in olive oil, the artichokes spread out during cooking and take on a dark color, so that they lie on your plate like flat black flowers. *Carciofi alla romana* are also made from completely edible young artichokes and exude a characteristic fragrance of Rome—that of wild mint, which goes into many Roman dishes. Mint leaves and cloves of garlic are tucked between the artichoke petals, and the vegetables are then cooked in a casserole with much olive oil over a low flame. Rome has a third way of preparing artichokes, not so widely known or so definitely associated with the city as the other two, *carciofi alla manticiana*, which are cooked on a grill.

These are the headliners of the Roman menu, but there is an almost limitless list of other Roman dishes. For instance:

SOUPS: The most Roman of soups is probably *stracciatelle* (little rags), which you may know as egg-drop soup; into hot consommé (in ascending order of goodness, vegetable, beef, chicken, or beef-and-chicken) you drop, just before serving, a thin batter of eggs, flour, grated Parmesan cheese and grated lemon peel, which splits up into little tatters in the soup—hence its name. Also very Roman is lentil and tomato soup, with the city's special flavoring, wild mint. However, chick pea (*ceci*) soup, into which elbow macaroni and tomato enter, is seasoned with rosemary. Bean soup *alla romana* also includes elbow macaroni and tomato, plus celery and a bit of chopped salt pork. *Brodetto* (a diminutive of *brodo*, broth) is a name which can be applied to any dish whose chief ingredient floats in a liquid (it is so old that the expression "*antico quanto il brodetto*" means "as old as Adam"); on the Adriatic coast, *brodetto* means fish chowder, but in Rome it stands for lamb broth with egg yolks and lemon juice, the floating elements being slices of round bread sprinkled with grated cheese and toasted. Such bread slices, called *crostini*, are often served with Italian soups.

SALADS: Italians, like Americans, have been accustomed

since the time of the Emperor Domitian to starting their meals occasionally with salad, unlike the French, who place it after the meat course. Italians, again like Americans, enjoy mixed salads, again unlike the French, who prefer lettuce alone, with a plain salad dressing, usually olive oil, vinegar, salt and pepper. I know of only one salad which can be put down confidently as specifically Roman, despite the existence of Romaine lettuce (called Paris lettuce in some places, though it was only introduced into France quite late, allegedly by Rabelais). This is *misticanza*, which is not a complete salad in itself, but the green which is the basis for various mixed salads, all of which become Roman through its presence. *Misticanza* is not appreciated in other parts of Italy. It is the plant known in English as rockets, eaten by the ancient Romans and the modern British. One common combination is *misticanza*, fennel, tomatoes and radishes, but whatever the formula, it appears on Roman menus as *insalata di misticanza*. The rest is incidental. Romans say it takes four persons to make a salad properly: a wise man to season it, a miser to put in the vinegar, a spendthrift for the oil, and a madman to mix and toss it (in dialect, *pe' condì bene l'insalata ce vonno quattro persone: un sapiente pe' mettece er sale, un avaro l'aceto, uno spregone l'ojo, e un matto che la mischi e che la smucini*).

PASTA: After *fettuccine al burro*, Rome's favorite pasta must be spaghetti, since it has so many ways of preparing it. *Spaghetti alla prestinara* is the simplest, seasoned only with garlic and oil; *alla arrabbiata* is accompanied by pimentos and tomatoes cooked on a very high flame; *alla carbonara*, a particular favorite, employs bits of bacon, beaten egg yolks, and grated Parmesan cheese; and *spaghetti a cacio e pepe* arrives with much pepper and the dry sharp pecorino, which is one of Rome's two oldest and most favored cheeses. The other, ricotta, turns up in *maccheroni alla ricotta*, again in the simple tradition. *Cappelletti* (little hats, from their shape) is a stuffed pasta. There is a miniaturized *fettuccine* of the same egg pasta sliced into strips no wider than a matchstick, called *tonnarelli*—in Rome at least; it is *trenette* in Genoa, where they are particularly fond of it, and *tagliolini* in Florence. Another thin ribbon pasta is *linguine*, which becomes *alla romana* when cooked with ricotta cheese and whipped unsalted butter. Finally the thick ribbed macaroni called *rigatoni* is much liked in Rome.

FISH: Rome has its own version of fish chowder, though it is not on the coast (but the sea is only 14 miles away). Ingredients vary, as they do almost everywhere, according to what is available, but a certain general pattern is followed. Roman fish soup, like Tuscan *cacciucco* or Marseilles *bouillabaisse*, requires some rock fish, the two most generally found being the only fish that *bouillabaisse* cannot be made without, *rascasse* (in Italian *scorfano*), and *capone* (which means big head)—the French *chapon*, also often included in *bouillabaisse*. *Pescatrice*, angler fish, is another common ingredient, but what makes this soup particularly Roman is the addition, whenever it can be had, of *murena*, a sort of lamprey (an echo of ancient Roman days) and octopus. Inkfish may go in too, plus mussels, clams, and a local variety of prawns from the Pontine Islands. Eels (the fat ones known as *capitoni*) are eaten traditionally on Christmas Eve; they are bought alive at the Via Ostiense market, normally for wholesalers, but open to the public for retail purchases on this one day of the year, when the Cottio—literally, "quoting" (of prices)—is opened at 2 a.m. December 24 by the mayor of Rome. For this holiday, the eels are roasted with oil, wine, garlic and bay leaves; the rest of the year they are cut into small chunks and cooked in a sauce containing white wine, olive oil, scallions, garlic and fresh peas. Squid is also cooked in this fashion. *Pagro* (porgy), when served in a similar sauce and accompanied by peas becomes *pagro alla romana*. The Romans cook many fish in paper bags, often with clams, shrimps or both. They serve sole simply, lightly floured, in butter sauce (*sogliola alla mugnaia*). Sardines are stuffed with spinach, rolled in beaten egg and flour, and fried in oil. The ugliness of the toadfish hardly prepares you for the delicacy of its grilled tail, *coda di rospo*. Most cities in Italy have their own ways of dealing with salt cod, and Rome is no exception. *Filetti di baccalà alla romana* is cod fillets dipped in thin batter and fried in olive oil. *Baccalà alla romana* on the menu may denote either cod with tomato sauce, pine nuts and raisins, or cod with tomato sauce and peppers. The tiny clams called *vongole* provide a favorite Roman dish. Rome grills the prawn-like *mazzancolle* with nothing but butter, or, alternatively, bathes them in a wine, cognac and tomato sauce.

ENTRÉES: In this grab bag category of unrelated miscellaneous dishes, Rome has a rich collection to offer. Foie gras, that invention of the ancient Romans, is still in favor with their descendants, who sauté slices of fresh foie gras in butter, nest them on bread also fried in butter, and nap the whole with an unctuous sauce containing pine nuts and little white raisins. Snails (*lumache*), another ancient Roman specialty, are eaten traditionally on St. John's Eve (June 24), in a sauce containing tomato, garlic, anchovy, rosemary, parsley and mushrooms. Eggs Roman style are little omelets, half-cooked separately and then finished in a previously prepared rich sauce of tomatoes, bacon, olive oil, garlic, bay leaf and sweet basil, over which is sprinkled grated cheese and (the Roman trademark again) freshly chopped mint. Roman pizza is soberer than the exuberant Neapolitan version, being made with oil and onions alone (no tomato). Amazingly, the Romans manage to produce quite a few dishes starting only with a slice of bread. *Panzanella* is a poor man's lunch—salad dressing on bread, producing a sogginess which accounts for its name (little swamp). *Pandorato* is what we call French toast—bread moistened with milk, dipped in beaten egg, and fried. *Crostini alla provatura* are also dipped in egg, and before being placed in the oven to cook are covered with a slice of *provatura*, buffalo milk cheese, which melts quickly and impregnates the bread. Finally there is toast soaked with oil and garlic, which the Romans call *bruschetto*, but other Italians refer to as *schiena d'asino*, ass's back.

MEAT: *Stufatino alla romana* is a rib-sticking beef stew made with lean meat, usually from the shin, simmered very slowly with onions, garlic, bacon and marjoram, and often served with stewed celery. Roast veal, served sliced, with *rigatoni*, is called *pagliata*. The head of Rome's famous suckling lamb provides a special dish apart from the rest, *testarelle di abbacchio*, well seasoned with salt and pepper, perfumed with rosemary, doused in oil, and roasted in the oven to a golden brown. Rome's favorite pork sausage is *cotechino;* cooked with lentils, it is a traditional New Year's dish. *Zampone*, stuffed pigs' feet, are also served with lentils, a combination which seems to be peculiarly Roman. *Coppa* is head cheese in Rome, though in other parts of the country the same word has some very diverse meanings. Most Anglo-Saxons, I imagine, would approach the thirst-provoking *coratella* with some misgivings; it is a workman's favorite, made of the heart, liver, lungs and spleen of lamb, heavily peppered, and cooked in olive oil with onions; a more appetizing variant adds tender young artichokes, which reach the right stage, conveniently, at the same season as lambs. *Trippa alla romana* makes this basically tasteless meat delectable by cutting the tripe into thin strips, first boiling it in water, and then simmering it in a thick tomato sauce containing chopped ham, garlic, parsley and (of course) wild mint; it is served sprinkled with grated pecorino cheese. Deep frying is exquisitely done in Rome, another culinary link with Tuscany, but the French poet Paul Valéry thought Rome does it better; he wrote that you have to visit Rome to experience the lightness and delicacy of Italian frying at its best. *Fritto misto alla romana* may contain sweetbreads, brains, kidneys, calves' liver, marrow, morsels of thinly cut veal scallops, minute lamb chops, rice croquettes, potato croquettes, béchamel sauce croquettes, little balls of ricotta cheese and eggs, asparagus tips, cauliflower, summer squash and tiny artichokes in season, most of them rolled in batter before being popped into the fat, some simply coated with flour, and others unadorned—not all of these at the same time, of course, but a selection of half or dozen or so from the varied possibilities.

POULTRY: There are several specifically Roman chicken dishes in addition to *pollo alla diavola*, for which the Roman mark seems to be the inclusion of green peppers—frankly in *pollo con peperoni alla romana*, surreptitiously in the case of *pollo alla romana*, which is sautéed with peppers and tomatoes. They are not included in Roman fricaséed chicken, which is cooked in red wine and stock with chopped *prosciutto* ham, tomatoes, garlic and marjoram. After the eels of Christmas Eve, the Roman family respectful of tradition sits down to roast capon on Christmas Day.

VEGETABLES: Rome is surrounded by market garden country, with results which you can see for yourself if you visit the crowded colorful cheerful open-air market of the Campo dei Fiori, a Babel of bustle and banter, whose often ribald quality may be lost on a foreigner unlikely to know that market wit is sharpened by the consciousness that "fennel" is slang for pederast and "fava bean" for the penis. These two happen to be among the many which Romans, great vegetable eaters, like to crunch raw, after dipping them into *pinzimonio*—only olive oil, salt, and pepper, but the finest oil locally obtainable, from Sabina or Tivoli.

Peculiarly Roman is *cipolline in agrodolce*, tiny new

spring onions in a thin tomato sauce whose sweet-and-sour effect is obtained by a careful dosage of the proportions of vinegar and sugar which go into it. Romans (like the Tuscans again) are particularly fond of the tender little peas called *piselli novelli,* and have been known to boast that theirs are the best in Italy; Venetians would certainly dispute this. Favorite ways of eating them are *piselli al prosciutto,* cooked with onions and the familiar paper-thin ham, and *piselli al guanciale* (on a pillow), with fat pork and bacon. Fava beans are cooked *al guanciale* too. *Fagioli con le cotiche* is akin to American baked beans, cooked slowly and lengthily in a thick tomato sauce with chunks of pork crackling. The Romans are also partial to chick peas (*ceci*). *Pomodori ripieni* are stuffed tomatoes anywhere in Italy, and when you add *alla romana* it indicates that the stuffing is of rice and mozzarella cheese. Peppers can be stuffed too, or combined in the patriotic combination of green peppers, red tomatoes and white onions, the colors of the Italian flag (*bandiera*), which is called *saltato alla bandiera* throughout Italy, but *saltato alla romana* in the capital. *Zucchini,* the long green bludgeon-shaped squashes, are stuffed with chopped meat, and often contain tomatoes and grated cheese as well. Eggplant is more widely used farther south, but there is a *melanzane alla romana* which combines it with a meat and tomato sauce and mozzarella cheese. *Broccoli alla romana* is sautéed in white wine and olive oil with garlic. Chicory *alla romana* is cooked with tomatoes, olive oil, garlic and chopped anchovy fillets. Spinach *alla romana* includes pine nuts, raisins, and bacon drippings. Rome does not believe in overcooking asparagus; in Rome, instead of "quicker than you can say Jack Robinson," the expression is "quicker than you can cook asparagus." Large mushrooms seasoned with oil, garlic and parsley are cooked on a grill or directly on red-hot coals. Finally, the Roman olives are small and black, and Romans prefer them to all others in *antipasto*.

CHEESE: The two cheeses most intimately associated with Rome are ricotta and pecorino, both made here since the days of the ancient Romans, and both of sheep's milk. *Ricotta romana* is a soft white cottage cheese, normally unsalted, although salted and even smoked versions of it exist. It is used extensively in cooking, and eaten by itself as a dessert, sprinkled with sugar, cinnamon, or coffee powder. Pecorino, the most widely consumed of all Italian cheeses, is made in many parts of Italy. Pecorino accounts for about one-seventh of the total cheese production of Italy, and Lazio and Sardinia between them produce half of it. *Pecorino romano*, considered the best, is a firm, sharp cheese, white or straw-colored, made from whole sheep's milk curdled with lamb's rennet, cooked, molded into cylindrical shape, and allowed to ripen for at least eight months. Romans often use it as a grating cheese rather than Parmesan. A special variety made in Lazio is *caciotta di pecorino*, frequently eaten with broad beans. Mozzarella, the soft buffalo-milk cheese, is associated more with Naples than with Rome, but Rome shares a fondness for it, and some of it is produced in the province of Latina, which borders Naples' Campania. Lazio also has its own buffalo cheese, *provatura marzolina*, like mozzarella, but creamier; also like mozzarella, it must be eaten freshly made—neither of them will keep. Other Roman cheeses are *caciotta romana*, semi-hard and bland in taste, and *caciocavallo*, "horse cheese," whose name is explained in various fashions. One is that it was originally made of mare's milk by nomads of the Middle Ages, from which this cheese evidently dates, since the first written reference to it appeared in 1335. Another theory is that it was designed to be carried on horseback, since it is usually sold in pairs, which could be fitted into the two sides of a saddlebag or slung over the horse's neck without benefit of saddlebags, a possibility opened by its peculiar shape. *Cacio-*

cavalli cheeses take the form of elongated figure 8s, the top loops only one-tenth the size of the bottom ones. Knot the two ends of a string around the narrow part between the loops, and all you need then is the horse. Whatever the origin of the name, *caciocavallo* as made in Lazio is a hard cheese made of whole cow's milk, with a thin smooth crust which varies from golden yellow to light chestnut in color, while the interior is white to pale straw. It seems bland enough on the tongue, eaten raw, but in cooking it develops a sharper, more flavorful taste.

DESSERTS: Romans, like other Italians, often choose fruit for dessert, but as fruit is much the same all over the country, there is nothing distinctively Roman to report on this count, except perhaps that a certain type of purple plum is irreverently called "nun's thighs" by Romans, or that watermelon, not particularly common in Western Europe, is so much liked in Rome that in warm weather the sidewalks of the Trastevere quarter blossom with stands where the red black-studded slices of dewy melon await the buyer on beds of ice. Italians are less committed than the French to fruit as the usual dessert, for they are tempted by their splendid *dolci* (sweets), irresistible, imaginative and weight-producing. For some reason, *zuppa inglese*, neither soup nor English (perhaps it owes its name to a certain family resemblance to the English trifle) is associated with Rome, and is certainly a favorite of Romans, though it does not seem to fit into the Roman culinary pattern; it should be Sicilian. Whatever its origin, it combines a rum-soaked cake with custard, in what one food writer has called "an exuberant joke." Many Italian cakes are impregnated with liqueurs, and often have luscious fillings or frostings; when these are chocolate, you are likely to be facing *crema romana*, which is a combination of heavy cream and melted milk chocolate. Macaroni is turned into a dessert in *pasticcio di maccheroni alla romana*, whose recipe seems very strange for a sweet dish, since it includes beef gravy, chopped beef, sausage, chicken livers and mushrooms, along with the *rigatoni* which is its base; the sweet element is provided by *pasticciera* cream and *pasta frolla*. There is a special Roman variety of the latter which differs from the ordinary flour-sugar-butter-eggs-grated-lemon-peel dough by using lard instead of butter for shortening and adding cinnamon. *Pasta frolla* is not a dessert in itself, but it can be used in different fashions in many kinds of desserts, as a crust for tarts, for instance. *Budino di ricotta alla romana*, cheese pudding, might be recognized as Roman without the tag because of the *ricotta*, with which are combined whole beaten eggs plus additional yolks, sugar, cinnamon and grated lemon rind. A good many Roman desserts are linked with holidays. *Pangiallo*, a sort of fruit cake containing raisins, pine nuts, candied orange peel, almonds, and spices, appears at Christmas. *Bignè*, deep-fried pastry puffs which may or may not be filled with cream, and *frittelle* (fritters) or *zeppole di San Giuseppe* are features, as you will have divined, of St. Joseph's Day. *Quaresimali*, dry cookies of flour, egg and toasted almonds, are Lenten fare, and *maritozzi romani*, small soft sweet buns made from egg dough studded with raisins are also particularly favored during this period, though they double as breakfast buns all year round. Finally, though Italy is a great country for ice cream, Rome is not particularly noted for frozen desserts. The most notable exception is *granita*, often described as sherbet, though it is not of the texture Anglo-Saxons think of as sherbet, but more like shaved ice. The favorite flavor is lemon, but there are many other possibilities—coffee, chocolate, strawberry, etc. *Granita* is not ordinarily an end-of-the-meal dessert, but is eaten alone, preferably on a café terrace on a hot day. Roman friends tell me you order it in the morning but not in the afternoon. There is also a *punch alla romana*, which is not, as in Tuscany, a drink, but real sherbet; it could justifi-

ably be described as a frozen drink, though, since its principal ingredient is white wine, to which are added water,
sugar, orange and lemon peel, and, after freezing, meringue;
it then undergoes a second freezing, and is served moistened
with rum.

Rome, like Florence, dominates its province gastronomically to such an extent that very few other places within it
have anything uniquely their own to offer, except produce.
One fertile area is the vast circle of extinct volcanos of the
Alban Hills, a great crater dotted with secondary craters,
now sparkling with pellucid lakes. Here are the Castelli
Romani towns, named for the 13 medieval castles which
dominated the villages clinging to their crests and slopes, a
region well known to tourists. The volcanic soil here is
propitious to vegetables, and it is from here that the first
young tender spring vegetables (*primaticci*) go to Rome.
Nemi is famous for its strawberries and holds a June strawberry festival, the Sagra delle Fragole, to celebrate that fact.
There is another wider tourist circle just beyond the
Castelli Romani towns, and if you follow it inland, counter-
clockwise, through ancient Velletri, with its 14th-century
tower, where the Emperor Augustus was born, and Palestrina, the birthplace of the 16th-century composer (it was
named Praeneste before him), whose ruined temple is one
of the oldest in Lazio, you finally arrive at Tivoli, the Roman Tibur, which not only harbors Hadrian's Villa and the
Villa d'Este, but also has two claims to gastronomic distinction: the local cooking, though not marked by any special
dishes, is reputed to be the best in the area; and the region
about it produces olive oil of high quality.
An important exception to the rule that other cities in the
province of Rome have nothing of their own to offer is
Ariccia, another town of the Alban Hills, which manages,
though only 15 miles from Rome, to challenge the capital

on its own grounds, with a private version of *porchetta*. Ariccia maintains that its housewives have somehow managed to keep its special formula for cooking suckling pig a secret, so I suppose that it was only an approximation of it that I ate at the autostrada restaurant of Frascati, where it was listed cautiously as *porchetta tipica dell'Ariccia al legno di faggio*, or Arricia-type suckling pig roasted over beechwood. Whether authentic, or only a reasonably accurate facsimile thereof, it was remarkably well seasoned, with garlic, parsley, rosemary and lots—*lots*—of pepper.

One other city in the province of Rome might be named for a local specialty, Anzio, which has devised a pasta pie (*pasticcio di maccheroni all'anziana*) different from the Roman *pasticcio* described above. It combines spaghetti with minced beef (or veal) and is often served with a meat sauce, though the dough is sweet and includes grated orange peel and cinnamon. This is simpler than the Roman version, whose complicated mixture of ingredients recalls the cooking of the Roman Empire. It ought to be the other way around, since Anzio, anciently Antium, was the birthplace of Nero. It is therefore the headquarters of the Order of Nero (Ordine Neroniano), whose ostensible object is to preserve the memory of ancient Roman cooking. I was shown menus there which indicated that serious efforts had been made to reproduce ancient dishes, but I fear that the evening I spent with the Neronians was an off-night. Decked out in a laurel wreath topping a business suit (the members of the Order wore togas) and seated enjoyably beside a toothsome starlet representing the Empress Poppaea (presumably fresh from a bath in ass's milk), I was served a meal which made less of an effort to retrace history. It began with spaghetti in a clam sauce, a dish I had eaten, better prepared, a few weeks previously in Novum Eboracum, continued with roast chicken pinch-hitting for peacock, but did end with a dessert that could have been authentic—celery cooked with honey and pepper.

Viterbo, the coastal province north of Rome, once part of Etruria, is mainly agricultural, and includes in its territory the largest lake of volcanic origin in Italy, Bolsena, and a smaller one, Vico. Both, along with Lake Bracciano in the province of Rome, were stocked by the Etruscans with sea perch, *orata* and other sea fish. The ancients apparently did not know that salt-water fish cannot live in fresh water, but neither did the fish, which adapted themselves to the new environment.

The Etruscans do not account for the eels in the lake, however. They swim up the Marta River, its outlet to the sea, in their migration from the Atlantic, and become so tasty in the waters of Bolsena that they led Pope Martin IV into the sin of gluttony. He was from the Touraine, where *matelote* of eel is a much appreciated dish; but this was not considered an extenuating circumstance by Dante (anti-French anyway) who punished him by placing him in purgatory in the *Divine Comedy*.

The specialty of the medieval town of Bolsena is lake trout. The city of Viterbo has its own local treatment for veal chops, while two towns of its province have developed pasta dishes, Canepina of macaroni, Borzacchi of *cannelloni*. It falls almost under the head of treason that Montefiascone, famous for a wine called Est! Est!! Est!!! should harbor a restaurant which makes its *scaloppine* sauce with whisky. The honor of the province is saved by another, in Aquilanti, which offers "Etruscan antipasto."

The coastal province south of Rome, the ancient land of Latina, Oscan before it was Roman, is a country of legend. Here Aeneas first set foot on Italian soil, according to Virgil, and here (if anywhere) Ulysses and his companions met Circe, at what is now San Felice Circeo, where he escaped being converted into *porchetta* by eating the magical herb, moly. The province was a summer vacation playground for the ancient Romans. Lucullus had a villa near Monte Circeo, where you can still visit the therapeutic spring called the Fountain of Lucullus, and the Emperor Tiberius maintained one at Sperlonga. This is the province of the Pontine marshes, which formerly covered 15 percent of its territory. The Romans drained the swamps and made the land fertile; but after the collapse of the Empire it reverted to marshland again. Nevertheless 600 land-hungry peasants from Padua moved into the area during the 17th century, and succeeded by their own unaided efforts in draining and cultivating some of the land. In the 20th century the government reclaimed all of it. Today, in an area once entered literally at the peril of one's life, 100,000 persons live on malaria-free territory.

The Paduans are still there. They maintain an enclave of Venetian cooking, surrounded by the cooking of Lazio. Did they also stock the waters with one of their region's gastronomic glories? If not, we have a biological mystery here: how does it happen that the same crustacean appears only in one small area on the northern Adriatic coast and another small area on the Central Tyrrhenian coast, but nowhere in between? Any Venetian will tell you that genuine *scampi* exist nowhere except in the waters around Venice. Nevertheless Latina's Gulf of Gaeta boasts of its *mazzancolle*, which are *scampi*, though they grow bigger here than in the Adriatic. The two principal cities on the Gulf, Formia (where Cicero is buried) and Gaeta, each has its own special method for cooking them.

Gaeta also has a local dish which combines cuttlefish and artichokes, *seppie con carciofi*. The mussel parks of the Gulf of Gaeta produce particularly succulent mussels, which go into the local *zuppa di cozze*, along with white wine. *Fritti misti di mare* is based principally on squid, mullet, shrimps and sole, but there are dozens of other fish which occasionally contribute to the tender deep-fried morsels of seafood on your plate. Gaeta also has a specialty unrelated to the sea, its glistening black olives. Off the coast lie the Pontine islands, Ponza, Zannone, Palmarola, Ventotene, Botte and Santo Stefano, of which the largest, Ponza, has an area of only three square miles. It is of volcanic origin, its high, jagged rocks are naked of vegetation, savage and almost nightmarish; perhaps that is why legend says that Pontius Pilate was once its governor. Many of the streets are stairways, carved out of the solid rock. Grottoes linked to each other with canals pierce the cliffs at water level; the ancient Romans used to keep in them that ferocious type of lamprey, the moray, considered an oracle, and sometimes decked out with jewels. Thirty-six miles from land, the islands command deep-water fishing grounds, where delicious spiny lobsters are taken and kept alive in submerged traps for marketing. The waters abound also in sea perch, mullets, *orata* (scientific name, chrysophrys), and sole.

Striking inland and moving northward, we come to Fondi, which still possesses considerable vestiges of its preRoman cyclopean walls. Olive trees surround it, and the vineyards which produce Cecubo and, in the shade of Monte Massico, Falerno wines. Orange groves surround its lake, behind which is Monte San Biagio, known for its smoked sausages. The stretch of coast between the lake of Fondi and the sea, from Sperlonga to Terracina, grows the Muscat grape. Terracina (Anxur before the Romans came, when it was a Volscian city), served the ancient Romans as an elegant vacation spot. Its port-canal receives the fishing boats which bring in their catches from the Pontine Islands. Behind it start the Lepini hills, their slopes covered with olive trees, the plains at their feet with fruit orchards. The hills constitute a separate gastronomic island, distinguished not by the creation of dishes of its own, but by a different fashion of preparing those of the general repertory of Lazio.

Behind Latina lies the inland province of Frosinone, a land of vineyards and olive groves (Acuto is noted for its oil). One of its most spectacular cities is Alatri, whose 4th-century cyclopean walls of massive stone blocks are largely intact. If you toil up through its medieval streets (some of which become flights of steps) between mansions whose doors and windows are Gothic arches, you will come out on an acropolis, the cathedral in its center, dominating the Frosinone valley. Alatri is the spiritual capital of the Ciociaria, despite the fact that this band of territory also includes the provincial capital, a far from negligible place itself, with its medieval aspect, and its remains not only of Roman, but of pre-Roman and megalithic times. The Ciociaria is a band of territory which starts northwest of Frosinone and runs across it, parallel to the coast, toward the Campania. Its back country, of which Alatri is more typical than Frosinone, is enchantingly venerable, robust in its eating, and unspoiled by tourists, whose migratory routes bypass it. It is also famous for its pasta, served with a sauce containing fat bacon, ham and sausage, so much appreciated that you will find *spaghetti alla ciociara* or *maccheroni alla ciociara* on many a Roman menu. Either of these dishes would be anathema to Ciociaria housewives, who, if they disdain to eat these tubular forms of pasta at all, buy it at the store. What they make themselves, and what they are famous for, are flat sheets of limp pasta, which are then cut up into ribbons, *fettuccine* style. They make wheat pasta and egg pasta, white, yellow or green, but almost never red—which is rare everywhere. If you drive through the Ciociaria, you will see pasta drying on wooden trays before the doors of most of the houses you pass; if you want to take some with you, you can buy it from your car.

If you elect instead to stop and eat it on the spot, try to work in a trout from the Posta Fibreno Lake.

Rieti, also a province of olive trees and vineyards—the farthest inland of Lazio—is the least dependent on Roman cooking. This is natural enough, since its separate history goes back to the ancient Sabines, whose country it was. Oddly enough, it is here, and not in the province of Rome, that one ancient Roman gastronomic custom has survived. During the December–January holiday period, when the olive oil of the region is still fresh, the people of Rieti regale themselves with flat coarse buns soaked in oil, often flavored additionally with garlic. The bun is called *bruschetta* today, but the ancient Romans called it *clustrum* or *crustulum*, and it was a holiday treat for them too. An ancient inscription preserved in the Villa Silvestri in Arca di Fara Sabina, to which it was removed from the forum of the vanished Roman-Sabine city of Curi, recalls the role of *clustrum*—it was distributed to the people together with *mulsum*, honeyed wine, on important holidays, like the Saturnalia, which came at the same season as Christmas now. Rieti has another Christmas specialty too, *nociata*, a lozenge-shaped confection of honey and ground walnuts. At Easter there is the rustic *pizza pasqualina*, a cake of ricotta, eggs and honey.

Amatrice, a pleasant little town on the slopes of the green Tronto valley, in the prong that pushes farthest inland, bounding Umbria and reaching The Marches, has a specialty often copied in Rome, *spaghetti all'amatriciana*. About half of the Roman restaurants which serve it, evidently ignorant of its place of origin, present it as *spaghetti alla matriciana*, but it is the same thing—unless the Roman cook has taken liberties with the recipe. In Amatrice, the spaghetti is served with a sauce of tomatoes, onions and bacon, cooked in oil, the whole sprinkled thickly with grated pecorino cheese. Rome has a habit of adding tiny hot peppers (or even ginger). Rome also differs from Amatrice by using spaghetti of normal caliber; Amatrice prefers *bucatini*, which is fatter, with a hole in the middle.

Antrodoco is another town with a local specialty—*stracci*, small disks of alternate layers of paper-thin pastry and, between them, ground meat, ground vegetables and grated cheese, doused with gravy, sprinkled with more cheese, and eaten as hot as your mouth can stand it. The tranquil noiseless medieval town of Fara Sabina is noted for its pecorino cheese. Two other towns in the province of Rieti, Accumoli and Vallecupola, also make pecorino. Leonessa, in good pig country, produces various types of salami, while its neighbor, Poggio Bustone, dares like Ariccia to challenge Rome by producing its own version of *porchetta*, celebrated annually at an October food festival.

All this falls into the Sabine-Rieti tradition of home cooking, simple, sturdy and healthy. So do such other local specialties as *agnello in guazzetto*, spring lamb stewed in the *stracciatelle* egg-and-cheese broth; *maccheroni a fezze*, thin threads of egg pasta with meat juice and cheese; and, this time with the merest hint of fantasy, *pollo spezzato alla sabinese*, chunks of chicken in a piquant sauce of olives, anchovies and capers.

Rome has no dearth of beverages to go with its multitudinous dishes, but for the last decade it has been deprived of a Roman pride—"virgin water." Romans considered it the purest drinking water of the city, to which it was delivered from the Alban hills by the aqueduct Censor Marcus Vipsanius Agrippa had built in 19 B.C., a marvel of engineering accuracy which drops only six feet in its 12-mile length. The name is explained by the legend that the location of the spring which provides this water was a secret jealously guarded by those who lived near it until a local girl fell in love with a Roman Legionnaire and gave it away. The ancient aqueduct still supplies the water for the Trevi fountain, the fountains of the Piazza Navona, and the Little Boat at the foot of the Spanish Steps, but the Department of Health, despite the indignant protests of Roman citizens, has ruled it unfit for drinking—after 2,000 years. The Vatican State, however, is still drinking water brought from Lake Bracciano by the Paolo aqueduct, built by Trajan and repaired in the 12th century by order of Pope Paul V.

Romans find ways of consoling themselves for the loss of their water, however pure. After all, it is a Roman dialect saying that *chi manga senza beve, mura a secco* (who eats without drinking—which doesn't mean water—builds without mortar). Lazio has plenty of wine, not the best in Italy by any means, but agreeable enough. It does not travel well, so almost all of it is drunk a few miles from where it is grown.

For foreigners, the best known wine in Lazio may well be Est! Est!! Est!!!, because of the story that goes with its name. German Cardinal Johann Fugger, a wine-bibber of sorts, on his way to Rome for the coronation of Emperor Henry V in 1110, sent his steward, Martin, ahead to scout for inns where the wine was good, with instructions whenever he found one to chalk on its door: *Est* (it is). At Montefiascone, the Cardinal found his advance man sprawled out on the ground dead drunk before a tavern on whose door was scrawled: Est! Est!! Est!!! The Cardinal missed the coronation. He did such homage to Montefiascone wine that in the churchyard of San Flaviano there you can see today the tombstone Martin erected to his memory:

> *Est. Est. Propter Nimium*
> *Est Hic Jo. Defuk Dominus*
> *Meum Mortuus Est*

(It is. It is. Because of too much it is here Jo. Defuk [the steward's or the stonecutter's spelling was weak] my lord, is dead).

Montefiascone wine does not seem worth the sacrifice today, but tastes have changed. It is a rather sweetish white wine, with an occasional natural tendency to sparkle slightly; we like drier wine now. A drier version does exist, not bad if drunk with fish from nearby Lake Bolsena, especially on a warm day, a light wine (no more than 10 degrees for the semisweet, 12 and usually less for the dry) which is far from being a great vintage. It is still quite popular in the region.

If Est! Est!! Est!!! is not the Lazio wine best known to nonresidents, then I suppose, thanks to Horace, Falerno is. This is the Falernian the poet celebrated, grown near Latina's Gulf of Gaeta, today a dry, white, 12-degree wine with a slightly bitter aftertaste if it has been grown between Formia and Massico, but red if it comes from beyond that area. What it was like in Horace's day we do not know. The same is true of another wine he praised, Caecubum for him and Cecubo for us, grown in an area whose corners are Formia, Fondi, Sperlonga and Gaeta. Tiberius and Nero liked it. It is dry, pale red, full-bodied, about 13 degrees, but hardly of imperial quality—at least, not now. The same area grows the fancifully named Sorriso d'Italia (Smile of Italy), a sweet red. There is another ancient wine in Latina, Setino, grown at Sezze, but neither Horace nor the moderns have given it any publicity, and it is all but unfindable today. Romans will tell you that the wines they themselves know best are the Castelli Romani vintages in general and Frascati in particular. The Castelli Romani towns, almost suburbs of Rome, cling to the crests and slopes of the extinct Alban volcanoes, whose soil is propitious to wine grapes. They make quite a to-do about their wine, especially Marino (a streetcar hop from Rome) which on the first Sunday in October puts on the liveliest of the various wine festivals in this area, with bands blaring, food vendors shouting the praises of their wares, amusement park attractions belching a bedlam of mechanical music, processions headed by the parish priest marching to the church, and the town fountain gushing wine instead of water. Not so many years ago the Castelli Romani wines used to be brought picturesquely into Rome by mule cart; but only a mule bent on suicide would affront Roman traffic today.

The typical Castelli Romani wine is white, quite dry, and from 11 to 14 degrees in alcoholic content, but there are numerous exceptions. Frascati, the best known, deservedly, for it is in general opinion the best, is as a rule extra dry, a little above average strength (12 to 14 degrees), and has a sharp clean taste. It is presented in a distinctive narrow funnel-shaped bottle. It also comes in semisweet and sweet varieties (the latter is sometimes labeled Cannellino), and there is even a red Frascati, but this you can ignore. The best place to drink Frascati is Frascati; it suffers noticeably even from the short journey to Rome.

Among other Castelli Romani wines, Colli Albani, 11 to 13 degrees, is usually rather dry, and so are Colli Lanuviani and Velletri. Velletri breaks the general Castelli Romani rule that whites here are better than their associated reds; Velletri red is more interesting than the white. Of the other Castelli Romani wines, the more recommendable include Marino, about as full-bodied as Frascati and fruitier, ubiquitous in Roman restaurants and protean in its forms (besides the standard dry white, there are semisweet, sweet, sparkling, rosé and red Marinos); Colonna, rare and lighter; and Montecompatri, 11.5 degrees. All these wines are apt to turn up on Roman restaurant tables in carafes, or in the attractive earthenware jugs called *brocche*.

Beyond the Alban hills, Palestrina produces a rather full-bodied white, while in its shadow Ottonese has a good dry white which you can only taste there, since all of it is consumed on the spot. Zagarolo makes a semisweet white and red. Farther back still, almost on the Frosinone border at

Subiaco (celebrated for its two monasteries) the extra dry full-bodied Cesana d'Affile and Cesanese del Piglio are produced, the latter perhaps the best of all Lazio wines; both also have sweet varieties. There are a number of reds and whites from the hills which hem in the Tiber north of Rome, of which the best known is probably Monterotondo, but you can easily pass these up. Finally, let us add Castel Bracciano, made on the shores of the lake of the same name, and Nettuno Bianco, from the Anzio region, whose better bottles are sometimes sold under another name, Cervicione.

The volcanic soil so propitious to the Castelli Romani wines appears again in Viterbo, around Lake Bolsena, where Montefiascone is located. There is another Montefiascone besides Est! Est!! Est!!!, Aleatico di Montefiascone. Aleatico is the name of the grape, so it appears elsewhere as well —for instance, there is an Aleatico di Genzano which, though grown in the Castelli Romani region, is not classed as a Castelli Romani wine because the Aleatico grape gives it a character completely different from the others. Aleatico is used to produce sweet liqueurish dessert wines, which is what the Montefiascone Aleatico is, and so are the Aleatico di Pitigliano and Aleatico di Viterbo, both from the same area. Viterbo also produces a dessert wine made from the Muscat grape, Moscato di Viterbo. Canaiolo is a grape name too, a red which is also sweet, very deliberately so, for it is made on the shores of Lake Bolsena from half-dried grapes, as though the grower had started out to make a Vino Santo and then changed his mind. Fortunately, it is light. On the far side of the lake from Montefiascone is a history-conscious wine, Colli Etruschi, Etruscan Hills. It comes in red and white, semisweet and light-bodied.

Latina wines begin immediately when you cross the border from the province of Rome, at Aprilia, which is right on it. Reds, whites and rosés are grown here on reclaimed marshland; they are dry and agreeable enough without breaking any records; the red is the best. The Lepini hills, which might be considered extensions of the Alban hills, produce wines not unlike the Castelli Romani vintages—for instance, Cori, which produces both red and white, drier than the typical Castelli Romani wines, and fuller-bodied. Monte Giove, near Terracina, is well above par; after a couple of years in the bottle (in the rare cases when it is allowed, contrary to local habit, to remain undrunk for so long), it becomes suave and flowery, with enough body to carry the pronounced flavor—12 to 14 degrees. Terracina is where the coastal belt of Muscat grapes begins, running southward to the Campania. Moscato di Terracina is a sweet golden dessert wine, lighter than is normal for its type, 10 to 12 degrees.

The two inland provinces, Rieti and Frosinone, produce humble wines drunk where they are made, just to dampen the meal, without much attention to their taste. I will call your attention to only one place in each: In Rieti, Fara in Sabina makes a pleasant white wine; Horace referred to "the little wine of Sabina." In Frosinone, Anagni produces both white and red. You can forget the latter, but the white, usually dry, 10.5 to 12.5 degrees, though a little rough, is drinkable enough. The real find here is Barbera di Anagni. The Barbera grape comes from Piedmont, where it goes into some of the finest wines of Italy, and even here, so far from its native habitat, it gives a rich red, 13 degrees or better, which is worth hunting for if you are in the neighborhood (you won't find it elsewhere, for it is all drunk on the spot).

Finally, let a man who is not partial to sweet liqueurs, especially if anise-flavored, recommend the one for which he makes an exception—Sambuca, the colorless after-dinner anisette of Lazio. It is produced principally in Civitavecchia, but also in the pasta-making Ciociaria country at Collepardo. Drink it *con le mosche* (with flies). You can order it also in the singular, *con la mosca,* but I like to get over the point that I want more than one fly in my drink—of this kind, that is. The "fly" is a coffee bean. Drop it into the Sambuca, sip the liquid, and crunch the bean at the same time. Its pleasantly sharp flavor takes the curse off the sweetness of the liquor—if there was any curse on it in the first place.

Umbria

"There would be no Tiber if the Nera did not give it to drink," goes an Umbrian saying. The Nera runs the whole width of Umbria, generously making its contribution to the Tiber, which traverses its whole length, at the precise point where the more famous river enters Lazio and ceases to be Umbrian. Inland water is important for this region, the only one in peninsular Italy which has no salt water, but thousand-valleyed Umbria does not lack rivers. It also has some sizable lakes, led, in ascending order of piscatorial importance, by Corbara, Piediluco and Trasimeno. Lake Trasimeno, one of the largest in Italy, shapes the life of the area which surrounds it, particularly its eating habits, not only directly because of its fish, but also indirectly through the fertility and the softer climate it induces.

The greater part of the Umbrians live in high-perched citadel towns, while the more thinly spread peasant population tills the valleys below. Umbria is everywhere mountainous, a land of swiftly rising heights and deep valleys, with landscapes alternately smiling and savage. The proportion of arable land is limited, but to make up for it the many small valleys are green and fertile, watered by the innumerable swift streams which run off the flanks of the hills; and though the hills are unsuitable for tilling, they provide good pasturage for sheep and goats. On lower ground, cattle graze in the region of Lake Trasimeno and pigs in the Tiber valley. Umbria has been noted as meat-raising country since antiquity, when it was also important for its oil, wine and spelt. Spelt has been replaced by wheat now, and the vineyards are in regression, but the olive remains important, for the yield is high and the oil of prime quality, especially when it comes from near Lake Trasimeno or from the slopes of the hills which hem the Tiber in between Assisi and Todi, whose oil is surpassed only by the very best of Tuscany and Liguria. The uplands provide much game, but the wild boars, once considered the tastiest in Italy, are in regression too, though they have not all disappeared yet. Since Umbria is landlocked, it has a continental climate over all of its area. There is a wide range of temperature between the greatest heat of summer and the sharpest cold of winter, and the autumns are rainy. The weight of the Italian sun is less apparent here, where it does not glint dazzlingly off the sea. I do not know if the name Umbria means, as it suggests, "dark" or "shadowy"; but in any case the more rigorous climate must have had its part in shaping the Umbrian character—less sunny, less volatile, less exuberant than in many other parts of Italy; steadier, more solid, harder-headed.

It must have been hard-headed practical businessmen

who in Renaissance times launched themselves into an enterprise which the timorous would have avoided. Umbria, like its former ruler, Tuscany, carried on banking, pioneering in a particular form of it—pawnbroking. It may be that the oldest pawnshop in the world is that established in Perugia in the middle of the 15th century, and it still exists, on the more respected level represented by the Banca di Credito e Pegno. The bank still has its old ledgers; one of them records a loan of "40 pieces" (value unknown) on a machine for catching thrushes, presumably for the table.

The Umbrian saying about the Tiber's debt to the Nera expresses more than just a literal observation concerning the flow of water courses. It is more essentially a veiled figurative assertion that Rome received other and more significant contributions to greatness from Umbria. "There is something of the *essence* of Umbria in Italy," wrote Cyril Ray in André Simon's invaluable *Wines of the World*, and the Umbrians would agree with him. They feel obscurely that Rome has only partly deserved the fame she reaped for qualities better exemplified in their own older and purer culture. Purer, because it held to the sober simplicity of ancient times when Rome succumbed to sybaritism. Older indisputably, for Umbria not only formed part of that Etruscan realm which taught civilization to Rome, but the Umbrians even antedated the Etruscans. Before the rise of Etruria their dominions reached east to the Adriatic and north to the valley of the Po; then the Picenese dislodged them from the east and the Etruscans from the north. When Herodotus wrote that the Etruscans originated in Umbria, he was perhaps misled by the fact that a considerable part of the *population* of Etruria had indeed originated in Umbria—Umbrians who remained on their former lands after the Etruscans conquered them. Even then the role of Umbria within Etruria was far from insignificant. Two of the twelve great confederated cities of Etruria were Umbrian, Perugia and Volsinii (Orvieto); and when, in 1444, a small-scale Etruscan Rosetta Stone, the Iguvine Tables (with an inscription in Latin and Etruscan), was discovered, the place of the find was Gubbio, in Umbria.

The cooking of Umbria is honest and natural, midway between the open-hearted gusto of Lazio and the refined simplicity of Florence. Condiments are used discreetly, with an occasional exception, like the popular peppery *porchetta*. The food is hearty, as mountain food usually is everywhere. Mountain climates make demands on the human body which only good stoking can meet, and mountain food resources usually provide it; running more to pasturage than to tillable soil, mountains require people to put rib-sticking foods into the larder. Living on its own products, Umbria eats more meat than many other Italian regions, because it *has* more meat. The Chiana River crosses the border from Tuscany into Umbria and so do the famous Chianina beef cattle. Perugia lies in their frontier region, which is why it is noted for its beef. The sheep of Perugia absorb tastiness from the wild thyme and sage on which they graze, the hogs from the acorns they find in the woods.

Of all the foods Umbria produces, the most noteworthy is the truffle. When Italian truffles are specified, many persons think immediately of white truffles since, as far as I know, they are found nowhere except in Italy. The white truffle is a specialty of Piedmont. The Umbrian truffle is black, and the tastiest I know. Spoleto exports large quantities of truffles to France, a successful sending of coals to Newcastle. Spoleto used to be the unrivaled truffle center of Italy (the ancient Romans preferred Spoleto truffles to all others), but now Umbria has two truffle cities, the other being Norcia, which has also become renowned for its black truffles, and supports its reputation by holding an annual truffle festival in November.

The Umbrian truffle has supplied a term to the Italian menu not always understood even by the professionals who deal with it—*trifolati,* which describes dishes of diverse kinds, pasta, kidneys, mushrooms, and many others. It indicates an effect so rich as to suggest truffles—*tartufi* in Italian, but *trifole* in Umbrian. It is an unconscious tribute to the Umbrian truffle that its dialect name is used to symbolize richness.

Besides truffles, Umbria produces a wide variety of mushrooms, which grow in the shade of beech and chestnut trees —especially the milky and orange agarics, the flap mushrooms which are the same as the French *cèpes,* and honey mushrooms.

Because Umbria is wheat-growing country, she makes (and packages for sale elsewhere) much pasta, and also cakes and cookies. This is only one department of a food-processing industry based on local products which is an important element in the region's economy. The cherries which Etruscan Perugia provided for the ancient Romans are still supplied to modern Romans. Many fruits are dried for export, especially plums. White figs are stuffed with walnuts and almonds. Refineries at Foligno produce sugar from beets. Vegetables supply local canneries, among them the onions of Cannara and the celery of Trevi—the latter, eaten fresh in tomato sauce, is inscribed on menus as *sedani di Trevi in umido.* The flavoring of many Umbrian dishes is provided by herbs which grow wild and fragrant on the mountain slopes.

Besides the trout of the mountain streams, Umbria enjoys many other fish from Lakes Trasimeno and Piediluco, especially the former. Trasimeno's great specialty is *lasca,* the European roach, considered so great a delicacy that ever since the Middle Ages it has been sent to Rome for the

Pope's Easter dinner. Both lakes also have trout, perch, fresh-water gray mullet, and Trasimeno has eels. There are others for whose names I have been unable to find any translation, perhaps because there are many local and dialect food names in Umbria, inscrutable even for other Italians. The *regina* (which means "queen," which should indicate a high regard for it) is a chunky somewhat greasy fish which is customarily fried in pork fat. There is also a king fish, *céfalo reale*, but this appears to be simply a mullet. *Luccio* is easy: pike.

Umbria is not especially notable as cheese country. Sheep's milk is favored for cheeses. The only two that need be mentioned are both made from sheep's milk, *ravigiolo* and *caciotto*. The most prized *caciotto* is that of Norcia, eaten fresh.

There is great variety from community to community in Umbrian cooking styles, the result of ethnic diversity. This stems from very ancient times, when to Umbrians were added Etruscans from the north, Picenes from the east, Latins and Sabines from the west, and Samnites from the south.

Perugia possesses the longest list of private specialties in Umbria, as one might expect from a capital city so many-faceted and vivacious, and so often in the forefront of history. The city retains many evidences of that history—for instance, an arch whose base is made of enormous stone blocks (Etruscan); above it a central portion of masonry (Roman); and surmounting the whole a 15th-century cupola—2,000 years of history summed up in a single monument. The remains of Perugia's Etruscan fortifications demonstrate that it was one of the strongest of all Etruscan cities. From later periods it has kept the narrow *rioni* (alleys) of medieval times, some magnificent Renaissance palaces, and a famous fountain. Everywhere one comes suddenly and unexpectedly on open terraces affording far-ranging views, for the city enjoys a most peculiar topography. Its center is constructed at a point where several mountain ridges converge from different directions along which its various quarters have flowed outward, separated from one another by deep valleys. Perugia lies sprawled out over its mountains like a drunken amoeba.

In Perugia, as in Rome, the list of gastronomic specialties starts out with *porchetta;* here the suckling pig is generously salted and peppered, and seasoned with a variety of herbs, not necessarily including the rosemary which is indispensable in Rome; it may be cooked either on a spit or in the oven. A treatment of *porchetta* not restricted to Perugia alone, *porchettini umbri ar girarosto*, does use rosemary, but also fennel, and as its name indicates is always spit-roasted. Costana and Bastia have their own particular varieties of *porchetta*, but they agree with the others in making liberal use of the pepper mill.

Fennel is a favored seasoning in Umbria. Not only does it go into *porchetta*, it is added also to *arista perugina*, which omits the rosemary Florence uses with this favorite cut of roast pork. *Scaloppine alla perugina*, tiny veal scallops, sliced thin and cut into pieces about three-inches square, are cooked in butter and served with *crostini di fegatini*, croutons with chopped chicken liver and ham. A dish I encountered myself in Perugia may not be officially considered as a local specialty, but I have met it nowhere else—a combination of veal steak and calf's liver. The game of the region is represented in Perugia first of all by *palombacci allo spiedo* (also called *palombe* or *colombe selvatiche*), spiced spit-roasted wild pigeon. If the menu reads *palombacci alla ghiotta*, it means the same thing, though the translation is then "gourmand's pigeons."

Cardi alla perugina are the same sort of cardoon (*chardons* in French) which are also eaten in France's Touraine; in Perugia they are first cooked in boiling water, then plunged into a thin batter, and finished in boiling oil. Perugian *torcolo* is touted as a local specialty—but it is simply our old friend, the festive Roman *clustrum*, here, as in Rieti, associated with holidays. Perugian cakes and cookies are numerous, and often unrecognizable by name to other Italians, since many of them are described by local words unknown elsewhere. Among them are *attorta*, a twisted pastry filled with almonds, chocolate and fruit. *Pinocchiate* are little sweet tarts whose ingredients include egg and pine nuts. *Torta col formaggio* is cheesecake. *Stinchetti di morto*, dead man's bones, is a rather grim title for a bone-shaped cookie. Then there are *frappe* (leaves, from their shape), *strufoli*, and such candies as *ciaramicole* and *tortion*, once convent specialties, which, according to one dithyrambic local gastronomic writer, accounts for their heavenly taste. Perugia is reputed to make the best chocolates in Italy, which must be pretty close to saying the best in the world.

One other city in the province of Perugia deserves special mention, Norcia. Lying in the middle of a tangle of some of Umbria's most involved mountains, it is the capital of Umbria's mountain climbers. Notwithstanding its truffle festival, its greatest gastronomic fame comes from another category of food—processed pork products. The woods of the region are thick with oaks, whose acorns are relished by pigs. This puts plenty of taste into the pork, and the *norcini* add a great deal more when they convert it into sausage. This specialty is so indissolubly identified with Norcia that in Rome a pork butcher, no matter where he comes from, is invariably called a *norcino*. Norcia makes practically everything in this line you can think of: various types of *salame;* many kinds of both fresh and cured sausage; cervelat; headcheese made from hogs which have fed on horse chestnuts (the region's appreciated fennel goes into this too); rolled pig's cheeks; and of course the Umbrian sausage made in many others parts of the region as well, *mazzafegati*—pig's liver sausages seasoned with garlic, pepper and coriander, which are served fried in oil. Though it is not pork, *testina di vitello alla norcina* (calf's head, Norcia style) seems vaguely related to these productions, if only because ham and fat pork go into the hashed mixture with which the diced pieces of the separately cooked calf's head are coated (it also includes mushrooms, butter, parsley and crustless bread); each morsel is then wrapped in pig's membrane, rolled in breadcrumbs, and finished by frying in olive oil. *Fagiano alla norcese* is pheasant stuffed with truffles and allowed to stand for 24 hours while their flavor sinks in before the bird is roasted; a stiff slug of *grappa* goes into the gravy. *Rigatoni alla norcina*, despite its name, is not necessarily called after its place of origin, but perhaps after the chief ingredient added to this heavy ribbed pasta—ground pork sausage. This is all that goes into it except butter, salt and pepper, and the inevitable Parmesan cheese.

The province of Terni, a local gourmet told me, is characterized by the "sober genuineness" which results from the quality of its raw materials and the simplicity of its cooking techniques. For the former, the purity of the water of the Nera and of Lake Piediluco is credited, most directly when it is a question of fish—trout, *coregoni* (a fish of the salmon-trout family which also exists in French Alpine lakes), pike, and crayfish. Fish are cooked here in the fashion called *pescati carbonaretti* ("the carbonized catch")— they are thrown into the flames and removed only when the outside is completely charred, apparently ruined. Not so; the burned scales are scraped off, the insides seasoned with oil and spices, and all is well. Crayfish (*gamberi*) are served with green sauce and *risotto*. (Terni crayfish are exported in quantity to France, where the local supplies are dwindling).

The Terni region is also good game country. Here wild pigeons are taken during their passage at the two migratory seasons, November–December and February–March, and cooked as a salmi or with a sauce based on its own cooking juices, but with what else I could not discover: "It's an ancient local recipe," was all anyone would tell me. Hare also get the salmi treatment. Other game of the region includes woodcock, quail, pheasant, thrushes—and tern (lake gulls!), all spit-roasted.

The local pasta is *ciriole ternane*, a sort of homemade spaghetti seasoned with a *soffritto* of tomato, garlic and olive oil, and served with a sauce of the strongly flavored local mushrooms—the red *sanguinacci, porcini* (like the French *cèpes*), orange *ovoli, prataioli* (chanterelles) and others. *Tagliatelle all'uovo* would be called *fettuccine* in Rome. Potato *gnocchi* is served with a meat sauce containing bits of kid or mutton. A combination popular in many parts of Italy is polenta with tiny spitted birds; in Terni they are cooked with mushrooms and salt pork. The region makes pork sausage, and hams and racks of pork are cured in the mountain air. Tiny mountain lamb and kid are spit-roasted.

Mountain lamb is also cooked in many other parts of Umbria as *agnello all'arrabbiata*, "angry lamb," so called because of the raging high flame over which it is cooked—very simply seasoned only with salt, pepper, and a sprinkling of vinegar. Among other unlocalized dishes which you may come across almost anywhere in Umbria is spitted thrush, served with thin slices of loin of pork flavored with sage. Umbria has many versions of pasta. The one which sticks most in my memory is *spaghetti ai tartufi neri*. As served to me in Perugia, it employed one very Umbrian ingredient— time. The truffles had been finely chopped the day before and allowed to marinate in olive oil, garlic and anchovy juice for 24 hours before being combined with the spaghetti. The effect was extraordinarily rich. *Spaghetti ad aglio ed olio*, spaghetti with garlic and olive oil, inexplicably fails to mention in its name the other ingredient, precisely the one which makes it Umbrian—ginger.

Umbrian wines could be disposed of with one word— Orvieto. It is the only one non-Umbrians know by name, the only one that is exported, and I think one might safely add, the only one in a class with well known wines of other regions. For most foreigners who drink it abroad (it is much exported) and for many Italians who drink it in other parts of the peninsula, Orvieto is a dry wine, 11 to 13 degrees, a clear transparent pale yellow, harmonious and delicately fruity, with an agreeable slightly sharp aftertaste. However, this Orvieto accounts for only about half of the million gallons made here every year. The other half is the Orvieto the Middle Ages knew, when it was a favorite of popes and cardinals, not to mention painters. When Luca Signorelli and Pinturicchio were working on the cathedral paintings, they took part of their pay in wine. It would have been normal if this had been given them in the local product, but Pinturicchio, being an Umbrian who knew his country's produce, took no chances. In his contract he stipulated that his wine must be of Trebbiano grapes. Orvieto wine was then made from Trebbiano grapes, and the majority of it still is.

Dry Orvieto was developed fairly recently, to meet modern tastes; but even the sweeter Orvieto, called *amabile* or *abboccato,* is not the sort of over-sugary wine that sets the teeth on edge. For one thing, it is lighter in body, 10 to 11 degrees, than is the dry version. For another, the process by which it is given extra sugar, though akin to that which in France produces the very sweet Sauternes, differs in one important detail: Sauternes grapes are allowed to rot on the vine before picking, producing the desired *pourriture noble;* Orvieto achieves its *muffa nobile* by allowing the grapes to start rotting in open barrels after they have been picked. Fermentation is stopped before all the sugar becomes alcohol, which explains the lighter body of the wine. Some persons think the quality of Orvieto, like that of Rocquefort cheese, depends largely on the caves in which it is aged. The cliff on which Orvieto stands is honeycombed with them, and it is in these caves in the porous volcanic rock that the grapes rot, ferment and mature. When ready, the wine is run into bottles of a distinctive shape—bulbous, but not like Chianti bottles; their bulge is wider and flatter, and the bottles hold 25 percent less than the Chianti bottles, though they don't look it.

Orvieto also makes an excellent Vino Santo, aged five years before bottling, rich, unctuous, and verging toward amber in color. There is some red Orvieto about, but it is not in the same class as the white. If the latter had not made the name of Orvieto famous, the red would probably be reaching the table in unlabeled bottles, like many other Umbrian wines. It does not surpass them.

The province of Perugia is a little richer in wines worthy of passing mention, though it has nothing to match Terni's Orvieto. Some very drinkable white wines are grown on the slopes of the hills around Marciano and Perugia itself. The reds of Lake Trasimeno are referred to by Umbrians, but not by Tuscans, as resembling Chianti. The Umbrians are not inexcusably wrong: these wines are not too far removed from ordinary Chiantis, either in taste or in distance.

Perugian wines could very well be left to anonymity, but I give you three, the first two for their merits, the last for its curious name. Greco, 13 to 14 degrees, straw yellow in color, sometimes deepening toward amber, which should be served cold, has a delicate and subtle flavor, and is on the sweet side. If the label reads Greco di Todi, it is all the way over in sweetness, a Vino Santo with a heavy fragrance and a golden color. Sacrantino is in a way its counterpart among reds—it has a light-bodied semi-sweet variety, 10 to 11 degrees, with a distinct fruity flavor, and a determinedly sweet one, 13 to 15 degrees.

The third and last of these Perugian wines I would hardly have bothered to list for its gustatory qualities—it is a heavy (13 to 14 degrees) headache breeder, almost unpleasantly tart nearly to the end of its drinkable life—you have to catch it practically on its deathbed to get it at its best. Perhaps that is why it is called *Scacciadiavoli*—"drive the devils out."

The Marches

The Marches (Le Marche in Italian) comprise four provinces—from south to north, Ascoli Piceno; Macerata; Ancona (whose capital city is also the capital of the whole region); and Pesaro, sometimes called Pesaro e Urbino in memory of the former greatness of the latter city. Put together, they are only three times as large as Rhode Island.

The inland border of The Marches runs along the outer edge of the spine of the Umbrian Apennines, from which minor spurs, perpendicular to the central chain and parallel to each other, divided by deep narrow valleys which break the land up into isolated compartments, descend in gentle slopes to the sea. A narrow coastal plain borders the Adriatic. The sea air, diffused through the valleys, gives the whole region a soft and equable climate. There is not much industry in The Marches except such ancient survivals as the paper manufactures of Fabriano, which date from the 13th century. The region lives on agriculture and fishing. The greater part of the population is concentrated along the coast, where enough fish are taken to satisfy local needs and to supply the markets of Bologna, Milan and Rome.

Agriculture also brings much money into the area. The wheat crop is important, and half of it is exported. The Marches sell much meat to other regions, for the soil is propitious to the raising of fodder crops for meat animals, including a special strain of the Chianina beef cattle which has been developed here. Sheep graze in the Sibilline mountains, which are also a good source of brook trout. Intensive exploitation of the land is the rule here, partly because this is an area of small holdings, whose tillers allow no fertile plot, however small and however inconveniently placed, to lie idle. Fruit trees and espaliered vines rise unexpectedly from wheat fields, wherever, for one reason or another, a patch of soil is difficult to plow. Besides food crops, the region also grows a good deal of tobacco, and raises silk worms.

It is all very quiet and self-centered. The coastal cities do not recall the bustling ports of call where seagoing vessels dock. The boats rolling idly on the swells are fishing boats, whose voyages last no more than a few hours at a time, after which they head for their sole destination—home. The interior is bucolic and calm. The peasants are pious and hardworking, open and tolerant. It is a country which manages to get along without violent emotions.

The Marches defy classification. Their different areas look back to different ancestral habits and have been subjected to divergent influences from their very beginnings. The Marches correspond only approximately to ancient

Picenum; when Ascoli Piceno, Macerata and that part of the province of Ancona inland from the capital city itself were Picenian, Pesaro was Umbrian. If the greater part of the territory may be considered to have been subject to Etruscan influence, lightly, and Roman influence, dominantly, the largest city of the region was originally Greek. Ancona, the best harbor of the northwest Adriatic, was founded about 390 B.C. by refugees from Syracuse. Its very name is Greek, from *ankon*, elbow, for it is built on a peninsula which curves elbow-shaped into the Adriatic, giving it the distinction of being the only city in Italy from which the sun can be seen to rise and set in the sea. Even after the Romans took over, Ancona continued to speak Greek and use its own coinage. The Gauls left their mark here too. Senigallia was once called Sena Gallica, and presided over the *ager Gallicus*, an enclave which the Gallic Senones had established here. Senigallia later entered into another special combination together with two other cities of The Marches, Pesaro and Fano (the ancient Fanum Fortunae, from the temple to Fortune which stood there), and two of Emilia-Romagna, Rimini and Ravenna, to constitute the Pentapolis, under the sovereignty of the Exarchate of Ravenna. Urbino was a separate duchy for more than two centuries. Macerata in Napoleonic times was, briefly, capital of a department of France.

Despite this patchwork background, the cooking of The Marches is not as heterogeneous as one might expect. One noted gastronomic writer has tried bravely to sum it all up in a single phrase as "rough and savory," but it is difficult to arrive at a description of The Marches cuisine which will apply everywhere, for The Marches do not have one cuisine, they have at least two. "Rough and savory" fits the inland cuisine (symbol, *porchetta*) which bows to Roman-Umbrian-Etruscan influence, but the coastal cooking (symbol, *brodetto*) casts a nostalgic glance toward Greece. Both main divisions of the regional cuisine appear in all four provinces, whose topographies are identical. They divide the region into parallel slices, each with its portion of seacoast, and each with a hinterland pushing back into the hills.

Ascoli Piceno, the Asculum of the Romans and the capital of Picenum before the Romans arrived, is also the capital of the inland cuisine, and very much aware of that fact. It must stick in the craw of Ascoli gastronomes to realize that the paternity of one of the most notable dishes in the repertory of The Marches belongs not to Ascoli but to Macerata. This is *vincisgrassi* (in local dialect *vinces-glasse*), a name so unusual and so impenetrable that many gastronomic writers have abandoned the attempt to unravel its meaning, and no wonder, for its source is somewhat curious. The dish was invented in 1799 by a chef of Macerata in honor of the commander of the Austrian occupation forces based at Ancona, and was named for him. *Vincisgrassi* immortalizes, not too efficiently, Prince Alfred zu Windischgrätz.

If the anonymous Macerata chef was weak in spelling, he was strong in cooking. This is how he made *vincisgrassi:*

First, a lasagna was concocted of a five-to-three dosage of farina and semolina flours, well-beaten eggs, much butter and—local Vino Santo dessert wine! A sauce was prepared of consommé, onions, mushrooms, chopped chicken livers, butter, and nutmeg, to which, after cooking, a thick béchamel sauce was added. Meanwhile, the lasagna had been cooked in boiling water. Its sheets were then disposed in a baking dish, layers of lasagne alternating with layers of sauce, and allowed to stand for six hours while the pasta soaked up the sauce. A lighter béchamel was then poured over it and it was baked in the oven until golden. "Serve piping hot (*caldissimo*)," the recipe ends, "with melted butter."

Vincisgrassi is not really indigenous in nature. It is clearly an enrichment of Bolognese baked lasagne, but borrowing seems typical of Macerata. Several dishes considered specialties of the province suggest foreign origins even in their names. *Petti di pollo trifolati* (breast of chicken with truffles) by using the Umbrian word for truffles suggests that the dish itself may have originated across the border. *Cannelloni all'adriana*, which includes ham with this form of pasta, refers itself to the city of Adria, in Venezia. *Quaglie al cognac* (quails in cognac) utilizes a foreign distillation, though the cognac is naturalized by an addition of local white wine. However, *testine di agnello al forno* (roasted lamb's head) bears no obvious outlandish stigmata, though of course it recalls Lazio's *testarelle di abbacchio*.

Ascoli Piceno disdains foreign influences and even seems to claim for itself some foods generally considered as having originated elsewhere, in an aggressive assertion of its own supremacy in inland cooking. A local pamphlet with a chip-on-the-shoulder attitude about Piceno cooking annexes *vincisgrassi* by illustrating its text with a map which adds the province of Macerata to that of Ascoli Piceno without indication that they are not one and the same, and takes over a few other dishes as well in a disarmingly casual fashion, in a footnote to a panegyric on Piceno sauces. "The preparation of sauces," it says, "is based entirely on the products of our soil: aromatic herbs, vegetables grown expressly for this purpose; unfindable elsewhere, these specialties are and remain exquisite as a result of their particular background and cannot become the patrimony of any other cuisine. It is this peculiarity which confers on our foods the signs of a sure authenticity, which does not permit their spreading or their exportation: *brodetto, porchetta, vincisgrassi*, olives, macaroni: if they are not from Piceno, they are bad imitations which hurt our reputation." It is doubtful if Naples would relish the idea that it cannot match Ascoli Piceno in making macaroni. Nor would Rome agree on *porchetta*, of which the pamphlet says, "Only the Marches—since medieval times—have known how to give *porchetta* a golden color and a delicate taste by skillful proportions of wild herbs. The whole secret of Picenian cooking is here: genuine fragrance, artful measure, new but natural flavors. In the characteristic foods of Piceno fragrance and taste, sobriety and vivacity, are harmoniously mixed."

It was the grammarian Enoch d'Ascoli, the pamphlet maintains, who first rediscovered the recipes of Apicius, so it is normal that "in Piceno, first above all other regions, ancient Roman cooking continues to be cultivated, and that it was transmitted and diffused elsewhere by our cooks, instructed by Enoch." It is difficult for the unbiased outsider to discern any particular traces of the extravagant sophisticated Apicius in the rustic cooking of Ascoli Piceno, and it is certainly preferable that one cannot. However, it would be appropriate enough that Ascoli Piceno should maintain links with ancient Rome, for it was bound to it by its umbilical cord, the Via Salaria, which runs right through it, crossing one of the city's two remaining Roman bridges, the Ponte di Cecco. Some Picenian produce moved along this road to Rome. In ancient Roman days, as in ours, a whole roast pig was customarily served with an apple in its mouth, and the apple was likely to be Picenian. Horace described Picenian apples as small but exceedingly tasty, whose like could be found nowhere else. A few centuries later another famous writer, Boccaccio, praised Picenian salame, whose superiority he attributed to the fact that the sausage casings were made from the intestines of the same pig which produced the meat.

The city of Ascoli Piceno has many specialties, of which the most widely known is its stuffed olives, *olive all'ascolana.* They are demanded throughout Italy, justifying the enthusiastic pamphlet's description of them as "definitely an exclusivity, not because the recipe for the stuffing is a secret, but because this fat fleshy olive, with its delicate

appetite-provoking aroma, can only be found in Ascoli."
Pizza rustica is made in Ascoli of egg pasta filled with green
vegetables, cottage cheese, sausage and herbs (Ancona pizza
is less complicated, simply a cheese tart, *pizza con formaggio
all'anconetana.*) Fennel-flavored snails are served salmi fashion in Ascoli, but elsewhere in the region *lumache alla marchigiana* means that they are cooked in a sauce containing
white wine, olive oil, butter, chopped onions, garlic, thyme
and tomato paste, and served on toast.

Many other localities in the province of Ascoli Piceno
have their own individual specialties—Offida its mushrooms; Montegiorgio its *calzoni* (small meat-stuffed ravioli, first boiled, then browned in the oven); Fermo (an
ancient Sabine city) its sweets, such as *casarecci*, a sort of
bun, and *ciambelle col mosto*, a ring-shaped wine-flavored
cake; Carassai its cheese, which must be eaten fresh; and the
whole Aso valley its fresh-water fish.

Certain cities in the other provinces also have their own
specialties of inland cooking. Fabriano, in the province of
Ancona, is the home of a sausage which once met Boccaccio's specifications, but no longer does. *Salame Fabriano* was
once all pork, but is now a mixture of pork and *vitellone*
(baby beef). Pesaro, though it is on the sea, presiding over
a hinterland of vineyards and orchards, has a specialty
which has nothing to do with seafood and is, indeed, something of an artificial creation, resulting from the accident
that this is Rossini's birthplace. Hence the local *tornedò
alla Rossini*—a round cut of steak cooked in a casserole with
ham, mushrooms, parsley, pepper and lemon. This is a far
cry from the classical *tournedos Rossini* known all over the
world, which is grilled and is distinguished by a slice of foie
gras balanced on top of the steak. *Tournedos Rossini* is a
French creation, named for the musician who was the idol
of Paris, where he lived for many years and where he died.
It is possible that Pesaro was spurred by the example of Paris

to produce itself a dish to honor its most famous citizen.

Another specialty of The Marches was not simply named for a famous man, it was created by him. The important personage in this case was Federigo da Montefeltro, Duke of Urbino, an ardent patron of literature and art, who created in his capital the atmosphere which would permit it to develop such great artists as Raphael and Bramante, the first born in Urbino itself, the second just outside it, in Fermignano. Duke Federigo was given to apprehension. When a falcon clawed out his right eye, he had a surgeon chop a hole in the bridge of his nose, so that his left eye could look through it and spy a possible assassin attacking from the right. He was also afraid of poisoners, so he ordered that everything served him should be left unseasoned. His theory was that the taste of poison would be detectable in unseasoned food before enough of it could be downed to prove fatal. However, he did not propose to spend his life eating flavorless food, so he created his own sauce, of secret ingredients, and after the first cautious exploratory bite of a dish placed before him, he would make the sauce himself at the table, and proceed with a sense of safety. The sauce disappeared with him, to be rediscovered nearly five centuries later (so the story goes) by a playwright named Paolo Serano, who stumbled upon the recipe while consulting old documents during research for a historical play. He made the sauce, tasted it, approved of it, and put it on the market. It is sold in bottles which bear the Duke's striking, if damaged, profile, but not the list of ingredients which compose it. They are still secret, except one—honey, whose taste, like that of poison, is difficult to conceal.

We need not continue with the interminable list of local specialties except perhaps to pay homage, in a region distinguished everywhere by the quality of its vegetables, to the particularly luscious ones of Iesi, especially its tiny tasty cabbages. Iesi (also often written Jesi), the ancient Aesis, was the birthplace of two famous men—Frederick II of Hohenstaufen in 1194, and Pergolesi in 1710. However, we might note a few other examples of the inland cuisine which are not attached to any one spot, but may be found almost anywhere in The Marches. *Pasta asciutta alla marchigiana* differs from ordinary pasta in that it is made from bread dough, which after it has been rolled into a flat sheet and cut into strips, like any ribbon pasta, is allowed to rise like bread before it is cooked. It is served with any of the sauces used on ordinary pasta. The standard pasta egg dough is used for *ravioli di ricotta*, stuffed with cottage cheese, and served with tomato sauce and grated cheese, and also for *pasticciata*, when it is seasoned with meat sauce and fresh buffalo-milk cheese and finished in the oven. The excellent meat and game of The Marches give rise to a series of pungently flavored pâtés.

Some Marches names are a trifle deceptive. *Olivette* have nothing to do with olives; they are small bite-sized morsels of veal, cooked in a white wine sauce flavored with herbs, but they do look a little like whole olives in their sauce. They are also called *bocconcini*, "mouth pleasers." *Pan pepato* is neither bread nor thickly peppered, as one might assume (nor gingerbread, as a Frenchman might think on the analogy of *pain d'épices*), but a sort of nougat including candied fruit, almonds and sultana raisins.

Ancona is the capital of the coastal cuisine, as Ascoli Piceno is of the inland cuisine, but, like Ascoli, it admits that it has been deprived of the outstanding dish of its repertory by the province of Macerata. As a former Greek city, Ancona ought to be the capital of The Marches' classic Greek dish, *brodetto*, but it is not. Six cities of The Marches besides Ancona—San Benedetto, Porto San Giorgio, Porto Recanati, Numana, Falconara and Senigallia—each insists that its *brodetto* is the best; but it is generally admitted that the palm goes to Porto Recanati. This is the seaport of Recanati, an important agricultural market for wheat, wine and other products from the food-rich province of Macerata, which raises meat animals on the mountains, fruit trees and vines on their slopes, and wheat in the plains.

The *brodetto* of The Marches (the very ancient and very rich fish chowder said to have been invented in Athens and in any case spread throughout the Mediterranean by Greeks) is the *cacciucco* of Leghorn, the *ciuppin* or *buridda* of Liguria, the *cassòla* or *ziminu* of Sardinia, the *ghiotto* of Sicily, and, going beyond Italy to include the most famous member of the family, the *bouillabaisse* of Marseilles. Something like 1,000 years before the Greeks brought *brodetto* to Italy, Achilles and Agamemnon, according to Homer, ate it beneath the walls of Troy. Something like 1,000 years later (in January, 49 B.C.) a very similar version of it was consumed in considerable quantity at Forum Livii (today Forlì) by Julius Caesar, who, fortified by it, proceeded to cross a stream called the Rubicon. Another 2,000 years and nobody knows how many wars later, another noted military man, Field Marshal Bernard Montgomery, sat down to virtually the same dish at virtually the same spot. It is also on record that Dante drowned the sorrows of exile in the *brodetto* of Porto Corsino, and that Napoleon downed a version of it, prepared for him by the fishermen of Porto-ferraio, before escaping from Elba to launch the Hundred Days.

To make a successful *brodetto*, an Italian culinary expert has written, "you must have a good sense of smell. You have to go to the seaside early in the morning and sniff the air to find out if it is going to be a good day for all kinds of fish, for if the *brodetto* lacks a fish, a single fish, a minute fish, a fish of no importance at all—well, the *brodetto* can't be a real *brodetto*."

This is all very well, but it seems to imply that there is a fixed invariable list of fish for *brodetto*, all of which must be present for genuineness, but this is just not the case. Every city, town, village and hamlet has its own version of *brodetto*, each has a different idea of what fish should go into it, and there is a tendency in every locality to assume that its own recipe has been communicated to it by divine revelation and all others are shameful, if not downright immoral. Yet the very places most convinced of the sacrosanct quality of their own special variety of *brodetto* sin regularly against it. Their ideal *brodetto* never gets made. The only element about *brodetto* which is always the same is that it is never the same. Its ingredients on any given day do not depend upon a theoretical recipe but upon what the fishermen happen to have netted. *Brodetto* is the child of happenstance —which raises the question, "If *brodetto* is simply the product of chance, if no locality honors its recipe, how can you distinguish one *brodetto* from another?"

The answer is that the local distinctions are based not on a complete invariable list of ingredients, but on a few key fish of the many which go into the *brodetto*. Each place has its own requirements for the fish—probably only two or three—which *must* be present in the *brodetto*, and usually one or two others which must *not* go into it. Once the fish that have to go in are present and those which must not have been sternly excluded, the rest can be filled in from a lengthy list of other admissible fishes, which also differs from place to place.

One fish, however, is on almost every list. This is the *scorpena* or *scorfano* (local form, *scarpena*), the hogfish, which is the French *rascasse*. You can vary the other fish in a *bouillabaisse*, but it isn't authentic without *rascasse;* and most Italians would agree that whatever other fish you put in or leave out, you must include *scorpena* to make an authentic *brodetto*. The *scorpena-rascasse* has poisonous spines, which might lead to the conclusion that a mild dose of venom is essential to the great Mediterranean fish chowders. This peculiarity led the late A. J. Liebling to rehabilitate the legend that Venus fed *bouillabaisse* to her husband Vulcan to put him to sleep whenever she expected Mars to call. The soporific effect of *bouillabaisse* had been attributed to its saffron. When saffron was proved not to be a soporific, Liebling, after tracking down the poisonous nature of *rascasse* and identifying it with the venomous stonefish of American waters, suggested that if *bouillabaisse* were sleep-inducing, it might be an effect, not of the saffron, but of the fish. "Venus," he wrote in *The New Yorker*, "may have known a thing or two about *rascasse* . . . an unduly large proportion of *rascasse* in the quick stew [he described it thus since *bouillabaisse*, whose name seems to mean "boil slowly," is actually cooked very fast] might have the same effect as a weak dose of the related stonefish poison. It could well have put even Vulcan to sleep . . . and it may have served as a catalyst, or latchkey, in many a meridional love affair . . . Proving saffron blameless does not exculpate *bouillabaisse* as a form of conjugal knockout drops, if *rascasse* is present. (It would be, incidentally, the kindest form of sedative yet invented, and a tribute to the savoir-faire of Venus, who understood how to keep husband and lover concurrently happy.)" There does not seem to be on record any case of *scorpena* having been used as a latchkey, but Adriatic fishermen, most of whom may be presumed to be married, do refer to it as *un pesce brutto*, a villainous fish. This may refer simply to its appearance, which is villainous enough, whether you are thinking of the reddish variety (*scorfano rosso*) or the *scorfano nero*, which is a gray-brown spotted with black.

Fish are not the only ingredients concerning which each locality has its own ideas. There is a story about a restaurant owner of Numana who, having heard that the best of all *brodetti* was made at Porto Recanati, determined to learn its secret. Dressed like a beggar, he entered a Porto Recanati restaurant on a cold winter day and snuggled up to the warmth of the stove—a convenient stance from which to follow the process by which the famous *brodetto* was made. When he saw a yellow powder added to the soup, he was reassured—not to say disdainfully delighted. He returned to his home town and aroused gales of scornful laughter among his fellow citizens by his report that the poor ignorant cook of Porto Recanati had known no better than to put saffron in his soup!

You can bring Marseillais, to whom it has never occurred to leave saffron out of *bouillabaisse,* to the verge of blows over the question of whether or not lobster should go into it, and you can bring Adriatic cooks, to whom it rarely occurs to put lobster into *brodetto,* to the verge of blows over the question of whether or not saffron should go into it.

There are three points on which all *brodetto* makers agree: (1) the olive oil used in this soup should be of the best obtainable quality; (2) only very fresh fish should be used; (3) in preparing the fish for the pot, they should be washed in sea water, never in fresh water. The last two stipulations make it impossible, even with the right fish, to produce inland a *brodetto* which the coastal dweller will recognize as the real thing.

Other details vary. The fish are usually cut up into chunks for *brodetto,* but in some places they go into it whole. Most recipes call for white wine, but not all of them. Certain cooks include crustaceans or squids, others abhor them. Some *brodetti* are made with onions, or garlic, or tomato; others are not. Cooking techniques and cooking times differ.

Porto Recanati *brodetto* is a thick chowder so full of fish of diverse sorts, especially rock fish, that you can hardly find the liquid. It is flavored with saffron and hotly spiced. This is evidently almost the same thing as the *bouillabaisse* of Marseilles. There are any number of slightly different local versions in other cities along the coast, including that of Ancona, which do not use saffron.

In ancient times, Ancona was a port accustomed to receiving ships from far away, and until recently it was still largely used by commercial intercoastal shipping. But the number of Adriatic lines has diminished under competition from automobiles and planes, so it is now almost exclusively a fishing port, where some 4,000 large-scale operators man 350 powered boats, while the rowboat fleet is uncountable. Their catch has given Ancona the opportunity to achieve a particular reputation for skill in grilling fish, which would seem to be a straightforward enough operation, but connoisseurs swear that *pesce ai ferri all'anconetana* are the tastiest that can be found anywhere. A markedly local specialty is *crocette*, sea snails, which are served in a hot sauce rich with herbs and spices.

Ancona presents cod with *potacchio anconetano*, an all-purpose sauce containing olive oil, local white wine, tomatoes, garlic, parsley and rosemary. This sauce is so highly thought of that on menus the sauce is featured, with the name of the food it accompanies appended as a sort of afterthought—*salsa di potacchio anconetano con agnello e pollo*, Ancona *potacchio* sauce with lamb and chicken, *salsa di potacchio anconetano con stoccafisso*, Ancona *potacchio* sauce with stockfish, etc. Among the other foods with which it appears are veal, rabbit and hare, sometimes with modifications to accord with the particular dish in question. Cod with this sauce is not the same thing as *stoccafisso all'anconetana*, for which the fried cod that looks like a piece of wood when you buy it, after being soaked back to limpness, is cooked with onions, tomatoes, garlic, olive oil, pepper, ground anchovies, and—rather curiously—a small amount of milk, added at the last moment. One food for which Ancona is noted seems to get us rather far from the sea—quail—but in a sense, at Ancona they come from the sea too. Great flocks of migrating quails pass over the city twice a year, in April and November, crossing the Adriatic from or to Yugoslavia.

Among dishes from the sea not particularly associated with Ancona, which are likely to turn up anywhere along the coast of The Marches, are squid in a white wine sauce given a tang by chopped-anchovy fillets, and a lift by red pepper. Mussels of the type called, from their shape, *datteri* (dates) are marinated in oil, vinegar, sage, and garlic before cooking. Ascoli Piceno adds *coda di rospo* to this list, with the observation, "a typically Picenian dish." It is a typically Roman dish too.

The Marches are not notable for wine. There are vineyards everywhere, but they produce small local wines, pleasant enough to drink with the food of the region—which indeed is how they are drunk, since they are consumed on the spot. There is one exception: Verdicchio dei Castelli di Jesi, which is exported and woos the foreign consumer by being put up in amphora-shaped bottles. As one might divine from the wine name, Iesi, like Rome, has its cluster of castle towns—Cupramontana, Maiolati, Spontini, Rosara, Castelplanio—and, like the Castelli Romani, they are wine producers. The typical Castelli di Jesi wine tests at 12 to 14 degrees, is a bright straw yellow, which sometimes verges toward amber, and has a sharp clean dry taste which improves greatly with age. There is also a semisweet variety which has less character, a *rosata* (rosé) which has almost none; and a sparkling variety which has character all right, but of the wrong kind.

The others you will not meet unless you happen to go to the places where they are grown. Bianco Piceno (11 to 13 degrees) and Rosso Piceno (10 to 12) are both a trifle tart, but Montepulciano Piceno (12 to 14) is a full-bodied bright-ruby-colored wine with a distinct nutty taste. Rosso Montesanto, also bright ruby, is recommendable, but is rather neutral in flavor. Agreeable but unsensational table wines are Bianchello Conero and Rosso Conero.

The Marches also make a Vino Santo which is highly thought of, the best coming from Urbino. There is also a *vin cotto* (cooked wine), which The Marches may have borrowed from neighboring Abruzzi, which also makes it. It is very sweet, like Malaga, and also very strong—20 degrees. Ascoli Piceno makes an anisette which is drunk throughout Italy.

Emilia-Romagna

Emilia-Romagna was created unintentionally by a man who never knew what he had done; by the time the achievement was consummated, he had been dead for many centuries. The author of the region was Marcus Aemilius Lepidus, who, in 187 B.C. built, and provided the name for, the Via Aemilia, the Emilian Way—which ran from Ariminum (Rimini), on the Adriatic, to Placentia (Piacenza), on the border of Lombardy.

Probably no other political entity of comparable importance has ever owed its formation so largely to a road. The trade artery provided by the Emilian Way held together throughout the centuries territories on either side of it, despite the powerful centrifugal forces exerted by their political oppositions and their disparate cultures. The same road, though nowadays it carries automobiles instead of chariots, remains the spine of Emilia-Romagna. Of the region's eight provincial capitals, all except two (Ferrara and Ravenna) lie on the Emilian Way. They mark the node points where important north-south roads, most of them dating also from ancient times, cross the east-west Emilian Way. Rimini, at its beginning not itself a provincial capital, was linked to Rome directly by the Via Flaminia, and indirectly by the Via Popilia, which prolonged the Via Salaria along the coast. At its end, the Via Aemilia was stopped at Piacenza by the Via Postumia, which crowned it like the crossbar of a T on its way from Genua (Genoa) to Concordia, in the neighborhood where Venice would rise later. Forlì stands where the Florence-Ravenna road crosses the Emilian Way; Bologna where the Florence, Prato, and Pistoia roads cut it on their way to Ferrara; Modena at the crossroads with the Pistoia and Lucca highways to Verona; Reggio nell'Emilia at the La Spezia-Mantua junction; Parma at the meeting with the La Spezia-Cremona road. Cities of minor but not negligible importance are interspersed between the capitals. From east to west the glittering beads threaded on the Emilian Way are named Rimini, Savigliano, Cesana, Forlì, Faenza, Imola, Bologna, Castelfranco, Modena, Reggio nell' Emilia, Parma, Fidenza, Fiorenzuola, Piacenza.

Man gave Emilia-Romagna economic unity by building the great road which runs for 125 miles through its center. Nature gave it geographic unity. The Emilian Way was constructed where it is because it bisects a rich plain running all the way from Piacenza to the Adriatic, which required a trade artery to drain its products toward outside markets. The regional limits are all natural—to the east, the Adriatic; to the south, the Tuscan Apennines; to the west,

LOMBARDY

to Turin
to Milan
Po River
to Cremona

Piacenza
RICE DISHES
GUINEA HEN IN CLAY
POULTRY
KID
COPPA ARROSTO
POLENTA E CICCIOLI
FRUIT AND
ALMOND TART
PROVOLONE
CHEESE

RICE

Busseto
SAUSAGE
POULTRY
SPONGATA

to Mantua

*Grazzano
Visconti*

Colorno
ROASTS

Luzzar
P

Fidenza
TOMATO EXTRACT

WHEAT

MAIZE

PIGS

COWS

PARMESAN
SCARPAZZO

GRAPES

Parma
HAM
PARMESAN EGGS
BOILED OR
BAKED VEGETABLES
FRIED FRESH-WATER
FISH
PASTRY
ICE CREAM

*Reggio
Emilia*

Rubiera

FRIED MUSHROOMS

Sandi

BURTLEINA

Canossa

Sassuo
SASSOLINO
LIQUEUR

GUTTURNIO WINE

MONTEROSSO WINE

TREBBIANINO WINE

to Genoa

to Genoa

LIGURIA

Parma River

to La Spezia

TROUT

GAME

T U S C A N

GAME
BURLEN
TIGELLI
CHESTN
MUSHR
WALNU
TROUT

to La Spezia

to Pistoia

EMILIA-ROMAGNA

Miles

0   25   50

Km.

VENEZIA EUGANEA

to Venice

Po River

Stellata
STURGEON
CAVIAR

Pontelagoscuro
ALMONDS
MACAROONS

Copparo
BUTTER
WHEAT

Mesola

Ferrara
SAUSAGES
PASTA
PAMPEPATO
CIAMBELLE

Tresigallo

Codigoro
EELS

Pomposa

Bologna
TORTELLINI
TAGLIATELLE
MORTADELLA
COSTOLETTA ALLA
BOLOGNESE
INVOLTINI
MAIALE AL LATTE
TRIPPA ALLA BOLOGNESE
TURKEY ALLA BOLOGNESE
FRITTO MISTO ALLA BOLOGNESE
TORTA DI RISO/
PANSPEZIALE
FRITTURA
PIGS

CHEESE
PEARS
GRILLED EELS

Lagosanto

Spina

FRUIT
SUGAR BEETS

Comacchio
BOSCO ELICEO WINE
EELS
FISH
SALT

Porto Garibaldi
CIUPETA BREAD

SOLE
TURBOT
SARDINES
TUNA
RED MULLET
GRAY MULLET
HOGFISH
DENTEX
ORATA
ANGLERFISH
SAN PIETRO
LAMPREYS
RAYS
CUTTLEFISH
DOLPHINS
LOBSTER
SQUILL
CRAYFISH
CLAMS
MUSSELS
SEA TRUFFLE

Massa
Lombarda

VALLI DI
COMACCHIO
SUGAR BEETS
WHEAT

Lugo
FROGS
ZUPPA ROMAGNOLA

Ravenna
BRODETTO
FRIED FISH
ASPARAGUS
POLLO AL LIMONE

A
D
R
I
A
T
I
C

S
E
A

SOGLIA FLOUR

Marzabotta

Imola

Russi

Faenza
ZUPPA AI SELLERI
CAPELLINI AL POLLO

Forli

Bertinoro
ALBANA WINE
SANGIOVESE WINE
TREBBIANO WINE

Cervia

Cesenatico
SEA FOOD
CIAMBELLE

to Florence

CATTLE

TORTA CAMPAGNOLA

LA SAPA

Cesena
BALSAMELLA
SAUCE

Rubicon River

BRODETTO WITHOUT EELS
FRIED SARDONE
PIADONE COI CICCIOLI

Rimini

Riccione

CLAM SOUP
ROAST CRAB

to Florence

VIA FLAMINA

VIA POPILIA
(prolongation of
VIA SALARIA)

THE MARCHES

Great Eating
Good Eating
Etruscan Cities

N

NOTE:
Map shows the modern Via Emilia,
parallel to the ancient road.
Designed purposely to bypass
urban traffic, it leaves off to
one side or another cities which
stood on the ancient road.

VIA EMILIA

the Ligurian Apennines; to the north, the Po.

If Emilia-Romagna possesses geographical unity, it has not been blessed by historical unity. It did not become a political entity until modern Italy was created in 1861. Until then, each city knew a separate crowded history of its own, often spectacular—Ravenna, Ferrara, Bologna, Parma are names which clang in the mind like great bells. The extraordinary complexity of the story of this region, its fragmentation, its local particularism, are fitted into an extremely small area. Its eight provinces—Ferrara, Ravenna, Forlì, Bologna, Modena, Reggio, Parma, Piacenza—are each a little larger than Rhode Island.

The history of Emilia-Romagna is a theme with variations. The different provinces provide the variations. All began with shadowy early settlers about whom little or nothing is known, Ligurians in the west, Umbrians in the center and east, and along the coast unidentified dwellers in buildings supported on piles. The Etruscans were present in the Bronze Age, but apparently not in force; they seem to have exercised overlordship, supplying a skeleton group of governors, without settling en masse. The Celts, represented by the Boii, dislodged the Etruscans, the Romans dislodged the Boii, the Goths dislodged the Romans, the Byzantines dislodged the Goths. By this time, the center of power had shifted to Emilia-Romagna, for when the Roman Empire declined, the Emperors fled from unsafe Rome to Ravenna, protected by its quagmires, and their successors stayed on. Part of the region was included in the Exarchate of Ravenna, which the Byzantine Empire set up to govern its overseas dominions. For every province, the Middle Ages were checkered. The great cities alternated between independence—as communes, republics, duchies or signories—and subservience, usually loose and often only nominal, now to the Holy Roman Empire, now to the Papacy, and occasionally even to both at the same time.

These phases were complicated by periods of domination by a constantly shifting series of family dynasties which passed their fiefs back and forth through conquest, marriage or purchase.

The double-barreled name of Emilia-Romagna is a product of its history. Romagna is the eastern section, which lies on the sea, with imprecise boundaries. The provinces of Forlì and Ravenna are indisputably in Romagna, which overflows into at least the southern part of the province of Ferrara and also into Bologna, extending at least as far as the capital itself; the adjoining province of Reggio Emilia expresses the opinion that *all* of the Bologna province is in Romagna by naming a town on the Reggio-Bologna border Finale Emilia, "the end of Emilia."

The name of Romagna results from centuries of close association between this area and Rome. It was an integrated part of Roman territory (under Augustus, part of the eighth region into which he divided his Empire) at a time when the cities of Emilia were still only colonies; it contained, as we have just seen, the capital of the declining Empire; and it was under the almost uninterrupted control of the Papacy while Emilian cities were undergoing vicissitudes which aligned them sometimes with Rome and sometimes against it.

Emilia is the western inland part of the region—indisputably all of the provinces of Piacenza, Parma, Reggio and Modena, and with less exactitude, parts of Bologna and Ferrara.

The long plain which runs the whole length of Emilia-Romagna is of alluvial soil, among the richest in Italy. Its culture is varied and intensive, requiring the bulk of the population to live in the lowlands. Hot summers are propitious to fruit trees; the production of table grapes is important. Emilia-Romagna leads all other regions of Italy in the production of wheat, tomatoes, sugar beets (especially in Ferrara) and hemp (Bologna and Modena). It is third for rice and cattle. Wheat and maize grown between the Po and the Apennine foothills account for two-thirds of the regional resources. Pigs are raised in large numbers. These products account for the numerous food industries on which the economy of the region is based. Wheat makes Emilia-Romagna the greatest pasta country in Italy. Pigs make it the greatest ham and sausage country. The cows give rise to milk products (Parmesan cheese especially). The vegetables and fruit support canneries.

The combination of abundant food resources and multitudinous separate histories and habits makes Emilia-Romagna the most complex gastronomic region of Italy. There are two underlying divisions of cooking: a coastal cuisine depending largely on seafood, and an inland cuisine. Each province, and in many cases every important city within each province, rings changes on one or the other—or both—of these two basic divisions. Those which reach for some distance into the Apennines display a second two-way division of cooking styles, lowland cooking and mountain cooking.

Despite this diversity, Emilia-Romagna displays certain general characteristics common to the whole region. First of all, it is a country of hearty eaters. One Italian expert describes its provender as "he-man's food," but it is for he-men who appreciate the fine points; quality as well as quantity are important here. "The people of Emilia and Romagna," says another Italian source, "are strong, hard working, warm blooded, and above all cordial and *bons vivants*. It follows that their gastronomy has a robust character, healthy and tasty, with a number of really typical dishes. Nothing is lacking." "The cuisine of the region," writes Cyril Ray, "is rich and hearty, and the Romagnoli are noted for their size and their appetites. Italians from other regions criticize the *cucina bolognese* as being *ingras-*

samento, fattening, but it is noticeable that they gladly patronize any restaurant in their towns that offers Bolognese cooking, and strive to be able to afford a Bolognese cook."

Consistent with a robust cuisine is the fact that, though all three of the principal cooking fats—butter, olive oil and lard—are used in the cooking of the region, the commonest is the heaviest—lard. It is possible that the cuisine has gained in heartiness since it was decided that the local soil is too rich to be wasted on growing olives. The country did produce olives until about two centuries ago, and such excellent ones that in former times the Visconti twice a year sent from Milan yokes of handsomely harnessed oxen to exchange not only for the famous sausages of Bologna, but also for its olives.

The existence of Ferrara is the result of the nonexistence of Spina. Spina, first Greek and then Etruscan, is today only a point on the map where archeologists dig for shards of pottery, but in its heyday, between the 3rd and 6th centuries B.C., it was an important harbor at the mouth of the Po, the principal port for the great Etruscan city of Felsina, now Bologna. The erratic Po ended Spina's period of brilliance early in the Christian era, when it shifted its course, leaving Spina inland, but not exactly high and dry. If the Po was now too far for commerce, it was too near for comfort. Its periodic overflowing changed solid soil to marshland, into which Spina gradually sank. After an unmeasured period of island hopping, the inhabitants grew tired of shifting from hillock to hillock in the mire, moved inland and settled Ferrara.

The earliest known documentary reference to Ferrara dates from 753 or 754, when it was listed among the dependencies of the Exarchate of Ravenna. In the same century it became independent, but two centuries later was destined to share the common fate of the great cities of the region and be tossed like a ball from one great family to another.

Several centuries of indecision were ended when the House of Este took over and gave Ferrara a period of relative stability almost unprecedented for those times—three centuries and a half under 15 sovereigns of the same dynasty. The Estes were a brilliant and glittering family, whose Alfonso I had the courage to marry Lucrezia Borgia, and whose two most brilliant women—Beatrice of Este, Duchess of Milan, and Isabella of Este, Marchioness of Mantua—surrounded themselves with a brilliant entourage of artists, writers and intellectuals, and kept Ferrara receptive to manifestations of the creative spirit. Nevertheless a contemporary description of the atmosphere of Ferrara in the latter half of the 15th century describes it as somber—a fitting background for the birthplace of the fanatic monk, Savonarola. No doubt it seemed somber to Torquato Tasso too, though in his case the gloom came from within rather than from without. Tasso was not a native of Ferrara—he was born in Sorrento—but when he entered the service of Cardinal Luigi d'Este and shifted later to that of Duke Alfonso II, he became a Ferrarese by adoption, and wrote most of his *Jerusalem Delivered* in Ferrara. He was a tormented soul, who died mad.

Ludovico Ariosto, the author of *Orlando Furioso*, who benefited also by the patronage of the Estes, was not born in Ferrara either, but in Reggio Emilia, where his father, who *was* from Ferrara, commanded the citadel. The family moved back to Ferrara when Ariosto was 10. He considered himself a native, and established there his *parva domus*, his "humble home." It is still there, open to visitors, and though Ariosto called it *parva sed apta mihi*—"humble, but right for me"—it is not as humble as all that. He had it built himself, sober in line and elegant in proportions. There was a kitchen garden behind it which has since vanished. Not many poets today could afford to live as well, but of course there are no noble patrons nowadays, only foundations. Ariosto needed neither. The success of *Orlando* was such that he was hailed as another Homer or Virgil. His portrait was painted by Titian, and he was honored even by high-waymen; a band of them once stopped his carriage, but when they found out who he was, they elected themselves an escort to protect him during the rest of his journey. "The roads are not very safe here," they told him.

It was Hercules I, the great builder of the Estes, who gave Ferrara its present appearance, though one kernel of buildings belonging to pre-Herculean Ferrara still remains, clustered about the cathedral. Hercules made Ferrara the first modern planned city, an example of Renaissance urbanism, by adding to it the Hercules Development (*Addizione Erculea*). It is to him that we owe the red walls which encircle the city to this day, the broad tree-lined avenues which make Ferrara so attractive and so open, and many of its magnificent buildings.

"This is Romagna," says the multi-authored *Mangiari di Romagna*, by Marcello Caminiti, Luigi Pasquini and Gianni Quondamatteo: "bread, wine, and whatever goes with bread. Between the sea and the mountain grow vines, grain and olives. On the green hills the herds graze in the shade of the leafy chestnuts (where they haven't been cut down). On the coast of Cervia, salt (after payment of the tax) offers itself for the seasoning of food. Fortunate land, which has the climates and the products of the whole country!"

The Po delta is rich in wheat, which is ground in Ferrara into a type of semolina flour called *soglia*, locally described as the best in Italy. This claim may not be accepted by all Italians, but most of them will agree that the bread made from it is the best. It is a specialty of Porto Garibaldi, named for the Italian patriot who landed there in 1849.

Ferrara bread is called *ciupeta*, a dialect word, and is distinguished by its peculiar shape—that of a ball with the crust drawn up into four points at the top, as though it had been molded over a crown. Its form has intrigued painters, so you may see it depicted not only in Ferrara itself—in Scarsellino's *Last Supper* in the Palace of Diamonds, and Achille Funi's frescoes illustrating scenes from *Orlando Furioso* in the Communal Palace—but even in Leningrad, in Garofalo's *Wedding at Cana*, in the Hermitage Museum. Ferrara bread is also represented in a form frowned upon by purists—a double sphere—in two scenes of the frescoes of Pomposa, the *Last Supper* and *The Miracle of Saint Guy*.

"Bread and whatever goes with bread." Nothing goes with it more indissolubly than butter, so it is fitting that a region which produces superb bread should also make some of the best butter in Italy—*burro di panna*, whose creamy texture is so much appreciated that it is snapped up everywhere throughout the country. It comes from an area north and west of Porto Garibaldi, which not only grows cereals, including the wheat which makes the bread, but also raises the cows which give the butter for it, and for good measure produces wine and tobacco too. The towns most noted for the quality of their butter are Copparo, Bondeno and Argenta, of which the last also makes two types of cheese indigenous to other regions—*provolone*, more commonly associated with Rome, and *grana*, which, if it came from a little farther west, would be marketed as Parmesan. The city of Ferrara makes *grana* too.

Salt, referred to in the quoted passage above as coming from Cervia (which is in the Ravenna province), is even more a specialty of Ferrara's Comacchio, where its history goes far back: in 854 Venice razed Comacchio to the ground to seize the salt flats and preserve her monopoly of this important product. Comacchio benefits today by a felicitous coupling like that which links butter and bread in

Porto Garibaldi. Its salt goes not only to Bologna and Milan for the curing of sausages, but is used also for the pickling of Comacchio's most important food product—eels. Eels are also ancient history in Comacchio, where they are raised in one of the most ingenious and unusual fishery installations in all Italy.

Comacchio would be worth a visit with or without eels. It is a sort of poor man's Venice, spreading over 13 islands as compared to Venice's 300, complete with canals crossed by humpbacked bridges, most of them small and picturesque, though not the modern monumental Trepponti, which, doing better than its name (which means "three bridges"), hops, skips and jumps across no less than five canals. A colorful backdrop is provided by the tinted sails of fishing boats. The population is 16,400, of whom 10,000 are fishermen who operate the elaborate system of dykes, canals, sluiceways and labyrinths. Since the Middle Ages they have been taking advantage of the migratory habits of eels, which leave the sea yearly to swim upstream into the rivers—but in Comacchio, they swim into a trap. Eels are not the only fish to be thus captured, but they are the most numerous and the most prized. Once captured, they are fattened and, according to the circumstances and the species, released to participate in their seasonal migrations, or fished out of the water to be killed and canned.

Comacchio lies on the great lagoon called the Valli di Comacchio, a name somewhat bewildering to foreign visitors, who see no valleys in this vast sheet of water; but *valli* in this context means fish breeding or storing reservoirs. The fishermen employed there are called *vallanti*, hardest worked in the autumn, when some eels are released to spawn in the Sargasso Sea and again in the spring, when the young elvers, moved by some mysterious instinct to seek the spot their parents left but which they themselves have never known, clamor to be let into the place of their destined deaths. The *vallanti* of today are much less harassed than their predecessors of the late 16th century, who were the serfs of Prince Torlonia, prisoners as much as the fish of a harsh system which gave them only bare subsistence. There were only 500 of them then, including the 120 who were policemen, assigned to keep the underfed fishermen from eating up the profits; nevertheless half the fish output was stolen every year.

Tasso knew the Comacchio labyrinth and used it in his *Jerusalem Delivered* to provide a simile for persons ambushed:

> *Like fish which in Comacchio's breast,*
> *Fleeing the boisterous billows of our sea,*
> *Seek in these placid currents peace and rest*
> *But by their own act are no longer free,*
> *Penned in a watery prison where their quest*
> *For wider spaces finds no remedy:*
> *The entrances are always open wide,*
> *The exits always closed against the tide.*

The eels taken here are eaten fresh in the region, usually grilled, especially at Lagosanto, which makes a specialty of this dish. But when they are to be preserved and packed for shipment to other parts of Italy or abroad, they are first roasted on spits, to get rid of excess fat, and then allowed to cool in wicker baskets similar to those used for picking grapes. They are then packed in wooden kegs filled with a good quality of wine vinegar, more or less strong depending on the size of the eels, or in tin cans. In the latter case, a bay leaf goes into the can along with the eels. This is the product you will find on the market labeled *anguilla ammarinata di Comacchio*. Comacchio eels are considered the best in Italy, though this might possibly be contested by the Ferrarese town of Codigoro, on another lagoon a little to the north, which underlines its own claims by holding an eel festival each September. Unfortunately the yield of Comacchio eels is diminishing, though not their quality. Land is being reclaimed from the lagoon for the more profitable pursuit of agriculture. Since this process began, the take has been cut in half, from 600 tons a year to 300. The 7,350 acres thus gained produce wheat and sugar beets worth much more than the lost 300 tons of eels. Altogether some 30,000 acres will remain of the original 73,500 covered by the water when the land reclamation is finished.

Drainage has also been applied beneficially to other areas in the province, including the immediate surroundings of the city of Ferrara itself; for when the inhabitants of Spina fled to Ferrara to escape the floods of the Po, they did not flee quite far enough. The altitude of Ferrara is only 35 feet, and it frequently found itself surrounded by bogs all the way to the sea, which is 35 miles away. Drainage was applied to this area long before the reclamation of the Comacchio lagoon started, revealing extraordinarily fertile soil, whose products, once again, are complementary to each other—not only bread and butter, as at Porto Garibaldi, but also fruit and the beets which provide the sugar for preserving it.

One hundred thousand acres of orchards on the drained land produce half a million tons of fruit every year. The leader in quantity is the apple, which accounts for 60 to 65 percent of the total acreage. The variety most widely grown is the Abbondanza, a winter apple which in refrigeration keeps from its picking (between September 15 and 20) to the following April, or even May. It is a heavy producer, but even better yields are obtained from the Imperatore and Rome Beauty trees. The Delicious group— Stark, Starking, Richard and Golden, the last sometimes called the banana apple—do not produce as lavishly, but their quality commands higher prices.

A much prized fruit of Ferrara is the Passacrassana pear,

a specialty of Tresigallo. A winter variety, picked about September 15, it will keep in refrigeration until the following summer without perceptible deterioration of taste.

The Ferrara area also grows excellent peaches, and the production of strawberries has increased since 1930, when new methods were developed for handling this fragile fruit so it could be shipped fresh without the excessive wastage which before that time had sent all of the province's strawberries not eaten locally straight to the canneries. Today fresh Ferrara strawberries reach tables all over Europe.

The complement to Ferrara's fruit is the sugar beet, which enables her refineries to turn out 125,000 tons of sugar yearly—one-fifth of the total production of all Italy. A large part of this is absorbed by the local canning, preserving and bottling industries, which produce large quantities of fruit juice. This is an important export item for Italy as a whole, since the peninsula produces a great deal more juice than it can consume itself; while Italians consume only about one quart of fruit juice per year per person (not including wine, of course) other nations drink much more—the West Germans, for example, eight quarts per person.

Apart from sugar beets, the most reputed vegetables of the Ferrara region are asparagus, zucchini and potatoes. Pontelagoscuro is known for its almonds. Game is plentiful, and includes deer, wild boar, hare and pheasant. The last is a local specialty, which is either cooked on a spit, roasted in the oven, or baked in an envelope of clay. The birds so treated are not all wild—15,000 domesticated pheasants are consumed every year. There is also an important chicken-raising industry. The province benefits both from the salt-water fish of the Adriatic and the fresh-water fish of the Po.

The Po also gives the province a specialty unique in Italy —caviar. The caviar center is the Po-side city of Stellata, strategically located where the river, approaching its mouth, swells to a width hospitable to the largest sturgeon. In medieval times the Italians of Ferrara were ignorant of the existence of caviar; but the Jews of their ghetto were not. The Ferrarese, when they discovered that Jewish fishermen were taking sturgeon from the Po at the time of year propitious for caviar, proceeded to follow their example, and fresh native caviar is now available there from April to June.

The Ferrarese varieties of processed pork products are many and tasty, the one which is most particularly its own being *salame da sugo*. This is a round pork sausage flavored with dry white wine, a splash of cognac, pepper, and cloves, which has to be aged for a year, half of this time under ashes. It must be cooked for a long while—preferably six to eight hours in a double boiler, but if you haven't that much time, four hours in boiling water. Hot, it is eaten with potatoes; cold, it is a great delicacy with iced melon.

Of the ham of the town of Volano, reproduced nowhere else, it is said locally, "If it isn't delicious, the pig had rabies." The *salame d'aglio*, garlic sausage, of Poggiorenatico, is shaped like an old-fashioned ridge-topped trunk; its name in the local dialect is *al zantil*, from the part of the pig's intestine used for the casing. It appears on the market at harvest time, and is a good durable winter sausage. Ferrara province also makes *salamelle* and *salame extra*.

Her abundant resources have permitted Ferrara to develop a cuisine of great richness and variety. The Estes gave the example early. They liked good food, and plenty of it. Duke Borso d'Este was so famous for his lavish entertaining that he was called Borso the Magnificent. The shopping list for a banquet offered the Infanta of Spain by another Este, Duke Alfonso, has survived; it includes among other items 500 pounds of different kinds of meat, 116 pullets, and 60 cockscombs. On May 20, 1529, Duke Ippolito II d'Este gave a banquet in the Palace of Diamonds in honor of Duke Ercole d'Este and his wife, Renée of France, second daughter of Louis XII, and Anne of Brittany. Among its 144 courses, particular honor was accorded to a dish which might not seem much of a highlight today, but it is interesting to meet it so early, for it is now the leading pasta specialty of Ferrara, *cappelletti in brodo alla ferrarese*. These are little hat-shaped envelopes of dough, whose stuffing is differentiated from that of other parts of Emilia-Romagna, for instance from the *tortellini* of Bologna, by a special ingredient, a neck gland of the pig. In the same category are *cappellacci con la zucca alla ferrarese*, pasta stuffed with squash; *pasticcio alla ferrarese*, a sort of round pasty with a filling of small elbow macaroni flavored with veal *ragù*, truffles, mushrooms, and a dash of nutmeg in béchamel sauce between two crusts, the top one being decorated with lozenge and leaf designs and glazed with egg yolk, and the whole served straight from the oven in the cooking dish, piping hot; and a similar dish made from lasagne—*lasagne pasticciate alla ferrarese*.

The two principal fish dishes of the province are its own variations on the theme of *brodetto*, and the marinated or spit-roasted eels of Comacchio or Codigoro. Porto Garibaldi has several fish specialties of its own, among them *calamari ripieni di calamaretti*—big squids stuffed with little squids. The *calamaretti* are chopped fine, seasoned with salt, pepper, garlic and grated Parmesan cheese, and mixed with boiled rice. This stuffing is then placed in the *calamari*, and the whole is cooked in olive oil and concentrated tomato extract. It was at Porto Garibaldi that a local restaurant offered during the war (for the delectation of occupying American soldiers) a dish called "Oysters Exarchate," unknown to local gourmets, who asked what it was. When they were told that it meant oysters cooked in milk, with cream, spices, salt, pepper, and nutmeg, they rose in indignation and forced the restaurant owner to swear never again "to mix holy water with the devil"—that is, to combine shellfish and cream. Oyster stew is now unknown at Porto Garibaldi, but it has *ostriche appetitose*, in which a batter of breadcrumbs, garlic, pepper, parsley and thyme covers the oyster in its shell, with its own juice carefully preserved; moistened with a drop or two of olive oil, it is cooked on a moderately hot grill, and served with lemon.

The subtle peculiarly Ferrarese desserts are headed by the delicate *mandorlini*, the macaroons which are a specialty of Pontelagoscuro, the almond town. The Christmas-New Year's holidays are marked by the appearance in pastry-shop windows of *pampepato di cioccolato*, a very old Ferrara sweet. It is a cake made of flour, cocoa, milk, honey (sugar if honey is not at hand), pepper, spices, almonds and lemon peel, with chocolate frosting powdered with sugar and tiny candies. It is of ancient lineage. Duke Borso d' Este served *pampepati* at a banquet on November 11, 1465, making them exceptionally appetizing by inserting a gold piece in each. Medieval Ferrara bakers used to send *pampepati* as presents to their overlords and to the Pope. The tradition was revived during the last war, when Ferrara gave an 11-pound *pampepato* to General Eisenhower.

While the *pampepato* marks Christmas, the ring-shaped *ciambella sfogliata di Ferrara* (*brazedela* in the local dialect) celebrates Easter. It is not nearly as sweet as *pampepato*, though its puff-paste circle is dusted with large grains of sugar and it is given a golden color with an egg-yolk glaze. It is served traditionally as a breakfast bun on Easter, accompanying fried eggs. It goes back at least as far as 1536, for which date a written reference to it exists.

The Adriatic is an arm of the Mediterranean, but it possesses certain characteristics of its own. Everyone knows the

Mediterranean is tideless; but the Adriatic, because of its long narrow shape and the conformation of its bed, does have tides. This shape, if you look at it on the map, might give you the impression that the Adriatic is a sheltered sea; but it is capable of whipping up violent storms. Adriatic waters, especially upper Adriatic waters, are less salty than those of the Mediterranean in general, for a large number of Alpine streams pour fresh water into its confined basin. Adriatic waters are also cleaner than those of the Mediterranean in general and of Italy's west Tyrrhenian coast in particular.

These circumstances make the Adriatic a prime source for food fish. The advantage of purer waters is evident. The existence of a zone between high and low watermarks, with its tidal pools and its life-protecting clumps of seaweed, is propitious to the propagation of shellfish and crustaceans. Even storms can be beneficial, for some forms of seafood become available chiefly when tempests wash them up onto the beach. The fresh-water streams vary the habitat (less salt close to the shore, more salt far from the shore) permitting fish of all kinds to find their optimum environments somewhere in the Adriatic. The inhabitants of the coast claim that their sea harbors a larger variety of fish than the Tyrrhenian. Whether this is true or not, it seems quite possible that the Adriatic may become the principal fish reservoir for all Italy, since many areas of the Tyrrhenian Sea are showing signs of being fished out, and the dwindling supply of fish is also vulnerable to depletion through pollution. Adriatic fisheries, foremost among them those of the province of Ravenna, are now shipping fish all the way to Rome, having plenty of surplus.

Ravenna lies in the center of the upper Adriatic, its most characteristic stretch, far enough south of Venice to avoid contamination of its waters by the factories which have recently sprung up on the mainland across from that city. It has consequently developed a fixation on fish, concerning which it is lavish with miscellaneous information and naive fables. I learned there apropos of nothing in particular that the sailfish is the world's fastest swimmer (among salt-water fish, I presume); it reaches 65 miles an hour, followed by the swordfish, 60; the tuna, 45; the dolphin, 37; and the tarpon, 35. The slowest swimmer is not, as you might expect, the whale (11 miles per hour maximum) but the eel (7½).

It is often difficult to match Adriatic fish names with fish names in English (themselves not always consistent), a process complicated by the existence of numerous species, subspecies, and sub-subspecies. Even when an Adriatic fish has been identified with a Tyrrhenian or a Mediterranean or an Atlantic fish to the satisfaction of zoologists, it is not always its gastronomic equivalent—habitat, available foods, water temperature and other ambient details alter taste. Thus one of the easiest identifications by name, that of the Adriatic *sogliola* (often aptly called *sfoglia*, which means leaf in Italian) with the English sole, does not take into account the difference in taste between the two varieties. Dover sole are famous among gastronomes, but the citizens of Ravenna insist that their sole tastes better, and point to the fact that they are shipped frozen to Denmark, a country nearer to England than to Italy. *Passera* is lemon sole, again with the reservation that in the ichthyological domain the same thing is not always the same thing when it occurs in a different place.

Rombo is turbot. *Rombo chiodato*, or *rombo maggiore*, may run to 70 pounds in the Adriatic, and a single female can lay 14,000,000 eggs. Its tastiness has caused it to be called "the pheasant of the sea," but a smaller variety, *rombo liscio*, is even tastier. It is called *suaso* locally; for some mysterious reason a political meeting is referred to, in dialect, as *suès arost*, roast *suaso*.

Sardina would seem to present no difficulties, but *sardone* is another thing again. It ought to mean a large sardine, but the name is often applied to the *acciuga* or *alice*, the anchovy. Some local gastronomes are outraged at this but seem unable to pin down the correct meaning of *sardone* themselves, except to say that the *sardina* is preserved in oil, while the *sardone* is pickled. To complicate things further, there are two subspecies of the anchovy known only by their dialect names, *sardunzêin* and *bagègg*. Finally, there is another species of sardine, the *cheppia* (dialect, *ceppa*), bigger than either the *sardina* or the *sardone*, which swims far up the rivers to spawn.

The tuna (*tonno* in Italian) is now found in Adriatic waters, but seems to be a newcomer (fleeing polluted waters elsewhere, perhaps). *Sgombero* (also called *sgombro*, *scombro*, *maccarello*, *luacerto* and *pesce-cavallo*, horse fish) is mackerel. These fish inhabit these waters in the summer, arriving in May in such numbers that the Ravennese in that month do not say, "I'm going fishing," but "I'm going mackereling"—"*a sgômbre*." At this season, the mackerel are ravenous; the spring schools devour everything in their path, like locusts of the sea, thereby adding a word to the Italian vocabulary—*sgombrare* means to sweep clean. Akin to the mackerel are the *aguglia* (dialect, *bicòn*), a kind of garfish, and the *sugarello* or *suro*.

Mullets offer a prime example of nomenclatural confusion. What fishermen and trenchermen call mullets belong to two distinct genera, the Mullidae and the Muglidae, both of which are found on this coast. The first are called red mullets, though they are not all red. The commonest species are the deep-water *triglie* or *barboni*, bearded mullet (the French *rouget*), which *are* red, or more exactly, especially when cooked, an improbable shade of pink which looks as if it had been concocted synthetically from chemicals, with delicious dry flaky white flesh; and the smaller, redder and even tastier *triglie di scoglio* (*rougets de roches* for the French), which live nearer shore. A local subspecies is called *russùl* in dialect. The gray mullets are schooling coastal game fish, which have no objection to roiled or brackish waters and are found in harbors, tidal pools and at river mouths. Their land-seeking habits extend even to their diet; a bait to which they succumb readily is boiled macaroni. The chief species here are *cefalo* and *bosega*, which run up to two feet or more in length and eight to twelve pounds in weight. They are best baked, but are also excellent in *brodetto*.

The *scòrpena, scorfano, scarpèna,* or (in French) *rascasse,* the hogfish, we have already met as indispensable for *brodetto* or *bouillabaisse.* The French consider *rascasse* inedible, except in *bouillabaisse;* but in Ravenna *scorpena* is sometimes eaten, boiled, for its own sake. As for the related *capone* or *gallinella* (dialect, *mazòla*), though it goes well in *brodetto,* it is excellent on its own, baked.

The Trachinidae are also edible though poisonous. Their venomous spines are lethal for other fish, and can cause acute local pain and inflammation for bathers who step on them, which is easy to do since some of the smaller species have the habit of burying themselves in the sand near shore with only their dorsal spines protruding. One of the most common is the *ragno* (spider) or *ragno pagano* (both are also called *tràcine*), a reddish gray with slanting brown stripes. The *pesce prete* (priest fish—dialect, *boch-in-chev*) is so called because its eyes are oriented upwards, toward heaven. It has a massive cubic head and a box-like chest, and is best in *brodetto.*

The Sparidae are voracious fish with sharp teeth and strong jaws, which enable some of them to break open oyster shells. One of them, the *dentice* (dentex) is named for its teeth, which impinge particularly on the fishermen's task in the case of this fish, because it uses them to rip its way out of nets. The large ones are boiled, preferably as a base for soup; the small ones are delicious baked. The *orata* (chrysophrys) is named for its delicate colors, gold and a brownish silver, which fade away as it dies. It is a hermaphrodite, with firm tasty white flesh, known to the ancient Romans and much appreciated by them.

The *parago occhialone* (dialect, *ucialòn*) is a spiny fish which gourmets prize, but of which the uninitiated are more wary, because its flesh has a bitter taste; it grows on you, the gourmets say, but not everyone sticks with it long enough to find out. It is usually grilled. So is the *sarago* or *sargo* (sar or sargo in English). Ditto for the *spigola*, also called *ragno* (confusingly, for the same name is also used for the quite different fish mentioned above), *spinola*, *branzino* or *lupo*, the French *loup de mer*, or sea perch, a fine food fish with delicate white flesh. The *cernia*—a highly parochial fish, restricted, in this part of the world at least, to the minute Tremiti Islands—seems to be a sort of sea bass. It can reach 90 pounds; fine-fleshed, it makes a very subtle soup.

Nasello is usually translated by the dictionaries as cod, but it appears to be more closely related to hake. Voracious, and with an enormous mouth, it is the terror of smaller fish. The flesh is fine and delicate, but without a great deal of flavor. Boiled, it is recommended for convalescents, but when roasted on live coals and eaten as hot as your mouth will take it, it is a dish for strong men. It is also often cut into small pieces and fried. Likewise in the cod family is the *mormora*, either roasted or broiled.

The gobies are represented here by a local variety called *guvàt*, of which there are at least 16 species. The commonest is the *guatto*, scientifically known as *gobius paganellus* (little pagan), because of a legend attached to the province of Forlì. When St. Anthony of Padua came to Rimini to preach, somewhere between 1221 and 1223, human auditors were lacking, so, the story goes, he preached to the fish.

They raised their heads from the water, except one, which refused to listen to the saint; it was, of course, the *guvàt*. A related fish, the *pignoletto*, used to frequent shallow water close to the beaches, but has now changed its habits and has to be sought farther out.

A de luxe fish is the *storione*, the sturgeon, which reaches the tables of well-to-do Ravennese from the Po, which it mounts to spawn. They have to be well-to-do, for its exquisite fine flesh is so prized that it is beyond the reach of limited incomes, and its caviar even more so. The *ombrina* or *corbello* (umbrine, umbra or meagre), which sometimes exceeds two feet in length, is excellent eating, and is sold on Adriatic markets by the slice.

The *rospo*, or *rana pescatrice*, is the angler fish, which reposes treacherously on muddy bottoms, assuming their color and dangling a little pennant of flesh over its gaping mouth to lure unwary prey. The favored way of serving it along the Adriatic coast used to be to cut it up into small pieces and use it to enliven a risotto; but nowadays its tail is roasted, following the example of Rome, where *coda di rospo* has long been an honored dish. The *San Pietro* (St. Peter's fish in Italian and French, but John Dory in England —the dictionaries say) gets its name from the legend that when the fisherman saint caught one of these fish, it uttered such plaintive laments that Saint Peter took pity on it and tossed it back into the water—leaving on its flanks the imprint of his thumb and finger, which are still visible. Fishermen today are less merciful, so the St. Peter goes into risotto. Finicky persons turn up their noses at *acquadella*, a schooling fish with a greenish black-spotted back and a shining white belly, but others relish it, fried, and eaten with a little lemon juice.

The eel-like fishes begin of course with the eel proper, *anguilla*—the same which is called *capitone* in Rome, in Naples and in Orbetello; *bisàto* in Venice; but simply *an-*

guilla (the dictionary name) in Ravenna and Comacchio. The conger eel (*grongo*) is also caught on this coast, and so is the *murena*, sometimes described as the lamprey of the ancient Romans, but the identification is open to doubt. Its scientific name is *muraena helena*, or Greek moray, but the lamprey is not a moray; whether the ancient Romans ate them or not, the modern Ravennese do, and call its flesh exquisite, although they believe its blood contains a poison —destroyable, happily, by cooking.

Selachians—sharks and rays—are not overly esteemed as food in Anglo-Saxon countries, but Ravenna has no such prejudices. *Gattucio* (dialect, *cagnulèin*), a name which here covers two species, *scyllium canicula* and *scyllium stellare*, is valued in many places only because its skin produces shagreen; but here it is eaten not only in *brodetto*, but for its own sake, grilled. *Palombo*, which in other circumstances means pigeon, is in this case a dogfish. The *pesce squadro* or *pesce angelo* (angelfish) is shaped like a ray, may exceed 100 pounds in weight, and is considered a food fish not to be despised. *Razza* means ray in general, of which there are several species—*raja asterias*, which is known locally as *baràccola*, *raja clavata*, *raja punctato*, and the favorite for the table, *razza di scoglio* (rock ray), also called *razza chiodata* ("nail-studded"). Even the torpedo ray (*torpedine* in Italian, *trèmul* in Romagnolo), which is capable of delivering a powerful electric shock, reaches the table, minus its voltage, usually in *brodetto;* its liver is considered a great delicacy.

Very popular on this coast, and for that matter much eaten in most parts of Italy, are the octopus-like fish. *Seppia* is the cuttlefish or inkfish, so called, of course, for its ability to lose itself in a protective cloud of ink spurted into the water (from which the pigment called sepia is derived). *Seppiola* (dialect *zotla*), fried, makes, in the local estimation, "a delicious morsel." *S-ciavòna*, known here only by this local name, is best spitted. There are many species of *calamaro*, squid, here called *totano*, many of which reach great size. The real octopus is *polipo* or *polpo;* local dialect sorts the *polipi* out by size. *Polipi grossi* are the big brutes. *Fulp* is the normal medium-sized octopus; *muscardèin* (*moscardini* in Italian) are smaller. The smallest are *polpetti* or *fragoline di mare*, sea strawberries, so called for their rosy color. Octopus and cuttlefish are the only occupants of the sea which are never eaten fresh; a couple of days out of water are required to reduce their toughness and make them edible. Even so, *polipi grossi* have to be pounded hard and long, and may remain rubbery all the same. Diogenes died trying to eat a *raw* inkfish.

Two items of seafood eaten here are not fish. One is a mammal, the dolphin (*delfino*) and the other is a reptile, the sea turtle (*tartaruga*). Some fishermen have compunctions about taking dolphins. Their comportment is almost human, and mothers have been known to follow boats which have taken young fish, lamenting, while sometimes a school of dolphins will try to rescue a captured comrade. But they are great raiders of catches, eating the fish and destroying the nets, so they finish on the table. No one objects to eating turtle.

The king of the crustaceans, here as elsewhere, is the lobster, which in these waters means the spiny lobster, *aragosta*, of which the best are taken in the Tremiti Islands. The Atlantic lobster of the American East Coast is not found in the Adriatic, or anywhere in the Mediterranean, for that matter. *Astice* is in principle a larger type of *aragosta*, but the name is also used, confusingly, for a smaller variety, which is either grilled or added to *brodetto*. The head meat is considered the choicest and is sucked out (the easiest way of getting at it) with devout assiduity. The *pregadio* is a miniature *aragosta*, the size of a small crayfish, taken especially when washed up from the sea by a storm; bright red, it is eaten fried. The squill (*cannocchia* or *cicala*) is so abundant in these waters that in less affluent times it was the chief lunch *and* dinner dish of the poor. It is most appreciated in winter, when the female is full of eggs. *Scampi* (shrimp), which Venice claims as its own, gets down the coast at least as far as Ravenna. The *gambero*, which might be described as a poor cousin of the *scampi*, also called *gamberetto*, *gamberello* and *gamberessa* when of smaller size, is a crayfish of protean manifestations. It is found either in salt water or in fresh; in small, medium and large varieties; and may be reddish, gray or transparent. The little ones are eaten raw, fresh out of the water; the big ones are served with risotto. *Granchio* means crab, of which there are many varieties. When eaten during the brief moulting period as a soft-shelled crab, it acquires the name of *mulèca*.

Mollusks are plentiful. The gently-sloping sandy beaches of the upper Adriatic encourage the proliferation of burrowing species. Other types cling to rocks or rocky bottoms in shallow water, while some are deep-water shellfish. The aristocrat of the bivalves is of course the oyster (*ostrica*), but this is not primarily oyster country. There are more clams, of which one of the commonest gets us into nomenclatural difficulties again.

This is the shellfish called *vongola* in many regions of Italy (Rome and Naples, for instance), which I have always understood to mean the cockle (in French the *coque*); it looks like a small rosy scallop. In Ravenna, the terms *vongola*, *cappa* and *poveraccia* seem to be used interchangeably by the untutored, but local experts insist they are not the same thing. Coherence ends at this point, for they never succeed in explaining what kind of different things they are. *Cappa*, which means cape, would seem to point to the scallop type of shell, whose ribs and wide spreading shape suggest the folds of a cape; and this is apparently identical with the *poveraccia*—which means "poor devil" and may indicate that it is poor men's food, unless it refers simply to the character of a shellfish described with approval by one local gastronomic writer as "cherished and modest." "The real *vongola*," this writer explains, "is found in the southern waters of Italy, and is oblong in shape, with a smooth shell and a greenish color." This certainly does not fit the cockle. Whatever the *poveraccia* may be, it has lately undergone an evolution in the kitchen. Today it is buried in spaghetti, but formerly, when large *poveracce* were available, they were cut into pieces and eaten by themselves. This detail confuses the identity of *poveraccia* again, for if it is the cockle, it would not be big enough to cut up. It does not help to learn that the *calcinello* is also called the *tellina*, two names which in normal zoological usage apply to entirely different types of shellfish, nor that the *calcinello* is described in one breath as a smaller version of *poveraccia* and in the next as having an oblong shell, which would seem to relate it rather to the "real *vongola*." Trying to untangle the identities of these clams may be a futile pursuit, for the Ravenna area appears to be the last stand of the *calcinello*, which is disappearing from the Adriatic, and the *poveraccia* may follow; at least the region is now suffering the indignity of having to import frozen and pickled clams of much the same sort from Spain, Japan and Thailand.

The largest shellfish in these waters is the scallop, here called *cappa marina* or *cappa santa*, the latter a reminder of the fact that the scallop shell is the symbol of St. James. The *canestrino* (little basket) is a much smaller scallop. What the *cuore di mare* or *noce di mare* (heart of the sea, walnut of the sea) may be in English I have no idea. It has a reddish humpbacked ribbed shell with spines protruding from it, and a red tongue-like appendage on which it moves. It is frequently washed up on the beach by storms, in clumps of seaweed. A curious one is the *cannolicchio* (lo-

cally the *cannelo*), a tube-shaped shellfish which buries itself upright in the sand, and is capable of burrowing deeper
with great speed to escape danger. It is best in soup, or
grilled after being salted, peppered, dipped in oil, and coated
with breadcrumbs. The *piede di pellicano* (dialect, *gara-
gòlo*), or pelican's foot, is esteemed as a fortifier, and somewhat tastier is the *nassa mutabilis*, or sea snail. A sea snail as
large as a baby's fist is called *bovolo*, which, in days when
people were less fussy, used to be cooked on hot coals
until charred, after the appropriate treatment with salt,
pepper, oil and breadcrumbs. The best part is supposed to
be the *mardulèina*, a dark creamy substance found in the
depths of its shell.

The *mitilo* is the common black mussel found all over
Italy under different aliases—*cozza* in southern Italy, *mus-
colo* in Genoa, *dattero di mare* (sea date) in La Spezia,
peòcio in Venice, and *pidocchio* in Ravennese dialect.
Some persons eat the *patella*, a barnacle which clings to the
rocks between high- and low-tide levels, but today there
seems to be little enthusiasm for it, except among small
boys who make a game of the attempt, invariably un-
successful, to pull the barnacles off the rocks with their
fingers.

One of the strangest foods from the sea is the *tartufo di
mare* or *uovo di mare*, sea truffle (not to be confused with
the type of clam so called in other regions) or sea egg.
Called *spônza* in the local dialect, it is a tuber, blackish and
roughly cylindrical in shape. A tough bark covers the edible
part, which is bright yellow with red streaks. It has a carbolic acid smell described by local gourmets as agreeable, as
no doubt it is to those who like carbolic acid. Its composition is 93 percent water, while the percent of solids breaks
down into salt, iodine, manganese, digestible iron and vana-
dium, which sounds either like medicine or something
which should clink in the stomach. "It is eaten raw, like oys-

ters," says *Mangiari di Romagna*, "and only the initiated are permitted to taste it; it provokes in others a sense of violent repulsion." It is difficult to understand how one becomes an initiate; perhaps it doesn't matter.

The province of Ravenna is so richly endowed with fish that it could hardly avoid basing its cooking largely on the sea. The king of fish dishes is of course *brodetto*, which, as in The Marches, is different in each place.

What you might call general Romagna *brodetto*, available in any locality too unimaginative to invent its own, is based on the following list of desirable fish (it is not exclusive and you would never find all of them simultaneously in any one stew): sole, angelfish, shark, red mullet, turbot, *ragno*, hake, *sardone*, mackerel, cuttlefish, squid, dogfish, anchovy, squill, *scampi*, crayfish—and, of course, the indispensable hogfish (*scorpena*). One local version which uses saffron is the *brodetto alla marinara* of Porto Corsina, the place where Dante feasted on it. The favored ingredients are hogfish, eel, lemon sole, gray mullet, red mullet, dogfish, squill, *calamari*, and *mazzole*, but almost anything else may be added. This also uses a tomato sauce, compounded with much olive oil and crushed garlic, with the addition of white wine.

Some persons refer to one-fish soups as *brodetti*, but the consensus is against them. It is true that a crab soup, by common agreement, was once called *brodetto*, but that was at a time when food was less plentiful than it is now, and it seems probable that this name was then used in a wistful attempt by the poor to forget that they could not afford a real *brodetto*. Yet crab soup was no mean dish. It was made in particular between the first of January and the middle of March, when the female crabs are succulent with eggs. Seasoned with salt, pepper, tomato extract, white wine and olive oil, the crabs were boiled violently for 12 minutes, and then simmered for half an hour more. "Since appetite is the best seasoning," one old cookbook apologized, "the humble crab" could thus be teased into giving the effect of having produced a tasty soup. The crab does not seem particularly humble nowadays, especially to inlanders, and it is recognized as tasty in its own right; it would seem that this presently neglected soup might be profitably resuscitated today.

Cannocchie used to be considered poor man's meat too, but now *cannocchie alla povera*, poor man's squill, is in style again. One dish they provide is *antipasto di cannocchie*, a specialty of Cervia, which claims that its immediate waters provide the best squill in the Adriatic. It is boiled in sea water, cleaned, cut into bite-sized pieces, served on a platter with a spoonful of the water in which it has been cooked and a little olive oil, and eaten as is, without adding anything else; even a drop of lemon, its appreciators declare, would falsify its subtle flavor.

After *brodetto*, the second most favored fish dish of the Adriatic is *fritto misto di pesce*, a mixed fish fry whose separate ingredients vary from day to day, depending on the fortune of the catch. Its more common components are mullet, sole, squid, shrimps and two small fish found only in these waters, and therefore known by untranslatable local names, *acquadelle* and *marsioni*. Cut into small pieces, they are sprinkled with flour and deep-fried in boiling oil. This is a particular specialty of Marina di Ravenna and Cervia. In Porto Corsino, instead of being simply sprinkled with flour, the pieces of fish are first bathed in a mixture of beaten eggs and milk and then floured, creating a crisp crust which locks in all the flavors of the fish. "Garnish the plate with slices of lemon," says a local recipe, "and put the cat out; the exquisite smell will drive him mad."

Another very popular way to cook fish is to grill it. *Sogliole in gratella* (grilled soles) are seasoned with salt,

pepper, and olive oil, and sprinkled with bread crumbs before being placed on a solid grill; they are turned by placing
a second grill over them. Baked sole (*sogliola arrosta*) is
also popular, coated with high-grade olive oil and preferably
cooked over charcoal. *Triglie* (red mullet) *sulla gratella*
are grilled like sole, but without the bread crumbs, and with
a morsel of garlic tucked into the gills—"a dish perhaps as
old as man," says my recipe; but in any case this was a favorite dish of the ancient Romans. *Rombo* (turbot) *in gratella*
is also prepared like the sole, but with some of the bread
crumbs inserted in the gills and in slits made in the flesh; it
is served hot, sprinkled with lemon juice, accompanied with
a cold green salad; *suàso*, the smaller turbot, is even better
so cooked than the more common larger variety. *Sardoni*
in gratella are cooked precisely like sole, and so are *sardelle*
and *saraghine*. Rossini was so fond of *sardoni* cooked in
this fashion that when he received a shipment of them in
Paris he asked a friend he had previously invited to Sunday
dinner not to come, because, he explained unblushingly,
when he ate *sardoni* he preferred to do so in peace, alone,
without distracting palaver; but he was magnanimous
enough to put aside for his wife (out of the mess of fish he
had received), *one*. *Cefali in gratella* are cooked like sole.
Seppie in gratella are cooked like sole and served with lemon
juice. *Sgombero in gratella* is cooked and served like turbot.

Dolphin is eaten much less now than it used to be, perhaps because pampered modern stomachs are likely to be
turned by the unappetizing aspect of the dolphin's very
bloody flesh. *Delfino alla Raul*, named for the restaurant
which created the dish, is made by cutting the meat into
large cubes and washing it for 10 to 15 minutes in running
water to get rid of the blood. It is then cooked in an earthenware dish for at least 15 minutes, without seasoning or other
ingredients, to dry it out. Incisions are made in the cubes of
flesh, into which pieces of bacon are inserted and, in one of

them, a clove. They are then cooked over a low flame in a sauce rich in oil and butter, with chopped onions, tomato extract and salt and pepper, for at least two hours. Allowed to stand for half an hour after being taken off the fire, the dish is then served in its own juice.

A dish not to be recommended is *scherzo del pescatore*, fisherman's joke. When the tiny *calamaretti* (which make only a mouthful each) are being served, they are popped whole into the mouth—which gives practical jokers an opportunity to plant on a chosen victim one whose purse has been filled with hot pepper.

Anguilla alla ravennate is a fashion of cooking eel several centuries old; it was once known as *anguilla alla Comacchio*. Skinned and cut into chunks, the fish is sautéed in butter with fresh tomatoes. Optional is the addition of truffles and crayfish. There are numberless other ways of preparing eel. One is *anguilla allo spiedo*, for which the skinned fish is cut up into small pieces and spitted, with a bay leaf between each two morsels of eel; but Sant' Angelo, a town a little north of Ravenna, prefers not to skin the eel, believing it retains more flavor unskinned. There are also eel soup; eel baked or fried with peas; fillets of eel; and *risotto adriatico all' anguilla*, in which the rice is enriched by bits of eel previously cooked in a *soffritto* containing garlic and parsley, and flavored after cooking with salt, pepper, and lemon juice.

There are many other rice and fish dishes. *Riso in brodo di pesce capone* is an old Ravennese dish in which *caponi* are put in cold water with spices and herbs, brought slowly to a boil, and left to cook for another 25 to 30 minutes, with chopped parsley added toward the end; the soup thus obtained is then sown thickly with rice. *Risotto con il San Pietro* serves St. Peter's fish stewed with celery, carrots and onion, together with rice boiled in a mixture of olive oil and the cooking juices left over from the fish. *Risotto con i gamberi* cooks crayfish with onion, garlic, celery, oil, and tomato extract; starts cooking the rice by sautéing it in butter; and then finishes it in the broth in which the crayfish were cooked. Halfway through the final cooking of the rice, the crayfish go back into the pot too. In *risotto con le poveracce*, the little *poveracce* clams, after having been browned in oil, onion, parsley, and tomato extract, are served with rice cooked in oil, butter and onion and finished in white wine. The liquid in which the clams have been cooked serves as the sauce. For *zuppa di poveracce* use extremely fresh clams, never *cadute* (windfall) clams, which is to say those washed ashore by a storm. They are left in salt water overnight to get rid of sand, or at least part of it, and washed in several waters the next day to remove the rest of it, if possible; these clams are great hoarders of sand. Garlic is pounded into a paste with parsley and browned in oil, extract of tomato is then added (or, better still, fresh tomatoes cut into pieces) and finally the clams. The soup made from this is poured over slices of bread placed at the bottom of the soup plates.

Despite the importance to Ravenna's cooking of the products of the sea, seafood is by no means all there is to the Ravennese cuisine. Its geography and its history prevent that. Fisheries are important to the province, but agriculture is too. The fertility of the rich alluvial plain which stretches from Piacenza to the sea increases from east to west as the proportion of coarse matter, stones and gravel from the Apennine streams diminishes, so that the best soil is just behind the sand of the coast. Ravenna lies in the center of this most fertile part of the plain, exposed neither to the detritus which Forlì, to the south, receives from the Appennines, nor to the disrupting floodings which Ferrara, to the north, suffers from the Po.

This natural situation fixes upon inland Ravenna a vocation for agriculture. There is little industry, and what there is depends on crops—the hemp which grows in the plains, or sugar beets, which supply a large refinery in Classe, on which in turn depends the jam and jelly manufactures of Massalombarda. Wheat grows in the plains and maize and grape vines on the hills. Ravenna, says a local writer, is a place "where abundant and flavorful munitions for the mouth abound."

As for the influence of history, that has given Ravenna a rich and diverse cuisine which draws on many other resources than those of the sea. It has been much refined since the days of the Emperor Honorius, who had transferred from Rome the over-elaborate precepts of Apicius and the extravagances which smothered natural flavors beneath the riot of highly spiced sauces to which the court had been accustomed in Rome. Perhaps it was the very quality of the original raw materials offered by both sea and land which first modified the imperial tradition in favor of letting natural flavors through. The descent of the Ostrogoths also worked against the excesses of Rome. A surface reversal toward extravagance occurred when Byzantine magnificence took over, but the Byzantine influence did not go very deep. A certain number of Ravennese dishes are still described as Byzantine, it is true (*tartufi con pollo alla bizantina*, truffles with chicken, Byzantine style), but it is probable that this name is not really a description of the origin of a dish, but simply one of those romantic titles with which misguided restaurant owners like to adorn their menus. This is certainly the case for *asparagi in consumato Teodora*, *filetti di sogliola Teodora*, and *pollastra all' Esarca*, which are simply asparagus in consommé, fillets of sole, and pullet, whose modes of preparation owe nothing either to Theodora or the Exarchs.

The one field in which the competition of the sea seems really to have eliminated the contributions of the land is that of meat. The Ravennese do not eat much meat, and when they do, they are content to reproduce dishes which originated elsewhere. Indeed, Ravenna might have had no meat dish at all to call her own if Lord Byron had not elected to spend 18 months there in 1820–21 pursuing the Countess Guiccioli (with apparent success if we may judge from the fact that he wound up occupying an apartment in her palace), though it is probable that *costolette di montone alla Byron* is just another example of romantic menu writing, and owes nothing to Byron, whose favorite room in a house was not the kitchen. He was, nevertheless, a great talker about food in the taverns of Ravenna, including some of the less respectable ones, of which he was an extrovert frequenter. It was there that he picked up a recipe he appreciated greatly—mashed potatoes mixed with butter and aromatic herbs from the pine woods beyond the beaches, lapped in béchamel sauce, thickly powdered with grated cheese, and finished in the oven. This could make an excellent accompaniment for mutton chop à la Byron, which is marinated for three hours in olive oil, vinegar, and spices, and then sautéed in butter.

Eleanora Duse and Gabriele d'Annunzio spent some time in Ravenna too, together; d'Annunzio was a good eater, but no one named any dishes after him, nor after another celebrated host of the city either—Dante—except one to which a foreign cook attached his name. Dante was a gourmet, and a great lover of fish, but with all the Ravenna fish dishes available to which his name might have been given, it was tacked, rather inappropriately, onto a consommé containing pigeon croquettes and the black truffles which are a product of the pine groves of Ravenna. They also appear with another of the province's chief food products—turkey. *Filetti di tacchino con tartufi* are browned, tenderized fillets of white meat in butter, seasoned with salt and pepper, and thickly powdered with grated cheese, covered with chopped truffles and melted butter, and then cooked in the oven.

Ravenna is not sausage country, but Castelbolognese used to be noted for homemade sausages, which were hung in the enormous chimneys of country homes, becoming impregnated gradually with the rich aroma of wood smoke. This is almost a lost art now, but Ravenna does make a sausage which tries to recapture the taste of the old ones; it is cooked on a griddle, after having been speared with a fork to let steam out, and served sliced on bread.

Pasta is plentiful, made from the wheat of the province, and served with the local *grana*, grated, which the Ravennese insist is as good as Parmesan; they use their own fresh cheese also for pasta stuffing. *Cappelletti* here are much larger than elsewhere in Emilia-Romagna, and are stuffed differently. In most places they contain bits of meat and sausage and are doused in sauce, but in Ravenna they are often stuffed with minced fish mixed with cheese and herbs, sometimes finished by browning in the oven, and are served with butter and grated cheese; this is *cappelletti di magro*, fast-day *cappelletti*. *Cappelletti alla cardinale* are stuffed with a purée of crayfish tails, mushrooms and sauce Suprême. *Pappardelle*, in consommé, or *asciutte* with sauce, is usually a rather uninspiring dish, but not when, as here, it is served with crayfish salad. *Ravioli all'uso di Romagna* is made of egg dough, stuffed with fresh cheese, and served with grated *grana* and meat juice from the dish it accompanies, for it is not served as a separate course by itself, but with braised beef or a fricassée.

Polenta is made in Ravenna of cornmeal. When served with meat, it is doused with the meat juice; when served with fish, the fish is placed on top of the polenta, its juices are poured over it, and both are eaten together; when served with game, it is anointed with the cooking juices; and when served with small birds, they are bedded on the polenta. As the poet Lorenzo Stecchetti put it:

> *I tordi, più di trenta*
> *In superba maestà,*
> *A seder sulla polenta*
> *Come turchi sul sofà.*

("More than thirty thrushes were seated in superb majesty on the polenta like Turks on a divan.")

The famous asparagus of Ravenna, praised in ancient times by Pliny and Martial, are utilized in *risotto con crema di asparagi ravennati* so subtly that, so far as the eye can see (but the palate is better informed) the asparagus disappears completely. A broth is first made by boiling asparagus at the same time as beef, along with a great deal of butter. When the mixture becomes creamy, the beef is removed. The rest is strained through a colander, and put to simmer. A cup of cream mixed with grated cheese and an egg yolk is then added; and finally the rice, which has been partly boiled separately, is turned into the broth, and the risotto finishes its cooking in a double boiler. If you prefer seeing your Ravenna asparagus as well as tasting it, a popular way to serve it is to boil it first, then soak the tips in melted butter, coat them with grated cheese, apply more butter, and finish them in the oven.

Ravenna has a considerable repertory of desserts. It lays particular claim to *offelle di marmellata*, though it is made elsewhere as well, maintaining that the very name comes from the Romagna dialect, which derives *offella* from the Latin *offa*, a sort of scone made of lightweight wheat (*offa al cerbero* is the sop thrown to Cerberus). *Offella* in Ravenna is a double round cookie with a filling of *marmellata*, which usually means any type of jam, but in this case means a sort of jam of apples, candied fruit, sugar and cinnamon. The filling is put in before the cookie goes into the oven, spread between the top and bottom rounds while they are still dough; the top cookie is then glazed with egg yolk and dusted with sugar before the *offella* goes into the oven.

Frittate dolci di pinoli (sweet pine-nut fritters) are made of pine nuts crushed to a paste in a mortar, together with butter, sugar and beaten eggs; after cooking, they are drenched with rum and served flaming. Also fritters are *castagnole*, which are anise flavored. *Casadello* is a cake of flour, water, milk, eggs and sugar, flavored with vanilla. Cookies shaped like dolls, hens or roosters are eaten at harvest festivals and are called, in the local dialect, *bambuzene d'Santa Caterina*, St. Catherine's dolls. Finally there is *'j jàbre* (dialect for *le labbre*, the lips), which are wedges of apple dried in the sun until they have been reduced to what looks like a lozenge with wrinkles. They have a tart taste, but are, says a local cookbook (not very enthusiastically), "preferable to American chewing gum."

Ravenna is not a gastronomically overwhelming capital. It does not impose its dishes on the other cities of the province; many of them have specialties of their own. Faenza naturally differs from Ravenna in its orientation, for it is pretty much cut off from the sea. It is an old city, once Roman (Pliny mentions the productivity of its vines), and Etruscan before that. It is highly appropriate that Faenza should have a school of cooking of its own, for it is important in the history of the table. The word faïence, for majolica ware, comes from Faenza, one of the first cities in Europe to produce porcelain for the table. Faenza started to make porcelain in the 12th century, and it does still. The peak came in the 15th and 16th centuries, and some of the fine pieces of that period may be seen in the city's International Ceramics Museum, which displays remarkable specimens of china ranging from medieval times to Picasso. Among Faenza's considerable list of specialties is *zuppa di selleri con formaggio*, slices of bread covered with grated cheese and submerged in a celery soup with a flavoring of aromatic herbs, derived from a very old recipe evolved by the nuns of the convent of San Maglorio di Faenza. *Minestra di passatelli antica*, a favorite of the Manfredi family when it ruled Faenza and of Gabriele d'Annunzio when he did his military service there, is a soup thick with bread crumbs, beef marrow and eggs, flavored with nutmeg. Another old soup is *minestra di lasagnotti e fagioli alla faentina*, which contains not only the pasta and the beans promised by its name, but also bacon, onions, carrots, herbs, and, of course, grated cheese. Duke Cesare d'Este insisted that it should be included in the menu of the sumptuous banquet he gave in Faenza on January 13, 1598 to celebrate the signing of the treaty with the Holy See which gave Ferrara to the Church, and the Duchy of Modena to the Estes.

Ravioli con formaggio fresco is a fast-day dish in Faenza, which conceals the fact that the ravioli is stuffed with humble cottage cheese by adding nutmeg, cinnamon, clove and saffron to it. Another pasta specialty of Faenza is *curziè*, extremely thin *tagliatelle*, half-boiled, drained, and then finished in capon consommé.

Capellini al pollo is another recipe which Faenza owes to the convent of San Maglorio. It is a fairly intricate example of the culinary art, inadequately described if you call it simply chicken with pasta. The chicken, cut into pieces, starts its cooking in a casserole, with butter, mushrooms and Madeira wine. Meanwhile the very finest *capellini*, pasta in hair-thin threads, has been boiled separately, and is combined with a sauce of butter, tomato juice and grated cheese. It is then worked into an omelet, which goes into a baking dish with the chicken. The whole is powdered thickly with grated cheese and is put into the oven, where baking turns the cheese into a succulent thick crust.

Lugo is another town with a mind of its own about cooking. Its triumph is probably *zuppa romagnola alla Lugo al vino*, one of the heartiest vegetable soups on record, since it contains leeks, tomatoes, peas, zucchini, celery, bits of beef, ham and white wine. This sounds like a full meal in itself, yet Salimbene da Parma, a monk whose *Chronicle* is a mine of precious historical material for the period between 1168 and 1288, reported that he had seen Giovanni da Ravenna, an obese glutton, stuff away a quantity of *lasagne* that no other human being could have absorbed—after preparing his stomach with an abundant helping of Lugo soup! *Costolette di vitello alla Lugo* are small slices of veal coated with egg and bread crumbs, fried in lard, and served lapped with a sauce of butter, egg yolks, consommé, fine flour and lemon juice. Another Lugo dish takes advantage of the fact that some marshes remain near it, providing the raw material for *rane in brodo al riso*. For this, a large number of frogs are boiled in water with leeks, onions, parsley and other aromatic herbs, including a bay leaf. The resulting broth is strained through a sieve and rice (or pasta) is then cooked in it. Frogs are not as plentiful near Lugo now as they were in the days when the city had a separate market which sold nothing else. But Conselice, between Santerno and Sillarco, is still so famous for its frogs that it is known in the local dialect as *tèra d'ranocc*, frogland.

Cervia may once have served as an ancient Greek port of call; no one is quite sure how old it is, but it was already important enough, under the name of Ficole, to have been worth destroying in the 8th century. It takes its present name from the stags which used to be plentiful in the vast pine forests which once surrounded it. Its chief special dishes are *pollo al limone*, tender young pullet cut into pieces, sautéed with seasoning and mushrooms, and doused with lemon juice toward the end of the cooking; and *frittelloni di Cervia*, fritters stuffed with spinach previously cooked in lard, sprinkled with raisins and with grated cheese, and then deep fried in lard and powdered with sugar. Cervia, like Venice, celebrates a marriage with the sea, and has been doing so since 1445. The two cities have something else in common—an interest in salt. Venice seized Cervia at one time to maintain her monopoly of this valuable condiment, but Cervia has proved the ultimate winner. Venice no longer produces salt, but Cervia does.

The capital of the southernmost province of Romagna is Forlì, once Forum Livii, founded in 188 B.C. by Livius Salinator after he had defeated the Carthaginian general Hasdrubal. Forlì presides over a rich agricultural district and plays host to the busiest cattle market in the area. Cesana, at the entrance to the fertile Savio valley, also derives much of its prosperity from agriculture, which supplies the raw materials for its important food-preserving industry. Bertinoro, "the terrace of Romagna" (its commanding situation on top of a hill gives it a view extending from the Apennines to the sea), is the place from which Italy obtains the unctuous Albana wine. There is something about wine making which promotes hospitality, a virtue which Bertinoro long ago institutionalized. From its old Column of Hospitality, which still stands in the center of the town, depends a series of iron rings. Each ring corresponds to a family—a "fire," as they phrased it then. The arriving stranger hitched his horse to one of the rings at random; and it became the duty of the family represented by that ring to take him in.

The best-known city of Forlì province is Rimini, older than Rome. It was originally Etruscan, peopled according to Strabo with Umbro-Etruscans, but first really important only with the arrival of the Romans, who named it Ariminum.

Rimini today is a pleasant resort in the center of the

Riviera del Sole, the Riviera of the Sun, a practically un-broken stretch of sandy beach 12½ miles long. The sea reaches deeply into the city through a canal which is also a port, picturesque with its confusion of fishing boats with colored sails festooned with the great square nets used to catch baby eels and other fish. In the early morning the Piazza Cavour offers the lively spectacle of a market teem-ing with every species of Adriatic fish.

A characteristic of the cooking of the province of Forlì is variety. Most of its cities have clearly marked specialties of their own—except the capital itself, a galling lack which may have goaded a near-native of the city (he was actually born in adjacent Forlimpopoli), Pellegrino Artusi, into becoming one of Italy's leading food writers. A full-fledged native was Olindo Guerrini, a poet who included a gas-tronomic book among his works and enjoyed a solid reputa-tion as a gourmet.

Among inland towns, Modigliana has a pasta specialty of *orecchioni,* so named from its ear-shaped form, stuffed with ricotta cheese, parsley and nutmeg, partly boiled, covered with butter and grated Parmesean cheese, and finished in the oven. Cesana claims as its own a creation whose origin is disputed. It is a sauce called *balsamella,* described as a *"salsa bianca di farina rosolata nel burro e nel latte"*—a white-sauce flour browned in butter and milk. This is clearly the classic béchamel, usually said to have been invented by the Marquis Louis de Béchameil, maître d'hôtel for Louis XIV. "Not so," says a Cesana brochure, "this sauce has been made here since the Middle Ages, and delighted Cardinal Albornoz when, in the 14th century, it was served him at a farewell banquet."

Cesana has a case. The post of maître d'hôtel for Louis XIV was held not by chefs, but by nobles, who were not likely to know much about cooking. Possibly some obsequious chef in the royal kitchens gave this name to a sauce already known to flatter the Marquis, or béchamel could have been a distortion of *balsamella* (some French authorities prefer to spell it *béchamelle*, which gets it a shade nearer to the Italian word while conversely Italians also spell it *besciamella*, obviously in attraction from French). Some citizens of Cesana are inconsistent when they maintain that the name *balsamella* is a salute to Cagliostro, whose real name was Giuseppe Balsamo; Cagliostro was two Louis later than the Marquis de Béchameil. However, Cagliostro was perhaps more of a culinary expert than the Marquis. When he became involved in the affair of the diamond necklace, his house was searched by investigators who were perhaps less interested in turning up evidence which would link him to this scandal than finding the formulas he was supposed to possess for making gold and diamonds. The only formula they found was a recipe for *boeuf en daube*. Whatever the origin of béchamel, the ancient Italian *balsamella* is virtually the sauce we know today; French béchamel as made in Louis XIV's time was somewhat different.

Moving from Cesana to Cesenatico brings us to the coast and, as might be expected, a local version of *brodetto*. Cesenatico also smothers pasta under seafood sauce, is renowned for its skill in frying sole, and offers as a dessert *ciambelle col buco*, ring-shaped fritters which might be described as a very distant relative of the American doughnut. The *ciambella*, a pastry ring of various sorts, is common throughout Italy, the peculiarity of the local variety being that it is flavored, in addition to a touch of lemon peel, with anise—"Romagna anise," specified Artusi, who betrayed his inland origin by paying less attention to the products of the sea than to those of the earth, "and I say Romagna, because this, by its agreeable taste and its strong fragrance, is without exaggeration the best in the world."

The *ciambella* is associated here with Easter Monday. By very ancient custom (it is mentioned in a document connected with the donation of Romagna to the Church by Pepin the Brief) the shell of the first egg which is to go into the *ciambella* is broken on the head of a boy to ward off bad luck. *Bracciatelli* are little *ciambelle* which street vendors sell at Easter threaded on canes. Even smaller ones called *biscottini* used once upon a time to be showered on wedding guests by the happy couple, but they have now given way to confetti, with bride and groom on the receiving end. *Piada dei morti* (dead man's dough) is made from bread dough (for which the Romagna word is *piada*), encouraged to rise with brewer's yeast, imbibed in olive oil, and studded with bits of walnuts, almonds and raisins. Some recipes add pine nuts and a dash of wine.

Many coastal cities share among them the credit for such regional specialties as *granzèvola arrosto*, large spider crabs roasted in their shells on hot coals (the females filled with eggs are the most prized), and eaten cold—an ancient dish much appreciated by Queen Christina of Sweden when the Duke of Mantua had it served to her. Others are *cannocchie fritte*, boned squill coated with a batter of flour, eggs, oil, white wine, and water, and then fried; *polpetta di mare*, highly tasty and nearly indigestible (which is probably why it has almost disappeared from circulation), for which a small octopus is stuffed with hake livers and eggs, *mormora* (a member of the cod family) and other fish, and spit-roasted whole, tentacles and all; *passatini*, bits of dough made with bread crumbs rather than flour, though occasionally a little semolina and farina flour is added, along with eggs, sometimes a little beef marrow, grated cheese, and a flavoring of lemon juice or nutmeg or both; gnocchi, which are made in some towns with a mixture of mashed potatoes and flour, and in others with semolina flour alone;

torta campagnola di sangue o migliaccio (a rustic tart of blood or blood pudding), available only at pig-sticking time since it requires the blood of the pig, which, cooked in a double boiler with an equal amount of milk, starts the preparation of the dish, to which eggs, sugar, grated orange peel and nutmeg are added, with the result strained into a dough-lined pie plate and cooked until the liquid filling solidifies; cooked green vegetable tarts and fritters, especially spinach, rustic also; tripe in nutmeg-flavored tomato sauce; and *la sapa*, a syrup made from grape must which in Romagna enters into recipes of very diverse kinds and is used in particular to make sherbet.

Since it is a coastal city too, Rimini, which has a reputation for good eating, naturally has its own version of *brodetto*. Its chief rule is no eels, for Rimini dislikes the eel, even hidden among other fish in a thickly populated stew. Another important identifying mark is that it always includes tomato. Rimini also claims as its very own not *piadone* in general, since these buns are typical of Romagna as a whole, but *piadone coi ciccioli*, which utilizes the morsels of meat left over when lard is rendered from pork (*ciccioli* in Italian, *i grasùl* in the local dialect). Dough is allowed to rise overnight. The following morning there are kneaded into it, bit by bit, equal quantities of lard and butter, eggs, sugar, orange or lemon peel, and the *ciccioli*. It is of course baked in the oven.

The colorful and ancient city of Bologna is the capital of Emilia-Romagna, both politically and gastronomically. Its culinary reputation has given it the epithet of Bologna the Fat (*Bologna la Grassa*). It is also known as *la città dei portici, Bologna la Turrita*, and *Bologna la Dotta*. It had two other official names before Bologna. Around 500 B.C. it was the Etruscan Felsina. The small province of Bologna includes at least one other Etruscan site, Marzabotto, which stands beside the ancient Misa, where Etruscan ruins can still be visited, and probably another in Imola, which seems to be an Etruscan name. In Roman times Bologna was called Bononia, a name sometimes described rosily by Bolognese as meaning "all good things"; it seems more likely that it came from the Celtic tribe of the Boii, who conquered the territory about 350 B.C. (They also gave their name to Bohemia.)

It is easy to see why Bologna is called *la città dei portici*. The *portici* are arches which roof 20 miles of its sidewalks from building line to curb, so that walking Bologna's streets is like passing through the covered soukhs of North Africa or the Near East. Above them rise the restfully colored walls of old rose, soft reds, sienna, and burnt orange, and magnificent churches and palaces.

Bologna la Turrita (Bologna the Towered) may seem less obvious, though you do find two towers, side by side, the Asinelli Tower, 317 feet high, and the Garisenda, which is under 160 feet—reassuringly no taller, since it is 10½ feet out of plumb, leaning more sharply than the Tower of Pisa. But when Bologna was given this epithet, it boasted more than 180 towers. Dante called the city *la selva*, the forest, for the tall slim towers bristled above the rooftops as thickly as trees from a wood.

The nickname *Bologna la Dotta* (Bologna the Learned) results from the fact that the city professes to have the oldest university in Europe. This depends largely on how you define a university. Organized study is said to have begun there in 425, but the date given oftener for the foundation of a university proper is 1088, though an old document attests that law lectures were already being given there in 1076. Whenever it started, university life was characterized by much banqueting. *Bologna la Dotta* lived in a state of symbiosis with *Bologna la Grassa*.

The epithet *Bologna la Grassa* goes back at least as far as the 13th century, when it was used in the *Roman du Comte de Poitiers*. Thereafter it appeared frequently. In the first half of the 15th century, Giovanni Schedel wrote in his *Chronache*, "Bologna is called the fat and the rich for the reason that it produces abundantly wheat, wine, and everything necessary to life." In the second half of the 16th, geographer Abram Oertel reported, "The territory is watered by rivers, to the convenience and advantage of the populations. The great abundance of all things is demonstrated by the popular saying, *Bologna la Grassa*."

The richness of its soil paradoxically deprived the Bologna region of one food for which it had been famous—the olive. In the 16th century, Bologna olives were renowned. P. Platina, a Cremonese author of those times, praised among the best olives of Italy those picked on the territory of Bologna. A Dutch witness, Andrea Schott, in his *Itinerario*, published in 1622, wrote: "Traveling through Romagna by the Emilian Way, five miles from Bologna, we came upon low hills, rich in olives," and after sampling some he added that "they are not inferior in flavor to those of Spain." In the 18th century, all travel guides to the area were still celebrating the Bologna olive. Yet today you can ride through the countryside and almost never see an olive tree. The reason is simple. Since the olive prospers on ungrateful earth, areas less richly endowed by nature can rival Bologna in olive production; but her fat earth makes her unbeatable for many more demanding crops. The land once devoted to olives has been converted to the cultivation of other foods.

But Bologna had become used to olive oil, and did not abandon it even after it had become clear that it was more profitable to buy it elsewhere than to produce it at home. The presence of those "large herds of red pigs," and, a little farther east, of the cows of Romagna, had made

Bologna an exception to the general rule that the character of the dishes in any given region is determined largely by the type of cooking fat available there. Bologna uses all three of the major cooking fats, cooking sometimes with olive oil, sometimes with butter, and sometimes with lard, so that here the character of the individual dish determines which cooking fat should be used. Some recipes even call for different fats in the same dish. Other things being equal, Bologna prefers lard, often perfumed with bay leaves.

If all this gives you the impression that Bolognese cooking is rich, you will not be in error. The citizens of Bologna are the Burgundians of Italy—hearty lusty trenchermen, who eat heavily and drink deep. They share with the Burgundians hearty appetites, the robust health that results from substantial varied nourishment, and a tendency to couple the pleasures of the table with those of the bed. "Wine is good for women when men drink it," says a Burgundian proverb, while the Bolognese credit to ardor for the female sex the inventions of *tortellini* and *tagliatelle*.

In his *Bologna a tavola*, Alessandro Cerbellati pays tribute to "the hearty appetite which characterizes our culinary ecstasies." Pellegrino Artusi, in *La scienza in cucina e l'arte di mangiar bene*, wrote: "When you speak of Bolognese cooking, make the bow it deserves. It is a rather heavy cuisine, if you like, because the climate requires it; but how succulent it is, and what good taste it displays! It is wholesome too, and in fact octogenarians and nonagenarians abound there as nowhere else"—except perhaps in Burgundy.

Bologna is renowned for banqueting. The university had no monopoly on feasting. The wealthy families whose spectacular repasts are described in the social histories of many parts of Italy were not wanting there. In Bologna as elsewhere, some of the most sumptuous banquets were associated with weddings. When Count Guido Pepoli

married Bernardina Rangoni in 1475, at least two contemporary writers marveled at the lavishness of the accompanying feast. Their accounts are preserved in the
library of the University of Bologna, a rich mine of gastronomic lore. It contains some hundred volumes, in manuscript, of the *Memorie antiche di Bologna* of Canon Ghiselli,
who reports that at the Pepoli-Rangoni wedding banquet
the guests stayed at table for three whole days, taking cat-
naps between courses. In his *Historia di Bologna*, Ghirar-
dacci tells what they ate. "The thousand diners passed cou-
rageously through roast kid, sausages, leg of boar in stew,
truffle-stuffed turkey, fried cockerel, and cheese, and lubri-
cated all these with eagle soup and the wines of Montedo-
nato and Bertinoro." I have been unable to find out what
eagle soup is, but I strongly doubt that it is soup made of
eagles.

Twelve years later Messer Annibale Bentivoglio married Lucrezia d'Este, natural daughter of the Duchess of
Ercole, but this time the guests stayed at the table for a mere
six hours. In this brief period, however, they managed to
get through a variety of roasts and of *fegatelli* (which in
those days included not only innards, like liver and kidneys,
but also, curiously, small birds), sausages, stews, and desserts
of every sort, including many made with gelatine—20
courses in all. The number of guests has not been recorded,
but you can make your own estimate from the statistic that
950 baskets were required to hold the famous white bread
of Bologna. This was only the wedding eve dinner. There
was a second banquet after the ceremony on the following
day; and on the day after that, preceded by traditional
games in the piazza, there was a third, distinguished by
trionfi di tavola so splendid that they were paraded around
the hall three times to permit the guests a good look at the
animals, castles, ships in full sail, fountains, chariots, dra-
gons, and other themes worked out in sugar and marzipan.

A century and a half later the banqueting tradition was still going strong. When one wealthy senator left the *gonfalonierato* (the magistracy) in 1639, he gave a banquet for the Council of Elders and other magistrates which not only did honor to all the local products, but also reached farther afield, offering all the edible fish of the Po and the lakes of Lombardy, along with wines and fruit from many foreign countries. It is recorded with awe that it cost the Senator 1,000 ducats, clearly considered a fantastic sum, though for what it would represent in modern money your guess is as good as mine.

Another century and a half, and Bologna was still at it. The feast given at his villa of Ceretolo by Count Ludovici Felicini to celebrate his marriage was marked by a fixation on family escutcheons. The meal started with a varicolored dish of gelatine which represented the arms of the Boschetti, the family of the bride. Then came a cold veal paté in the shape of the Felicini blazon, with supporters of a leopard and a lion in armor modeled in marzipan. A pheasant paté figured the arms of three other proud families, after which heraldic fantasy ran out, and other types took over. There was an "imperial tart," whatever that may have been, which imitated a garden, with what success was not reported; dough built up to form a pyramid; peacock in bright unbedraggled plumage; what Bologna called Spanish bread and France calls Genoese bread—vanilla-flavored almond cake imbibed with liqueurs; and blanc mange molded into the shape of the Ghirlandina of Modena (the cathedral tower).

The name of Bologna has contributed a word to the English language. The type of sausage called boloney in the United States is so named because it is a pale reflection of Bologna's own special sausage, mortadella. A great deal of mediocre sausage is misleadingly referred to as mortadella, but as made in Bologna, mortadella is one of the great sausages of the world, which well deserved the accolade accorded it in 1661 by Ovidio Montalbani, a doctor and a gourmet, who called it "the noblest of all pork products." Many other experts, before and since, have agreed, and have praised other Bolognese sausages as well. Toward the end of the 16th century, Andrea Schott noted that Bologna was making "salami and sausages of which there is no equal in the whole country." François Deseine in 1669 wrote in his *Nouveau voyage d'Italie*, "The *salumi* of Bologna are renowned in the whole world." (Salami are sausages, *salumi* is the general word for processed pork products, including sausages, and also, for instance, ham.) Toward the end of the 17th century an Englishman, E. Veryard, reported that "the Bolognese trade extensively in silk, velvet, linen, puppies, but above all in sausages, which are sent to all parts of Europe."

A dissenting opinion was expressed by Anatole France, who found mortadella unpleasant in taste and indigestible for the stomach; "but he had with him, during his visit to Bologna," wrote Alessandro Cervellati, "his tyrannical friend, Madame Caillavet, which was certainly no help to the digestion."

Mortadella is made of finely hashed pork, kneaded well together, highly spiced, and packed tightly into sausage casings. The flesh is even and smooth, the flavor subtle and delicate. Sometimes the casing is the skin of a whole suckling pig, into which the meat is stuffed with such artistry that no incision is visible—unless you pull up the foreleg and look under it, which is where you will find the hole through which it was inserted. This trick was known to the ancient Romans, and some authorities are of the opinion that mortadella was first made by them and has been manufactured continuously since, a theory which they buttress by another concerning the origin of its name. They point out that the Romans made a sausage called *murtata* because it was flavored by myrtle berries, *mortella* in modern Italian—hence, mortadella. The only trouble with this theory is that it is not myrtle berries which provide the spiciness characteristic of mortadella, but whole peppercorns, and these are so much the indispensable mark of mortadella that its heavy peppering is recorded even in the 15th century, when pepper was so precious that it was used as money.

The ancient Romans apparently did make a sausage which was a precursor of mortadella, but it disappeared from public view with the fall of the Empire. It either took refuge in the monasteries or was reinvented there. In any case, it emerged from them about the 14th century, when the Corporazione dei Salaroli (the guild of sausage-makers) was organized in the Bologna region in 1376. The monks achieved the fine uniformity of the seasoned pork which still distinguishes this sausage by crushing it painstakingly with mortar and pestle, using a mortar especially made for this purpose. It was called the mortar for pig's meat— *mortaio della carne di maiale*, which, foreshortened, produced the name mortadella.

Mortadella is not the only ware of the Bolognese *lardaròl* (the dialect word for a sausage merchant), for the province makes many other sausages, and has been doing so for centuries. It was in the 16th that Ortensio Lando wrote in his *Commentario delle più notabili e monstruose cose d'Italia ed altri luoghi*, "I do not want to forget to signal that in Bologna are made the best sausages ever eaten, whether they are meant to be eaten raw or cooked, which sharpen the appetite at any hour of the day; they make wine seem tastier." But the other sausages, though long made in Bologna, probably originated in other provinces of Emilia-Romagna. What is definitely peculiar to Bologna is the habit of eating plump sausages with lentils on Christmas Day.

* * *

Bologna is the capital of *pasta tirata*, northern pasta (archetype, *tagliatelle*), as Naples is that of southern pasta (archetype, macaroni). Northern pasta dough usually contains egg, southern pasta usually does not, but neither rule is invariable.

The supremacy of Bologna for pasta is a function of the wheat grown here and more directly of the kind of flour milled from it. This is *soglia*, the same semolina flour we have already met in Ferrara, which Bologna uses to make bread which is certainly not far behind that of Ferrara, and perhaps equals it. *Soglia* is also credited with enriching the flavor of thick soups; but its primary purpose here is providing pasta.

To the quality of the flour is added the skill of Bolognese pasta makers. *Pasta tirata*, rolled pasta, can be made by machine, but the Bolognese would rather not. They hold that no machine can duplicate the hard hand labor of skilled women pasta makers, who knead and roll their dough interminably until their haunches are bathed in sweat, which, it is locally agreed, is the sign that the pasta is ready. It should be rolled so thin that when a sheet of it is held up, the person holding it can be seen through the dough.

The Number One gastronomic specialty of Bologna, in the estimation of many, is *tortellini*. Bolognese are capable of becoming impassioned about this dish. "If the first father of the human race was lost for an apple," a Bolognese poet once wrote, "what would he not have done for a plate of *tortellini?*" "*Tortellini,*" a dithyrambic writer of the *Gazzetta di Bologna* pronounced about a century ago, "is more essential than the sun for Sunday, or love for a woman." The archives of the city of Bologna contain the record of a case brought against a student in 1289 for being abroad at night without a torch, against the law since prowlers in unlighted medieval streets could be assumed to be up to no good. He was acquitted because he explained that he had hurried out to buy *tortellini* to offer some friends who had arrived unexpectedly; the court considered this a reasonable justification. *Tortellini* has also appeared in court records in our own times. A case judged on June 23, 1909 concerned a postman who, in a Bologna restaurant, had assaulted a visitor from Venice imprudent enough to have run down *tortellini*. The Venetian wound up in the hospital and the postman in jail, sentenced to six months—without *tortellini*, the court specified, from which it may be assumed that Bologna had no statute forbidding cruel and unusual punishments.

"*Tortellini* is a happy marriage between the envelope and its stuffing which is a paste of prosciutto, mortadella, veal, and Parmesan cheese, with a dash of nutmeg," a Bolognese food writer explains, but for at least three centuries, the Bolognese imagination has been titillated less by the nature of its stuffing than by its shape. To make *tortellini*, you take small circles of the standard thin egg pasta dough, dispose your stuffing in the center, and roll them into bulgy tubes, twisting the two ends together to form a ring. For this process, there is good reason for preferring hand to machine work—from the point of view of the eater, at least. I have watched girls stuffing *tortellini* rings, and marvelled at their speed, which permits a single girl to turn out 6,000 to 6,500 of the little rings every hour; but a machine makes 65,000 in the same time, without developing sweat around the haunches. Man-made *tortellini* contains 50 percent stuffing, the machine-made variety only 30 percent. The customers know the difference. In the shop where I watched the *tortellini* makers, both kinds are sold. Many buyers insisted on the handmade pasta, though it costs more; stuffing is more expensive than dough.

The ring shape of *tortellini* suggests to the Bolognese mind the human navel—or more exactly the feminine navel, for it does not seem to have occurred to anyone that the male umbilicus possesses inspirational qualities. Obsession with this resemblance has produced a number of stories about the origin of *tortellini* which contribute little to history, but do shed some light on Bolognese psychology. A 17th-century story is the simplest; it maintains that *tortellini* was born when a cook molded his pasta directly in the navel of a Bolognese woman. The image is fetching, but the exact process by which edible pasta could thus be arrived at is not easy to figure out. Another picturesque but dismissible account is provided in a parody of Tassoni's *Rape of the Bucket* by a Tuscan author named Ceri who depicts Venus as stopping like any mortal at an inn in Castelfranco, whose cook, having had the great good luck to catch a glimpse of her nude, was moved to model her navel in dough.

More down to earth is the version of the poet-journalist Ostilio Lucarini, who wrote a play in Bolognese dialect called *Quèll ch'ha inventà i turtlein*, or The Man Who Invented Tortellini, which was first produced at the Teatro del Corso on December 3, 1925. Laid in the 17th century, this comedy tells how Minghèn, a rich junk dealer, in the middle of the night calls in his father-in-law, who is, conviently for the plot, a judge, to charge that he has just surprised his young cook, Pirulèn, in the bedroom of his wife, Laurina. Laurina denies it, but the cook confesses that, having returned to the house late after too much to drink, he had blundered by mistake into the wrong room, where, overcome by the beauty of his young mistress's unveiled charms, he had sunk to his knees beside the bed to gaze at her in rapture. However displeased Minghèn may have been at this, he was deterred from discharging the cook by a practical reason comprehensible to any good Bolognese—he was giving a Carnival banquet for the notables of the city, and he needed Pirulèn in the kitchen. For the banquet, the cook devised the first *tortellini* in the shape of Laurina's navel, and contrived to have them served to her, a love letter which she perspicaciously understood; so the play—for Pirulèn and Laurina at least—had a happy ending.

It was probably no accident that this opus was first produced in December, since Christmas dinner in Bologna traditionally starts with *tortellini*. "Christmas should be celebrated in Christian fashion," the *Gazzetta di Bologna* wrote in the article already cited above: "that is to say by eating until you burst, drinking until your head spins, and in general loading down the human machine with choice wines and edibles of all sorts, varieties and origins. But precede everything with a great dish of *tortellini*. Without *tortellini* there can be no Christmas in Bologna." How far back this association between *tortellini* and Christmas goes nobody knows, but as long ago as the end of the 12th century it was customary to make gifts of *tortellini* to priests and monks at that season—and eggs at Easter. Thus *tortellini* antedates considerably the 17th century, which seems to have been hit upon by the fanciful creators of legends as its time of birth. The date of 1410 has been ascribed to it in what otherwise might have seemed a credible story of its origin: this account says that *tortellini* was invented by Pietro Filargo da Candia, the anti-Pope Alexander V, who benefited by divine inspiration; he is buried in Bologna's church of San Francesco.

A recipe for *tortelli* or *tortelletti* (a larger size of *tortellini*, while *tortelloni* is the largest of all), dating from about Alexander's period, since it was found in a 14th-century manuscript, is very close to that used today. Its seasoning is based on *enula*, a medicinal herb no longer used, which is *liôla* or *lella* in Bolognese dialect. To this are added, for the stuffing, lean pork, grated cheese, eggs, spices (especially nutmeg), and much salt, all of which is ground into a paste. This was partly cooked before going into the pasta, which was probably much like that of today, and finished its cooking wrapped in its ring-shaped envelope of dough, in chicken or beef consommé. "These *tortelli* should be well salted and potent with spices," the recipe insists. Their closest modern cousin would be *tortellini d'erbette,* in which modern herbs replace the *enula.*

The variety of *tortellini* stuffings is endless. Although the first one given above is the classic combination, there are so many variations that it is almost rare to come upon the original. One favorite alternative mixture includes chopped pork, turkey, veal, egg, beef marrow, cheese, and spices. Another complicates this by adding ham, mortadella, calves' brains, and increasing the dosage of nutmeg, with the optional substitution of capon for turkey. A third variant hashes together fat and lean pork, mortadella, beef marrow, beef brains, eggs, grated cheese, salt, pepper, and nutmeg, wrapping this stuffing in an egg pasta which differs from the ordinary recipe by containing a little olive oil.

Tagliatelle asciutte (*tajadèl sôtti* in the local dialect) is another Bolognese pasta favorite. As is the case for *tortellini,* the origin of *tagliatelle* is ascribed to feminine influence. *Tagliatelle* is ribbon shaped and often golden in color from the eggs in the dough, enhanced when it is served with melted butter. Gastronomic writer Nasica (real name, Augusto Majani) says in his *Nei regni della gastronomia* that Mastro Zafirano, the Bolognese cook of Giovanni II of Bentivoglio, presided over the banquet Giovanni gave for Lucrezia Borgia when she arrived in Bentivoglio on May 28, 1487 to marry Ferrara's Duke of Este, and was so taken by her long flaxen hair that he invented *tagliatelle* in imitatation of it.

Tagliatelle, unlike *tortellini,* is never cooked in consommé, but is boiled in salted water. It is so thoroughly Bolognese that it would be superfluous to designate it as such; hence when you read *tagliatelle alla bolognese* on a menu, the adjective does not refer to the pasta, but to its sauce. It means that the pasta is doused with Bolognese *ragù*, an unctuous blend of onions, carrots, finely chopped pork and veal, butter, and tomato. You may expect to find this almost always when you encounter the label *alla bolognese* attached to pasta of any kind, and sometimes with other dishes as well. *Ragù* is a corruption of the French *ragoût*, stew, which in turn comes from *ragoûter*, meaning to arouse or enhance the taste—a service which *ragù* performs admirably for pasta. Often *ragù* is richer than the basic recipe given above.

Ragù goes well also on green *tagliatelle*, whose color results from mixing chopped spinach with the dough. But it is naturally absent from *tagliatelle col prosciutto*, whose whole idea is to avoid smothering the taste of the *tagliatelle* under a rich sauce. For this dish you cut the prosciutto (uncooked ham) into thin strips, sauté it separately in butter, and pour it over the pasta on serving along with its cooking juice—adding, of course, grated Parmesan cheese.

Lasagna, the pasta which comes in broad sheets, is also claimed by Bologna as peculiarly its own. "Lasagna is our own word," Alfredo Panzini, a native of Emilia-Romagna, wrote in his modern dictionary, but he evidently did not mean it to be taken quite literally, for he immediately called it "a survivor of the culinary glory of ancient times," and proceeded to discuss the derivation of the word from Latin. Lasagna was indeed known to the ancient Romans, who called it *laganum;* it is still called *lagana* in Calabria. It is believed to have been derived from *lasanum*, a cooking pot.

The preferred way to cook lasagna is to bake it in the oven (*lasagna al forno*) after, of course, preliminary boiling, and apparently it always has been. A 14th-century recipe in the library of the University of Bologna describes its making as follows: "Take good white flour and knead it with lukewarm water to make your dough. Then roll it out thin and let it dry. Cook in chicken consommé, or consommé from other fat meats; then put it in a platter with grated *cascio* cheese, layer after layer, as many as you please," to be finished by baking. You will notice that this is not an egg pasta; modern lasagna is made from dough with egg in it. Nowadays the layers of lasagna are not alternated simply with grated cheese, but with *ragù*, butter, and cheese (and sometimes béchamel sauce). While green *tagliatelle* are comparatively rare, green lasagna is common. The first person who thought to add spinach to lasagna dough, Mario Sandri wrote in his *Guida Gastronòmica di Bologna*, "was undoubtedly a great man, a true benefactor of humanity."

These three make up the great trinity of Bolognese pasta, but they are far from exhausting the list. A leading pasta center like Bologna could hardly be content with so few samples of the tremendous variety offered by Italian pasta. A few years ago a Dr. Rovetta listed more than 600 different shapes of pasta; and when you consider that each shape can be produced in different types of dough; cooked in different fashions; and served, in *brodo* or *asciutta*, with different stuffings, accompaniments or sauces, it becomes obvious that the possible variations run into the thousands. Italians insist upon this variety. Shortly after the war a Marshall Plan official, horrified at the waste involved by the making of 250 different forms of pasta by the same factory, persuaded it to cut its offerings down to 50. The company went bankrupt.

Passatelli in brodo, little dumplings of finely shredded spinach, egg dough, and cheese, cooked in consommé, is widespread in Emilia-Romagna, but there is a special variant, *passatelli alla bolognese*, in which bread crumbs and beef marrow replace the spinach. Since *passatelli* are served in consommé, this dish violates the general rule that the *alla bolognese* tag applied to pasta means with *ragù*. There are even *pasta asciutta* dishes which violate it too, for instance *pasticcio di tagliatelle alla bolognese,* which is dough in dough, for the *tagliatelle* is used as the filling for a pie whose crust is enriched with egg. This can be served with *ragù* if you want to, but it's not obligatory. Another exception to the rule is *maccheroni alla bolognese,* in which the macaroni, after boiling, is finished in the oven with truffles, chicken livers and chicken giblets, over which fresh cream is poured.

There are many humbler less sophisticated pasta dishes —the modest unadorned *strucchetti* (dialect, *strichêtt*); *pappardellini* (*papardlén*), meaning little squares, since the dough is cut into this shape; and *minestra del Paradiso,* made from bread crumbs dipped in oil, egg, and grated cheese. Often encountered in Bologna, but also in other cities of Emilia-Romagna, are *cappelletti,* little hats, describing the shape of their dough envelopes, which are stuffed with cottage cheese, minced turkey, egg, spices, and Parmesan; sometimes they are served on their own with melted butter, *ragù,* and grated cheese, or they may turn up in turkey soup. We must put an end to the listing somewhere, so suppose we finish with the Bolognese type of *anolini,* which stuffs the little pasta rings with bread crumbs mixed with egg, grated Parmesan, and concentrated meat gravy, the dough itself being often seasoned separately with onion or nutmeg; they are served in beef or chicken consommé.

Pasta and sausage are important on the Bolognese menu, but they by no means dominate it. One of the most widely known local meat dishes is *costolette alla bolognese,* a cousin of the Roman *saltimbocca.* Bologna arrived at this dish by evolution from an earlier version which combined pork fillets dipped in beaten egg with breaded veal. It was eventually decided that the pork made this too heavy even for Bolognese, so it was replaced by ham. The Bolognese fashion of cooking *costolette* starts with coating thin slices of veal in beaten egg and bread crumbs and sprinkling them with grated Parmesan. They are browned in a frying pan, some cooks using butter and others lard. A slice of ham is then pressed firmly down on the half-cooked veal, more grated cheese is shaken over the combined meats, and it is moistened with a little white wine, soup stock, or meat juice, according to the whim of the cook. It is finished in the oven. Sliced white truffles are sometimes added, and the dish is accompanied by mashed potatoes or green vegetables —braised endive is a favorite.

Bologna also does a good many other things with veal. *Scaloppine alla bolognese* means small slices of this meat cooked with alternate layers of prosciutto and previously boiled potatoes, accompanied by meat juice, butter, and Parmesan cheese. *Scaloppe farcite* is a sandwich of two slices of veal enclosing a filling of one slice of ham, with chopped sautéed mushrooms (or truffles) and grated cheese; a thin slice of Gruyère-type cheese is laid on top, and the whole is then moistened with meat stock. For *umido incassato*, veal is cooked with chicken giblets, sweetbread, beaten egg yolks, truffles, and mushrooms in béchamel sauce. *Involtini* are made by rolling slices of veal into a cylinder around a stuffing of highly spiced chopped meat and cooking them in *ragù* sauce.

Manzo alla Certosina may have been developed at the Charterhouse (*Certosa* in Italian) just outside the city, like many other dishes which were the products of monastery cooking; it is a beef pot roast, whose local peculiarities are nutmeg seasoning and the rather unexpected ingredient of chopped anchovy fillets. Also a little unusual is *maiale al latte alla bolognese*, since it simmers pork in milk, sometimes with pieces of white truffle. *Trippa alla bolognese* is made by first heating olive oil, bacon, onion, garlic and parsley over a moderate flame; the tripe, cut into small squares and moistened with a little bouillon, is then added; and after lengthy cooking (about an hour and a half) egg yolks with meat juice, powdered with Parmesan, go into the pan for the last five minutes.

Bologna's most famous poultry dish is *filetti di tacchino alla bolognese*, turkey white meat cooked with ham in exactly the same way as *costolette alla bolognese;* roast turkey is a favorite dinner-party *pièce de résistance. Petti di pollo alla bolognese* is the same thing with chicken. *Canestrelli di pollo* does not quite come under the heading of genuine regional cooking, since it was the creation of one man, but we might as well describe it here, since it was invented by a Bolognese chef—a "white bear," they would say in Bologna, where *orso bianco* means a chef, while his aide is a *gerla,* which is a hod, like the one grape pickers carry on their backs. *Canestrelli* is a complicated show piece, which starts by scalding strips of chicken in boiling water to keep them firm. They are then enveloped in a paste of chopped mutton, chicken giblets, mushrooms, truffles and béchamel sauce, and after cooking are served bedded on prosciutto and onions crushed together, laid on an infrastructure of purée of spinach. The dish is served surrounded by a ring of *tagliatelle* or some other form of pasta.

Fritto misto alla bolognese is composed of brains, liver and zucchini, each enveloped in bread crumbs; little cream puffs stuffed with cheese; and *bocconotti ripieni,* which are little balls of pasta filled with chopped chicken giblets and truffles. You would not expect an inland city to have a special fish dish, but Bologna has one—fresh-water fish, though. This is *frittura,* small fish fried in oil. They come from the Reno River, which flows by Bologna on its way to the Po.

Bologna benefits by a bewildering richness of desserts. Alas, one Bolognese sweet justly popular at the turn of the century seems to have disappeared from circulation—*bigné alla Margaretta,* also called *alla Menini,* from a pastry cook famous for them. They were a sort of sweet ravioli, whose dough contained eggs, sugar, butter, lemon peel and Rosolio cordial, stuffed with vanilla-flavored cream, and deep fried in oil. Menini's success with this dish was not so much the result of the scrupulous care with which he prepared these delicacies from the purest ingredients, as of his fashion of selling them. Piling his *bigné* in an enormous basket mounted on a barrow, he hawked his wares through the streets of Bologna, to the accompaniment of a running fire of hilarious stories bellowed at the top of his voice, most of them highly scurrilous anecdotes about the grandees of the city. There was such a sense of loss when his lusty personality disappeared from the Bolognese scene into which it fitted so well that his fellow citizens stopped eating *bigné* in an instinctive sign of mourning.

Another Bolognese sweet with a role in the local folklore has managed to survive. This is the *mandléina*, almond-flavored and almond-shaped. It was associated especially with the *addobbi*—the "decorations," a name given to the religious festivals which different quarters of Bologna hold every ten years. On these occasions rivalry among *mandléina* makers was strong. To demonstrate that its *mandléine* were the best, Bolognese families invited cognoscenti in to sample them; and most persons living in the district where an *addobbo* was going on left their doors open to permit all comers to taste their *mandléine*. This hospitable custom has disappeared. *Addobbi* are still celebrated, but they have become rowdy. The doors of homes where they are going on are more likely nowadays to be kept tightly closed than open to all. The *mandléina* is not the only sweet associated with these feasts. "An *addobbo* without *torta*, like a political banquet without speeches, cannot exist," a humorous weekly of Bologna once wrote. This referred to *torta di riso*, a cake of rice, almonds, milk and sugar.

Some other Bolognese sweets are also associated with

holidays, for instance *panspeziale alla Certosina*, special bread Charterhouse style, which was created by the friars of this monastery. It is a *ciambella*, another of those ring-shaped pastries. There is also an everyday *ciambella bolognese*, which makes do with only lemon peel and sugar for its flavoring, but *panspeziale*, a feature of the Christmas-New Year's season (also called *pan pepato*), is something else again. Brown in color, it is made of flour, sugar, honey, sweet and bitter almonds, pine nuts, sultana raisins, and orange and lemon peel, boiled in wine and chocolate, and strongly spiced with cloves and cinnamon. St. Joseph's Day is marked by the appearance of *ravioli di San Giuseppe* (*raviol* in dialect), for which the ravioli are stuffed with marmelade or marzipan.

Among other sweets worthy of attention are *sfrappole* (dialect, *sfrapel*), also called *crespelli*. These are ribbons of dough fried in oil, dusted with vanilla-flavored sugar, and capriciously twisted together. They were once considered so inexcusably luxurious that a sumptuary ordinance of 1294 forbade them. *Pinza*, which means "stuffed," is a Bolognese cake with a sweet filling. The Bolognese *semifreddo* is ice cream with custard (trifle), doused with thick chocolate sauce. A favorite ice cream flavor in Bologna is strawberry, and it is made there with an incomparable lightness, making it the perfect conclusion for a heavy Bolognese meal.

Modena's first appearance in written history was Pliny's account of an earthquake which occurred there in 91 B.C., which "killed a multitude of animals," for Modena was already producing meat; the nearby Campo Macri was a great wool market. It was already an old city in 91 B.C., a former Etruscan settlement called Mutina. What Pliny called its "Roman knights" were probably Etruscans, descendants of noble families who had been made knights when Rome took over because their property status entitled them to that rank. Their holdings were not large, five acres ordinarily, but this was enough for prosperity on the fertile plain between the Secchia and Panaro rivers. In Pliny's time much of it was covered by oak forest, whose acorns fattened the prized pigs of the region. The forests are mostly gone now, but the pigs are still there. They antedated the Romans, and, for that matter, the Etruscans too; Ligurians were raising pigs here before the Etruscans arrived. But they must have waited for the Romans to acquire the name by which they are still known, *maiale*, for it was the Romans who sacrificed pigs to the goddess Maia, mother of Mercury.

The medieval history of Modena resembles that of the other great cities of Emila-Romagna, with perhaps less turbulence. The modest scale to which fighting, so deadly in other areas, was confined in Modena, is symbolized by a wooden bucket, probably the humblest triumphal trophy in military history, still preserved in the Ghirlandina, the tower of the 11th century cathedral. Modena wrested it from Bologna during squabbling between the two cities, inspiring Alessandro Tassoni to compose his mock epic, *The Rape of the Bucket.*

Modena's military history was not spectacular, but her gastronomic history makes up for it. It begins with the pigs whose existence had been noticed by Pliny. To the south, in Tuscany, Lazio, Umbria and The Marches, pigs provided *porchetta*, but Modena preferred to make sausage from them. She is famous today for her own particular type of sausage, *zampone*, stuffed pigs' feet, which no one denies was invented there. Modena may already have been making sausage in Pliny's time. He praised the quality of Modena pork in terms which cause some authorities to conclude that he sampled it in the form of sausage. There is nothing inherently unlikely in the theory that Modena was making sausage even before the time of the Romans. The Romans learned how to concoct it from the Gauls, and the Gauls were in Modena before the Romans were.

There is no doubt that Modena was making sausage at least by the 1500's. Ortensio Lando, a poet of this period, described Modena in one of his verses as "the fecund mother of sausages." Also in the 1500's, the chronicler Tomasino Lancilotto listed some current dishes, and included among them the *salamo* [sic] of Modena. In the 1600's Tassoni called Modena "the city of fine sausages," and in *The Rape of the Bucket* attributed their invention to one Sabbatino Brunello. Brunello was almost certainly a creature of Tassoni's imagination, but Modena has named a street for him all the same. None of these old writers mentions *zampone* specifically, so it has often been assumed that *zampone* did not appear on the scene until fairly recently. The Modenese poet Enrico Stuffler even wrote that *zampone* was invented for a culinary contest in the 1800's and won first prize. *Zampone* may very well have won a first prize on this occasion—it has won many others at food fairs since—but it was certainly not as a novelty. *Zampone* may not yet have acquired the reputation it has today, but it was definitely in existence in the 1500's. The proof is there for all to see in the Modena municipal museum, which contains an anonymous 16th-century painting of the Piazza Grande, the market place. Look closely, and you will spot a detail which escaped the attention of those who believed *zampone* was invented in the 19th century. A sausage shop is clearly depicted in this old painting—and its display contains two *zamponi*.

Zampone was even being cited by name a century before the date Stuffler gave for its invention. In the 1700's a Ferrarese poet named Frizzi mentioned in his *Salameide* "*zampetto*" and its sister sausage, *cotechino*, ascribing them both to Modena. In the same century Alfonso Coccapani wrote a whole poem in praise of *zampone*. Early in the 1800's the satirical poet Giuseppe Giusti seems to have had *zampone* in mind when he remarked that "the existence of Modena sausage makes up for the existence of the Duke."

By this time *zampone* had reached the zenith of its fame. It was the king of the Piazza Grande, a bustling and colorful place which still deserved to have its portrait painted. The public scales stood there, in charge of the weigher— *al balanzer* in the local dialect. In the center of the square, sheltered by enormous umbrellas, vegetable merchants shouted the merits of their wares. Their area was surrounded by the stalls of the fruit vendors, and beyond them were the poultry mongers. The place of honor, under the clock, was reserved for the sausage sellers, whose *zamponi* were prominently displayed. The Modenese climate was rugged a hundred years ago, and in winter the market was often covered with snow. Itinerant vendors pushed their barrows through the crowd and sold marketmen and customers slices of hot roast meat from great smoking caldrons.

Zampone by now was being exported to Paris, London and other appreciative capitals. It was eaten in London in 1837 by the politically exiled proponent of national unity Giuseppe Mazzini and in Paris by the self-exiled ambassador of Italian opera Gioacchino Rossini. The house of Bellentani, still making sausage in Modena today, preserves in its files a letter in which Rossini ordered *zamponi, cotechini* and *cappelli da prete* (priests' hats, a sausage so named because it is shaped like a biretta), and though his handwriting was clear enough, drew little pictures of them to insure against error. Also attributed to him (erroneously, for it was actually written by Paolo Ferrari) is a letter acknowledging receipt of an order, with a piece of doggerel.

> *Ricevetti lo zampone e lo mangiai*
> *ricevetti il lambrusco e lo bovei:*

The Food of Italy:

squisito il primo e di Rossini degno,
degno il secondo degli dei d'Omero.

Which might be rendered freely thus:

The zampone came, I have eaten it up.
The Lambrusco came, I have just drained the cup.
Of Rossini was worthy the exquisite first,
While the second was fit to quench Homer's gods' thirst.

Another letter carefully kept in the Bellentani files is dated December 18, 1867, and reads: "I have tasted your *zampone*. It merits its reputation of being the best. Nowadays it is difficult to find anything with so exquisite a taste as your product. With gratitude which comes truly from the heart, Yours, Giuseppe Garibaldi." On May 24, 1895, Zola, with characteristic excess, wrote that he had been completely conquered by *zampone*, "a delicious and divine dish [capable] of bringing to the saddened soul a breath of joy for poor suffering humanity." The poet Norberto Rosa, who was setting out to write one, asserted in a footnote that "the *zampetti* of Modena are the only ones worthy of a poem in twelve stanzas."

The centuries-old process of making *zampone* in Modena begins with a double selection—careful selection of the right pigs for the purpose, careful selection of the right parts of the pigs. The animals most prized come from the hills of Castelnuovo, Castelvetro and Vignola, where there are still stands of ancient oaks. Their acorns build up flesh which is firm but not fibrous, tender but not flabby. The porkers are allowed to forage among the oaks until they reach a weight of some 375 to 450 pounds. They are then fed on grain, especially corn and bran.

The pig-slaughtering season opens traditionally on All Saints' Day, November 1. The choicest of these choice pigs are reserved for *zampone* and their choicest parts only are retained for the *zampone* stuffing. Ordinarily this means meat from the shoulder, the neck, the throat, the ears and the shank; but the decisive criterion is that the meat should contain the exact proportion of lean to fat which centuries of experience have shown to be ideal for *zampone*.

Big *zampone* manufacturers necessarily use machines, even in Modena, but the purists insist that to make the best *zampone* there is no machine which can substitute for man. Salt, pepper, nutmeg, cinnamon and cloves are crushed together with mortar and pestle, along with other seasonings which each maker has developed for his own product, whose secret he guards jealously. Modena sausage-making is in the hands of family dynasties; the secret seasoning formulas are passed down from father to son, and are divulged to no one outside the family.

Some of the pig's skin is cut into the finest possible pieces with a half-moon chopper on a board coated with a film of garlic. The skin, the spices and the carefully selected pieces of meat now go into the mortar all together, to be battered and crushed into a fine smooth paste. Getting this just right is Secret No. 1 of perfect *zampone*-making. It is a long arduous process; the grinder is exhorted not to tire until he succeeds in producing a mixture which is *bein tacleint*. This dialect phrase is untranslatable by any single word; it means gelatinous, sticky, light, and delicate, all at the same time. It is then ready to be tamped tightly into the pig's feet, previously boned, cleaned, scraped and steamed.

In the old days, after the pork had been processed, the *zamponi*, and the hams and other products made from the same pigs, were hung in wells to preserve them until their sale. There were icehouses in those days, but they were reserved for fresh meat. Cured pork products would keep for a long while anyway without refrigeration, easily through the winter after their making, and usually much longer. Nowadays Modena has running water, and wells are not available; but hanging and aging in well-aired warehouses works quite as well.

Cooking *zampone* properly is almost a liturgical rite. To begin with, a special cooking utensil is required, the *zamponiera*, long and narrow; it is barely wide enough to take the *zampone* in. The idea is to keep the *zampone* completely covered during its long slow simmering, but with a minimum of boiling water, so that the cooking juices suffer the least possible dilution. Before being put into the *zamponiera*, a cross-shaped incision is made in the *zampone* to let steam out, and it is wrapped in a heavy oiled cloth tied firmly around it to prevent water from seeping in and making the interior soggy; only enough of the hoof end is left protruding to allow later probing with a fork. This protective wrapping is all the more necessary for cooks who follow the practice of putting the *zampone* in the *zamponiera* and letting it stand overnight, covered with water, before starting to cook it the following day. How long *zampone* should cook is a much disputed point—probably the longer the better. An old-fashioned rule of thumb followed by many housewives is that a *zampone* should cook an hour for each kilogram of weight (2.2 pounds); as the family-size *zampone* would be likely to weigh about two kilograms, this would mean only two hours, which is not enough. Another formula is to cook it three hours for the first kilogram and one more for each additional kilogram. This would allow four hours for a two-kilogram *zampone* (it should be kept barely at the boil), and more does not hurt. The test is to prick it with a fork. If the tines penetrate as if into soft butter, without meeting resistance, the *zampone* is done. It should then be served immediately, as hot as possible, sliced, and accompanied by white beans (the type known familiarly as "old woman's teeth") or lentils and mashed potatoes.

Three other Modena sausages are made from the same

stuffing as *zampone*—*sassolini*, the least known; *cappello da prete*, the kind Rossini ordered; and, the most important, *cotechino*. The name of this cylindrical sausage comes from *cotica*, pig's skin, but, inconsistently, it is not wrapped in pig's skin, but in ordinary sausage casing. The name dates from earlier times, when a rectangular sheet of skin, coated with lard, was rolled around the sausage meat, and held in place by a network of thread. *Cappello da prete* is still enveloped in pigskin.

Cotechino is usually served with lentils, but there is also an elaborate way of presenting it known as *cotechino in galera* (in prison). For this, a *cotechino* weighing about a pound is boiled until it is half cooked, wrapped in a slice of raw ham which is itself then wrapped in a very thin slice of beef, the two being held in place by thread wound around the whole. A small onion, finely chopped, is now cooked in an earthenware dish in plenty of oil. The wrapped *cotechino* goes into this and is covered with consommé and dry Lambrusco wine in equal quantities. The cooking is finished in the earthenware dish, with the addition of more consommé if necessary. The *cotechino* is served sliced in the cooking dish, bathing in the dense gravy which results.

For outsiders, *zampone* is the great gastronomic specialty of Modena. For the Modenese themselves, there is another which many of them consider more precious. This is *aceto balsamico*, a fine wine vinegar flavored with herbs. You can find a commercial version of it (at which Modenese who make their own at home would probably turn up their noses) under the labels of *aceto modenese* or *aceto del duca*. The latter refers to the Dukes of Este, and intimates that the bottle contains the sort of vinegar made for these august consumers; but Modena was making *aceto balsamico* centuries before the Estes moved in. The earliest written reference to it dates from 1046, when Bonifacio di Canossa (father of Matilda, the Great Countess) presented a barrel of it to the Emperor Henry III as a coronation gift. In Bonifacio's opinion, an ordinary keg was not worthy to transport this precious liquid. He had a special one made, decorated with repoussé designs in silver. This was placed on a cart drawn by two white oxen, and delivered to the Emperor at Piacenza, where he had stopped on his way to Rome.

In the 16th century this vinegar was considered so precious a commodity that it was disposed of specifically by will, figuring among the more important bequests. In 1944, when the frantically clanging bells of the Ghirlandina warned Modena that American bombers were approaching, thousands took to bicycles and pedaled desperately out of the city. Many of them had taken time to scoop up money, jewels and other easy-to-carry valuables; and on dozens of luggage carriers small kegs were securely strapped. They contained vinegar.

"For me," wrote Franco Vanni, a native of Modena, "*aceto balsamico* does not simply recall salad. It recalls boyhood: the gates of my school; the avenues between the Storchi theatre and the victory monument (excuse me, I don't remember what victory it was); the booths where watermelon and ice cream were sold; the outdoor cinema and the cyclists passing by; my schoolmates, whom I have not seen for years, and everything else that existed when I was ten years old—a little girl with freckles on her white skin, another who was studying philosophy, a blonde who lived in my neighborhood (I don't remember the name of the street, but by the Almighty I could find it with my eyes shut!). All this floods my mind, you understand, from a simple whiff of *aceto balsamico*. It invokes echoes of the jingling bell of the tram turning the corner to enter the Via Giardini and of the soothing night sounds of my infancy; the old attic, with apples spread to dry on the floor; the

cherry jam, the tomato preserves cooked in a double boiler
—a whole world, peaceful and slow-moving, soft and quiet,
in which we tried to learn to live without knowing anxiety
or anguish. It evokes the Sunday dinners, with the bulbous
black bottle enthroned in the center of the table amid the
perfume of fresh bread. The salad seemed seasoned with
coffee and its bitter-sweet aroma rose from the bowl to fill
the air."

The "bulbous black bottle" was the traditional shape for
the vinegar recipient and every other detail about the making, storing and serving of *aceto balsamico* is traditional too
for the Modenese families which for generations have been
perpetuating their own vinegar, stored in casks in the cellar.
They make it with as much care as if it were wine; and so
do the few remaining artisans who turn it out for sale on a
small scale. The mass manufacturers claim that their product is as good as homemade vinegar. One can only hope
they are right. But in any case, suppose we turn our backs
on the factories, and go down into the cellar of a private
family which makes *aceto balsamico* for its own use.

A line of 12 kegs is standing on some sort of platform.
Why 12, I do not know; it is traditional. The first keg in
the row contains newly made herb-flavored wine vinegar.
Its qualities are still a mystery. It is too young to have developed its own character. It will reach full potentiality
after a journey from barrel to barrel, during which it will
enter into different blends and absorb other perfumes. This
is the process into which the vinegar in the other casks has
already entered. As you move along the row, each barrel
is richer than its predecessor; the last is the acme of what
this cellar has so far been able to produce. It may have had
a long life—in some of Modena's cellars you can find kegs
containing vinegar 50, 60 or even 70 years old. It was
started with the encouragement of a vinegar mother at least
ten years old, in a keg of red oak, and in the course of years

has been transferred from one keg to another—of oak, of chestnut, of mulberry and of juniper wood. Each of these added new fragrances to the liquid. This is traditional too, but nowadays it is also obligatory; the law stipulates that only casks made of these woods can be used for *aceto balsamico*. At the end of several years of blending, of moving, and of aging, the vinegar is a dense dark brown, almost black, with a pleasing characteristic aromatic odor, and a taste which is a mixture of tart and sweet. Acidity is not less than 6 percent, alcoholic content is not more than 1.5 percent. The cask lies on its side; the bunghole, facing upward, is covered by a smooth flat slab of stone from the banks of the Secchia River—traditional too. As for the handsome old-fashioned bottles from which the vinegar is eventually served, not many remain. They are impressive—massive dark-blue spheres, drawn out below into a thick foot and above into a heavy neck, whose old glass picks up reflections of purples, greens and russet reds.

Modena claims that its vinegar has medicinal as well as gastronomic qualities (as though it mattered), and confirmation has been supplied by that ubiquitous 24-karat gourmet, Rossini, who turned to it for relief from scurvy and reported that in a short time this decoction had restored him to "health and tranquillity."

If you should be lucky enough to find yourself in the province of Modena between April 10 and 20, leave the Emilian Way at Castelfranco and strike southward to Vignola. The object is not to visit Vignola itself, though it is a worthy city which was culturally capable of producing such distinguished citizens as Giacomo da Vignola, the architect who built the Villa Giulia and the Gesù in Rome, and Ludovico Antonio Muratori, "the father of Italian history," known for many works weightier than his youthful *Carmen macaronicum*, a eulogy of *soglia* flour and the pasta

made from it. It is for the countryside surrounding Vignola
that you should head in its direction at this particular season.
You will pass through a sea of rosy cherry blossoms extending in every direction as far as you can see, tossing against a
clear blue sky in the never failing soft spring breeze, fragrant with perfume. A month later the first cherries will be
ready for picking, and from then on the harvest will continue at a breakneck pace which seems likely to exhaust the
energies of the whole region (for everyone here lives from
growing, processing or selling cherries) until August 1.
Only then is it possible to stop for breath.

Vignola cherries are not only the earliest to reach the
market, they are also the best in Italy—"the best in the
world," the region boasts, which was also the opinion of the
ancient Romans.

According to the growers, Vignola cherries are superior
to all others for firmness of flesh, richness of flavor, fragrance of odor and brilliance of color. Half the total Italian
production comes from Vignola. In an average year, the
area produces 45,000,000 pounds of cherries, but in some
years it has passed 60,000,000. They are far from a negligible item in Italian foreign trade. In most years 20 to 30 percent of the crop is sold abroad, in peak years 50 percent.

Alas, since 1962 the production of these superb cherries
has been decreasing. The chief reason is the exodus of the
population from country to cities, causing the cities to ex-
pand. Urban building has been pushing southward from
the Emilian Way into the cherry territory, and splendid
cherry trees are cut down to make room for jerry-built
suburban housing. But Vignola cherries have been supreme
for 2,000 years, so we may reasonably expect that they will
not disappear overnight.

Cherries are the most important fruit export of Modena,
but there are others—strawberries, apples, peaches and
pears, especially the famous William and the Principe Al-

berto pears, which supply the large canneries of the province. Even more important for canning are pedigreed vegetables dignified with fancy names: Pascal, a wide-ribbed celery; Borlotti di Vigarano, marble beans; and Nano Ricciuto, parsley with deeply indented leaves. Potatoes and onions are anonymous. Vegetables are canned not only for their own sake, but to compose complicated mixtures—for instance, Modena exports great quantities of canned minestrone containing at least seven different vegetables.

The economy of Modena has always leaned largely on the export of food. An early exporter—on the individual scale, it is true, but a lavish individual scale—was Cesare Borgia. During a visit to Modena in November 1494 he sent a gift package to his wife, Carlotta d'Albret, who was being detained in France at the Château of Nérac by Louis XII. It included 180 ducats in cash; a quantity of fine white sugar from Venice, which was almost as good as cash; a large amount of pure white wax, in those days nearly as valuable; 20 sheets; six kegs of Malvasia wine; oranges and lemons; and from Modena itself, three caskets of preserved fruit, and other fruits in syrup. It is almost a certainty that the last item included Vignola cherries.

"Those who are born in the shadow of the Ghirlandina," wrote Franco Vanni, who was one of them, "are more Emilian than all the other inhabitants of Emilia. Naturally those who come to Emilia from abroad are not able to understand this. For a foreigner, we are like the Bolognese and even (God forbid!) like the Ferrarese. However there is a subtle but enormous difference, a difference of taste, of palate. We are simultaneously better and worse. Nowhere on the surface of this earth can you find an individual who succeeds in being as rude as a Modenese when he wants to be—this is the worst, but it is also the best. A Modenese is recognizable in any latitude, differentiated from a Bolognese, from a Reggian, or from any other Emilian. For one reason or another, we Modenese are different: we are *more* —more upright, more petty, more timid, more heroic, more stingy, more generous; it depends on the circumstances. More villainous, more dirty-minded, more innocent; we are as improbable as a genetic accident."

It would be too much to expect the Modenese character and the Modenese cuisine to correspond exactly at every point. There is hardly complete congruence between the former, as described above by a Modenese man, and the latter, as described by a Modenese woman:

"Skilled rather than sparkling, charged with temperament rather than with fragrance, a cuisine which aims at satisfying the desires of the palate and does not indulge in the display dear to the eye: how to describe it?" asks Luciana Leonelli. "It is not refined, in the sense in which we think of the refinement of the *haute cuisine;* but it balances deftly the proportions of its varied and indispensable elements, which demand an equilibrium of sensitiveness and care. Behind our cooking one perceives the woman's influence. I daresay that it is not possible to think of it as being confined exclusively to masculine hands. It is perhaps for this reason that it evokes the image of solid tables, of united families, failing to extend its limits to a conception more vast than that of the home. The times have become frenzied, but within the haven of our homes, the crescendo of the chopping knife on the board sings a song of solidarity, of security. So do the flour-dusted hands of the women, the vast white aprons, the rapid hammer blows of the knife cutting the sheets of pasta into strips, the frowns of preoccupation and of time pressure, and the rapid to and fro between table and stove. For the Modenese, cooking is not an improvisation; it demands assiduous care and slow cooking."

Modenese cooking is also the fruit of long experience. It

is great today and has been great for as far back as the records go. "It is not possible for anyone who has eaten even a single meal in Modena to think of this city without recalling its cooking," a current tourist publication remarks—which was already true for Pope Leo X, who visited Modena in 1513. Many years later he was still recalling nostalgically "the very good things of the Modena table." Three and a half centuries later, Professor Giosuè Carducci, the poet who won the Nobel Prize for Literature in 1906, testified to the continuing quality of the Modenese cuisine by coming to Modena every Christmas ten years running for the sole purpose of enjoying a superb meal. The Grosoli restaurant where he ate it is called the Carducci today, and still has the letter in which he announced his 1885 visit: "Arriving a week from today. Here's the menu: *tagliatelle; zampone* with lentils and sauerkraut[!]; roast chicken and game; fruit and cheese; coffee and anisette; Lambrusco of the best quality." At the end of this meal he pushed back his chair and exclaimed feelingly, "This is the best day of the year!"

The earliest Modenese recipes which have come down to us appear in a book published in the 1500's, *Compositions and General Pomp of the Table*, which its author, Christoforo Messisburgo, dedicated to "the most illustrious and most reverend lord, Don Hippolito d'Este, Cardinal of Ferrara"—appropriately, for the Cardinal was more renowned as a gourmet and as the builder of the Villa d'Este at Tivoli than as a man of piety. The recipes in this book presumably mirror the food which was set before the Dukes of Este. They are written with a breathless imprecision which would make them the bane of modern housewives— interminable sentences of unpunctuated directions linked by a series of "ands"; no quantities given for ingredients which are themselves often described in the vaguest terms; no cooking times—following them must have been a case of every cook for himself. The recipe for "Fish in brown sugar" begins: "Take the fish [type unspecified] which has been well scaled and washed and cut it in pieces large or small as it pleases you and take good white wine and strong vinegar and a handful of salt and put these things to boil with the fish and when it boils drop in a sprig of sage and let it cook and when it is cooked it can be eaten hot but it is better cold." As for the brown sugar mentioned in the name of the dish, it is never heard of again.

Similarly the recipe for "Fish soup, Hungarian style," forbears from listing fish among its ingredients, though it does call for onions, olive oil, white wine ("and if it is sweet it will be better"), white vinegar, saffron ("enough to give it color"), slices of bread—and, believe it or not, honey, cinnamon, grapes and apples cut into small pieces! "Let it cook thus, *piano piano*"—already the slow cooking characteristic of Modena.

Skimming through these ancient recipes, one gathers that a common ingredient of the times was elbow grease. A great many of them demand the preliminary crushing of obdurate materials like veal into paste with mortar and pestle. Examples include *minestra di carne* and *ravvivoli di polpa di capponi*. The first was made of slices of veal steak and beef kidneys ground in the mortar with much pepper, ginger, cloves and orange juice, boiled in consommé, and served with one hard-boiled egg with three cloves stuck in it per person. *Ravvivoli* was what ravioli was then called. Its stuffing was made of white capon meat ground in the mortar with pecorino and ricotta cheese, after which egg whites, fine flour, and sugar were added. Stuffed with this, the ravioli were cooked in consommé and served on a plate powdered with mixed pepper, while the ravioli were dusted with cinnamon, grated cheese, and more pepper.

As these recipes indicate, there was a strong liking for spices in those days, and there was also a well-developed sweet tooth. Cinnamon seemed to go into everything, cloves and ginger were frequently employed, and saffron, though it was very expensive, was nevertheless much used. Some seasoning ingredients turned up in what we would consider the wrong places. Sugar, honey, the ubiquitous raisin, and verjus (green grape juice) appeared early in the meal; many soups were sweet. Saffron, on the contrary, which we would be inclined to employ early, often turned up at the end, in cakes and cookies. Modenese cooking has cooled off since; but the medieval taste for spices lingers in a considerable use of nutmeg, rare in the old recipes because nutmeg was the last of the major spices to reach Europe.

It would be difficult to imagine a modern housewife starting out the meal with the Duke of Este's sweet Royal Golden Soup—consommé containing egg yolks, saffron, almonds crushed together with their shells, orange juice, grapes, verjus, rose water, sugar and cinnamon, served by pouring it over slices of bread fried in oil. Even plain consommé in those days might include egg yolks, sugar, cinnamon, ginger and rose water.

Pasta existed in those days, but did not enjoy a great vogue. Today it is highly important on the Modenese menu, though most of it is probably a borrowing from Bologna rather than a local flowering. Modena's stuffing for *tortellini* grinds together veal, raw ham, a touch of mortadella and more than a touch of other sausages, browns the resulting paste lightly in butter, allows it to cool, then adds grated cheese, eggs, bread crumbs and nutmeg, and stuffs egg dough *tortellini* with the result. The *tortellini* are then cooked in capon consommé, and when done are removed from the consommé and dried briefly in the oven before serving. Alternatively, after the *tortellini* have been taken out of the consommé, they are placed in a pastry shell, lapped with cream, powdered with grated cheese, and finished by a few minutes in a very hot oven. *Tortelli di*

zucca are also called *tortelli di Novi*, which marks them as
the creation of the town of this name in Modena province.
Their dominating ingredient is *zucca gialla*, yellow squash,
which is not yellow (until you cut it open), but dark green.
The hard-skinned variety used here is called *marina*, and is
curiously shaped—a hardly rounded flattened cube. The
squash is first baked, then peeled and crushed together with
dry macaroons, grated cheese, bread crumbs and nutmeg,
and moistened with egg. Stuffed with this mixture, the
tortelli are boiled in salted water, and served with *ragù*,
chopped chicken giblets and grated cheese.

Modena also shares lasagne, *cappelletti* and *tagliatelle*
with Bologna, and like Bologna, serves them with *ragù*, in
this case made with celery, carrots and onion cooked in oil
and butter, to which minced beef, veal and pork, previously
lightly braised, are added. When this mixture is half cooked,
a little milk is poured over it, and, when this has boiled
away, a generous portion of tomato extract thinned with
water. The cooking is finished at a simmer so low that the
boiling is barely perceptible—slow Modenese cooking
again.

More definitely Modenese is *maltagliati con i fagioli*—
maltagliati, "badly cut," because a sheet of *tagliatelle* dough
is divided into pieces of irregular size; the pasta is accompanied by beans cooked with tomato and bits of pork crackling, seasoned with a sauce of oil, butter, bacon, celery,
onion, garlic and parsley. *Quadretti in brodo* are little
squares of dough cooked and served in consommé; after the
bouillon has been taken off the fire, diced chicken from a
separately cooked bird is added. Allied to the homemade
pasta family is *calzagatti*, a sort of cornmeal polenta boiled
in the cooking water of the beans served with it, themselves
seasoned with butter, onion, tomato and bits of lean pork.
It is eaten hot, in a mush-like state. The Modenese housewife purposely makes more polenta than she expects to need

for the meal. What is left over hardens when it cools, and is sliced and fried in lard for the next repast.

Calzagatti is a rustic dish, and though it appears in the plain, is related to the considerable number of dishes made from dough in the extensive repertory of Modenese mountain cooking, found in the southern part of the province, which penetrates into the Apennines. A shared characteristic of these mountain dough dishes is that they are fried; and another used to be, for many of them, at least, that they were made of chestnut flour, since chestnuts grow plentifully here. *Castagnaccio*, a sort of scone, still is, but for the others wheat flour has replaced chestnut, producing such variants as the hearthcake called *focaccia*, the Italian version of the ancient *fougasse, fouasse* or *fouace* of France, mentioned by Rabelais. These fried breads or buns or scones or biscuits or pancakes or flapjacks were once described by Modenese writer Franco Ferrari as "the nourishing basic dishes of a poor and isolated population." The population has become less isolated and less poor, so these rustic confections nowadays tend to be served less and less as the basic provender at mealtimes and more and more as between-meal snacks—an important role in the bracing appetite-provoking mountain air. They are indeed wonderful outdoor food, and the king of them all, *borlengo*, is most likely to be served you at open-air meals in the Modenese Apennines, possibly because there isn't enough room to make it inside. This is as it should be, since the very name recalls the origin of this dish, first cooked in the open to feed the famished merrymakers who crowded the public squares during medieval festivals. Pleasantries crackled like firecrackers among the festive throngs on these occasion. Everything was a joke (*burla*), including the giant pancake associated with them, which was therefore nicknamed *burleng* in the mountaineer's dialect, later citified into *borlengo*.

Borlenghi are no jokes for the cooks who have to produce them. They are made in a cartwheel-sized frying pan, so large and heavy that the chef has to use both hands to lift it from the stove, like an old-time warrior brandishing a two-handed sword. Into this great pan a liquid batter of vigorously kneaded flour, eggs, milk, water and salt is poured, covering its whole surface. When this has been cooked on one side, some supermen succeed, unwieldy though the pan is, in tossing the outsized flapjack into the air to turn it. When both sides are done, one of them is buttered with bacon fat, garlic, and rosemary, and dusted with grated cheese. The *borlengo* is then cut into four pieces and folded into convenient size for eating in the hand. It is filling all by itself, but if you are ravenous, you fold it around a slice of prosciutto or a few strips of fried bacon.

These mountain dishes, Franco Ferrari put it a little flamboyantly, are "without pretension, though *borlengo* wears the crown of a king and *crescentina* that of a queen; one exists through honesty, the other is a Cinderella with a heart of gold." *Crescentina* is literally a Cinderella, since it is a hearthcake cooked in the ashes or on the hot coals of the hearth. Tourists, impressed by its spectacular dimensions, usually remember *borlengo* as the archetype of this category of mountain dishes, but the natives give top billing to *crescentina*, which is probably the older of the two. They do not ordinarily call it *crescentina* though, nor *piedone*, another name for the same thing. The local word is *tigella*, which outrages purists, since it really means not the dish itself, but one of the clay disks between which it is cooked. The dough, of flour, baking soda, a minimum of milk, olive oil and salt, is shaped into a round cake, chestnut leaves are applied to both sides, and it is placed between two of the disks, which are laid directly on the red coals. Like *borlenghi*, *tigelle* are rubbed with fresh bacon, oil and rosemary, and are eaten hot, right off the fire (but not overcooked), so that the delicate evanescent flavor derived from the chestnut leaves will not be lost, as it will be if the cake is allowed to cool. This is what you should get wherever the sign *tigelle montanare* is displayed, but unless you are in the Modenese Apennines, you are not likely to find the real thing.

Gnocchi in this area are not what you would expect if you have already sampled gnocchi elsewhere. Again it is a question of fried dough—of flour, milk, salt and brewer's yeast, allowed to rise overnight, and fried in small cakes in a mixture of oil and lard. For *ciacci montanari*, the dough is a mixture of cheese and flour, cooked on an iron griddle, and eaten hot with prosciutto or sausage. *Stria*, exceptionally, is cooked in the oven, perhaps because it is already greasy enough without being subjected to frying. It is made from ordinary bread dough, usually when some is left over from other baking, to which is added a generous amount of olive oil; this is worked well into the dough, and it is then larded with bits of bacon.

To these dishes, the mountain menu adds the natural products of the Apennines: finely flavored trout from the clear swift mountain streams; chestnuts—which are not only made into flour, but (especially on St. Martin's Day), soaked in wine must and roasted; wood mushrooms; and game in autumn, especially hare. For the rest, the fare is much like that of the plain.

One of the favorite dishes of lowland Modena is *bollito misto*—not a local specialty, for it is met everywhere in Emilia-Romagna, and indeed is not confined to that region—but the best I have ever had was that of Modena's Fini restaurant, for which a whole tongue, a calf's head, a large cut of beef, a ham, and a chicken had all been boiled together, and at serving were combined with a large *zampone* which had been cooked separately. It is a dish for trenchermen, which, after all, is what the Modenese are. Modena also does other things with pork besides making sausage of it. *Costolette di maiale alla modenese* are pork chops rubbed with a mixture of rosemary, sage, garlic, salt and pepper, simmered in a cup of water in a covered greased frying pan until all the water has evaporated, then browned in their own fat, and finished with a half cup of dry white wine. Veal chops are soaked in egg beaten with salt and pepper, coated with bread crumbs, fried in butter, and then finished in the oven with a slice of prosciutto and another of cheese on top.

With the dessert course, Modena really comes into its own. It is famous above all for its *amarelli* or *amaretti*, macaroons, which it exports in great quantities; they are made with both sweet and bitter almonds (more of the sweet), flour, sugar and egg whites. In second place come *benzone* (or *bensone*), sweet pastries baked in the form of a spindle or of the letter S, whose egg-glazed crust is sprinkled with powdered sugar; it is no longer made as it used to be, when one-third of the fine wheat flour which goes into it was potato flour instead, to produce a smoother dough. *Erbazzone dolce* might seem somewhat curious for a dessert, since the ingredient which gives it its name is finely chopped chard or young beet leaves, but the greens are overpowered by sweet tastes in a cheese tart which employs as much sugar as it does ricotta cheese, along with crushed sweet and bitter almonds, egg, rum and grated lemon peel. Pasta becomes a dessert in *torta di tagliatelle*, which adds sugar to the *tagliatelle* dough of the crust, and fills it with more sugar, butter, sweet and bitter almonds, chocolate, and lemon juice, flavored with any subtle and delicate liqueur which suits the fancy. Bits of candied citron are stuck into the surface after cooking, and the whole is powdered with sugar. It is eaten cold, the day after cooking. Another case of pasta converted into a dessert is *tortelli fritti e al forno* (fried-and-baked *tortelli*); the *tortelli* are made of sweetened dough and stuffed with a mixture of chestnuts which have been boiled in milk and mashed into a paste together with chocolate, almonds, and *mostarda di Carpi*, a relish made by a complicated process which involves filtered partly fermented red wine must, walnuts, sweet apples, pears, quinces and orange peel. The *tortelli* are first fried in much lard, drained, glazed with egg and powdered with sugar while still hot, and then placed, carefully separated from each other, on a greased plaque for finishing in the oven. *La bonissima* is a cake of flour, butter, sugar, egg, grated lemon peel and vanilla flavoring, with a filling of crushed walnuts, honey and rum, and chocolate or sugar icing. *Colomba di pavullo* is a sort of multi-layer cake of raised egg dough containing Marsala wine, pine nuts, and bits of lemon peel, with a filling between the layers of a jam of pears and sweet apples, the whole glazed with egg and powdered with sugar.

Torta nera (black tart) certainly has enough dark-colored elements to justify its name—both chocolate and coffee, not to mention *crème de cacao* and rum, along with sweet and bitter almonds crushed into a paste, butter, sugar and eggs, of which the yolks and whites are beaten separately, the latter with the rum and *crème de cacao*. The most striking characteristic of *straca dent'* (dialect for "strong teeth") may be divined from its name; yet this hard cookie has in it only the finest farina, sweet almonds, sugar and egg whites. You can take the curse off its hardness by dunking it in *saba*, filtered but unfermented white wine must, boiled down to one-third of its original volume and then bottled. It is often poured over desserts or even polenta, and is drunk diluted with water. *Saba* is also poured over the rich bun called *pan ed Nadel* while it is still hot; this is dialect for *pane di Natale*, or Christmas bun, a complicated sweet of flour, yeast, eggs, bits of walnuts and almonds, whole pine nuts, fennel seed, sugar, butter, chocolate, coffee, and Sassolino liqueur. *Zuc-*

cherini di zocca are rings of anise-flavored dough, slit on the side to make them swell during a preliminary baking in the oven, after which they are finished in a syrup also flavored with anise. The rings are then frosted with egg whites beaten together with sugar, and studded with tiny silver-colored pellets.

Making these desserts often requires staggering amounts of time. The dough for the *colomba di pavullo* is kneaded and allowed to rise three times, the first time alone requiring eight to ten hours; and the marmalade filling has to cook for 24. *Mostarda di Carpi* (Carpi is a town north of Modena), only one of the ingredients of *tortelli fritti e al forno*, stays on the stove 14 to 18 hours. Many of the desserts require several operations, with different ingredients cooked separately, and added at varying times. Usually the cook cannot go away and leave things to cook by themselves; they require constant stirring or other manipulations —for instance, *zuccherini di zocca* are cooked in a two-handled kettle, so that it can be picked up and shaken from time to time, to insure thorough impregnation of the *zuccherini* by the syrup before hardening.

Reggio nell' Emilia (or Reggio d'Emilia or simply Reggio Emilia) has kept for its present name the least meaningful part of its old one. When Marcus Aemilius Lepidus built a forum there, it was known as Lepidi. This became Lepidum Regium, the Domain of Lepidus, and finally just Regium.

The province of Reggio Emilia is one of the richest agricultural districts in Italy. It produces grapes both for the table and for wine. It is a center of pig breeding (and therefore of processed pork products) and of cattle raising (and hence of cheese making). After Reggio's hogs and cows have been fed there is enough fodder left over for export to other regions. The Apennines are rich in game, and trout of exquisite flavor are found in the lakes of Cerreto and Calamone and the rivers Enza, Dolo, Secchia (shared with Modena) and Po (shared with Lombardy). The name of the town of Luzzara, on Reggio's side of the Po, is said to have been derived from one of its food fishes, *lucci*, pike.

The most important product that Reggio derives from its resources is cheese. Parmesan cheese, despite its name, originated not in Parma but in Reggio, though Parma also makes it now. The birthplace of Parmesan is the fertile Enza valley, between Parma and Reggio, but in the province of Reggio the lush pasturage enables cows to produce what is reputed to be the richest milk in Italy (with the exception of that of Padua, which makes *grana padana* from it, essentially the same type of cheese). The Enza valley still makes the best Parmesan, and it may be that the best of the best is that of a town which lives from cheese alone, Montecchio, just south of the point where the Enza crosses the Emilian Way.

Parma was not really a usurper in attaching its name to Reggio's cheese, for Reggio Emilia was once part of the Duchy of Parma. Today the makers of what has become by legal definition genuine Parmesan have agreed on a compromise name, Parmigiano Reggiano, which may seem a contradiction in terms, but does describe more inclusively, though not completely, the area deemed worthy of using the name of Parmesan. This area, as carefully delimited as a wine region, includes all of the provinces of Parma, Reggio and Modena, the province of Bologna as far east as the Reno river, and even a piece of Lombardy, that part of the province of Mantua which lies south of the Po. Curiously, it does not include any of Piacenza or of Ferrara, though these provinces produce *grana* cheese on territory contiguous to the Parmesan area; understandably, it omits another *grana*-producing area of Lombardy, Lodi, which

228

is separated from the Parmigiano Reggiano district by intervening territory less skillful with cheese. Yet Lodi was already producing so much *grana* about 1850, when Alexander Dumas passed through there, that he maintained incorrectly in his *Grand Dictionnaire de Cuisine* that Parmesan was the particular specialty, not of Parma but of Lodi, where in his time 30,000 cows were assuring the production of "Parmesan." Lodi today does not describe its product as Parmesan, but as *formaggio lodigiano, formaggio di grana*, or *grana lodigiano*. In Italy the designation Parmesan is now jealously protected, and a few years ago a national scandal was provoked by the discovery that certain supermarkets were selling as Parmesan a product of their own making which included such unorthodox ingredients as ground banana peels.

Parmesan is a very old cheese. The people of the region claim it has been made there for 2,000 years. It was already well known in the 14th century, when Boccaccio, in the third story of the eighth day of the *Decameron*, poked fun at the gullibility of one of his characters named Calandrino by having him believe that in Bengodi, in the Parmesan country, "there is a mountain consisting entirely of grated cheese, on which live people who do nothing but cook macaroni and ravioli, which they roll down the slopes so that it arrives at the bottom coated with fragrant cheese."

In 1516 Francesco Maria Grapaldo, in his *De Partibus Aedium*, wrote that "in our day, Italy's greatest glory comes from Parmesan cheese, though in older times it came from the abundance of wool." Pepys reported that during the great fire of London, in 1666, cheesemongers dug a deep pit in which to bury their Parmesan to save it from the heat. Diderot and d'Alembert, in their 18th-century encyclopedia, described Parmesan as "a strong cheese highly appreciated by Italians, produced in the region of Parma, and from there exported to all European nations." There were times when Molière almost lived on it, and Sainte-Beuve referred to it several times in his works. Parma preserves preciously a letter dated March 19, 1767, thanking the Duke of Parma for the present of a Parmesan cheese. The letter is signed by Cardinal de Bernis, possibly more perspicacious about cheese than about men, considering that he allowed himself to be hoodwinked by Cagliostro, who by a feat of legerdemain doubled the size of the diamond in his ring. The original smaller stone had the advantage of being genuine.

Grated Parmesan is ubiquitous in Italy, where its uses are universal and its season endless; unlike most cheese, it is equally good all year round. It appears almost invariably on pasta, often on rice, and frequently in minestrone. It is sprinkled before cooking over meat or vegetables or anything else which requires a *gratiné* crust. It is superior for this purpose because it is almost the only cheese which melts without degenerating into long rubbery threads, like the streamers which wrap themselves around the chin when you eat a *gratinée* onion soup made with other types of cheese. Most persons who know Parmesan only in its grated form would be astonished to see a whole Parmesan cheese. The fine particles of grated cheese which the consumer usually encounters only in small cellophane envelopes come from enormous cartwheels which weigh about 66 pounds each (trade standards refuse the name of Parmesan to any cheese falling below 52.8 pounds). The crust of these great cheeses often glitters with a fine dew. Cut open, the cheese is a pale straw-yellow, crumbly and coarse-grained, the rough texture accounting for the name of *grana*, which means grain. In this form, ungrated, it can be sliced and eaten on its own like any other cheese, and is delicious—provided, that is, that you have a real Parmesan at hand and not one of the many vapid tasteless imitations.

The production of Parmesan begins with the raising of the mixed grasses and clover which is the basic diet of cows whose milk makes Parmesan cheese. Thus fed, the animals produce the thick milk essential for it. Parmesan is made only between April 15 and November 15, when the feed is at its best and the milk at its richest. Skimmed milk is used, but it is not necessary to resort to mechanical means to skim it. The density of the milk causes the cream to separate naturally. The skimmed milk is then treated by an acid fermentation process and cooked for half an hour or so until the curd has separated. The whey is put aside to feed the pigs which will produce Reggio sausages, while the curd goes into the great cartwheel forms, where it undergoes various processes—drying, draining, pressing, coloring, washing, brushing, scraping and rubbing with oil. Then the aging begins. Parmesan, like wine, improves with age, and like wine it is brought to its maximum perfection with the greatest of care. For a year, the semi-fat firm-fleshed cheese is kept in a damp cool chamber. It is then sealed from the air with a coating of *fumo nero*, literally "black smoke," in reality burnt umber earth, applied over a coating of wine or oil pressed from grape seeds. It is now transferred to an aging chamber which is warmer and has higher humidity. After another year there, it is known as *vecchio* (old), and is for the first time ready for consumption. Real fanciers demand at least three years in the warm chamber, when the cheese is called *stravecchio*, and preferably four, when it becomes *stravecchione*. Parmesan cheeses may keep for as long as 20 years, and the older they are, the better they get.

During the aging process, the cheese is under constant surveillance. A short flat broad knife is thrust into a sample cheese from time to time, and its degree of progress judged by smell. The cheeses are also tapped with a hammer, to diagnose possible disease—for unfriendly bacteria may multiply in their interior. When a hollow sound from the hammer blow reveals the presence of a cavity—an abscess, one might say—surgery is called for. The cheese is opened, the cavity is scraped to remove all bacteria lurking there, and it is then cauterized with a hot iron to kill any that may have escaped. Thus healed it continues to age along with its unscathed brothers.

Aside from Parmesan, Reggio offers little in the way of peculiarly local food. It makes excellent dishes from the produce of its territory, but they belong to the general cooking of Emilia and are not unique to this region. The preserved pork products are of high quality but of familiar types—a good prosciutto is made here, and the preferred sausages are *salame da sugo* and *cotechino*, for which the capitals are, respectively, Parma, Ferrara and Modena. For pasta, the favorites are *tortelli d'erbe*, stuffed with spinach, and *tortelli di zucca* (stuffed with squash), both served either with melted butter or *ragù* (and of course grated Parmigiano Reggiano); and *cappelletti*, the little hat-shaped envelopes, filled here with a stuffing of chopped meat, chicken giblets, cheese, and nutmeg, served either as dry pasta, with *ragù* or cream, or in a mixed beef and chicken bouillon. *Scarpazzone* is a vegetable tart, baked in the oven with cheese and bits of bacon. Local breeding supplies a heavy demand for beef and pork.

The name of Parma means "shield." It was given to the city by the Romans, who fortified it as a buckler against enemies to the north and west. But those who date its beginning at 183 B.C., when Marcus Aemilius Lepidus is said to have founded it, are shortening its history. There had been a settlement here since the Bronze Age, when Etruscans inhabited the region. Unlike most of the other capitals on the Emilian Way, Parma is not located at a point where that highway was crossed by a north-south road in

Roman times, but where it is crossed by the Parma River on its way to the nearby Po. Since the Parma is a torrent, difficult to cross in those days, it provided a natural obstacle which explains its choice by the Romans as a defensive position.

The famous Parma violets, alas, have become extremely rare; but the perfume industry they inspired still exists. Parmesan cheese, as we have already seen, did not originate in Parma. Parma ham does not come from Parma either, if when you think of Parma you think of the city; but it does come from the province of Parma and, unlike the violets, is not shrinking away. The production of ham (prosciutto) remains the most important industry of the province and seems likely to remain so. The ingredient which gives Parma ham its particular quality is not readily duplicatable elsewhere—the air. The town of Langhirano, south of Parma, has proved to have the ideal atmosphere for the curing of these hams. Nobody has ever been able to work out exactly what conditions are best for ham, but empirical observation has located Langhirano as the place where they exist. For one thing, Langhirano is in the hills, but not too high up in them, which experience has indicated is important. Mountain air has always been effective in the curing of meat. The famous *jamón serano* of Spain is a mountain product, and so is the *Bundnerfleisch* of Switzerland, beef dried in the Alpine air.

Langhirano's whole existence is based on the care and curing of hams, which are sent here for finishing from all over the province of Parma, and even from Lombardy. During the drying season, from September to March, private homes are pressed into service. In every room of every house, even the bedrooms, hams hang thickly, suspended from the ceilings three or four layers deep. The inhabitants sleep beneath a ceiling of ham and breathe a ham-flavored atmosphere. What Langhirano cannot accommodate goes as overflow to neighboring villages, but the result is never quite the same.

Parma ham enjoys a symbiotic relationship with Parmesan cheese. The first secret of its quality is the feeding of the hogs. A diet of acorns is good enough for sausage, but for fine ham something richer is needed. It is provided by the whey left over from the making of the cheese. The other secrets of Parma quality appear during the processes of treating and curing. The hams are boned, and undergo an esthetic operation—they are molded, smoothed and rounded to give them a pleasing contour, like a great fruit; pounded with a thick wooden paddle to eliminate wrinkles in the thick skin; and brushed energetically to polish the surface. The ham "rests" for a few days in a cold place, and is then salted. This is a delicate operation. Most hams are too heavily salted, from the eaters' point of view, a precaution to insure their preservation. The object with Parma ham is to salt as lightly as possible, to keep the ham sweet, and this is abetted by the mountain air, which discourages multiplication of the bacteria which provoke decay; Langhirano hams may safely be treated with a minimum of salt. The salting is done simply by laying the hams in wooden trays filled with rock salt, turning them every week or so; the process takes from a month to seven weeks, depending on the size of the ham. Loose salt is then washed off, and the hams hung to dry—in a warm draft for the first week, then at about 20° Centigrade for a month, at 15° for another month, and at 10° for the rest of the curing period, which may last anywhere from three to six months more.

The cured ham is of a pale salmon pink, mild, sweet and tender. Its even velvety texture, one of the signs by which you can recognize genuine Parma hams, is the result of the feeding of the pigs. Parma ham is served in paper-thin slices. It is a wonderful start for the meal with melon or figs, but lacking these, it makes a first-rate hors d'oeuvre eaten alone with bread and butter.

Ham is of course by definition made from the rear legs of the pig. Parma also treats the shoulders, which are smaller and greasier, but not to be disdained. The shoulder is marketed as *fiocchetto*.

Prosciutto alone would be enough to support a flourishing food packaging industry—Parma sells 150,000 hams a year—but there is a good deal else. One great specialty of the province of Parma is associated for most persons with Naples; but Parma does it better. This is tomato paste, for which the leading center is Fidenza. Tomato paste has been produced there in commercial quantities since the beginning of the century; but on a smaller scale the product preceded the can which now contains it. In earlier days, the cooked tomato sauce was set out to dry in the sun. The result, as described in a local gastronomic publication, was "loaves the color of dark mahogany, of the consistency of stucco, cylindrical in form, well oiled, and wrapped in oiled paper. In the winter it was . . . eaten, spread on bread, by children." Today's tomato paste is called *concentrato*, which is already a rich tomato extract. But there is also a doubly concentrated variety, *doppio concentrato*, whose strength may be divined from the fact that it takes 250 tons of tomatoes to produce 35 tons of *doppio*. There is even *triplo concentrato*, for which the same amount of fruit produces only 32 tons of tomato extract.

Other Parma food exports include cakes and cookies, and, most important, pork products other than ham—various cuts of the pig, and sausages. These are often specialties of individual villages and towns. The leader in this field is probably Felino, which, being not far from Langhirano, is a runner-up for the making of ham. The *salame da sugo* of Felino, often called simply *salame di Felino*, is renowned throughout Italy. Made of pure lean pork, with no more than 15 to 20 percent fat, enlivened with whole pepper-corns, white wine, and a touch of garlic, it is high priced and hard to find except in luxury stores.

In the northwestern corner of the province, a concentration of sausage-making towns, Busseto, Roccabianca, San Secondo, Zibello, Soragna and Fidenza produce *culatello*, made from cured pork shoulders; *spalla*, cooked or raw, also of shoulder meat; *coppa*, from the pig's head, muscles, feet and rind (also called *lonza*) and its cousins, *bondiola* and *capocollo; cotechino;* and *pancetta*, from the stomach.

Other reputed local specialties are the mushrooms of Borgotaro; the fish of the Po towns (catfish, carp, chub, pike, sturgeon, eel and perch); and much game (hare, quail, pheasant).

The cooking of the different towns, and of Parma itself, is standard Emilian cooking; but there are marked local preferences for certain items of the Emilian repertory, and many towns apply twists of their own to dishes which originated elsewhere. *Anolini* are highly popular in Parma; *tortelli alla panna* and *tortelli d'erbette* are frequently served in Parma, Colorno and San Secondo; the latter in particular is a summer specialty of Parma, where the stuffing is made of spinach, chard, or young beet leaves. The best *tortelli* of my experience were those served me in Parma's Filoma restaurant, stuffed with ricotta cheese, chopped meat, greens and *zucca* (squash). Many towns of the province have their own particular favorites in the pasta category—Busseto likes *cappelletti* and *lasagne verdi*, Colorno *agnolotti* and *lasagne*, Fidenza *lasagne* and *tortellini*, San Secondo *cappelletti* and *lasagne*.

The description *alla parmigiana* on a menu does not always denote a Parma dish; it may mean simply that it is sprinkled with Parmesan cheese. For instance, it is doubtful whether Eggs Parmesan originated in Parma or are so called because they are sprinkled not only with finely chopped prosciutto, but also with grated Parmesan cheese, after which they are doused with melted butter and baked in the oven. *Asparagi alla parmigiana* is authentically local—asparagus tips with grated Parmesan and melted butter. *Spinaci alla parmigiana* begins cooking the spinach by boiling it, then draining it, chopping it fine, and finishing it in a saucepan with butter and Emilia-Romagna's favorite spice, nutmeg, stirring in eggs at the last minute, and, of course, powdering the whole with grated cheese. *Sedano alla parmigiana* is subjected to a similar double cooking process and works in two Parmesan specialties, grated cheese and tomato paste; the celery is first boiled with onion, cloves and bacon, then placed in a buttered casserole in alternating layers of celery, tomato sauce, grated cheese; celery, tomato sauce, grated cheese; and so on until the dish is full. It is then baked in a hot oven. Double cooking again for artichokes, minus their stems, bases of leaves, and the chokes: after a preliminary boiling, the artichokes are finished in the oven in a buttered casserole, covered with a cream sauce containing egg yolks, shredded prosciutto, nutmeg, and, of course, grated Parmesan.

The Parma River is responsible for another local specialty, a *fritto misto* of fresh-water fish. *Trippa alla parmigiana* is a specialty of San Secondo as well as of Parma itself. The Parmesan way with veal cutlets is to coat them with beaten eggs and bread crumbs, brown them in butter in a frying pan, and finish them in the oven doused in tomato sauce with slices of soft cheese on top.

The skill of Parma pastry cooks is legendary throughout Italy. It accounts not only for an endless variety of tarts, cakes and cookies, but also for non-sweet pastry. It is rare in Italy to find cafés serving cheese or anchovy allumettes, but not in Parma. Pizza is supposed to be a Neapolitan specialty, but nowhere are the small individually-sized pizze called *pizzette* better than in Parma. As for sweet pastries, there are too many to be listed. Almost every community in the province has its own (gourmet Busseto produces one of the best known, *spongata*, and Salsomaggiore is famous for its little almond-sized macaroons—the macaroon was invented in Italy, perhaps here). As a natural accompaniment to its little cakes, Parma offers the lightest, most luscious ice cream imaginable.

Piacenza occupies a location predestined to produce a city even before the Romans made it the junction of the Postumian and Emilian Ways. It stands where the Trebbia flows into the Po. There was a settlement here in prehistoric times; the Etruscans once controlled the territory, and the Romans made it a colony in 218 B.C. after the remnants of their army took refuge there from Hannibal, who had just administered a drubbing to it. A university city from 1248, Piacenza suffered the usual vicissitudes of the Middle Ages —a brief period of independence in the 12th century followed by a succession of overlords.

Despite many surviving medieval buildings, it is a very modern city now, with a business activity which depends in considerable part on the discovery at Cortemaggiore of oil and methane. It is also a center for agricultural products, for this is still farming country. The most important crop of the province is grapes, mostly for eating, though some are used for wine.

Piacenza is on the stretch of the Po where rice is grown, and its menu shows it. *Bomba di riso* is a classic Piacenza dish—boiled rice pressed into a round mold around boned pigeon in mushroom sauce, coated with bread crumbs, spotted with rosettes of butter, and finished in the oven. *Risotto in padella* is rice simmered slowly in a vegetable sauce, to which tomato sauce or fresh tomatoes are added, while small amounts of consommé are poured over it from time to time to replace evaporated liquid; it is served lapped in a second sauce made from mushrooms.

The rice for these dishes is grown just across the Po, in Lombardy, and the Lombard influence is apparent in other dishes too. Thus *faraona all creta*, guinea hen flavored with aromatic herbs roasted in an envelope of oven paper itself enclosed in a coating of clay, is a dish of the ancient Longobards, which persists in the territory where their last colonists held out until their diminishing population was absorbed. The Longobards are usually associated with Lombardy, but it happens that the geographical center of this last Longobard holding falls somewhere between Fiorenzuola and Castell' Arquato in the province of Piacenza. The links between Piacenza and Lombardy forged by this ancient people, whose domains here straddled the Po, has been maintained ever since. Lombardy is great polenta country, and Piacenza has borrowed from it a specialty called *polenta e ciccioli*, in which pork crackling and onions are worked into the polenta toward the end of its cooking, which should leave it soft, but firm enough so that it can be sliced for serving, powdered with grated cheese. The cheese used for this purpose is of local manufacture and is hardly distinguishable from Parmesan; but since Piacenza is just outside the officially defined Parmesan belt, it is called not Parmesan, but *grana piacentina*. However, it is made like Parmesan, and like it improves with age. Very old *grana* is specified with *pisarei e fasò*, minute gnocchi made of stale bread crumbs, flour and milk, served with a tomato-and-bean sauce, and heavily powdered with this cheese. Piacenza also makes a hard cheese of the provolone type.

The sausages of Piacenza are of the same types found in Parma. *Culatello* is made especially in Castelmaggiore and Monticello, *pancetta* in Piacenza, and *coppa* in Carpeneto, but there is one preparation of the last, *coppa arrosta*, which differs from *coppa* elsewhere. Instead of being made from salt meat from the pig's neck, it uses fresh meat from the same part of the animal. This is marinated for several days with spices and herbs, rolled up around salame, and baked, basted copiously with dry white wine. *Gambon* looks like the French word *jambon*, ham, and that is what it is—the boned thigh of a young pig, marinated with salt and spices, pressed between two boards, and hung in the cellar to dry. It is served with mashed potatoes.

If you get away from the big restaurants, which is almost always a good thing to do in Italy if you want to taste real local cooking, you may need a smattering of dialect to read the menu. Thus the most popular form of pasta here is *anvein*, which you might not recognize under this alias as *anolini*. *Anvein* is a very old word and so is the Piacenza version of this dish—the stuffing is made of bread crumbs soaked in gravy obtained by braising beef, with *stravecchio* (old) grated Piacenza *grana*, and egg for a binding agent. This is the original formula, but nowadays many persons add bits of the beef which has produced the gravy. Castell' Arquato modifies it the other way around by leaving out the beef gravy; but it adds nutmeg and cooks the pasta rings in double consommé. *Anvein* is eaten either *in brodo* or dry, sometimes with melted butter and cheese, sometimes with a tomato-and-mushroom sauce. *Mezze maniche ripiene* (stuffed half-sleeves, so called from their shape), are filled with the classic *anvein* stuffing, and the open ends of the pasta tubes are plugged with white of egg. *Tortei con la cua* is *tortelli* stuffed with ricotta cheese and chopped herbs; the pasta is not twisted into the *tortelli* navel shape, but is given the form of a butterfly—"hence its name," the locals explain, which does not seem quite evident, since the Italian word for butterfly is *farfalla*; we are here faced with dialect again. *Paglia e fieno* is not dialect, but it is a disrespectful description of a delicious combination, egg *tagliolini* and *tagliolini verdi*, in a cream sauce containing shredded prosciutto and peas. The two colors of ribbon pasta account for the name, which means "straw and hay." Other forms of homemade-type pasta popular in Piacenza resemble those found elsewhere—*cappelletti,* "little hats," stuffed with chopped meat; *cannellotti;* and *tagliatelle.* For the last, there is a special variant, *tagliatelle alla salsa di noci,* which means that the *tagliatelle* are served with a dressing of oil, butter, fresh ricotta cheese, grated *grana* and crushed walnuts.

This, as the walnuts might lead us to expect, is mountain food, spreading from the Apennine area around Genovesato, in Liguria, across the regional border into Emilia-Romagna. Here the province of Piacenza, like that of Modena, possesses a separate school of cooking in the uplands, including even an echo of Modena's famous *borlengo.* Here it is called *burtleina* (Italian, *bortellina*), and it does not assume the heroic dimensions of *borlengo. Burtleina* is a large thin fritter made from a batter of dough, flour, water, eggs and salt, fried in lard, and eaten hot—either alone or with slices of *coppa.* The town of Bettola makes a special kind, *bortellina della nonna* (Grandma's *bortellina*), which uses raised dough and a filling of prosciutto. Another mountain dish, the specialty of Groppallo di Farina d'Olmo (the smaller the place, the longer the name), is *funghi fritti:* the heads of the large flap mushrooms which the Italians call pig mushrooms (*funghi porcini*) are cut into quarters, blanched in boiling water, drained, floured and fried.

Poultry is much eaten in Piacenza—roast turkey, roast duck, potted chicken, guinea hen. Meat is frequently served braised or in stews. *Capretto alla cacciatora* is kid cut into chunks, doused with dry white wine, and cooked in an onion *soffritto,* basted at frequent intervals with splashes of consommé; toward the end of its cooking it is sprinkled with chopped parsley and garlic. A game dish is *lepre sfilata,* hare boiled in salted water, boned, and then fried, with crushed bacon, onions, basil, and parsley, in some of the liquid saved from its boiling.

Emilia-Romagna is frequently compared to Burgundy. So far as its lusty food is concerned the comparison is apt. Great eating country is usually also, when the climate permits, great wine country. Here the comparison breaks down, for if Burgundy is great wine country, Emilia-Romagna, in my opinion, is not. Plenty of wine is grown here, but it falls below the Burgundy level.

This judgment is bound to bring howls of rage from the citizens of Bologna, who wax dithyrambic about one of their wines, Lambrusco. Unless my palate is lying to me, not only is Lambrusco a mediocre wine, but it is not even the best wine of Emilia-Romagna, whose inhabitants seem to have been blinded to the merits of their other vintages by the fanatic devotion they give to Lambrusco.

Frank Schoonmaker, the American expert, found Lambrusco "as nearly undrinkable as a well-known wine could be." His opinion (which is mine) is far from unanimous even among non-Emilians (some English connoisseurs like it).

Certainly Lambrusco lacks qualities which are generally considered to be characteristic of great wines everywhere. Great wines usually enjoy a long life, improve with age, and are best drunk some years after bottling; Lambrusco can be drunk immediately and is in fact usually consumed within a year or two of bottling—a wise precaution, since it goes off quickly after that. Great wines usually have considerable body, with an alcoholic content of 12 degrees or more; 11.5 is the top for Lambrusco, but 10 to 10.5 is more usual (consequently it does not travel well). Great wines usually (but this is a rule with many exceptions) complement the food of their own regions. It is my opinion that

Lambrusco does not. It is maintained by the Bolognese that it is the ideal accompaniment for *zampone*, the theory being, apparently, that since *zampone* is heavy and Lambrusco light, they compensate for each other's failings. My feeling would be, on the contrary, that they cancel out each other's merits. A lusty dish deserves a lusty wine. I suspect that the Lambrusco-*zampone* coupling has arisen fortuitously, simply because both are produced in the same area.

Lambrusco is a light dry slightly sparkling red wine. When poured into the glass, it boils up into a burst of foam of a pinkish color which, for one about to drink it, is disconcertingly reminiscent of synthetic chemical hues. This eruption immediately subsides. Bubbles do not continue to rise in the wine, as they do in champagne, and to all appearances it has become still; but it still provokes a slight prickling sensation on the tongue. Lambrusco is, in short, not a forthright sparkler (*spumante*), but only a *frizzante*—fortunately, for since sparkling red wine is an abomination, the less it sparkles the better. *Spumante* is ordinarily made to sparkle by artificial means, while *frizzante* normally indicates a natural sparkler, which takes some of the curse off it.

Every Lambrusco I have ever tasted has been thin and tart, perilously close to vinegar. Since the best Lambrusco comes from Modena, as does the best vinegar, one might wonder whether the Lambrusco grapes which produce wine have not missed their real vocation. These would be fighting words in Bologna, but perhaps not in Modena, despite its reputation as the leading Lambrusco area.

Lambrusco is named from the grape of which it is made, whose chief characteristic is that it imparts a violet flavor to the wine. This is strongly pronounced in the finest Modena variety, Lambrusco di Sorbara, which is 11 to 11.5 degrees, a brilliant ruby red, and normally dry, though a sweet type exists. It is credited with aiding digestion.

I consider Sangiovese superior to Lambrusco, which does not mean I would class it as a great wine; but it is a welcome one. I find in my notes that at Bologna's Pappagallo restaurant I drank a Sangiovese which I set down as "warm and comforting, more body than Lambrusco"; and at the Chilo in Ravenna I rated another as "a full-bodied generous red." But Alexis Lichine, in his *Encyclopedia of Wine and Spirits*, warns that Sangiovese is not steadfast in quality. "It is variable in the extreme, sometimes slightly bitter and hard, sometimes mellow and warming. It is always, however, available, is always red, and is always dry." Sangiovese has a higher alcoholic content than Lambrusco, between 11 and 13 degrees, and it ages more slowly, needing at least a year in the bottle before it is drunk, and preferably four to five. There is a violet flavor in Sangiovese too, but with a tart agreeable aftertaste. Sangiovese is the name of the grape, which is one of those which goes into Chianti.

Excellent with roasts, Sangiovese would seem to accord better than Lambrusco with hearty Emilian cooking, yet it has incongruously invaded precisely that part of the region where the cuisine is least heavy—Romagna, the coastal section, where seafood dominates a lighter menu. Sangiovese Romagnolo may come from almost anywhere in Romagna, but for the two localities whose Sangiovese is most prized, the labels will read Sangiovese del Ravennate or Sangiovese di Forlì. The name of Sangiovese has become almost interchangeable with the word wine in Romagna, as in an anecdote about Lorenzo Stecchetti, whose many books include one on 18th-century cooking. Asked by a friend during a typhoid epidemic what to do about water feared to be infected, Stecchetti answered: "Here's my system: First, boil it for an hour; second, sterilize it; third, drink Sangiovese." This story hints at popular affection for Sangiovese, but the name of a specific vintage in a popular saying does not always denote fondness for it. When the Bolognese say, "*Al gi' a in di' Alionza*," to mean that a man drinks too much, their evocation of the heady local white wine so named is not complimentary. It implies that only a really obstinate winebibber would persevere with Alionza, a wine distinguished by lack of distinction.

Romagna has not only Sangiovese. It produces at least two other outstanding vintages, which makes it better wine country than Emilia. One is Albana, a sweetish wine for which I have a certain fondness, though ordinarily I do not much care for sweet wines. The capital town for Albana is Bertinoro, reputed to owe its name to this wine.

The story is that Galla Placidia, regent of what remained of the Western Roman Empire, passed that way in 435 A.D. She was offered a mug of Albana and found it too good for the rough cup in which it had been served. "I would drink thee in gold!" she exclaimed—"*Vorrei berti in oro!*", and lo and behold, Bertinoro had been christened. The tale does credit to the ingenuity of the wordsmith who invented it, but he seems to have neglected a minute detail: Galla Placidia spoke Latin, not Italian, which did not yet exist.

As I recall the first Albana I ever drank, in 1928, it was unctuous, rich, mellow, velvety and amber in color. It may have changed in 40 years, or my memory may be at fault; my taste buds were relatively uneducated then. The samples I have had recently were paler, a golden yellow, and the wine was thinner than I remembered it. On one occasion it had a slight taste of flint, and on another it was definitely dry, which is uncharacteristic. In principle Albana should be full-bodied, with its 12 to 13 degrees of alcohol; one Italian gastronomic book in my library describes it as "limpid and perfumed." In spite of its sweetness, Albana can be drunk pleasantly with fish, perhaps because it has no added sugar but derives its sweetness from the fact that some of its natural sugar does not enter into its fermentation.

Another Romagna wine which, like Sangiovese, seems to be in the wrong place is Bosco Eliceo, or Vino Rosso del Bosco, which is produced near Comacchio, the eel breeding center. It is consequently touted as an excellent accompaniment for eels and other fish, another case of mistaking propinquity for compatibility, as for *zampone* and Lambrusco. Bosco goes well with meat dishes, but the ideal wine for fish, even the oily eel, would hardly seem to be a full-bodied (11–12 degrees) dry red—so dark that it is almost black, with a certain bitterness, and a resinous taste which results from growing it along a sandy littoral from which pines have disappeared, leaving the soil impregnated with their fragrance. With age Bosco becomes smoother. It is a wine which ought to go better with the Burgundy-like food inland than with that of the coast, and it is indeed a Burgundy by descent. The grape from which it is made is called the golden grape, *uva d'oro*. Even experts have been puzzled by this, since the fruit is black. The explanation is that it was imported from Burgundy's great wine region, the Côte d'Or, the Golden Slope. The vines were brought to the province of Ferrara toward the end of the Estes' rule at the instigation of Renée of France, daughter of Louis XII.

The Trebbiano grape provides another example of the greater oenological alertness of Romagna as compared to Emilia, blinded by its infatuation with Lambrusco. The Trebbia River, which gives its name to the grape, is in the Emilian province of Piacenza, but Romagna has gotten hold of it, and the Romagna Trebbianos have today surpassed those still grown on its native ground, despite the very considerable head start enjoyed by the latter. Trebbiano goes back in Emilia at least to Roman times, when Pliny the Elder spoke highly of Trebulanus, of which he appreciated the medical virtues as much as the gustatory qualities. He described it as a dry white *frizzante,* which, except for the last word, would fit today's wine well enough. Lambrusco existed then too, for Pliny wrote of autumn leaves "which like Lambrusco undergo changes of color before settling on blood red." He also mentioned a black grape called *pruxinia,* "whose rosé wine, after four years' aging, has the magical power to become golden." Ignoring the long Emilian past of Trebbiano, Romagna seems to have forgotten the origin of the wine and considers it typical of its own area. Trebbiano di Romagna may come from anywhere in the district, Trebbiano di Forlì is perhaps the best, and the label Trebbiano Ravennate covers not only wine grown around Ravenna, but also that of Faenza, Russi and Lugo. The Trebbianos are dry whites, pale straw yellow, of 10 to 11 degrees.

Most Italian regions are content to have one or two special liqueurs to their credit, but Emilia-Romagna has a long list of them, probably because of its fragmentation into eight provinces of individual habits and histories. It sometimes seems as if every town in the region had its own private afterdinner drink, not to mention every monastery, for in the Middle Ages it was common for monasteries to develop their own liqueurs and cordials, keeping the recipes secret, and supporting the monastery in considerable part from their sale.

The province of Modena has built up a considerable distilling industry from the many liqueurs of Emilia-Romagna, reproducing most of them, regardless of where they originated; Modena even goes outside of the regional boundaries to make such drinks as Sambuca, which was developed in Lazio. The province does not depend on other people's creations alone; it is the birthplace of many fine liqueurs of its own, of which the greatest is the walnut-flavored Nocino, developed in the region between Sassuola and Formigine, in the foothills of the Apennines—walnut country.

No one who has ever tasted Nocino is likely to forget it. Chocolate-colored, it suggests chocolate also by its rich velvety sweetness. It is not cloying, because it has a slight bitterness, so well masked by the sweet taste that you are not likely to notice it unless you happen to be giving the flavor analytical attention. It is reputed to possess tonic and digestive qualities.

Nocino was first produced in monasteries, and emerged from them to be made in private homes. It was then taken over by mass production distilleries, chiefly those of Modena and Sassuola, and is not quite the same for any two of them. Each company has its own carefully guarded formula, most of them dating back for more than a century. However, the big distilleries are not too happy nowadays about Nocino. They have discovered that the process by which it is produced is not propitious to large-scale handling. Small manufacturers do better with it, for they can start at the very beginning, superintending the picking of the nuts themselves, and thus getting them at exactly the right stage for best results. Nocino is made from green walnuts; the local superstition is that they must be picked on Midsummer's Day. Actually, though the pickers hold approximately to this date, they may pick a few days earlier or later, depending on the state of the nuts. Twenty-four hours' difference one way or the other can give a totally different taste to the finished product. This is one reason why Nocino does not adapt itself to mass production. The quantities of walnuts required by big distilleries make it necessary to accept nuts picked over a large area at various stages of ripeness. Now comes the next difficulty for a machine-dominated operation: the walnuts must be shelled and picked very carefully; a single rotting nut could spoil a whole distillation. This means hand labor. These two hurdles passed, the walnuts are soaked in alcohol for two years, together with their empty shells. They are then transferred for aging to casks of brown oak, where they spend another year; the rule is three years from picking to bottling. Distillation follows the aging process, whatever secret ingredients the manufacturer's recipe calls for are added, and the Nocino is ready to be bottled and sold. The next difficulty is for the Nocino fancier, who will have trouble finding it. The supply does not begin to meet the demand, and it is decreasing. Production in Modena has dropped to only 30,-000 bottles a year.

As a result Sassolino, which normally should play second fiddle to Nocino, is more widely known, for more of it is made. It is the specialty of Sassuola, a town noted for its liqueurs (and also for manufacturing ornamental tiles). Sassolino is made from star anise, imported mostly from China, and goes back many centuries; some experts believe the ancient Romans knew it, or something very much like it. It had gone into a decline until early in the last century, but after the unification of Italy enriched the bourgeois families of Emilia-Romagna, it was much demanded for their well-furnished tables and enjoyed a period of maximum favor. A slight decline was followed recently by another boom, and today Sassolino is the fashionable liqueur to drink in the bars of Milan, Rome and other cities far from Sassuola.

Ancione is made from anise seeds imported from the Middle East. Apart from this nothing is known of its formula, which was devised in 1814 and since then has been the secret of the Cassoni family, which produces it in Finale Emilia, also in the province of Modena. It is suspected, however, that part of its secret lies in the calcium and other mineral salts contained in the underground water of Finale Emilia. In any case, the result is described by local experts as "pure, dry, and deliciously perfumed."

Eaux de vie are made from a wide variety of fruits—especially apples, plums, apricots and pears, of which the last is the most prized; it is distilled from the reputed William pear, or pears of comparable quality, and is a specialty of Formigine. These drinks are velvety and dry, not sweet, and have a high alcoholic content. They are setting a new style in drinking; instead of appearing only after the meal, they are nowadays sometimes drunk during it, following the pasta. Many of them are made by simple distillation without other treatment for export to foreign countries, which use them as the base for more sophisticated concoctions, which pass as the native products of their own regions. The distillation of Vignola cherries, for instance, provides the raw material for many bottles of German *Kirsch*, whose drinkers never suspect that this beverage was supplied by Italy.

There are any number of other after-dinner drinks—Rugiada di Flora (Dew of the Flowers); the ancient Rossioli, made in Porretta Terme in the province of Bologna; *grappa di Vinaccia*, a Romagna brandy which I drank in Bologna, and found to be on the level of a run-of-the-mill French brandy; and any number of digestive drinks made from herbs of one kind or another, bitter in taste, but not disagreeably so. They are reputed to have medicinal qualities, but they manage not to taste like medicine.

THE
DOMAIN

OF THE
TRIBES

Lombardy

Lombardy owes its name to the Germanic Longobards, who left nothing else behind except the iron crown of their kings, legendarily beaten out of one of the nails of the Crucifixion, and the technique of roasting birds in a ball of clay. They were latecomers, arriving only at the end of the 6th century. Among their unrecorded predecessors were some Etruscans—though nobody knows just when they came, nor just where, nor in what numbers, nor how long they stayed. Although this is not generally considered to be Etruscan territory, some savants think that Melpum, one of the 12 major cities the Etruscans set up in the north, in imitation of the 12 principal cities on their original territory, was Milan. In any case, Mantua was an Etruscan city, named possibly for the Etruscan war god Mantus, and was founded in the 5th or 6th century B.C. Some blocks of the Etruscan walls are still there.

Some of the clues which suggest an Etruscan presence are alimentary. Lombardy is polenta country; but it seems likeliest that Lombardy did not get polenta at first-hand, from the Etruscans, but at second-hand, from the Romans. More significant is the recorded fact that among the cereals which those great growers of grain, the Etruscans, provided for Rome was millet from Cisalpine Gaul, a territory which included Lombardy. Millet has always been associated with Lombardy. A document dated 1589 notes that millet was one of the three most widely consumed foods in Milan; and Milan was still noted for its millet-flour bread at the beginning of our century. *Pan d'angiol* (bread of the angels) was sweetened bread of millet flour; *pan de mistura* was a mixture of millet, barley and sorghum; soaked in wine it became *pan moin*, which is why Milanese today order a garment dyed by saying, *"Fà pan moin."*

The long and complicated history of Lombardy, and especially of its capital, Milan, strikes from time to time a gastronomic note, sometimes no more than a grace note, as in the theory that ambrosia, the honeyed beverage of the gods, was named, because of his eloquence, after St. Ambrose, who became Bishop of Milan in 375, the first of the many churchmen who ruled the city from the 6th to the 11th centuries. Unfortunately for this assertion, Homer had written of ambrosia more than a millennium earlier.

Of greater importance to the future gastronomic history of Lombardy was the reaction of the indomitable Milanese when the Emperor Frederick I, Barbarossa, destroyed the city in 1154. As though rebuilding Milan were not enough, the Milanese began at the same time to construct an ambitious waterway, drainage and irrigation system, the Na-

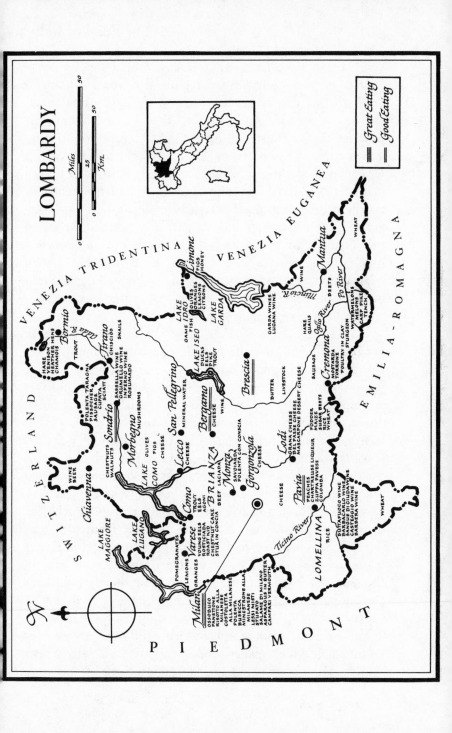

viglio Grande, still important today. Collecting the stag-
nant dispersed waters of the region, it drained marshland
and irrigated dry areas, providing at the same time an artery, safer than the bandit-infested roads, over which the
produce of the improved soil could be transported to market. It took 278 years from the time when the first section
was opened, on August 5, 1179, connecting Milan with the
market town of Abbiategrasso, to its completion, when its
northern branch attained Bereguardo, nearly on Lake Maggiore. Its southern terminus had already reached Pavia, on
the Ticino, just above its junction with the Po, so when
Leonardo da Vinci's invention of the lock made the Po
navigable and extended the reach of the Naviglio, it brought
into Milan rich cargoes of cream, butter, *mascarpone*
cheese, honey, vegetables and fruit.

Barbarossa destroyed Milan again in 1162, but she took
her revenge, with her allies of the Lombard League, by de-
feating him at Legnano on May 29, 1176. It was a victory
not only for the League, but also for the Papacy, and was
appropriately marked by a sign of celestial approval. Two
doves, symbolizing, the Milanese were sure, the Holy
Ghost, alighted during the battle on the altar of the Carroccio (the war chariot of medieval cities, which carried
their standards and an altar). The Carroccio's starting
point was the church of San Simpliciano, where to this day
a mass is celebrated yearly on the anniversary of the battle,
during which two live doves are released from the altar.
The event is also recalled by the appearance at the Easter
season of the *colomba pasquale*, the Easter dove, a cake in
the shape of a bird made from the same dough as Milan's
famous *panettone*, plus toasted almonds and a powdering of
sugar.

Pavia makes *colomba* too, and has a different story to account for it which makes it 600 years older. It relates how
Alboin, King of the Longobards, taking Pavia after a siege

of three years, ordered the city sacked; but as he entered it, a beautiful girl offered him a cake in the form of a dove, a symbol of peace since Noah. Whether in appreciation of the gift or of the giver, Alboin canceled his order and made Pavia his capital.

In the 14th century, an offbeat gastronomic note was inserted into history by one of the less admired members of the powerful Visconti family, then ruling Milan. This was Barnabò, who had been excommunicated by the Pope. The bull of excommunication was delivered to him by two Benedictine monks whom he accompanied on their way back as far as the middle of a high bridge across a torrent, where he stopped to demand threateningly whether they preferred to eat or drink. Gazing at the torrent below, they had little doubt what would happen if they chose to drink, so they opted for eating; Barnabò made them swallow the bull, parchment, ribbons, seals and all. They were not poisoned by it, but Barnabò was poisoned, though somewhat later, in 1385, by his nephew, Gian Galeazzo, the most eminent of the Visconti. The succeeding Sforzas had their black sheep too—Galeazzo, who so endeared himself to his subjects that in 1476 three of them murdered him for the public good. Yet he had one tremendous achievement to his credit: he introduced the cultivation of rice into Lombardy. It is not certain that the territory then possessed saffron to convert the rice into *risotto alla milanese*. This may have had to wait until 1535, when Charles V made his son Philip Duke of Milan, initiating nearly two centuries of Spanish rule. In this case, *risotto alla milanese* is a descendant of *paella*. Saffron, once discovered, became almost too popular in Milan. It was put into so many dishes by one Milanese cook that he was nicknamed Zafferano; when he married the daughter of the master stained-glass maker Valerio da Flandra in September 1574, the wedding feast was enlivened by joking friends who slipped saffron into every dish which could possibly stand it, and some which couldn't.

When the Austrians took over, they were regarded as oppressors, but their *censimento* land tax produced a more even division of wealth, and agriculture, always the backbone of the region's economy, flourished under measures which encouraged small landholders.

In spite of the industrial importance of Milan and one or two other large cities, Lombardy is primarily an agricultural province. Its principal resources are raising livestock, and exploiting its mountain forests. Lombardy has the reputation of employing the most modern methods of food production in Italy—highly developed agricultural machinery, scientific breeding techniques, carefully handled irrigation and fertilization, exploited by hardworking farmers one of whose chief characteristics is perseverance. This, as much as the soil and the climate, accounts for high yields. Lombardy gets more wheat per acre than any other region of Italy. On the artificially enriched flooded meadows of the Po valley, Lombardy farmers count on cutting seven crops of fodder every year; sometimes they get eight harvests of hay. Not surprisingly, Lombardy leads the country in production of fodder, and also of maize, and consequently also of cattle. Mountain pasturage is good too; Lombardy produces every year more than half a million pigs, about half as many sheep, and not far short of 2,000,000 cattle, half of them milk producers.

One of the most important crops of the lower plains along the Po is rice; the same rich alluvial soil produces sugar beets, maize and wheat; these cereals are grown in the higher plains too, together with green vegetables and fruit, which are also found beside the Po. In the hills, agriculture is concentrated in the valleys, especially the Valtellina and the higher valley of the Adda River in the province of

Sondrio, where small properties are the rule, and the principal products are honey, fruit, wine grapes (which grow as high up as 2,400 feet), and in the woods, walnuts, chestnuts and mushrooms. Game is plentiful here, and trout are fished in the mountain streams as well as the lakes, which also give eels and *agoni*. The Po offers sturgeon, tench, carp, pike, perch and other fish; the town of Vorana specializes in preserving fish in vinegar. Poultry and eggs are specialties of Badia Pavese, Borgofranco, Mezzana Bigli, Quingentole and Mezzanino, which also raises pheasant. All this makes the region self-sufficient for food; it imports almost nothing except exotic products like spices, tea, coffee and tropical fruits.

Lombardy's importance as a milk producer accounts for the fact that it is one of the rare regions of Italy which cooks almost entirely in butter—and also for the fact that one of its great glories is cheese.

The most widely known Lombardy cheese is undoubtedly Gorgonzola. Many persons think of it as an Italian Roquefort (which it resembles because of the greenish streaks in its light-colored flesh) but there are many differences between the two, of which the most important is that Roquefort is made from sheep's milk, and Gorgonzola from fresh whole cow's milk. Roquefort, apart from its streaks, is practically white; Gorgonzola shades toward yellow. Roquefort is dry, and often crumbly; Gorgonzola is creamier.

If you buy Gorgonzola outside of Lombardy, it will almost certainly have been made by a large company, which is to say that you will not be getting the best in the opinion of those who are fussy about Gorgonzola. For them, the ideal Gorgonzola can only be had from small cheesemakers, who still exist, but whose wares are usually eaten on the spot. Purists insist that a Gorgonzola should be the product of a single milking, or at most two, a stipulation which necessarily limits the scale of the operation. Assuming the maximum two milkings, the first is the evening milking, after which the curd is heated (not cooked) and then left to cool overnight. The following morning, the curds of the second milking are likewise heated, and a layer of warm curds poured into the mold. A layer of the cooled curd of the night before follows it; and it is the difference in temperature between the two which encourages the formation of the mold which streaks the cheese with green. Nowadays this mold is often produced by inserting copper wires into the cheese, but this is not necessary if the process just described has been employed. Also nowadays the aging of the cheese, which requires a cool storage place, usually takes place in the warehouses of big producers; formerly Gorgonzola was aged in the natural caves of the Valsassina, still the best place for it.

Gorgonzola is a little town, about ten miles from Milan; it was more or less by accident that it developed a famous cheese. It was here that the herds stopped to rest during their annual pilgrimage from summer pastures in the mountains to the plain; every year Gorgonzola found itself suddenly submerged in a flood of milk which it could not possibly consume; so it was turned into cheese. How long ago this started, nobody knows; perhaps even as early as ancient Roman times, for the Romans seem to have known this type of cheese. In any case, foreign lands learned of its existence about the time Columbus was discovering America— French soldiers returning from Charles VIII's Italian campaigns brought Gorgonzola back with them. Even so it was not until the second half of the 19th century that Gorgonzola began to be exported commercially.

Because the cows that stopped at Gorgonzola were tired from their long trek, their cheese was at first called *stracchino di Gorgonzola*, from the Lombard word for "tired" —*stracco*. Eventually the name *stracchino* was dropped for

Gorgonzola, but it has survived for another cheese, probably without thought for its original meaning. Today's *stracchino* is a soft runny cheese, a bit on the sharp side.

There is also a white Gorgonzola, little known outside its area of origin, sometimes called *Gorgonzola bianco* and sometimes *pannerone*.

The second best-known cheese of Lombardy also originated in the province of Milan, in the region of Melzo. This is Bel Paese (Beautiful Country), made of cow's milk, yellow, soft but not runny, and so bland in taste that sometimes it almost seems not to have any. *Pastorella* is a smaller sized Bel Paese, and the same type of cheese turns up in Lombardy under the names of Bella Milano and Bel Piano Lombardo, and in neighboring provinces as Cacioreale, Bel Piemonte, Bell' Alpina, Fior d'Alpe, Savoia and Vittoria.

Lodi, still in Milan province, makes more *grana* (Parmesan-type cheese) than Parma does, marketed as *grana lodigiana*, or *grana padana*, *grana* of the Po. The latter name covers all cheese of this type made not only in Lombardy but also in Piedmont, Venezia, and those parts of Emilia-Romagna not entitled to use the name Parmesan. *Grana padana* goes back to the 10th century, but the earliest extant reference to it in Lombardy dates from 1494, when the accounts of the Milanese Abbey of Chiaravalle recorded that the *cacio duro* (hard cheese for grating), the ancestor of *grana*, made by its monks at Cascina Pecchione, had been exported to Flanders in exchange for goods from that country.

Lodi may also have been the birthplace of *mascarpone* (or *mascherpone*), a fresh cream cheese which comes in little individually-sized muslin-wrapped cylinders, and is eaten for dessert—with sugar (alone or with maraschino); with powdered chocolate; or with liqueurs.

The uplands of Lombardy are also good cheese producers. Bergamo produces *branzi* and *taleggio*, soft and runny, with a stronger variety called *taleggino*. Lecco, in the province of Como, makes a sheep's milk cheese and ripens it in the caves of the Sassina Valley. Sondrio's Bitto valley makes one from a mixture of cow's and goat's milk. Other Lombardy cheeses are the soft mild *crescenza* and the runny *robiola*, with its sharper version, *robiolina*. The region also imitates some cheeses which originated elsewhere—for instance, *groviera italiano*, Italian Gruyère, and Rome's favorite provolone, which is copied in Cremona.

The importance of cheese in Lombardy has given rise there to a unique institution—the cheese bank. Backed by the Lombardy Cassa di Risparmio, which does general banking, there are cheese banks in Cremona, Novara, Pavia, Lodi, Montava, Pegognaga and Villa Po. Their function is to provide producers with liquid cash during the long periods when their capital is tied up in ripening cheese; the cheese is the security for their loans. They are like no banks you ever saw in your life. Their most important feature is cold-storage rooms. Here the cheese makers deposit cheese and withdraw money; you might say they discount their cheese, as other businessmen discount notes. At the beginning of 1969, the banks had taken in 15,000 tons of cheese and had loaned 25,000,000 lire on it.

Another symbol of the importance of cheese in Lombardy is the existence in Milan of what may be the world's greatest cheese shop, opened in 1892 by a Czechoslovak named Franz Peck. Today the Peck company owns a restaurant and a lavishly stocked delicatessen in the same street, but its pride is its House of Cheese, the Casa del Formaggio, which offers hundreds of different cheeses from Italy and abroad, along with products made from them, such as a bewildering number of different kinds of cheesecake.

The area which produces these foods is composed of nine provinces, of which Milan is the keystone; the nine divide themselves into three groups, each topographically and historically congruent. The southern tier occupies the valley of the Po—from west to east, Pavia; Milan, of which an arm pushes southward to the river; Cremona; and Mantua. The history of the first three is closely interlinked, but Mantua might be considered a special case, since it was for a considerable period an independent state, politically divorced from Lombardy. To the north are the lake-and-mountain provinces, Varese and Como, which border on Milan, and Sondrio, which continues them. Finally there are the two provinces of mixed geography, neither alluvial plain nor high mountains: Bergamo, which touches Milan, and Brescia beyond it, differentiated historically as having been part of Venezia. All nine provinces put together cover an area of only 9,191 square miles, less than that of New Hampshire.

The gastronomic influence of Milan is strong in the other provinces, and there is often a tendency to speak interchangeably of Milanese cooking or Lombardy cooking as if they were synonomous. They are nearly so, but not quite. To represent to yourself graphically the extent to which Milanese cooking overshadows that of Lombardy in general, think of those photographs of total eclipses of the sun. Milan's proportion is that of the black central disk; the share of the other provinces may be represented by the thin fringe of the corona, encircling the penumbra. The solar corona is brilliant, and so, sometimes, is the corona of the Lombardy cuisine. Milan's influence is least strong in the mountainous areas; it is most strong on the shores of the Po. If we consider first the cooking of Milan, we shall have made acquaintance with the major part of the cooking of Lombardy.

Milan is industrious, perhaps the hardest working city of Italy. The tempo is dynamic. It is the second city of Italy for population and the first for economic activity: the wealthiest manufacturing and industrial complex; the center of the European silk industry and consequently of the Italian textile industry; the nexus of steel, metallurgical and mechanical enterprises, of chemical manufactures, of the production of electrical energy and of electrical appliances; the capital for hats and shoes—and also for the food industries, particularly those based on milk from the rich pasturage of Lombardy. Milan is a great market for cereals, fruit, vegetables and livestock. As New Yorkers are accustomed to think of their city as the real capital of the United States, despite the technicality that Washington harbors the government, so Milanese think of their city as the real capital of Italy—and indeed it was, for just under a century, the capital of the Roman Empire.

Milan never lost the sumptuous habits the ancient Romans gave it, which apparently included an expansive attitude toward food. So far as I know, Milan is the only place in the world which has ever based eligibility for public office on food qualification. At one period in the Middle Ages, its parliament, the *consiglio grande*, was made up of all those who produced their own bread or wine. There turned out to be too many of them. Their numbers were first reduced to 2,000, then to 1,500, and finally to 800, by which time the definition of a legislator as a food producer had become so restricted by other considerations that it was abandoned altogether.

Perhaps the most ungrateful guest in Lombardy's gastronomic history is Galvano Fiamma, who attacked the Milanese as *magni commestores*, big eaters, after having been invited to the dinner given for the marriage in 1368 of Violante Visconti to the Duchess of Chiarenza (another guest was Petrarch). No doubt its 50 lavish courses were shocking to a preaching friar (who could have spared himself the agony by not attending), but he might have had the good grace to remark that the lords of Milan did not mo-

nopolize their luxury but permitted the people to participate whenever they gave a feast. The tradition of the *corte
bandita*, or open house, seems to have been set on July 7,
1261, when Napo Torriani celebrated the visit of Pope
Innocent IV with festivities which lasted for a week. The
example was so successful that similar public rejoicings followed in 1273, 1300, 1348, 1368, and 1395, this last date
being that of the great banquet given on September 5 to
celebrate the coronation of Gian Galeazzo Visconti as Duke
of Milan. While the guests were wolfing down eel, lamprey,
sole, trout, pullet, capon, quail, partridge, pheasant, peacock, boiled and roasted pork and veal, lamb, kid, rabbit,
hare, venison, deer, meat tart with cooked pears, and marzipan (most of it gilded to assure 24-karat indigestion), there
stood untouched in the middle of the floor an impressive
display of gilded sturgeons, pigs, calves, deer, and bears, all
in their natural pelts, though they had been seasoned,
stuffed and cooked. They were designed for distribution to
the people.

One Renaissance banquet of Milan is of special interest
because of the emphasis it accorded to a food which it was
at the moment fashionable, even snobbish, to serve— the orange. "In 1529," wrote John McPhee, in his fascinating
book on this fruit, "the Archbishop of Milan gave a sixteen-
course dinner that included caviar and oranges fried with
sugar and cinnamon, brill and sardines with slices of orange
and lemon, one thousand oysters with pepper and oranges,
lobster salad with citrons, sturgeon in aspic covered with
orange juice, fried sparrows with oranges, individual salads
containing citrons into which the coat of arms of the diner
had been carved, orange fritters, a soufflé full of raisins and
pine nuts and covered with sugar and orange juice, five
hundred fried oysters with lemon slices, and candied peels
of citrons and oranges."

The days of the great lords and of ducal feasting passed,

but the wealthy Milanese maintained the tradition. Witness, for instance, a banquet given in May 1851 for authors from many countries, whose menu included 80 kinds of antipasti, galantine, crayfish, liver paté, ham, tongue, five different soups, turbot, red mullet, salmon, filet of sole, fish croquettes, lamb, mutton, beef, chicken cooked in two different fashions, duck, 15 jelly desserts, 20 cream desserts, and a countless variety of pastries. The 18th and 19th centuries were a brilliant period in Milan. Gibbon had found its people's manners were polished and liberal in 300 A.D.; they were still polished and liberal in those elegant centuries. Stendhal lived in Milan for seven years during this period and described them as "the flower of my life." He asked that his tombstone be inscribed, "Henri Beyle, Milanese."

The city's animated social life gravitated around two main poles. One was the glass-roofed Galleria off the cathedral square, with its cafés and restaurants, an informal forum where women went to gossip in the ice-cream parlors of Motta or Alemagna (still purveyors of these same wares, and many others, throughout Italy), while men read the *Corriere della Sera* at café tables and talked politics over steaming cups of coffee from the most perfected percolators in the world. The other was the opera house, La Scala, the rendezvous of artists and intellectuals as well as socialites. Music lovers who enter La Scala nowadays with the appropriate feling of awe would have been astonished at its atmosphere in the preceding centuries. The audience combined opera with dining. The boxes had sitting rooms (the Duke's even had a bedroom, in case the opera bored him), and boxholders used them as dining rooms, eating meals they brought with them, warmed up by a restaurant established for that purpose on the premises. On some occasions, minestrone and veal steaks were served during the performance, and the music could not be heard for the clatter of knives and forks, or so Berlioz complained; but it would stop when arias were attacked.

The Teutonic Longobards ruled Lombardy for some two centuries; the Austrians were present for hardly more than two-thirds of a century. This is not much, measured against more than 2,000 years of Lombard history, yet a certain affinity seems to subsist between Germanic and Lombard cooking. Some of it may be accounted for by the sharing of a continental climate, which made both Germans and Lombards heavy eaters. Then there is the circumstance that part of the northern frontier of Lombardy abuts on German-speaking territory and that trade currents, with all the other interchanges they inevitably provoke, have always flowed between Milan and Central Europe. Perhaps the most important fact is that modern Lombard cooking is comparatively recent. Despite the survival of many individual old dishes, the present cooking methods and eating habits of Lombardy developed after the fall of Napoleon —in other words, during the period of Austrian domination. One thing that happened then was that Milan prospered; so Milanese cooking is a cooking of plenty. The whole population could afford to participate in the lavishness formerly restricted to the aristocrats and the rich. "As well-being spreads," wrote Melchiorre Gioia, the 18th-19th-century liberal priest, politician and author who, though born in Piacenza, lived and died in Milan, "as the standard of living rises, artisans and workmen will eat white bread instead of the traditional indigestible mixture of coarse grains; and meat; and olive oil will replace the perfidious linseed oil." (Linseed oil has not always been considered perfidious in Lombardy; between the two World Wars, when it was scarce, it became a precious rarity sought desperately for the seasoning of Lombardy potato salad). Some of the most widely known specialties of Milan resemble German dishes. *Ossobuco* reminds us that neither Lombards nor Germans care much for roasts and steaks, preferring their meat braised or stewed (*stufato, pfefferpotthast*) or even boiled (*lesso misto, Tafelspitz*). *Panettone* is essentially *Kugelhof*, plus bits of candied fruit. *Costoletta alla milanese* is related to *Wiener Schnitzel*. Finally, Milan is famous for its *lattemiele*, whipped cream, as Vienna is for *schlagobers*.

If Milanese food recalls that of Germanic countries, it is not prepared with the heavy-handed touch often encountered in Germany, partly, no doubt, because of the corrective skill of the fine Italian hand, but also because of a second, counteracting, foreign influence—that of France. The prestige of French culture, French elegance and French cooking moved the Milanese to emulate France. This was all the easier since Milan uses butter as its principal cooking fat, and so does the French *haute cuisine*. Paolo Mantegazza, the 19th-century doctor and anthropologist, coupled French and Milanese cooking in his *L'igiene del piacere*, placing them together "at the summit, above all others." Fashionable Milanese restaurants of the 18th and 19th centuries served French food rather than their own, and so did the more pretentious private homes. Raffaele Calzini, in *Milano fin de siècle*, told of a wealthy Italian who took advantage of a lengthy visit to Paris to bring along his cook and place him as assistant chef in a Paris restaurant so that he could acquire a repertory of French dishes.

French influence is reflected in the Milanese dialect, which contains a considerable smattering of French, particularly in the gastronomic vocabulary. This apparently did not occur to the many food experts who for the last hundred years were puzzled by a frequently recurring but never explained word in old Milanese recipes, *corbuglione*; it is simply *court-bouillon*. The Milanese *aj* (garlic) is nearer to the French *ail* than to the Italian *aglio; armàndola* (almond) is nearer to *amande* than to *mandorla; articiocch* (artichoke) to *artichaut* than to *carciofo; cocumeritt* (cucumber) to *concombre* than to *cetriolo; pever* (pepper) to *poivre* than to *pepe; grass* (meat cooking juices) to *graisse* than to *sugo; pomm* (apple) to *pomme* than to *mela; sciress* (cherry) to *cerise* than to *cilegia; sèller* (celery) to *céleri* than to *sedano; tomàtes* (tomato) to *tomate* than to *pomodoro*.

The most potent influence in preserving Milanese food from Germanic heaviness was probably the skill of Milanese cooks. In 1895, G. A. Sala wrote in *The Thorough Good Cook* that "the Milanese are undoubtedly the best cooks in Italy." This is a debatable statement; one thinks immediately of Genoese, Venetian and Modenese cooks, for instance, but we will be on safer ground with Pellegrino Artusi, who wrote that "Milanese cooking has to be handled by Milanese." There is little opportunity for outsiders ever to learn the fine points of Milanese cooking, for it developed not in public professional kitchens, but in private homes, the focal points of Milanese life. Milan is a bourgeois city, where the comfort and intimacy of home is preferred for eating and cooking. The *borghesia agiata*, the well-to-do bourgeoisie, can very well afford restaurants, but when they entertain (and, being a hospitable people, they entertain a great deal) they would rather do it within their own walls.

The basis of Milanese home cooking was the family cookbook, handed down from mother to daughter, enlarged from generation to generation by the addition of new private recipes, many of them acquired by swapping favorite formulas with other housewives. A well-filled cookbook was as good as a dowry.

After World War I, Milanese home cooking seemed to be in danger; women stopped paying much attention to cooking; but after World War II they returned to the kitchen, more or less as a hobby, and began hunting up forgotten and often mislaid cookbooks as the best source for the old recipes which had been disappearing under the conditions of modern life—lack of time, shortage of servants, and the shift from wood and coal to gas and electricity. Milanese cooking was vulnerable to these changes, for the Milanese style calls for slow careful painstaking cooking, almost incompatible with contemporary habits. "This healthy and even delicious cooking," wrote Léon Daudet, the fiery pre-war French Royalist, who also had a substantial reputation as a gourmet, "is the result of taking pains and exercising judgment, as well as of finesse in taste."

"Only fried dishes, *scaloppine*, and soups are ordinarily cooked over a high flame," wrote Ottorina Perna Bozzi in *Vecchia Milano in cucina*. "In general, the prevailing usage is slow cooking, over a low steady fire. . . . The idea is not to dry up meats or vegetables, making it necessary to add water, but to cook them as far as possible in their natural juices, to preserve flavor and tenderness." And again: "The basic principle of the Milanese cuisine in its practical application is that everything should be cooked slowly, covered, and for a long time. Boiled meats should be simmered, roasts should not be strongly pre-browned, but you should wait for them to brown spontaneously at the end of the cooking. Otherwise how could you attain that magnificent juice, a little greasy, which should always be placed in a gravy dish . . . the principal basis of all cooking."

Why are many Milanese dishes cooked covered? "The natural humidity is the quantity necessary for cooking. Therefore never lose it by lifting the cover, but let it fall back into the cooking vessel: '*Mai scoeud via l'acqua del coverc*' "—a familiar maxim in dialect: "Never shake off the water on the cover."

A good deal of fat is used in Milanese cooking, which

causes Italians from other regions to describe it as difficult to digest; perhaps it is in summer, but in winter the climate demands warming foods. By far the most important cooking fat for Milan is butter; it dominates Milanese cooking; when used for frying, it is heated alone first before the food to be cooked is placed in it. Bacon comes second and lard third; but there is a present tendency to replace lard with bacon. Fourth place is held by cream. After this comes meat juice, with all its fat left in, further thickened by long cooking; whatever meat juice is left over from any given meal is carefully saved for future use; every Milanese kitchen has a jar of accumulated stock at hand.

Olive oil comes a long way after the first five as a cooking fat in Lombardy, but is gaining in popularity because of the influence of other parts of the country; linseed oil is liked in Lombardy but has become extremely difficult to find, though Lombardy grows a great deal of flax. Milan used to consider as a cooking fat, though it is rather more complicated than that, a local specialty called *cervellada* (in dialect *cervellàa*)—now, regrettably, all but extinct. With luck, you might find it in Monza, where some housewives still make it for their own private use. It is a sausage, made of pork fat, marrow, cheese and spices, in a casing of pig's intestines; originally it also included pig's brains, which accounts for the name, from *cervello*, brain. This was a prescribed ingredient in many old Milanese dishes, not because they wanted sausage in it, but because its presence provided the necessary cooking fat; if *cervellada* was called for, no other fat was used. When modern cooks use old recipes calling for *cervellada*, they replace it with pork fat and marrow.

Milanese seasoning is often rather complicated. The principal herbs, spices and vegetables (used rather for seasoning other ingredients than for their own sake) are, in the order of their popularity: parsley, sage, rosemary, onion, celery, carrots, garlic (always used in small quantities and usually removed from the dish before serving), tomatoes (usually just enough to give a rosy, not a red, color to the dish), pepper, saffron, fennel, cinnamon, nutmeg, bay leaves, thyme, marjoram, juniper, anise, and elderberries. When a Milanese recipe calls for mixed spices, the approved local formula puts together three parts each of cloves, white pepper, dried bay leaf, basil and thyme, with ten parts each of nutmeg and queen cinnamon; this is so finely ground that it can be strained through silk. The Milanese housewife keeps it in a tightly closed jar so that it will lose none of its fragrance.

Of the hundreds of local dishes in the Milanese repertory there are, I should say, nine which are particularly widely known. They are, in about this order:

OSSOBUCO, a thick slice of veal shank, meat, bone and marrow, for which I find seven different recipes in seven Italian cookbooks; if I consulted seven more, I have no doubt that I would wind up with 14. All but one begin by browning the veal shank in butter; the other uses a mixture of oil and lard. Three of them direct you to sprinkle the meat lightly with flour; the other four do not. Four counsel cooking it with tomato pulp; three eschew tomato. The one point on which everyone agrees is that it is accompanied by *gremalada* (Milanese) or *gremalata* (Italian) sauce; but there are seven different opinions on how *gremalada* is made. The only ingredient on which everybody agrees is grated lemon peel. Parsley is so common that one would expect all the recipes to include that too, but only five of them do. Most Milanese would include crushed anchovy fillets, but four of the seven omit it (the four whose authors are not Milanese). In the face of this confusion, here is a formula which should be authentic since it comes from an old Milanese cookbook: The meat is not floured; it is browned in butter and then cooked slowly, covered, for an hour and a half. The *gremolada* goes into the cooking juices during the last five minutes; it is made of parsley, garlic, crushed anchovies, rosemary, sage and grated lemon peel, all chopped or ground together. To this recipe, others add bouillon, carrots, celery and marjoram for cooking with the veal, and fennel seeds to the *gremolada*, while omitting other ingredients. *Ossobuco* goes very well with pasta, but though I have had pasta served with it elsewhere, I have never known it to be so accompanied in Milan. Mashed potatoes and peas do occasionally turn up with it there, but traditionally it should be served with *risotto alla milanese*. This is rather rare, for rice is not ordinarily a side dish in Italy. It is eaten separately, for its own sake.

PANETTONE is a deliciously light porous-textured egg-yellow cake containing seedless raisins and bits of candied citron and orange, in my opinion the world's best accompaniment for breakfast coffee. It remains fresh for a long time—exactly how long I cannot say, for I have never been able to resist even the largest *panettone* long enough to find out.

Panettone lends itself to fabulation. The simplest fable connected with it states that its bulbous top is meant to honor the domes of Lombardy churches. One might as well maintain that Lombardy churches were given domes in honor of *panettone*. Cook any raised dough in a cylindrical tin and you will get a dome-shaped top.

A more complicated fable is put forward to explain its name. *Panettone*, it alleges, was originally called *pan de Tonio*, Tony's bread. The Tony in question was supposed to be a poor 15th-century baker. A wealthy young man interested in marrying his daughter staked Tony at the Christmas season with enough money to buy the finest flour, the freshest eggs, and, as an added value, sultana raisins and candied citron peel; as a result, *pan de Tonio* sold like hot cakes, and has been doing so ever since (Tony's backer, of course, married Tony's daughter). Unfortunately for the story, *panettone* is simply the word for bread plus an Italian suffix which denotes bigness (like *tortelloni* from *tortelli*); it means simply "big bread," bigness in this case referring to quality rather than quantity—"enriched bread," if you want. Indeed the old name for *panettone* was *pan grande*—big bread, using a word for "big" with a definite connotation of quality. The Tony's bread story connects *panettone* with Christmas, and on this count is in step with tradition. *Panettone* is involved in a very old Christmas ceremony. At this season, the head of each family used to cut three large slices from one of these cakes, and each member of the family ate a bit of each to insure good luck. The Duke of Milan himself used to perform this rite, in the Sala dei Fagioli (Bean Hall) on the third floor of the Castello Sforzesco. *Panettone* is eaten all year round now, but it is still associated especially with Christmas; every December the big Motta and Alemagna food packing companies sell between them a quarter of a million *panettoni* throughout Italy. Apropos of holiday dishes, if you hear "camel soup" mentioned in Milan at New Year's, don't take it literally. It means bread soaked in water, which Milanese children put on window sills on New Year's Eve to feed the camels which bring from afar the Gesù Bambino (Christ Child), bearing gifts.

RISOTTO ALLA MILANESE. "They bring you at dusk," wrote the late Edouard de Pomiane, the French doctor-biologist of the Pasteur Institute whose studies on gastric juices seem to have stimulated his own, "a preparation which seems to you to be made of grains of gold, and you are delighted already by nothing more than the sight of those grains of rice, each one distinct, each one gilded." He was writing of *risotto alla milanese*, which has been called "the national dish of Lombardy," and which is typically Milanese in that it is cooked slowly, in a small amount of liquid, a difficult trick with rice, but more is added little by little during the process as the rice absorbs it.

The invaluable *Vecchia Milano in cucina* quotes two old recipes for *risotto alla milanese* and gives its own contemporary version. From *La cuciniera che insegna a cucinare alla casalinga*, published in 1809, it reproduces this one: "An onion, chopped and puréed, fried in butter until it is the color of a hazelnut, *cervellato* [the no longer available sausage described above], a good consommé, a little meat juice, let it boil for half an hour and pass the broth through a strainer; in this broth put the rice and saffron; cook it until the rice is dry; put in plenty of *grana* cheese, a little pepper and a lot of fresh butter." An 1821 recipe from *Il cuoco senza pretese* runs: "Put a finely chopped small onion in butter, add marrow and butter in proportion, and when the onion has taken on a good golden color without browning, put in the rice and simmer until it has absorbed the liquid. Then add the *cervellato* and immediately the boiling consommé. When it is two-thirds cooked, color it with the saffron dissolved in the consommé; and put in a little mushroom or truffle cut in slices, mix in at the same time some good cheese, and finish the cooking."

The modern recipe is derived from these older ones, using more meat juice than the 1809 recipe "instead of the *cervellato*, which is no longer to be found." Otherwise it is closer to the 1821 recipe, adding beef marrow, which is chopped and cooked separately in the meat juice while the onion is being gilded in butter. The rice is cooked in both of these with the addition of consommé, but the saffron is added, not two-thirds of the way through the cooking, but almost at the end, in order not to dissipate any of its delicate flavor. At the *very* end, a piece of butter is added, for which milk or cream may be substituted. On serving, chopped dried mushrooms or white truffles, cooked separately in a double boiler, are poured over the rice, and the whole is covered abundantly with grated cheese. "The risotto should remain somewhat liquid," says the recipe, "and the grains should be well separated, but light and at the same time creamy. Your true Milanese eats it with a spoon." He also drinks red wine with it, though for most other meal openers he prefers white. Usually he eats it separately, as an independent dish capable of standing alone, as it magnificently is, for *risotto alla milanese* is not a mere side dish, despite its exceptional coupling with *ossobuco*.

It is difficult to stray far from the classic *risotto alla milanese* without discovering that you have produced some other already known and labeled rice dish, there are so many of them. The following are all Lombardy rice dishes, but they are not *all* the Lombardy rice dishes:

Ris con la luganega, rice cooked in comsommé with chopped lean Monza sausage, served heavily peppered with much grated cheese; *ris e corada*, rice boiled in consommé with calf's lungs, bacon, onion and sage; *ris e erba savia*, rice boiled in consommé with onion and sage; *ris e erbion*, rice cooked in consommé with peas and parsley; *ris e erborin*, rice cooked in consommé with parsley and sage, served with much grated cheese; *ris e latt*, one of the simplest dishes imaginable, rice boiled in a mixture of one part of water to five of milk and served, after a ten-minute resting period, with a lump of butter on top; *ris e lentigg*, rice boiled in water with celery, onions and lentils, served with chopped bacon and butter; *ris e lovertis*, rice boiled in consommé, to which is added at the last minute hops browned in butter, served with much grated cheese; *ris e rav*, sliced turnips browned for two minutes in butter, then cooked in consommé, to which the rice is added when it boils, with chopped parsley put in at the last minute; *ris erborin e fideghin di pullaster*, the same as *ris e erborin* with the addition of chopped chicken livers; *ris e spargitt*, young asparagus tips added to rice boiled in consommé ten minutes before the cooking is finished; *ris e verz*, small onions browned in butter, to which is added first chopped bacon, and then a whole cabbage which after browning is covered with consommé, to which the rice is added for the last 15 minutes of cooking, the whole being served with much grated cheese; *ris e zaffran*, onion browned in butter and rice boiled in consommé, to which saffron is added at the last moment, so cooked as to come out creamily semi-liquid (for which reason it is sometimes referred to affectionately in the feminine as *la risotta*), a quality which it will lose if it is not eaten piping hot immediately after cooking; *ris e zucca barucca*, chopped onion and yellow squash, of the type known as *marina*, first browned in butter, then cooked in milk to which the rice is added when it boils; *ris in cagnon*, fried rice with butter, garlic, sage, and much grated cheese, so called because a minute drop of the butter blackened in the frying clings to each grain of rice, making it resemble a certain type of small white black-headed worm called in the local dialect *cagnott*; *risotto alla certosina*, with crayfish, mushrooms and peas; *risotto alla paesana*, a rustic dish from Brianza, in which pieces of crackling are added to a vegetable consommé, after which crushed bacon and onions are browned in butter, followed by the rice, over which the consommé is poured little by little, served with slices of bread coated with grated cheese previously cooked in the consommé, plus much more *grana*; *risotto al salto*, leftover cold rice patted into little cakes and fried in butter; *risotto bianco*, rice boiled in consommé with onion browned in butter and much cheese, an exception to the rule that rice is not a side dish, for this serves as an accompaniment to boiled chicken; *risotto con le rane*, rice and boiled frog's meat pounded into pulp in a mortar, cooked in consommé, with butter, oil, onion, garlic and chopped parsley; *risotto con rognoncini trifolati*, not really a single dish, but a combination of two, since a hollow is made in the top of a *risotto alla milanese*, in which are placed separately cooked veal kidneys; *risotto trifolato*, rice boiled in salted water, drained, and coated with grated cheese, over which a mixture of oil, butter, chopped parsley, garlic and pepper is poured while it is still boiling, producing a foamy effect; *ris, porr e erbett*, the white parts of tender young spring leeks and Swiss chard, cut into pieces, lightly browned in butter, cooked in consommé with rice, and served with much grated cheese; and *verzata di riso alla lombarda*, much the same as *riz e verz*, plus peeled diced tomatoes.

COSTOLETTA ALLA MILANESE (or *cotoletta*) is commonly reputed to be the same thing as the familiar Wiener Schnitzel and to have reached Milan from Vienna, which is wrong on both counts. Vienna got it from Milan, and though Wiener Schnitzel developed from *costoletta*, they are not the same dish. Both are breaded veal, but they are not the same cut. Wiener Schnitzel comes from the fillet (or, for the economically minded, from the leg) and so is never accompanied by bone; the *costoletta* is a loin chop and is therefore served usually, though not invariably, with the bone (purists insist that the bone should be left on). The reason why Milan insists on the loin chop for this dish is that it is felt that only there does the meat provide the proper proportion of fat to lean. Wiener Schnitzel is fried in lard (though sometimes melted butter is poured over it just before serving), *costoletta* is fried in butter.

There is a certain rustic quality about this dish; it may have originated in Brianza, a food-conscious rural region north of Monza; in any case, the ultimate refinement for contemporary *costoletta* fanciers is that the meat should come from a very young Brianza calf. This gives you a small chop, making practical a return to a habit of former times which explains why a frilly paper collar is placed around the projecting bit of bone of the *costoletta*. This is not a mere decoration; it is intended to make it possible to pick up the chop and eat it with the fingers without getting them greasy.

The first step in preparing a Milanese breaded veal chop is to flatten it by pounding it with a wooden paddle. This is to discourage it from curling up in the pan, which makes for uneven cooking, particularly of its crust. In the old days of numerous tireless servants, kitchen maids rose unusually early on *costolette* days to pound the meat in slow regular rhythm for hours on end until all the fibers were broken. Pounding is less persistent nowadays, but the same end is achieved by making incisions all around the edge of the chop, which minimizes curling. It is then soaked in beaten unseasoned egg; some recipes advise putting salt and pepper in the egg, but gourmets insist on the fine point that any seasoning should be applied to the crust after it is formed. The chop is next rolled in bread crumbs before being put into already heated butter, over a high flame to promote quick formation of the crust, after which the flame is lowered. The swiftly established crust thus seals in the juices and keeps the meat inside humid and tender. *Costoletta* is served with lemon wedges.

Costoletta is a very old dish in Milan, dating from long before the time when there were Austrians about. The menu of a banquet served there in 1134 lists *lombolos cum panitio*, breaded loin chop. This alone would make the story that it was copied from the Wiener Schnitzel seem unlikely, but it is not necessary to rely on a simple probability; we have documentary evidence. The Austrian General Joseph Radetzky von Radetz, who became enamored of Milan, of its people, and of its cuisine, discovered *costoletta alla milanese* there, and imported it to Vienna;

he said so in one of his letters.

POLENTA, passed in its earliest forms from the Etruscans to the Romans, is most popular, curiously, in the northern regions of Italy, where Etruscan influence hardly penetrated—hence it is probably a legacy from the Romans. This area grows much maize, unknown to the Romans in the days of *pulmentum,* which has proved ideal for polenta. The dish is so important in Lombardy today that every properly equipped family owns a special copper pot reserved solely for the cooking of polenta, along with a similarly dedicated long stick for stirring it.

Polenta was once considered the lowliest of peasant foods, humbler than bread; but then a polenta cult developed, and by the 18th century Domenica Batacchi of Pisa was introducing it into poetry by describing its preparation in *La rete di Vulcano,* an example followed in the next century by the most famous of Italian novels, Alessandro Manzoni's *I Promessi Sposi*—whose scene is laid in Lombardy.

Polenta is indeed a very simple food—cornmeal mush. Toss a fistful of cornmeal into violently boiling salted water, stir it more or less constantly for an hour, and you have polenta. If you use a quarter more water than the normal proportion (normal is a quart of water per each cup of cornmeal), the result is *polentina,* a thin gruel eaten with milk and, if you like, sugar, for breakfast, like oatmeal. It is clearly not a sophisticated dish, though there are degrees of refinement, depending for instance on whether the meal is coarsely or finely ground, on whether it is removed from the fire while still relatively liquid or allowed to thicken, and above all on the intuition of the cook, which determines whether it emerges from the pot sulky and soggy, or light and, after drying, flaky.

Polenta may be eaten immediately, hot and creamy, or allowed to harden, when it can be sliced like cake. In this form, it serves as the basis for further complications which introduce more interest into what is fundamentally a far from subtle food. One of these is *polenta coi osei*, particularly popular in the provinces of Bergamo and Brescia —natural enough, since this dish is fancied even more in Venezia than in Lombardy, and Bergamo and Brescia were once Venetian. It consists of tiny songbirds, spit-roasted, each wrapped in a band of fat for cooking. Sometimes they are brought to the table with each bird separately bedded on its own slab of polenta moistened with the carefully caught cooking juices; or slices of hardened polenta may be laid under the spit to catch the drippings directly, after which the whole spit is brought in, with its chaplet of little birds skewered together on it, their beady eyes fixed reproachfully on the diner, a sight which has been known to indispose Anglo-Saxons. The birds are too small for successful shooting. They are taken in Italy by luring them into large circular wire enclosures, where flat boards are shied at them; they dash themselves in panic against the wire, in which they become enmeshed by the hundreds, like fish in a gill net.

You can do a limitless number of other tricks with cold polenta slices, using them to accompany various dishes, moistened with whatever they may happen to provide in the way of liquids. Pan juices, tomato sauce, or meat sauces may be poured directly over the polenta (rather uninspiring) or applied to the slices after they have been fried in butter or oil, toasted, or baked; or a filling hot sandwich can be made by placing a thin slice of Gruyère and another of ham between two of polenta and frying the whole. Gnocchi can be made from polenta, starting either from its hot liquid or its cold solid state; or it can produce the relatively elaborate *polenta pasticciata*, polenta pie. To make this, you put into a buttered earthenware oven dish alternating layers of slices of cold polenta and of butter with grated cheese, the top layer being a cheese-butter one, so that when it is baked in the oven a rich golden crust will form on top. It is served hot in the cooking dish. A more sophisticated version cooks mushrooms in their own juice in a double boiler while chopped onion is being browned simultaneously in butter. The mushrooms and onion are then combined with sausage cut into small pieces; as before, layers are built up in an earthenware dish, the cold polenta slices this time alternating with the onion-mushroom-sausage sauce, plus grated *grana* and morsels of Gruyère. This is sprinkled with nutmeg and baked very slowly, an hour being allowed to melt the two sorts of cheese thoroughly. Lately some cooks have taken to adding tomato pulp or extract to the sauce layer. An even richer variety, still based on the alternate layer system, uses béchamel sauce with a little nutmeg, plus sliced mushrooms which have been separately browned in butter (white truffles are often substituted when they are in season), while the top layer is thickly covered with grated cheese or Gruyère. This version is cooked more quickly, 30 minutes in a hot oven, and served like the others in the cooking dish.

BUSECCA is a typical Milanese dish of which foreigners are not particularly conscious, but Italians are so much aware of its importance that they call the Milanese *busecconi*, tripe eaters. *Busecca* is to the Milanese what onion soup is, or used to be, to Parisians: the latter, in the days before the Central Markets moved out of the city, repaired to Les Halles at any time between midnight and dawn to eat onion soup; the Milanese, after the theatre, especially on Saturdays, flock to the restaurants of the Porta Garibaldi and the Porta Ticinese to eat *busecca*.

Busecca is not indiscriminately from any sort of tripe, but from two very precisely defined ingredients, called in dialect *la ciappa e la francese* (in standard Italian, *cuffia* and *ricciolotta*). The dialect phrase means "the cap and the

Frenchwoman." The "cap" is the caul, the animal membrane which covers the brain; the "Frenchwoman" is that section of the stomach lining called curly tripe; since the same word is used for curled hair, the reference is to the elegant coiffure of Parisians. These two are cut into small pieces, boiled lengthily (four hours for veal tripe, six for beef), flavored with onion, celery, carrots and sage, and served on slices of French bread, thickly peppered and covered with grated cheese.

This is the prototype, but the popularity of *busecca* accounts for the existence of a host of vaguely related dishes, some with only a slight resemblance to the original, also called, abusively, *busecca*, or something like it—for instance, there is a type of sausage called *el busecchio*, which contains no tripe, but does have a casing of intestines, which are also included in Milan in the meanings of *busecca*. Occasionally apology is implied for improper use of the word—thus the egg dish (with no tripe) called *busecca matta di uova* means "make-believe *busecca* of egg," and a soup (without tripe) is *busecca matta in brodo*, "make-believe *busecca* in consommé." This latter has at least all the ingredients of *busecca* except the tripe, plus half a cabbage and an increased proportion of celery and carrots, all cooked in consommé and served poured over slices of coarse mixed-flour country bread or polenta. Closer to the original is *busecchin de corada*, which, as it is made in Milan, is more of a sauce than a dish in itself. It substitutes lungs for the tripe, boils them in consommé for an hour with the real *busecca* seasoning plus tomato, and sprinkles them with grated cheese on serving. Also sometimes improperly referred to as *busecca* is the closely related Milanese dish whose correct dialect name is *foijoeu* or *fasoeu de Spagna*, for the Spanish beans which dominate the dish. *Foijoeu*, like *busecca*, uses two specific kinds of tripe, but not the same couple; the curly tripe appears in this dish also, but the other is *fogliolo* (also called *centopelli*), the lining of a cow's third stomach. The dish is cooked very slowly, and by successive stages. First the *fogliolo* is simmered in consommé and meat juice for an hour, together with onion previously browned in butter, diced bacon, tomato, salt and pepper. Then the curly tripe goes in, for another hour's cooking. Carrots and celery are now added, and the cooking continues for two hours more, extra consommé being added from time to time to replace what boils away. The Spanish beans, cooked separately, go in only for the last few minutes of the cooking. The sage of true *busecca* is omitted from this dish, and the amount of consommé used is kept to a minimum so that the result is a thick, barely liquid dish, which is eaten with much grated cheese.

MINESTRONE ALLA MILANESE is identified by that ubiquitous Milan trademark, rice. Other parts of the country put pasta in minestrone, but Milan abhors it. Almost any combination of fresh or dried vegetables can go into the soup, but if it doesn't have rice it isn't *alla milanese*. Its other distinctively Milanese characteristic is slow cooking over a low flame. Four hours are allowed for the formula which follows, with the rice going in last, 20 minutes before the end, and the cabbage an hour before the end; "but," says the recipe, "the result will be better if you cook it on the hearth for six to seven hours." The ingredients called for besides the rice are: cabbage, zucchini squash, carrots, celery, potatoes, beans, tomatoes, bacon, crackling, sage, parsley, rosemary and garlic, simmered in water. The eater sprinkles grated cheese over it abundantly before attacking a soup so thick it is almost a stew.

LESSO MISTO is the familiar Northern dish, of different kinds of meat boiled together, elsewhere usually called *bollito misto*. There is another very important difference. In Lombardy, the better cuts of meat are used for boiling, for the primary consideration is to end with tasty meat, to be eaten alone; in some regions where the main object is to produce a rich bouillon, the meat being almost a by-product, cheaper cuts are used. There the first course of the meal is the soup, the second is the meat, along with any vegetables which have been cooked with it. In Lombardy, no vegetables go into the bouillon; anything served with the meat is prepared separately. Preoccupation with the meat rather than the bouillon means that it is put into water which is already boiling, so that the heat quickly seals in the juices; when a rich bouillon is desired, you start with cold water, allowing the juices to escape into the liquid.

The soul of Milanese boiled meats is beef—indeed, sometimes beef is boiled alone, larded with bits of bacon and a small piece of garlic; or it may be accompanied only by a calf's head. The Milanese are particular about the sort of beef they use. They try to make sure that it has come from an animal which has been adult for at least a year, and which has spent the last six months of its life shut up in a stall being fattened. Thus they can hope to arrive at *"mostos de mangià cont el cugiàa, che' el se sfruguja en boca,"* as the dialect phrase puts it—"meat which can be eaten with a spoon, and dissolves in the mouth."

The real *lesso misto* contains several kinds of meat. A favorite New Year's combination adds to the main chunk of beef the special cut of *biancostato*, which comes from the breast; a calf's head; a capon (this is preferred by the Milanese, but they make do with chicken when capon, obtainable only from November to March, is out of season); and a Modena *zampone*. The amount of water used is barely enough to cover the meat, but more is added from time to time to maintain the level as it boils away. The pot is kept at a steady low boil; violent boiling would cause the meat to disintegrate. The main cut of beef, weighing perhaps 3½ pounds, is cooked for four hours. The *biancostato* (about 2 ¼ pounds) and the capon go into the pot an hour and a half after the beef, and the calf's head (2 ¼ pounds) an hour after that. The *zampone* is cooked separately and only joins the rest when the various meats are sliced and arranged side by side on the diner's plate. A little bouillon is spooned onto each slice of beef, which has been cut across the grain so that it absorbs the liquid immediately. There are a number of standard side dishes to serve with boiled meat—spinach cooked in cream, mashed potatoes, potato salad—but many eaters prefer nothing but a sauce or relish to provide a sharp flavor. The favorites are *salsa verde*, a piquant green sauce, and Cremona *mostarda;* often both are offered.

STUFATO. The favorite meat of Lombardy is beef; most other Italian regions, with the exception of Tuscany, put veal or pork first. Hence another important Milanese dish is *stufato*, well seasoned beef cut into chunks and stewed slowly in a covered pot with white wine and vegetables, usually tomatoes, carrots and celery. There are also pot roasts, in which case the beef is cooked in one piece: *manzo alla lombarda* gives it a preliminary braising in the fat of diced bacon, and then simmers it for 1 ½ to two hours with red wine, chopped parsley, carrots, celery, and onions, in a minimum of stock or water.

The nine most famous dishes of Milan come far from exhausting the city's rich repertory. Here are some others worth noting:

ANTIPASTI: In old Milan, the hors d'oeuvre course consisted solely of cured meats—sausage, smoked tongue, ham and the like, with the occasional addition on special occasions, such as birthdays, of something more elaborate, like a galantine. This was curious, since Lombardy is not really sausage country, with minor local exceptions, such as Monza, the Brianza region north of it, and some of the Al-

pine valleys where local sausages are made and usually consumed on the spot. Sausage is made in Lombardy, of course;
it is made everywhere in Italy; but the types manufactured
in different Lombard towns are usually not original with
them, but are imitations of those made across the southern
border in Emilia-Romagna, which *is* sausage country, with
a vengeance. Mantua does have one sausage of its own,
crespone, otherwise known as *salame di Milano*, which on
being sliced open looks as if it contained grains of that famous Milanese specialty, rice. They are actually pearls of
pork fat, which goes into this sausage in equal quantities
with lean pork and beef, the other ingredients being white
wine, garlic and pepper. It is not, to tell the truth, a particularly notable sausage, no better than par for the course. One
might also add the intestine-encased sausage therefore called
el busecchin (*sanguinaccio* in Italian), though it is hardly
original, being simply a form of that widespread and very
ancient confection, legendarily invented by the Phoenicians, blood pudding, served hot.

Nowadays the antipasto list has lengthened, including
notably pickled or smoked herring, another link with Germanic countries; *giardiniera di sottaceti*, which is onions,
celery, carrots, beans, and yellow and red peppers, boiled
in vinegar, and served cold with more vinegar; *paté di magro* (fast-day pâté), which is tuna, anchovy and butter converted into a paste by being forced through a sieve, mixed
with lemon juice, and chilled before serving with an accompaniment of raw celery; and a variety of preparations
which are likely to appear on the menu in dialect, causing
confusion even among Italians: *la bisetta*, marinated eel
served with lemon wedges; *cocumeritt e peveron in l'asée*
(in Italian, *cetriolini e peperoncini sott'aceto*), pickled
peppers and tiny cucumbers, often served also as a side dish
with boiled meat on All Souls' Day; *gnervitt in insalada*
(*cartilagini lesse in insalata*), pork from the leg ligaments

which has been cooked with *lessi misti* to absorb its flavor, cooled, pressed, seasoned with oil, salt, pepper and sliced raw onion, served sprinkled with chopped parsley; *pessitt cunscià (pesciolini fritti in carpione)*, tiny fish, breaded and fried whole in butter, accompanied by carrots, celery, onion, garlic, sage and pepper, likewise cooked in butter plus oil, with a little vinegar, the whole served cold, sometimes with a slice of polenta; *remulazz e tonn (remolacci col tonno)*, the same as the above with tuna replacing the small fish, plus chopped parsley; *remulazzitt ross e tonn (ravanelli col tonno)*, shredded tuna and sliced radishes with olive oil, pepper and salt.

SOUPS: Lombardy does not offer much variety in soups, except in its minestrone, which offers plenty of variety all by itself; but attention might be called to a group of extremely simple bread soups, all of which begin by soaking bread in water. They range from very liquid soups to a thick gruel, depending on the proportion of water used. *Pancòt (pancotto* in Italian, which means cooked bread) is the simplest, just bread soaked lengthily in water, broken up with a fork, and cooked in the same water with the addition of butter, oil, beef extract, and plenty of salt; it is dusted with grated cheese on serving. *Pancòt maridà* (married) adds an egg or two, beaten together with grated cheese and put uncooked into the tureen, after which soup is poured over it. *Pantrid maridà*, or *panada*, is a variant of this, traditionally served at Easter: finely grated bread is soaked for a quarter hour in consommé, and then cooked in it for five minutes, along with a lump of butter; meanwhile, as before, eggs beaten together with grated cheese have been placed in the tureen; but this time, after the soup has been poured in, it is stirred vigorously, which avoids the formation of lumps but fills the soup with little shreds of egg, so that it looks like the Roman egg-drop soup (*stracciatelle*).

ENTRÉES: Lombardy does not go in much for pasta, preferring rice, a not very marked exception being provided by the provinces of Brescia and Bergamo, probably because of their distance from the rice-growing Po valley. There is a *tortelli alla lombarda*, which is the familiar Emilian dish, with a different and somewhat curious filling—pumpkin, eggs, grated cheese (so far, so good), but then ground macaroons, Verona mustard, finely chopped candied citron and nutmeg! Over this is poured, on serving, melted butter—flavored with sage!—plus, of course, more grated cheese. The Middle Ages could have done no better. Gnocchi are made with white flour, bread crumbs and eggs (*gnocchi di farina*); or with flour and egg yolks (*gnocchi alla gratiroeula*); or with flour, mashed potatoes, and very little egg (*gnocchi di patate*). *Mozzarella milanese* is something of a misnomer; it was probably so named in reference to the Neapolitan *mozzarella in carrozza*, which is made with mozzarella cheese, while the Milanese dish is made with Bel Paese. The cheese is cut into slices which are sprinkled with flour, dipped into beaten egg, coated with bread crumbs, fried on both sides, and eaten as hot as your mouth can stand it. *Crespelle* are pancakes rolled around chopped meat and served with a cheese sauce. Snails are prepared by a complicated process which involves three cookings—brief boiling in salted water with vinegar; browning, coated with cornmeal, in oil and crushed garlic; and finally, baking in the oven in the fat used for the browning, to which are added butter, crushed anchovy fillets, chopped parsley, onion, fennel seeds, nutmeg, and white wine. Frogs, a by-product of the flooded rice fields, are cooked in several ways: fried (*rane fritte*), either very simply, coated with flour, or more elaborately, after being marinated in dry white wine, wrapped in a dough of flour and water, and served with lemon juice; *rann in sguazzètt*, sautéed with dry white wine thickened with flour, butter, and a little water; and *frittura di rane e gamberi con panna e mascarpone*, fried frogs and crayfish with cream and *mascarpone* cheese, which, believe it or not, is a recipe given in a book called *Cooking for Weak Stomachs* (*La cucina degli stomachi deboli*).

FISH: *Agoni*, a local variety of shad, is cooked in sage-flavored butter. *Tinca carpionata* is tench, fried in oil, and served cold after having been marinated in vinegar and white wine, with onion, garlic, sage, and much pepper. Pike from the Po are floured and stewed slowly in fish stock and red wine with celery, carrots and onion. Perch fillets *alla milanese* are rolled in flour, dipped in beaten egg, coated with bread crumbs, and fried on both sides in butter.

MEAT: *Scaloppe alla milanese* seems to mean, outside of Milan, thin slices of veal cooked in the same way as *costoletta alla milanese*, and possibly this does exist in Milan, but I have never happened to meet it there. What I have encountered is *scaloppine*, protean in the diversity of its forms, beginning with the kind of meat used. Unless the menu tells you the contrary, you may assume that *scaloppine* is veal, but in Milan the term may apply also to pork or beef. *Scaloppine* is an exception to the rule that Milanese dishes are cooked slowly, but it is only a half-exception. There are two main techniques for *scaloppine: mezza cottura*, literally, half-cooking, and *cottura completa*, complete cooking. Veal or pork may be cooked by either method, but beef must always undergo *cottura completa;* otherwise it will be too tough.

It is *mezza cottura* which is the exception to the Milanese rule of slow cooking. This means using a high flame for five to ten minutes, the idea being to sear the meat quickly and lock the juices inside, so the interior will be tender and juicy, after which cooking may be finished over a moderate flame. In *mezza cottura* the meat is salted before serving, not before or during the cooking, to prevent it from drying up any of the natural moistness. For *cottura completa*, on the contrary, the meat is seasoned beforehand, and after preliminary browning, the flame is lowered to minimum intensity, and the cooking is finished slowly in a covered pan, usually with the addition of some liquid, for the natural juices of the meat are unlikely to suffice for prolonged cooking.

Among the myriad Milanese treatments of *scaloppine* are the following (all but one are breaded): *scaloppine con i capperi*, cooked in butter and oil, with capers and onion, plus consommé for *cottura completa; scaloppine al formaggio*, moistened with a little white wine, covered with a slice of bland cheese, and cooked in butter; *scaloppine di manzo*, beef, cooked slowly and lengthily (about two hours) in butter and red wine, with tomato extract, cloves and other spices; *scaloppine di manzo all'aceto*, again beef cooked slowly in butter, vinegar and consommé, with onion and bacon; *scaloppine al marsala*, cooked in butter and Marsala wine, plus consommé for *cottura completa; scaloppine con olio e limone*, the one which is not breaded, marinated in peppered oil and lemon juice and cooked in its own juices, to which the marinade is added before the meat dries; *scaloppine alla panna*, sprinkled with white wine and cooked in butter and cream; *scaloppine al pomodoro*, cooked in butter with onion and cut-up tomatoes; *scaloppine al prezzemolo*, cooked in butter, white wine and lemon juice with an abundance of chopped parsley; *scaloppine in salsa piccante*, cooked in butter, plus consommé for *cottura completa*, with pickles and pickled peppers and mushrooms; *scaloppine con la salvia*, cooked in sage-flavored butter; *scaloppine al sedano*, cooked in butter with a slice of prosciutto on top (like Rome's *saltimbocca*) plus celery; *scaloppine all'uccelletto*, veal or pork, sprinkled with white wine and cooked in butter and oil with cut-up tomatoes, plus consommé for *cottura completa*. The list is not complete, nor does it include similar dishes made from different cuts of veal, such as *rostin nagàa (arrostini bagnati col vino*), in which a lightly floured cut from the round, browned in butter with bacon and rosemary, is cooked in white wine.

The list of *polpette* (meatballs) and *polpettone* (meat loaves) is also long: *polpett cont i fasoeu de Spagna*, leftover roast veal or pork, *cotechino* sausage, and *zampone*, served with Spanish beans; *polpett de la serva*, veal and pork with parsley, garlic and egg; *polpett di verz*, beef or pork with cabbage; *polpette di maiale*, pork and pork liver with bread crumbs, grated cheese, parsley, sage, garlic, tomato and egg; *polpette della nonna*, spiced pork and ham; *polpettine Campari*, pork or veal ground together with sausage, bacon, bread, cheese, egg, onion, garlic, parsley, grated cheese and spices; *polpettone di cotechino*, veal or pork with *cotechino* sausage; *polpettone di fegato*, beef, with liver, raw ham and egg; *polpettone di rognone*, veal, veal kidneys, raw ham, sage and rosemary; *polpettone con gli spinacci*, veal with spinach, raw ham, egg, sage and rosemary; *polpettone tritato arrosto*, beef, pork and veal with egg, sage and rosemary; *polpettone tritato a lesso*, beef with mortadella sausage; *polpettone di vitello tartufato*, beef and veal with truffles.

A curiously named dish is *messicani con risotto*, "Mexicans with *risotto*." It consists of strips of veal rolled around a hash filling; this suggests the Mexican habit of wrapping tortillas around various foods, or enclosing them in cylindrical *tacos*, and very possibly accounts for the name. Crustless bread is soaked in milk, the surplus liquid being pressed out of it with the hand, and the bread is chopped together with lean pork, ham fat and garlic, which is then pre-cooked with grated cheese, lemon peel, nutmeg and an egg binder before the veal is wrapped around it. The cylinders of veal with their stuffing are then spit-roasted, basted during the process with white wine and consommé, and are served bedded on *risotto alla milanese* moistened with the cooking juices, another exception to the rule that *risotto* is usually served alone.

Cazzoeula, or *cassoeula*, is pork, pig's foot, crackling and *lugànega* sausage stewed together with cabbage, carrots, celery and onions. A dish traditionally served on All Souls' Day is *ceci con la tempia di maiale del giorno dei Morti*, meat from a pig's head boiled with dried chick peas, onions, carrots, celery, sage and rosemary. *Fritto misto*, often called *frittura mista* in Milan, deep fried in olive oil in most regions, is fried in clarified butter here, all its ingredients being previously coated with egg and bread crumbs; they are chosen from among a list of possibilities of which the most favored are small veal escalopes, calf's liver, brains, cockscombs, artichokes, cauliflower, zucchini, veal sweetbreads, celery, marrow and calf's lungs. Milanese liver (*fegato di vitello alla milanese*) is also breaded, after having been marinated in its seasoning of salt, pepper, chopped parsley and lemon juice; it is fried in butter. Somewhat similarly, calves' brains (*cervelle dorate alla milanese*) are seasoned with salt and pepper, dipped in beaten egg, rolled in bread crumbs, and fried in butter.

POULTRY: Turkey is popular in Lombardy. *Tacchino ripieno alla lombarda* is turkey roasted with a stuffing of the giblets, chopped beef, *lugànega* sausage, bacon, eggs, chestnuts, grated cheese and nutmeg; it is cooked wrapped in slices of ham, with a dusting of sage and rosemary, and is basted with white wine and stock. It is often served at Christmas (when it becomes, in the local dialect, *el pulin natalizi*) traditionally with a somewhat different stuffing— the beef, bacon and eggs are left out, but apple quarters and prunes are added; the overlay of ham slices is also omitted. Milanese families used to keep a special copper pan for this dish alone, *el padelot del pulin*. The fruit in this stuffing recalls a special Milanese fashion of stuffing roast chicken, now, sadly, almost forgotten, *pollo col pieno di noci*, "chicken with its fill of walnuts"; the stuffing is of sausage, apple slices, prunes and a wealth of walnuts.

VEGETABLES: Lombardy shows less interest in vegetables than do many other parts of the country; nevertheless it was here that Julius Caesar discovered, and recorded his appreciation for, asparagus with butter, which is what the Milanese serve it with today. The butter is browned to a dark hazelnut color before being poured over the asparagus, which has been cooked in a specially shaped pan in which the thicker ends of the stalks are submerged in water but leaves the tips protruding, to be cooked by the steam. There also used to be a special serving dish for asparagus, with hollow sides filled with boiling water to keep it warm. *Asparagi al burro* is served nowadays with grated cheese, not the case when Julius Caesar tried it. It is also sometimes accompanied by a fried egg.

Sedano alla milanese is celery served with béchamel sauce and grated cheese; *broccoli o cavolfiori alla milanese*, broccoli or cauliflower first boiled in salted water, then allowed to cool, soaked in egg beaten with grated cheese, coated with bread crumbs, and finally fried in butter. Chard is cooked with cream, spinach with milk or cream, in the latter case in the form of a purée. Onions are served *in agro-dolce* (sweet-and-sour sauce) or in their own cooking juice plus butter, chopped bacon and sage. Peppers, onions and cut-up tomatoes are stewed together, producing an effect like that of the French *ratatouille*. *Scarpazza* is a vegetable tart made from such vegetables as spinach, chard or cabbage, separately or in a mixture, while *scarpazzitt* is a vegetable fritter—for example a ball of previously cooked chopped spinach, which after cooling is floured, dipped in beaten egg, coated with bread crumbs, and deep-fried in butter.

SAUCES: Besides the standard sauces found everywhere in Italy, Milan has a few of its own to accompany its fish, meat and vegetables. What is known simply as Milanese sauce (*salsa alla milanese*) is made of finely chopped ham and veal cooked in butter with a little flour, fennel, Malaga wine and vinegar, plus, if necessary, enough consommé to keep it liquid. This is passed through a sieve and served hot or cold, depending on the dish it goes with. *Salsa di capperi* is made of capers with chopped onion and crushed anchovy fillets cooked slowly with plenty of butter, to which vinegar and thyme are added; it is served hot or cold with fish. *Salsa di cren* is grated horseradish worked into a paste with vinegar, to which salt, or, strangely, sugar, can be added according to taste. *Salsa di pignoeu* is based on pine nuts, to which are added cream, sugar and cinnamon; it accompanies boiled meat, and can be made sharper by adding crustless bread soaked in vinegar, chopped together with anchovy fillets in egg yolk, in which form it is recommended with vegetables. There are also relishes based on somewhat unusual ingredients, like dogberries (*salsa di cornàa*) or wild rose bays (*conserva di grattacù*), arse scratchers, from the aggressive behavior of this thorny plant as you stroll through the woods.

DESSERTS: That Lombardy likes rich desserts might be guessed from the fame of its whipped cream (*lattemiele*). It is less immediately associated with ice cream, as Sicily and Naples are, but in my personal experience the best ice cream I have ever eaten was served me in the Galleria of Milan. Milan also makes a variety of creamy chilled puddings: *bonett de latimel*, of cream and vanilla; *budino al caffé*, mostly egg yolks and coffee; *budino di cioccolato*, chocolate pudding; and *cavollatt* (in Italian, *crema d'uova*, egg cream), made of egg yolks, sugar, cream, and milk, with grated lemon peel, served in a cup.

To attempt to list all the different types of Milanese pastry would be a hopeless task, but here are a few: *Crostata di pere alla milanese* is pear tart enriched with apricot jelly and a dash of rum. *Pastine fantasia alla milanese* are cookies of almonds, egg whites, whole eggs and sugar, seasoned with vanilla and rum or a liqueur, decorated with a half walnut, almonds, candied fruit peel, or jam. *Biscutin d'anis* are anise-flavored cookies. *Charlotte di farina gialla* is an apple tart in a crust of mixed flour and cornmeal. The round puff-paste ring-shaped cookies called *ciambelle*, made in many parts of Italy, turn up in Milan made with cornmeal, either ring-shaped or in the form of the letter S (*offell e ess de pastafrola*); a variant known as *pastafrola de melgon* is made in the S shape only, of a mixture of cornmeal and white flour, with butter, sugar, egg yolks and grated lemon peel.

Milanese desserts often carry picturesque names. Nuns' Chatter (*ciàcer di monegh*) is sweetened ribbon-shaped egg dough flavored with Marsala wine, cooked in boiling oil, and sprinkled with sugar. The Prince's Sweet (*dolce del principe*) is almost an intoxicant: a shell of plum cake and anise-flavored cake soaked in a mixture of alkermess (a liqueur based on cloves and cinnamon), rum, and cognac, is filled with beaten egg yolks, sugar, and *mascarpone* cheese drenched with more rum; it is served chilled. The Princess's Sweet (*dolce della principessa*) is another chilled dessert, rich with egg yolks, cream and ladyfingers, powdered with cinnamon. The *Epouvantable* (frightful; the word was borrowed from French) is another chilled dessert, with layers of ladyfingers moistened with cognac (or coffee) separated by a filling made of egg yolks, butter, sugar, and bitter chocolate. Dead Men's Beans (*fave dei morti*) are little nut-shaped almond-flavored confections with a touch of grappa (Italian brandy), grated lemon peel, and cinnamon. There is also Dead Men's Bread (*pan di mort*), a rich cake of white flour, sugar, chocolate, cocoa, and white wine, in which are embedded bits of almond, pine nuts, candied citron and orange peel, and various spices. *Oss de mord* (in Italian, *ossa da mordere*) might sound as though it belongs to the same funereally named category, but it means only "bones to bite;" they are stick-shaped almond cookies with a little lemon peel.

Mascarpone cream cheese is not only eaten as a dessert on its own, but also enters into a variety of combinations: with zabaglione; as a chilled filling for a mold of spongy cake; in *mastrich*, a mixture of *mascarpone*, egg yolks, and sugar, flavored with rum and grated lemon peel, anointed with olive oil, and served chilled with a thick chocolate sauce; or as a soufflé, of *mascarpone*, sugar, cinnamon and eggs, with the whites and yolks beaten separately.

Milanese, like other Italians, often end the meal with fresh fruit for dessert, but don't ask for figs. They have been a painful subject for Milanese ever since 1162, when the Emperor Frederick Barbarossa subdued a revolt during which his wife had been driven ignominiously out of the city, seated backside-to on an aged mule. Having captured the ringleaders, Barbarossa gave them their choice of being hanged or saving themselves by presenting a fig to the executioner as a ransom—a fig which had to be obtained in somewhat special fashion. It was stuck into the rear of the Empress's mule. The prisoner had to extract it with his teeth, bring it to the executioner with the words, *"Ecco il fico,"* and then return it to its place in the same fashion, ready for the next comer. The story says that some of the prisoners let themselves be hanged. In any case, if you want to get into trouble in Milan today, glare at a Milanese and execute a familiar Italian gesture—make a fist with your thumb thrust out between the index and middle fingers and bite the thumb. This sign is known as "making the fig." It was an insult in Shakespeare's time (*Romeo and Juliet*, Act 1, Scene 1) and it is an insult in Milan today.

The Milanese repertory is long, but it does not cover quite all of the specialties of Lombardy. Different conditions of climate and terrain, and above all, differing historical backgrounds, account for these additions to the cuisine of Lombardy, some of which exist even in the province of Milan itself. Lodi, the ancient Laus Pompeia, lying in a grazing district so rich that the Romans called it *fertilissima*, enjoys a partly independent style of cooking, based on the lavish use of the milk and milk products which it possesses in such plenty. Monza, although it is only ten miles from Milan, has also managed to retain a certain culinary individuality despite the formidable influence of the capital. Its gastronomic importance results largely from the fact that it is on the edge of a food-originating territory, the Brianza, but the city itself deserves credit for at least two inventions—its sausages and *savoiarda*. This is a sort of catchall meat-and-fish salad, which combines the meatiest morsels from a calf's head, boiled pork, and cured tongue, with tuna fish and salty anchovy fillets, seasoned with pickles, pickled red and yellow peppers, capers and chopped parsley, the whole doused with plain salad dressing.

The Brianza starts north of Monza and pushes into the province of Como as far as the two southern tips of its lake. It raises the best beef in Lombardy. Determinedly rustic, its contributions to the menu are almost all country fare. Brianza has its own fashion of serving polenta, *polenta cunscia*. A layer of hot semi-liquid cornmeal polenta is poured into a soup dish. A film of crushed garlic cooked in much butter is then poured over this, and it is sprinkled with grated cheese; then comes another layer of polenta, of garlic butter, and of grated cheese; and so on, until the eater decides he has had enough. This is surely rustic, and so is *laciada*, a hearthcake studded with a few grape seeds and fried in linseed oil; this is traditionally eaten at corn husking bees. *Laciaditt* is a variant fried in butter, and dusted with lemon-flavored sugar and spices, such as cinnamon or nutmeg.

The Po-side provinces offer fewer dishes of their own than one might expect from their frequently independent and always very charged histories. The province of Pavia, for instance, might reasonably have been expected to contribute more than it has, both because of its agricultural importance and because of its long and brilliant history. Its capital city has been important ever since recorded history began, and there was a period when Pavia seemed more likely than Milan to lead Lombardy.

More than its history, the geography of Pavia should have turned it toward gastronomic greatness. The life of the province is shaped by its watercourses. Italy's largest river, the Po, cuts west to east across the center of the province. The Ticino cuts north to south on its way to the Po, passing through Pavia, where it is joined by the Naviglione, so important for irrigation and the transportation of crops. The eastern boundary of the province is formed by the north-south Sesia, which also ends in the Po. These rivers split the province into three parts. The northwest corner, boxed in by the Sesia, the Ticino and the Po, is the Lomellina area, named for Lomello, a town on another Pavese river, the Agogno, but it is Mortara which is the agricultural market for the great crop of the Lomellina—rice. Pass here in May, through a boundless drowned countryside, and you will think the famous film, *Bitter Rice,* is being re-enacted before your eyes. Hip-booted women advance slowly in long lines through the flooded fields, herons and green ibises wade in them; you may even catch a glimpse of a water buffalo. On the other side of the Ticino, the northwestern corner of the province is the Pavese Plain, highly fertile land which produces much fodder and other crops as well. This is the home of the Pavia peach, a firm-fleshed clingstone fruit, of which some varieties are white and others red. The pointed southern half of the province is the Oltrepò, which means "across the Po," an exact description of its location. It grows a good deal of wheat, and is one of the best wine-producing areas in Lombardy—faint praise, since Lombardy is not top-notch wine country.

Yet this rich agricultural region has only two original food specialties sufficiently important to need mention here. One is a sausage, *salame di Varsi*, one of the few Lombardy offers; the other, more widely known, is a humble dish which spread into private homes throughout Italy, until fairly recently the only place where you were likely to meet it; but it has now emerged onto restaurant menus. This is *zuppa pavese*, whose origin is supposed to be historical. The story goes that when François I was being held prisoner after the battle of Pavia, a peasant girl who had been told to take a bowl of soup to the king improved it by adding an egg to it. However that may be, Pavia soup today is consommé plus an egg. Slices of bread are first fried in butter and sprinkled thickly with Parmesan cheese. One slice is placed in each soup plate, with the yolk of an egg on it. (Persons inexpert at separating yolks from whites often use the whole egg). The hot consommé is then poured over the egg, carefully, in order not to break it (pour it through a fine strainer and the risk is less). The only cooking the egg gets results from the heat of the consommé, which means that it is nearly raw. Those who don't like raw egg yolks can always poach the egg in the consommé before placing it on the bread.

Cremona, the city of the violin, has played its history tremolo. Jumping from one string to another, it has frequently changed sides, or tried to be on both at once or on neither, and as a result has been razed with excessive frequency. It still retains the oval form and medieval fortifications of its embattled days, of which another reminder in its province is the square dungeon at Zighettone in which François I was confined after the battle of Pavia.

The province of Cremona has a vocation for agriculture, carried on here in a fashion more modern than anywhere else in Italy—including even the rest of Lombardy—with the aid of the finest agricultural machinery and the most advanced techniques; the town of Crema is particularly noted as the spearhead of avant-garde agriculture. Butter and cheese are among the province's leading food products. The Po provides it lavishly with sturgeon, carp and tench; the fields leave enough space for ground cover to endow it generously with small game, especially hare and quail. It casts a gastronomic eye across the river to Emilia-Romagna on the other side, which it emulates in the making of sausage (including such otherwise localized types as *zampone* and *cotechino*); and in its cooking it imitates both Emilia-Romagna and Milan, for Cremona curiously has no cuisine of its own—curiously, for it is the birthplace of Bartolomeo Sacchi, alias Platina, author of that earliest of post-Roman cookbooks, *De Honesta Voluptate et Valetudine*, of which the first manuscript edition, also curiously, is in Boston. Cremona may have been gastronomically important in Sacchi's day, but now it has only two specialties to its credit, neither of them in the mainstream, since one is a relish and the other a dessert which actually comes more under the category of candy.

The first is *mostarda*, which apparently can be made successfully nowhere else. Other cities have tried to reproduce it, but with no more than mediocre results, either for lack of know-how, or perhaps only because the public is unwilling to accept it from anywhere else. It is a mixture of fruits preserved in sugary syrup, whole or in chunks, depending on their size—cherries, grapes, figs, plums, pears, apricots, melons (and pumpkin!) with mustard oil and other seasonings, all stirred together with wooden paddles. It seems an alarming combination at first blush, but think of chutney, which, indeed, *mostarda* resembles. It marries best of all with *lesso misto*, providing a welcome piquancy to offset the blandness of boiled meat. It takes the curse off the greasiness sometimes noticeable in eel; and for the benefit of Americans, it may be added that in general it is appropriate whenever cranberry sauce is.

Mostarda goes far back in time, and is apparently a development of the process of making ordinary mustard. In antiquity, the use of mustard began in the form of mustard seeds preserved in vinegar. Then the seeds were crushed into a sort of flour and preserved in wine must—the first step toward the fruit-mustard combination. There is a recipe in that early cookbook of Platina which reads: "Ye mustard thou wilt crush wetted with water before, and then thou wilt add in this almonds, and immediately thou wilt crush all together with ye soft part of ye moistened bread; finally, everything dissolved in verjuice or strong vinegar, thou wilt make it to pass through ye strainer."

You can buy Cremona *mostarda di frutta* in glass jars or cans anywhere in Italy, but it is never as good as when ladled out of an open wooden tub in a grocery store in Cremona or Milan.

Cremona's other contribution to the Italian repertory is *torrone*, a rich, not to say cloying, form of nougat made from egg whites, honey, sugar, toasted almonds and candied fruit, consumed with particular avidity at the Christmas season. The name, and perhaps the origin, of *torrone* dates from a banquet given in Cremona to celebrate a most memorable event, the inception of a new dynasty by the wedding of Bianca Maria Visconti and Francesco Sforza. Its high point was a dessert which reproduced, in egg whites, honey, sugar and almonds, the 12th-century campanile of Cremona's triple-naved cathedral, the highest (374 feet) in Italy. It is called the Torrazzo—hence *torrone*. Or at least this is the way the Cremonese tell it. Some other parts of the country provide different accounts both of the origin of the dish and of its name.

The ancient city of Mantua has been inhabited since Neolithic times. It knew the Etruscans and the Gauls before the Romans arrived and made it a municipality. The one fact everyone knows about Mantua dates from Roman times, that Virgil was born there, which is not quite true, though Virgil himself composed the epitaph containing the assertion: *Mantua me genuit*, Mantua gave me birth. Actually he was born a few miles away, at Andes, which ceased to exist when Napoleon razed it to the ground; its ancient site is now occupied by Pietolo.

Mantua is an agricultural center whose province grows beets for its sugar refineries, mulberry trees for the production of silkworms, wheat, and wine. At Gonzaga, the Fiera Millenaria, first opened in 1580 by Duke Guglielmo, continues to be held yearly, the second week in September, and remains one of the most important agricultural fairs in the Po valley, with special days devoted to bread and to wine. But Mantua's agricultural importance has not inspired an independent cuisine, though Lombards familiar only with their own province's cooking often credit Mantua with originality. The fact is that while Mantuan cooking departs considerably from that of Lombardy in general, it does so not because of local originality, but because Mantua has escaped from the gravitational pull of the Milanese kitchen only by becoming a satellite of Emilia-Romagna. Mantuan cooking is basically Emilian cooking; and the only specialty we need to note for this province proves it. It is *salame dell' Oltrepò*, a sausage which imitates those of Emilia, not surprisingly, since the Oltrepò (across the Po) area of Mantua is on the Emilian side of the river, geographically though not politically associated with Emilian territory.

We move from Emilian to Venetian influence in the

provinces of Bergamo and Brescia, which were ruled by Venice for nearly three centuries; but its positive effects were less marked in cooking than in culture. The two provinces did not adopt the Venetian cuisine, but their subtraction from Milanese domination encouraged latitude in local modification of Lombard tendencies.

Brescia, *città delle belle fontane* (it still has 72 public fountains), is the ancient Brixia, a city of the Celtic Cenomani before it submitted to the Romans in 225 B.C. It shares with Bergamo a common fondness for *polenta coi osei*. Brescia has its own variant of *manzo alla lombarda*, much more rustic than the ordinary version, with its citified accompaniment of celery, carrots and chopped parsley. *Manzo alla bresciana* leaves all of these out. It is a pot roast for which the beef, after being braised in bacon fat, is cooked in red wine with chopped salt pork, garlic and butter. What is true of this dish is true in general of Brescia and Bergamo cooking; it is made up of Lombard dishes cooked in a more rural style.

Countrified cooking, and independence of the influence of Milan, is even more marked in the northern provinces, subject to the isolation always found in mountainous country, while less fertile soil and a sharper climate also make for differences. These are less evident in the province of Como, whose lake imposes a moderating influence on temperatures over its whole territory, while its popularity as a vacation spot makes it more urban than other lake resorts. Varese, west of Como, is affected to some extent by the climatic effects of its lakes also, but is less frequented by outsiders and therefore freer of the influence of Milan. Sondrio, the northernmost, is the most individualistic in its cooking.

Varese, the smallest province of Lombardy, is fortunate in having almost no history. In the neighborhood of Lake Varese, a prized specialty is *risotto* with eels, cooked in a highly spiced sauce, made, when they are in season, with the young eels of the lake. A January dish is *rostisciada*, strips of pork and sausage in a herb-and-spice onion sauce. Kid is marinated in a mixture so rich in herbs that it looks as if it has been coated with a green moss. *Lo stuà in cônscia* is a local variety of *stufato*, for which the beef is marinated in wine, herbs and spices for five days before cooking. Desserts utilize the chestnuts of the province, which turn up either in an unctuous cream eaten with milk and sugar, or in flour used to produce a variety of cakes and cookies.

Como is more frequented, and has been since Roman times, when it was called Comum. Its cooking does not differ much from that of Milan, except when it utilizes its own special foods. Examples are *missoltitt* and *scigollitt*, both evidently dialect names. The first is called in Italian *agoni seccati all'aria;* this is the shad-like fish of the lake, dried in the sun and the lake breezes, and heated, rather than cooked, before serving with vinegar. The other is *cipolline sott' aceto* in Italian, tiny onions grown on the shore of the lake, which are steeped for at least a week in vinegar perfumed with bay leaf, thyme, cloves, cinnamon, pepper and garlic before eating.

Sondrio, backed up against the towering wall of the Alps, has even less history than Varese. In its torrents, ponds, and the river Adda, Sondrio fishes trout of exquisite flavor; and its wild Alpine country is rich in game, some of it of kinds not plentiful elsewhere—not only hare and deer, but also heather hen and chamois. The mushrooms grown in the valleys around Morbegno are reputed to be among the tastiest in Italy; they are cooked fresh in a variety of ways, and are also one of the products which furnish Morbegno's flourishing canning industry, along with the fruit, especially pears and apples, grown here. In this area, curiously, is a population island, a community of French descent, refugees there since Carolingian times.

Sondrio boasts first of all of two special dishes, *polenta taragna* and *pizzòcher*. *Polenta taragna*, a specialty of the Valtellina valley, is made with a large amount of buckwheat flour and a little cornmeal, for buckwheat, less productive than other grains on rich bottomland, grows excellently on poorer hilly soils, like those of central Asia, where it originated (which is why it is called Tartar wheat in some countries, though in Italy it is Saracen wheat). To make *polenta taragna*, you bring salted water to a boil; the buckwheat flour, mixed with a small amount of cornmeal, is then poured into it little by little; you wait for each handful to become absorbed before adding the next. It is stirred constantly until it has become quite thick, for it is destined to harden and be sliced for eating, with melted butter and grated cheese poured over the slices.

Pizzòcher is made mostly of buckwheat flour too, but this time with a slight admixture of white wheat flour. A dough is made with this plus water and salt, rolled into sheets, and cut into small pieces. These are then boiled in water, along with potatoes and cut-up leeks, until they are half done. A layer of the dough, potatoes and leeks is then placed in a buttered oven dish, covered with a layer of grated cheese in melted butter, then with another layer of pasta, of cheese, and so on until the dish is full.

Other Valtellina specialties are *malfàtt o strozza pret*, a local form of pasta; *lumache alla cappuccina*, snails boiled with olive oil, salt and pepper; and *chisciòo* or *cicc*, a specialty of Tirano, an unsweetened tart of buckwheat flour, filled with any semi-fat cheese cut into strips, eaten hot. With Valtellina meals you are likely to be served *brazadèl*, bread made of barley; dark-colored and tasty, it keeps well and is palatable even dry.

Pastry desserts are popular. *Biscieùla* is a less rich version of *panettone*, but it does not play *panettone's* Christmas role; this falls to *cupeta*, made of white flour, honey, sugar and crushed walnuts, combined to make a soft bun. *Sciatt*, which means "tails" in the local dialect, are tail-shaped fritters of buckwheat flour with a touch of *grappa* in it, rolled around a strip of cheese, fried in lard, sugared, and eaten as hot as you can stand it.

The province of Sondrio is one of those rare regions of Lombardy which has created its own sausages—homemade *salame*, *mortadella di fegato* (mortadella with liver in it), and *bondiola*.

Wine is grown almost everywhere in Lombardy, but it is not remarkable for its quality, a fact to which Lombardy growers have resigned themselves, for wine production there is decreasing. Vineyard acreage is being reduced especially in the Po valley plain, which is simply common sense: wine likes hills; flatland does not produce particularly good wine; so the Po valley winegrowers are well advised to pull up vines from soil which can never produce anything but thin vintages and use it instead for crops to which it is better fitted.

There are, however, three areas in Lombardy which produce better wine than the regional average. Two of them, Pavia and Brescia, are prolongations of wine-producing areas more important on the far side of the Lombardy border. But the third, and best, is purely Lombard. This is the Valtellina valley in the province of Sondrio, which owes nothing to outcroppings from alien territory.

Wine has been cultivated here for a long time if it is true, as has been claimed, that the almost unknown Retico comes from here and that it is the same wine which was much appreciated by the Emperor Augustus. In any case, really ancient or only moderately so, the wines of Valtellina are interesting. Most of them are reds.

The best is probably Sassella, the name of a grape, which is somewhat misleading, for 85 percent of the juice which grows into Sassella wine comes from the Nebbiolo grape, the favorite here as in Piedmont; and of the other 15 per cent, not all is Sassella either—three other types of grape may enter into it in varying proportions. At any rate, Sassella contains 12 to 13 degrees of alcohol, is a bright ruby red which throws off orange reflections as the wine grows older, and has a delicate fragrance of roses. It should be aged at least three years, and is better after six. Grumello is a close second; it is made from the same blend of grapes, grown on territory adjacent to that of Sassella, and is barely distinguishable from it after four years in the bottle, when it is at its best. Inferno comes third in the same family, a little lighter-bodied (11 to 12 degrees), with an aftertaste of hazelnuts; it requires three years to mature. The other Valtellina wines are less distinguished—Villa (or Perla Villa) 12 to 12.5 degrees, tart, *frizzante;* Fracia, 12 to 13 degrees, of which a white (12.5 to 13 degrees) also exists. Valgella is only so-so. Forzato di Valtellina is that abomination, a sweet red dessert wine. Recently a more recommendable white dessert wine has been coming into favor, Sfurzat, which requires long aging to reach its full 15 to 16 degrees of alcohol, its almost orange color, and its rich full sweet flavor. The Valtellina ages and stores its wine in the many cool natural caves of the area.

You may be offered, in the Valtellina, if you ask for a glass of wine, a *rosumado.* Before you accept, you might want to know what that means. It is red wine into which an egg yolk and sugar have been beaten. Possibly it is not ideal from the gourmet's point of view, but it's a wonderful pick-me-up.

One of the reasons why the cooking of Pavia often shows affinity with that of Piedmont may be that both are influenced by the same winegrowing area. Why the wine is so much better on the Piedmont side of the border than across it, in the Oltrepò region of Pavia, is a mystery. The Pavese wines cannot touch those of Piedmont, but they are never-

theless not at all bad. Often they are made from the same
Barbera grape as some Piedmont wines, but there is also a
local grape, called *ovattina, bonarda,* or *uva rara,* the rare
grape. The region goes in for picturesque names: Barba-
carlo (or Barbagallo), Charlie's Whiskers, a heavy (12 to
14 degrees) bright red, which goes well with poultry; But-
tafuoco, firebug, 13 to 14 degrees, bright red, a natural
sparkler which makes a noise when poured like the crackling of a fire, hence its name; Sangue di Giuda (Blood of
Judas), 12 to 13 degrees, bright red, a little sweet, and,
again, a natural sparkler.

Casteggio is a center for light dry white wines: the better vintages are sold under a modernized form of the town's
Latin name, Clastidium, which has been Italianized into
Clastidio; it comes in white, rosé and red. A very sweet
dessert wine made here goes all the way back to Roman
times, and is known as Clastidium Gran Riserva. Near
Casteggio also are the vineyards which produce the recommendable Frecciarossa vintages: a delicate tart pale yellow
wine, 12 to 12.5 degrees, which improves with age; an amber yellow demi-sec, 12 to 13 degrees, with a fruity bouquet; a pleasant rosé, 11 to 12 degrees; and a smooth fragrant bright ruby-red wine of 12 to 13 degrees, excellent
with game.

Just as the Oltrepò region of Pavia lies on the edge of the
renowned Piedmont wine country, so that of the Brescian
Lake Garda region is on the fringe of the Venetian territory
which produces the reputed Bardolino and Soave wines.
Chiaretto del Garda, 11 to 12 degres, is a rosé, almond-
flavored, with a slight but not disagreeable bitterness; Rosso
Riviera del Garda, 11 to 12 degrees, a bright clear ruby in
color, is dry, also with an almond flavor and a slightly bitter aftertaste; Tocai del Garda, 13 to 14 degrees, is a sweetish greenish-yellow wine; Pusterla Bianco, 10.5 to 12.5
degrees, is a dry white; and Lugano, possibly the most

agreeable white wine of Lombardy, 11 to 12.5 degrees, is a pale golden yellow—a perfect accompaniment for the fish from its lake.

Sondrio makes excellent beer, a result of the purity of the water of its mountain streams.

It is Piedmont which is usually thought of as *aperitivo* country, but Lombardy has one with a world-wide reputation. This is Campari, made in Milan since 1867 by the family of that name, scarlet in color and a trifle bitter in taste. And for a stirrup cup, here is a drink invented in the same year as Campari—citron peel and small pieces of the fruit itself, steeped lengthily in heavily sugared eau de vie with a dash of cochineal dye for coloring. Its name is *Perfetto Amore*—perfect love.

Piedmont and the Valle d'Aosta

I f Milan is not the hardest-working city in Italy, then
Turin is. The capital of Piedmont, Turin (Torino in
Italian), like Milan a northern city possessed of northern
dynamism, has thrown the major part of its energy into
business; but Turin diverted some of it into politics. "Piedmont gave birth to Italy," its citizens claim. It is true that
when Italy was finally united after centuries of fragmentation, its first king was Vittorio Emmanuele II, of Piedmont's
House of Savoy, which originated about 1000 A.D.; and the
architect of unification was Piedmont's Prime Minister,
Count Camillo Benso di Cavour, "Anglo-Saxon in his
thinking and Gallic in his language."

Good Eating

N

SWITZERLAND

LOMBAR

LAKE
MAGGIORE

Novara

LAKE ORTA

PIEDMONT

POLENTA GRASSA
GLANDUIA

TENCH
TROUT IN BIANCO

Vercelli
GATTINARA WINE
GHEMME WINE

RISO E CECI
RISO TO WITH QUAIL
RICE AND MILK SOUP

Aosta

DISHES
SOUPE À LA VALPELLINENTSE
RICE AND CHESTNUT SOUP
SOUPE À LA COGNEINTZE
SELUPA DE STAMPATO ALLA VALDIEROSE
COSTE DE STAMPATO ALLA VALDIEROSE
IBEX MARMOT
LO SPELL
PRESERVED PORK HEAD MEAT
CHILLE
CARBONNADE
PIANDOLEIN
FAVÒ
PLANTZÉ
BLANC MANGE

DRINKS
CAREMA WINE
DONNA WINE
TORETTA WINE
ENFER WINE
BLANC DE MORGEX WINE
MONTOUVERT WINE
MASCATO DE CHAMBAVE WINE
GRAPPA (BRANDY)
BEER

HIGH
GROWING
RYE
AND
BARLEY

Monte Rosa

TORCETTINI
TOMÉ
CHEESE
BUTTER

Valtournanche

VALLE D'AOSTA

SNOW LETTUCE
SALIGNON CHEESE
REBLÉQUE CHEESE
SERAS CHEESE

FONTINA CHEESE
FONDUTA

GRAN PARADISO RANGE

Great
St. Bernard
Pass

CHAMOIS
HARE
PHEASANT
QUAIL

BOUDINS
POTATOES

CHESTNUTS
SAUSAGE
MORTZETTA
HONEY
IBEX

APPLES
PEARS

Mont Blanc

WILD BOAR
CHOCOLATE
KISSES

Little St. Bernard Pass

SAVOY OMELETTE
SAVOY TROUT

BOLLITO MISTO

FRANC

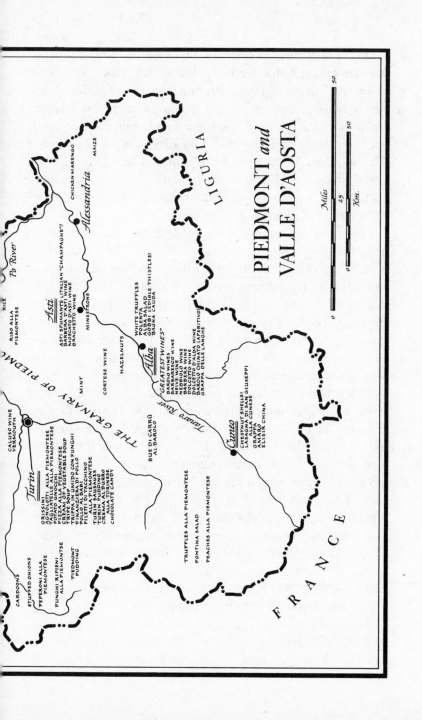

PIEDMONT *and*
VALLE D'AOSTA

LIGURIA

FRANCE

Po River

RICE

RISO ALLA
PIEMONTESE

Asti

ASTI SPUMANTE (ITALIAN "CHAMPAGNE")
BARBERA D'ASTI WINE
MOSCATO D'ASTI WINE
BRACHETTO WINE

MINESTRONE

CHICKEN MARENGO

Alessandria

MAIZE

WHITE TRUFFLES
ALBA SALAD
GOBBI (EDIBLE THISTLES)
BAGNA CAUDA

Alba

"GREATEST WINES"
BAROLO WINE
BARBARESCO WINE
NEIVE WINE
NEBIOLO WINE
BARBERA WINE
DOLCETTO WINE
DOLCETTO D'ALBA WINE
BAROLO CHINATO (APERITIVO)
GRAPPA DELLE LANGHE

CORTESE WINE

HAZELNUTS

MINT

Tanaro River

Cuneo

CHESTNUT SHELLS;
LASAGNA DI SAN GIUSEPPI
ALLA CUNEESE
GRAPPA
ELISIR CHINA

Turin

CALUSO WINE
VERMOUTH

THE GRANARY OF PIEDMON

GRISSINI ALLA PIEMONTESE
AGNOLOTTI ALLA PIEMONTESE
TAGLIATELLE ALLA PIEMONTESE
POTATO GNOCCHI
PIZZA ALLA PIEMONTESE
CREAM SOUP
TRIPE SOUP VEGETABLE SOUP
TRIPPA IN UMIDO CON FUNGHI
FINANZIERA DI POLLO
POLLO AL BABI
FILETTI DI TACCHINO
ALLA PIEMONTESE
TURIN SAUSAGES
TURIN PUDDING
CREMA ALBURRO
ALLA TORINESE
CHOCOLATE CANDY

BUE DI CARRÙ
AL BAROLO

CARDOONS

STUFFED ONIONS

PEPERONI ALLA
PIEMONTESE

FUNGHI RIPIENI
ALLA PIEMONTESE

PIEDMONT
PUDDING

TRUFFLES ALLA PIEMONTESE

FONTINA SALAD

PEACHES ALLA PIEMONTESE

Miles

Km.

0   25   50

0   50

The pre-Roman history of Piedmont is practically unknown. It was Celtic territory, but which tribes were there is by no means certain. Presumably the Taurini dominated when Augustus set up a colony there (the future Piedmont was part of Cisalpine Gaul, not Roman territory), otherwise he would not have named it Augusta Taurinorum, which would become Turin. As for the name Piedmont (Piemonte in Italian), that goes back only to the 13th century, when the territory was called Pedemontium, or Pedemons in Low Latin.

Piedmont is dominated by mountains. One-third of its area, the north, is high mountain country; the central third is hilly; only the south is plain. This would not seem to leave much scope for agriculture, but Piedmont has developed the art of making crops climb hills. Wine grapes are grown up to 4,000 feet, rye and barley up to 6,000, and good pasturage exists even 9,000 feet up. True, we are on the southern side of the Alps here, protected from northern winds by the highest mountain wall in Europe.

What plain there is is fertile, for the Po starts its course here, with Piedmont's private river, the Tanaro, flowing into it. As in Lombardy, the Po valley is rice country; and as in Lombardy, one of the by-products of the flooded rice fields is frogs, eaten fried or in soup. Another by-product is carp, which are bred artificially in the same waters. Trout are found of course in the swift mountain streams. Maize is an important crop and so is barley; wheat, rye, oats, potatoes, sugar beets, other vegetables and forage crops follow. Characteristic of Piedmont is the large farm which does not belong to a single proprietor; its cluster of farm buildings is inhabited by several families, each working its land from the common headquarters.

Mountain country, because of its compartmentation, makes for individualism, and the Piedmontese character has been so deeply stamped by it that local concentration on single products seems peculiarly marked here, exemplified by the small sweet russet *renette* apples and *Martin secco* pears of the Aosta valley, the cherries of Cereseto and Pecetto, the peaches of Canale, the strawberries of San Mauro, the mushrooms of Rifreddo and Sanfront, the hazelnuts of Alba, the walnuts of Feisuglio, the chestnuts of Garessio—and several much more unusual specialties. Nizza Monferrato produces *gobbi*, edible thistles, while several other towns offer the related white cardoons. Between Carmagnola and Pancalieri, in the province of Turin, there are a solid seven or eight miles of fields which grow nothing but mint. The most curious of all is Cuneo, where there is a picturesque market dealing only in chestnuts shells—not chestnuts, just the shells.

Piedmont consists of seven provinces, including the Valle d'Aosta, whose special character is recognized officially by the fact that it is politically an autonomous district. The southern tier, west to east, is composed of Cuneo, Asti and Alessandria. The topography of Cuneo is curious: fourteen fertile valleys fan out from the capital city. The area from Savigliano, north of Cuneo, to Chivasso, which is is in the province of Turin, is known as "the granary of Piedmont." The name of Asti will no doubt remind most persons of Asti Spumante, the sparkling sweetish white wine which comes from here, the nearest thing Italy has to champagne; it is not very near. Alessandria is chiefly agricultural—maize on the plains, vines on the hillsides.

The next tier, to the north, is composed, still west to east, of Turin, Vercelli and Novara, the last two being long narrow provinces which push up into the high mountains, especially Novara, which reaches the Swiss frontier. Turin is where most of the industry of the region is concentrated, though the big grain-growing area which starts in Cuneo reaches up into it from the south. Despite this, Vercelli and Novara outdo it as cereal farmers. Between them they produce three-quarters of all the rice grown in Italy, with Vercelli (from Wer-Celt, its name when it was founded by Celts in 600 B.C.) well in the lead; it grows all by itself 45 percent of the entire national production—350,000 tons of rice per year, plus another 125,000 tons of maize, oats and rye. Local industries husk and package these grains for export.

Piedmont goes in for food festivals. This is polenta country, so Monasteri Bormida and Bubbi, side by side in the Asti district, attract great crowds every year to the festival of the Polentone, or Big Polenta, a Homeric banquet of polenta with various meats. Morozzo (Cuneo) holds a capon festival on Christmas week. In the Asti area there are corn husking bees, as in the United States, and barn dances at vintage time.

To speak of Piedmontese cooking is misleading; the gastronomic and political frontiers do not coincide. There are two main cuisines in Piedmont. One is the cooking of certain of the larger cities and of the lower altitudes—say the areas east of Cuneo but not including it, and south of Turin, which does include the capital. Foreigners are likely to think of this as typical of Piedmont, for it is found in the most traveled parts of the country; but it embodies a minimum of local inspiration. It leans heavily on the cooking of Lombardy and more lightly on that of France, whose example is admired and emulated in Piedmont. The cooking of Turin is the most affected of all by these outside influences (Turin has been called "the most Italian city of France"), which is why you will find more interesting and more characteristic Piedmontese cooking in Cuneo, Asti and Alba than in the capital.

North of Turin, as you get deep into the mountains, you meet a different cuisine, which is really native. It depends on food resources peculiar to the region (white truffles) or concoctions born of the local genius and found nowhere else (*bagna cauda*); and when there are echoes of dishes from across the border, they are not so much borrowings as sharings with adjacent areas whose similar geography has produced similar culinary results (*fonduta*). Given that geography, this indigenous Piedmontese cuisine is, of course, mountain cooking—solid food to provide fuel for men who work hard at energy-burning altitudes and for much of the year have to combat cold—hence, roasts and boiled meat, lively seasoning, a goodly amount of garlic, the filling rib-sticking polenta, and a yearning for sweets, since sugar is a quick energy provider; it is no accident that Piedmont is famous for its confectionery. The nature of Piedmontese mountain dishes has also been shaped by what might be called a mechanical accident—it took form at a period when in the mountain areas few persons had ovens. They were dependent first of all on the frying pan and after that on the kettle (for boiling meat or making thick warming soups).

Piedmontese mountain food is heavy but Piedmontese are not heavy eaters. They are preserved from gluttony because they are of sober northern stock, relatively reserved, lacking the exuberance of more southerly peoples, and not given to excess. Their cooking is not sophisticated; it is tasty and (this is the key word) healthy.

The most exclusive food product of Piedmont is the white truffle, whose highly local character is indicated by its name, *trifola d'Alba*, for the region around Alba, especially south of it, is the home ground of the white truffle. It is a rarity, found, so far as I know, nowhere else in Europe, though there are some white truffles in Morocco.

In most truffle-growing areas, the tuber is associated especially with oaks, but the Piedmont white truffle is versatile, growing not only around oaks, but also within the root systems of willows, hazels, poplars, and some other trees. They are less versatile in the matter of altitude, appearing only between 1,300 and 1,950 feet. Some black truffles are found in Piedmont too, but the white ones are more highly prized because they have a stronger flavor. To taste them fresh, at their best, you need to visit Piedmont between November and February. In France, the favorite discoverer and rooter-up of truffles is the hog, but Piedmont prefers dogs—dogs with a college education, for there is a "university" to train truffle hounds at Rodi. Often truffle hunting is done at night; their odor is stronger then, making it easier to detect a fungus which may be as deep as a foot underground. Some human truffle hunters seem to be able to sniff out truffles unaided, but dogs are better at it.

The white truffles of Piedmont go into many of the region's dishes, including what is perhaps its best known speciality, *fonduta*. This is an Alpine melted cheese dish, found also in the French and Swiss Alps. Piedmont is good cheese country. Roccaverano and Murazzano make a sharp but creamy goat cheese called *robiola*. *Paglierino* is made from cow's milk. The Gressoney valley (in the Valle d'Aosta), which makes the best butter in Piedmont, also produces *tome*, a heavy cheese with a reddish hue, of which the natives say, "It has three virtues: it sates hunger, quenches thirst, and cleans the teeth."

None of these goes into *fonduta*. For this Piedmont uses *fontina*, which comes from the Valle d'Aosta, taking its name from Mount Fontin, at Quart. It is a cheese of respectable age. As long ago as 1477 Pantaleone di Confienza wrote in his *Summa lacticinorum: "Vallis Augusta casei boni sunt"* ("in the Valle d'Aosta the cheeses are good"). The rich fatty orange *fontina*, which comes in great cartwheels, is made with infinite pains, but the finishing touch comes from a process with which human skill has little to do—its aging in well-aired stone buildings nearly 10,000 feet up.

VIII · *Piedmont and the Valle d'Aosta*

If *fonduta* is related to the French and Swiss *fondues*, it nevertheless has highly individual characteristics. The melted cheese which is the base for all three is mixed in *fonduta* with butter, milk and beaten egg yolks, none of which appear in the French and Swiss dishes, and is sprinkled liberally with white pepper. Swiss *fondue* uses white wine and kirsch; French practice on alcoholic additions varies; but *fonduta* uses none at all. Finally, *fonduta* is crowned with a layer of white truffles sliced paper-thin, a touch which neither France nor Switzerland can match. Both in France and Switzerland, the bowl of *fondue* is usually placed bubbling over a heater in the middle of the table; the diners spear cubes of bread on their forks, plunge them in the common pot and twirl the bread around to coat it with the melted cheese, and then pop the result into their mouths, repeating the process ad infinitum. In Piedmont the *fonduta*, which has the consistency of a thick cream, is served in individual plates, like soup, or may be poured over slabs of polenta.

Uniquely Piedmontese is *bagna calda* (*bagna caôda* in dialect), which means "hot bath." I have never encountered it anywhere else in Italy. Perhaps you have to be born in Piedmont to be able to make it successfully; a Milanese cook told me he had tried to produce it, but always wound up with a slimy thin unappetizing liquid. Yet it seems simple enough. You heat olive oil and butter, about a quarter more butter than oil by weight, together with a generous amount of chopped garlic, in a saucepan, without browning the garlic. When they are well combined, the saucepan is taken off the fire and finely chopped anchovy is stirred into it, along with a bit of salt. The last step is to add thinly sliced white truffles. It is usually placed on the table in little individual bowls over heaters, to keep it hot, particularly important since the vegetables which are dipped in it before being conveyed to the mouth are cold and raw. In Piedmont, the favorite vegetable for *bagna calda* is that local specialty, the cardoon, or edible thistle, but if cardoons are not at hand, you make do with whatever is available—celery, fennel, bits of red or yellow peppers, cauliflower, coarsely chopped cabbage, artichokes, or strips of carrot, singly or in combination.

There is one Piedmontese specialty which you surely know, though perhaps not where it came from—what most people call "Italian breadsticks." Italian, yes, since Turin is in Italy, but actually breadsticks (or *batonnets*, as Napoleon, who was fond of them, called them), are purely Turinese even if, like Milan's *panettone*, they have since gotten around. On their home ground these long narrow fingers of a wheat bread that is all crust are called *grissini* and are held to be the most digestible form of bread. Their usual function is to be munched with something else, but if you can lay your hands on a can or jar of white truffles, you can convert them into tasty hors d'oeuvres with the greatest of ease. Mince a truffle fine, crush it in a mortar with a tablespoon of butter, cream a little more butter separately and then mix the crushed truffle with it, with a pinch of salt. Spread this over two-thirds of the length of the breadstick, leaving the other third bare for a handle, and wrap a strip of prosciutto around the truffled spread. This goes nicely with cocktails, but it is perhaps safer served on a plate with other hors d'oeuvres, unless your guests are careful people. The spread acts like paste to hold the ham in place, but there is always danger that it will unwind itself when manipulated by a standing eater whose other hand is occupied by a glass.

One dish that some persons whose geography is good put down as Piedmontese because of its name, though first produced on the soil of Piedmont, was made by a French cook who was only passing through, and does not belong to the Piedmontese school of cooking; for that matter it belongs to no other, including the French, unless you want to create a school of dishes which make do with anything you can find at a moment of near famine. This is chicken Marengo, which has given birth also to veal Marengo. Having defeated the Austrians on June 14, 1800 at Marengo by a miracle of improvisation, Napoleon pursued them with such vigor that he left the commissary, but not his cook, Dunand, far behind. Dunand was desperate. Napoleon as was his habit had not eaten before the battle, to keep his mind clear, and was certain to be famished; and when he called for a meal he demanded immediate service (and bolted it down in a few minutes when he got it). Foragers were sent out and turned up only meager booty—a scrawny chicken, four tomatoes, three eggs, a few crayfish, a little garlic—and a frying pan, for Dunand was also without his cooking utensils. They had been unable to find butter, but had managed some olive oil. The cook cut up the chicken with a sabre and fried it in oil, crushed garlic, and water made more palatable with a little cognac filched from Napoleon's own canteen, together with some emergency-ration bread supplied by one of the soldiers, with the eggs, fried in the same liquid, on the side, and the crayfish, also fried, on top. A measure of Dunand's desperation was the unholy combination of chicken and crayfish; he must really have felt that all the food he had been able to scrape together was none too much. Napoleon found the dish excellent and ordered that it be served him after every battle. On the next occasion Dunand tried to improve the dish by substituting white wine for the water, adding mushrooms, and leaving out the crayfish. Napoleon noted the disappearance, and demanded that they be restored to the dish—not for gastronomic reasons, however. Chicken with crayfish was associated in his mind with victory and he was superstitious. "You left out the crayfish," he told Dunand angrily. "You'll bring me bad luck." Most French cooks today leave out the crayfish, but in Piedmont, where restaurants responsive to French influence put it on their menus for historical reasons, they respect the tradition by including crayfish. Sometimes they add what Dunand's foragers might have found in this area, but didn't—truffles. Chicken Marengo today is chicken cut into pieces, browned in oil, and then cooked (slowly, not as Dunand did it) with peeled tomatoes, crushed garlic, parsley, white wine and cognac, seasoned with crushed pepper, and served with fried eggs on the side (with or without crayfish, also on the side) and sometimes croutons, doubling for Dunand's army bread.

Although Piedmont produces more rice than Lombardy does, rice has not driven pasta off the menu in Turin as it has in Milan—and this despite the quality of Piedmont rice, already so famous in 1787 that it was there that Thomas Jefferson smuggled some out of the country. This was an illegal act. Piedmont was producing the best rice in Italy, possibly the best rice in the world, and it intended to keep its monopoly. Jefferson got hold of two bags of rice, however, and thus brought the first Piedmontese rice to America.

Though Piedmont has not gone in so exclusively for rice dishes as Lombardy, it nevertheless has a number of local rice dishes. *Riso alla piemontese* proclaims its nationality by including Piedmont's most ubiquitous ingredient, the white truffle, here chopped and combined with a meat sauce, which is poured over the rice; the same sauce also converts *tagliatelle* into a Piedmont dish. *Riso e ceci* is the sort of country fare consistent with the mountaineer tradition, rice and chick peas, seasoned with tomato sauce and hotly spiced. Vercelli has a specialty of risotto with quail. What is called rice and milk soup is not really soup, for the rice is boiled in milk until all of it has been absorbed, when it is served with grated cheese.

VIII · *Piedmont and the Valle d'Aosta*

The favorite pasta of Piedmont is *agnolotti*, an egg-pasta ring-shaped dough envelope, cooked in boiling water, whose stuffing seems to vary with each cook. The item which appears most consistently in the filling is chopped meat; second is nutmeg; third is spinach; but of three recipes of *agnolotti alla piemontese* which I consulted the first omitted the nutmeg, the second the spinach, and the third the chopped meat. For one which combines all three, try chopped chicken (or veal), chopped prosciutto, chopped purée of spinach, white wine, a little flour, and nutmeg. At the last *Quindicina Gastronomica Piemontese*, the Piedmont gastronomic festival which occurs only every 15 years, an *agnolotti alla piemontese* had stuffing of minced veal, minced ham, onion, egg, grated cheese, nutmeg—and a minute quantity of finely ground walnut shells! *Tagliatelle* is served not only as noted above but also in a number of other local fashions, for instance cooked in chicken consommé and served with chicken livers. Lasagne become so specialized that there is not only a recipe for the lasagne of the town of Cuneo, but even for St. Joseph's Day in Cuneo; it is something of a letdown to discover that *lasagne di San Giuseppe alla cunese* is no more exotic than the familiar oven-baked sheet pasta with a combination of chopped meat sauce and béchamel, with grated cheese and butter on top to provide a crust. Piedmont makes gnocchi with potatoes and also with *fontina* cheese, for which semolina flour gnocchi are first cooked in spiced milk to which the cheese is added, and then dipped in beaten eggs, breaded and fried. Much polenta is eaten, especially in the form of *polenta grassa*, a mountain dish of alternate layers of peppered polenta and *fontina* cheese baked in the oven until well browned on top.

From the long list of Piedmont specialties, here are a few tempters, chosen almost at random:

ANTIPASTI: Alternate cubes of polenta and *fontina*

323

cheese, dipped in beaten egg, breaded, fried in oil and speared on cocktail sticks; little tart shells filled with a paste of ground truffles, butter, and béchamel sauce; canapés spread with a mixture of *fontina* cheese, crushed truffles and butter; *pizza alla piemontese*, little pizza shells filled with a mixture of tomatoes, peppers and anchovies.

SOUPS: *Crema di legumi con crostini al burro*, a cream soup of mixed vegetables with buttered croutons; Asti minestrone, fresh shelled beans, cabbage, potatoes, carrots, celery, rice, bacon, grated cheese, garlic, basil and parsley, all in one rich thick soup; tripe soup, for which strips of tripe are boiled in water plus meat stock, with chopped onions, diced potatoes, chopped celery, cabbage and leeks.

ENTRÉES: *Rane dorate*, skinned frogs dipped in egg and fried in olive oil; Savoy omelet, with diced potatoes and grated cheese; *finanziera di pollo*, which combines chicken livers with sweetbreads, truffles and mushrooms in a thick meat or tomato sauce in a pastry shell.

FISH: The exquisite mountain brook trout are best cooked in the simplest possible style, whether boiled (*in bianco*, common in Piedmont), fried or grilled, but *trota alla Savoia* is nevertheless well worth a try; it is floured trout first fried in butter, then bedded on mushrooms which have been fried in butter and oil with parsley, the whole sprinkled with butter and bread crumbs and finished by baking in the oven; it is served with chopped scallions in melted butter. Another favorite Piedmontese method is to fry the trout in sage-flavored butter. Tench is cooked in red wine and water with clove, marjoram and garlic, and served with a sauce made of the cooking juices, flour, butter, and a dash of lemon juice.

POULTRY: *Pollo al babi* is young chicken cut into pieces, salted, peppered and doused with olive oil, and cooked for 20 minutes in a frying pan. Capon is roasted, wrapped in strips of ham and bacon, on a bed of chopped celery, diced

324

carrots, bay leaf, thyme and marjoran, basted with Marsala wine and stock, and served with a sauce containing sliced truffles. *Filetti di tacchino alla piemontese* means that the turkey fillets are seasoned and floured, browned briskly in butter, and then placed in a buttered oven dish; they are covered with sliced truffles, powdered with grated cheese; a sauce is poured over them made of the browning juices, with Marsala wine, bouillon, and butter, and they are finished rapidly in a hot oven, for just the time necessary to melt the cheese.

MEAT: Piedmont likes *bollito misto*—for instance, beef, chicken, veal and ham, all cooked together, served with potatoes, cabbage and onions with green sauce and a dab of jelly on the side. *Bue di carrù brasato al Barolo* is a thick slice of beef first browned and then cooked very slowly (three hours) in Barolo wine, to which beef consommé is added from time to time as the liquid boils away. Roast veal is larded with bacon, pepper, and bits of truffle. Turin sausages are cooked in tomato sauce, with snails and chicken livers. *Trippa in umido con funghi* is stewed tripe with onions, tomatoes and grated cheese in white wine, to which separately sautéed mushrooms are added at the end.

VEGETABLES: *Panizza* is a specialty of Vercelli, which combines white beans, rice, tomatoes, onions and bacon. *Fagioli della regina alla panettiera* is a complicated name for baked beans, and so is *fasoeil al fùrn*, which is a richer version usually eaten on Sundays after all-night cooking, of dried red or white beans soaked for 12 hours, and then baked with pork rind or bacon, crushed garlic, pepper, cinnamon, crushed cloves and mace. The famous Piedmontese thistles are prepared in a number of ways: rolled in flour and beaten egg, fried in oil, and finished in the oven with butter and grated cheese; or baked in a flour, milk and butter sauce; or, of course, raw with *bagna calda*. Summer squash is stuffed with chopped meat, *fontina* cheese, egg and grated cheese. *Sciule piene* (*cipolle ripiene alla piemontese* in Italian, Piedmont stuffed onions) sounds almost like a dessert, for onions are stuffed with bread soaked in milk or stock, macaroons, beaten eggs, raisins, and grated cheese; Ivrea, north of Turin, does a simpler job on onions, cooking them in oil, butter, stock and white wine, with a bay leaf. *Peperoni alla piemontese* are peppers stuffed with tomato, anchovy, garlic, butter and oil, baked in a moderate oven. The heads of large mushrooms are stuffed in *funghi ripieni alla piemontese* with the chopped stems, parsley, onions, anchovies, egg and bread crumbs, baked with a sprinkling of olive oil. Truffles are cooked in Asti Spumante, or *alla piemontese*, which means that each slice of white truffle is covered with a thin slice of *fontina* cheese, flavored with olive oil, lemon juice, salt and pepper, cooked until the cheese has melted into the truffles, and served with slices of lemon. *Fontina* salad is made of yellow peppers, green olives, fresh cream, mustard and condiments and *fontina* cheese; and Alba salad (*insalata alla moda d'Alba*) is a bed of white lettuce on which repose asparagus tips, celery, and slices of white truffle, with a dressing of olive oil, lemon juice, salt and pepper, and a touch of cream.

The sweet tooth of Piedmont is served by *gianduia*, a chocolate pudding involving crushed hazelnuts and lady fingers, served chilled; Piedmont pudding, a creamy lemon-flavored dessert; Turin pudding, vanilla-flavored chestnuts and chocolate; Savoy cake, which has the peculiarity of being made with a mixture of potato flour and pastry flour, the other ingredients being egg yolks and whites beaten separately, vanilla and grated lemon peel; and *crema al burro alla torinese*, a cake icing and filling of cream, egg yolks, sugar, vanilla, potato flour, chocolate and almonds. Chocolate candies are a Piedmont specialty. And to end the dessert list on something less cloying, here is one way Piedmont serves peaches:

VIII · *Piedmont and the Valle d'Aosta*

Wash, dry, peel and stone five peaches. Scoop out a hole in the center of four of them, and mash the pulp you have removed together with the fifth peach. Mix this with two tablespoons of sugar, 1 ¼ ounces of butter, four crushed macaroons, and one egg yolk. Fill the scooped-out hollows in your four peaches with this mixture, and cook in a moderate oven for about an hour. You can eat the result either hot or cold.

It has always seemed to me rather pointless to try to name the "best" wine (or for that matter, the best anything else) of a region, a country or a continent. Best under what conditions? with what food? in what weather? and in any case, what is "best"? Wines are different, and therefore incomparable.

Yet if I were pinned down to naming the best wine-growing region of Italy, I suppose I would nominate Piedmont; and for the best wine, Barolo. If there is any such thing as the greatest wine in Italy, this is it. It was at La Morra, in the Barolo area, that Julius Caesar drank wine which so impressed him that he digressed from recounting his military exploits long enough to describe it as marvelous. In the 16th century, François I imported this and other Piedmont wines into France.

Piedmont wines are predominantly red—about 90 percent—but among the whites is the one best known to foreigners, Asti Spumante. The naming of these wines is somewhat confusing. Most of them are named for the grapes from which they are made—Nebbiolo, Barbera, Bonarda, Freisa, Brachetto, Cortese, Dolcetto, Erbaluce, Grignolino—but some are place names—Barolo, Barbaresco, Asti, Carema, Gattinara.

The greatest Piedmont wines are grown in the region around Alba. The Tanaro River flows through the town, and also through this major wine area. It misses being an all-Piedmont river by two or three miles of its 170-mile length, rising just beyond the Ligurian frontier, but remaining for all the rest of its way within the region of Piedmont until it empties into the Po. In the neighborhood of Alba, its valley is limited on the north by the Monferrato hills and on the south by the Langhe hills; it is on their slopes that the great wines grow.

The Nebbiolo grape is king here. The name is supposed to be derived from *nebbia*, fog, but just why is not clear; one suggestion is that it is because the season of mists has set in by the time the grapes are picked. Its chief characteristic is that it imparts a violet taste to wine. It is known to have been cultivated at least since 1300, and while this vine is not a prolific producer of grapes, those it does ripen are of high quality.

Barolo, grown in a small minutely defined territory south of the Tanaro, is made from the Nebbiolo grape. To have the legal right to call itself Barolo, wine must not only come from this area and be made from the Nebbiolo grape, it must also have spent at least three years in the wood; actually this is usually not enough. The wine is so rich in tannin and acids that it is almost undrinkably sharp when young, and requires ripening from four to seven years in the cask, after which it continues to age in the bottle. Some Barolos take 12 years or more to attain maturity. The corollary of slowness in maturing is long life; a good Barolo will hold out as long as a good Bordeaux, perhaps longer.

When it is good, it is very, very good. It is a rich, full-bodied generous wine, unequaled in Italy as an accompaniment for roasts, game, and dishes with rich sauces. At its earliest permissible age, it is a brilliant ruby color, which when poured into the glass shows a brownish onion-skin edge; as it gets older, its color deepens, first to a reddish brown with glints of orange, and finally almost to black. It also becomes mellower and more velvety. The alcoholic content, at least 13 degrees to begin with, may rise to as much as 16. There is a whisper of violets in its flavor, followed by a slightly resinous aftertaste, often described as recalling tar, though this gives a false idea of the effect. It should be served at room temperature or a little above, and it is advisable to uncork the bottle to let it breathe at least an hour before serving it, taking care not to shake up the wine, though it throws no visible sediment.

Two other notable wines in the same area are made from the Nebbiolo grape. One is Barbaresco, also grown south of the Tanaro, in the smallest of the six wine divisions of the Alba district. The town of Barbaresco clings to a steep slope, and is dominated by its ancient tower, which appears on the neck label of bottles of genuine Barbaresco. Although Barbaresco is probably the second best wine of Piedmont, the old Roman town of Neive, in the Barbaresco area and hence entitled to that appellation, often prefers to put out its exceptional wine under its own name. Barbaresco, like Barolo, is a "big" wine, but a trifle less overwhelming, a younger brother of Barolo. It is less rugged, and when young lacks the rasp of Barolo at the same age (a quality which, however, pleases certain winebibbers); it has a lower alcoholic content, 12.5 to 13 degrees, and matures more quickly—it is drinkable in its second year, but is better after three or four. It is also good with roasts.

The third wine made from Nebbiolo grapes is called, simply, Nebbiolo, and grows north of the Tanaro. It is to Barbaresco as Barbaresco is to Barolo—lighter, running from 11 to 12.5 degrees. It can be drunk young, but is best at three to four years, and is better suited to the first course of the meal or to white meat than to roasts of red meat or game. Ruby-red in color, it manifests, like its two elders, the violet fragrance of the Nebbiolo grape. There is also a sweet Nebbiolo, usually naturally sparkling, 9 to 10 degrees, which ages to a pinkish tint with yellow reflections.

Stick to the dry variety.

Oddly enough, the three Nebbiolo grape regions are all separated from each other by the region which straddles the Tanaro immediately around Alba and produces Barbera. While it is not the best wine of this area, it is the Piedmont wine grown in the greatest quantity, no doubt because it produces grapes more abundantly and is therefore less dependent on quality to be profitable. Half of all Piedmont wines are made from the Barbera grape, 20 times as much as from the aristocratic Nebbiolo. The Barbera wines produced in this particular area of *vini pregiati*, precious wines, are neverless not the best Barberas of Piedmont; the best is probably the Barbera of Asti, and there are other respectable Barberas in the provinces of Alessandria and Turin. Barbera is best after, say, four years in wood and six months in the bottle; it is then a vigorous full-bodied wine, 12 to 14 degrees, ruby-red, with an aftertaste midway between cherries and violets.

There are two other wine areas in this major region. The southernmost grows the Dolcetto grape, a name which suggests sweetness. The grape itself is indeed sweet, but the wine made from it, usually drunk young, is dry and tart. It is a quick ripener, and needs to be, for it grows up to 2,000 feet. Dark red and light in body, it also comes in artificially provoked slightly sweetish and sparkling versions, which to my mind are no improvements, and there is also a white Dolcetto d'Alba, dry and a trifle bitter.

The last of the six areas is a white wine region, growing Moscato d'Asti, a light (6 to 7 degrees) golden yellow wine, fruity, naturally *frizzante* and sweet, allowing you to divine that it is made from the yellow Muscat grape. This region extends north into the province of Asti (the area we have just examined is in the province of Cuneo, or Coni). Here is found that special superior case of the Moscato d'Asti, the famous Asti Spumante. It has been described by at least one expert as one of the great white wines of the world, but I fear I cannot go along with him. Those who refer to it as "Italian champagne" do it no great service, for this provokes an inevitable comparison in which Asti Spumante comes out a very distant second best. It is not even on the level of a minor champagne; in France, it would be only a *mousseux*—like a sweetish sparkling Vouvray, perhaps. Naturally sparkling when poured, its bubbles quickly exhaust themselves; it is a pale yellow, 7 to 10 degrees, fresh, but with only a slight flavor, masked by excessive sweetness, and an efficient headache producer. Since present-day taste is away from the sweet, some manufacturers are now making a drier version, using the French champagne manufacturing technique, which is not applied to ordinary Asti Spumante.

The other Piedmont wines, though often interesting, can be disposed of briefly. The rare usually sparkling red Brachetto, with a perfume which suggests roses, grows in the Asti area. Freisa also appears in the neighborhood of Asti, but the best comes from around Chieri, in the province of Turin; it is a dry red, with a slight raspberry flavor, which requires some aging; a sweeter (*amabile*) version and a sparkling Freisa are also made. The nutty Grignolino, grown around Asti and Alessandria, light, dark garnet in color, 11 to 13 degrees, is a very acceptable table wine, which improves with age—it was the favorite of King Umberto I and Queen Elena, not, we may assume, in its sweet sparkling version.

The Nebbiolo grape appears again in the Vercelli region, where it is called *spanna*, and produces several excellent reds: the noble tannin-rich Gattinara, the finest wine of this province, 13 to 14 degrees, rather sharp in taste, especially when young; Ghemme, runner-up to Gattinara, which is not made exclusively from Nebbiolo grapes but mixes them with Bonarda and some others, a slow ripener, which needs four to five years to mature; Lessona, Gattinara in a minor key; and Mottalciata, very much the same.

Among the few Piedmont whites, notable are Cortese, a pale straw-yellow with green highlights, 10 to 11 degrees, good with fish. Caluso, northeast of Turin, makes white wine, especially *Caluso passito*, golden to amber in color, a sweet dessert wine, 13 to 15 degrees, made from a grape with the romantic name of *erba luce* (grass of light). Other *passito* wines are made in Piedmont; the term means that the grapes have been dried in the sun after picking, producing a high concentration of sugar.

So far as Piedmont is concerned, the most important derivative of wine is vermouth. Despite the exceptional presence in Lombardy of Campari, it is Piedmont which is the great vermouth producer of Italy, with such big companies as Cinzano, Martini e Rossi, Cora, Carpano, Gancia and others. Etymologically and historically, the Piedmont vermouth industry presents some surprising facets.

Etymologically, the localization of vermouth in Piedmont seems all wrong, for the name comes from an archaic German word—*Wermuth*, which means wormwood, from which absinthe is made. Its foreign character for Italy is demonstrated by a lack of agreement on how to spell it; you will find Italian bottles labeled vermouth, vermout and vermut. To make it even stranger, authorities declare that there is no wormwood in Piedmont vermouth, though this assertion has to be taken on faith, since no maker of vermouth reveals what he puts in his beverage; in any case, no one labels his product as *assenzio*, which would be the Italian equivalent for *Wermuth*. The explanation seems to be that long ago a drink of this type, which did include wormwood, was made by private families in Central Europe; but now that it has gotten into big-scale commercial production, Germany usually buys any vermouth it requires from the two big makers of this drink, France and Italy.

Historically, the most curious thing about the modern Piedmont vermouth is that Antonio Benedetto Carpano should have found it necessary to go to France to learn how to produce vermouth, as he did, for it should have been possible to find out everything he needed to know in Italy. The wine museum in Passione, only a few miles from Turin, the capital of vermouth, which displays the complete history of wine, inexplicably neglects vermouth; but it is known nevertheless that vermouth, or something very much like it, is literally ancient history in Italy. Pliny and Cicero both refer to aromatic wines; and the *vinum absintiatum* of the ancient Romans, unless it is misnamed, should have had wormwood in it.

In the 1300's a vermouth-type drink of wine, cinnamon, cloves and aromatic herbs was being made. In the Middle Ages beverages of this sort were taken as medicine, and indeed vermouth is held to have medicinal value today; it often includes ingredients also used in medicine, for instance quinine. The Rosolio of those times was in essence vermouth, and today's Ratafià is a descendant of the Rosolio di Torino, which included orange blossoms, cinnamon and cloves. Many parts of Italy were making drinks of this sort in the 17th century; why did Italians have to look to France in the 18th for instruction in the art of making vermouth?

Nevertheless, it was a French technical publication which first signaled the beginning of Piedmont's modern vermouth-producing industry by printing in 1733 a recipe for Rosolio di Torino; apparently industrial production of vermouth, hitherto made chiefly by private individuals, had begun in Piedmont about 1700. Italian documentary evidence exists for the commercial manufacture of vermouth by herb dealers and liqueur makers in 1736. One of them was named Giovanni Alberto Rovere; his son went to work for Giuseppe and Luigi Cora, and thus was founded the house of Cora which is still operating today. It was this company which made the first recorded export of vermouth; it shipped a case to Montevideo, Uruguay. Latin America is still Italy's best client for vermouth, taking a major part of the exports which bring into Piedmont every year $14,000,000 to $15,000,000 in foreign currency (the domestic sale is about 2½ times as much). Vermouth today is clearly big business; it began to be that when Carpano initiated the first large-scale operation in 1786. He quickly became furnisher to Vittorio Amedeo III, King of Sardinia; and the shop he opened in Turin's Piazza Castello was one of the city's leading *salotti*, the public equivalent of the French private *salon*, where the leading politicians, artists and scientists of the day used to gather, along with the city's socialites and businessmen.

The Piazza Castello shop was near the Stock Exchange, which accounts for the name of one of Carpano's most popular products. A harassed stockbroker who came in at the end of a hectic day's trading sank with relief into a chair, raised his arm and called to a waiter, and as he repeated the gesture he had been making in the Exchange all day, instead of ordering a bitter Carpano, he automatically pronounced the call which went with the gesture: *"Punt e mes!"*—"point and a half!" The mistake amused one of the Carpano family, Ottavio, who was present, and Punt e Mes vermouth was christened. It happens that this is usually the vermouth I order myself, if I order any at all—I am not much of a vermouth drinker—because it gets rid of the cloying sweetness characteristic of many Italian vermouths by adding a larger proportion of bitter ingredients.

Once Piedmont took vermouth up, it is not surprising that it held the lead, for it has close at hand the two main ingredients essential for it—a plentiful supply of more or less neutral wine, without too much assertive character of its own to interfere with smooth blending (Moscato d'Asti is excellent for this) and the aromatic herbs which supply the flavor. The chief French vermouth centers have the same combination of natural resources in the lower Rhone valley and at Chambéry in the French Alps, but they make on the average a much drier beverage from them. Piedmont does make what it calls dry vermouths, but it also makes some so sweet that they almost make the teeth ache; the Piedmontese are more likely to take the edge off sweetness by adding bitter ingredients to a sweet base than to make a dry vermouth to begin with.

But what *is* vermouth exactly? Essentially, it is white wine (preferably from white grapes) flavored with herbs, spices, roots, woods, etc. (Red vermouth acquires its color not from the wine used, but from caramelized sugar.) The two main elements—the wine on one hand, the flavoring on the other—start on their ways separately. The various flavoring ingredients (flowers of artemisia, flowers and leaves of balm, pungent sage, the bitter leaves of dittany, the aromatic flowers of Roman camomille, oily coriander seeds, lemon peel, the peel of bitter oranges, vanilla beans, sandalwood, cinnamon and quinquina bark, rose and violet petals, sweet calamus root and bitter gentian root, sarriette, centaury, cardoons, marjoram, cloves, juniper [perhaps, sometimes, even wormwood?]—and tea!) go into the long lines of curiously shaped retorts paired with cylindrical tanks which look modern enough but are in essence the alembics in which medieval alchemists may have made early vermouths, in intervals between searches for the Philosopher's Stone. In these are distilled the fragrances and essences from these varied flavorings, poignant or bland, tingling or velvety, sharp or mild, aromatic or delicate, assertive or subtle; they become readily soluble in alcohol, in various dosages which open infinite possibilities of taste. So that the alcohol in which they are next steeped may absorb their perfumes more easily, it is sometimes heated, though not always. In any case, the essences remain in the great drums of alcohol, which hold 250 to 300 gallons at a time, for between three to six months; for half an hour each day, the drums promote mixing by turning slowly, say three revolutions a minute.

Meanwhile the wine has been treated in another fashion. Piedmont vermouth production has long outstripped the capacity of the Piedmont vineyards producing the particular type of neutral wine which can carry the carefully concocted flavors without contradicting them by the rivalry of its own. Piedmont now imports great quantities of such wine from Emilia-Romagna, Apulia and Sicily. The wine is mixed with sugar syrup, or with unfermented grape juice fortified with brandy, in great vats containing perhaps 1,300 to 1,400 gallons of the limpid liquid. To this the flavoring is added gradually, two or three parts to a hundred of wine, with a little extra alcohol to promote blending. It takes about two days to perform the mixing operation. The vermouth then "goes to school"—it is alternately frozen and heated. The freezing precipitates insoluble impurities so that they can be filtered out, while the heating kills any taste-altering bacteria. Graduated from this process, it is ready to flow to the swift smoothly operating machines which fill, cork and label 20,000 bottles an hour.

The finished product is an unctuous 32 to 36 proof, about one-third the strength of whisky. The legal definition says that vermouth must contain at least 70 percent natural wine; if it does not meet the legal conditions, it cannot be labeled vermouth. But there are on the market any number of worthy apéritifs which the palate would call vermouths though the law does not—the Amaro and Elisir China (*china* means quinquina) of Cuneo; the Ratafià d'Andorno and Elisir d'Oropa of Vercelli; and above all, Barolo Chinato, four- or five-year-old Barolo wine combined with tonic and digestive herbs and spices.

When the famous vermouth companies of today were started, they were small family affairs. Now they are giant family affairs. The reason why single families continue to dominate monster manufactures which should have outgrown such narrow control is simple—the need for secrecy. Italians are strongly family-minded. They entrust important secrets only to persons who are in the family; and vermouth making is based on secrets. The vermouth maker's most essential property is the formula to which he mixes his flavoring. In great vermouth companies employing thousands of persons, you can count on the fingers of one hand the number of persons who know the formula—in almost every case, members of the owning family. For the Cinzano company there are said to be just two. As a safeguard, however, every company has one copy of the formula locked up somewhere in a notary's strongbox. This is the great secret, but it is not the only one. Vermouth companies are as sensitive to the dangers of industrial espionage as the possessors of secrets of synthetic textile production or of electronic military equipment. ENTRY STRICTLY FORBIDDEN, says a sign on a door in one Turin vermouth factory. What is behind that door—the room where the formula is put together? Not at all; it is simply the place where the sugar is caramelized; the company does not want anyone else to know how it performs this operation. Even when an Italian vermouth company sets up a bottling plant abroad, as many of them have done, it does not communicate its secrets to the branch establishment. The flavoring is mixed in Italy and sent in sealed cans to the foreign bottling plant, to be mixed there with local wine and brandy. Some manufacturers think you get a better result by using wine grown in the region of consumption, but others create special dosages to please foreign tastes and make in Italy vermouth designed especially for Spain or Puerto Rico or Canada—

but not for the United States; Americans prefer to drink Italian vermouth as the Italians drink it.

The small family businesses which because of secrecy have remained family businesses despite thousandfold expansion are empires today. The Cinzano company was founded in Turin at the turn of the century by Francesco Cinzano. Its beginnings were modest. There is now a whole village named Cinzano, attached to the town of Santa Vittoria, on the banks of the Tanaro River in the province of Cuneo. The company's reception building was once a royal hunting lodge used by King Vittorio Emmanuele II. A hill at Santa Vittoria has been hollowed out to make a natural vat for Cinzano vermouth; you could float an ocean liner on its contents.

The vogue for vermouth continues, though some other apéritifs, particularly the sweeter ones, are falling into disfavor. But 50,000,000 bottles of Italian vermouth are consumed every year, most of it made in Piedmont. If there were nothing else to keep vermouth in the forefront, there is always the fact that it is an ingredient in the most classic, and probably the most favored, of all cocktails, which has taken its name from one of the Turin vermouth companies —the Martini.

A curious fact about the French-speaking Valle d'Aosta is that it has never been French (though it was occupied by the Franks in Carolingian times). If it speaks that language, it is because it was held by the Dukes of Burgundy before Burgundy became part of France; Burgundy spoke French. Aosta then became the fief of the House of Savoy, which gave Italy its kings. There is a French Savoy too, whose dialect is almost identical with that of Aosta; it was once part of the realms of the Italian house, along with a sizable section of southwestern Switzerland. Aosta displays one of the most complicated language patterns in Italy. As Italian merchants moved in among the original French-speaking inhabitants, the two populations, which did not intermarry, divided the territory between them—the Italians took over the towns and the French retired to the surrounding mountains. The most curious situation is that of the valley of the Lys. This was colonized by German-speaking Swiss from the Valais; but within the German-speaking island thus formed is the village of Gaby, which speaks the French dialect! It makes one think of a set of Chinese nested boxes —a French-speaking kernel within a German-speaking container, itself within a French-speaking territory, surrounded by a Celtic-Gallic-Italian patois area, the whole within an Italian-speaking nation. No wonder the cooking varies from town to town!

It is in the Valle d'Aosta that cereals are grown at high altitudes, near Valtournanche. In its all but inaccessible upper reaches game animals are still found which have disappeared or become rare elsewhere in Europe: a wild goat whose age can be read by the number of knots on its crescent-shaped horns, no longer found anywhere else in the Alps; the chamois, less rare here than in France or Switzerland (there is a town named Chamois in the Valtournanche, 5,450 feet up); the white hare; the wild boar; the less rare pheasant and quail; and among inedible animals, the otter, the ermine, and a sort of lynx called the lynx wolf.

Although other high-lying regions of Piedmont produce typical mountain cooking, nowhere is it as determinedly rustic, even coarse, as in Aosta. The sharpness of the climate is met by the heaviness of the food, and, on occasion (in the case of game, for instance) its richness. Two elements in particular are basic to Aosta cooking: bread, country type, often black, usually made of a mixture of barley and hard wheat flours, the basis of the peasant diet; and the stock pot always simmering on the back of the stove. The bouillon it contains is the start of the region's many soups (some of them so thick as to remain soup only in name) and goes into many other dishes which are meant to be non-liquid. It is made from the broth saved when meat is boiled, into which are put garlic, bay leaves, clove, rosemary, and a variety of other seasonings to give it flavor; no bouillon is considered ready for use until it has had at least two weeks to inhale these fragrances, preferably in a much-used copper pot—*viëlle marmitta, bouna seupa*, say the natives—"the older the pot, the better the soup."

Soupe à la Valpelleunentse starts with such a bouillon, but by the time it is done, the bouillon has practically disappeared and the word soup seems somewhat inappropriate. A layer of slices of wheat bread is laid on the bottom of an oven dish. On top of this goes a layer of finely chopped green cabbage, the white parts only, which has already been boiled in salted water. Then comes a layer of *fontina* cheese slices. Hot butter is poured over this, it is then covered with bouillon, also heated, and the whole is placed in the oven for 30 or 40 minutes.

A mountaineers' version of the lowlands rice and milk soup is, again, like its prototype, not really a soup at all, since all the liquid in which it has cooked boils away before the dish is served. This is *la soupe di latte, riso e castagne*, for which freshly gathered peeled chestnuts are boiled in water until they are well cooked. They are then transferred to milk, salted, and allowed to boil for ten minutes more. A handful of rice is thrown in, and the mixture is stirred constantly until the milk has been absorbed, leaving a sort of mush. *La seuppa de l'ano*, ass' soup, also called more discreetly *seuppa freida*, is not soup either. It is a very simple dish—slices of black bread soaked in red wine with much sugar. Really a soup, however, is *la soupe à la cogneintze*, another dish which smells of the mountain, simply rice in beef consommé, poured over slices of black or white bread spread with melted *fontina* cheese.

After the staple basic foods of the region, the outstanding food category in this area is game. If you want to taste chamois, you will have to come here (or to the highest reaches of Novara or Vercelli); there is not enough for it to trickle down to the lower, more urban, centers; but it is worth the trip. Even rarer is ibex. This Alpine wild goat is almost extinct. It still exists in only two spots—in the Swiss National Park, a nature preserve where hunting is forbidden, and in the Gran Paradiso range, the southern border of the Valle d'Aosta. There is a nature preserve here too, which is not only closed to hunters, but also to fishermen and even to botanists, but occasionally a few ibex may stray imprudently beyond the confines of the park; there is also an institution known as poaching. The Swiss are stiffer than the Italians about enforcing game laws, so it may be that the Valle d'Aosta is the only place where, with luck, you might get a taste of ibex. In any case, the trip to ibex country, whether it produces a dinner or not, is an enchanting one. The key to the region is Cogne, at the end of a valley which pushes into the Gran Paradiso, whose houses are tossed casually onto the meadows like brightly colored rugs placed haphazardly on a green lawn. In the middle of the settlement, an archaic cross rises above a wrought-iron grill. Dusk falls, and in the distance the dancing bonfires lighted by the gamekeepers sparkle in the mountains. Here any food would taste superb. Chamois is cooked in the Valle d'Aosta in Barolo wine, laced with a glass of *grappa*, and among the ingredients for its seasoning and sauce are garlic, carrots, celery, thyme, juniper, parsley, bay leaf, onions, cloves, cinnamon, olive oil, consommé, cream, and tomato extract. If you can't get to the chamois country, you might be able elsewhere to find kid, cooked in the same way. Another way of cooking chamois is *camoscio stufato alla Valdierese*, which is a cut of chamois soaked in wine for a week, braised for two hours in a covered dish, and served with white truffles.

Gradually disappearing, since the animals from which it is made are disappearing too, is *motzetta*, made from chamois when it is impossible to get ibex. *Motzetta* is cured meat from one or the other of these animals, of which some of the tenderest cuts are heavily salted and steeped for two weeks in brine containing garlic, bay leaves, sage and rosemary. It is placed in a cylindrical recipient and covered, under weights which press it compactly together, and kept thus for another month in a dry well-aired place. It is then ready to be sliced and eaten, with mountain butter spread on rye bread. The *motzetta* of Cogne is famous.

An even rarer, and on the whole less recommendable dish than chamois or *motzetta*, is marmot, an Alpine rodent related to the American woodchuck. The natives claim its meat has aphrodisiac qualities, which may account for the trouble they take with this little-eaten animal. First it is scalded for a few minutes in boiling water with a little vinegar in it. Then it is put in a bath of fresh water rich with green vegetables, onions, celery, carrots, garlic, rosemary, and sage, and marinated for two days. Cut into pieces, it is cooked in water in a covered pot over a low flame until all the fat has been boiled out of it. Next it is browned in butter, after which it is ready to be roasted in the oven or on a spit, or made into a stew. It is described as tastier than hare, but I do not know that we are obliged to take the word of persons who also describe as better than hare the cats apparently especially raised for the table at Pont Saint Martin and Donnaz, which are hung for 48 hours to give them a gamy taste, and consumed as a Christmas treat.

We return to less uncharted game with *fagiani al vino di Neive*, pheasant braised in wine, with a final dash of *grappa* or some other drink for strong men, served with mashed potatoes and white truffles; *lepre tartufata al Barbaresco* is hare treated the same way.

A good deal of sausage is made in the Valle d'Aosta. The typical local sausage is a hard, air-dried mixture of lean beef, pork, and fresh lard, sharply seasoned with salt, pepper, various spices, garlic, and bay leaf, to which some makers add cloves for hotter spicing. The local *boudin*, blood pudding, is made of pig's blood, boiled potatoes pressed through a colander, lard, and spices, in a casing of pig's intestine; some persons make it with steer's blood, but this produces an inferior product. To get the best, ask for the *boudins* of Morgex or Gignod; they are served fried in oil, or boiled, with potatoes. The town of Bosses is noted for its ham. Pig's head cut into small pieces and preserved in lard, with rosemary, bay leaf and other herbs is another local specialty.

Ham provides one rustic dish, *lo speck*, in which ham in the process of being smoked is removed from the smokehouse when it is seven-eighths done, and boiled with potatoes, carrots and sauerkraut, which sounds as though this should be a contribution from that German island in the middle of the Valle. As though this were not enough for one sitting, it is often served with *chnolle*—cornmeal gnocchi cooked in consommé.

Some other Aosta dishes are nearer to the beaten path. *La costoletta di vitello con fontina* is a veal chop with the bone left on, cut through horizontally as far as the bone so that a slice of *fontina* cheese can be sandwiched into the meat, after which it is seasoned, dipped into beaten egg and bread crumbs, and fried in sizzling butter. *Il fricandeau* is veal cut into cubes and braised in white wine with bacon, bay leaf, rosemary and any other herbs or spices the cook may fancy.

La carbonnade is a very old traditional dish so named because it is supposed to have been invented by charcoal burners seeking some means to improve the monotonous fare provided by the dried meat they carried with them into the woods; if so, they must also have taken along quite a bit of cooking equipment and condiments, for this is how the dish is made: Cut beef fillet which has been preserved in salt for 12 days into small cubes. In a saucepan, cook smoked fat bacon slowly with much garlic, until the latter is golden in color. Meanwhile heat dry white wine and the yolk of an egg into which a tablespoonful of flour has been stirred, seasoning it with cinnamon, cloves, and pepper. When the garlic is ready, pour the contents of the frying pan into the saucepan, simmer them together for seven or eight minutes, and then put in the diced meat. Cover, cook for another ten minutes, and serve with rather firm polenta.

Potatoes, not the most favored vegetable of Italy, are eaten daily in the Valle d'Aosta, because they marry well with the strongly flavored and almost always fatty dishes, and also because they grow well in the poor mountain soil, where they are found up to 5,500 feet. They are small, tortuously shaped and floury, but tasty; one feels a certain affection for this simple food behind the complaint of a poet writing in the local dialect:

> *Poure dzen di campagne*
> *No careimen tot l'an;*
> *Et trifolle et tsatagne*
> *Fan noutro camentran.*

Or, translated freely:

> *Pity us poor country folk;*
> *Lent all year is not a joke!*
> *Potatoes, chestnuts—they are all*
> *That we have for Carnival.*

Lettuce too grows at high altitudes in Aosta, at the very limit of cultivation, in the strip of land just below the snow. This "snow lettuce," like the potatoes, stays very small;

lately it has met competition through the introduction into the region of other types of lettuce, endive and chicory, grown a little lower, but not much; for instance, a high Alpine endive is eaten with relish in the late spring. These greens are served both raw, in salads, and cooked.

High altitude accounts for the exceptional quality of some other Aosta products also—for instance, the butter, of which that of Gressoney is the most reputed; it comes from the milk of cows which feed in summer 4,000 feet up. From it, only partially skimmed, is made the Gressoney *tome* cheese, rich in butter fat. Whole milk is used for *reblèque*, a fresh cream cheese which children like to eat, sugared, from a cup. *Serò*, or *seràs*, is a cottage cheese eaten fresh with polenta, which forms the almost daily food of the herdsmen; it can be converted into a hardened form (*cacio magro*) which they carry with them to the pastures. There is also a variety called *salignon*, studded with minute bits of pimento and the dried flowers of aromatic mountain herbs.

Herbs also account partly for the superb quality of Aosta honey, though the bees draw nectar from many other plants also, from rhododendrons to evergreens. There are some 500 apiaries in the Valle d'Aosta, but there are no big honey producers; it is all homemade. Sometimes herdsmen and shepherds take hives with them to the mountain pastures for the summer, bringing them down again with the first cold weather. Alpine honey is more transparent and whiter in color than that of lower altitudes. It crystallizes normally in October; but even when filtered to keep it liquid, it throws off a certain amount of half-crystallized half-liquid sugar, called "sugar of manna," which is the proof that you have genuine Alpine honey.

Honey sweetens many of the mountain desserts, which also draw often on another local product, chestnuts, of which the best are grown between Aosta and Ussel. An example of the first is provided by the *torcettini* of Saint-Vincent, little cupcakes rich in Alpine butter, sweetened with sugar; of the second, the Ussel combination of chestnuts cooked together with sweetened black bread—not to mention the chestnut cream which put an end to the Challant family when its last surviving member, Giulio Giaconito, died at the age of 12 from a surfeit of a dessert which proved too succulent.

Bread is the basis of many of the coarser desserts of the Aosta region. For instance, *fiandolein* is a cream made of milk, plenty of beaten egg yolks, much sugar, a dash of rum and a little lemon peel, cooked with constant stirring without being allowed to boil, and then poured directly from the pan into a cup filled with bread broken into small pieces. *Brochat* is also a creamy dessert, of milk, sugar and wine, a sort of zabaglione, eaten tepid with black bread. *Flantze* are sweetened round flat cakes made when bread is being baked, half bread dough and half squash.

Aosta also boasts some desserts of considerable finesse. The natives claim that blanc-mange was invented here. What Deorsola calls *panettone* has little relation to the Milanese cake—it is made of leaves of almond pastry covered with a soft finger-sticking chocolate frosting. The finest chocolate of all Aosta is probably that which goes into *baci*, chocolate kisses, from Courmayeur, well laced with West Indies rum.

The Valle d'Aosta does not produce distinguished wine, though it makes much use of the Nebbiolo grape. "The wines of the Valle d'Aosta are difficult wines," writes Sergio Canavese, a local gourmet. "Difficult by their basic nature, slightly irritating, which risk degradation from the temperature of the place in which they age and from a warm season too short for the ripening of the grapes. They are also difficult to find on the market." Nevertheless Carema, made from the Nebbiolo grape, here called *picotener*, or *picotendro*, grown up to 2,000 feet, can have a good deal of finesse; it suggests a lighter version of Barolo, clearer in color, with an alcohol content of 12 to 13 degrees; the natives think enough of it to hold a grape festival every year at harvest time. The runner-up is Donnaz, also a Nebbiolo product, bright red, 12 degrees, with a slight bitter almond taste, locally reputed to be lightly aphrodisiac; it is drunk with pasta when young, and with roasts as it grows older. *Vin de l' Enfer*, Hell's Wine, grown in the French-speaking region between Aosta and Mont Blanc, is not so called from any quality of the beverage, but because it grows among rocks which throw back the heat of the sun, which is what makes it possible for the grapes to ripen nearly 4,000 feet up. The result is a small wine, but a quite drinkable one, 12 degrees, clear ruby-red, and a trifle sharp in taste. Toretta is a red dessert wine.

Whites include *Blanc de Morgex*, another high-growing wine, pale straw-yellow, 8 to 10 degrees, dry and quite acid, with a hint of Alpine herbs in its aftertaste, and several dessert wines. Montouvert, 13 to 14 degrees, an unctuous product of white Muscat grapes, owes its sweetness to fruit picked after the first frosts. The once widely known Malvasia di Nus continues to exist through the efforts of the parish priest of Nus; 11 to 12 degrees, a golden yellow, it is not over-sweet. Another wine which owes its continued existence to a single producer is Moscato di Chambave; it was widely produced before the phylloxera epidemic, which discouraged everybody else. It is of a rare type, a dry dessert wine—one might almost dare say a dry sweet wine, for its liqueur-like texture and high alcoholic content (15 degrees) suggest sweetness; but actually it is dry, though it does take on some sweetness with age. Young, it is often drunk with pasta; matured, it is taken with dessert, chilled, or as an *aperitivo*. It is made by a very ancient method. The grapes, picked when they are barely ripe, are hung up to dry in a room well aired but protected so that they will not freeze. They are then freed of skins and seeds, producing a must which ferments slowly and quietly—accounting, probably, for the slight aftertaste of must in the finished wine. It is aged four years in the wood, the first year in mulberry wood casks, before bottling. There is also a Grand Cru de Chambave, a dark red wine, 11 to 13 degrees, dry, with a rich bouquet, which, say the inhabitants of Champlan, who make it, forms a marriage of love with *carbonnade*.

The wine of the Valle d'Aosta is much inferior to that of the Alba region; but inferior wines often make superior brandies; Aosta wines do, and have been doing so for centuries. The brandy was called *acqua ardens* in the 13th century, and nowadays Aosta considers it the only Piedmont distillation worthy of the name of *grappa;* other Piedmontese eaux de vie are referred to disdainfully as *branda,* (the English brandy). The rest of Piedmont does not agree, so Cuneo dares produce *grappa piemontese stravecchia* and Alba makes a *grappa delle Langhe.* These are looked down upon by Aosta, especially when it is a question of the very special type of *grappa* made in this region, called *génépy.* In it are steeped the small yellow flowers of the herbs *artemisia genipi* and *artemisia glacialis,* found above 8,000 feet; it has a strong pungent flavor of aromatic herbs, and is 80 proof. Another wine by-product of the region is red wine, cooked in an earthenware vessel with cinnamon, cloves and sugar until foam begins to appear on its surface. Finally, one of the oldest, smallest and most famous breweries in Italy is that founded in Gressoney in 1837 by Antonio Zimmermann; the secret of the quality of its beer is the pure water of the mountain streams.

Liguria

The International Institute of Ligurian Studies, whose headquarters are at Bordighera, is not unanimously sure that the subject it studies exists. Writing in its official publication, the *Cahiers Ligures de Préhistoire et d'Archéologie*, F. C. Octobon remarked that "the origin of the Ligurians remains enshrouded in so much mystery that excellent authors have come to ask themselves the question, 'Was there ever an ethnic group or at least a people of that name?'" The French historian Pierre Belperron, in *La Croisade contre les Albigeois*, referred to the Ligurians as "a primitive aboriginal substratum which it is preferable not to try to identify, under pain of being shot down in flames by the ethnologists"—or, he might have added, by the archeologists; as the dean of British archeologists once put it: "Archeology is not a science, it's a vendetta." The Ligurians, says the Larousse encyclopedia, "were divided into numerous branches and did not constitute a political unit. Practically nothing is known of their civilization or their language." Some students think they did not constitute an ethnic unit either. The Encyclopaedia Britannica does not go this far—apparently it takes the existence of the Ligurians for granted—but refers cautiously to "the Ligurian ethnica," which is a plural, and might suggest that not all the tribes referred to at one time or another as Ligurians belonged to the same race. It produces nevertheless a description of the Ligurians as "thin and wiry, short of stature and dark complexioned, hardy and warlike." This comes from classical writings, but for the ancients, did "Ligurian" mean anything more precise than a convenient label to designate peoples living along the northern coast of the western Mediterranean whom they had not succeeded in identifying? Michelet did come pretty close to the ancient description when he called the people who occupy in Italy what the old writers considered the last stand of the Ligurians "a strong, small and hardy race." This would fit a good many Celts too, and is hardly conclusive proof that a Ligurian race ever existed. Perhaps the best evidence that it did, since it is so heart-felt and so devoid of doubt, is the very old popular simile: "He lies like a Ligurian."

Whether or not there were ever any Ligurians, there is a Liguria, a boomerang-shaped narrow strip of the northwest coast tucked into the curve where the Italian peninsula swells into the mainland, the size of Delaware. A simple look at the map would lead you to suspect that the sea is Liguria's hinterland; and if you have ever passed along its coast, by car or train, you know that it has to be. On the Riviera di Levante, the eastern stretch, the Apennines

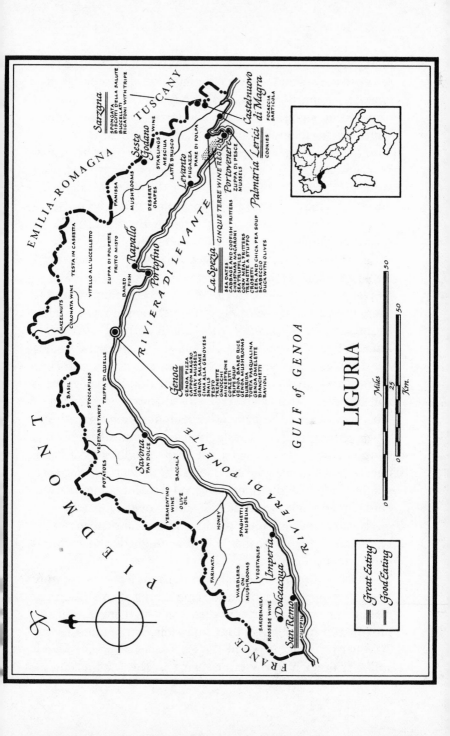

march right up to the sea. Going by car, much of the time the road runs along a shelf clinging to cliffs dropping precipitately beneath you to the water. By train, the railroad seems to be running through one long tunnel from which windows open briefly and brilliantly from time to time. This is perhaps the most spectacular way to make acquaintance with the Ligurian coast. The periods of darkness are tantalizing, but they are worth it for the contrast which intensifies so mightily the flood of light during the open intervals, when the view plunges down the dark flanks of those perpendicular mountains, with bright patches of color clinging to their sides, for flowers bloom everywhere here, down to the clear bright blue sea.

The provinces of Liguria are four. Starting from the French frontier, at Ventimiglia (which comes from Album Intimilium, or Capital of the Intimilian tribe), they are Imperia and Savona, on the Riviera di Ponente, and Genoa and La Spezia on the Riviera di Levante. Since they form a narrow and largely mountainous strip along the coast, it is not surprising that their agricultural importance is slight. Only a quarter of the population is employed in agriculture, a proportion unique in Italy; and of this small number, a considerable part is engaged not in the production of food, but of flowers, particularly along the Riviera di Ponente, where the production of olive oil is decreasing because commercial flower growing is taking over land from the olive groves. Liguria once produced more oil than any other region of Italy; its quality is still renowned, and it dominates the local cuisine.

The low proportion of farmers in Liguria results not only from its topography, but also from strong competition for manpower from other activities. One of them is tourism; one-quarter of all Italian tourism is concentrated in Liguria. Another is the industries of the sea. Genoa's genius today is still maritime. It is the largest port in the Mediterranean, and the outlet to the sea for landlocked Switzerland. Its shipyards and drydocks employ a large proportion of the population; and there are of course many sailors, though not as many fishermen as you might expect, for the Ligurian coast is not particularly rich in fish—at least not nowadays, for industry has polluted these waters. There may have been more fish in earlier times, as at least two place names indicate. Santa Margherita was once called Pescino (little fish), apparently because of the abundance of fish in its gulf; and Portofino, according to Pliny, was originally Portus Delphini, because of the large numbers of dolphins accustomed to taking refuge from storms in its sheltered bay. Liguria now produces less oil than it consumes, and consequently imports it. It produces wine, but of unremarkable quality, and consequently imports it. Honey is a natural by-product of flower cultivation, and it consequently exports it.

The chief products of the land are fruit, especially oranges and lemons, green vegetables in Imperia and Savona especially, and potatoes. A feature of the Genoa street scene is vendors of *resta*—strings of hazelnuts. Special mention should be made of a table grape grown in Niassa, in the La Spezia area, the *uva di bosco*, oval and golden. And of course Liguria is famous for the herbs which grow on the slopes of its hills so thickly that in the days before natural scents had to compete with the fumes of automobile exhausts, fuel oil, and the exhalations of chemical factories, ships beating into port against an offshore wind counted as their first landfall the fragrance of sweet basil, blown far out to sea.

If the Ligurian sea is less rich in fish than the Adriatic, it nevertheless provides most of the familiar fish of the Mediterranean, and in particular one specialty of the Gulf of La Spezia, *datteri di mare*, sea dates. This is a mussel named for its shape, not confined to this region, but for some reason most luscious when pried from the rocks to which it attaches itself on Palmeria Island, and at Portovenere, where it has a particular affection for the dike. Its scientific name is unusually accurate in its description—*lithodomus dactilus*, rock-dwelling finger. The Emperor Frederick Barbarossa was particularly fond of these mussels. He stipulated that his vassals of La Spezia should include in the tribute they brought him from time to time a large shield heaped with sea dates. The region is also rich in the more common everyday mussels, *mitili* or *muscoli* (*mytilus edulis*), which it exports in quantities second only to the great shellfish hatcheries of Taranto. They are eaten raw with lemon juice and pepper; or floured and fried in oil; or are used to make soup; or go with tomato and parsley into a sauce for pasta or rice. Genoa boasts another curious mussel—the *cozza pelosa*, so called because its shell is covered with hair.

Given the geography of Liguria, which offers little space for large-scale raising of pigs, one would not expect this to be sausage country, and it is not. Nevertheless there is a tasty *salame genovese*, half veal and the other half two parts pork to three parts pork fat. It is strongly spiced, and is a favorite hors d'oeuvre with raw broad beans and Sardinian sheep cheese. This is the favorite cheese of Liguria, which does not go in for cheese making itself, for the same reasons which prevent it from being sausage country; where there is little room for hogs, there obviously cannot be much for cows, sheep or goats.

It was not the bankers or the merchants of Liguria who shaped its cooking, it was the sailors. They did it long ago, and it has not altered substantially since. It is still a sea-inspired cuisine dating from the time of sailing ships, and to understand its anomalies, you must envision shipboard life in those days. Voyages lasted for weeks or months, and were often lengthened far beyond expectation by contrary winds or dead calms. Except for a few days after each stop at a port, the fare was restricted, monotonously, in those days before refrigeration, to foods which would keep indefinitely even in the heat of the tropical seas which Genoese ships so often visited. This often meant, chiefly, salt meat; dried beans; and sea biscuit, devised not for its appeal to the taste buds but for its comparative immunity to mold and weevils.

The cooking of Liguria was tailored to fit the desires of the returned seafarer.

The most salient feature of Ligurian cooking is a presence—of aromatic herbs. Its second most important characteristic is an absence—of spices, so freely used elsewhere in Italy. The extensive use of herbs resulted from the yearning of the deep-sea sailor for freshness (the dietician would say for vitamins). Liguria makes almost a cult of one of them, sweet basil, *basilico* in Italian, from the Greek word, "kingly." It was indeed considered in antiquity as a sacred plant, which was cut only with an instrument of some noble metal (iron was considered too base for this task) by a person who had previously performed purificatory rites, and in the absence of anyone in a state of impurity, for instance women during menstrual periods. A Christian legend says that Saint Helena, mother of the Emperor Constantine, received a divine revelation that the true Cross would be found where the air was sweet with perfume; she found it under a patch of basil. Whether they believe the legend or not, Genoese have a special cult for basil. Those who have no plot of land in the suburbs to raise it for themselves place old tomato cans in sunny spots on their windowsills, filled with carefully selected soil rich with humus, in which they grow their own private supply of basil.

Basil is by no means alone in the Ligurian herbal. Among other favorite flavoring elements in Ligurian cooking are bay and laurel, oregano and sweet marjoram, fennel and mint, sage and rosemary, wood mushrooms and garlic, borage and parsley, olives and capers, pine nuts and walnuts. Their fragrance in the dishes offered him when he returned home restored for the old-time sailor the charm of the damp woods, of the verdure of the fields, of the sun on the mountain slopes, of the freshness of riverbanks.

This explains the presence of herbs; but what explains the absence of spices? Until the Portuguese rounded Africa in 1488, Venice and Genoa were the great providers of spices for the Western world. The Venetians consumed a good deal of spice themselves; the Genoese sold it to others. It was not simply because the Genoese were merchants that they preferred to convert into cash the most precious commodities of the medieval world; Venetian mercantilism was well developed too. The different seasoning habits arose primarily because the Genoese were deep-sea sailors, the Venetians church-steeple navigators. Venetian ships were never long out of sight of land. They sailed down the Adriatic, guiding themselves by landmarks on shore, turned eastward when they left their own sea, and threaded the islands of Greece to Asia Minor. They breathed continually the offshore breezes with their fragrance of the soil. The Genoese spice carriers, in their long voyages beyond sight of land, breathed day and night (rising through the hatches which covered their holds) the nauseating odors of pepper from India, cloves from Zanzibar, cinnamon from Ceylon, pimento from the West Indies. By the time they docked, the Genoese sailors needed an antidote. They neutralized these heavy fragrances by the lighter scents of herbs. The last thing in the world they wanted was more spice. There was one exception. The Genoese consumed, aboard ship but not ashore, ginger. It staves off scurvy.

Several other characteristics of Ligurian cooking stem also from Genoa's vocation for the sea. Two of them originated from the nature of the situation when the sailor returned, after months or years of absence, to his family. It was a moment of festival, of celebration. No pains were too great to be taken to please the wayfarer, so that Genoese cooking is distinguished by patience. Minestrone becomes velvety through long slow cooking (it is *confeto*, the Genoese put it, local dialect for *crogiolato*, simmered), a process during which it develops a symphony of tastes and smells; pot roasts are cooked lengthily and braised beef is referred to as *stracotto*, "overcooked," constantly tended while it smokes over a few glowing embers of coal; the juices are slowly sweated out of meat, so that they become syrupy and are used as the base for the sauces with which ravioli and lasagne are flavored. For the same reason, Genoese cooking became elaborate. Every dish had to be a festive dish. Even if it were as humble as a vegetable tart, it was brought to an apotheosis as *torta Pasqualina*. Stuffed breast of veal became the complicated *cima genovese*. Fish salad developed into a work of art, or of architecture, in that peculiarly Genoese confection, *cappon magro*.

The tradition of festive elaboration accounts in part for the prevalence in Ligurian cooking of stuffings. Everything is stuffed—pasta, meat, fish, shellfish, vegetables, mushrooms, even fruit. Stuffings permit the subtle combination of ingredients to produce an exultant final result. Each stuffing by itself is a work of art. Most Ligurian stuffings are dominated by vegetables, whose attraction for the seafarer has by now become clear. They are likely to be made on baking days; after the bread has been taken out of the oven, the stuffing goes in, to be lightly cooked in a cooling oven. In this form it may be eaten alone, hot; ordinarily it is even better cold the next day. But usually it has been designed to finish its cooking as a filling for something else. There are unlimited varieties of stuffing, each concocted with an eye to the food it is to enhance, with which it should achieve perfect harmony and homogeneity. There is also another almost contradictory reason for the prevalence of stuffings in Ligurian cooking—economy, a shipboard habit, as we shall see when we reach ravioli.

Finally, what appears to be an anomaly of Ligurian cooking: though seafood dishes are not lacking, fish plays a much less important role in the diet than might be expected from a territory which is virtually all coast. The eating habits of sailors explain this too. On long voyages, the only fresh food available was fish. They had a surfeit of it. It was not what they wanted when they reached land.

Of the many specifically Ligurian or Genoese dishes, two stand out particularly for precisely opposite reasons— *pesto*, because it is so sharply localized, unfindable elsewhere; ravioli, because it has spread around the world, and is eaten everywhere by persons who have no idea that it originated in Genoa—or more exactly, on board Genoese ships.

The statement that *pesto* is not found outside of Liguria requires one qualification. On the French Riviera, adjoining Liguria, there is a local variant of *pesto* called *pistou*. It marks the former presence of the Genoese in this area. *Pistou* is much milder than *pesto*. The Genoese sailors, who found in its basil and garlic the green freshness and the earthy pungency they craved after their long odysseys, wanted those qualities in strong, even exaggerated, form. The *pesto* of Genoa is sharp and challenging. When the cookbook of Luigi Carnacini was translated into French, the recipe he had given for *pesto* in the Italian version was toned down because it was "too aggressive" for the French. It is not always aggressive, even in Liguria. The *pesto* I ate in Genoa's excellent La Santa restaurant seemed to me unaccustomedly mild, and I asked the chef why. He told me he did not use the traditional recipe of Genoa, but that of Nervi, smoother because it adds cream. This is a good example of the localism of Italian food; Nervi is just seven miles south of Genoa, yet it manages to escape the culinary magnetism of the capital and have ideas of its own. Almost every Ligurian town of any importance has developed its own variant of *pesto*.

What is *pesto?* You will often find the name alone on a bill of fare along with the soups; and if you order it, soup is what you will get—usually a thick minestrone. But *pesto*, properly speaking, is not the soup, but the sauce which is added to it at the last moment. The same sauce is also often applied to pasta, in which case the favorite vehicle for it is *trenette*, the local variety of ribbon pasta. After that, *pesto* appears oftenest on gnocchi, of which the two favorite varieties in Liguria are *gnocchi alla genovese*, made with potatoes, and *gnocchi verdi*, made with spinach.

The soul of *pesto* is basil, and the patience and care characteristic of Genoese cooking appear from the very start of *pesto* making in the meticulous preparation of the basil. It is first deprived of its stems and central veins; only the deveined leaves go into the mortar in which it will be ground. *Pesto* makers are adamant on this point: no one can chop the ingredients fine enough; they must be ground, and, it is specified, in a marble mortar (with a pestle "of good wood," one recipe adds, but does not insist on any specific sort of wood). You begin by crushing the basil leaves carefully with coarse kitchen salt and a clove of garlic. The tender green color of this mixture is your guide for the rest of the process. It should be maintained as the other ingredients are added; if it weakens, put in more basil. Next you add equal parts of young Sardinian pecorino cheese and old Parmesan (if you want a stronger taste, increase the proportion of the sharp Sardinian cheese; if you want it milder, decrease it). As you grind this with the rest, add olive oil (preferably Ligurian) drop by drop, until you have achieved the desired density (you may want it thicker for soup than for pasta). The last ingredient is pine nuts (some persons use walnuts instead), which must also be crushed so thoroughly that they become an indistinguishable part of the whole pungent creamy mass.

When *pesto* goes into minestrone, it must not be cooked with it. This would destroy the fresh sharpness of the sauce. Every recipe I have ever seen says that it should be added at the very end of the cooking, and stirred into the soup—the stirring is indispensable, one of them adds, to prevent the *pesto* from sticking to the bottom of the pan. This contradicts my own experience, which is that I have always been served *pesto* in soup floating raft-like on the surface, like sour cream on borscht or *rouille* on *soupe aux poissons*. Perhaps I was supposed to stir it in myself, but I didn't.

The minestrone with *pesto* which I sampled at La Santa contained peas, potatoes, a little onion, olive oil, garlic, and a few herbs, rather a restrained selection for Genoa. Usually minestrone in Liguria is much richer. One recipe I have, in a Ligurian cookbook, describes *minestrone alla genovese* as containing not only all the ingredients mentioned above, but also squash, cabbage, zucchini, fava beans, red beans, string beans, a ripe peeled pitted tomato, diced eggplant and celery. It also offers a choice of several varieties of pasta to add to the soup, just to make sure it is thick enough—vermicelli, *maccheroncini rigati*, *ditalini* or *penne*, but recommends *tagliatelle*, a rather filling variety.

As for ravioli, its Genoese origin seems confirmed both by the story of its invention and its name. Until the beginning of the 19th century, this form of pasta was called *rabiole*, which is a Genoese dialect word meaning things of little value—rubbish, say, or, in the kitchen, leftovers. On shipboard, at least in the days of sail, making use of leftovers was important; if they were thrown away, a ship might risk running out of food if the voyage were unexpectedly prolonged. The story is that on Genoese ships anything left over at one meal was chopped up together, whatever it might be, stuffed into envelopes of pasta, and served at the following meal. The contents of shipboard ravioli could not have been very exciting; but Genoese ravioli today are often highly elaborate. To begin with, the pasta envelope is made with the finest wheat flour and with eggs. The stuffing called for by my Ligurian cookbook to produce *ravioli alla genovese* is lean veal, heifer's udder, calves' brains, sweetbreads, egg, bread crumbs, grated Parmesan cheese, chopped chard, borage, and nutmeg. This formula can of course be varied, but apparently not very much without losing the right to the name of *genovese*. Another version replaces the veal, including the udders, by chicken and sausage meat or ham, but maintains all the other ingredients. Whatever goes into the ravioli, it is eaten in Liguria either in soup (*pasta in brodo*), or as *pasta asciutta* with a variety of sauces or accompaniments—meat or tomato sauces, mushroom sauce, with truffles, or simply with butter and grated cheese.

Ravioli is an exception in the Ligurian list of dishes, one of the rare travelers. Most Genoese dishes do not turn up elsewhere in Italy. Ligurian cooking is perhaps more distinct from northern Italian cooking in general than that of any other single region of the North, to such an extent that even Italian "international" restaurants which offer a hodge-podge of regional dishes from other parts of the country generally let Ligurian dishes strictly alone. In some cases, it may be suspected that an impelling reason is that only Ligurians have the patience to make some of their specialties—for instance, *cappon magro*.

Cappon magro means, literally, "fast-day capon," a deceptive name for two reasons: it contains no capon, and the person who tackles it is not exactly going to fast, for it is "a dish worthy of Homeric heroes," according to gastronomic writer Achille Noli. It does meet the literal definition of the foods permitted during periods of fasting by containing no meat. It is a fish and vegetable salad, possibly the most elaborate salad in the world.

It is understandable that non-Ligurians have not been tempted to engage in the complexities of preparing this dish. In the first place, it contains so many different ingredients that it is not practical to prepare it for a small number of persons. Eight would be the absolute minimum, but it really isn't worth the trouble for fewer than 12. Then it demands that practically each ingredient be cooked separately, which can tie up every saucepan in the kitchen. Finally, a large number of separate operations are involved, which break down into four general groups, as follows: (1) preparing the foundation for a finished structure which is going to be a towering pyramid or cone; (2) cooking and seasoning the ingredients with which the pyramid is to be built; (3) doing the same for other ingredients whose function is decorative; (4) making the sauce. To these one might add (5), putting the whole thing together, which is less the work of a cook than of an architect.

To complicate the situation further, *cappon magro* is one of those dishes for which there is no fixed invariable list of ingredients, though there is one without which, some (but not all) Genoese authorities insist firmly, *cappon magro* cannot really be considered *cappon magro*. This is *scorzonera*, or Goat's Beard, whose absence from a mess of *cappon magro* would probably not greatly distress most American eaters, since it is a form of salsify, a vegetable not highly esteemed in the United States; it also has the disadvantage that after being peeled it has to be put into water containing vinegar or lemon juice to keep it from turning unappetizingly black. The name is curious. It comes from the Catalan *escorzo*, a type of viper; the plant also grows in Catalonia, and may very well have been imported into

Italy by Catalans. The Catalans gave it that name because it was supposed to counteract viper venom, as whisky is sometimes held to be sovereign against rattlesnake bite. The efficacy of both is probably roughly equal. The ingredients I give below for *cappon magro* are taken from the formula of a Genoese expert who does not insist on *scorzonera*, since it strikes me as the most authentic, on the basis of my own personal eating experience. I have marked with an asterisk (*) those ingredients which appear in every recipe known to me; I imagine they can be considered as basic to genuine *cappon magro*.

Operation 1: The base of your structure is going to be sea biscuit.* It is first rubbed with garlic,* and then put into salted water mixed with vinegar* to soften it. It may be that this element, rather than the whole dish, accounts for the name *cappon* (capon). The French also sarcastically call *chapon* (capon) a slice of bread rubbed with garlic, sometimes moistened also with olive oil or a bit of consommé, placed in the bottom of a salad bowl or in a soup plate.

Operation 2: You boil separately the following vegetables: cabbage, green beans,* celery,* carrots,* beets* and potatoes.* The vegetables are cut into pieces (the potatoes and beets into thin slices) and each is seasoned separately with olive oil, vinegar and salt. You also boil a fish of firm white flesh* (dentex, chrysophrys, *capone*, sea bass, or the like) and, separately, a lobster. Both the fish and the lobster are treated like the vegetables—cut into pieces and seasoned with olive oil, vinegar and salt. This list is subject to considerable individual variation—I have even heard of oysters being added to *cappon magro*, a rather horrible idea.

Operation 3: Some of the decorative elements of your *cappon magro* you will be able to buy already prepared: green olives,* anchovy fillets, *botargo* (tuna roe), capers, pickles and button mushrooms preserved in oil. In addition, you boil crayfish, small artichokes, which are cut into quarters, and hard-boiled eggs,* also quartered.

Operation 4: The sauce for *cappon magro* is more standardized than the salad itself. It is made by grinding together in a mortar parsley,* garlic,* pine nuts, capers,* anchovy fillets,* the yolks of hard-boiled eggs,* crustless bread soaked in vinegar (those who omit this usually replace it with bread crumbs), and pitted preserved green olives.* (Some cooks add fennel.) When this has been reduced to a smooth creamy paste, vinegar and olive oil are added, the latter drop by drop while the mixture is being stirred constantly and vigorously, as in beating mayonnaise.

It is now time for the cook to become an artist.

To build the pyramid of all these ingredients, some timorous cooks use a mold, but it gets in the way of the composition; most chefs scorn it. They simply lay their sea biscuits on a large round platter, and pour some oil over them for a beginning. Now they take their main materials (all except the lobster) and begin to build up the pyramid, layer on layer. One basic technique is to make each layer of the same ingredient, with alternating layers of fish and vegetables; but there is no invariable rule, and some pyramid builders prefer to variegate the layers, which does have the effect of making it easier to serve each individual eater with a sample of everything that has gone into the salad. Each layer as it is built up is doused abundantly with the sauce, but not so abundantly as to allow it to run over the sides and obscure the pattern. The decorative elements can be used to stud the pyramid with spots of color here and there, or they may be arranged to run up and down the pyramid in gay bands. Now at last comes the turn of the lobster. It constitutes the top layer, with its scarlet coral on top. No sauce should be poured over this culminating glory; the coral is meant to be seen, for the finished dish is essentially a work of art. Striped with green (cabbage, beans), white (fish, celery), orange (carrots), sombre red (beets); crowned with scarlet on white; high-lighted with the rich red of crayfish and the yellow of egg yolks, it looks almost too good to eat. It takes a brave man to plunge the first spoon into this creation and initiate its destruction.

Cima alla genovese is also a dish which you are not likely to find reproduced elsewhere, though it does have near relatives. In essence it is simply stuffed breast or shoulder of veal. Genoa does it with more sophistication than else-where. The chief ingredients of the stuffing are chopped veal (recipes that call for pork have probably originated elsewhere than in Genoa), sweetbreads, brains, peas (and artichokes in season), pistachio nuts, grated cheese, marjo-ram and garlic, the whole moistened in enough beaten egg to cover the stuffing completely. Whole hard-boiled eggs go into the middle of the stuffing. Both stuffing and pocket of veal have been partly cooked separately before the veal is filled with the stuffing, and the whole is boiled slowly for about an hour and a half in water in which a bay leaf, onions and carrots have been placed. After cooking, the *cima* is pressed under weights in a cool place, and is eventually served sliced.

Also particularly Ligurian, but not confined to that area, is the vegetable tart, which reaches its highest, and most typically Genoese, form at Easter, in the *torta Pas-qualina*. The region seems particularly conscious of reli-gious holidays, as is evident from the many dishes listed in two versions in local cookbooks, one for fast days and the other for everyday use—for instance, there are *ravioli grassi*, with meat in the stuffing, and *ravioli magri*, which contain only vegetables. Among dishes tied to holidays are the cabbage with codfish fritters which La Spezia eats on Christmas Eve, followed in the same city on Christmas itself by *i maccheroni di Natale*, which is the thick ribbed variety called *rigatoni*, with a meat sauce. Sarzana also eats *rigatoni* for Christmas, but with tripe. La Spezia has a special pastry for Christmas, a honey-flavored fritter. In Pegazzano the feast of the Madonna dell'Acqua Santa Selvatica is marked by the appearance of *mescina*, a dish of chick peas, beans and wheat, flavored with olive oil. There are many other specialties which appear on holidays, especially in the pastry department.

The *torta Pasqualina*, as befits its celebrational character, is richer than ordinary vegetable tarts, both in its filling and its crust. The latter is of puff paste; the former is a creamy mixture of leeks, curds (*quagliata* in Italian, *prescin-seua* in one Ligurian dialect, *sairas* in another), eggs (with a small piece of butter placed on each egg), milk, olive oil and grated cheese. The tart is not open-faced, as it so often is in Italy, but covered with crust, as for an American pie. After baking in the oven, it is allowed to cool off slightly before eating; it is also excellent cold. Similar tarts, using ordinary pie crust, also including curds and eggs, are made of various other vegetables—for instance, spinach, artichokes, and one rather unusual combination of chopped flap mushrooms and zucchini squash, with a little chopped onion and parsley thrown in for good measure.

ANTIPASTI AND ENTRÉES: A favorite start for the meal in Liguria, especially in the province of La Spezia, is the sea truffle, eaten raw with lemon juice. This is one example of the confusing nature of Italian food names, especially of shellfish (for instance, the type of clams called *arselle* in Genoa—and Sardinia—are *vongole* in Rome and Naples, *capperozzoli* in Venice, *calcinelli* or *telline* in Ravenna). The *tartufo di mare* of Genoa (*Venus verrucosa*), a small clam, is no relation to the sea truffle of the Adriatic (*microcosmus sulcatus*), a tuber. These clams were formerly used in soup, or in sauces for pasta; but lately they have become rare, and when fishermen are lucky enough to find a mess of them hidden in the sand of the beaches, they prefer to benefit by the opportunity to savor their subtle taste unveiled by mixture with other ingredients.

In the processed meat category, there is *cotichelle*, a pigskin casing stuffed with mixed chopped pork and fat, with egg and grated cheese, cooked in gravy. Snails (*lumache alla genovese*) are served with a minimum of disguise, simply salted, floured and fried in olive oil. *Funghi alla genovese* are heavily peppered mushrooms cooked in olive oil on grape leaves, and eaten with cloves. The Ligurian way with scrambled eggs (*imbrogliata di uovo con pomodoro*) combines them with bacon and tomatoes. *Frittata genovese*, Genoa omelet, mixes the eggs with grated cheese, basil, and chopped spinach. *Riso arrosto alla genovese* is pretty substantial as an entrée; it can also very easily be the main dish. It is a timbale of rice with sausages, peas, artichokes, mushrooms, onions and grated cheese, baked in the oven; this is a comparatively modern development from an older form of this dish which used chopped veal instead of sausages, only parsley instead of peas and artichokes, and no mushrooms (some cooks still omit the mushrooms). *Riso arrosto* is not the same thing as *riso alla genovese*, which is only boiled, not baked afterwards, and adds nothing to the rice except a sauce including chopped beef or veal, carrots, celery, onion, herbs and white wine; it is served with grated cheese on the side.

There are various kinds of pizza, a dish ordinarily thought of as Neapolitan, but the definition of pizza is simply tart or pie; any flat round crusty dish can be called a pizza, and as in Italy it plays the role of the sandwich elsewhere (a snack that can be picked up conveniently and eaten from the hand) it is found in some form or other almost everywhere in the country, though not always under that name. It *is* called pizza in Liguria (at least, most of the time; but it *can* also be called *focaccia* and there are many possible fillings for it). Fairly standardized are *pizza alla genovese*, which contains mussels, mushrooms and ham, and *pizza alla Liguria*, which is mostly onions, with highlights of black olive and anchovy fillets. The *sardenaira* of the Riviera di Ponente is also a pizza, whose ingredients, besides the crust, comprise tomato, anchovy, onion, olive oil, marjoram, garlic, capers and black olives.

When we reach the doughy dishes of the province of La Spezia, we experience a feeling of familiarity. Where have we encountered before that specialty of Sarzana, *buccellato*, a thin pancake which may reach four feet in diameter? Where the *fugazza* of Levanto, cooked on chestnut leaves on a hot earthenware disk? One immediately thinks of the giant *borlengo*, and the *tigella* of Modena. (*Tigella* is called *tosco* or *tosto* in La Spezia.) Why, you may wonder, have these dishes skipped from Modena over Reggio Emilia, Parma, Piacenza, Tortona and Genoa to reach La Spezia? The answer is that they haven't. This is the way it looks if you think of the route you take between these two cities by the automobile roads. But these are dishes, not of the city of Modena, but of the mountainous southern section of the province of Modena, in the Apennines. If you pushed your way on foot from Modena straight across the Apennines toward the coast, you would come out in the province of La Spezia, most precisely at Sarzana, home of the *buccellato*, which is in the mountains too. We have here a gastronomic island which straddles two regions, determined not by political boundaries but by the nature of the terrain. La Spezia offers many other examples of this family of doughy dishes, typical of mountain fare. Levanto has not only *fugazza* (which is made of maize flour, while Modena's *tigella* is of wheat), but also *pane di polpa*, an oven-baked bun of raised dough mixed with the skins and pulp left after the pressing of olives for oil. A rustic specialty of La Spezia is cornmeal fritters with chopped onions in the dough, while another type of fritter, of chestnut flour with pine nuts and raisins, comes pretty close to qualifying as a dessert. *Panigacci* are leaves of pastry cooked on earthenware disks with grated cheese and olive oil spread over each layer of dough. *Farinata* is a Ligurian form of polenta made of chick pea flour; if it is allowed to cool, is cut into lozenge-shaped pieces, soaked in olive oil with chopped onions, doused with mushroom sauce and grated cheese, and put back into the oven to develop a crust, it becomes *paniccia* or (the popular term) *panissa*. Very Ligurian is *il latte brusco*, literally sour milk, though it isn't; its more formal name, *frittura di crema*, cream fritter, is closer to the reality. You start with a *soffritto* of finely chopped parsley and much onion browned in 2½ tablespoons of butter. A cup of flour is stirred into a quart of milk, or even cream, added to the *soffritto*, salted, and cooked over a very low flame for about half an hour, constantly stirred. The saucepan is now taken off the stove, four egg yolks are beaten into the rest, and it goes back onto the stove for another half hour, being stirred constantly. Now you pour it into a large plate or bowl, with a few drops of olive oil in the bottom, and let it cool and harden. It is then cut into small bite-sized morsels, dipped in the beaten whites of the four eggs and then dipped in bread crumbs (or coarse semolina flour), deep-fried in boiling oil, and served hot and crusty.

The province of Imperia is noted for its many pasta companies, so it is not surprising to find here, at Pontedassio, the fascinating Spaghetti Historical Museum. It is housed in an early-19th-century building which is presented as having been at one time the first commercial spaghetti factory, an assertion which I permit myself to doubt. In any case the museum disposes of the fable that Marco Polo brought pasta back from China, for it traces its history from Etruscan times. Written documentation begins with the 13th century, and includes Papal bulls fixing standards of quality for spaghetti. Perhaps this vigilance had been relaxed by the 16th century, when Dr. Giovanni da Vigo wrote a learned article, on display here, warning of the dangers to health involved in eating spaghetti; however, both pasta and pasta eaters have survived. Exhibits of pasta-making machinery demonstrate that even the ancients had mechanical devices for producing it. Schopenhauer's anti-spaghetti views are given prominent position, and so are cartoons dealing with the difficulties of eating spaghetti. The museum offers counsel on this point: You should not raise a forkful of spaghetti over the head and attempt to lower the slippery strings into your mouth at the risk of wrapping them around your chin. You should not roll the spaghetti into a ball around your fork in a large spoon. You should use only the fork, pressing the tines against the bottom of the plate, perpendicular to it, and turning it to twist a few strands around the fork. It should not be cut, and dangling ends should not be bitten off and allowed to drop back into the plate. They are disposed of instead in another fashion, enshrined among the museum's exhibits: "Spaghetti can be eaten successfully if you inhale it like a vacuum cleaner." The name of the authority affixed to this piece of advice is Sophia Loren.

Trenette, married with *pesto*, is, as we have already seen, the favorite pasta of Liguria. La Spezia also offers *trenette a stuffo*, which is served with a bean sauce, and the same province also makes several other local varieties of pasta, some of them inspired by the region's consciousness of holidays—for instance, a specially rich stuffing for ravioli at Carnival. From La Spezia also come *crosetti*, of leavened dough, stamped with traditional patterns, and served with meat sauce. Genoa has *corzetti alla polceverasca*, egg pasta in the form of the figure 8. *La pasta con gli ovoli* can only be served in September and October, for it is necessary to have at the same time the milky orange agaric mushrooms and green walnuts; the latter, crushed into a paste with garlic, olive oil and grated cheese, forms the sauce for the pasta, along with the minced mushrooms.

SOUPS: Liguria claims to have invented minestrone, though it does not really seem likely that any single place stumbled alone upon the idea of putting whatever happened to be in the kitchen into a pot and converting it into soup. A story told locally about the origin of this soup is apparently intended to support Liguria's claim to paternity, but it is not particularly convincing. For what it is worth, the story is that Genoese soldiers serving in the First Crusade under Godfrey of Bouillon provided a meal for their leader by requisitioning from the local inhabitants vegetables and herbs from which they cooked soup in their helmets. The theory that this is why consommé is also called bouillon can be taken with as much salt as would go into the bouillon; it is obviously our word "boil," which derives from the Latin *bullire*. However, the story recounts that in drumming up their ingredients, the Genoese Crusaders explained that they were "for Bouillon"—in their dialect, *pro Buggiun;* and to this day a simpler version of Genoese minestrone is known in Ligurian country districts as *pre-buggiun.*

Besides Genoese minestrone, two soups require mention: the leek and chick-pea soup of La Spezia, which also contains garlic, olive oil, celery, onions, and tomato extract, and is served during Lent; and a very old Genoese dish, *sbira,* tripe soup. The dish takes its name from *sbirri,* policemen, who were reputed in medieval times to feed almost exclusively on this dish. It consists of beef consommé containing a few pieces of braised beef and a great many pieces of tripe, flavored with rosemary and garlic, and served with grated cheese. There is also a *zuppa di polpette,* containing croquettes of the same filling which goes into Genoese ravioli (not the fast-day variety, of course).

As for fish soups, once you dispose of special cases, like *zuppa di datteri*, mussel soup, you are faced with a problem of nomenclature. What is the difference between *burrida*, which seems to be a generalized name for fish soup in Liguria; *zuppa di pesce*, which literally means simply "fish soup," and is the term favored in La Spezia; and *ciuppin*, a dialect word? They seem to change in meaning from town to town, and in many places to be used interchangeably. Whatever a Ligurian fish stew is called, it starts out the same way, with a *soffritto*, in this case of olive oil, onions, garlic, celery, carrots, and parsley, to which, after this has been lightly browned, peeled seeded tomatoes and white wine are added. When it has cooked for a quarter hour, the fish go in, scaled or skinned, whole (so only relatively small fish are used), the firm-fleshed varieties (hogfish, *capone*, priestfish) on the bottom, the softer ones (henfish, *tracine*) on top, and are simmered slowly for about an hour. Slices of bread fried in oil are placed in the bottom of the soup plates, the liquid (strained) poured over them, and the fish heaped on top.

A common characteristic of *ciuppin* seems to be eclecticism; the principle is that every kind of fish found in the catch is used. La Spezia, however, which prefers to use the Italian term *zuppa di pesce*, goes to the opposite extreme, almost to austerity. It uses only rock fish, and the *soffritto* is reduced to its bare essentials—olive oil, parsley and garlic (no tomato), to which white wine is added. It is a great specialty here, and La Spezia claims it makes the best fish soup of the region, especially at Portovenere, which is also famous for its mussel soup.

Finally comes *burrida*, apparently covering all fish stews, perhaps including *ciuppin* or *zuppa di pesce*. The most authentic recipe I have for *burrida* uses the same *soffritto* as *ciuppin*, including tomatoes, but adds pine nuts and anchovy fillets to it, and omits the white wine; it also uses only rock fish. Another is identical, but does use white wine, and permits the addition of clams, removed from their shells. The most permissive of all also admits, optionally, clams and mussels, *in* their shells, shrimp, mushrooms, and all sorts of fish, including members of the octopus and eel families.

FISH: If Liguria does not put as much emphasis on fish as might be expected from its geography, it is far from ignoring the products of the sea which washes its shores. Indeed, it was in Genoa that I made one of the most delightful discoveries of my life in the realm of seafood. It was a very simple one, *bianchetti*, extremely tiny white fish; they must have been taken immediately after hatching. They were so small that there were a few hundred in my portion, and I felt somewhat guilty about contributing so massively to the depletion of Mediterranean fisheries. My conscience was quickly silenced, for the fish were delicious, with a quite indescribable delicacy of flavor. The cook had wisely done as little as possible to them. If they were cooked at all, it could have been no more than a swift light poaching; and they were served with the lightest possible sauce of extremely fine olive oil and lemon juice. This is not the way *bianchetti* are served everywhere. They may be breaded, lowered briefly in a sieve into violently boiling oil, drained, salted and served piping hot and crackling, when they are called *rossetti*. This is good too, but far from as subtle as the *bianchetti* I tasted in the simpler fashion.

Some other sections of Liguria are more given to fish specialties than Genoa itself. La Spezia has one called *scabeccio*, which is fried mullet pickled in vinegar flavored with sage and rosemary; this is obviously the same word as the Neapolitan *scapace*, which also refers to pickled fish. Along the coast of the Tigullian Gulf, roughly from Portofino to Sestri Levante, there is a specialty of baked fish, marinated in olive oil and lemon juice for an hour, put in the oven in this liquid, basted from time to time with a mixture of olive oil and white wine, and enriched ten minutes before the end of the cooking with a mixture of three parts chopped pickled mushrooms to one of capers. "If it isn't good," goes the local saying, "change your cook." Fresh anchovies are stuffed with a mixture of bread well moistened with milk, eggs, grated cheese, garlic, marjoram and parsley, baked in an oiled pan in the oven, with a little more olive oil poured over it; anchovies stuffed in the same fashion are also sometimes dipped in beaten egg, rolled in bread crumbs, and fried in oil. In the months of April and June, when anchovies are particularly good, the stuffing is often dispensed with, and after the fish have been scaled and their heads, tails and fins cut off, they are dipped in egg and bread crumbs and fried in oil without other additions, as are fresh sardines, considered, however, less choice than anchovies.

In Genoa eels are cut into chunks and cooked in white wine and olive oil with onions, mushrooms, peas, anchovy fillets, garlic and tomato sauce. Squid, also cut into small pieces, is cooked in water and olive oil, with chopped onions, mushrooms and parsley, tomato sauce, garlic and rosemary. Small fish called *signorini* are breaded and fried. There are the hard-shelled *moscardini* clams, which look like stones, and *calamaretti*, also called sea strawberries because of their color when cooked. And like other Italian coastal areas which, in spite of their access to fresh fish, make use of dried or salted cod, Liguria has its specialties of *stoccafisso* or *baccalà*. *Stoccafisso* (*stocchefisso* in the local dialect) is soaked in milk for 12 hours, and then cooked very slowly in olive oil, or it is stewed, also very slowly, with mushrooms, parsley, onions, carrots, celery, anchovy fillets, olive oil, garlic, tomatoes, potatoes, pitted green olives and pine nuts. *Baccalà* goes into fritters, for which the salt cod, softened by soaking and cut into pieces, is mixed with flour and fried in oil; or it is cooked somewhat like the *stoccafisso*—first soaked in water for 24 hours, then in milk, while chopped celery, carrots, garlic and much onion are being browned in oil, to which chopped parsley and anchovy fillets are added later; dried mushrooms, capers and pine nuts are then crushed into a paste in a mortar and added to the rest, after which the pieces of cod, floured, are put in; slices of boiled potato, not too completely cooked, are then placed in an earthenware oven dish, the cod and its accompanying juices poured over them, and the whole is finished in the oven over a low flame, and served in the cooking dish.

MEAT: Because of the high quality of Ligurian olive oil, it is natural that the most typical meat dishes of the region should be those fried in oil. *Fritto misto* is one of those dishes which comes in two versions, *grasso* and *magro*—for normal usage and for fast days. The varied foods which go into a Ligurian mixed fry, coated with batter before they go into the bubbling oil, seem often rather curious—chopped sage, wisteria petals, the hairy leaves of borage, edible roots, salsify stalks, squash flowers, and mushrooms. These would come under the head of *fritto misto magro*, and most such ingredients are intended to flavor the batter rather than to be eaten for their own sake. *Fritto misto grasso* may include pieces of veal, liver, brains, sweetbreads, kidneys, etc. *Fritto allo stecco*, or *gli stecchi*, are tidbits of different suitable foods spitted on little wooden sticks (*stecchi*) in batter, egg, and bread crumbs, and fried in boiling oil; this sounds simple enough, but not as they make it in Genoa, by a subtle and painstaking process too complicated to explain here, which employs such recondite ingredients as truffles and cockscombs. *Fritti ripieni nell'ostia* are large round crackers with a sandwich filling made of finely chopped exotic variety meats (the only one found in Anglo-Saxon cooking is sweetbreads), béchamel sauce, beaten egg yolks, and little fresh peas; once filled, the crackers are dipped in egg and bread crumbs and deep-fried in hot but not boiling oil.

Vitello all'uccelletto or *vitello alla genovese* is veal cut into small thin slices, or very small pieces. It appears in various guises, of which the chief common factor seems to be that it is cooked in white wine; apart from that, the chief variations are (1) a mixture of olive oil and butter for the cooking fat, and bay leaf to give it flavor; (2) butter for the cooking fat, and artichokes; (3) whatever the cooking fat, sage as the flavorer. *Stufato* is made either with beef or mutton, cut into pieces and braised in oil and butter (some cooks add marrow or kidney fat) and red wine, along with peeled and seeded tomatoes, and garlic and rosemary to perfume it; the classic accompaniment of this dish in Liguria used to be turnips, but nowadays it is more likely to be potatoes. *Testa in cassetta* is meat from a pig's head, boiled, salted, pressed, and eaten cold. The Genoese fashion of cooking liver (*fegato di vitello alla genovese*) starts with a *soffritto* of butter, olive oil, onions, parsley, and garlic, into which, after the garlic has been removed, is put the liver, along with dry white wine, wine vinegar, and consommé. The liver is sprinkled with bread crumbs while cooking, and with grated cheese just before it is removed from the stove. *Trippa alla genovese* is tripe, first boiled for two hours in water (unsalted, to keep it tender), then browned in a mixture of olive oil and butter, with chopped onions, carrots, celery and dried mushrooms, to which are added peeled and seeded tomatoes, meat gravy and consommé. The tripe and its accompaniments then go into a covered dish for the end of the cooking, along with sliced potatoes (some cooks prefer broad beans). *Trippe di quelle*, a classic Ligurian dish, is seasonal; it can only be made in the spring, when the vegetables which go into it are obtainable. It differs from *trippa alla genovese* in that (1) it contains no tomatoes; (2) more butter than oil is used, and more consommé than meat gravy; (3) white wine is added; and (4), halfway through the cooking, spring peas, fava beans, new potatoes, and chopped parsley. It is served sprinkled with grated cheese.

POULTRY: *Fricassea di pollo* is chicken cut into pieces, and cooked slowly in a covered pot with butter, onions, beaten egg yolks, lemon juice and parsley. The creative province of La Spezia offers *anitra alle olive*, duck stuffed with olives and cooked in a pot with a rich sauce of beef gravy, liver, and the duck giblets hashed together with onions and olives.

GAME: La Spezia is also the inventor of *storni in salmì*, the starling, a bird not ordinarily thought of as edible by Anglo-Saxons, cooked in a rich sauce of olive oil, herbs, various vegetables and olives. *Beccafichi al nido* (warblers in the nest), are small birds cooked differently in Liguria than in most other parts of the country, where they usually appear spitted, a half dozen or more on each spit. Here each bird is cooked separately, bedded in the head of one of the large local red mushrooms, seasoned and doused with olive oil. In the days of coal, wood or charcoal cooking, Liguria had a special utensil for cooking this dish—a cast iron pan whose lid was shaped to hold live embers; placed over the flame with the embers on top, the bird was cooked evenly, with heat above and below. Nowadays gas and electricity have banished this technique, and the birds are cooked in the oven in a covered pan.

VEGETABLES: The Ligurian penchant for fresh green herbs leads naturally to a similar fondness for fresh green vegetables; and the liking for stuffings combines with this to produce a number of stuffed vegetable dishes. *Zucchini pieni* are small summer squash split in half, filled with a mixture of their own flesh with garlic, dried mushrooms, cottage cheese or bread without its crust soaked in milk, grated cheese, chopped marjoram and beaten eggs, moistened with olive oil before being baked in the oven. Eggplant and peppers are cooked in the same way. La Spezia calls one of its dishes, served traditionally at Easter, stuffed lettuce (*lattuga ripiena*), but it is not really stuffed, simply cooked in beef consommé, and served with beef gravy. Genoa bakes Swiss chard combined with olive oil, onions, garlic, chopped parsley, beaten egg and grated cheese in the oven with a crust of bread crumbs. *Polpettone* of various vegetables are large croquettes, like *polpettone di zucca*, seeded squash, diced and boiled in salted water, ground in a mortar, put in a *soffritto* of olive oil, butter, chopped dried mushrooms and garlic, mixed with curds, grated cheese and eggs to permit molding into croquette shape, and finally baked in a hot oven with a crust of bread crumbs dampened with olive oil; similar croquettes are made of eggplant, cardoons, string beans, spinach, artichokes, onions, black mushrooms and potatoes, and are often served with cold Brody sauce, a name which sounds Anglo-Saxon, but whose origin is unknown to me. In any case it is made by boiling red wine until it has been reduced to half its volume, to which are then added lemon peel, cloves, and whole peppercorns, simmered for a few minutes over the lowest possible flame, then enriched with a little butter, and cooked for five minutes more before the lemon peel, cloves and peppercorns are removed and thrown away. Raw chicken liver is then forced through a strainer, and stirred into the mixture until it has the consistency of mayonnaise. On serving, it is sprinkled with a few drops of lemon juice. Finally, mushrooms are cooked in a wide variety of fashions, particularly in the neighborhood of Varese Ligure, which specializes in mushrooms and exports large quantities of them, both fresh and dried. *Tocco de funzi*, mushroom sauce, is a popular condiment for polenta or pasta. *Tocco*, incidentally, is defined in some Italian dictionaries (published elsewhere than Genoa) as "Genoese tomato sauce," but in Liguria it can mean any simple sauce, especially meat gravies.

DESSERTS: Ligurian pastry takes off from different forms of sweet bread which are less desserts than coffee cakes, ideal with breakfast. Street vendors in Genoa sell the ring-shaped *canestrelli*. *Pan dolce* is a Ligurian version of Milan's *panettone*, studded thickly with raisins, candied citron, pine nuts, and, in some places, fennel seeds as well. Castelnuovo di Magra makes a simpler sweet bread in the form of a bun, *focaccia castelnovese*, of cornmeal, olive oil, butter and pine nuts, eaten especially at Christmas and Easter, which the religious fraternities used to distribute among the processional carriers of the Cross. The *biscotti della salute* of Sarzana resemble it. The same town makes *spongata* containing candied fruits and a jam filling; it dates from ancient Roman times, when the filling was of honey. La Spezia makes apple fritters for Christmas, while San Giuseppe produces *friscieù*, a fritter of apples, currants, and sultana raisins. In the cookie category, La Spezia is known for macaroons and *biscotti de a bricia*, studded with fennel seeds; Varese Ligure is known for monastery-made *sciuetta*, of almond paste in the shape of brightly colored flowers, mushrooms, fish, fruit, etc. The most famous cookies are those of Lerici, near La Spezia, a food-conscious town which celebrates gastronomic Saturdays every year from mid-January to mid-March, with local and visiting chefs vying with each other to see who can produce the most notable meal. *Ravioli dolci*, sweet ravioli, is a name which gives an inadequate idea of the exquisite flavor of these little envelopes of sweetened egg dough with a filling of orange (or lemon) peel, beef marrow, candied squash, citron and sometimes egg yolks, all crushed together into a paste with mortar and pestle.

Most cakes are variations of *pasta genovese*, the basic raised dough upon which all sorts of complications are built. Roughly, it is composed of equal quantities (by weight) of flour, butter, sugar, a number of eggs prohibitive at modern prices unless you raise hens, and a flavoring. Originally this last used to be almonds, but nowadays it is more likely to be rum. The French, who have adopted *pâte à génoise*, use vanilla for an ordinary *génoise*, but, like the Genoese themselves, sometimes go in for extravagance, as in *Génoise fourrée à la normande*, Normandy Genoa cake (!), which is a two-layer cake, soaked in Calvados (applejack), with an apple filling and Calvados-flavored frosting studded with bits of apple, almonds, and angelica. The Genoese themselves can hardly do better, though they are certainly elaborate enough in *meringhe genovesi*, for which the basic dough is cut into cupcake-sized circles, bathed in rum or a liqueur, set one round on top of another with apricot jam between the two, and topped with vanilla-flavored méringue. A full-sized chocolate three-layer cake is made of the basic dough, dampened or not by liqueurs, finished by spreading a chocolate cream filling between the layers, and covering the whole with chocolate frosting. Mocha cake is made similarly. A return to simplicity is achieved with *pan di Genova*, a sweet bread which gets back to the original almond flavoring, plus kirsch, but is more economical than the standard *pasta genovese*, calling for only half as many eggs. *Sciumette* (or *latte*) *alla grotta* is approximately a Ligurian Floating Island, with pistachio-flavored cream, and cinnamon sprinkled over the stiffly beaten egg whites which rise from it. A fruit dessert is *pesche ripiene*, stuffed peaches. The stuffing is made of the nuts of the peaches themselves, crushed into a paste with candied citron, candied squash, and some of the flesh of the peaches. The latter, cut in half and slightly hollowed out, are filled with this stuffing, and cooked in the oven with low flames above and beneath, in sugared white wine. They are served either hot or cold.

* * *

IX · *Liguria*

On the coast of the province of La Spezia, between Levanto and Portovenere, lie five villages which are all but cut off from the rest of the world. They are accessible only by boat (or on foot, if you are a mountain climber). The Cinque Terre (the Five Lands), Monterosso, Vernazza, Corniglia, Manarola and Riomaggiore, cling to steep cliffs dropping perpendicularly to the sea. About all you see is bare rock. It would be hard to imagine terrain less propitious to growing anything at all; yet this is where the best wine of Liguria comes from. The wall of rock which cuts the five villages off from civilization protects the vines from north winds and provides a sun-drenched exposure to the south. Thus they are able to prosper in tiny patches of soil in fissures or on cornices of the rock, often in places almost impossible to get at. Some plots have to be harvested from boats; to tend others, men let themselves down on ropes or ladders, and when the grapes are gathered, they are lowered in baskets to waiting dories below, which ferry them to the wine presses. Vines growing under such circumstances, sucking their food from such minute parcels of earth, do not produce heavy yields of grapes —only enough, say, to make about one-fifth as much wine as is sold under Cinque Terre labels.

When you do get genuine Cinque Terre, you may hit some quite interesting bottles. Corniglia has the reputation of producing the best, followed by Manarola; hence, while most of this wine is sold simply as *Bianco secco delle Cinque Terre*, you will sometimes find the name of Corniglia on the bottle. Or the label may identify the wine by its local name, Schicchetrà, which also serves as an epithet for drunkards. It is made from small white grapes, *rosco*, *albarola* or *vermentino;* is a light straw yellow when young, darkening as it grows older, and is delicate and fruity. The must from these grapes is naturally rich in sugar, and requires processing to produce a dry wine, but to tell the truth, it never becomes really dry. When the opposite course is taken, and the grapes are briefly sun-dried, increasing the concentration of sugar, the alcohol content rises from the normal 12 or 14 degrees to 18, and you get a very sweet dessert wine, so sweet, indeed, that the natives claim it is the only Italian wine which can be drunk with ice cream. This used to be marketed as Vernaccia, but nowadays it is often called *vin dolce* or *vino rinforzato*. There is also a sparkling red Schicchetrà dessert wine, 14 to 15 degrees, which, like the white, takes two years to mature and is best only after six; so little is produced that it is practically a confidential beverage.

Pliny very probably did not know about the Cinque Terre when he wrote that Genoese wines are the best of Liguria. This was not overwhelming praise, since Ligurian vintages set no records—not even those of the Cinque Terre, though they have been praised by such appreciators as Boccaccio and Gabriele d'Annunzio. If the Cinque Terre wines are set aside, the modern verdict would undoubtedly be that wines of La Spezia are the best in Liguria, which may not be foreign to the fact that La Spezia, after Genoa, is the most fruitful deviser of local dishes. In La Spezia is the Val di Vara, which produces some wine resembling that of the Cinque Terre, and the Val di Magra, where both reds and whites are made, the best known being those of Sarticola, northeast of Castelnuovo di Magra, straw-yellow, fruity, slightly *frizzante*, rather sweet, 10 to 11 degrees. There is also a sweet dessert variety, 13 to 14 degrees, and a red, of which not much is produced; most Ligurian wines are whites, for that matter, and in areas where both red and white are produced, the whites are almost invariably better than the reds. Also in La Spezia is Varese Ligure, where some comparatively dry full-bodied fruity whites are made, 11 to 12 degrees, agreeable with fish, the most reputed of which comes from the Cornice di Lovara in Sesta Godano.

Pliny notwithstanding, the only wine of the province of Genoa which needs to be mentioned is Coronata. It is white, very pale, with a flavor so delicate as to be almost imperceptible, despite its 11 to 13 degrees of alcohol. The Genoese call it dry, and no doubt it is by Ligurian standards, but to me it seemed not sufficiently so to harmonize with its slight flintiness; and it was rather thin. But it goes agreeably enough with fish, or for that matter with antipasto and, for the Genoese taste, with pasta.

The province of Imperia produces Rossese (the name of the grape), often encountered under the label of Dolceacqua, the town reputed to make the best. It tests 11 to 13 degrees of alcohol, but, though warming, does not strike me as heavy; it sometimes has a slight peppery aftertaste. Pomegranate red, it improves with age; more long-lived than most Ligurian wines, it needs four or five years to be at its best. Its makers boast that it was a favorite with Napoleon.

The remaining province, Savona, joins with Imperia in producing Vermintino, a fresh, relatively dry, slightly *frizzante* light-yellow wine, 12 to 13 degrees.

For the record, two other names may be noted, for reasons other than the quality of the wine. One is the *rosato* Barbarossa (red beard) so called because its red grapes grow in long bunches, so that they look like beards hanging from the vines. The other is Campochiesa Bianco, a dryish fruity white; its producers claim it is long-lived for a white wine; and to prove it, they lay down a supply of that year's wine on the birth of a son, to be consumed at his wedding. He will do well to marry young.

THE
DOMAIN

OF THE
VENETI

Veneto

The protohistoric people called the Veneti have bequeathed their name to the three northeasternmost regions of Italy. Modern ethnologists are of the opinion that
they originated between the Baltic and the Carpathians, in
what is today Poland, and migrated to northeastern Italy.
This would account for the fact that there were also Veneti
in northwestern Gaul, resulting from a migration in a different direction; for the Veneti provided a name not only
for Venice but also for Vannes, in Brittany.

The theory of the ancients is more romantic. It held
that the first settlers of Veneto were refugees from Troy.
Homer, who called the Veneti *Henetoi*, put forward as

AUSTRIA

SWITZERLAND

Brenner Pass

CHAMOIS DEER
TRALENDAL BREAD

POTATO, TRIPE AND SPLEEN SO

SPARKLING WEISS BURGUNDER

WHEAT-AND-BARLEY BREAD
GOULASH

Merano

SNAIL SOUP

Bressanone

ELEPHANT PLATTER
HAUSPLATTE

Adige River

Isarco River

A L T O   A D I G E

CHA
DEE

LAGREIN WINE
SANTA MADDALENA WINE

_Cort
d'Amp_

SPECK
WHEAT
MAIZE
RYE

Bolzano

KREN
SAUERKRAUT
TIROLER KNÖDELN
NOCKERLN

TROUT
GROUSE
HAZEL HEN

• _Termeno_

C A D O

VENEZIA TRIDENTINA

_T R E N T I N O_

GRAPPA

TRAMINER WINE
TEROLDEGO WINE
CALDARO WINE

SCHMORBRATEN
KALBSRAGOUT

Bellu

BARLEY
OATS
WHEAT
MAIZE

PIATTO DI VE
PASTIZZADA
BARLEY POP
CAZZONZIE
TORTA DI PO

Trento

BOLLITO MISTO
ROAST PORK
RAVANADA
POLENTA
TÜRTELN
STRUDEL

Lamon

BEANS

PROSECC

MARZEMINO WINE

Valdobbiaden

TRENTINO WINE

GARDA WINE

VENEZIA EUGANE

LAKE GARDA

Malcesine

FOCACCIA
SNAILS

Breganze

PIGEON

Cittadella

SOARE

Padua

PAN PADOVA
MUSETI
POLLO
ALLA PADOV
ZALETI
COARI
BRUSTOLÀ
PASTISSO DI
PIEDI DI MA
PETRARCH S
SQUASH FLO
FRITTERS

BARDOLINO WINE
VALPOLICELLA WINE
VALPANTENA WINE
GARGANOSA WINE

Vicenza

MUSHROOMS
PEACHES

BACCALÀ ALLA VICENTINA
TURKEY WITH
POMEGRANATE
DUCK WITH PASTA

Verona

PANDORO
POTATO GNOCCHI
PEARÀ SAUCE
SOPPRESSE SAUSAGES

SOAVE WINE

MIRTILLI
GRAPES
STRAWBERRIES

CHERRIES
PEACHES

Adige River

L O M B A R D Y

R O L E S I N

CUTTLEFIS
STURGEO
CAVIAR
ETRUSCA
GREEK R
WILD DUC
COOTS
HERONS
EELS

RICE

Rovigo

SUGAR BEETS

EMILIA-ROMAC

Miles

0   25   50

0   50

Km.

VENEZIA EUGANEA, VENEZIA GIULIA
and VENEZIA TRIDENTINA

A U S T R I A

CARNIA
GAME
CHEESE
VENEZIA GIULIA

Tarvisio

...SEEDS

CELERY SOUP

POTATO SOUP

CIALZONS

SGUAZETO

PORK CHOPS
WITH CABBAGE

SPIT-ROASTED PORK

BROVADA

F R I U L I

Tarcento
LUGANICA SAUSAGE

LADIN-
SPEAKING
AREA

San Daniele
di Friuli
HAM

Cividale
GUBANA

Udine
VEGETABLES
ASPARAGUS
ARTICHOKES

REFOSCO WINE
CABERNET WINE
MERLOT WINE

Y U G O S L A V I A

Codroipo
MUSETTI

Cormons
TOCAI WINE
MALVASIA WINE
RIBOLLA
GIALLO WINE
BUZOLAI

Gorizia
PLUM GNOCCHI
BLOOD PUDDING
SLIVOVITZ BRANDY

...LIANO

...VERADA
...OSE WITH CELERY

MAIZE

Aquileia

TOCAI WINE
FRIULANO WINE

Prosecco
WINE

C A R S O

...V150

...CCHIO
FISH
...COADA
...EGA SAUSAGE
...A ALLA
VISANA

RABOSO WINE

Grado
BROETO

Trieste
IOTA
MOCNIK
SGUAZZETTO
BRUSCANDOLI
LIPTAUER
GOULASH
STROCCOLI
PRESNITZ
TERRANO WINE
REFOSCO WINE

...no

...Lido

G U L F o f V E N I C E

...oggia
...TO ALLA
...OGIOTA
...A GIALLA
HIOGGIA

Venice

LIVER WITH ONIONS
POLENTA
RISI E BISI
BLACK RICE
RISOTTO DI SECOLE
RISOTTO ALLA SBIRRAGLIA
BACCALA MANTECATO
VENETIAN OYSTERS
COPPA
PASTA E FAGIOLI
ZUPPA DI TRIPPA
BROETO
SGUAZETO
BISATO IN TECIA
SFOGI IN SAÖR
PASTIZZADA
BAICOLI

═══ *Great Eating*
─── *Good Eating*

confirmation of this theory the reputation the Veneti enjoyed as breeders and trainers of horses, a talent also possessed by the Trojans. Polybius and Titus Livy also subscribed to the idea that the Veneti were Trojans.

Whoever they were, the Veneti seem to have been more civilized than was normal for the time and place. They are described as devout, loyal to the community, and respectful of family ties. They were skillful farmers who improved the land they exploited. They developed religious rites and administrative institutions. As artisans, they were skillful and industrious, and exported many of their manufactures —the first indication that the Venetians were destined to become great traders, importers as well as exporters, for the Veneti brought in amber from the Baltic.

Though they fastened their name on the region, the Veneti were not its first settlers; but the identity of their predecessors is even more shadowy than their own. The region was settled sparsely in Neolithic times (by the "Ligurians?"), and in the Bronze Age the population was increased by the Euganei, sometimes described, in the absence of fuller information, as an offshoot of the "Ligurians," and at other times as Umbrians. Their capital was Ateste, today Este, which gave a great family to Italy. The same name also lives on, distorted into almost unrecognizable form, in that of the river which dominates the geography of Venezia, the Adige. Names were about all the Euganei left. Their pre-Alps are still called the Euganean Hills and the region of Veneto is also known as Venezia Euganea. The Euganei seem to have been driven into the mountains about 800 B.C.—into the Rhaetic Alps, according to some savants, which would mean northwest, toward or into eastern Switzerland. This is where Rhaeto-Romansch, a Ladin dialect, is spoken. One unsolved linguistic mystery is how it happens that there are three separated islands of peoples who speak Ladin dialects in Switzerland, northwest of the

Este-Padua-Vicenza area once inhabited by the Euganei; in the Alto Adige, north of it; and in Friuli, northeast of it. It might seem logical to suspect that the Euganei, in process of being pushed northward, split into three groups and ended up in these three different regions.

Around the proud city of Venice, three Venezias have gathered, by a process of accretion. Veneto, or Venezia Euganea, of which Venice itself is the capital, joins to the province of Venice those of Rovigo, Padua, Verona, Vicenza, Treviso and, reaching all the way to the Alps, Belluno. To the west is Venezia Tridentina, also called Trentino-Alto Adige. This is made up of two provinces, Trento and Bolzano, the latter being the Alto Adige, before World War I the South Tyrol of Austria. Venezia Giulia, also called Friuli-Venezia Giulia in recognition of the importance of the Ladin-speaking population of Friuli, is the farthest east. It is made up of the provinces of Udine, Gorizia and Trieste.

Venice is a stage setting for an extravaganza. Its buildings look as if they were painted on theatrical flats, and when you walk around the edge of one, you almost expect to see a backing of canvas stretched between wooden slats; but no, they are quite solid. All the same, their builders must have thought of them as façades, which they decorated brilliantly, paying scant attention to how they looked from the rear. They are not meant to be viewed from all angles or to be walked around, and indeed in many cases they can't be. Almost the only building in the center of Venice you can really walk around is the Campanile. Even the Doge's Palace has only two sides meant to be looked at. St. Mark's has two and a half if you count what you can see of a third above the courtyard of the Palace, to which it is attached because originally it was the Doge's private chapel. Goethe called the Grand Canal "the most beautiful street in the world," but he should have called it the most beautiful pair of facing backdrops, through which the visitor runs a gauntlet of brilliant façades.

Venice's fascination with the façade may be related to the ubiquity of reflections in a city set in water; mirrors reflect only surfaces. (Venice had a monopoly on the manufacture of looking glasses in Renaissance times.) This could account for the city's brightness too, and for the lavish use of gilt, thrown back so brilliantly from water tossing under a blazing sun. This gilt was also a symbol of the richness of Venice. It was a richness derived largely from trade in exotic spices, so it was fitting that Venetian palaces should be exotic too. Their almost garish colors were imported from the East along with the spices, Byzantine booty both, the nutmeg and cinnamon, the gilt and the mosaics.

No date can be given for the foundation of Venice, for it was never founded. Venice was a city of refuge. The early inhabitants took to its islands to escape raiders. The islands were unattractive and their sparse inhabitants too poor to tempt passing invaders to pursue them to their retreats. In the days of the Romans, the islands of the lagoon supported only a few fishermen; but as wave after wave of Barbarians poured into Italy, more and more mainlanders joined them. When the Longobard invasion of 568 occurred, the refugees took root on the islands for good. It is not certain when they realized that they had become sufficiently numerous to constitute a city; but in 460, twelve townships of the region had already taken the first step toward it by setting up a sort of intercommunal council. Venice was thus one of the rare great capitals of Italy which was not important in Roman times. It was to gain an even rarer distinction as the only city in Italy which would succeed in remaining independent of Pope and Emperor and of escaping the domination of great families. The free state of Venice maintained its independence for a thousand years. Its power extended inland over all northeastern Italy, and along the valley of the Po into part of what is now Lombardy; and for some 200 years it was the world's greatest maritime power. From fishermen, the Venetians had become sailors. From coastal traders, they had become navigators, sailing especially toward the ports of the Levant. From dealers with the East by sea, they became importers from the East by land; the most famous example of their expansion in this direction was the journey of Marco Polo to China.

It was after the year 1000 that the Venetian fleet acquired control of the Adriatic and dominated the route to the Holy Land. From the first three Crusades, Venice acquired exclusive trading rights in the Near East. For the Fourth, leaving the fighting to others, she furnished the transport, at a profitable price: 4,500 horses, 9,000 knights, 20,000 foot soldiers, and their provisions for a year. By 1280, her riches were already fabulous, and the Venetian gold ducat was accepted everywhere. In the 1400's she held the Dalmatian coast to Ragusa (today Dubrovnik, Yugoslavia) and beyond; many Greek islands, including Crete and Cyprus, and a piece of the mainland; and her trading counters were established in Egypt, Turkey, other points in Asia Minor, on the Black Sea, and in the Asiatic hinterland. Her ships returned from the East loaded with all its precious products; the most precious of all were spices.

The supremacy of Venice in supplying seasoning began with the humblest of all, salt. The power of Venice, like the power of Rome, began with this. Salt gathered from the coastal marshes was sold to inlanders. Venetian salt sellers pushed westward along the Po, and where commerce entered, political power followed. Venice had a monopoly of salt in this area, and defended it fiercely, by force of arms when necessary—she made war on Comacchio to eliminate that city's competition.

Venice needed her hinterland not only as a market for the goods she imported from the East, but also as a supplier of staple foods like wheat which could not be raised on her small islands; this freed her from dependence on foodstuffs brought in by sea, and made her invulnerable to blockade.

Salt was followed by more esoteric seasonings, many of which had been known to the ancient Romans but had disappeared from Italy after the Empire's communications with the East broke down. The Crusaders brought them back, mostly in Venetian ships, and also provided consumers for them, for they had acquired a taste for high seasonings in the East, and passed it on to their own peoples. For several centuries the Middle Ages and the Renaissance weltered in a veritable orgy of spice-eating, which, for the greater glory of Venice, kept demand strong and prices high. Pepper was worth its weight in gold. In a period when the value of many coinages was dubious, spices often served as foreign exchange, to make payments abroad, or to pay tribute. When a sovereign visited a city, spices were usually among the presents he received. A gift of spices to a judge was sometimes as effective as eloquence in winning a case. Spices were also in demand, before the days of refrigeration, as preservatives for food. Nor did the fact that many spices were reputed to have aphrodisiac qualities hurt their sale.

Pepper was the basic spice, and of this Venice had a monopoly in transport and distribution from the 12th century on, picking it up in eastern Mediterranean ports, especially Alexandria. It probably originated in India and Indochina; its name is believed to be derived from *pippali*, a Sanskrit word. It had been widely used in the Near East for as far back as history goes, and had been much appreciated by the ancient Romans; but after the fall of the Empire, it seems to have stopped reaching western Europe. The last references to it in old writings report the paying of tribute to Attila in the form of pepper. After Venice reintroduced it to Europe, it was consumed both as black pepper, picked before ripening and dried in its own envelope, and white pepper, allowed to ripen and then husked, providing a product less strong but more subtly flavored. In the Middle Ages, the wealthy considered it essential to keep an abundant supply of pepper in the house; it was a sign of solvency. One way to say that a man was poor was to say that he lacked pepper. It was a sad day for Venice when Portuguese sailors splashed ashore at Calcutta, shouting, "For Christ and spices!" But Venice still controlled the sales outlets she had established, and for a century more continued to make fortunes from pepper. The market was in any case big enough for everybody. Europe at this time was consuming nearly 3,300 tons of pepper a year.

From another direction, the east coast of Africa, just north of the Equator, Venice also brought in a different type of pepper, which the Romans had somehow missed— Melagueta pepper, named for Méléga, which produced it, also called Guinea pepper or grains of paradise, the last term confusing, since it was also applied to other spices. It is not really pepper, though it looks like it, and is hot on the tongue. The first written mention of it comes appropriately from Veneto, more precisely from its city of Treviso, where the celebration of Carnival included a sort of mock battle in which twelve ladies of the nobility held a fortress which was attacked by assailants whose arms were flowers, perfumes and spices—one of them *pepe di Guinea*. This was in 1214, but the spice is referred to as though it was then already well known.

The 12th century saw the arrival in Europe, thanks to the Crusaders and the Venetians, of a number of other seasonings from the East. One was saffron, which was now making its third appearance in western Europe. It had been known to the ancient Romans, but disappeared from sight after the collapse of the Empire. Then the Arabs, presumably the first producers of saffron (since its name comes from a Persian-Arabic word, *zahfaran*, crocus) introduced it into Spain about 960, but again it faded away. When the Crusaders returned, with a taste for it acquired in the Holy Land, it came back with a vengeance. A separate Office of Saffron was set up in Venice to handle the trade, and Verona charged a duty on it of 10,000 ducats for 2.2 pounds. No doubt an atavistic yearning for it awoke in those once-Greek cities which had added it to their *brodetti*. The demand was not purely alimentary. It was used to perfume theatres (the Romans had used it for this too), and it was deemed good for the health, especially (a potent consideration in those times) as a remedy for, or protection against, the plague. A French apothecary, Nicolas Lémery, called it "the friend of the lungs" and "the king of vegetables". It was so ubiquitous in the public mind that it gave birth to a host of popular expressions. The legend that Venus used it to put her husband Vulcan to sleep when she expected a visit from Mars, caused saffron to become a symbol of cuckoldry, and the color yellow to stand for cuckolds. Either because bankruptcy in love was compared to bankruptcy in business, or because men whose affairs were going badly were considered to risk jaundice from chagrin, those in money difficulties were said to be "in saffron," and Rabelais applied the epithet *safranier* to two of his characters who were plagued by debt. A glutton was a *safrette*.

Tarragon (Arabic, *tarkhoun*), one herb which the Romans had not known, was brought to Europe by the Crusaders in the 12th century too; but the attribution to them of another importation is probably incorrect. The story is that shallots were also a gift of the Crusaders, and that the name is derived from the city of Ascalon, in ancient Judaea. This seems to have been an error of Pliny, which dictionaries and reference books have repeated diligently ever since. Actually the shallot has never been found in a wild state in Judaea or anywhere else. It was probably developed from the already domesticated onion, and it did not have to wait for the Crusaders to introduce it to Europe. It was being raised there long before the Crusades, notably in the vegetable gardens of Charlemagne.

It was probably not the Crusaders either who introduced into Europe a spice which is first heard of at the end of the 12th century—nutmeg, and mace, which is the seed covering of the nut (for botanists it is not a nut, but a seed). Nutmeg was apparently introduced into Europe directly by the Saracens themselves, and if so must have been slow in capturing the fancy of Italians, for the first reference to it is dated 1190, when the streets of Rome were perfumed with it to celebrate the entry of Emperor Henry IV. Nutmeg is a polygamous plant, which botanists refer to in their playful moments as "the pasha of tropical flora." Each male tree is surrounded by a small grove of female trees, which it fertilizes. Both bear nuts, but those of the female trees are smaller and tastier.

The value of the spices in which Venice was already dealing in the 12th century attracted the attention of Marco Polo, and when he pushed into Asia in the 1270's, he recorded frequently the presence of spices in the places through which he passed. He noted at Hormuz, at the mouth of the Persian Gulf, that this was where Arab ships from India arrived loaded with spices. He reported also on the spices of Ceylon, though it is not certain that he ever went there himself, nor did he reach Tibet, but he got very close to it and would have liked to go farther, for he had heard that Tibet knew "many spices which have never been seen in our country." Borneo he described as "an island of very great wealth in spices." In China, he found pepper and cinnamon, and appears to have been, for post-Roman Europe, the rediscoverer of ginger. He was in any case the first European to describe its culture, but he said little about the edible rhizome itself, a gap which was filled by another far-ranging Italian, the missionary Monte Corvino. Though Marco Polo found it in China, it originated in India, as is indicated by its name, which is from the Sanskrit *sringavera*, Latinized into *zingiber*—for the ancient Romans knew ginger, though it disappeared from Europe for something like eight centuries until Marco Polo found it again. Ginger appeared in three forms in those days. The run-of-the-mill variety was *baladie;* inferior to it was *michino,* which yielded unpleasantly under the knife like rubber; *colombino,* the most appreciated, was consequently the most expensive. This last was used to make the Venetian specialty of *gingembras,* which should probably be classified as medicine rather than food, since it was vaunted as a fortifier of the stomach. But *gengibretum* was definitely on the alimentary side, a confection, candied ginger. Also popular in the Middle Ages was an ancestor of today's nougat, in which ginger was combined with sugar, crushed almonds and egg whites.

Ginger must definitely have waited for Marco Polo to reappear in Europe, but some of the other spices whose presence has been recorded in the 13th century may already have reached Venice before he met them in Asia, such as cinnamon, though this is far from certain. The ancient Romans had cinnamon, but not much of it, and they didn't know where it came from. In the Middle Ages, the best was that of Ceylon, with China second.

Cloves were probably a 13th-century arrival also; the earliest known reference to them after classical times is dated 1228, when they were five times as dear as nutmeg. The early Romans apparently did not know it, but by 335 the Emperor Constantine was able to make a present to Sylvester, Bishop of Rome, of 150 pounds of cloves, more precious than the gold and silver containers in which they were delivered. Cloves then disappeared from European history until the Middle Ages, when St. Jean d'Acre became the trading center for them, a convenient place for Venetian ships carrying Crusaders to this strong place of theirs to pick up the valuable spices. The Arabs who delivered the cloves to St. Jean d'Acre succeeded in keeping their origin a secret, and the Venetians who had been trading in them since the 13th century did not find it out until the 15th. Then Niccolò dei Conti, appropriately a Venetian and the most important traveler of the times after Marco Polo himself, learned from Arabs that cloves came from the Molucca Islands of the Malay Archipelago. About 60 years later the Portuguese found out too when one of Magellan's men, Serrano, touched in 1511 at Ternate, one of the five small islands where the cloves grew; and Magellan's historian, Pigafetta, gave the first description of the living plant (more accurate than his identification of the banana as a giant fig).

Venice imported other food products from the East too, one of which has provided a saying for the French, *mi-figue, mi-raisin* (half fig, half raisin), which might be translated, "neither fish, flesh, nor good red herring," though the meanings of the two phrases are not quite congruent. The expression is said to have originated when Venice imported the famous grapes of Corinth (a place which gave its name to the currant). The Corinthians, who were sharp traders, often delivered baskets apparently filled with the expensive grapes, but whose lower layers were composed of cheap figs.

The Venetians created a brilliant society with the riches brought them by spices and commerce. Was it the effect of the exotic nature of their merchandise? "The intellectual faculties seem to have soared in an enduring exaltation under the influence of spices," Alexandre Dumas wrote in his *Grand Dictionnaire de Cuisine*. "Is it to spices that we owe Titian's masterpieces? I am tempted to believe it." Yet the Genoese dealt in spices too. They were trades-men too. They were sailors too. They were rich too. Yet when they decided to spend their money on art, they had to seek painters elsewhere. The Venetians developed their own artists. It may have been the light, reflected softly and subtly from the water, a temptation and a challenge to painters. (The light of Tuscany might account for the Florentine artists too.) In Titian's painting we may see at least one aspect of the light. The "Titian blonde," the "Ve-netian blonde," was born when Venetian women took to wetting their hair with a bleaching solution and then sitting out in the sun on the *altane*, rooftop terraces built on the *palazzi* for that specific purpose.

The distinctive feature of Venetian art was its colorful-ness. There was first the brilliance of mosaics, of tinted mar-ble, of Byzantine gilding; and then the more subtle effects of easel paintings, when the Venetians divorced painting from the walls and confined it within a frame from which the light and warmth of Venice illuminated the room.

Venice in its heyday was possibly the most brilliant city then in existence. The Doges gave lavish feasts, and it was in Venice that forks and glassware appeared on tables for the first time. Venice developed the art of making glass after the Portuguese reduced its predominance in the spice trade, and also went in for the manufacture of cloth, espe-cially luxurious stuffs of exclusive colors, like a purple dye imported from the East in the 13th century. The gondolas were brightly colored too before the 15th century, when an austere Senate ordained that they should all become black.

The brilliance of Venice did not black out as early as the gondolas did. This was the period of Giovanni Bellini, with Giorgione and Titian still to come. It was in 1494 that a great printing house was established in Venice by Aldus Manutius, who gave his name to a font of Italic type widely used today. But with the end of its monopolies, Venice began its decline. Sumptuary legislation was enacted to restrain extravagance and ostentation in dress. It met with the customary lack of success, but it was a symptom of the changing spirit of the times. The light was slowly paling. All the same, as late as 1750, when London had only six theatres and Paris ten, Venis had 16. Today, no longer a power of any kind, with little industry except that of catering to tourists, the monuments of its past glory still give it a splendor unequaled elsewhere. The visitor to Venice can feel with Byron that it was "the revel of the earth, the masque of Italy."

What sort of food accorded with the contradictory characteristics of the Venetians? They were earners (the men) and spenders (the women), combining an acute respect for the value of money with readiness to dissipate it lavishly on luxury. Solidity and extravagance: they managed to marry in Venetian society and they managed to marry (and happily at that) in Venetian cooking.

The busy merchant, often, no doubt, eating his food in haste, with scant regard for its flavor, preferred simple uncomplicated foods. After *scampi*, Venetian by a whim of nature, the most widely known specialties of Venice are liver with onions; rice with peas; polenta—all humble dishes. But then the other side of the Venetian character intervenes. Nowhere else has liver with onions become so refined, nowhere else has rice been treated with such subtlety and taken on such varied and imaginative forms, nowhere else has polenta been made from such fine grain. The high coloring of Venice has been transported to the table too. Venetians even eat flowers (a habit inspired by the East?)—candied violets, squash-flower fritters, acacia flowers in *bei grappoli dorati e odorosi*, fritters too. Nature has conspired in this. It seems almost a deliberate symbolization of Venetian colorfulness and the Venetian character that the *radicchio* chooses to grow in Veneto alone; a member of what is essentially a simple unassuming family of foods, lettuce, it has become, in its Veneto metamorphosis, a beautiful flower.

An observer with a sensitive eye, Elizabeth David, has described the impact of Venetian color on the table in her *Italian Food*, when she writes of "a restaurant where the colors of Venetian painting are translated to the kitchen:"

"Saffron-colored polenta is cooking in copper pans next to an immense dish of artichokes, purple and dark green, stewing in a bath of white wine and olive oil. On the other side of the stove is a deep pot of red-brown Venetian bean soup [another case of a humble dish here refined to perfection] and simmering in a *bain-marie* is an orange and umber sauce of tomatoes, clams and onions. Translucent little squids sizzle on the grill; on a marble table are rose-colored *scampi* and vermilion Adriatic crabs, and coils of pale-gold *fettuccine* are drying in plaited baskets. In the coolest part of the larder the oranges shine, luminous with their sugary coating."

The color is there even before the food reaches the kitchen. To quote Mrs. David once more:

"Of all the spectacular food markets in Italy the one near the Rialto in Venice must be the most remarkable. The light of a Venetian dawn in early summer—you must be about at four o'clock in the morning to see the market coming to life—is so limpid and so still that it makes every separate vegetable and fruit and fish luminous with a life of its own, with unnaturally heightened colors and clear stencilled outlines. Here the cabbages are cobalt blue, the beetroots deep rose, the lettuces clear pure green, sharp as glass. Bunches of gaudy gold marrow flowers show off the elegance of pink-and-white marbled bean pods, primrose potatoes, green plums, green peas. The colors of the peaches, cherries, and apricots, packed in boxes lined with blue paper matching the blue canvas trousers worn by the men unloading the gondolas, are reflected in the rose-red mullet and the orange *vongole* and *canestrelle*, which have been pried out of their shells and heaped into baskets. In other markets, on other shores, the unfamiliar fishes may be vivid, mysterious, repellent, fascinating, and bright with splendid color; only in Venice do they look good enough to eat. In Venice even ordinary sole and ugly great skate are striped with delicate lilac lights, the sardines shine like newly minted silver coins, pink Venetian scampi are fat and fresh, infinitely enticing in the early dawn."

The color of Venetian foods, seen in the soft light of Venetian skies, no doubt inspired Venetian cooks, while Venetian wealth gave them the means to delight the palate as well as the eye. The renown of Venetian food spread at the same epoch as the renown of Venetian riches and power. It took a little time for it to move from the kitchen to the printed page, so it was only in 1610 that the Alessandro Vecchi printshop of Venice published Bartolomeo Scappi's *Manual of the Art of Cooking for the Education of All Cooks, Carvers or Master Chefs*, an encyclopedic work in six books.

In the region of Veneto, less than in the city of Venice itself where cooking was more of a professional occupation than in the surrounding countryside, family life revolved around the fireplace, for it was on the open hearth that meals were cooked. Fireplaces grew ever larger, becoming, with their surrounding working areas, separate rooms in the houses, their concave paunches filled with spitted birds, meat, or game turning slowly above a fire of wood. When gas and electricity arrived, fireplace cooking became associated with peasantry and poverty, so it was a matter of pride to substitute the new *cucina economica* for the fire-place. During the last 35 years, many magnificent old fire-places disappeared. But snobbishness has now turned in the opposite direction. The old hearths which remain are being put to good use again, while in new buildings old-fashioned fireplaces are being installed.

There is also today a return to the sound old Venetian traditions of a cuisine basically sane, delicately executed, and highly varied. A land running from the sea to the high mountains, Veneto is gifted with diverse climates, and each has produced its own eating habits. Add to this the divergent histories of the many proud and noble cities which make up Veneto and Venezia, and you have here a wide gamut indeed.

Almost any Italian, asked to name the one dish most firmly associated in his mind with Venice, would answer *risi e bisi*, rice and peas, known all over Italy by this Venetian dialect name. In the spring, it is the Venetian *minestra* (first course) par excellence; and like many other cherished local specialties it can give rise to heated arguments: is it a soup or a vegetable dish? Restaurants listing it among soups nevertheless give you a fork with which to eat it.

The Italian gastronomic writer Giuseppe Mazzotti points out that *risi e bisi* is only a special case of the characteristic Venetian way with rice. "There is not always much difference in Veneto between a risotto and a rice soup," he wrote in *Le Vie d'Italia* for April 1965. "The people of Veneto, and especially the Venetians, like *risotto all'onda* [wavelike risotto], a fashion of naming a dish which could only occur to a people of navigators. That means that the risotto should not be too dry, but rather creamy, if not almost liquid—in a word, wavy"—*ondoso*.

Rice and peas may not sound like a particularly inspiring combination, and it is not as it is so often made outside of

Veneto, where boiled peas are simply poured over boiled rice. Only Venetian cooks can succeed in capturing the delicate springtime essence of this dish. A real *risi e bisi*, Mazzotti says, "can only be found in Venice, in its season. To make it well, you must follow all the rules, especially this one: the peas must be fresh, sweet, tender (and hence from Veneto), shelled at the last minute." (Purists add that the peas must come from vegetable farms between Chioggia and Burano, which means those which border the lagoon of Venice itself.) "You prepare a *soffritto* with oil, butter and chopped celery (there are those who add garlic, onions and parsley: but the taste of the celery must predominate); when it is browned, put in the rice. You boil the pea pods separately, to give flavor to the water. Moisten the rice with this water and a few tablespoons of beef and chicken bouillon. After seven or eight minutes' cooking, add the peas, stirring them until the rice has finished cooking. Two minutes before the end, add grated Parmesan cheese, and serve with solicitude"—which in this case means as soon as you take it off the stove.

Risi e bisi is the most celebrated Venetian rice dish, but it is only one of an uncountable list, which is natural for a city which for centuries controlled the major part of the valley of the Po, the greatest rice-producing area in Italy, which is the greatest rice-producing country in Europe. Nobody seems to know just when Veneto started to eat rice. The Saracens apparently introduced it into Italy themselves, rather than through the intermediary of the Crusaders, but it may have taken a little time to work its way up to the northwest. In any case, it goes far enough back so that Veneto has had time to combine it with almost any other food you can think of. True to Venetian tradition, many rice dishes appeal to the eye by adding a touch of color, in addition to the two colors which are not colors, black and white. Black rice, *risotto nero*, otherwise *risotto di seppie*, is made from inkfish, which dyes the grains black. *Risotto nero*, Mazzotti admits, "causes the brows of novices to knit suspiciously, and their noses to wrinkle, but nevertheless, at the second mouthful, they almost always allow themselves to be conquered by the rare flavor of this dish, alarming as its aspect is." As for white rice, there are two main kinds, whose names are so much alike that it is easy to confuse them. *Riso in bianco* is undebatably a soup, rice in consommé, a variety recommended for those with weak digestions, called "white" because it is devoid of tomato. *Risotto bianco* is made with fish, and is also called *risotto di pesse*, *pesse* being the Venetian dialect form of *pesce*, fish.

The variety of rice and fish dishes is infinite—rice with eel (*risi e bisati*); with sole; with fresh anchovies (*minestra di riso alla cappuccina*); with *gò* (Venetian for the fish called *gobidi* or *guvàta* farther south); with *branzia*, Venetian for *spigola;* with *ociàda*, Venetian for *occhiata*. There are risotti with crustaceans (*scampi*, shrimp) and shellfish (mussels, *peòci* in Venetian); others which would be lumped together in English under the vague heading of "clams": *cappe* (*vongole* elsewhere), *poverasse* (*poveracce*), *capparozzoli, masanète, bòsega, schie;* and even oysters. *Risotto di mare* (sea *risotto*) combines spiny lobster, salt-water shrimp and squill, and is not to be confused with *risotto alla marinara* (sailor style) which is with clams.

There are risotti with vegetables—spinach, asparagus tips, beans, fennel, potatoes, mushrooms, cabbage—and even with grapes. This last is *risi co' la ua* (dialect again), made with fresh Malaga grapes, which might lead you to expect a dessert until you hear the other ingredients—garlic, oil and parsley, with a blanket of grated Parmesan over the finished product. There are risotti with frogs' legs, with tripe, with chicken livers, with stewed chicken, with quail. There are risotti with meat, several of which deserve separate mention. *Risi in cavromàn* (dialect) is with diced mutton, a meat not often used with rice, though there is a younger edition, with lamb, *risotto in capro roman*, Venetian despite its name. Both cook the meat in consommé with tomato, but cinnamon is put into the mutton dish to counteract its gaminess, while the more delicately flavored lamb is gratified by a touch of white wine. *Risotto di secole* utilizes the scraps of meat (*secole*) which remain on the bones after beef or veal has been boned; they are sold separately in Venice for this purpose. If you find *risotto alla bechèra*, butcher's risotto, on the menu, this is the Venetian dialect name for the same thing. Finally, there is *risotto alla sbirraglia*, with chicken cut into small pieces. The name, which dates from the 19th century, when Venice was ruled by the Austrians, is supposed to suggest that Venetians would be happy to see the alien police (*sbirri*), like the young suitor in W. S. Gilbert's *Gentle Alice Brown*, chopped particularly small.

After *risi e bisi*, the Venetian specialties most widely known are probably *scampi*, *fegato alla veneziana* and *baccalà mantecato*. *Scampi*, as everyone knows, are the shrimp so peculiar to this region that they are known throughout the world by their Venetian name. *Scampi alla veneziana* marks the classic way of presenting them in Venice. It means boiled, cooled, and served with a dressing of olive oil, lemon juice, salt and pepper. Venice does not limit itself to this treatment. Sometimes *scampi* are served as an hors d'oeuvre, rolled in thin slices of prosciutto. They may appear alone in a risotto, or combined with other sorts of seafood. *Scampi* can make a soup by themselves, or go into other seafood soups. They can be fried. They can be baked in the oven. Or, as I prefer them myself, they can be spitted and grilled.

Fegato alla veneziana is simply liver with onions, a dish the Venetians claim they invented, though it seems so natural a combination that it need hardly be pinned down to any single point of origin. It is true, however, that nobody does it better. Venetian success in this case results perhaps from the contradictory elements in the Venetian character —it is necessary to be slow, patient and painstaking for the onion, but quick and alert for the liver. There are two secrets for cooking a perfect *fegato alla veneziana*. One is to gild (not brown) coarsely chopped onion very slowly in olive oil, taking half an hour or more to do so. The other is to choose extremely tender liver and slice it as thin as possible, so that when you put it in the onion-flavored oil, it will cook in the fastest possible time—three minutes at the most, one at the best. It is sometimes accompanied by the very special polenta found here, which is not yellow but almost white, made from the fine white maize of the Friuli region. Venezia is polenta country; and goes into such complicated dishes as *polenta pastizzada*, concocted of alternate layers of polenta and of minced veal, mushrooms and cockscombs, cooked with onion, celery, carrot, parsley, tomato sauce and salt pork in white wine and butter.

Veneto does a good many things both with *baccalà*, salted cod which has been dried on rocks in the sun, and *stoccafisso*, air-dried unsalted cod, a Norwegian specialty whose name means literally "stick fish," since the cod are suspended from racks of sticks for drying. The cod dish most completely associated with Venice is *baccalà mantecato*, which loyal Venetians insist was invented there, though it is almost identical with the French Provençal *brandade de morue*, and it is probable that both countries got it from Spain, where it is called *bacalao al ajo arriero. Mantecato* means "worked," the working consisting of long crushing together of cod, milk and oil, with more than a touch of garlic, until the final result is a creamy mixture with the consistency of rather liquid mashed potatoes, in which the flesh of the fish has been completely absorbed. Another dish with cod is *baccalà alla veneziana*, for which the fish is browned in oil and onions, cooked with a mixture of butter, milk and flour, and given piquancy with a bit of shredded anchovy fillet.

The chances are that a meal in Venice will start with antipasto drawn from the sea, *scampi*, shellfish of one kind or another, *bottarga* (tuna eggs seasoned with oil and lemon juice, or lightly toasted), or that very local dish, *ostriche alla veneziana*. This is oysters with caviar from the sturgeon of the Po. You coat the opened oyster with caviar, flavored with lemon juice and pepper, and put it in the refrigerator for an hour or two to allow the flavor of the caviar to be absorbed by the oyster. In the same luxury category are hard-boiled quails' eggs, nowadays rather rare. Among prepared meats, Veneto produces *coppa*, which would be headcheese elsewhere in Italy, but here is a cold meat loaf composed of alternating layers of ham, tongue and mortadella.

The ubiquity of rice has reduced pasta and its cousins to relative unimportance in Veneto. It is true that one widely known Venetian dish is called *pasta e fagioli* (in dialect *pasta e fasioi*) but it is basically bean soup, with the pasta playing only a subordinate role. Bean soup sounds like a simple dish, but it is a little more complicated than you might expect. It can be made with either fresh or dried white beans, but most Venetian cooks prefer the dried beans of Lamon, in the Veneto province of Belluno, which is famous for them. They are soaked in tepid water overnight to prepare them for cooking, which begins when chopped onions are sautéed in olive oil until they begin to take on color. The beans are then added, and a plentiful amount of lean beef consommé is poured over them, enough to hold out for a very slow cooking which takes about four hours. After the first hour, a small amount of tomato extract is stirred in. Toward the end of the cooking, part of the beans are fished out and forced through a sieve before being returned to the soup, in order to thicken the liquid. The pasta goes in only for the last quarter hour. Whatever kind is used, it should be of hard wheat flour, without egg. Venetians frown on the practice of using flour instead of strained beans to thicken the soup, but are tolerant about occasional additions of other items to enhance the flavor—a marrow bone, for instance, or rosemary, parsley or garlic.

Among Venetian soups is *zuppa di trippa*, traditionally the start of the meal on market days, for which the tripe, cut into strips, is cooked together with tomatoes, potatoes, bacon, onion and celery. Venice has its own versions of chicken soup (*zuppa di pollo*), frog soup (*zuppa di rane*) and lentil soup (*zuppa di lenticchie*). There is of course a Venetian *brodetto*, but it does not seem to be taken quite seriously until it is called by its dialect name, *broèto*. I cannot swear that it is an invariable rule, but in my experience, whenever the word *broèto* has appeared on the menu, the fish contained in it has always included the orthodox rock fish, especially *scorfano*. *Brodetto di pesce* did indeed contain a mixture of fish, but a more or less random one; and it had tomato in it, which *broèto* did not. Another difference between the two was that the flavoring elements in *broèto* were mild (onion, carrot, celery and—the strongest—garlic), letting the taste of the fish come through, whereas *brodetto* was dominated by the pungent odors of thyme, sage, bay leaf, and pimento, with garlic the mildest element, except for onion. Neither version used saffron. A queer soup is *sguazèto*, ox pluck with aromatic herbs; if this alarms you, you should be informed that if you encounter the same word on a menu in Friuli, it will be something more familiar, lamb stew served with polenta. *Zuppa de peòci*, mussel soup, is really only a soup by courtesy; a simple concoction of mussels cooked in olive oil with garlic and chopped parsley, it does not have enough liquid to give the impression of soup. It might more accurately be called sautéed mussels.

Another way of preparing mussels is *peòci al pangrattato*. The mussels are first put into the oven to oblige them to open their shells, and into each are put a little finely chopped garlic, parsley and a coating of bread crumbs, moistened with a few drops of olive oil and consommé. The mussels are left in the oven long enough for the bread crumbs to form a crust, and are then served hot, or put aside to be eaten cold later.

Venice has many ways of serving eel—*anguilla allo spiedo*, cut into pieces and threaded on a spit between cubes of bread and bay leaves, coated with bread crumbs after it is partly cooked, and served with slices of lemon; *anguille al limone*, which uses small eels, also cut up, but cooked in a pan with lemon juice and bay leaves; and what should be the classic Venetian fashion, since it is called *anguilla alla veneziana*, for which the eels are cooked in a sauce including not only lemon juice, but also tuna worked into a paste. However, I would be inclined to consider more typical a Venetian eel dish known only by a name in local dialect, and not known at all outside its own area. This is *bisato in tecia*, *bisato* being dialect for eel, and *tecia* for frying pan. For this dish, pieces of eel are marinated in oil, vinegar, bay leaf, salt and pepper for several hours before being breaded, and cooked in the frying pan in oil and butter, moistened with Marsala wine, together with tomatoes pressed through a sieve.

Many other Venetian fish dishes attest to their local origin by their dialect names. *Sardoni a scotadeò* are spitted fresh sardines basted with lemon juice, while *sardelle in saòr* is the favorite dish of Venetian fishermen, who often make it aboard before they return to port, and eat it on their boats. *Filetti di sgombro alla veneta* is translatable as mackerel fillets, Venetian style, but the *sgombro* is a very special type of mackerel. In the Adriatic, it mates in Venetian waters, before moving south to gain a bad reputation off the coasts of Emilia-Romagna as an omnivorous devourer of everything in its path. It is cooked very simply in Venice, salted and simmered for ten minutes in dry white wine. But it is then served with the rather elaborate *salsa veneta*, which demands for its confection butter, flour, egg yolks, lemon juice, wine vinegar, dry white wine, minced onion and cooked strained spinach. *Sfogi in saòr* is a dish traditionally eaten for that great Venetian holiday, the Feast of the Redeemer; it is fillets of sole, floured, partly cooked in oil, and then transferred to an earthenware oven dish. The oil of the first cooking is poured over it, and chopped onion, carrots and celery are added, together with bay leaves, plus equal quantities of vinegar and dry white wine. The fish is served cold with pine nuts and Malaga grapes. *Filetti di sogliola in crema di gamberi* is sole, partly boiled in fish stock, and then finished in the oven with crayfish tails and a sauce whose dominant ingredient is the rest of the crayfish crushed in a mortar and passed through a sieve.

Mullet are eaten hot elsewhere in the Adriatic. In Venice, though they can also be eaten hot, they are frequently served cold; gray mullet after having been poached, and red mullet after having been floured, fried in oil, and marinated in a sauce of oil, chopped onion, white wine and wine vinegar; it is served with parsley and lemon or orange slices. The varieties of mullet are legion. *Cefalo* is a mullet too; *cefalo bollito in salsa aromatica* is boiled slowly in salted water with a dash of vinegar and a little parsley, and served with a sauce made by creaming together in a mortar crustless bread, anchovy fillets, pitted preserved olives, capers, chopped parsley, an egg yolk, vinegar, and a little pepper. Smaller fish of the same type are pan-fried in olive oil in which garlic has previously been browned but then taken out, with salt, pepper and chopped parsley, and served with lemon juice (*cefalèti in padela*). *Orata* (chrysophrys), cooked with mussels and crayfish, seasoned with marjoram, nutmeg and capers, with a discreet amount of tomato extract and a mere whisper of curry, is a dish which has lingered fondly in my memory ever since it was served me years ago in Venice's Colomba restaurant. *Coda di rospo* (toadfish tail), a fish often associated with Rome, is a favorite in Venice, which is closer to the source—Rome imports its *rospo* from the Adriatic and grills it; in Venice it is either grilled or baked. *Pesciolini marinati* are little fish of almost any species, breaded and fried in olive oil, after which, in most parts of the country, they would be eaten hot; but in Venice, which seems to have a special taste for cold fish, they are cooked in a mixture of white wine and vinegar, richly perfumed with finely chopped garlic, onion, and carrot, together with bay leaf, basil leaves, marjoram, sage and whole peppercorns, doused with olive oil, cooked together for 15 minutes, and poured boiling over the fish, which are left in it for 24 hours before eating.

The fish of the cuttlefish family are much eaten in Venice. *Seppie alla veneziana* (or *seppioline* for the little tender ones) are inkfish stewed in their own black juice and olive oil in which garlic, later discarded, has been browned, with a little white wine (some cooks add a dash of cognac and a little chopped parsley). They are usually served with polenta. Inkfish also go into *insalata di seppie e fagioli*, which is not a salad in the sense of being a lettuce dish, but simply a combination of cold boiled beans and inkfish (previously boiled with aromatic vegetables and herbs), with a dressing of olive oil, some of the cooking juice, lemon juice and chopped parsley; it is often served surrounded with segments of hard-boiled egg. *Insalata di polipetti* is a combination of these very small cuttlefish with potatoes and tomatoes, chilled in the refrigerator before serving. For this dish, the *polipetti* are left whole, except for the parts customarily removed before cooking, but for *polipetti e fagioli in bordura di polenta* they are cut into pieces, cooked with oil, wine, crushed anchovies and tomato extract, and served hot with boiled beans in a crust of yellow corn meal polenta. Finally *granzevola alla veneziana* is not called a salad, but in Anglo-Saxon eyes it is, since leaves of lettuce are placed in emptied lobster shells to form a bed for cold boiled lobster, cut into pieces, and accompanied with diced potatoes and celery stalks, under a rich sauce of mayonnaise, cream, ketchup, Duke of Urbino sauce (for which Worcestershire can be substituted if necessary), and cognac. Hardboiled egg crushed with a fork is sprinkled over the sauce, and the dish is garnished with pitted black olives.

Venetians are not really meat eaters. They rarely eat meat in its most pristine forms as genuine meat lovers do, roasted or grilled (the one exception that comes to mind is grilled pork chops). They do not even keep it in one piece as a rule, which allows the flavor of the meat, rather than its accompaniments or seasonings, to dominate the taste of a dish. Here again one exception comes to mind, *pasticciata alla veneta* (*pastizzada* in dialect), which is beef marinated overnight in wine vinegar, with slivers of garlic stuck into incisions in the flesh, lightly floured, browned in butter containing chopped onion, seasoned and moistened with wine, covered with buttered oven paper, and cooked in a covered pan very slowly (an hour for a pound of meat). It is served sliced, with the cooking juice for gravy, accompanied by whatever vegetables may be in season. Otherwise, Venice prefers to chop its meat for hashlike treatment, or cut it into chunks to stew it or even cook it on spits, a favorite practice in the Veneto ever since the days when most cooking was done in open fireplaces. When kitchens replaced fireplaces, they were still arranged to reserve a prominent role for the revolving spit. The persistence of old habits still leads Venetians to spit even meats that are eventually cooked in the oven, like *polenta e oselèti scapài*, for which pieces of veal, chicken liver, bacon and fresh mushrooms are threaded on the spit, with a leaf of sage between each two morsels of the other ingredients, after which the adorned spits go into the oven in a dish of butter, to be eventually served on slices of hot fried polenta. *Scapai* (English, escaped) makes the name of this dish mean "polenta and the little birds that got away." There are no birds in this dish. The joke is that its ingredients are what the frustrated housewife might find at the last minute to substitute for the birds she expected to put on her polenta if her husband had not returned from the hunt empty-handed.

Montone or *agnello alla veneziana* is mutton or lamb cut into pieces and cooked in milk; *stufato di castrato* is mutton stewed with oil, wine, onion, carrots, celery, parsley, garlic and sage.

Polpette di carne are meat balls, of beef and salame chopped together, with egg for a binder, and a high seasoning including bits of candied citron, pine nuts, Malaga grapes, and a dash of cognac; after being fried in butter they are served dusted—with sugar! *Frittura secca* is another chopped meat dish, the mixture this time being of previously boiled veal and chicken, salame, eggs, chopped parsley, grated cheese and nutmeg. This is shaped into little balls the size of a walnut, which are floured and fried in butter.

Calves' liver is not cooked solely with onions in Venice. There is also *fegato garbo e dolce*, fried in butter after having been dipped in beaten egg and coated with bread crumbs, and served with sweetened lemon juice. Goose livers are cooked in butter with sage, the seeds of fresh white grapes, chopped parsley, cognac and pitted black cherries. The dish ought to be called, it would seem, liver with cherries, but, on the basis of their seeds, it is called, perversely, liver with grapes, *fegato d'oca all'uva*. Tongue is served with a sauce of white wine, capers and chopped anchovy fillets (*lingua in salsa*).

Venetians are much fonder of poultry than of meat. They

eat a great deal of this, of all available kinds. Chicken may become, as in Rome or Florence, *pollo alla diavola;* or be cooked on a spit and eaten with boiled beans; or, again spitted, served with rice cooked with the chicken liver, oil, anchovy fillet, garlic and onion (*pollo allo spiedo con riso in pevarada*); or cut into pieces, browned in butter and white wine, cooked with onion, celery, carrots, tomato passed through a sieve, fresh mushrooms, cloves and cinnamon, and served with polenta (*polastro in tecia*). *Capòn a la canevèra* is a capon sewed into a pig's bladder with pieces of beef and guinea hen, with a hollow bamboo stem thrust into the bladder to let the steam out; when no more steam escapes from it, the bird is done.

Dindo alla schiavona (Slavic style turkey—*dindo* is the Venetian word, recalling the French *dinde;* it is *tacchino* in Italian), is stuffed with chestnuts, prunes and celery, spit-roasted, and served with fried potatoes. Roast duck (*anitra ripiena*) has a stuffing of its own liver, lean bacon and veal, crushed into a paste with grated Parmesan, bread crumbs, egg, thyme and tarragon. Duck also appears as *anitra alla salsa piccante,* duck with a piquant sauce, in which it is allowed to soak for half an hour before serving. The king of duck dishes may well be *màsaro a la valesana,* which gets us into the category of game, for *màsaro* is wild duck. It is first marinated for twelve hours in vinegar with thyme and tarragon, then buttered, barded with bacon, cooked for 15 minutes in a moderately hot oven, then cut into pieces, and finished in butter, wine, chopped anchovy fillets, chopped onion, and capers. Most game dishes are found farther inland, but on the spits of Venice small birds and pheasants often turn slowly, dripping into the receptacles set to catch it, drop by drop, the fat from the bacon in which the birds are wrapped. The hare found in the uplands is replaced nearer the sea by rabbit—*coniglio bollito al sale aromatico,* cut into pieces and stewed with rosemary, sage, lemon peel and garlic, or *coniglio fritto dorato*, also cut up, marinated in oil, lemon juice, chopped onion, salt and pepper, soaked in beaten egg and floured, then fried in boiling oil.

The market gardens of the Veneto coast are famous. God knows how long they will hold out against the pall of pollution which is threatening the area, but at the time of writing they were still producing tender luscious peas and artichokes, tomatoes and onions, cabbages and the oddly shaped brightly colored "baroque squash," of which roasted slices are served scalding hot from booths in the market of Venice, as are pears fished out from great steaming kettles, and boiled chestnuts. Another kind of squash, *zucchini* or *zucchine* (this word appears in both genders and means the same thing in both), are prepared very simply, cut into pieces, seasoned only with salt and chopped parsley, and cooked in oil; at the last minute beaten egg is stirred in, and grated Parmesan added; this is called Grandma's squash, *zucchine della nonna*. Venice uses both the root and the leaves in cooking kohlrabi (*cavolirape*), cutting the former into quarters, boiling it for five minutes in salted water, and then stewing it for half an hour in a covered dish, heavily peppered, along with the leaves, in a mixture of butter, consommé, chopped onions and a little flour. *Cavoli-cappucci agrodolci* is Brussels sprouts in sweet-and-sour sauce, containing caraway seeds. Lentils are half-cooked in water, then seasoned with salt, pepper and a bay leaf; a mixture of chopped garlic cooked in butter with small pieces of bacon in it, thickened with a bit of flour, is then added, vinegar is poured over the whole, and the cooking finished in a covered dish, producing *lenticchie stufate*. Yellow peppers cut into strips are stewed in a covered dish with oil in which garlic has been cooked and then removed and tomatoes, added halfway through the cooking; it is sprinkled with chopped parsley on serving (*papriche stufate*). *Fagioli in salsa* is a salad of boiled beans eaten cold, with a dressing of garlic-flavored oil, chopped anchovy fillets and vinegar. *Carciofi alla veneziana* use the small totally edible dark purplish-brown artichokes; only the tired outer leaves are peeled off before the artichokes are stewed slowly in a covered pan for an hour, covered with a mixture of olive oil, white wine and water, in equal proportions, after which you take off the lid, raise the flame, and wait until all the liquid has boiled off except the olive oil, when your artichokes are done.

It is only natural that Veneto should have a sweet tooth; after all, it was Venice that first introduced sugar into Europe, which at first called it "Indian salt," with characteristic nonchalance about Eastern geography. The result is a really bewildering assortment of pastries—cakes, tarts, cookies, everything you can think of. To walk from the Rialto Bridge to the Campo Santi Apostoli, keeping as close to the Grand Canal as the topography will permit, is a mouth-watering experience. Your way is lined with pastry shops, diffusing a spicy odor into the air. These are the *scaletèri*, a name which comes from a pastry called *scalete*, popular in the 1400's. When the pastry cooks of Venice formed a guild in 1493, they did it under the name of *scaletèri*, and many of the streets of Venice bear today the names of the *scaletèri* who had shops in them. In the 15th century *scalete* drove out the hitherto very popular *storti*, a specialty of Dolo, on the Brenta River, a pastry of flour, sugar, eggs and lemon peel, covered with bits of almond, given a twisted shape—hence *storti*, twisted. Because of this "deformity," *storti* became a synonym for physical weakness. This may account for the decline of the name and the pastry, and its replacement by the similar *scalete*. Likewise *pandoli*, popular at the same time as *storti*, a symbol for slow-wittedness, disappeared from circulation too, possibly because customers grew tired of the not very brilliant witticisms provoked when they asked for them; but there was no lack of replacements. If one had to name the top Venetian specialty in this category today, it would probably have to be what Giuseppe Mazzotti described as "the superb very Venetian *baìcoli*, more worthy than any other sweet to represent the cuisine of Veneto." *Baìcoli* have a history too. Little biscuits of flour, yeast, sugar, salt, butter, and orange flavoring, they stocked the galleys of the medieval Venetian sailing ships because they lasted a long time without becoming moldy, crumbly or flavorless. They are favored for dunking, in coffee and milk, or even better in the rich chocolate for which Venice is famous—minor figures in several canvases of Luigi Longhi are pictured in this act. Another dunking biscuit is the *fugassa de Pasqua*, the *focaccia* whose origin reaches so far back that no one knows when it was first invented, but, as its name indicates, it was the Venetian version of the hearth cake found all over Europe in the Middle Ages. As its name also indicates, it is an Easter dish. There are other pastries similarly attached to holidays. Shrove Thursday sees *galani*, egg dough fritters whose only unusual ingredient is white wine, eaten cold, powdered with sugar. A cookie in the shape of a mounted knight appears on St. Martin's Day. I do not know whether any specific type of dough is prescribed for this, but it may well be the same as for *veneti*, Venetian cookies, an ordinary enough combination of flour, butter, sugar, salt and egg, which are cut into squares, frosted with an icing of confectioner's sugar, egg white and lemon juice, and then decorated with an X of apricot jelly on top.

Other typical Venetian pastries include *fagottini di Venezia*, "Venetian little bundles"; they are stacks of round wafers flavored with lemon peel, with a filling of butter, sugar, flour, egg yolk, sultana raisins, candied orange peel, rum and stiffly beaten egg whites between the wafers. Chocolate macaroons are described locally as *bruti ma boni*— ugly but good. *Pan di sorgo* is made of mixed cornmeal and wheat flour, two parts cornmeal to one of flour, both butter and lard for shortening, again in a two to one proportion, a good deal of egg, Damascus grapes, lemon peel, and, of course, sugar. *Crema fritta veneziana*, Venetian fried cream, does not sound like pastry, though it is, but it starts with a thick cream made by mixing sugar into beaten egg yolks, then flour, lemon juice and milk; it is brought to a boil, and poured out onto a cold surface, lightly oiled, and smoothed out with a knife blade to a thickness of a little under an inch, and left to harden. Cut into lozenges the next day, it is dipped into egg whites and bread crumbs, and deep-fried in boiling oil. *Frìtole* are little fritters whose flavoring includes cinnamon, sultana raisins, pine nuts, lemon peel, vanilla and rum. *Giallettini* are small biscuits made mostly from cornmeal, with a little wheat flour, the other ingredients being milk, eggs, plus extra egg yolk, butter, sugar, raisins, pine nuts, lemon rind, and any liqueur you fancy for flavoring; they are presented in various fancy shapes—little squares, rings, half moons, horseshoes and the letter S. *Favette* are tiny liqueur-flavored fritters powdered with confectioner's sugar. The list could be extended indefinitely, but space is lacking to describe other Venetian pastries, most of which betray their authentic local origin by dialect names—*zaletti, castagnole, pinsa, cotognata, presniz, sbréghe*, etc.

Outside the pastry category, I cannot forebear from paying tribute to one dessert which is the specialty of a single restaurant—the delicate ice cream that Florian's in Venice makes from wild strawberries. To skip from the most sophisticated to the most rustic, here is a countryman's dessert (indeed its very name is *paesana*, peasant style), white raisins soaked in eau de vie.

The city of Venice dominates the province of Venice gastronomically; what the city eats, the province eats. One small assertion of independence is achieved by the city of

Chioggia. The lagoon of Venice occupies the northern part of a half-moon-shaped push of the sea into the land; Chioggia is on the point that marks its southern limit. It is a fishing port of about 50,000 population, which has earned the right to have some independent ideas about food by supplying a good deal of it to Venice. Some of it is vegetable, but more comes from its colorful fish market, surrounded by fishing boats with long funnel-shaped nets floating from their masts, while from the windows of the houses in the port hang long strings of cuttlefish, drying like the weekly wash. Chioggia has two dishes of its own particularly worthy of note. For *risotto alla chioggiota*, local fish, especially *il gò*, are first boiled and then passed through a sieve to produce a paste. This fish paste is stirred into boiled rice with bits of butter and grated Parmesan, and the whole doused with white wine. *Zucca gialla di Chioggia in marinata* is peeled yellow squash, cut into slices moistened with olive oil, and baked in the oven, after which the slices, with basil leaves between them, are covered with barely boiling vinegar in which oil, salt and pepper have been cooked; the squash is marinated in this liquid for several hours and then eaten cold.

If you follow the main auto road south from Chioggia, you will come, just after it has swung westward through Loreo, to a town of perhaps 25,000 inhabitants called Adria. It was this apparently insignificant place which gave its name to the Adriatic. It is not on the Adriatic, which is 13 ½ miles away (though only 13 feet lower than Adria). It isn't even on the Po, which is 2 ½ miles away. Once, however, it was on both. In 600 B.C. Adria (formerly Atria) was a flourishing Etruscan port, the Venice of antiquity, with wide canals but narrow streets. In the 3rd century B.C. it was important enough to attract the attention of Aristotle, who noted that it was famous for having developed a particularly luscious breed of chicken. Adria lasted as a port until the Roman imperial period, although by then it was silting up and a canal had to be dredged between the harbor and the open sea. Then the silt won, and Adria was left stranded, inland.

The fate of Adria was geographically ineluctable. It is in the province of Rovigo, otherwise known as the Polesine, which comes from a Low Latin word, *policinium*, meaning land which has emerged from the sea. The soil of Polesine did not exactly do that; instead it was carried down to the coast and deposited there by two great rivers, the Adige, which forms most of Rovigo province's northern border, and the Po, which forms most of its southern border. The capital city of the province appeared much later than Adria. It was founded by the Romans, who called it Rhodigium, hence Rovigo.

The province of Rovigo has a curious shape, long and narrow, like a leg from the knee down bathing its toes in the sea. Since the whole province is composed of fertile alluvial soil, it is rich agricultural country. It grows wheat and, even more important, rice—the motion picture *Bitter Rice* was filmed in the Polesine. Among fruits, the region's melons and watermelons are especially prized. The most important crop is sugar beets, which produce more than 100,000 tons of sugar a year.

The Polesine area is obsessed by water. Its two major rivers fragment toward their mouths into a crisscrossing labyrinth of smaller streams, which do not draw enough water from the Po to prevent its main branch, the Po della Maestra, from reaching a width of 600 yards at the point near Adria where it leaves the second largest branch, the Po di Goro. The Po della Maestra widens even more as it ends its course through a maze of islands, promontories, isthmuses, peninsulas and other formations in which land and water become thoroughly confused with one another.

This maze is constantly changing as the Po carries down silt, so that every year its main stream has to flow 282 feet farther to reach the sea. It is not surprising that the *cucina polesana* is founded on foods which depend in one way or another on water, whether it is rice, which needs flooded fields in which to grow; river fish, like the sturgeon of the Po; salt-water fish; or waterfowl.

The most distinctive feature of the *polesana* diet is its large proportion of game, all of the same kind, water birds. A bewildering variety of species winters in the delta of the Po. For most of them, the open season lasts from October to March, but the locals are sniffy about taking them after February, which is the mating season, when their flavor falls off. They are hunted from huts of reeds built in the marshes of the delta. The inhabitants of the Valle, as they prefer to call their region, rarely refer to ducks, except in cookbooks where the word *anitra* serves to indicate that the recipe which follows can be applied to various types of duck. Otherwise, they specify the particular bird they have in mind by the word identifying its special species. "Duck" covers too much ground for people familiar from childhood with every minute deviation in the large group of birds which less tutored persons lump together indiscriminately under that name. They know how to cook each type in the fashion that will best bring out its particular virtues (or hide its particular faults), extending this skill to some birds which Anglo-Saxons consider inedible.

One of the most prized birds for the table is dignified with the word "royal"—*germano reale*, in dialect *anara* or *mazorin*, which is the spoonbill duck—"royal" in this case because it is a larger and more colorful variety than the ordinary *germano*. The female is preferred for boiling (it gives richer bouillon), the male for roasting; but even when it is to be roasted, the bird is boiled in slightly salted water for 15 minutes before going onto the spit or into the oven.

Germano reale al sugo means that it has been boiled, boned, and marinated after cooking, to be eaten cold with fried polenta. *Germano reale rifreddo* is roasted, boned, pressed and jellied, to be eaten cold. *Germano reale* is also often used for *filetto di anitra,* a preparation applied to various ducks, for which the fillets are cut from an already roasted duck, and then sautéed separately in oil or butter and served with fresh local mushrooms.

These methods of cooking are employed also for *canapiglia* (dialect, *pignola*), the gadwall duck; *codone* (dialect, *asiao* or *colanzo*), the pintail duck; and *fischione* (dialect, *ciosso*), the widgeon, except that the last two are never boiled. They are usually either spit-roasted or cooked hunter's style, *alla cacciatora*—skinned, cut up, and sautéed with oil, butter, onion, parsley, consommé, white wine, a little flour and bay leaves.

Less highly thought of are the *moriglione* (dialect *magasso* or *magasson*), which I think is the tufted duck; the *moretta* (dialect, *magasseto* or *moreton*), which I think is the mussel duck; and the *quattr'occhi* (four-eyes; dialect *quatroci* or *campanato*), which I am completely unable to identify. Whatever they are, all three are served in one or another of these fashions: (1) *alla valligiana,* in the manner of the Valley, which means stuffed with their innards, bacon, onion and parsley and boiled; (2) *minestra di fagioli al magasso,* with beans; (3) *minestra di fagioli al magasso con noci,* with beans and walnuts. In all three cases, the bird is likely to be accompanied by rice or pasta.

Less reputed still is *messolone* (*fòfano* or *palettòn* in dialect), and what it is in English I have no idea. If it were as good to eat as it is to look at, it would be the top game dish of the Valley; alas, it isn't, but sellers take advantage of its splendid appearance to pass it off on the unwary at the price of other varieties of wild duck, which means at about twice the price it brings from the knowing. Connoisseurs recognize (and avoid) it by its wider, flatter, bent beak; those who do not succeed in doing this are advised to sauté it with heightened seasoning in order to give it a palatability which it does not naturally provide.

Alzavola (dialect, *sarzegna* or *zarzegna*) provides another problem in identification. It is teal, but it is defined in the dictionaries as "winter teal," and its open season, longer than that for most other water fowl, is from August to April. "Summer teal" (according to the dictionaries) is *marzaiola* (dialect, *rocheto* or *crècola*), and does not appear to be the same bird. In any case, it is much appreciated because it is a fast-day dish. It is usually sautéed with butter, oil and consommé, boned, and combined with rice to produce *risotto di sarzegna*, or baked with pasta in a *pasticcio di maccheroni colla sarzegna*.

We reach more exotic meats with *folaga* (dialect, *fòlega*), which is coot, usually served *alla cacciatora* with polenta, but it is also spit-roasted, served with rice or pasta; or cooked like *magasso* with beans or beans and walnuts; or like *sarzegna* as a *pasticcio* (it is also fast-day food).

Airone (dialect, *garzo* or *sgarzo*) is heron, "mediocre even when it is young, the only time when you are likely to be tempted to eat it," writes Antonio Tenani, the gastronomic expert of the Valley, who suggests that if you try it, you should throw everything away except the thighs and the breast meat, soak it in wine for a couple of hours before cooking it, and then do so in a saucepan with white wine, lemon juice, consommé, tomato, bay leaf and sage, apparently to kill the taste of the heron. The same treatment is applied to the *chiurlo* (dialect, *arcaza* or *arcada*), which is curlew, the idea being to drown the fishy taste which comes from the bird's diet of mollusks, small crustaceans and seaweed.

The *chiurletto*, from its Italian name (the dialect is *taragnola*), ought to be a young curlew; but apparently it is a different bird (the lesser curlew, perhaps)? In any case it brings us into a category described as not really birds of the Valle, meaning that though they pass through, they are not regular winterers. Among them are two I have not succeeded in identifying in English terms—the *pettegola* (dialect, *tòtano*), a word meaning gossiper, so it would seem that this should be a bird which chatters a lot; and the *pittima* (dialect, *vettola*), which is probably a noisy animal too, since the word means whiner or grumbler. Two others are recognizable: the *pivieressa* (dialect *barosala*) is plover, the *piovanello pancia nera* (dialect, *biseghìn*) is snipe.

One game bird that has now become extremely rare is the wild goose. It is usually roasted on a spit, barded with bacon, and cooked with a bay leaf and some flavoring vegetable as stuffing—celery, carrots or cabbage.

After water fowl, the second great category of *polesana* food is fish. The same cooking methods are applied more or less indiscriminately to all kinds of fish. They are frequently boiled, especially when they are to appear with rice, either in a soup or as *risotto di brodo di pesce*. *Pesce arrostito* can mean either grilled for small fish, or baked in the oven for big fish. *Pesce all'umido*, fish in sauce, is preserved fish (sun-dried or smoked in the fireplace). It is cooked in white wine and tomato extract, with a bay leaf, before being put away for future eating within the next two or three months, which is as long as it will keep. *Friggere in padella* means that the fish is cooked in a frying pan, in a fashion peculiar to this region; the pan stands on a high tripod over the flame from a soft-wood fire, which is allowed to envelop the whole pan.

One of the favorite fish of the Polesine is eel. It may be boiled; fried, cut into chunks, each rolled in cornmeal; cooked *all'umido*, in tomato extract and white wine, with a bay leaf; *arrostita*, grilled; *al girarrosto*, spitted; or, in a local manner, *alla valligiana*, split open lengthwise and cooked in its own fat with much pepper. Another favorite is *capa tonda*, little cuttlefish, cooked with oil, onions, garlic and parsley, and served with polenta, risotto, or pasta.

The great specialty of the Polesine, however, is a fresh-water fish—the famous sturgeon of the Po. Here again the natives, who know them well, distinguish variations imperceptible to outlanders, some of them with names which elsewhere would suggest quite different fish. The best eating is provided by the river sturgeon, *storione fluviale*, a white-fleshed fish of delicate flavor, but, local connoisseurs will warn you, only up to the weight of 55 pounds, after which the taste coarsens. A river sturgeon weighing 205 pounds was once taken from the Po; a fish this big makes a fine trophy for a fisherman, but not for a cook. The *storione minore*, with a blunter, fatter head and an enormous mouth, is not such good eating; you can spot it on the plate because the fatty part of its meat is yellowish in color, in contrast to the unbroken white of the river sturgeon. The *ladano* is also rated excellent up to 55 pounds only, and some persons think it is because of its flavor that it is also called the "royal fish," or "king fish" (*pesce reale*). More probably it is because it is a voracious feeder on other fish. Finally there is the *ladano tonnina*, with an even bigger mouth than the *storione minore*, which is not eaten much in the Polesine, but is sold easily to the Piedmontese, who are less knowledgeable about sturgeon, and provide Rovigo's principal market for this fish.

The caviar from Po sturgeon is not preserved in the same fashion as in Russia. The eggs are lightly cooked in oil, and then put up in glass or earthenware containers, in which they will keep under refrigeration for at least a year, or in tin cans, in which they will keep at least two. Po caviar has one characteristic in common with Russian caviar: it is extremely expensive.

* * *

The province of Padua insinuates itself between Venezia and Rovigo with just a toehold on an indentation of the coast between them. Its capital (Padova in Italian, Patavium for the ancient Romans) is a very old city, legendarily founded by Antenor, a companion of Aeneas, an echo of the theory that the Veneti were Trojans.

The Roman historian Titus Livy was born in Padua, and St. Anthony of Padua died there, having somehow reached this country from his native Lisbon. The University of Padua was established in 1222, and harbored some illustrious professors, including Galileo. The beauty of the Euganean Hills has attracted poets: Petrarch, who died among them, in Arquà, and in later times Byron and Shelley. Paduan menus recall the names of two of its great guests: *piedi di maiale alla Sant'Antonio* is breaded pig's feet with cucumbers and truffles, while Petrarch salad is a combination of tomatoes and potatoes. Galileo inspired no cooks.

The Paduan plain has been an important agricultural region at least since the times of the Etruscans, whose engineers supplied it with a network of canals and irrigation ditches, producing wheat so abundantly that Athenian ships touched at the nearest ports to buy grain for Greece. Today Padua has an important food processing industry founded on its own products, and stresses stock breeding and agricultural machinery at its annual fair, held on the anniversary of St. Anthony's death, June 13, 1231. The Euganean Hills are crowned with vineyards and peach orchards. A wide variety of mushrooms grows there; they should be gathered by experts, for there are several poisonous varieties among them. The chestnut trees in this area are descendants of those planted by the Romans.

The traditions of good eating go far back here; the memoirs of visitors to Padua through the centuries repeat like a litany the praises of its inns, restaurants and cafés, and of the gaiety of its society, which owed a great deal to

Venetian influence—in Padua, as in Venice, women were prominent in public social life, frequenting the cafés along with the men, not the habit in most of the rest of Italy. Their independence extended even to those members of their sex whose business it was to please, so that the young courtesan Zulietta did not hesitate to make fun of the sentimentality of Jean-Jacques Rousseau, advising him to "give up women and study mathematics."

The names of some famous old-time eating establishments have remained in Padua. The university is in the Palace of the "Bo," a slangy shortening of the name of a famous inn, the Sign of the Ox (ox is *bove* or *bue*), which formerly stood on the site. It was called the best in Italy by Savonarola, though it may be doubted whether this ascetic monk was a qualified judge. The Pedrocchi Café, famous among other things for the political plots which used to be hatched there, still exists. When Alfred de Musset was studying at the university, he turned out a bit of doggerel affirming that he preferred its polenta to the university's courses, as indeed what student wouldn't.

> *Moi, j'aime mieux la polenta*
> *Qu'on mange aux bords de la Brenta*
> *Sous une treille.*

Many Paduan specialties are local variants of Venetian cooking, especially in the seafood department. Others are reminiscent of Bolognese cooking, especially in the pasta department (Bologna is only 75 miles away). There does not seem to be much left to Padua itself except fantasy—a fondess for such unusual ingredients as cockscombs and marrow, oddities like squash-flower fritters (*fiori di zucca alla padovana*)—and of course the favorite cakes and cookies, highly localized everywhere in Italy. The imports and the original dishes divide themselves into two sharply distinguishable groups, city cooking—chiefly that of the capital—and the rustic cooking which reaches its apogee in the Euganean Hills.

The close relationship between Paduan and Venetian cooking goes so far that Padua even dares contest the paternity of Venice's most characteristic dish, *risi e bisi*, which in Padua (but nowhere else) is presented as an invention of (in dialect) *Venezia bela e Padova so sorela*—lovely Venice and her sister, Padua. In any case, rice and peas is a favorite dish in Padua, and so are many other rice dishes—rice with celery and tomato for instance, and of course above all *risotto di pollo alla padovana*, for which the risotto, cooked in consommé, is accompanied by chopped chicken and dried mushrooms, celery, carrots, onion, tomato sauce, and both of Padua's two gastronomic trademarks, marrow and cocks' combs. Venetian influence is clearly present in *minestra di pasta e fagioli*, the pasta-beans combination we have already encountered both in Venezia and Rovigo. *Minestra di zucca gialla*, the yellow squash of which Venice is so fond, here in a soup, also falls into this category. Two dishes whose names attribute them to Veneto in general are nevertheless specifically Paduan—*lepre alla veneta*, spitted hare, and *pomodori alla veneta*, breaded tomato halves or slices fried in onion-flavored olive oil, with much pepper and parsley.

Padua also shares general tendencies with Venice, for instance, scant interest in meat, which when it does appear is usually cut up to disguise its unappreciated nature. About the only beef dish which one automatically associates with Padua is *pastisso de carne* (dialect), which might be described as an oven-baked hamburger with grated cheese on top. It is customarily served with a salad of that very special kind of lettuce, *radicchio*, from Treviso. Also like Venice, Padua replaces meat with poultry. *Pollo alla padovana* is chicken cut up and sautéed, though I have encountered (but not in Padua) grilled chicken flavored with aromatic herbs under the same name. Guinea hen is treated in much the same fashion, in *faraona al vino rosso*, when the bird is again cut up before being stewed in red wine with a touch of *grappa* along with various seasonings, including nut-meg—the Paduan touch of fantasy again.

When it harks back to Bologna, Padua injects its note of fantasy too. *Bigoli coi rovinazzi* (*bigoli* is dialect for a kind of pasta) adds Padua's favorite cockscombs to the sauce, and throws in a touch of sage. Gnocchi are made with bread instead of dough, with morsels of chopped ham. The Bolognese touch may be glimpsed also in what Padua does with prepared pork products. The town of Montagnana, hidden behind its ancient ramparts, is noted for its ham. *Museti a la padovana* is a local sausage, served hot with boiled potatoes and, curiously, sauerkraut, which suggests seepage from the Alto Adige, with which, however, Padua has no common frontier. *Soppresse* is a sausage of pork, or pork and beef.

This gets us into rustic products, chiefly from the Euganean Hills, often uniquely Paduan, a fact betrayed by the dialect names which appear to be the only ones they have. The country origin may be less marked for *torresani*, a dish made from pigeons, or *pevara alla padovana*, which is Padua's favorite beef marrow, well spiced, and served with salad. Get into the hills and you will at once hear the praises of homemade bread. "Paduans," remarks a local writer, "with incredible modesty, sing the praises of Vicenza wine, Treviso tripe, and Venetian women, but are limited themselves to *pan padovan* (Paduan bread). It's enough." In the same category of foods, Padua goes in for polenta, also Venetian (especially, in the hills, *polenta e osei*, since the little birds served with it are plentiful there) and is determinedly in favor of corn for its flour, a rustic enough preference which is carried over into other fields, such as sweets. A dialect name is given to fresh polenta eaten with cheese at the end of the meal, in lieu of plain cheese or dessert—*brustolà*. The cheese may be local too, *grana padano*, a cousin of Parmesan (the Bolognese influence again), and is eaten less often for its own sake than grated, on other dishes. *Funghi dei Colli Euganei*, the mushrooms which have been famous since antiquity, are prepared in a variety of ways: roasted, with garlic, oil, salt and pepper; fried; or sautéed, either chopped or whole, with garlic, oil and parsley.

Most rustic of the "sweets" is a sort of hearth cake, which isn't normally sweet at all, but is eaten at times when sweet cakes or cookies are ordinarily called for, *coari*, nowadays baked in the oven, with bits of pork and bacon sprinkled through the dough. Corn turns up in several sweet pastries, such as *zaletti*, elongated oval buns with lemon peel, raisins and pine nuts in them. *Smejassa* is made of polenta and cookies crumbled together, mixed with milk and molasses, filled with raisins, pine nuts and candied citron, and cooked in oil in an earthenware dish. A non-pastry dessert is *persegi in guasso* (dialect), lightly cooked halved peaches, preferably from Monselice, which is noted for them, flavored with almonds and liqueurs.

As is true elsewhere, many sweets are holiday fixtures. *Zaletti* and *pazientina* turn up during Carnival, and at Easter there is a bun called *focacce* at Este and *polentina* at Cittadella, a town in the extreme north of the province which has a sweet specialty all its own—*soare di Cittadella*, a sort of marmalade made from grape must, pears, and apples.

If the food of Italy is a function of history, no city symbolizes that fact better than Verona, whose market, the oldest in the country, is established in a square which epitomizes the history of the area from ancient Roman times on. The Verona market is in the Piazza delle Erbe (Vegetable Square) thus named for its function, though it might have merited some more august appellation on the basis of the history with which it is impregnated. It is on the site of the ancient Roman forum. In its center is a 14th-century fountain, bearing a statue now called the Madonna, which is actually a pre-Christian Roman statue. Before the 15th-century column, the Capitello, the decrees and sentences of the governing tribunal were read. To one side rises the 16th-century Column of St. Mark, with the winged lion of Venice on top of it. The square is surrounded by notable buildings—the 14th-century House of the Merchants; the baroque 17th-century Maffei Palace, surmounted by six shining statues representing the working days of the week; the Mazzanti houses, built when the Scaligers were lords of Verona; the Romanesque 12th-century Communal Palace with its exterior Gothic staircase; and, towering above it all, the 275-foot Lamberti Tower, which was nearly three centuries in building, 1172 to 1464. Its bell is still rung to summon the city council to meetings.

All this splendor is pretty much invisible when the market is functioning. The Piazza delle Erbe is then a sea of umbrellas, gay with bright colors, beneath which vendors hawk their wares, vegetables to take home or hot snacks to consume on the spot. It is a noisy animated fascinating spectacle.

Verona was fated to be a city of history as well as of legend by its position at the crossroads of two great routes: from Milan to Trieste (from Mediolanum to Aquileia in ancient times), and from the south to the Brenner Pass. After the Romans had displaced the Cenomani Gauls in the 2nd century B.C., Verona became a Roman city so important that to this day it has more Roman remains than any other northern Italian city.

The province of Verona is an important agricultural

region, noted especially for its fruit—peaches, strawberries, cherries and grapes. Vegetables are exported even as far as northern Europe. Its International Agricultural Fair, held in March, attracts 600,000 visitors yearly; more modest is its Peach Fair in August. Its products are the basis for the largest refrigeration plant in Europe. They take on greater variety due to the presence of Lake Garda on the western boundary, whose moderating influence on the climate provides a different sort of vegetation, including the celebrated Bardolino vineyards.

If any one food specialty of Verona is singled out as most representative of the city, it has to be *pandoro*, "golden bread." It is a rich dome-shaped vanilla cake, dusted with confectioner's sugar. There is another dessert which for me is particularly connected with Verona—a small red berry which I ate in the famous restaurant of the Twelve Apostles (*Dodici Apostoli*). I have spent a good deal of time trying to identify it with something in English, without great success.

The menu called it *mirtillo*, which the dictionaries turn into bilberry—but the bilberry is blue. At a guess, it was our mountain cranberry, or a close relative of it, an acid red fruit which is a cousin of the bilberry. The scientific name of the former is *vaccinium vitis-idaea*, of the bilberry *vaccinium myrtillus*. Even in Latin it is very good on vanilla ice cream.

Verona is not otherwise rich in specialties, following chiefly the lead of Venice, with some borrowings from Lombardy. It is known for its addiction to gnocchi, here made from potatoes, which everyone eats on Good Friday, often referred to in Verona as Gnocchi Friday, *venerdi gnoccolaro*. In Rione di San Zeno, there is even a procession in 14th-century costumes on that day, at the end of which the Father of Gnocchi for the year is chosen. There is also a special sauce, *pearà* in the local dialect, *peperata* in Italian, of marrow, butter, stock, bread crumbs, grated Parmesan and a great deal of pepper, which is served especially with boiled meat to give it more personality; Treviso calls almost the same thing *pevarada,* but uses it for roasts, which need heightening less than boiled meat. The Veronese would be more likely to use their mushroom sauce (butter, olive oil, chopped onion, chopped parsley, garlic, sliced mushrooms and flour) with roasts or grilled meat, or even with chicken or on pasta. *Pasticciata* does not mean a doughy dish in Verona, as it does in other places; here it is a meat stew. *Risotto alla veronese* is with chopped ham, smothered in this mushroom sauce; rice with chicken livers, hardly restricted to Verona, is popular here too. Spit-roasted kid and fish from Lake Garda are also well liked, but are by no means unique. The list may be closed with *soppresse,* the same pork-and-beef salame already encountered in Padua.

Vicenza, the Vicetia of the Romans, does not loom very large in history, even though it did manage to achieve the feat of establishing an independent state early in the 12th century and maintaining it for some 200 years. It did not develop a sufficiently marked individuality to resist the stamp of Venice, when that city gained domination over it in 1404. Instead, it became so thoroughly imbued with Venetian habits and customs, and so colorful, with its Gothic buildings and frescoed façades, that it was described as "Venice on dry land." A symptom of the harmony of spirit between Vicenza and Venice is the fact that the outstanding architect of Vicenza, Palladio, is represented by outstanding works in only one other province, Venice.

The influence of Venice also dominates the cooking of Vicenza. Except for one reminiscence of its Longobard period, poultry cooked in a casing of clay, the cuisine echoes that of Venice, in spite of the fact that, lying inland, it has a different list of local raw materials to draw on. Venetian shunning of meat is partly attributable to the abundance of salt-water fish, which landlocked Vicenza does not possess (it does not even have a large lake). Nevertheless, Vicenza follows the lead of Venice in preferring birds to meat, and also in cooking them most often on spits.

Among the local products of the province of Vicenza are the reputed cherries of Castello di Marostica, the fat asparagus of Bassano del Grappa, and the strawberries and mushrooms of Montello. Pasubio makes a much appreciated *soppresse* sausage. The hilly northern part of the province is cheese country. "The *forme di Vèzzena*, princes of Venetian cheeses," writes Giuseppe Mazzotti, "descend each year from the huts of the shepherds scattered over the high pastures to compete in knightly competition in some locality of the Vicenza plain"—less poetically, to vie for prizes at agricultural fairs. *Asiago*, of partially skimmed cow's milk, is a little sharp in flavor, but agreeable. Cheeses are also produced in the Grappa area.

The dependence of the Vicenza cuisine on that of Venice is demonstrated by the fact that the most famous single dish of Vicenza, *baccalà alla vicentina*, is simply a variant of the Venetian *baccalà alla veneziana*. It is made by putting olive oil, a little butter, and chopped onion into a braising pan, and after the onion is browned, putting in boned skinned cod, which is covered with milk and cooked *piano piano*—very slowly. Some cooks add other touches to this dish—garlic, or chopped anchovy fillets, or parsley, or white wine, or cinnamon, or other spices, or grated cheese, or combinations of these ingredients. It is often served with polenta. Polenta also accompanies tiny spitted birds, a dish found everywhere in Venezia (and in Lombardy too), but never better than in the form of *polenta e osei alla vicentina*, which is flavored with sage.

The favorite bird of the province of Vicenza is the turkey. "*Quando in novembre el vin no xe più mosto, la paeta xe pronta par el rosto,*" says one maxim in dialect—"When the wine has stopped fermenting in November, the turkey is ready for roasting." "*La paeta gà un destin che finisse a San Martin,*" says another—"The turkey has a destiny which ends on St. Martin's Day" (November 11). *Paeta,* of course, is the local name for *tacchino,* turkey. Castelgomberto holds a turkey fair each year, when prizes are awarded to the breeders of the best birds. A turkey contest which used to be held at Montebello during the three-day festival of Santa Maria Assunta, beginning the first Sunday in May, has now, happily, been forbidden. Blindfolded contestants armed with long rods tried to knock off the heads of the unfortunate birds. Nowadays all that Montebello does to turkeys is to spit-roast them basted with pomegranate juice (*paeta arosto col malagragno*). Another local specialty is *torresani di Breganze,* the young rock pigeons of this locality, spit-roasted, basted with olive oil, and flavored with wild bay leaves, herbs and spices. They are ordinarily served with fried polenta and a green salad. Vicenza, Castello di Marostica and Thiene incorporate duck into pasta, in this case a sort of cannelloni, *bigoli con l'anara.*

Also popular in Vicenza are *bovoloni,* fat snails with olive oil, garlic, parsley, salt and pepper, eaten especially at the Christmas season; *pappardelle alla panna,* ribbon pasta cooked in consommé, served with cream and meat sauce; and *focaccia vicentina,* cookies which appear at Easter, made from a recipe whose origin is lost in antiquity.

One of the pleasures of eating in this region is to do so in Palladian villas or other magnificent mansions, which often combine delightful natural settings with man-made luxury —like the Taverna de Marostega, a medieval castle at Marostica; the Villa Eolia at Costozza, where 16th-century frescoes look down upon you as you dine; or the Ca' 7, in the 17th-century villa of the Counts of Sette at Bassano, whose specialties are trout from the Brenta delicately perfumed with sage, and egg *tagliatelle* with mushrooms.

The province of Belluno lies farthest of all the Veneto areas from the glittering port of Venice, and participates least in its riches. It penetrates deeply into the Alps, extending to the Austrian frontier, where the savage bare rocks of the Dolomites thrust abruptly upward from the valleys.

Belluno is poor country, which became poorer still after the destruction of the first World War. Although it had been Venetian since 1420, with a capital which can boast fine buildings dating from the 15th century, Belluno was not much visited by outsiders until the vogue of winter sports set in. Now Cortina d'Ampezzo and other meccas of skiing bring thousands of tourists and a flood of dollars, pounds, francs and marks into the province every year. This has helped the local economy, though it has not quite enriched it. Outside of the resorts, life in Belluno remains simple, and the food humble if hearty—typical mountain fare. Appropriately, the single food for which it is most famous is the homely bean—a vegetable with solid virtues, but subtlety is not among them. The best beans in Italy are those produced at Lamon, near Feltre, which give rise to many of the most popular dishes of the Bellunese: *riso all' uso di Lamon*, for which the beans are worked into a paste with potatoes and celery, pointed up with bits of bacon cooked in oil, served with rice doused with melted butter and grated cheese; *zuppa di fagioli di Lamon*, which is, of course, bean soup; and *minestrone alla bellunese*, which is bean soup too.

The other products of the soil are in the main unsophisticated also, the only one which would be likely to be ranked among luxurious foods being the asparagus of Vas. In general, the broad valleys of Belluno are given over to woods and pasturage. Excellent cinnamon pears and russet apples are grown here; the Feltre region is noted for walnuts and that of Fener for chestnuts. Trout are in honor, as is natural in mountain country threaded by swift clear streams—especially those of the Livenza, at the foot of Mount Cavallo, and the red-speckled variety found near Misurina. Game is plentiful. The area produces many preserved meat products, salted or smoked, notably the *soppressa bellunese*, here a pork sausage (usually served hot with polenta) and *sappada,* smoked ham.

Belluno is not abashed by the humble nature of its cuisine and does not need to be. In a world too often given to a pretentious, tortuous complication of cooking, it is refreshing to discover an oasis capable of appreciating the honest virtues of simple food. Bellunese food is not so simple as to be without art, but it is the art of the housewife who loves to cook, and would rather achieve a tasty result than astound the neighbors. Though Bellunese cooking has succeeded in retaining its ancient virtues, especially in the highest northernmost region of the province, the Cadore, one might wish it had retained even more. The mountaineers have succumbed to gas and electricity, which do of course lessen drudgery, but there is a loss of cheer in the disappearance of the *caminazze,* the large fireplaces where polenta was made daily in a great kettle hanging from a hook over the open fire where the loaded spits turned slowly in the fireplace, while fragrant odors rose from the wealth of copper and earthenware vessels disposed about the hearth.

Polenta, however it is made today, remains a mainstay of the Bellunese diet, despite a local ditty which goes something like this: "In the old days, we had polenta Monday, polenta Tuesday, polenta Wednesday, polenta Thursday, polenta Friday, polenta Saturday, and on Sunday, for a special treat, in real Bellunese style, polenta and bread; now times have changed, and we have bread Monday, bread

Tuesday, bread Wednesday, bread Thursday, bread Friday, bread Saturday, and on Sunday, for a special treat, in real Bellunese style, bread and polenta." Polenta remains ubiquitous in Belluno and serves as the basis for elaborations of various kinds, like *torta di polenta*, which might be described as a mountaineer's club sandwich. Between two round slices of hardened polenta laced with meat sauce are placed ham or sausage, slices of tomato, and cheese, and the whole is fried in boiling oil. The Cadore region uses polenta as the basis for gnocchi.

Tagliatelle del cacciatore, a specialty of the Cordevole Valley, is egg ribbon pasta with a sauce made of bits of rock partridge and chopped mountain mushrooms, a dish for a king if a king could afford it anywhere else. *Gnocchi alla Cadorina* are made from the excellent potatoes of the Cadore region in one of three fashions—with melted butter and grated smoked cheese; with butter, cinnamon and sugar; or with butter, sage and aged cheese. *Calzonzei* is a very old dish, a ravioli-like egg pasta envelope stuffed with two kinds of cheese, smoked *ricotta* and sharp cheese, squash and egg, served with melted butter, hare sauce and grated cheese. Old also is *lasagne da fornel*, served on Christmas Eve in the valley at the start of the meal, though from the ingredients it sounds like a dessert: the pasta, before being cooked in the oven, is moistened with melted butter, and covered with crushed walnuts, poppy seeds (poppies are grown in this valley especially for their seeds, used in a number of dishes), raisins, grated apple, bits of fig and a sprinkling of sugar.

Timballo di riso is very simply made, with butter stirred carefully into the rice, until each grain is glistening, the timbale then being served with meat, fish, or vegetable sauce. More substantial is *riso con salsicce arrosto*, when hot sausages, sliced horizontally, are served with the rice. *Minestra di latte e riso* is a cross between rice with milk, and a rice-milk soup. *Crema d'orzo al latte* is of porridge-like consistency—oatmeal without oats, but with barley instead. An excellent thick minestrone is one containing beans, squash, potatoes and herbs, with either pasta or rice.

If you do not start the meal with pasta, rice or soup, there are two other possibilities always present in mountain country—sausage or cheese. Fresh sausage meat is often served grilled. One local sausage contains horse meat as well as pork. Cured tongue is also popular. The local cheeses, some of cow's milk, some of goat's, which may be fresh or smoked, ordinarily come at the end of the meal, but may be worked into dishes which serve as entrées. *Tosella alla panna*, also called in dialect *formaio schiz*, is a mountain dish of a fresh cheese rich in fat, which is sliced, browned in butter, and combined with the butter and cream to be served with polenta. *Caduta di formaggio* crushes ⅔ Gorgonzola and ⅓ butter together, puts them through a potato masher, flavors the result with a dash of brandy, and serves it on a pyramid of vermicelli. Another possible entrée is breaded snails cooked in a celery-flavored sauce.

Belluno does not share with the rest of Veneto a distaste for meat, which it likes to grill over the flames when open fireplaces are available. Otherwise the province often follows the example of Venice by cutting its meat up, as in meatballs about the size of a walnut, of chopped veal, diced ham, egg yolk, grated cheese and parsley, cooked in butter and a little Marsala with carrots and (a vegetable not often called for specifically in Italian, or for that matter, European, recipes) sweet potatoes. *Carne pastizzada* also cuts up the lean beef from which it is made into small pieces, reversing the practice of Venice, which exceptionally does not cut up its *pastizzada* before cooking, slicing it only on serving; it is probable that Venice borrowed, and modified, *pastizzada* from Belluno, where it seems to have originated a good many centuries ago. As made in Belluno, the meat is browned in a mixture of butter and pork fat in a covered pan, and then boiled slowly with a little wine vinegar, much freshly ground pepper, a clove, and a twist of lemon peel. *Nodini di vitello*, recommended locally for persons with delicate stomachs, cuts the veal into small pieces and stews it in butter for two hours in a covered pan with mealy potatoes, also cut into small pieces, the long cooking producing a sort of creamy mixture at the end. For *stufato*, the beef or veal is sliced before cooking and coated with a paste of bacon, anchovy fillets, grated cheese of the Emmental type, ground meat, egg, Marsala, sage and bread crumbs before stewing for several hours in a covered pan with oil, butter, onion, consommé and red wine. Finally, Belluno goes in for boiled meats, *bollito misto*, as Venice does not.

Galletti minorenni is made chiefly from the breast meat of young roosters, cut into pieces, and marinated in dry white wine plus a little cognac, together with celery, carrots, onions and a whisper of garlic, then dipped in beaten egg and flour, and fried slowly in butter. But Belluno is apt to neglect domestic poultry, for when it reaches the category of birds it thinks at once of game, which abounds in its high valleys—grouse, hazel hen, quails, the tiny game birds cooked threaded on a spit, hare, deer, and even the rare chamois. Indeed, game is so plentiful that it is often used simply to make consommé, *brodetto di selvaggina*, though I should think most persons would find it difficult to resist eating also the discarded meat which produced the bouillon. For those of us to whom game is a rare treat, it must also seem prodigal to reduce hare to a purée, *minestra alla purea di lepre*, but Belluno does it. Several kinds of game are served sliced, breaded and cooked in a sauce of butter, onion, consommé, Port wine, cloves, whole peppercorns, a touch of Cayenne pepper—and gooseberry jam; this is *spezzato di selvaggina*, and it is served with more gooseberry jam and fresh gooseberries on the side. Quails are presented with risotto or *alla cacciatora*. Venison (*capriolo*) usually comes in the form of a salmi, and hare often in a civet. Pheasant is stuffed and roasted, or cooked on a spit and served with a hot pepper sauce or sweet-and-sour (*agrodolce*) sauce. Chamois, if and when you come across it, will probably be spit-roasted, as is domestic kid.

The vegetables that come with this are likely to be on the rustic side, like potatoes or cabbage—*verze e patate*, cooked together in oil, onions, and tomato juice. More imaginative is a dish not considered as an accompaniment for meat, but served for its own sake, often as a first course. This is potatoes (not a mealy variety), turnips, carrots and celery root, all diced to the same size, cooked in consommé with a little oil added, and served with a touch of curry. *Zucchine della nonna* are cooked with beaten eggs, parsley, olive oil and grated cheese. The famous beans of Lamon substitute for the salad course in *fagioli in salsa*. The sauce is made of olive oil in which garlic has been browned and then discarded, chopped anchovy fillets, and vinegar. When still hot, this is poured over the beans, which have been cooked separately with salt, pepper and chopped parsley for seasoning, and is put in a salad bowl. They are allowed to stand for several hours before being served cold in the dressing.

Belluno is the only province of Veneto which does not have a variety of sweets for the end of the meal. The mountaineers generally finish with cheese or fruit. When a dinner does end with pastry, it is likely to be some form of strudel (sweetened, perhaps, with the fragrant honey made by bees which feed on mountain herbs and flowers). Austrian influence has crept across the border.

In summer, the canals of Venice were inclined to smell. The Doges, the aristocracy, and the wealthy found the city unhealthy. For the hot weather, they left their islands for the mainland, crossed an insignificant stream curiously named the Zero, and established themselves in splendid villas in and around Treviso, "the garden of Venice," 10 miles away. The habit gave Italian a new word: *villeggiatura*, meaning vacation. The villas were splendid. The Terraglio road from Venice to Treviso, which was lined with them, aroused the admiration of Goldoni, "lengthy and united, thronged with people, with palaces of city folk and sovereigns." In the light and cheerful atmosphere of holidays, the villa dwellers did not allow themselves to become bored. The Marca Trevigiana, the March of Treviso, became known in the Middle Ages as the *Marca gioiosa et amorosa*, the March of Joy and Love; and Treviso threw itself whole-heartedly into the chivalric games of the times, including the famous Courts of Love, usually associated with France; but Treviso had a Castle of Love in 1214.

These were the great days of Treviso, the Tarvisium of the Romans, whose apogee was the 13th century. In the 14th, Treviso accepted voluntarily the political rule of Venice, which had already occupied it economically. Sharing in the riches of Venice, Treviso came to resemble in man-made works a city it already resembled naturally. It had canals of moving, even rushing, water, fed by the mountain streams descending from the north. It had islands, carved out by its two rivers, the Cagnan and the Silo. Bridges in the Venetian style were thrown across the water courses; private mansions and public buildings, also in the Venetian style, rose along the streets, with painted frescoes on their façades; the 15th century walls were strengthened and restored in the 16th. Some Italians insist that Treviso has maintained the traditions of Venetian good living even more strongly than has Venice itself. This may be especially true for eating.

Treviso is a city conscious of the pleasures of the table. Each December it holds a festival of Treviso cooking, and it is not simply a festival of Venetian cooking as executed by Treviso. The city has adopted many Venetian dishes, but it also has its own, which Venice does not reproduce.

One indication of Treviso's interest in food is the fact that some of the best, simplest and most characteristic cooking is found not in the large bustling brightly lighted restaurants, but, as in Rome, in the *trattorie*, one-man establishments known by the names of the geniuses operating in the kitchen—Alfredo, which looks out on a canal; Nerina, whose sisters serve graciously at the tables; Lino, who has chosen a rustic site outside the city proper, and perhaps pushes folklore a little far by putting his waitresses in the ancient costumes of the region; and Nando, who has chosen also to set himself up among groves of trees rather than among city streets. Another indication is the animation, the color and the variety of the markets, among the most picturesque of Italy. Pass behind the Palace of the Three Hundred, where the governing council used to meet, and you find yourself in the mushroom market, which sells nothing else, with emphasis on the little twisted orange mushrooms that grow in the shade of the pines of the nearby hills. Next comes the long narrow fruit and vegetable market, a tumult of hawkers' cries, of bustle and of brilliance; and after that the fish market (conveniently located on a branch of the Cagnan, into which refuse can be tossed) displaying a bewildering number of fish, shellfish and crustaceans.

If you pass through the vegetable market at the right season—the very best time is the beginning of December, but I have seen it displayed in September—your eye cannot fail to be caught by the most spectacular vegetable of the province of Treviso, which may fairly be described as its gastronomic trademark, since it was originally peculiar to this region, and Trevisans still insist that the real thing is grown nowhere else, though a very passable version is found nowadays not only in other parts of northern Italy, but even as far away as France. This is *radicchio*, a red winter lettuce—*un fiore che si mangia*, a flower which is eaten, they say locally. There is a little jingle about it too.

> *Se lo guardi, egli è un sorriso;*
> *Se lo mangi è un paradiso*
> *Il radicchio di Treviso.*

Or:

> *If you keep it, that is nice;*
> *Eat it, and it's Paradise:*
> *The* radicchio *of Treviso.*

Actually there are two kinds of *radicchio*. Around Treviso itself, you have the type which grows in a tall tight bunch, in the shape of Romaine lettuce, with white stalks, like celery, and narrow ruby-red white-veined leaves. They are crisp under the teeth, and the taste is agreeably sharp. The other, which comes from Castelfranco Veneto, about 20 miles to the west, is prettier to look at but less interesting to eat. It is lighter in color than the Treviso lettuce, pink rather than red, the color sometimes almost solid, sometimes in delicate streaks against a nearly white background of tightly folded petals; the shape is that of a camellia. The taste is more neutral. In some surrounding regions, near enough to import *radicchio*, the two kinds are served together and called "Treviso salad," but not in the province of Treviso, which considers the two as separate vegetables, which should not be mixed; indeed, purists call the Castelfranco plant *rose*, and give the name of *radicchio* to the Treviso variety alone. If any mixing is done, either variety of *radicchio* is combined in a salad with fennel, rather than with the other.

Radicchio is a traditional Christmas dish in the province of Treviso, and at that season it graduates to a separate market of its own in the loggia of the Palazzo dei Trecento at Treviso, while at Castelfranco it is sold in the shadow of the medieval walls, under the protection of the statue of Giorgione, a native of the city, whose palette, it has even been suggested, was affected by the color of the Castelfranco *rose*. Its short late growing season may account for the fact that it has never been duplicated successfully elsewhere (*imitata sempre, non è uguagliata mai*, "always imitated but never equaled," the Trevisans say scornfully of attempts to do so), for it is cultivated after cereal crops have been harvested, on the same ground, and it may be that only here do the exact climatic conditions necessary for success at this season exist. There are also secrets to enhance what is called "whitening," but should be called "reddening," of the crop after it has been gathered and is being readied for market, which are not known elsewhere.

"The king of salads," a title given *radicchio* on the theory that it is the finest salad of Italy, is nevertheless not always eaten as a salad. It is sometimes cooked. The outer leaves are stripped off and the inner leaves broken into halves or quarters, depending on their size. These pieces are then washed, drained, floured, dipped in beaten egg and bread crumbs, and fried in oil. They are also cooked *alla giudia* (like artichokes in Rome) in boiling oil, as accompaniments to a main dish; or seasoned with oil, pepper and salt, and roasted on a grill; or cooked like mushrooms.

If the gourmet cannot think of Treviso without recalling *radicchio*, it does not follow that Treviso would be gastronomically poor without it. The area on the contrary is particularly rich in local dishes, quite independently of those it has annexed from Venice. A listing which I have before my eyes as I write includes 30 hors d'oeuvres; 60 entrées (the influence of Venice may be seen in the fact that there are 33 rice dishes against 12 pasta dishes); 52 boiled and roasted meats (24 of them are poultry, and of the meat dishes only eight are cooked in large pieces, the Venetian influence again); 45 variously classifiable dishes which might appear among entrées (egg dishes, for instance) but are here called, a precious indication of the Trevisan spirit, "pastimes"; 33 fish dishes; 55 vegetable preparations; 16 different kinds of bread; eight local cheeses; 57 desserts; and 41 kinds of fruit and nuts. Ignoring such necessarily indigenous products as cheese and fruit, I should say that at least half of the dishes in this impressive list are native to Treviso.

Among dishes indisputably and famously Trevisan, are the following:

CRAYFISH (*gamberi*). These succulent fresh-water crustaceans have long been a traditional specialty of the whole water-threaded region northeast of Treviso along the Piave River, but they were inexorably localized by an unidentified artist of the 1400's who painted a fresco in the small church of San Giorgio at San Polo di Piave showing the Last Supper with crayfish displayed prominently on the table. This small village thus became the capital of crayfish, and by common consent its headquarters is the Gambrinus restaurant, which was foreordained for the role by the presence of what I imagine was formerly a mill race flowing along one side, supplying water for the tanks behind the building covered with wire grills through which you can view the live crayfish (and in some other tanks, trout, eels, and frogs as well). The place has a mildly zoo-like quality, since in addition to its kitchen aquarium it has, scattered about its yard, a few cages containing decorative birds and a few small mammals (inedible). In the interior, the decorative element is provided by the bright darting flames of the open hearth in the middle of the kitchen, where it is frequently located in this region. It provides an atmosphere of light-hearted gaiety abetted by the directions for eating crayfish handed to the diner in his native language, or even in local dialect, if he can read it. The house's English version goes thus:

THE 10 COMMANDMENTS
or
THE RIGHT WAY TO EAT CRABS OF SAN POLO

1) *Put a (big) table-napkin on.*
2) *Lay the fork and the knife on the table (because they are not used).*
3) *Take the whole crab with the fingers and snatch the feet away. The big ones squash with the teeth, to eat the pulp wath is in it.*
4) *The crab is now without feet. Turn to the head the big crust wath's on the back. To do that, press the nail where the crust ends and the tail begins and lift so the crust up. You will see now the "best piece" of the whole crab but jou must leave it for later.*
5) *Squash now the tail between two fingers, beginning from the end to the head.*
6) *Suck your fingers.*
7) *Turn the crab and clean the tail. Open the rinds on both sides, just like a prown.*
8) *Suck the rinds (and again the fingers).*
9) *Hold the poor crab—now in a so bad condition— with the fingers of both hands, turn it over and eat "the beste piece," together with the rest in the tail.*
10) *Put the polenta in the gravy—eat—and lick again cleanly your fingers ab.*

The last word is perhaps an example of onomatopoeia. It should be added that Gambrinus' crayfish is better than Gambrinus' English, in which was omitted a final exhortation which appears in the dialect version: "Suggestion for those who are never satisfied: put the feet and shells in a jug of white wine and drink the wine."

EELS. To remain in the fish category, the town of Quinto sul Sile specializes in eels, not simply one fashion of cooking them, but eels in general, of which you can get a whole meal here, beginning with eel risotto, followed by boiled eel, roast eel, fried eel—as much as you can take. San Polo di Piave does this too.

SOPA COÀDA is not soup, despite its name. Consommé does go into its making, but in essence it is composed of alternate layers of bread and boned pigeon, with its giblets. This is a very old dish, and though the bread is less subtle than the delicate pastry leaves of the Moroccan *pastilla*, it is reminiscent of this famous dish, so that one wonders whether it did not enter Veneto when this area was the chief window on the Moslem world.

RISO ALLA LUGANEGA is strictly Trevisan. This is a highly spiced sausage produced in the Treviso area, cooked in a thick rice soup without tomato. You may find it on local menus spelled in one of the two dialect versions, *iugànega* or *xuganega*.

OCA DI TREVISO is goose cooked with celery. In the same category is *faraona con pevarada*, guinea hen roasted and served with a rich heavily spiced sauce made from oil, vinegar, lemon juice, garlic, anchovy fillets, chicken livers, grated Parmesan, bread crumbs, peppercorns, lemon peel and ginger. It is really the *pevarada* sauce (also used on boiled and roasted meats and game) which makes this a specialty of Treviso.

TRIPPA ALLA TREVISANA is tripe given flavor with butter, bits of bacon, onion, and rosemary, spread steaming over slices of bread, and doused with grated Parmesan cheese. It is eaten traditionally on market days.

LIÉVERO IN TECIA is hare, a particular dish from the town of Vittorio Veneto cooked in *pevarada* sauce, but in this case the formula is different from that given above. It includes the hare's liver, sausage, butter, lemon juice, cloves, cinnamon, salt and pepper.

"*Chi no ghe piase el vin, Dio ghe toga l'acqua,*" say the Venetians—God will take water away from him who does not like wine. The inhabitants of Veneto are in little danger. The three Venezias vie with Apulia for first place in the quantity of wine they produce, but while Apulia's is usually rather ordinary, the Venezias, and especially Veneto, have some very fine vintages. Indeed, Veneto runs the whole gamut in quality—everything from almost the tops in Italy to simple table wines which slip down without announcing their presence.

It has been my observation in Veneto that the nature of the grape assumes relatively more importance here than in most other wine-growing areas; perhaps it is because there is less difference in the desirability of various locations on the more or less homogeneous plain which stretches from Lake Garda to the sea. Location is of course always important, including, as it does, nature of the soil, basic climate, amount and times of rainfall, exposure to sun, etc.; and that it is a factor by no means negligible in Veneto is evident from the fact that as soon as you have passed the first tier of vineyards lying right along Lake Garda, you hit the best wine of Veneto and thereafter, as you move eastward, the quality declines more or less uniformly, though happily not too much. It is also notable that in two areas where wine production has developed in recent years (the Breganze region and the province of Padua) improvement in the quality of the wine has been achieved by introducing superior strains of grapes. The considerable differences which can be produced on the same soil in this region by changing the grape were demonstrated to me forcefully during a meal which I ate at the Gambrinus in San Polo di Piave, accompanied by wines which harmonized perfectly with each other, no doubt because they had all been grown locally in the same area by the same producer, though they were considerably different in character. We had been served as an *aperitivo* a light white wine, agreeable but no more than that, which had no name ("It's just the ordinary wine we grow here"). Then came the first course, *agnoletti* stuffed with ricotta cheese and spinach, served with a cream-and-butter sauce. With this we had local wine from the same place, but it had more body and this time bore a label, Prosecco, the name of a grape. With the crayfish, we had an even more authoritative wine, still from the same place, named Verduzzo, a deformation of Verdiso, again the name of a grape; it had a good deal of character, was fruity, and a trifle on the sweetish side, while the first two had been rather dry. With the dessert came a liqueur, Sangue di Raboso (still the same place, but derived from a different grape, Raboso of course), a rich syrupy digestive, not a type I care much for, but I sampled it out of curiosity before switching to a Tocai Scelto 1961 (same place, different grape), which brought us back to the whites; it was *frizzante* and compared well enough with a minor champagne. We finished with a *grappa*, a little too sweet, made from the same grapes that had gone into the opening bottle of wine. The sequence was highly educational, and fortunately I was not driving.

The importance of the type of grape used in Veneto wines accounts for the fact that minor vintages are very often sold under varietal names—that is, the name of the grape —rather than under place names.

The westernmost vineyards of Veneto lie along the southern bulge of the shore of Lake Garda, in the province of Verona, one of the two top wine-producing provinces of the region. The Sona-Custoza wine of the southern part of this area is a light red, about 12 degrees, which is only so-so and is generally drunk on the spot within a year of its making. The northern half of this area, however, centered around the town of Bardolino, produces the wine of the same name, one of the three principal red wines of Verona, or for that matter of all Veneto, Bardolino, Valpolicella and Valpantena, all of them light and dry. They are less robust, but also less austere, than the Piedmont wines, and their color is less intense. They are made of a blend of grapes, utilizing in varying proportions Molinaro (also called Rosara), Corvina Veronese (obviously, from its name, a local variety), Negrara (local too, named from the town of Negrar, in the Valpantena district), and, to a lesser degree, Rontinella and Rossignola. They can all be drunk young, but are better after two or three years.

Bardolino is the lightest of these wines, 10 to 11 degrees, and consequently is better drunk young, when it is refreshing and (a word which recurs regularly in descriptions of this wine) charming. It is a clear bright ruby red in color. Different growers have different formulas for their wine, but all of them lean heavily on grapes developed in this area. Inhabitants of the region, carried away by local pride, are likely to maintain that Bardolino goes well with roasts, but it is really too light for that; poultry, pigeon, and rabbit are its best accompaniments.

Moving eastward across the plain, we cross the Adige and come to the Valpolicella vineyards, nestled in its curve, which produce the best red wine in Veneto. It has more body than Bardolino, probably because it is grown in heavier soil, for it is made from about the same grapes. Consequently it ages better. It is a dark red, velvety in the mouth, with a delicate, slightly bitter aftertaste of almonds, and runs from 11 to 12.5 degrees, exceptionally sometimes to as much as 13. This is the description of the superior dry Valpolicella which is the one you should insist on when it matters. There is also an ordinary table wine sold under the same name, which is more variable—usually lighter in color, with an alcoholic content which may drop as low as 10 degrees, usually dry and sometimes a little too bitter for agreeableness, but also occasionally sweetish and even naturally *frizzante*—in short, undependable, though for run-of-the-mill feeding it may serve well enough.

The next area to the east is that which grows Valpantena, which stands between Bardolino and Valpolicella in character, but a little closer to the latter; it is usually made of the same grapes. It ages more quickly than Valpolicella and goes off more quickly too; the best time to drink it is when it is about a year and a half old. A clear ruby red, 10.5 to 11 degrees, it is a well balanced wine, dry, fresh and a little tart, which makes it a good appetite arouser.

Our eastward movement now brings us through a series of red wine areas of the Colli Veronesi district—Val Squaranto, Val Mezzane, Val d'Illasi and Val Tramigna, which might be described as lesser Valpantenas—and leads us into the vineyards producing the finest white wines of Veneto, and possibly of Italy, Soave; it is not a great wine, but I cannot think of any Italian whites which are. The Italian word *soave* means "suave," and the wine might be so described; but this is not the reason for the name, which comes simply from the town of Soave, in the center of the district where it is grown. It is a pale limpid straw-yellow wine with greenish reflections, dry, light, delicate, and velvety, with just enough acidity to give it character. It runs from 10.5 to 11.5 degrees, and is made chiefly from the Garganega grape, with an admixture of Trebbiano. It goes wonderfully with hors d'oeuvres and fish, especially in summer, when it should be drunk chilled and preferably young. A warning: more Soave is drunk in Italy (and abroad, for it is often exported) than is made; in other words, there is a lot of non-authentic Soave about. Look for the Veronese neck label, which identifies the real thing. In the Soave neighborhood, you have also a minor wine,

Colognola, which is made from the Valpolicella blend of grapes, and may be either red or rosé.

The province of Verona thus produces, all by itself, the three most reputed reds and the one most reputed white of the whole Venezia region. Before we leave the province, we might note two others produced there, and also elsewhere in Veneto, named for their type rather than for the place where they are grown.

The first of this pair is produced mostly in the province of Verona, but it may be made elsewhere. This is Recioto, which takes its name from the local dialect words for ears, *recie* (Italian, *orecchie*). Only the "ears" of each bunch of grapes are used to make this wine, which means the grapes on the outside of the bunch, which have been most exposed to the sun and are consequently the sweetest. Even after this selection, they are sweetened further by being sun-dried. There are several varieties of Recioto in Verona, of which my personal preference goes to the Recioto Bianco (or Recioto Soave, if it is grown in the Soave area, in which case, like Soave, it is made chiefly from the Garganega grape), a sweet white dessert wine rating from 13 to 14 degrees. But Recioto is produced through the whole breadth of the province; and in the Bardolino-Valpolicella-Valpantena area, you get a sweet *red* dessert wine, made from the same grape blends as those wines. It has a pomegranate color, a fruity bouquet, and runs from 13 to 14 degrees in alcoholic content. A rarity, because it is made only in small quantities, is Recioto Amarone, bitter Recioto, which, exceptionally for a Recioto, is dry and does indeed have an agreeably bitter aftertaste. Some connoisseurs consider this the best, and drink it with red meat and game. There is also a "noble" Recioto, Recioto Nobile, a sweet red sparkler, with a heavy alcoholic content, 13 to 14 degrees, which is praised by those who like sweet red sparklers.

The other widespread wine is Raboso, from the name of

the grape. A few years ago the best known Raboso was Raboso del Piave, produced mostly between the Piave and Livenza Rivers. But the Piave Raboso is rather coarse, dark ruby in color, with considerable acidity but enough body to carry it, and, it seemed to me, close to a cherry taste. Modern taste has grown away from heavy wines, so Piave Raboso has tended to be displaced by Raboso Veronese, which is not confined to the province of Verona but also comes from the Padua area. This version is lighter, using less of the Raboso grape, and more Merlot, Cabernet, Italian Riesling and Italian Tokay, which also go into the Piave wine, but in lesser quantities. As would be expected, the Piave version needs more aging, and can be drunk ten years after bottling, which is a long while for Italian wines; Raboso Veronese should be drunk young.

The Soave wines are grown up to the border of the province of Vicenza, and just across it Vicenza has a wine which resembles Soave, without its finesse, Garganega di Gambellara; it is possible that some of it gets sold under the Soave label. Garganega is the name of the grape, but some Trebbiano goes into this wine too. It is a dry white wine, pale yellow to golden in color, 10 to 11.5 degrees, with a delicate light perfume. There is also a Gambellara Passito, which is a heavy sweet dessert wine, and a Gambellara Rosso, a red.

Just across from the Garganega country are the Berici Hills, which produce a number of interesting wines—almond-flavored whites and rather tart reds, which may be offered under the generic label of Colli Berici or Riviera Berici, or perhaps—and these should be the better bottles—under their specific place names: Arcugnano, which comes in both red and white; Barbarano, red and white; Brendola, only white; Costoza, red and white; Orgiano, white only; and several others. In the Breganze area, where the altitude increases, there is another cluster of vintages which rise above routine quality. The Breganze whites (11 to 12 degrees) have a nutty taste and a slight pleasing acidity, the reds (also 11 to 12 degrees) are smoother, but sometimes have a sharp aftertaste. There is much variation from these norms, since a wide range of grape mixtures is used. This is in part a recent development, for Breganze wines are being improved, those of lower quality being replaced by new vintages produced by the addition of foreign grapes, like the French Pinot Noir and Pinot Gris. Cabernet grapes are also often used here nowadays, producing a red wine of higher alcoholic content, sold under the grape name. Merlot is another grape name found here and everywhere else in the region.

Finally, if you want a Vicenza dessert wine for digestive qualities, move out of the Breganze region for Malvasia di Nanto, if you don't mind the Oriental method of easing the stomach (this wine is reputed to promote belching).

The wines become less striking as we move east, and in this case a little south, so that the province of Padua might have little to boast about if it were not for the Euganean Hills. They are volcanic in origin—there are still hot springs in the area—and volcanic soils are often good wine producers. Hence the slopes and valleys of this area produce some interesting Vini dei Colli Euganei. This is a very old wine-producing region, with a reputation going back to the Middle Ages, which until fairly recently had been content to coast on its reputation and continue to use outmoded unimproved grape varieties—Pattaresco, Corbinella and (the roughest of all) Friularo. This confined Padua to carafe wines, but lately producers have been introducing other grapes in an attempt to improve the quality—Merlot, Cabernet Franc, Garganella, Pinella, Serpina, Pinot Blanc, Sauvignon and Riesling. The Euganei wines are mostly whites, 10 to 11 degrees, and the region sometimes boasts of its Moscato d'Arqua, a sparkling dessert wine of surprisingly low alcoholic content (8 to 9 degrees) for its sweet-ness.

Padua still produces a Friularo, but not in the Euganean Hills. It comes from the south of the province and is appreciated by those who like the sharp acidity of this old red light (10 degrees) wine. The grape, as its name suggests, came originally from Friuli. An even lighter red is Clinton, also named for its grape, which was imported from America; it gets down as low as eight degrees, and ten is its top.

A little Clinton is also drunk in the department of Rovigo, but here, close to the sea, the importance of local wines is almost zero. This is true also for the province of Venice, which produces a little easily ignored wine from a mixture of Cabernet and Merlot grapes, and equally forgettable Italian Tokay, around Portogruaro. This is about as far north as you can get in the province of Venice, on the border with Treviso, and as you move into Treviso and push north, into mountain wine territory, the picture becomes very different. Treviso produces no famous wines, but it produces a great many, of considerable variety, and though they may not provoke cries of enthusiasm from winebibbers, they are eminently drinkable. The program of one of the yearly gastronomic festivals of Treviso which I have before me lists 120 local wines, 71 of them whites, 44 reds and five rosés, which were served during a ten-day period. It may be assumed that there are many others. Treviso is self-conscious about wine. It was at Conegliano, in this province, that the first school of wine raising and producing in Italy was established, and it is still functioning. True to its vocation, Conegliano produces a wine of its own, Blanco di Conegliano, 10 to 11.5 degrees, golden yellow, dry and tart, excellent with fish.

Generally speaking, Treviso produces white wines on its hills and reds in the flat stretches. Generally speaking also, Treviso wines are low in acidity. Generally speaking once more, they should be drunk young. Generally speaking again, the labels here are more often grape names than place names. Prosecco, though it is found everywhere in the Venezias, is particularly abundant in Treviso; the grape from which it takes its name has been popular here for about a hundred years. The typical Treviso Prosecco is a golden yellow, 8 to 10 degrees of alcohol, refreshing and fruity, with a slightly bitter aftertaste. Conegliano makes a Prosecco Spumante which is not bad. The best Prosecco is reputed to be that from the Valdobbiadene in the neighborhood of the Vittorio Veneto battlefield. Cartizze, which also makes a well known sparkling Prosecco, is in the Valdobbiadene. Another good wine area is the Asolo-Maser region, which produces both Prosecco and Verdiso. It produces a pale yellow wine, 11 to 12 degrees, which has to be drunk young, as it ages badly. When you meet the Tokay grape here (spelled locally Tokai or Tokaj), it is not a producer of heavy sweet liqueurish wines, like the Hungarian grape for which it is named; Tokai Italico is a native grape which produces whites excellent with fish.

Once the farthest north is reached, in Belluno, climatic conditions become unfavorable to wine, and though a few reds are made in the neighborhood of Rocca and Rocca d'Araiè and whites at Fonzaso, they do not get beyond the regions which produce them. For the rest, native beverages are confined to beer and a vegetable juice concoction. However, the mountains do produce materials from which to distill or flavor eaux de vie and liqueurs. *Grappa* is made from grapes, plums, or juniper berries (Kapriol), distillations from such ordinarily inoffensive plants as camomile and passion flower (*Passicamo*). Vedana makes a Genziana of good repute and syrupy liqueurs are flavored with Cansiglio raspberries (a rare fruit in Italy), walnuts, chestnuts, apples, pears and even asparagus. Perhaps the strangest digestives of all are those made from wild olives, tea roses, or the sap of the eglantine.

Treviso has its after-dinner drinks too. The Valdobbiadene region, and the town of Fagaré, are noted for *grappa* (called *graspa* in the local dialect). Cornuda makes an orange-flavored eau de vie, which is called Curaçao, after the Dutch product from the West Indies which it imitates. Sangue del Piave is a liqueur made from the Raboso wine. Similar to the digestives of the same names in other regions are Ratafià, Rosolio and China.

Venezia Tridentina

The most spectacular feature in the landscape of Trent (in Italian, Trento) is the great rock west of the city, on the right bank of the Adige, rising above it to a height of 308 feet. This is the Doss Trento, on which were built the scattered cabins which harbored the first inhabitants of this area, a handful of human beings described by disagreeing authorities as Ligurians, Veneti, Illyrians or Italiots. The reference to Italiots, meaning Greeks settled in Italy, so far from the coast and even farther from their normal territory in southern Italy, sounds like another echo of the legend that refugees from the Trojan War settled in Venezia. This list omits the Euganei, but if it was this shadowy race that engendered today's Ladin-speaking populations, some of them must have reached Venezia Tridentina, for there are three Ladin islands here: one near Bolzano; a second south of Bressanone; and the third southwest of Bressanone.

Whoever the first settlers were, Gauls seem to have moved in by 222 B.C., when the Romans conquered the region, or rather occupied it, for they met with no resistance. The Gauls were living in what were little more than camps, which under the Romans would grow into villages—Ala, Rovereto, Riva. The Romans also took over the Doss Trento, which they called Verruca, and founded Tridentium, today Trent.

Trent is the capital of the Italian-speaking Trentino, the southernmost province of the two that make up Venezia Tridentina. But there is an anomaly in the beautiful region of small isolated lakes not far from Trent, of two pockets where old Germanic dialects are spoken—not the result, as is the case for the northern province, of the transfer of Austrian territory after World War I. In a section of the Fersina valley live the *mocheni*, speaking a dialect called *mochens*, descendants of miners who settled here about 1000 A.D. Nowadays many of them become migratory agricultural workers during the growing season. They retain many of their old customs, such as a choral spectacle at Carnival time, and the distribution during wakes for the dead of rye bread and salt, which is repeated for the first five anniversaries of the death. The Luserna region speaks *slambrot*, and its inhabitants are supposed to be all that remains of the ancient Cimbrians, which would date their stay here from about 100 B.C.

The northern province, largely German-speaking, is Bolzano, also called the Alto Adige—the South Tyrol of Austria before the first World War. The region is dominated geographically by the high Alps which shut it off to the north, and the Adige River, the most important in Italy after the Po, which runs from north to south through the whole region, receiving all its other streams in a fishbone pattern. The valley of the Adige, and the larger valleys of the rivers that empty into it, are fertile; it is in these valleys that the basic crops of the area are cultivated. North of Bolzano, the chief cereal grown is rye, followed at some distance by maize and wheat. South of Bolzano, maize is the most important crop, with wheat, oats and barley following. Cattle raising and dairy farming appear on the lower hills and on the slopes of the valleys. Vines are grown extensively on hillsides, and fruit trees produce up to an altitude of 4,000 feet. A heavy proportion of the land is given over to forests—one-half of the two provinces taken together, with the larger proportion of forest land in Bolzano. Forest acreage and the high pastures connected with it are held largely by very large property owners, whose estates cover one-third of the territory. The rest is so minutely broken up that the average holding is only a third of an acre. To prevent further fragmentation, special inheritance laws are applied here, under which the eldest heir retains all the land, indemnifying brothers and sisters for their shares.

Among the many migrants who passed along the road to the Brenner Pass was an elephant named Solomon. This happened in 1551, when John III of Portugal decided that Solomon would make a suitable gift for Maximilian of Austria, and dispatched him to that monarch via shank's mare. It is a long trek from Lisbon to Vienna, and Solomon had only made it to Bressanone when word came that the Brenner Pass was snowed shut, and would normally remain so until spring. Solomon's keeper put him up for the winter at the Heberge am Hohen Feld, an inn that had been in business for 131 years without attracting any particular attention. Solomon brought it fame. No one in the region had ever seen an elephant and everyone wanted to. The Hohen Feld enjoyed a wave of prosperity, and when the thaw came and Solomon departed, its grateful owner changed the name of his hotel to the Elefante. It is still there, five and a half centuries after the original Hohen Feld was built, and to commemorate this high mark in its history, it serves (for not less than four diners, and six are recommended) a specialty called the Elephant Platter.

The Elephant Platter is actually a three-course meal; the main plate is preceded by a lavish collection of hors d'oeuvres and followed by an offering of cheeses, desserts and fruit which is likely to be taken back to the kitchen untouched if the guests have done honor to the main platter. This is a staggering heap of meat and vegetables, varying with the season and the butcher's stock; the basic principle is that it must contain six different kinds of meat (at least) and 12 different dishes of vegetables (at least).

On one occasion, when the management let itself be talked into serving the *piatto elefante* for only two persons, here is what it included: On the hors d'oeuvre tray were prosciutto, sardines, assorted minor antipasti, hard-boiled eggs with mayonnaise, tuna, salame, several salads, and sliced tomatoes. The main platter was crowned with three thick steaks, two hamburgers, and a gaggle of pork chops, veal steaks, mutton chops and lamb chops. Hiding under this were slices of grilled liver, grilled milt, boiled ham, spitted kidneys, chunks of suckling pig, thick slices of *Speck*, and several kinds of hot sausage. The handmaidens of the meats included raw and cooked sauerkraut, rice, fried potatoes, potato chips, souffléed potatoes, roast potatoes, noodles, macaroni, spaghetti, peas, carrots, asparagus, spinach, grilled tomatoes, beans, zucchini, lettuce, and cucumbers. The dessert tray carried various cheeses, three kinds of cake, and stewed and fresh fruit. It sufficed for a couple.

The present proprietors of the Elefante do not know

who hit upon the idea of presenting an elephantine dish in memory of Solomon, but suggest that its composition might have developed from the *Schlactplatte* served at pig-sticking time, when all sorts of pork products—ham, blood pudding, liverwurst, smoked meats, sausages, etc., appear with enormous helpings of boiled potatoes and sauerkraut. There is another possibility. A dish resembling the Elephant Platter exists in the cuisine of a nearby region which, like the Alto Adige, was until World War I part of the Austrian Empire. This is the Serbian national dish, *Balkanska plosca,* a pilaff of rice buried beneath pork, beef, veal, chicken, liverwurst, frankfurters, tongue, calf's head meat, and various meats smoked, boiled, roasted or spit-roasted, accompanied by sauerkraut, potatoes, peas, beans, red cabbage, salsify and carrots. Whether the dish is Balkan or German it is certainly not Italian, nor is Alto Adige cooking in general. The German-speaking Austrians who make up the greater part of its population have kept up their own cooking traditions. They may have added some Italian dishes—particularly those, like *bollito misto* or *maiale arrosto* which are in harmony with their own heavy cuisine—but in general cooking remains Teutonic. The temptation to lighten it by adopting some Italian techniques is not very strong in mountainous country, where rib-sticking food fits the climate.

The dominant element in Alto Adige cooking is the pig and the ultimate in pork preparation is *Speck,* which in general means smoked bacon, though in some localities this name is given to boned smoked ham. The guiding principle in producing first-rate *Speck* is to take one's time. The meat is smoked slowly and intermittently—two or three hours a day. The whole process takes three months. The theory is that if the smoking were done all at the same time, only the outer layer of meat would be really smoked, whereas the slower process smokes it through and through.

Taking time is not the only secret for making good *Speck*. Altitude and a cold climate are also part of the recipe. The Passirin valley is considered the best place; it is for *Speck* what Langhirano is for Parmesan prosciutto.

Alto Adige cooking lacks a middle class. It offers heavy, not to say coarse, dishes for the peasantry, and delicate ones, like trout from the Alpine streams with almonds for the aristocrats, but there is nothing for the bourgeoisie.

Italian authorities are not inclined to stress the fact that the Alto Adige was formerly the Austrian South Tyrol, but restaurant menus are less reticent, listing dishes like *gnocchi tirolesi di magro, canederli tirolesi, gnocchi tirolesi neri, camoscio alla tirolese* and *krapfen tirolesi*. There is at least one common dish which announces its origin as being another part of Austria—*gnocchetti di Salisburgo*, or *Salzburger Nockerln*. This is specified to distinguish this vanilla-flavored soufflé from non-dessert *Nockerln* (noodles). But even without identifying labels, one finds in Alto Adige cooking other echoes of the Austro-Hungarian Empire even beyond the confines of the Tyrol, for instance *Kren* (which in the Trentino changes its name to *ravanada*), pork with horseradish, of Bohemian origin. When the names of Austrian dishes are transliterated into Italian, they sometimes take on forms which may give you pause. *Gulasch* you will certainly recognize. You may have to think a moment about *crauti* before recognizing sauerkraut. *Canederli* could make trouble; it is the closest Italian can get to *Knödel*. *Knödel* provides another problem: it sometimes turns up in Italian as gnocchi, though as a rule gnocchi, and even more consistently *gnocchetti*, are the equivalents of *Nocken*. The two words are clearly the same. Apparently the Austro-Hungarian Empire adopted gnocchi from its Italian subjects; but when they became *Nocken*, they also became thoroughly naturalized and assumed the characteristics of Austrian cooking. For instance *gnocchetti di fegato*, *Lebernocken*, are liver dumplings. What could be more Teutonic?

It is evident that though Alto Adige cooking exists within the political boundaries of Italy, it is not Italian cooking; and since it is an alien element, we need not look at it here in great detail, nor at that of Venezia Tridentina as a whole. The Austrian influence is more unadulterated closer to the frontier, but it remains strong also in the province of Trent, once under Austrian rule. Nevertheless, some dishes have been borrowed from Italian cooking and rebaptized with German names for local use (*spezzatino di vitello* becomes *Kalbsragout*, *arrosto stufato*, *Schmorbraten*). They are more numerous in the Trentino than in Alto Adige.

Every region of Italy is of the opinion that its bread is the best, and Venezia Tridentina is no exception. Highly touted is the bread of Merano, molded into fat cylinders, dark in color because it is made from a mixture of wheat and barley flours. *Schüttelbrot*, "shaken-up bread," is so called because of the violence of its kneading, and the *Tralendal* made in the mountains of eastern Bolzano gets even rougher treatment, being beaten by the fists or a mallet; it is a long-keeping bread meant to go into soups, often so used in this region instead of pasta. *Vorschlagbrot* is also made from vigorously pummelled dough. In all of these caraway is likely to be found, partly, perhaps, because it is believed locally to possess aphrodisiac qualities.

Filling, substantial soups are typical of mountain country, and there is no lack of them here. *Einbrennsuppe* is a sort of gruel made of flour cooked in butter, diluted with hot water, laced with wine, and adorned with boiled potatoes; use tripe instead of potatoes, vinegar instead of wine, and you have *Saueresuppe*, reputed to be just the thing to get the digestion back into shape after excessive drinking. *Backerbsensuppe* is consommé flavored with parsley and chives in which floats a shower of drops of egg batter; *Schwammerlsuppe* is cream of mushroom; *Schnecken-suppe* cream of snail. *Griesnocken* are egg dumplings flavored with nutmeg served in consommé; *lebernocken*, liver dumplings, are also eaten in bouillon; and if rice is substituted for most of the flour in the dumplings, it becomes *Leberreis*. *Mus* is a sort of porridge of milk and two parts of wheat flour to one of cornmeal, *Zwiebelsuppe* is made with a paste of flour cooked in butter, in equal quantities by weight, diluted first with cold and then hot water, into which chopped onions are stirred; then the mixture is poured into boiling salted water and simmered for half an hour, with the addition, toward the end, of wine vinegar and sugar. *Milzeschnittensuppe* is made of little sandwiches of bread and a paste of ground spleen, eggs, garlic juice, marjoram and nutmeg, first browned in butter and then cooked in beef-and-vegetable consommé flavored with chives.

As in all mountainous regions, doughy dishes are in great favor, with innumerable variations rung on the themes of dumplings and noodles. The Italian names for some of these dishes spot their Tyrolese origin, but in German it is often considered unnecessary. *Canederli tirolesi* (with diced *Speck* and sausage), does come out as *Tiroler Knödel*, but *gnocchi tirolesi neri*, which is based on rye bread and buckwheat flour, is simply *schwarze Knödel*, and *gnocchi tirolesi di magro, Fastenknödel* ("fast day" because it contains no bits of meat, as so many kinds of *Knödeln* do). Polenta has been pretty thoroughly Teutonized by filling an earthenware oven dish with alternate layers of meat sauce and polenta, covering the top layers with sliced frankfurters, and baking it in the oven under a thick layer of béchamel sauce. So has ravioli in *Türteln*, in which rye flour is used for the envelope, while the stuffing contains spinach, or cabbage, or even sauerkraut, flavored with marjoram, chives or chopped onions, and caraway.

Meat dishes are very much on the Teutonic model—various types of goulash, which German-speaking peoples adopted enthusiastically from the Hungarians, stews, pot roasts. *Hausplatte*, a traditional dish of the Alto Adige, is another which recalls the Elephant Platter: a tremendous oval plate is heaped with boiled cabbage buried under a mound of smoked pork, smoked tongue, boiled beef, liver dumplings, and boiled potatoes, quartered, moistened with melted butter, and sprinkled with parsley. Game is important—venison, cut into pieces, marinated in red wine with herbs, breaded and sautéed, and served with a rich cream sauce accompanied by dumplings and *mirtilli* jelly; or chamois Tyrolese style, which requires plenty of time (five or six days), two cookings, at the start and the finish of the process, and the use not only of some fairly pungent herbs, but also of cloves and ginger.

Vegetables are of the coarser varieties—potatoes, turnips, kohlrabi, cabbage—including red cabbage, which comes out in German as blue cabbage (*Blaukraut*).

Finally, the Austrian sweet tooth is much in evidence. There are all kinds of strudel—ordinary strudel, fruit strudels, with apple, of course (*Apfelstrudel*), but also with pears, cherries, etc; *Rahmstrudel*, with sour cream; *Germstrudel*, which uses yeast in the dough, and has a complicated filling involving cream, milk, butter, sugar, lemon juice, honey, raisins and crushed poppy seeds. The pancakes of Austria (*Schmarren*) appear here, served with cooked fruit—plums, apples, cherries, etc. *Presnitz* is a durable sweet of marzipan enriched with chopped walnuts, almonds and hazelnuts, with bits of citron and pine nuts imbedded in its cinnamon-sprinkled surface. *Kastanientorte* and *Erdbeertorte*, chestnut and raspberry tarts, are natural derivatives of the local products, the raspberry being almost a monopoly of this region because of the curious lack of interest in this fruit in the rest of Italy. *Mohrenköpfe*, Moor's head, uses chestnuts too, but also chocolate, is drenched in a liqueur, and is decorated with a maraschino cherry—a dessert where Italian and Austrian cooking join hands. *Guglhupf mit Germ* is the spongy cake, in this case dotted with raisins, which turns up in all Germanic countries. The Viennese cream puffs, *Krapfen*, are a Carnival dish in the Alto Adige, *Faschingskrapfen* (but the *mirtilli* fritters, *frittelle di San Candido*, are not feast-day sweets, as the name might seem to indicate; it comes from the name of the town of San Candido, where they are made). Apple fritters (*Apfelküchel*) and sweet plum dumplings (*Zwetschgenknödel*) are popular too. *Zoof-Krapfen*, flavored with ground poppy seeds, is an Alto Adige specialty; this area produces poppy seeds expressly for the table. *Tiroler-Krapfen* are filled with jam.

The cooking of the Alto Adige is the cooking of the Tyrol; its wines often imitate German vintages. They conform so exactly to Germanic tastes that the rest of Italy hardly knows them. Many are excellent, and are exported, but not to the peninsula. The best market is Germany (the bulk of the wines here are reds, and Germany, being chiefly a white producer, craves reds); the second best is Switzerland; Austria comes third.

The two provinces of Venezia Tridentina, not sharply different in their cuisines, do show considerable independence when it comes to wine. Bolzano is Germanic; the Trentino is Italian. Bolzano has imported many foreign vines. The original tendency was toward German grapes, but once the habit of importation had been established, a good many French grapes were brought in also—*cabernet, merlot, pinot noir, blanc* and *gris*.

One of the grapes used here is Traminer, which I had always associated with Alsace. It was a surprise to me to discover that here it is not listed among imported vines, but is held to be native, named from the village of Termeno (in German, Tramin) halfway between Bolzano and Trent. It gives perfumed and fruity wine in Bolzano as in Alsace, white, dry and velvety, with a taste which varies from that of almonds to a faint reminiscence of vanilla. In the 18th century the renowned doctor Guarinoni di Hall advised his patients to drink it, but in moderation. It has exciting qualities. "It stimulates the nervous system," writes Felice Cusolo, a local expert, "and makes women expansive"— *espansive*. (I would have appreciated his private definition of this word, but he failed to give it.)

Red wine from the same area is named from the place, not the grape—Termeno. It is dry, light (10 to 11 degrees), and is drunk young.

Sylvaner is another grape found in Alsace and also in Germany. It is said to have been introduced into the Alto Adige in 1142, when Augustinian monks from the Abbey of Neuberg, on the Danube, joining those of Bishop Artemanno in the Abbey of Novacella, above Bressanone, brought the vines with them. It is described as related to the German Liebfraumilch, which does not pin it down particularly, since Liebfraumilch is variable. Sylvaner is grown all the way from Bressanone to the Austrian frontier, sometimes as high as 2,500 feet, and produces a straw-colored wine with greenish highlights, fairly dry and a little acid, but not too much so.

Riesling is another grape name found also in Alsace and along the German Rhine. The Alto Adige has two Rieslings—Rhineland Riesling, *Riesling renano*, of fairly recent importation (about 1850) and *Riesling italico*, which presumably goes far enough back to have developed qualities of its own. Actually it is difficult to distinguish between them; both produce pleasant refreshing white wines, which, however, do not reach the heights the same grape achieves in Alsace or Germany.

Among other white wines of Bolzano are Valle Isarco, a greenish-yellow apéritif wine, delicate, light and sharp, 11 to 12 degrees, which needs two years of aging to be at its best; the dessert wines, Moscato Giallo, 13.5 to 16 degrees, made of course from Muscat grapes (Moscato in Italian); and one produced from the imported *pinot blanc* grape, known here variously as Pinot Bianco, Borgogna Bianco, or Weissburgunder. In its ordinary form, this last is a full bodied (12.5 to 13.5 degrees) pale greenish-yellow apéritif or fish wine, with a delicate perfume and a slightly bitter taste. It is also converted into a sparkling wine which is possibly the best in Italy; in any case its most prized variety, Ferrari di Trento Riserva, costs three times as much as the most expensive Asti Spumante, the one which for most foreigners represents Italian "champagne."

The whites above account for less than one-quarter of the Alto Adige production. The rest are reds (with a few rosés). A link between them is Terlaner (Terlano), of which both reds and whites exist. This is an old wine too, for in the 14th century it was a favorite of the "Ugly Duchess," Margaret Maultasch—Maultasch is not a surname, but a nickname which means "pocket mouth," a tribute to her expressive features, which inspired Tenniel for his drawings of the Duchess in *Alice in Wonderland*. Terlaner is somewhat unpredictable, for the wines grown here, all marketed under the same name, are made of different blends of grapes, depending on the whim of the individual grower. Generally speaking, the whites are a clear brilliant greenish-yellow, which becomes deeper as the wine ages; it also becomes mellower, 11.5 to 13 degrees, developing more fully its refreshing taste and slightly fruity color. The reds are light, 10 to 12 degrees, should be drunk young, and are not particularly interesting, except Terlaner Merlot, which is specifically identified by the kind of grape which goes into it precisely because it is superior to the others.

The finest red wine of the Alto Adige is Santa Maddalena, made from *schiave* grapes grown on the abrupt and picturesque hills which dominate Bolzano, with the Dolomites as a magnificent backdrop in the distance. The slopes face south, getting full sunlight, intensified by reflection from the surface of the Isarco River. The result is a rich pomegranate-red wine, mellow and velvety, 12 to 14 degrees. Like most full-bodied wines, it ages well, and after three or four years is at its best, developing an interesting aftertaste recalling almonds. It goes well with red meat and game. Santa Giustina di Bolzano, from the same area, also goes with roasts, but is less assertive—12 to 12.5 degrees, bright ruby-red, with a tart aftertaste sometimes mollified by a slight hint of vanilla.

Lagrein or Lagarina, named for its grape, also grown close to the city of Bolzano, is generally thought of as a rosé, light and fresh, with a tendency to sparkle naturally. It is agreeable, especially in summer, and is reputed to be mildly aphrodisiac, which may account partly for the popularity of Lagreinkretzer (Lagarina Rosato), as it is called when the label spells out the nature of the wine—which, regrettably, is driving out the more serious red Lagrein, 12 to 13 degrees, a ruby-red which turns light pomegranate with age, subtle, mellow, exhilarating, and again with that merest hint of vanilla in its aftertaste, characteristic of so many wines of this region. Lagrein is hard to find in Italy, except on the spot where it is grown, since most of it is shipped to Germany and Switzerland.

A wine that does stay in Italy, and is known to connoisseurs throughout the country, but only to connoisseurs, since the general public has never heard of it, is Marseiler. It grows on the slopes of the hill of Colterenzio, near Cornaiano, and there isn't much of it. It is worth hunting for.

A generous wine (13 degrees), it is a clove-red, dry but with a slight exotically spicy taste. It can be drunk within two years, has developed its full quality by three, and after that continues to age gallantly.

An exception to the rule that Bolzano wines outdo Trent wines is Merlot Trentino. Bolzano produces some Merlot too (named for the grape, of course), but the Trentino succeeds better with it. This is another wine much appreciated in Germany and Switzerland. It runs from 12 to 13.5 degrees of alcohol, is ruby-red in color, of well balanced acidity, and reaches its prime in about three years. There is also a rosé.

The most distinctive wine of Trent is Teroldego (or Teroldico), highly appreciated in its own country, but not always by those accustomed to suaver wines. Teroldego can be rough, which is the way its fanciers like it. It is grown where the Noce River runs into the Adige, in an area called the *Campo rotaliano*, a name you will sometimes find on the label. The vines are grown on arbors—the renowned "trellises of Trent"—and *Teroldego* is the name of the grape. In color, Teroldego is an intensely bright ruby-red, and its penetrating taste, when it has been sufficiently aged, say two or three years, recalls a mixture of raspberry and violet. It runs between 12 and 13 degrees.

The other best-known name of the Trentino is Marzemino, again a grape name. It was given immortality by no less a person than Mozart (or more exactly his librettist, da Ponte, who cites it in *Don Giovanni*); and lest anyone assume it was chosen there only because it is a name easy to sing, it should be reported that it is described in the text as "the excellent Marzemino." It is a bright ruby, 11 to 12 degrees, a little astringent, with a subtle slightly tart taste which does not allow itself to be fully captured at the first swallow, but grows on you as the meal progresses. The flavor becomes more pronounced and the color lighter as the wine ages. Forget the rosé.

Trent makes a Vin Santo, the sweet dessert wine found in many parts of Italy, which compares very favorably with those of other regions. The chief rosé is Casteller, dry and with considerable body; there is also a red, with a delicate perfume, light in tannin. Finally, with Garda Trentino, red, rosé or white, the Trentino vineyards along the northern shores of the eastern side of Lake Garda adjoin the famous ones of Verona on the southern shores; but they are far from matching the Verona vintages.

A region which looks toward Germany gastronomically and bibulously should have good beer. Venezia Tridentina has, especially in Bolzano. Light and dark beers are made, and they are both excellent.

Venezia Giulia

"O*ce biel ciscjel a Udin,*" sing the Friulani ("Ah, the beautiful castle of Udine!"), and if it were not there, occupying an elevation which Venice, flat as a pancake, cannot duplicate, you might for a fleeting instant think yourself in the Piazza San Marco instead of in Udine's Piazza Contarena, rebaptized the Piazza della Libertà after the war. The graceful Renaissance arcade before the church of San Giovanni substitutes for the ground-floor arches of the Doge's Palace, and though there is neither campanile nor Grand Canal, there are twin columns as in the Piazzetta San Marco, one of them supporting the winged lion as in Venice, and on the square clock tower, which

bears St. Mark's lion too, colossal statues stand on either
side of a great bell and strike the hours with their hammers,
like the two Moors of Venice. They are supposed to represent Hercules and Cacus, but the Friulani refer to them
irreverently as Florean and Venturin, two characters of
the rustic spectacles staged at country fairs. Here is the
heart of the "little fatherland," the *piccola patria*, as its
inhabitants call Friuli; the heart is Venetian.

The spirit of Venice triumphed in a land which through
the centuries was swept by successive waves of invasion
and as a result has known no less than three capitals: Aquileia, which was Roman; Cividale, which was Longobard;
and Udine which was, and is, Venetian. Yet when the
ancient Veneti entered this territory, it was already solidly
occupied by people who are still there, the Ladin-speaking
Friulani. Despite the overlay of Venetian culture, they are
so distinct that Venezia Giulia has been made an autonomous
political unit. There are 800,000 Friulani, all of them
represented as Ladin-speaking by local boosters, though
outside linguists put the number at more like 450,000; this
represents 90 percent of the Ladin speakers of the planet.
The Friuli culture has survived because of the strong unifying influence not only of a common language, but of common customs and traditions, and a common problem, mis-
ery, which, as everybody knows, loves company. Today, as
improved communications probe deeper into remote districts, Ladin is retreating before standard Italian; and as
individuals become more mobile, emigration is sapping the
population of what, with the Polesine, is probably the
most underdeveloped region of northern Italy.

Udine is three capitals in one: of its own province of
Udine, one of the largest in Italy, a third the size of Ver-
mont; of Venezia Giulia as a whole, which adds the province of Gorizia and the territory of Trieste to Udine; and
of Friuli, which is not a political unit, but a cultural one,

almost, but not quite, congruent with the province of Udine. The population of Friuli does not extend into Carnia, which is the northern fringe of the province in the Carnic and Julian Alps, some of which are 9,000 feet high; nor west of the Tagliamento, Udine's largest river; but on the southeast it spills over the borders of Udine to cover the better part of Gorizia.

Venezia Giulia is chiefly agricultural; but it has little arable land, permitting only limited farming and little cattle raising. Mountains cover 40 percent of its area, where the only possible exploitation is lumbering and grazing, but the forests are sparse and the pasturage poor. More or less sterile hills, the *colline povere*, account for 19 percent more. Of the 37 percent that remains, only the not very extensive plain of Friuli is fertile, and it is here, consequently, that the population is most dense. There is a great difference between the two banks of the Tagliamento. The soil on the western side is alternately arid and soggy from the heavy spring and autumn rains, usable only for pasturage; the soil on the east bank is better constituted to handle its precipitation, so here cereals are grown, principally maize, and forage crops for animals. The Carso, which is the strip of territory bordering on Yugoslavia, is an arid stretch of limestone, where sheep and goats are raised on small farms; the chief produce is wine, root crops and a little maize. The unproductive soils of these areas reduce the proportion of useful agricultural land to 20 percent, and even here the yield is not high. The brightest spots are the area around Udine, where vegetable growing is feasible (Tavagnacco is noted for asparagus); the coastal plain, which cultivates fine white maize that makes especially delicate polenta; and the Carso for fruit. Even so, the region is incapable of raising enough food to feed its own population, and this situation has been further aggravated by the splitting of properties into ever more minute fractions through successive inheritances; there are about 300,000 small farms with an average area of less than three acres.

Unpromising though much of this territory is, Venezia Giulia does enjoy certain natural resources, apart from the fish of the Adriatic found along its coast. The mountains provide a good deal of game, and, as is normal in mountain territory, trout. From the Alpine cattle, Carnia and Montasio produce cheeses, some resembling coarse-grained Gruyère, others small-holed Emmental. Also characteristic of mountain country are preserved pork products. Tarcento, called from the bleak beauty of its Alpine landscape "the pearl of Friuli," makes a special sausage, *lujanis* (the same word as *luganega*, but here not exactly the same thing), long, thin and spicy, which has to be cooked before eating—fried, grilled on a spit between pieces of bread, or sautéed in tomato sauce. The village of Codroipo produces *musetti*, pork crackling, while *muset*, which looks like the same word, is not the same thing, but the type of fat sausage known elsewhere as *cotechino*. The most famous of all Friuli food products is the *"molto dolce e giustamente celebrato"* San Daniele di Friuli, the only prosciutto more prized than the best from Langhirano. Not much of it is made, so it is as rare as it is precious; if you see a prosciutto with the whole foot left on, pounce: it may be a San Daniele. Do not be put off by its ashen crust; as you cut into it, its subtle aroma rises in your nostrils, and it curls away from the knife, pink, sweet and fragrant. Appreciated all over Italy, San Daniele ham is served as an appetizer with figs or melon, included in antipasti, or used for sandwiches, going easy on the bread in order not to smother the delicate taste of this ham.

In spite of the poverty of food resources and of the country in general, the Friulani are quietly hospitable, welcoming visitors into homes where the patriarchal family has not yet disintegrated. Friulani families are large and cohesive; their size is evident in the generous dimensions of the farmhouses. Within them, ample space is allotted for the *maie*, the flour bin, for the family stock is kept permanently in the house. The housewife would hardly feel secure if her supply of the most basic of all foods were not always at hand. She does not buy her bread from a bakery, but makes it at home, the dough being kneaded and compressed in a special wooden trough known as the *panaria*.

The focal point of the house, where the family gathers and guests are received is the *fogher* (*focolare* in standard Italian, a word which carries in its stomach the title of the Lares, the ancient household divinities who presided over pantry and table and symbolized the protection and comfort of the family). Elsewhere the familial spirit is breaking down nowadays, but in Friuli it remains strong and the *fogher* is its altar. In its classic form the *fogher* is a hearth in the middle of the room, with an open flame whose smoke is carried away by a hood above it funneling into a chimney. Around it stand heavy wrought-iron supports, with spits turning between them, or kettles hanging from heavy chains, the *alari*, which would make the mouths of antique dealers water. Fortunately there are not many antique dealers in Friuli, and the potential market is far away, but all the same modernism is taming the *fogher*. Nowadays it may be pushed back from the center of attraction into a sort of dining nook. The hearth is hidden within a cube of masonry with a circular hole in its top, which has all the aesthetic appeal of a toilet seat. When in use, thin tongues of flame rising from the hole replace the magnificent roaring fire of the old-fashioned *fogher*, while the sturdy wrought-iron *alari* (*ciavedal* in dialect) have shrunk to a squat grill standing over the flame and perhaps a hook in the ceiling from which a kettle can be slung. It may be more practical (though I am inclined to doubt it), but it is certainly less picturesque.

The peasants of Friuli are limited to what they can raise themselves. Rarely can they afford meat; poultry is more within their means, since it is home-bred, geese and guinea hens especially. (Goose liver is a specialty of Pieve di Soligo.) The soups are therefore not of consommé, but of vegetables. *Sopa friulana*, a celery soup, is traditionally served on Christmas Eve. *Minestrone friulano* is a potato soup flavored with onion and tomato sauce. *Cialzòn* or *cjalsòn*, a local variety of pasta, resembles *agnolotti* stuffed with cottage cheese and other ingredients which vary with the cook, but never include meat; it is usually served in soup, but may be eaten without liquid. Risotto appears with asparagus tips, or with *luganega* sausage, or beans. Omelets are enlivened with aromatic herbs, or vegetables, or sausage, or, on the coast, shrimps, shellfish or even fish.

On the rare occasions when a Friuli family gets to eat meat, it is likely to be *sguazeto*, lamb stew in thick tomato sauce, served with polenta. A treat is *costolette di maiale con verze*, pork chops with cabbage. On the rare occasions when the family can afford a rack of pork, it is not roasted in the oven (ovens are rare in the rural districts) but on a spit.

Usually such luxuries are not available, and the family has to fill up on bread and vegetables. The typical vegetable dish is *brovada*, whose principal ingredient is the lowly turnip, cut into strips and marinated lengthily in vinegar and water. You begin the dish by heating olive oil, into which you then put crushed garlic and onions, followed by a little flour. When this has become well integrated, the prepared turnip goes in, along with caraway seeds. It is usually served with *musett*, Friuli sausages;

you might call it a turnip sauerkraut. *Carciofi alla Venezia Giulia* are breaded artichokes. The standard Friuli salad, *insalata al lardo*, is made of two kinds of lettuce and bits of hot bacon.

Friuli relieves the coarse nature of its main dishes by letting itself go on desserts. The *gubana* of Cividale is really a *ciambella*, a ring-shaped cake, of *millefeuille* pastry, in its simplest form stuffed with crushed walnuts, pine nuts, almonds and spices, but which will lend itself to almost any fantasy of the cook—one recipe I have adds to this sultana and Damascus raisins, chopped dried figs and prunes, candied citron, orange peel and chocolate, and douses the whole in rum and eaux de vie. I have even seen frosting on the inner layers of this cake. Pisino makes its own version of *ciambella*, with honey, almonds, pine nuts, coriander, lemon peel, saffron, coffee, white wine, cinnamon, and nutmeg adorning the basic pastry. Martignacco is known for its dry cookies.

The Carnia area north of Friuli proper has nothing specific to add to the general menu; its favorite dishes, barring a touch of Germanic influence in the Tarvisio area, are borrowed from the Venetian repertory; pasta with beans, for instance, or small birds spit-roasted and served with polenta. It is great game country, serving almost all of it with polenta—quail, partridge, pheasant, hare, chamois, deer and wild boar.

Gorizia, called before World War I "the Nice of Austria," because of its mild climate, is on the Yugoslav frontier (so close, indeed, that it lost some of its suburbs to Yugoslavia by the World War II peace treaty). It is the capital of the eastern province of Venezia Giulia and its cooking is very much akin to that of Udine, plus a Slavic touch in the Natisone valley. The food is simple, tasty and even in restaurants more like home cooking than professional cooking. The region likes its meat grilled, when it can afford it, and slices of it, or of the *luganega* sausage of Cragno, between slices of home-made bread baked on the embers of old-fashioned hearths make robust sandwiches. Coinciding with the vintage season, game from the hills is abundant. This is also a fruit-growing area.

One of the most noted dishes of the province is *broèto*, the fish chowder of Grado, noted for its good eating, at the tip of a peninsula which stretches out into the Adriatic like an elongated big toe. *Broéto* is dialect for *brodetto*, and there is also a famous *brodetto* at Monfalcone. Another town of Gorizia with a widely known specialty is Cormons, celebrated also for its wine, but in this case the reference is to a dessert, *buzolai*, a pastry of the simplest ingredients, flour, sugar and butter, particularly rich in egg. Gorizia makes gnocchi of potatoes and plums, bakes its ham, serves hare and deer as salmis, and embeds blood pudding in crust.

When we come to the Trieste neighborhood, we have rounded the head of the Adriatic and started down its eastern shore. This minute district, which is officially referred to as a province, is little more than a city and its suburbs. Lying on the border of Yugoslavia, of which, under the name of Trst, it was momentarily a part, it has, as would be expected, a mixed cuisine, englobing reminiscences of the Austro-Hungarian Empire (goulash, here called *golas*, for instance, considered a local specialty) and seepages from the basically Byzantine cooking to the east, Hungarian, Greek, Slav and Jewish. In spite of this, the cooking of Trieste is much more Italian than that of the Alto Adige, which after all is not surprising, since the Latin character of this region was established long before there was a Yugoslavia or a Serbia or an Austria.

The cooking of the Carso (an Italicization of the German *Karst*, meaning the inland area of Slovenia and Istria), is basically peasant cooking, heavy and robust; as a result, dishes described as *alla triestina* are often of this type. Such is *jota* (or *iota*) *triestina*, a thick soup of beans, potatoes and cabbage, sometimes with bits of pork crackling or smoked pork. *Mocnik del Carso* is a soup thickened with flour and eggs. Trieste potatoes are first boiled, then sliced and fried with chopped onion in oil or butter plus a lacing of consommé. Consommé is also used to give added richness to calves' liver, *fegato di vitello alla triestina*, flavored with onions, celery, carrots, parsley, cloves and lemon juice. The Trieste area also has its own version of *brodetto*.

Venetian influence is apparent in the importance of rice on the Trieste menu—in many soups, in a variety of risotti, and in the appearance here of *riso e piselli*, Venice's famous *risi e bisi*, of which a revised version crushes the peas and rice together into a purée and serves it with egg ribbon pasta. There is a German or Austrian air about *gnocchetti di fegato*, liver dumplings flavored with onion, parsley, marjoram and nutmeg. *Sguazzetto* here is not lamb stew, but a mixture of pork and veal, served with polenta. *Bruscandoli* is wild asparagus with an egg sauce.

Liptauer is described on the menus as a cheese, but it is a little more than that. It is a fashion of mixing and seasoning cheeses, and when it is done as in Central Europe, the ingredients are brought to the table and the diner combines them himself, to suit his own taste. In Trieste, the ingredients are Gorgonzola and Mascarpone, a cream cheese, butter, crushed anchovy, caraway seeds, chopped leeks, mustard, paprika, capers and onion. Mash them together in the proportions which please you.

There are many types of rich pastry, which vary from town to town even when they carry the same name. Thus the fairly simple *strùcoli*, in local dialect, a pastry rolled into cylindrical shape and sliced to provide individual pieces, is simply flavored with honey, or cherries, or cottage cheese in what is presumably its original form, but suffers a slight change of name and a considerable change of nature when it becomes *stroccoli alla Carsolina,* including in its makeup vanilla, cinnamon, pine nuts, raisins and acacia flowers. *Presniz,* also spelled *Presnitz,* a name of obviously Germanic origin, recalls strudel, and includes in its ingredients bits of walnut, sultana raisins and candied citron. You will excuse me, I trust, for not describing the other desserts listed in a Trieste cookbook I have before my eyes; there are 285 of them.

"Our wines," laments a writer from Friuli, "are more exquisite than renowned." Friuli has always been proud of its vintages, and it must be admitted that many of them are very pleasant, drunk on their own territory, which is chiefly where you find them. There is no exportable surplus.

Certain Friuli wines do deserve a wider reputation than they have—especially one white and one red whose acquaintance is worth making. The first is Tocai Friulano, pale lemon-yellow, a little tart, with 11 to 12 degrees of alcohol, while Tocai del Collio, from the province of Gorizia, always drunk young, is a little spicy. The name Tocai causes first-time tasters to expect something like the famous sweet liqueurish Hungarian wine, and in their surprise at finding a refreshing dry one, they often accept explanations which are plausible but inexact. One is that the Italian wine is made from the same grape, but by a different process. Another is that Italian wine is made from a different grape, but one developed from the Hungarian Tokay vine. This is not correct either, for the unexpected fact is that the similarity of the two names is pure coincidence. The word that gives Italian Tocai its name simply means "here," so its sense is "local wine, our wine," an example of local pride, which in this area crops up fairly often—for instance, not to leave the field of wine, in the label Refosco Nostrano, "our Refosco," to distinguish Friuli wine made from the Refosco grape from that produced from it elsewhere. However, it was perhaps because of the example of the famous Hungarian dessert wine that Friuli set out deliberately to produce something of the same sort, using a special strain of grape called *piccolit* because of the small size of its seeds. Friuli attempted to approximate the great Hungarian Tokaji Aszu, whose secret was legendarily discovered by accident when a battle delayed the grape harvesting until the grapes had apparently spoiled on the vines; but the Tokay made from the "spoiled" grapes turned out to be rich, sweet and smooth. Friuli allows the grapes to wither before pressing them, which results in a heavy-bodied wine of 14 degrees or more, very sweet, highly perfumed, velvety and golden in color, which requires three to four years to reach maturity.

The possibly underrated red is Cabernet, a grape name of course, which is a "bigger" wine than the vintage of the same name of Venezia Tridentina (to even things up, the Merlot is less good), especially that of Buttrio. It is full-bodied and slow to mature (three to eight years in the bottle), often a characteristic of superior wines.

Among other Friuli wines, grown mostly in the province of Udine, though some extend over into Gorizia, are names familiar from their appearance also in Venezia Tridentina—besides Tocai, Traminer and Riesling, and also Sauvignon, Pinot Blanc and Pinot Grigio; the straw-yellow color of the last sometimes becomes a grayish pink; it is excellent with fish and is also particularly recommended with hors d'oeuvres composed of sausage or other pork products. Typical reds are the Refoscos, already mentioned above—Refosco Nostrano, or Refosco dal Peduncolo Rosso (red-stemmed Refosco), has a dark ruby color, with plenty of body, and a sharp flinty taste.

The vineyards of Gorizia were badly hit during the

war, and their production was greatly reduced, though the province is making a valiant effort to recover. Besides the Collio Goriziano made from the Tocai grape mentioned before, the area produces the white Riesling Italico, Pinot Blanc, Pinot Gris, Sauvignon, Traminer and Malvasia, a Malvasia somewhat different from the more aromatic grapes of this name, probably a strain developed in Istria; and the red Merlot, Cabernet Franc and Pinot Noir. The Yugoslav influence appears in Gorizia in Slivowitz Friulano, the local version of the famous Yugoslav plum brandy. Similar eaux de vie are made from pears and peaches, and there are several types of *grappa*.

Trieste wines do not differ greatly from those of Gorizia, but special mention should be made of Terrano, light-bodied, 9 to 10 degrees at the most, bright red, with a flavor that combines hints of nuts and mountain raspberries. It is drunk young and, exceptionally for a red, chilled. Zolla and Rupingrande are especially noted for it, but they may not be much longer. It is gradually disappearing under the relentless pressures of competition; the vines do not provide a large yield, and there is more money to be made by replacing them with bigger producers. It is not a great wine, so its disappearance will not be a tragedy.

Other prized wines of the Trieste area are the red Refosco of San Dorligo della Valle, and several whites: the Malvasia of the same town, the Pinot of Sant'Antonio in Bosco, the Sauvignon of Prebenico, and the Prosecco of Santa Croce. The last requires a word of explanation. Prosecco is a town in the Trieste area which has developed a special grape called, on its home grounds, Gerla. The rest of Venezia has adopted the grape and calls the wine made from it by the name of its birthplace. In Trieste itself, however, this name on the label means, not the grape, but the place. Prosecco Triestino (of which that of Santa

Croce is a special case) means wine made in the Prosecco area, no matter what grape has gone into it. As a matter of fact, most Trieste Prosecco does contain some Prosecco (or Gerla), but it contains more Malvasia, Sauvignon and Garganella. It cannot be said that the labelers have done much to help the hapless tourist identify these wines.

THE
DOMAIN

OF THE
GREEKS

The Campania

I t is a common assumption that the name Campania means "countryside" or "field"—the same word as the French *campagne*, from the Latin *campania*. Nothing could be more reasonable, but as a matter of fact the word is not Latin, but Oscan. The Campani were the inhabitants of Capua, and the Romans extended the pre-Roman word that described them to cover the district of which Capua was the chief city. It was possibly from this beginning that the word *campania* entered the Latin vocabulary, for one of the qualities Rome associated with the land of the Capuans, the Campania, was fertility. It was true then, and is true now, of the part of this region the Romans knew best, the coastal strip from Naples to Lazio; but it is far from true of Campania as a whole, or at least of modern Campania, which covers more ground than the territory to which the ancients applied the name of Felix Campania, Fortunate Campania.

In ancient times, the Romans marveled at the fertility of Campania, for their own soil was heavy and hard to work. The loose black volcanic soil (*terra pulla*) of Campania offered its fruits almost without effort. Depending on the product, there were two to four crops per year, and for each the yield was greater than from the earth of Lazio. The Campania produced pears, apples, cherries, figs, melons (the tiny ones the Romans knew), pomegranates, quinces, almonds, chestnuts, all sorts of vegetables, spelt, millet, barley and wheat. Excellent oil was made from the olives growing on the slopes of the hills behind the coastal plains. The wine was good, especially that from the Mons Massicus and the Ager Falernus.

The picture is much the same today for the coastal country between Naples and Lazio. Despite 2,500 years or more of exploitation, the soil remains extraordinarily fertile and the region is consequently the most densely populated in Italy: 3,000 inhabitants per square kilometer. Maize has been added to the cereal crops. Zucchini grow to a length of six feet. The land is capable of nourishing several different crops at the same time: beans, cabbage, broccoli and tomatoes are planted between rows of olive or fruit trees, grapevines are draped over trees, which serve as living trellises (usually over poplars, not over fruit trees, as that would cut off the sunlight from the fruit). Cultivation is not confined to the plain, but is pursued up the hillsides, to a height of 650 feet. The growing season is practically all year around.

This, however, is not the whole picture. Along the coast, south of Naples, where the plain disappears and cliffs rise abruptly from the sea (to the despair of farmers,

Good Eating
Greek
Settlements

LAZIO

MOLISE

APULIA

N

Volturno River

FRUITS
CEREALS   OLIVE
WINE   OIL
VEGETABLES
FALERNO WINE

Capua

Caserta

Benevento
NOUGAT
SOLOPACA WINE
STREGA

APPIAN WAY

BASILICATA

Aversa
ASPRINIO WINE

Avellino
CHESTNUTS
TAURASI WINE
GRECO DI TUFO WINE
FIANO WINE

ALICI
ALL'ISCHIANA
OLIVE OIL
MAIZE
FISH
DIANCOLELLA
D'ISCHIA WINE
EPOMEO WINE

Cuma

Pozzuoli

Herculaneum

Mt. Vesuvius
LACRIMA CHRISTI WINE

Pompeii

OLIVES

Ischia

GULF
of
NAPLES

Vico
Equense

Castellammare

BUFFALO
CHEESE

Salerno

CEREALS
FRUIT

Sele River

Amalfi

Sorrento
GRAGNANO WINE
RAVELLO WINE
CONCA WINE

TRAMONTI WINE
FISH-STUFFED CANELLONI
FURORE DIVINA COSTIERA WINE

Naples

PIZZA
CALZONI
MACARONI
SPAGHETTI
MOZZARELLA
SARTÙ
TOMATO SAUCE
PIZZAIOLA SAUCE
FISH FRY
OCTOPUS
MUSSELS
CLAMS
STUFFED PEPPERS
PASTRY
ICE CREAM
SALAME NAPOLETANO
MINESTRA MARITATA
CONCH
ROAST LAMB'S HEAD

Capri

FRUIT
OLIVE OIL
CRAYFISH
GOAT CHEESE
ZUPPA DI PESCE
ALLA CAPRESE
CAPRI WINE
TOTANI
ALL'ANACAPRESE

GULF
of
SALERNO

Paestum

WINE

OLIVE OIL

SORRENTO
PENINSULA

ORANGES
LEMONS
WALNUTS
OLIVES
ALMONDS
WINE
LOTUS FRUIT
MACCHERONI ALLA SORRENTINA
ZUPPA DI SOFFRITTO
LASAGNA

Miles

0   25   50

0   50

Km.

CAMPANIA

but this is what produces the breath-taking beauty of the Amalfi Drive), oranges and lemons still flourish, the vines that cling perilously to the steep slopes give highly agreeable local wines, and Sorrento makes walnuts its specialty. But many areas have been completely disinherited by nature. The situation is improving in the low valleys, once subject to constant flooding from rivers pinched into narrow clefts, but now responding to reclamation projects, so that they support great herds of the enormous white buffaloes which give the Campania one of its most characteristic foods, mozzarella cheese. Poor or mediocre soil covers extensive areas in the mountainous areas. Cereals are grown there, but with difficulty; while the northern coastal plain gives several crops a year, the earth in the mountain regions must lie fallow for long periods after each crop to replenish its feeble store of nutrients. This part of the Campania has been largely abandoned by its population, attracted to what they expect will be an easier life in Naples. Many of them must be disappointed. Naples is overcrowded, competition is fierce. That is why there are so many Neapolitans in the United States, and why American ideas of Italian food stem from Naples.

The *regione* of Campania is divided into five provinces, Naples, Caserta, Benevento, Avellino and Salerno. It is the first, and smallest, that the world knows best. Much of the history of Campania is concentrated here, and so are the dazzling towns which attract visitors, except those of the Sorrento peninsula, which are in the province of Salerno, although the tourist, who customarily visits it from Naples, does not realize he has crossed boundaries. The city of Naples, despite the destruction it suffered during the bombings of World War II, has conserved numerous relics of its varied history—nothing much of its Greek past, except in the character of its inhabitants, though there is a name which hawks back to it, that of a coastal town, Torre del Greco, the Greek Tower, smack in the center of the Bay of Naples, a logical place for a lookout or a lighthouse, so we may assume that the name refers to a distant reality. For Roman remains also, you will do better to leave the city itself, unless you are willing to content yourself with the National Museum, and visit Pompeii and Herculaneum (or Capri). From then on, Naples itself will offer you a cross-section of its history.

On my first visit there, in 1929, I acquired a distaste for macaroni, at least in Naples, for its insalubrious courtyards were jungles of it. Limp strands hung over clotheslines to dry, dirt swirled through the air, flies settled to rest on the exposed pasta, pigeons bombed it from overhead, children invented games to play with it, and the large dog population, finding itself short of lampposts, put up with what it could find. But have no fear today: macaroni and spaghetti are now made indoors in spick-and-span automated factories.

Naples ranks high in the decibel count, it is full of life and bustle, partly resulting from the fact that it is the second port of Italy, led only by Genoa. It is also a cheerful city, which seems to have banished dullness and boredom.

There are Neolithic remains on the island of Capri, which closes the Bay of Naples on the south; it must have been a place of security then, easy to defend, with its steep cliffs rising precipitously from the sea. There was probably no lack of food, either, not only because the surrounding waters teem with fish, but also because there was plenty of game. It is natural to think that the name of the island refers to goats, coming from the Latin *capri*, but it does not; it is derived from the Greek *kapros*, wild boar, an animal which abounded on this island when the Greeks arrived. Capri has always been propitious to the growth of living things, many of them edible. The island supports on its four square miles 850 different species of plants, plus 133 varieties of some of them, a consequence of its mild equable temperature, and produces olive oil, fruit and highly pleasant wine.

The larger island of Ischia (18 square miles), which closes the Bay of Naples on the north, is volcanic in origin; its towering Mount Epomeo (the name is derived from *epopeus*, viewpoint) is the principal crater, surrounded by 12 smaller ones. The Eritreans and Chalcidians who had colonized the island abandoned it about 500 B.C. after a particularly destructive eruption, but the island has grown calm with age; the last recorded explosion was in 1301, though there was a bad earthquake in 1883. It produces olive oil, fruit, maize and, especially, wine, which has made its town of Forio a flourishing wine trading center.

Caserta is the northernmost provincial capital of the Campania. Its province contains what was once the second city of the Roman world, whose inhabitants were renowned for their haughtiness and their indulgence in luxury, Capua. It is in a sadly diminished state today.

East of the provinces of Caserta and Naples is that of Benevento, whose history was often distinct from that of the territories surrounding it because, whoever nominally ruled the region, Benevento was usually accorded a special status as the particular fief of the Pope. It first entered history as the capital of the Samnites, which hardly accords with a local legend that it was founded by Diomedes, a hero of the Trojan war who is more often associated with the Adriatic coast. In any case, Benevento, though considered today as an area of mediocre resources, was an important agricultural center under the ancient Romans, who in 268 B.C. had changed its name to Beneventum from the former Maleventum, a name, in their opinion, of evil portent.

South of Benevento and east of Naples lies the province of Avellino, in ancient times Abellinum, really back country. The tourist does not know it today, and neither, to any great extent, did the ancient Romans, though Virgil did refer in the *Aeneid* to Batulum, which is in the Irpino mountains, thickly covered with chestnut trees. South of Avellino is the largest of the Campanian provinces, Salerno, nearly as big as all the rest put together, a place of ancient and honorable history.

This is pure Greek territory, where the Roman hand rested lightly. Paestum displays ruins as impressive as anything in Greece itself. Was it the liveliness of Greek culture which made Salerno (anciently Salernum) the site of what is generally regarded as the first university in Europe? Or was it the eclectic character of the city? For legend has it that the university was founded by "the Four Masters," a Greek, a Latin, an Arab and a Jew.

After Salerno itself, the best known cities of its province are Sorrento, where Torquato Tasso was born in 1544; Positano, once a fishing village and now a sort of Italian St. Tropez, whose Moorish-style houses, clinging to the steep hillsides which rise from the sea, recall the intermittent presence of the Saracens; and Amalfi.

Amalfi is a story all by itself. The tourist who visits it today, glittering and beautiful but minute, finds it difficult to believe that it was once a great naval power; nevertheless it was. An outpost of the Byzantine Empire, it became the most important center for exchanges between southern Italy and Constantinople; made itself a free republic in 839; fought against the Saracens (not always with success, if one may judge from the survival today of a Saracen tower on its territory); and helped ferry Crusaders to the Holy Land. Its shipyards were capable of building galleys for 120 oarsmen. The apogee was reached in the 11th century, at the period when its citizen Flavio Gioia was credited with inventing (or re-inventing, for the Phoenicians may have known it) the magnetic compass. At this period maritime traffic in the Mediterranean was regulated by the Amalfitan Tables, still preserved in the City Hall, which remained valid until 1570.

If we may judge from the evidences found at Pompeii and Herculaneum (both once Greek), the ancient Campanians showed an interest in food transcending by far the simple necessity of sustaining life. Fortunes were made from it. Baking seems to have been a particularly lucrative occupation; one of the richest houses uncovered by the excavators of Pompeii, fittingly in the Street of Abundance, was that of Publius Paquius Proculus, who had become rich as owner of an important bakery. In one Pompeiian bakery, an oven was found containing 81 round loaves baked on August 24, 79 A.D., the day of the cataclysm. They reveal that the bread of those days, made of hard wheat and barley flour, came in large round loaves scored across the middle, like the country bread made throughout southern Italy today; sometimes the scoring divided the loaf into eight wedge-shaped segments, easy to break apart into individual portions.

It was not far from Pompeii that the ancients set up what was perhaps the first oyster hatchery in the world, or at least, since China may have been ahead of Rome, the first in the Occident. That the Greeks ate oysters everyone knows who remembers the story of Aristides the Just scratching his own name on an oyster shell for an illiterate who wanted to vote against him, a use of the oyster which has given us the word "ostracize" (a less radical way of employing it to eliminate an undesirable than was used against St. Blaize, patron saint of Bradford, England, Ragusa, Yugoslavia, and, of course, of shellfish gatherers, who was scraped to death with oyster shells).

XIII · The Campania

The ancient Greeks seem to have contented themselves with wild oysters, as nature provided them. Aristotle records that it had been discovered that oysters attached themselves to broken pottery and similar objects thrown into the sea at Rhodes, and that some fishermen had moved oysters from one spot to another, where they fattened better. But the Greeks seem to have made no systematic effort to raise oysters from scratch. The Romans did.

The first oyster promoter was Sergius Orata, a big business operator of pre-Christian times, who established an oyster farm in Lake Lucrinus (now Lucrino), already famous for its tame lampreys. Breeding oysters in fresh water may sound like a strange proceeding to the layman, but the water of Lucrinus, which was linked to the sea by underground water courses, was brackish rather than fresh; and the mingling of fresh and salt water is often beneficial to oysters. Orata's oyster beds were a great success, and had a ready market nearby at Baiae, with its wealthy pleasure-loving residents and vacationers; it has even been suggested that there is a relationship between the proper noun Lucrinus and the common noun lucre. Oysters were still flourishing in Lucrinus in 37 B.C., when Marcus Vipsanius Agrippa, who was building for Octavian the fleet that would enable him to win the battle of Actium, established a naval base by linking Lucrinus with Avernus, whose sulphurous waters promptly killed the oysters. Oyster cultivation was later resumed there, but in 1853 a volcanic eruption wrecked the lake. Oysters continued to be raised in the nearby Lake Fusaro, but sulphur polluted the water and once again the oysters were the victims.

The Pompeiians also ate pizza. It was pizza without tomatoes, of course, for 1,500 years had to elapse before the first tomato would be seen in Europe—according to local legend, when Neapolitan sailors brought the first seeds back from Peru. There is no evidence to support this belief, except that Naples makes lavish use of the tomato; but in any case the antiquity of pizza as a Neapolitan dish is firmly established. It is probably the single food most firmly associated with Naples.

I once read that 27 different kinds of pizza are made in Naples. I have not attempted a census myself, but I would guess that this is an underestimate. There is no limit to the number of combinations which can be put into a pizza shell, sometimes several at the same time. The pizza I remember most fondly was the size of a large pie, divided into six wedge-shaped compartments, each containing a different filling more luscious than the last; oddly enough it was served to me, not in Naples, but at the Capricciosa in Rome. This was a husky pizza, but in size it was beaten by one made at Vico Equense, across the bay from Naples, in a place which advertises "pizza by the meter," meaning that you get a slab a yard long.

Pizza basically means pie, and can be applied to any flat round bakery product; but it is generally understood to mean the familiar Neapolitan circular tart. It is the direct descendant of the ancient Roman breakfast, "bread with a relish," made easier to handle by giving the round slice of bread a raised rim to hold the relish. In its pristine form it is a poor man's dish; the dough is rough, the filling inexpensive; it can be picked up and eaten from the hand, without waste of time or the use of utensils, particularly if it comes in the form of *pizzette*, little pizzas, the size of a small saucer. This is what foreigners tend to think of as pizza, but in Naples a pizza is generally pie-sized, big enough to serve several persons as an entrée with a full meal, though it is often consumed entire by one eater when it constitutes his whole repast, as it often does. Served with a meal in a restaurant or at home, it is likely to be made with pastry crust replacing the classic coarse dough, and if so becomes *pizza casalinga*, homemade pizza.

The classic *pizza alla napoletana* is a disk of rough leavened dough, saturated with olive oil, and filled with diced *mozzarella* cheese, bits of fresh tomato or tomato paste, oregano (or, sometimes basil or other herbs), and usually anchovy fillets. Many cooks add garlic. This basic pizza should be eaten, if possible, hot from the oven, before it hardens and becomes unappetizing. Drink a rough red wine with it, nothing refined; a suave wine would be wasted on pizza. It wouldn't help the pizza and the pizza wouldn't help the wine.

The variations of pizza are infinite. *Pizza alla francescana* uses a filling of sliced mushrooms, chopped ham, cheese and tomato. *Pizza con cozze* replaces the anchovies of *pizza alla napoletana* with mussels. Though pizza is usually associated with Naples, other cities have developed their own varieties—with onion and without tomato in Rome, while in Genoa pizza means only the unfilled crust, often spread with cheese; and there is also the Ligurian pizza with its filling of onions garnished with anchovy fillets and black olives.

Eating pizza from the hand becomes even easier when the crust is folded around the filling into a sort of turnover, though it is a trifle greasy, since it is fried in oil. This treatment gives you *calzoni*, also very Neapolitan. They are made most often with the standard pizza filling (mozzarella, tomato, anchovy), but here also there is no limit to the possibilities. One recipe calls for chopped chicory hearts, unsalted anchovy fillets chopped fine, capers, pitted sliced black olives, currants, garlic and an egg yolk. Another wraps the dough around an intact slice of ham, along with preferably sticky cheese. A third employs diced *mozzarella*, fine strips of prosciutto, similarly cut-up salame, tomato paste, and grated cheese. When these tidbits are made not in the half-circle turnover shape, but in tubular form, they become *calzone*, which means "trouser leg," an apt description of their shape.

Also definitely associated with Naples is macaroni. Here we are south of the great dividing line for pasta, no longer in the land of soft sheet or ribbon pasta, often made in the home kitchen, but in that of machine-made tubular pasta —macaroni, spaghetti and the like. Naples started to manufacture macaroni in the 15th century; it is today the undisputed capital of this form of Italy's national staple. "The good Lord gave macaroni enough substance to make of it a whole meal," said a 19th-century writer, and in the South that is very frequently what it is. Here pasta is classified as *paste lunghe*, long pasta, which includes macaroni, spaghetti (from *spago*, cord), *bucatini*, and their fellows, or *paste corte*, short pasta—*rigatoni*, *penne*, *maltagliati*, *stelline*, etc. Long or short, it is always accompanied by sauces promising to the eye and piquant to the tongue. It is not here that you will find the restraint of the North. This is the South, exuberant, colorful, sybaritic, Eastern, Byzantine, Greek. Spaghetti and macaroni are served in many ways, most commonly *al sugo*, with meat sauce; *alle vongole*, with a clam sauce enlivened with tomato; or *al pomodoro* (with tomato), the most popular fashion, and one which admits of innumerable variants. A favorite type of tomato sauce is *pommarola*, in the local dialect *pummarola 'ngoppa*, which besides fresh tomatoes includes carrots, onions and celery. *Alla marinara* is with tomato sauce too, in which the tomatoes are almost raw, scalded rather than cooked. *Alla napoletana* uses little oval tomatoes, a mixture of butter and olive oil, in the proportion of three to two by volume, and basil.

Peculiarly Campanian and especially Neapolitan is mozzarella, buffalo milk cheese. The animal it comes from is a true buffalo, descended from the Indian water buffaloes imported into Italy about 600 A.D. When I first visited

XIII · *The Campania*

Naples, more than 40 years ago, great herds of buffaloes were encountered all along the Campanian coast. Now they seem to have retired inland, and there are not nearly as many of them, with the result that genuine mozzarella is becoming rare. To make it clear that they have the real thing, shops display signs reading *mozzarella di bufalo;* if it is the same type of cheese made from cow's milk, which has less flavor but is cheaper, they should call it *fior di latte* or *scamorza,* but they sometimes neglect to do so. Even genuine mozzarella, to tell the truth, has not a great deal of flavor eaten fresh by itself; to enliven its blandness it is often sprinkled thickly with black pepper.

When mozzarella is to be eaten fresh—connoisseurs say it should be eaten the day it is made—it goes off to the retail shops at once in an almost liquid state. You will see it in bowls in grocery windows, dome-shaped, swimming forlornly in a small puddle of its own buttermilk. It is highly perishable. Almost your only chance of eating it in this form is to be near the spot where it is made.

Mozzarella which is not to be eaten on the spot is molded by hand into various shapes—cubes, balls, eggs (*uova di bufalo*) or plaits (*trecce*), left in cold water for several hours to harden, and then wrapped in waxed paper and packaged for shipping. Even then it should be eaten fairly young, and as a matter of fact is now used chiefly for cooking. Mozzarella is sometimes given longer life (and added flavor) by smoking it. *Provola,* another Campanian buffalo cheese, is also often smoked, over burning straw, and is also eaten fresh. *Provolone,* made either from buffalo's or cow's milk, also comes either smoked or fresh, and is made in two varieties, the mild, which has a buttery flavor, and the strong, which is sharp and piquant. The difference is in the type of coagulant used—rennet from calves for the mild, and from kids for the strong. It should be eaten very fresh after ripening, which takes two or three months for the bland cheese and a little longer for the sharp one, when it is covered with a thin smooth shiny crust running from yellow to brownish, and has a creamy center, near-white to straw-yellow. It is attractively put up for sale in all sorts of shapes—pears, melons, cylinders, sausages (I have even seen *provolone* piglets)—which are molded by hand, after which the cheese is tied together with a network of fine cords or red tape. An interesting taste combination is provided by *burriello*, designed to give more interest to the near flavorlessness of *mozzarella*; a center of some more sharply flavored cheese is enveloped in a ball of mozzarella, so that when you bite into it, you get the mingled tastes of bland and sharp at the same time.

Though mozzarella does not seem to have much taste to the uninitiated, in cooking it has the gift of enhancing the flavor of other ingredients. One explanation for the excellence of real Neapolitan pizza is that it contains mozzarella, whereas pizza made with other types of cheese lacks a certain authority. The most widely known and most distinctively Neapolitan dish dominated by this cheese is *mozzarella in carrozza*, "buffalo cheese in a carriage." It is simple enough, in the same category of inexpensive rather coarse food as the unsophisticated types of pizza, simply a slice of mozzarella placed between two slices of bread, soaked in beaten egg, and fried in olive oil. Like pizza, it should be eaten as hot as your mouth will take it. Other mozzarella dishes are *mozzarella impanata* (breaded), *mozzarella ai ferri* (grilled), and *mozzarella e uova* (with egg). Mozzarella also goes into *sartù*, a complicated timbale of rice (a cereal not much eaten in Naples) in which memories of lavish Oriental feasting triumph over the present poverty of the South. The rice, first boiled, is then placed in the oven, in the same dish in which it is to be served, richly combined with diced mozzarella; *polpette*, little meat balls made of chopped veal, bread, and egg flavored with garlic, parsley, nutmeg and grated lemon peel; a tomato sauce that includes onions, bacon, garlic and basil; chicken livers cooked with onion, carrot, celery, bacon, garlic and bay leaf; and mushrooms.

The Campania does not eat much meat, and its beef in particular is not of high quality, yet one of the best known dishes of Naples is steak—*bistecca alla pizzaiola*. The main attraction is the *pizzaiola* sauce, of tomato, garlic and wild marjoram; the beef, generously drenched with olive oil, is stewed in a saucepan with the *pizzaiola*. Although *bistecca* or *costata* is always cited when this dish is mentioned, in practice you will often find veal substituted for beef, either a chop or an escalope; your chances of getting tender meat are better with veal than with beef.

The rarity of meat in the Neapolitan diet is compensated by a richness of fish. Even *fritto misto*, which in other parts of the country is usually composed of breaded deep-fried morsels of various types of meat as well as vegetables, in Naples turns out to be made of little pasta balls which contain not only liver, calf's brains, cauliflower, potato, and ricotta cheese, but also fish (a three-course meal in one dish), and there is in addition the *fritto di pesce*, which is all fish—bits of sole, hake, red mullet, squid, shrimps, etc. Neapolitans go in heavily for mussels (*cozze*) and clams (*vongole*), and also for members of the squid-cuttlefish family. *Polpi alla Luciana* is octopus cooked lengthily, to make it tender, in a sauce of oil, parsley and hot red peppers; some cooks use tomatoes instead of peppers, and I have heard of ginger being added, but this sounds a little out of tune for Campanian cooking; it would be more normal farther south. All of the common Mediterranean fish are available in Naples, which seems to know no other way of cooking them than frying, exception made for soups. The classic Neapolitan fish chowder is *zuppa alla marinara*, made with whatever fish are at hand, stewing them with tomato, garlic and parsley; the mixture is poured over slices of fried bread or toast on serving. *Zuppa di vongole* or *di cozze* treats clams or mussels the same way, but makes the result hotter by adding small red peppers.

Almost as ubiquitous as tomatoes in Neapolitan cooking are peppers, whether in other dishes or by themselves— *peperoni gratinati*, stuffed with tomato, spices, anchovy and mozzarella, rolled in bread crumbs and baked in the oven; *peperoni imbottiti*, stuffed with olives and capers, and baked similarly. Eggplant does not appear as often in Naples as it does farther south, but the city does offer *melanzane alla parmigiana*, for which the eggplant is cut into thin slices, which are seasoned with olive oil, herbs, mozzarella and tomato, dusted with grated Parmesan, and baked in the oven.

The tendency to extravagance which in Neapolitan cooking is often thwarted by poverty of means breaks forth when the desserts are reached—especially pastries. At this point the operatic spirit invades the kitchen. A Neapolitan lets himself go even when baking bread—he gives it a polished egg-white glaze and embellishes it with decorative patterns. Gratified by the opportunity to allow his fancy free rein with cakes and cookies, he invents fantastic shapes and brightly colored frostings. The variety is endless: *pastiera*, a crumbly cake with a filling of cottage cheese and candied fruit; *pastiera napoletana*, puff pastry made of barley or wheat flour, buttermilk, sugar, and candied fruit, which appears especially at Christmas; *sfogliatelle*, flaky pastry in a fan- or shell-shape, with cream, chocolate or jam, delicately flavored with lemon, orange, or rose; *rasprato*, sponge cake; *babà*, also of spongy consistency, the Neapolitan equivalent of the well known French *baba au rhum*; *crostata alla napoletana*, a chocolate cream pie with apricots; *pignolata* (also called *strufoli*, "wads of cotton," because of their shape), little balls of pastry with grated lemon and orange peel, dipped in honey; *zeppole alla napoletana*, brandy-flavored fritters; *bignè di San Giuseppe*, also fritters, eaten on St. Joseph's Day; and the crisp *croccanti*. *Sanguinaccio* is a creamy chocolate-vanilla flavored dessert whose name comes from an ingredient which may sound forbidding to Anglo-Saxons, cooked pig's blood, probably unavailable in American supermarkets, but on sale in Neapolitan butcher shops.

Is it necessary to call attention to the frozen desserts? All around the world people ask for Neapolitan ice cream. *Spumone*, misspelled spumoni in the United States, has gotten around too; but such local varieties as *stracchini* and *mattonelle* are found only on the spot. The quality of Neapolitan ice cream results from the subtlety with which its ingredients are mixed. Elsewhere it might be considered sufficient to use strawberries to flavor strawberry ice cream; but *gelato di fragole alla napoletana* contradictorily but successfully adds tartness to the crushed strawberries with lemon juice and balminess with vanilla; only then are they considered worthy to go into the cream.

These are the highlights of the Neapolitan menu, but there is much else. In the antipasto category, you have the local sausages, especially *salame napoletano*, which combines equal amounts of beef and pork, highly spiced with both black and red pepper, and the smoked sausages of Secondigliano. A conspicuous exception to the rule that most Neapolitan soups are of fish is *minestra maritata*, rich with *pezzentelle* (pork sausage), a winter dish. Perhaps you should be cautious about ordering *zuppa napoletana*, whose chief ingredients are chopped portions of the pig you have very probably never eaten before, except the heart, the others being the lungs, the esophagus and the windpipe; there is also strained tomato, bread, chopped onion, hot red peppers, a bay leaf and *nzugna* (dialect for cooked butter). Leftover spaghetti is used up by being worked into an omelet. In the fish category, the Neapolitan way with fresh sardines is to fry them with parsley and marjoram in olive oil, along with tomatoes. An appreciated shellfish is *scungilli*, dialect for *conchiglie*, conch, which is boiled and served with a highly spiced sauce. *Capozzella*, Neapolitan for "little head," is roasted lamb's head, while lamb's brains are sautéed in oil with capers and black olives, sprinkled with bread crumbs, and finished in the oven in a baking dish. Pork chops are *alla napoletana* when cooked with peppers, mushrooms and tomato paste. *Insalata di rinforzo alla napoletana* does not involve lettuce, but cauliflower, with anchovy fillets, capers and black olives, moistened with the standard oil-vinegar salad dressing; it is traditionally eaten in Naples for Christmas dinner, often with slices of eel left over from Christmas Eve, a traditional holiday dish too.

Campanian cooking is very nearly synonymous with Neapolitan cooking, but a few localities have special dishes of their own, or at least special products—Castellammare is proud of its sleek black olives, Sorrento of its oranges and lemons (it is also noted for the quality of its fish), Anacapri of its round purple figs.

Capri has a number of specialties of its own, some of which may be suspected of being artificial productions encouraged by the presence of the international tourist set rather than of pure native inspiration. One such is ravioli stuffed with cheese, which is not the Campanian type of pasta, while another is *riso al curry con gamberi*, curried rice and crayfish. Crayfish are a specialty of the island, but curry certainly is not, and as we have already remarked, rice is infrequently eaten in the Campania. Other dishes of the island seem more authentic: *quaglie con piselli*, quail with peas; *crespolini al formaggio*, thin pancakes rolled around cheese, of which the island has its own variety, *caciotto*, made from goat's milk; the Capri *calzoni*, whose filling is of tomato, cheese and ham; and *zuppa de pesce caprese*, a chowder of squid, mussels in their shells, the large prawns here called *massancolle*, *tonnetto*, a sort of cross between tuna and mackerel, tomatoes, white wine and olive oil. Small as the island is, the settlement of Anacapri manages to have a separate dish all its own, *totani all'anacaprese*. The *totani* (small inkfish) are cut up into rings, boiled briefly in vinegar, and then preserved in olive oil flavored with wild marjoram. This is a Christmas Eve dish in Anacapri. Also popular on the island is *spaghetti ai totani*, which combines these fish of the squid family with a very Campanian form of pasta.

The other principal island of the Bay of Naples, Ischia, makes less of a pretense of originality, except for the abundance of its fish dishes and its wines. One dish, however, is known by the name of the island, *alici all'ischiana*, which is fresh anchovies, moistened with olive oil and lemon juice, sprinkled with wild marjoram, and baked in the oven.

"Does the marvelous strength of soul of the Campanian people, which permits them to support all the adversities of life with a song on the lips, come perhaps from the wines, superb and generous, fiery and ardent, of this volcanic soil?" a local writer asks, with true Neapolitan enthusiasm. "It is from this region that the most celebrated wines of ancient Italy spread throughout the Roman world. It will suffice to remember Falerno, which was judged superior even to the famous Cecubo. Pliny gives Falerno the first place in his scale of great wines; Horace describes it as robust, ardent and generous; Martial has said that it is immortal."

Yes, but was the Falerno Pliny, Horace and Martial were talking about the wine still grown on the coastal plain of the Campania north of Naples, or was it the Falerno of Lazio, which also still exists? The Campanian Falerno is a dry white, made from its own special grape, the *falanghina*, variable in alcoholic content from 11 to 14 degrees, straw-yellow with golden-amber highlights. It is unassertive when young, but develops a more pronounced though still delicate flavor as it ages, which makes it a fine accompaniment for dry-fleshed fish. Though the white is ordinarily thought of when Falerno is mentioned, there is actually more red Falerno. It is a dark ruby-red, heavy, from 13 to as much as 16 degrees, dry, but with a flowery bouquet and a fruity taste; but it is often tart because of its high tannin content. It goes well with game, roasts and even poultry when well aged, but it is not often allowed to age as long as it should (it is a slow ripener) and would profit by more attention. The easygoing character of southerners does not encourage the sort of meticulous painstaking care given to wine in Tuscany, Veneto or Piedmont, which may be one of the reasons why the passage quoted above strikes me as a little too exuberant. I have drunk some extremely agreeable wines in the Campania, but I do not recall a great one.

There is no very accurate information on the antiquity of the grapes of the Campania, though some of their names hint at an origin going back to Greek times. There are several varieties of a grape called *greco*—the famous Lacrima Christi is made from *greco del Vesuvio;* an Avellino grape is called *greco di tufo* (*tufo* means volcanic rock), but it was probably so called from the village of the same name; some Benevento wines come from *greco bianco;* and the local grape known as *aglianico* flouts a modernized spelling of *ellenico,* Helenic.

I must confess here to a dereliction of duty. I am unable to offer you a reliable first-hand report on the most widely known wine of the Neapolitan area, Lacrima Christi, Tear of Christ, because when I first visited Naples, more than 40 years ago, I naturally tried it on the spot, and was bitterly disappointed. It was thin and tart, and I have never ordered it since, partly, I suppose, because I put it down automatically on the lengthy list of wines which have achieved popularity solely because they have pretty names. The Lacrima Christi name comes from a legend that Lucifer, caught in the act of stealing a piece of paradise, was cast out from heaven and fell, with his rebellious angels, in the Bay of Naples. The stolen bit of paradise is the island of Capri; and the fallen angels converted the Neapolitan area into such a realm of wickedness that Christ dropped a tear on Vesuvius, watering the vines on its slopes. I suspect now that what was served me under the name of Lacrima Christi may have been ordinary Vesuvio, which by general agreement is a wine one could do without, for there is much mislabeling in this area, and I imagine the practice was even more cheerfully uninhibited in earlier days. I can therefore only pass on at second hand the general opinion of experts acquainted with it—Giovanni Dalmasso, president of the wine academy of Siena, seems to sum it up well enough as "a fine dry white wine distinguished by its golden-yellow robe, its subtle perfumed bouquet, a velvety savor, and a moderate alcoholic content" (12 to 13 degrees), while Cyril Ray, in the André Simon *Wines of the World*, describes it as dry, delicate, with a hint of sweetness, like a German wine, or a dry white Bordeaux, but with a flowery fragrance peculiar to itself, and hard to define—of elder flowers and broom, suggests Bruno Bruni. It is a good wine to drink in the excellent fish restaurants of Naples, but it is rather headier than it seems.

The average Neapolitan would as a rule choose neither Falerno nor Lacrima Christi, prestigious though their names may be, but Gragnano. This is the wine Neapolitans have taken to their bosoms. In their Punch and Judy shows, Punch never asks for wine; he calls for Gragnano. It is grown on the Sorrento peninsula, particularly around Castellammare di Stabia, and its popularity seems to be a local phenomenon, like the fondness of the Bolognese for Lambrusco. Outsiders are apt to find Gragnano a trifle sweet (there is a drier variety, however), its dark mulberry color a little dispiriting, and the slight purplish foam it produces rather unappetizing. Yet it has a distinctive interesting nutty taste, with a faded violet perfume, and it isn't a bad accompaniment for the coarser Neapolitan snacks, like pizza or *mozzarella in carrozza*.

The non-average Neapolitan, the connoisseur looking for a better than average bottle, would not be likely to order Falerno or Lacrima Christi either. He would be more likely to pick Capri, which produces a first-rate white wine, clear and fragrant, refreshing and dry, pale straw-yellow, 11 to 13 degrees, which marries wonderfully with the island's shellfish. You will probably never get a chance to taste it except on the island itself. Capri does not produce enough wine to meet the local demand, and you may even drink wine on Capri labeled Capri which actually comes from the mainland; some Sorrento peninsula wines are allowed to carry that label. There is also a little red Capri wine, not as well thought of as the white, with a slight violet taste and a well-balanced flavor.

The other important Bay of Naples island, Ischia, produces creditable wine too, a light, slightly sharp, but refreshing white, of which a superior variety is called Biancolella d'Ischia. Epomeo, named for the island's extinct volcano, has a faint hint of iodine, the taste of the sea.

There are a host of other wines in the Campania, but these are the ones you are most likely to want to remember. A few other names to keep in mind, in case you find yourself on the spot where these wines are produced, are these: north of Naples, around Aversa, the very light (7 to 8 degrees) white *frizzante* but acid Asprinio dell' Aversano, kept in caves out of the summer heat, and served refreshingly cool, a drink appreciated by Pope Paul III in the 16th century. In the Benevento region, the reds, whites and rosés of Solopaca. Around Avellino, Taurasi, which can be an excellent vigorous red, but is another example of Southern *laissez-faire*—a little more care, especially in allowing it to age sufficiently before putting it on the market, would do it no harm; Greco di Tufo, dry and semi-dry whites, sometimes *frizzante*, named for the grape from which they are made; and Fiano, a light white which comes in dry, still, sparkling and sweet dessert versions, also named for its grape, Fiano being a distortion of its Latin name, *vitis apiana*, given to it because it attracts bees. The Sorrento peninsula offers a number of recommendable wines—besides Gragnano, the Neapolitan favorite, Ravello, which comes in red, white or rosé, the last being a little sweetish; the red Conca, rather harsh but not bad with pasta; Tramonti, from the hills back of Amalfi; and, also from the Amalfi region, the flamboyantly named Furore Divino Costiero, which exists in both white and red varieties. Finally, the province of Salerno offers Corbara, Monte Julio, and Cilento, which, when properly aged, are exported to South America, where they are popular.

The South is not *grappa* country; the Southern climate and strong drinks do not mix; but Benevento has a reputation for liqueurs to round off your meal. One of them you certainly know—the renowned sweet Strega. Benevento must have a sweet tooth. Its other specialty is *torrone* —nougat.

Abruzzi e Molise

Whatever the region of Abruzzi e Molise has retained of the spirit of Greek Italy was gained by osmosis. It does not appear that the Greeks themselves ever penetrated this difficult country. True, it has a 100-mile stretch of coast on the Adriatic. But it is 100 miles without a single good harbor, and even if landings had been made there, only mountain goats would have enjoyed penetrating the interior. The coastal strip is so narrow that even today only one important city of the region is established on it, Pescara; there are others which offer magnificent views of the sea, but from the heights which rise swiftly from the coast to the highest mountains of peninsular Italy. These mountains blocked inland progress by Greeks from

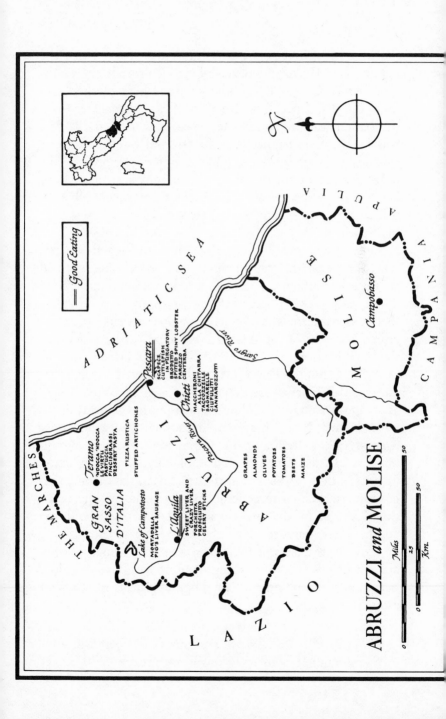

= Good Eating

THE MARCHES

GRAN
SASSO
D'ITALIA

Lake of Campotosto

Teramo
'NDOCCA 'NDOCCA
LE VIRTÙ
PANPUGLIA
PANCISENT PASTA

PIZZA RUSTICA
STUFFED ARTICHOKES

L'Aquila
SWEET LIVER AND
CRAZY LIVER
PROSCIUTTO
CELERY STICKS

MORTADELLA
PIG'S LIVER SAUSAGE

A   B   R   U   Z   Z   I

ADRIATIC SEA

Pescara
SCAPECE
CUTTLEFISH
IN PURGATORY
BRODETTO
SPITTED SPINY LOBSTER

Chieti
MACCHERONI
ALLA CHITARRA
TACOZZELLE
SAGNARELLE
CIUFULITI
CANNAROZZETTI

PAROZZO
CENTERBA

Pescara River

GRAPES
ALMONDS
OLIVES
POTATOES
TOMATOES
BEETS
MAIZE

M   O   L   I   S   E

Sangro River

Campobasso

APULIA

CAMPANIA

LAZIO

ABRUZZI and MOLISE

Miles
0   25   50

Km.
0   50

the west coast, but at the same time they assured that the region would remain politically and culturally in southern, that is, Greek, Italy. The presence here of the Gran Sasso d'Italia, "the Great Rock of Italy," 9,560 feet high, the culminating point of the Apennines, caused the Via Salaria, the frontier between North and South, to curve around it. Abruzzi by latitude ought to belong to the northern half of the country, but the physical obstacle of heights unrivaled except in the Alps has erected here a wall against the North and thrown Abruzzi e Molise into the South.

Some observers see traces of a Greek passage at Scanno, where the women wrap themselves in black robes ascribed to Oriental influence; but to *which* Oriental influence? The costume could be Greek, but it seems more probable that it is Saracen, and the steep vaulted streets recall the covered soukhs of the Arabic Near East. Apart from this, the basic heritage of the country is neither Greek nor Roman, but Samnite. These early settlers, related to the more cultivated Sabines, were described in ancient Roman times as savage mountaineer looters, and they gave the Romans a tough time. It was they who ambushed the Legions in a narrow gulley leading from Campania into their mountains in 328 B.C. and inflicted upon them the humiliation of the Caudine Forks; not until the year 290 did Rome succeed in establishing some semblance of authority there. To this day, the inhabitants are described as rough and uncouth. They stage some of the most spectacular festivals of Italy for the days of their favorite saints, mingling their ancient beliefs in evil-working demons with Catholic doctrine, and their observance of religious rites is spiced with a touch of sorcery.

Abruzzi consists of four provinces; Molise has only one. The capital of the region is L'Aquila, farthest from the sea of the four provincial capitals. History says it was founded in 1240 under Emperor Frederick II, but this is too prosaic for the inhabitants, who claim that it appeared miraculously, complete with 99 quarters (*rioni*), containing 99 châteaux, 99 squares, 99 churches and 99 fountains. However this may be, L'Aquila remains obsessed by the number 99. The city fountain spouts 99 jets and going to bed early is discouraged by the clock on the old tower of the Palace of Justice, which chooses 2 a.m. as the appropriate hour to strike 99 times. The fountain dates from 1272, the city walls from 1316, and the massive citadel from 1535, when it was built by Don Pedro of Toledo, whose body lies in the church of San Bernardino of Siena, as does that of the saint himself.

This is high mountain country; the tallest peaks are snow-covered most of the year. It is normal that ancient traditions should have been best preserved in mountain fastnesses; Scanno is in this province, near the Abruzzi National Park, where chamois and bears abound in undisturbed liberty—both the ordinary brown bear and a species called locally the horse-bear, because of the speed with which it runs. In the area around Scanno and Sulmona, herds of gray cows and black sheep graze on the high plateaux. Their milk is converted into *latticini*, milk products, chiefly cheese, by the shepherds and herdsmen themselves; the most common is *scamorza*, a pressed white cheese molded into an egg or pear shape, for which the town of Rivisondoli is the principal market. Sulmona and L'Aquila are marketing centers also, for the grapes, olives and almonds grown in the valleys nestled between their high mountains, while Avezzano serves the same purpose for the fertile region once covered by the drained Lake Fucino, where potatoes, tomatoes, maize and sugar beets are now grown.

The other three provinces all have their quota of narrow

coast. North to south, they are Teramo, Pescara and Chieti. The city of Teramo lies far inland. Its mountains are clothed with forests where large herds of swine roam, feeding on acorns and other taste-creating forage, which accounts for the fame of Abruzzi ham and sausage. Pescara, on the site of the ancient Aternum, is the region's one coastal city of any size, and marks the fact by a regatta on St. Andrew's Day, a fisherman's fete. It is the birthplace of d'Annunzio, whose house is still there. Chieti, capital of the last province, again is set back from the sea, on the summit of a hill carpeted with olive groves, surrounded by gardens filled with acacias, cedars and Judas trees. It was the Theatre Marrucinorum of the Romans. Today its fame rests on the quality of its macaroni and spaghetti, which depends on the pure water of the mountain springs used in their manufacture. The principal pasta factory here, that of Fara San Martino, is nearly a century old, having been founded in 1887. At the foot of the mountains, so that it can receive its water directly, it is fussy also about the quality of its flour, which it assures by buying durum wheat from Basilicata, to the south, and grinding it itself.

Not many foreigners get to Molise (whose capital is Campobasso) unless they are shopping for church bells, which are made at Agnone, or studying Oscan, which they can do at Sepino. Sepino is described by the local tourist bureau as an "almost intact" Roman city (it is the ancient Saepinum), which underestimates its interest for archeologists. Roman remains abound in Italy, but Sepino was an ancient Samnite city, where a considerable proportion of all the known Oscan inscriptions were found.

There are two main cuisines in Abruzzi e Molise, that of the coast, dominated, naturally, by fish, and that of the interior, dominated by pig, though lamb, veal from the high pastures, and poultry are also important. A detail is the fondness of the Abruzzi for cheese, which is eaten for its own sake, and also used frequently in cooking. Just as Emilia-Romagna sprinkles grated cheese on any dish which can take it, Abruzzi incorporates cheese into its cooking whenever it can.

Another detail is a fondness for strong flavoring. The Abruzzi like to lace their soups with hot red pepper. They make liberal use of the sharp mountain herbs, like wild thyme, or poppy seeds. This is the only region in Italy where saffron grows, on the high plateau of Navelli.

The coastal cuisine is relatively uniform, but that of the interior is compartmented and localized, as a result of the regional geography, which divides the population into small groups, each shut up in one of the boxed-in areas of the honeycomb terrain. Every town, however small, has its own specialties—the pork products of Campotosto, the polenta of Pettorano sul Gizio, the turkey of Canzano, the roast suckling pig of Campli, the *stracci* of Sella di Corno, the chick peas of Navelli, the lentils of Santo Stefano di Sessanio, the white beans of Capestrano, the pancakes of Teramo. Teramo and L'Aquila enjoy the longest lists of special local dishes, and it is probably no coincidence that these are also the two provincial capitals set most deeply into the mountains.

L'Aquila has a tradition which should appeal to all trenchermen—the *panarda*. This is a banquet of many courses whose characteristic is that it so presented that each time you think you have reached the end of the meal, it starts all over again. It is given when an emigrant returns to his birthplace; when a young man is called to military service, or when he returns; at pig-sticking time; when somebody wins a prize, a promotion or an election; when there is a religious festival, a national holiday or a country fair; when a program of public works is begun or finished; when there are bachelor dinners or business conventions, gatherings of students or family get-togethers, reunions of friends or birthdays, baptisms or weddings—in short, whenever anyone can find an excuse for giving a party.

A *panarda* is not really a *panarda* unless there are at least 30 courses, and they have been known to run to 60. Here is what was served at one given in 1962, described as comprising 35 courses; a good counter could undoubtedly make it more. It began with a prelude which apparently didn't count. Too meager, no doubt; it included only three fish dishes; mountain ham, country bread and mountain butter; double consommé; and boiled meats. Having thus worked up an appetite, the guests were ready for the official first serving, which included: mortadella from Campotosto, guitar macaroni, fritters in celery sauce, grilled trout, roast kid, potato omelet, and artichokes fried with *scamorza* cheese. A slight pause to take breath, and the second serving began: sausages, cardoon soup, veal rolls with beans, eel country style and grilled mutton with salad rich in mountain herbs, to refresh the taste buds and ready them for the third service. This consisted of baked artichoke hearts, broccoli in sauce, galantine of chicken in jelly, pickles and artichokes in olive oil, deep-fried brains and utility meats, veal with tuna sauce and capers, chicken hunter's style, and lamb chops. By now things were slowing down, so the fourth serving was one of lightness and whimsy: sweet-and-crazy pig's liver, kidneys, rock partridge with ham, veal scaloppine with truffles, and peas with ham. The final flourish was composed of toasted *scamorza* cheese, pecorino cheese from Pizzoli, dry and fresh fruits, cake, cookies and *noci attorrate* (call them Jordan almonds, if you like). The meal was washed down with local wines and liqueurs.

This list includes a great many characteristic Abruzzi dishes, but omits what is perhaps the most striking of all. It is true that the *panarda* described above was served in

L'Aquila and the missing dish is primarily a specialty of Teramo. It bears the strange name of *le virtù* (the virtues) which is obscurely explained by the allegation that an offer of this dish will make a suitor more welcome to a lady than if he sang her a serenade. The theory might also be advanced that after getting through a good helping of it, the eater would be too well stuffed to go in even for serenading, let alone any more energetic attempt on his Dulcinella's virtue. An alternative explanation might be that only a woman of great virtues would be willing to launch herself into the preparation of a dish which requires at least six separate cooking operations, and the washing afterward of a formidable number of pots and pans. But the most probable reason for this name, I venture to hazard, is that the dish contains all "the virtues" of the gardens of its season.

Le virtù appears in the month of May, since that is the season when the fresh young vegetables providing one of its series of ingredients become available. These must include fava beans and peas, but you can add any other spring vegetables that may be available; they are boiled along with dried beans, lentils and chick peas in pot number one. In pot number two, you boil together endives, leeks, young beet leaves, celery and fennel. In pot number three, you boil ham, cut into substantial chunks, and pig's crackling, ears and feet. In pot number four (which is a pan), you fry bacon with parsley, fresh onions and fresh garlic. In pot number five, you cook some factory-made pasta (macaroni, spaghetti or any other kind) and some homemade egg pasta. In pot number six (a saucepan), you fry meatballs.

You now have six pots and pans bubbling, steaming and sizzling on the stove, and things are about to get complicated. Take pot (pan) number four (bacon, etc.), pour its contents into pot number one, and add salt, marjoram and mint. Take the pig's feet out of pot number three, bone them, return them to its pot, and then add its contents to pot number one. After a decent interval, empty the greens from pot number two into pot number one, add tomato, and let everything stew together for a while in what is becoming a pretty crowded vessel. Now empty pot number five, whose pasta you have timed to be still a little undercooked at this juncture, into pot number one. You still have pot (pan) number six waiting with its meat balls. They go in last. And serve.

The most typical dish of the coastal cuisine is *scapece*, which the interior can enjoy too, since it is pickled fish, first fried and then preserved in the prized fine white vinegar of the region, flavored with saffron. It is the local claim that this dish goes back at least 200 years, but the presence of saffron raises the question of whether it is not very much older, drawing its inspiration from the Greeks, who must have touched this coast, since they penetrated much more deeply into the Adriatic. However, the local *brodetto* is flavored with tomato, onion, garlic, parsley and bay leaves, plus the local white vinegar, and not with the saffron which goes into this fish chowder in some other places where the Greek influence was direct. Perhaps Spanish influence accounts for the saffron in *scapece*, which could still make it older than 200 years, for the Spanish ruled this area in the 15th century. They may have planted the saffron of Navelli.

Polpi in purgatorio is an example of the high spicing of the Abruzzi; it is cuttlefish cooked in a rich sauce of oil, tomato, garlic and such quantities of pepper as to explain the reference to purgatory in its name. Not only mackerel, but also fresh herring, anchovies or sardines are cooked according to the formula for *sgombri con pan grattato*, mackerel with bread crumbs: the mackerel (three or four pounds for four or five people), are halved, boned, placed in an oven dish with three to four teaspoons of olive oil, a little chopped garlic, a few capers, two cups of water, two teaspoons of white vinegar (or good wine vinegar), a few drops of lemon juice, salt and pepper; this is started over low heat on top of the stove for a few minutes, then coated with bread crumbs and baked in the oven until the bread crumbs turn brown (about 20 minutes), taking care that the fish does not stick to the dish. This is a Teramo coastal recipe and so is *triglie ripiene*, boned red mullets stuffed with bread crumbs, rosemary, chopped garlic, salt and pepper, placed in olive oil already heated with chopped garlic, and cooked in the oven for 30 minutes at 250 degrees, basting from time to time. Pescara has a specialty of spiny lobster fillets cooked on a spit.

The interior is of course not devoid of fish either, especially trout. L'Aquila boasts of the savor of its *trota del vera*, which is tasty enough to carry seasonings which would drown the delicate flavor of ordinary trout, like *trote al pomodoro*, cooked in olive oil with tomatoes, garlic and parsley, or *trote del Sangro al forno* (from the river of that name), oven-baked with garlic, capers and parsley, moistened with olive oil and coated with bread crumbs. The tench of the small Lake Caporciano are delivered alive to the cook so that it can be purged by being made to swallow strong vinegar, producing a sort of sweat which rids the animal of the muddy taste which tench, carp and similar sluggish fresh-water fish often have. After being cleaned and dressed, it is breaded and fried in boiling oil; onions are cooked separately in oil with a leaf of sage and one clove of garlic, which is removed when the onions are browned; salt, pepper and strong wine vinegar are added, and the whole is boiled together over a low flame. This sauce is poured over the fish, which is allowed to stand in it until the next day, when it is eaten cold. This is *tinche carpionate*. Mountain territory is also quite as well placed as the coast to employ salt cod, so Teramo has its *stoccafisso alla Corropolese*, stewed slowly in olive oil with fresh tomatoes, onions, pimento, celery leaves, and parsley, and served with boiled young turnip greens on the side.

The importance in the inland cuisine of what Abruzzi calls "the 13-flavored pig" is exemplified by the fine sausage and other preserved pork products of the area, but there are also excellent fresh pork dishes, such as *porchetta*, roast suckling pig, probably borrowed from the adjacent Marches, and cooked in much the same fashion, with a trifle more emphasis on the herbs with which it is stuffed; or the thoroughly local *'ndocca 'ndocca*, a Teramo specialty. This is made at pig-sticking time, in December or January, when the feet, ears, snout, a few chops, and some of the pig's skin, cut up into small pieces, are boiled for three or four hours in water flavored with bay leaves, garlic, pimentos, rosemary, salt and pepper. Tomato is added at the last moment, and the meat is served hot in its own juice. A similar mixture bears the dialect name of *nnuije*. Pork chops are cooked accrding to an old Teramo recipe by browning them in oil, then cutting away the fat, and finishing the cooking in a mixture of two parts of wine to one of vinegar, salting and peppering only at the end.

Whether or not the saffron of *scapece* is a Spanish contribution to Abruzzi cooking, the ham of L'Aquila, *prosciutto aquilano*, certainly is. For the last 500 years it has been cured according to methods learned from the Spaniards, and not surprisingly recalls the *jamon serrano* (mountain ham) of Spain. Is there a Spanish touch also in the orange peel which, along with garlic, flavors the Abruzzi *salsicce di fegato*, pig's liver sausage? This is fried before serving, but not until it has dried thoroughly, which brings it into season in February, at least a month after the pig killing season. L'Aquila has two very special variations on pig's liver sausage, *fegati dolci* and *fegati pazzi*, sweet liver and crazy liver. The first is combined with honey, the second with the very hot *diavoletto* (devilish) pimentos, which leave a burning sensation on tongue and palate. Another L'Aquila sausage is *mortadella di Campotosto*, made from pigs raised near Lake Campotosto, at an altitude of 4,500 feet, reputed for their especially tasty pork. The sausage produced from their meat differs from the classic *mortadella* of Bologna in being drier, more highly spiced, and having a strong garlic flavor. Teramo uses sausage in one of its specialties which dates from medieval times. This is *pastuccia*, a bun impregnated with beaten egg cooked around slices of sausage, made nowadays of cornmeal, not available, of course, at the time of its creation, when other grains had to be used.

The humane ideas of modern times have banished one famous dish of L'Aquila—*capretto incaporchiato*, "trapped kid." At birth, the young goat was imprisoned in a sort of wicker basket attached under the belly of its mother, so that it could reach the udder but could not begin to graze. Nourished only by milk flavored at this season by the new grass and the first herbs and flowers of spring, unable to move and develop tough muscles, the flesh of the kid, killed after a few brief days of existence, was of an incomparable tenderness and delicacy. Suckling kid is still available, but the abandonment of this method of producing particularly succulent meat has made lamb, freed of the competition of *incaporchiato*, the second most important meat source of Abruzzi, in spite of the local saying, "The meat of sheep is the shame of the kitchen" (because there is such a high proportion of bones). Teramo favors *agnello con cottaceti*, which is chunks of lamb, from the leg or chops, cooked in a saucepan with olive oil, white wine, garlic and rosemary, to which, toward the end, chopped vegetables pickled in the region's white wine vinegar are added— carrots, cucumber, pimentos, cauliflower, celery, etc. A fine leg of lamb eaten anywhere in Italy may have come from Abruzzi, whose animals are renowned, but it is not necessarily cooked elsewhere in the local fashion, like *cosciotto d'agnello all'Abruzzese con fettuccine*. Garlic and rosemary are inserted in slits cut into the leg of lamb, which is then moistened with olive oil and put into an oiled saucepan. It is salted and peppered with freshly ground pepper. Several slices of fresh bacon from the breast are added. The leg of lamb is browned, then rinsed with half a glass of white wine, and two unpeeled cloves of garlic are put in. When the wine has boiled away over a high flame, tomato pulp, parsley and oregano are added, and the cooking finished over a medium flame, which takes about 20 minutes. It is served with *fettuccine* seasoned with the cooking juices. Typically Teramese, traditionally eaten for Easter, is *mazzarelle d'agnello*, a dish foreign to Anglo-Saxon eating habits, since it is made of lamb pluck, flavored with parsley, marjoram, onions and fresh garlic. wrapped in a leaf of chicory or Swiss chard, and cooked with bacon in oil and white wine. In the same category falls the *marro* or *marritti* of L'Aquila, a rustic dish for strong stomachs, made of lamb's intestines flavored with rosemary, garlic and bacon. Another holiday dish is *rosticini*, which you will see cooking along the roadside if you drive through L'Aquila on a holiday or during a fair, in a sort of iron trough across which are laid wooden spits threaded with cubes of mountain-raised lamb or mutton over a smoldering coal fire. When the animal gets too old for these dishes, it goes into stew—*ragù abruzzese*, mutton simmered *adagio adagio*, with bacon, onion, rosemary white wine and tomato, served with pasta doused with the cooking juices.

Veal is a poor third among Abruzzi meats. Penne, in the province of Pescara, cooks it in milk with sausages and kale. Veal rolls (*involtini*) are wrapped around a filling of mortadella sausage and of onion cooked in oil and vinegar in which sugar has been dissolved, the whole being finished in oil and wine. This is *involtini saporiti,* a dish of L'Aquila, which admits many variations, provided only that it is veal from a young calf which has grazed on mountain herbs and gives lean meat without fat.

Pollo con olive (chicken with olives) must be modern, at least as made at present, for it requires the presence of a refrigerator. The chicken, cut into pieces, is put into a bag with olives, chopped garlic, lemon peel, salt, pepper, sage, rosemary and a little nutmeg, and left in the refrigerator overnight. It is stewed slowly for 40 minutes, in olive oil for the first 10, plus white wine thereafter. The same dish is made using pimento cut into strips instead of olives. This is a Teramo dish, and so is *tacchino alla canzanese,* turkey in the style of Canzano, a small town of which this is a specialty. It is boned turkey (but you must keep the bones). You rub it with salt, pepper, rosemary, a bay leaf, sage and garlic, place it in an oven dish barely covered with water, into which you put also the bones (broken), two calves' or pigs' feet, two cloves of garlic, a bay leaf, rosemary, sage, carrots and salt. Cook for about two hours at 350 degrees, when the turkey should be golden brown and cooked through. Remove and allow to cool. Strain the liquid through a cloth and put it in the refrigerator to jell; the turkey is served cold, sliced, with the jellied broth.

All this may sound as though Abruzzi is a well-nourished country, but though its inhabitants like filling food, they do not eat dishes like these every day, and some of them rarely eat meat at all, except such as they raise themselves and can afford not to sell. Dishes like *mazzarelle* and *marro* probably owe their existence to the fact that they are made of parts of animals which the poor peasant breeder can keep for himself, yet still have a whole carcass to sell. Otherwise he is likely to live largely on vegetables and pasta;

Abruzzi is not as poor as much of the territory farther south, but it is not rich either, and the ordinary family diet is hardly luxurious.

Pasta is not always bought at a store; it is made at home too, and in the country almost everyone can manage to hold out a few eggs now and then from the family chickens. Hence there is egg, in a proportion equivalent to one per serving, in one of the most typical types of pasta of the region, *maccheroni alla chitarra*, guitar macaroni, whose well kneaded dough also contains a little olive oil. Abruzzi claims to have invented this, though it is widespread in the South. It takes its name from the "guitar" with whose aid it is made—a rectangular wooden frame with steel strings stretched across it, against which a sheet of dough is pressed and thus cut automatically into strips. A common way of serving it in the Abruzzi is with meat sauce and grated pecorino cheese, and it is sometimes promoted into a more substantial dish by adding an accompaniment of small meat balls or chicken giblets.

Meat balls also appear among the layers of the baked pasta dish called *pincisgrassi*, which, like *porchetta*, has slipped across the border from The Marches, undergoing a change in spelling in the process, for this is the *vincisgrassi* of that region. There are endless other varieties of pasta, almost all made of durum wheat and without egg, many of them with local names, some of them picturesque: *gnocchetti cacio e ova*, cheese and egg dumplings, which also contain bits of bacon, are called more familiarly *strangolapreti*, priest strangler, in Molise (and *strangolapriéviti* in Naples); *stracci*, irregularly shaped pieces of pasta, served with tomato sauce in which bits of mutton are sometimes included, go also by the popular name of *carte da giuoco*, playing cards, which may puzzle you if you think of their shape, but not if you watch them being cooked, since the pieces are thrown one by one into boiling water like a player dealing cards. Others are *taccozzelle*, rectangles of pasta eaten with cottage cheese and tomato sauce; *sagnarelle*, with wild asparagus; *nocchette* and *pizzichi*, which contain egg, and are sometimes called *farfalline*, little butterflies, from their shape; the short ribbed *cannarozzetti*, served with potatoes in tomato sauce; *sagnettine*, called *linguine* elsewhere, which is eaten with meat sauce; the cylindrical *ciufulitti* of Antrodoco; the *maccheroni con gamberi* (with crayfish) of Bussi, in the coastal cooking area of Pescara; and the *panzarotti* of Teramo, large ravioli with a stuffing borrowed from the recipe for *pizza rustica*. *Pizza rustica* is a sort of meat-and-cheese pie of considerable complexity. The dough is made with self-rising flour, beaten eggs, milk, a generous dosage of olive oil, grated Parmesan-type cheese, some sugar, a little cinnamon and a touch of nutmeg. The filling requires three kinds of cheese (mozzarella, soft pecorino and Emmental), chopped ham, sausages cut into small pieces or sausage meat, and the yolks of hard-boiled eggs. The upper crust, pierced with holes to let steam escape, is brushed with egg yolk and melted butter before the pie goes into a slow oven for 40 minutes. Less elaborate, but in the same peasant tradition, is the very old *pastuccia*, a sort of cornmeal scone (it must have been made from some other grain in medieval times), whose dough is enriched with egg yolks, studded with raisins and bits of bacon, rubbed with lard before being cooked between two burners, above and below, and eaten hot.

In earlier times, those who could not even afford these dishes filled up on *parozzo*, a sort of poor man's bread, made of cornmeal and boiling water. Today almost anyone can manage to eat pasta, so *parozzo* has become the name of a Pescara dessert, of mixed corn starch and wheat flour, eggs, crushed sweet almonds with a few bitter ones to enchance the flavor, butter, sugar, and chocolate frosting. Finally, to continue the roster of cereal dishes, it may be noted that while polenta is primarily a Northern dish, there is an Abruzzi tradition of *polenta sulla tavola*, polenta on the table. This is placed on the table, doused with a sauce containing morsels of hare (*polenta con la lepre*) and everyone attacks the common dish in a contest to see who can eat the most, thus flattering the hunter who provided the hare and the housewife who made the polenta.

The importance of vegetables in the Abruzzi diet has given rise to a great number of local dishes: *carciofi ripieni*, artichokes stuffed with hashed tuna, capers, garlic or parsley (meat when tuna is not available), coated with egg and bread crumbs and fried in plenty of olive oil; *piselli al guanciale*, the first tender peas of spring, cooked in olive oil with equally tender young onions and bits of bacon; *ceci di Navelli*, chick peas soaked overnight in salted water, boiled, and served on slices of bread fried in oil with a sauce of olive oil, rosemary, a little onion, and salt and pepper (this is *ceci scriti*, or chick peas alone; but when they are served with pasta and meat sauce, they constitute a New Year's Eve dish); also eaten on that night is *ceci e castagne*, for which the chick peas are again soaked overnight in salted water, or, a delicate refinement, in the same water with salt cod, which does not otherwise appear in the dish, and cooked with roasted chestnuts; *volarelle e fagioli bianchi di Capestrano*, the renowned cinnamon beans of this town, soaked for 12 hours, and served with *quadrucci* pasta (called *corarelle* as well as *volarelle* in Abruzzi) and tomato sauce (the best beans of this type are served cold with uncooked olive oil in Capestrano, also noted for the quality of its oil, and much pepper); *fagioli con le cotiche*, beans with pork crackling, tomato, celery, onion, parsley and olive oil, eaten in many towns January 17, the day of Sant' Antonio Abate; *lenticchie di Santo Stefano di Sessanto*, the excellent tiny lentils of the small town of this name, classically simmered with oil and unpeeled garlic in just enough water to cover them, though they are also cooked in many other fashions; *ghiotta*, strips of peppers and slices of potatoes, tomatoes, and zucchini baked together in the oven and eaten lukewarm or cold, the usual beginning of the evening meal in summer; and *patate sotto il coppo*, a specialty of the minute town of San Pio di Fontecchio, legendarily the birthplace of Pontius Pilate. This last can only be made in farmhouses where the fireplace burns night and day in winter, heating the hearth stone thoroughly. It is swept clean, spread with sliced potatoes, and covered with a heavy rectangular iron lid (the *coppo*), on which live coals are heaped. A tantalizing odor fills the air for half an hour before the potatoes are cooked, to be served with a salad dressing of oil and vinegar. Potatoes cooked in this fashion, the natives say, are light and easily digestible.

The most important cheeses in Abruzzi are made from the milk of the large herds that summer in mountain pastures, descending along the western slopes to Lazio or the southern ones to Apulia in the fall. The favorite cheese, both for eating alone and for cooking, is pecorino; the ricotta cheese is a secondary product for this region. The export of cheese has been a source of wealth for Abruzzi for centuries, but the pattern is changing. Large scale cheese making has been dropping off, but many small localities make their own distinctive types of cheese.

The *scamorza* of Rivisondoli is made from the milk of cows which graze on pastures nearly 4,000 feet up. It provides a very old Abruzzi dish, *scamorze allo spiedo*, for which small *scamorza* cheeses, well dried on the exterior, but soft inside, are threaded on spits and revolved over the embers of a wood fire; the cheese takes on an amber color, and the interior becomes creamy and tasty. *Fritto del così*, or *pane in carrozza*, is an Abruzzi version of the Neapolitan *mozzarella in carrozza*, and indeed *scamorza* is often called mozzarella in Abruzzi, though in the Campania it means a cheese made from buffalo milk; cow's milk is used in Abruzzi. (There is a buffalo milk cheese, however, made in Pescocostanzo, strong and highly spiced, here called *caciocavallo*, a name applied to quite different cheeses.) The Abruzzi *mozzarella in carrozza* consists of little pieces of bread, soaked in consommé, dipped in beaten egg, and spread with fresh cheese. Two pieces are placed together, cheese sides touching, and they are fried in olive oil. Fresh cows' milk cheese is also used for *calzonetti col pomodoro*, a cheese omelet with an onion-and-tomato sauce—a special case of what is here called *frittate maritate*, married omelets, which means one in which other foods have been added to the eggs—chopped sausage, bits of tuna, anchovies, or, instead of fresh cheese, little cubes of matured *scamorza*. A common dessert combination is a slice of sharp pecorino with a pear; they enhance each other's flavor.

Other popular Abruzzi dishes are *scrippelle 'mbusse*, thin pancakes flavored with parsley and nutmeg, wrapped around a grated pecorino filling, served in hot chicken consommé; the same pancakes are also sometimes stuffed with chopped ham, peas, and cubes of soft cheese in a white sauce, covered with meat-and-tomato sauce, and baked in the oven. *Timballo* is also based on pancakes, built up in layers with fillings between each two pancakes of previously fried tiny meat balls, small pieces of chicken, peas, mushrooms which have been pre-fried in butter, diced ham, bits of mozzarella cheese, chopped hard-boiled eggs, milk with beaten eggs in it, meat-and-tomato sauce, and nutmeg. Soups include *zuppa di cardi*, made from cardoons (edible thistles), which grow particularly large and white in the Abruzzi mountains; celery and potato soup; *cannarozzetti* and potato soup (*cannarozzetti* are short ribbed pasta, called more generally throughout Italy *ditalini* or *tubetti*); *zuppa reale*, royal soup, of flour, with egg yolks and whites beaten separately; and of course the local version of minestrone, which is rich and complicated. The exact ingredients are not fixed; they vary with the season. But they must include fresh vegetables; dried vegetables of the bean-pea group (haricot beans, broad beans, chick peas, lentils, split peas); aromatic vegetables (celery, chard, fennel, spinach, etc.); seasoning vegetables and herbs (onions, carrots, sweet marjoram, etc.); any sort of pasta which happens to be at hand; and some substantial additions like ham, pig's feet, or pig's ears. The green and aromatic vegetables are half-cooked separately. The feet and ears, if used, are scalded separately, and then go into the pot at the same time as the ham and dried vegetables; the feet are later fished out and boned, and feet and ears are cut into small pieces before being put back into the pot. The pasta is added last, beginning with the largest if several types are combined. The soup is sprinkled with grated cheese at the end. It is good either hot or cold.

For everyday purposes, dessert in Abruzzi e Molise is likely to be simple—often fruit, for instance in season the small tasty figs for which the Abruzzi is noted. But there are plenty of cookies, buns and little cakes, some of them attached to holidays and others specialties of different towns. One dessert which is both, not in the pastry category, is the nougat of L'Aquila, which claims, improbably, to be the homeland of this sweet (possibly introduced by the Spaniards) and which makes it, of honey, sugar, nuts and egg whites, particularly at Christmas time; if the old traditions are followed, two members of the family relay each other during the night before Christmas, stirring the mixture in its kettle throughout the night without a break. They may already have worked hard the previous day, making *cauciunitti* to give to friends Christmas Eve or Christmas Day, though the modern tendency is to buy them from a bakery, so you no longer find in every Abruzzi kitchen the enormous stone mortar once used to grind into a fine paste the almonds flavored with honey, cinnamon and lemon peel used to stuff a sort of ravioli made with flour, eggs, sweet white wine and much sugar, which are then deep fried in very hot oil and powdered with confectioner's sugar. This is primarily a dish of L'Aquila; Teramo has Christmas ravioli which is filled with a paste of chestnuts (or sometimes chick peas), grated chocolate, crushed almonds, tiny bits of citron, honey, cinnamon, sugar and plenty of rum. The Carnival period is marked by the appearance of *mignozzi*, little cognac-flavored fritters made from eggless dough nowadays usually sweetened with sugar, but in earlier times with honey; *mignozzoli di donna enrichetta* add eggs and wine to the dough. They should be eaten hot from the oil, before they harden. *Pizza di Pasqua*, Easter pizza, used to be made Easter Saturday, sprinkled with holy water by the parish priest, and eaten Sunday with hard-boiled eggs and salami; it is a sort of raised bun containing egg, with lard shortening, glazed with beaten egg yolks. *Zeppole di San Giuseppe* are cinnamon-flavored fritters eaten on St. Joseph's Day. Ascension sees *cacio ricotta*, again not a pastry dessert, but coffee-flavored junket made from sheep's milk in which a bit of citron peel, ultimately removed, has been boiled; this is a festive version of ordinary junket, an Abruzzi specialty there called *quagliata*, the local word for rennet (*caglio* in standard Italian).

Local dessert specialties include the sugared almonds of Sulmona, the snowy celery sticks of L'Aquila, and "seven-eyed pizza" (*pizza sette occhi*) from San Pio di Fontecchio, three narrow strips of sweetened crunchy pizza dough tressed together in a length which leaves seven holes between their intersections. Less localized are the biscuit-like sugared *taralli*; *bocconotti*, tarts containing a filling of jam, grated chocolate, grated lemon peel, chopped mixed candied peel, coffee, vanilla, rum, sugar and a little flour; *pepatelli*, honey-sweetened biscuits of whole wheat flour, with chopped almonds, grated orange peel and pepper; various confections made from dried figs; and soft chocolate nougat. Finally there is *crema della mia nonna* (my grandmother's cream), a cream of milk, egg yolks, sugar, caramel and bits of citron, a very ancient dessert, since it was in the 6th century (when it was sweetened with honey, not sugar) that Saint Fortunatus, Bishop of Poitiers, thanked Queen Radegunda of the Franks for sending him some.

The rocky slopes of the Abruzzi are not propitious to wine; the vintages tend to be bitter, sharp or acid. Grape production is not very important here, coming chiefly from the narrow coastal strip, and two-thirds of those grown are for the table. Of wine grapes, 40 percent go into reds, and 30 percent each into whites and rosés. You will not find them outside the region, since almost every other part of Italy can do better.

The three top names of an undistinguished list are Montepulciano d'Abruzzo, the best of the reds, with a bouquet suggesting the wild flowers of the region and a nutty flavor; the often sweetish Cerasuolo d'Abruzzo, made from the same grape (*Montepulciano d'Abruzzo* is a grape name), whose light cherry red color, almost pink, results from the special process used for the fermentation of the grapes; and the very dry white Trebbiano d'Abruzzo. For the first and third, the better bottles are those labeled Giulianova, identifying the wine as coming from the coastal area north of Pescara, which produces the best Abruzzi wines, such as they are. There is, however, one white from the inland province of L'Aquila which is drinkable enough, Peligno, from the little village of Pratola Peligna.

The aromatic mountain herbs of Abruzzi e Molise compensate to some extent for the weakness of the local wines by providing the basis for various digestives. Perhaps the best known is Centerbe, a specialty of Tocco Casauria, in the province of Pescara. The name means "a hundred herbs," which seems a lot. It comes in two types, *forte*, strong, and *dolce*, mild. Both have a high alcoholic content; it is the herbs which are relatively strong or mild. The first is brewed for its tonic, medicinal effect, and in fact, though it is served at the end of a meal like other liqueurs, its taste is strong and bitter, perilously close to that of medicine. The *dolce* is designed for easier drinking. One of the herbs it contains is wormwood, the base for absinthe, grown in the Abruzzi and, so far as I know, nowhere else in Italy. Aurum, also from Pescara, is an orange-flavored liqueur, amber in color. Nocino is made here much as it is in Modena. Rosolio di Anice is a liqueur flavored with anise seeds. Vino di Genziana is based on gentian root, but has as well a good dose of the absinthe-making wormwood, in a decoction of Marsala wine. Civitella Alfedena makes a liqueur from a strongly flavored mountain plant of tonic properties called *zeppino* locally and *genipì* in standard Italian, which we have already met in Aosta. Liquore di Cerasoli and Ratafia di Cerasoli are cherry brandies. Quinces are the basis for Liquore di Mele Cotogne, which also has rum, cinnamon and bitter almonds in it. Finally, to keep out the winter cold, there is *ponce*, which combines orange and lemon peel with caramelized sugar in alcohol.

Apulia

In Apulia there is no doubt about it: we are in Greek Italy. Greeks may have settled around the Bay of Naples a few years before they began establishing colonies in the foot of Italy, though this is not certain; but the Greek stamp in the far South remains more firmly marked than in Campania, perhaps because the former is farther from Rome, and was thus less exposed to obliteration of the Greek spirit by the Roman spirit. It was more resistant too. The Greeks of Naples accepted the profitable influx of wealthy pleasure-seeking Romans at Baiae, Pompeii and Herculaneum, but the Greeks of the far South supported Pyrrhus and Hannibal against the Romans. The Romans scattered a few amphitheatres around the foot, but other-

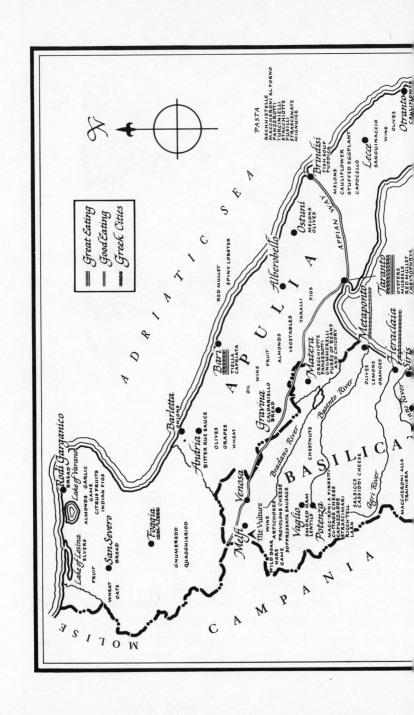

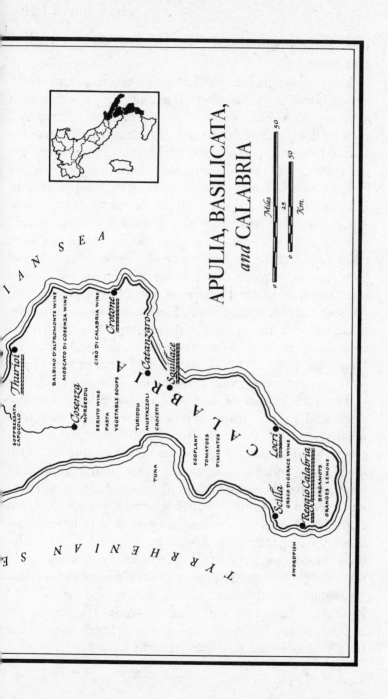

APULIA, BASILICATA,
and CALABRIA

Miles
0   25   50

Km.
0   50

IAN SEA

TYRRHENIAN SE

SOPPRESSATA
CAPOCOLLO

Thurioi

BALBINO D'ALTROMONTE WINE

MOSCATO DI COSENZA WINE

CIRÒ DI CALABRIA WINE

Crotone

Cosenza
MORSEDDU

SERUTO WINE

PASTA

VEGETABLE SOUPS

TURIDDU

MUSTAZZOLI

CROCETTE

Catanzaro

Squillace

C A L A B R I A

TUNA

EGGPLANT

TOMATOES

PIMIENTOS

Locri

Scilla

GRECO D'GERACE WINE

Reggio Calabria

BERGAMOTS

ORANGES LEMONS

SWORDFISH

wise their heritage is barely noticeable. That of Greece is visible everywhere.

Many of the great cities of Magna Graecia, a term which covers Greek-settled southern Italy, but not the Campanian area, are in Apulia. Taranto, settled first by Cretans and then by Parthenians driven out of Sparta, was the wealthiest and most important city of Magna Graecia after the destruction of the brilliant but short-lived colony of Sybaris, which lasted only two centuries, disappearing in 510 B.C. Gallipoli, the capital of Greek *brodetto*, is in Apulia too. Bari was under Greek influence from the 3rd century B.C., of which one evidence is the wealth of Greek coins found there. Otranto was of Greek origin. Monte Sant'Angelo, a place of Christian pilgrimage today, was once the spot where Podaleirius, son of Aesculapius, and the seer Calchas were adored. Foggia was founded by the inhabitants of the ancient city of Arpi, fleeing from a scourge of malaria. Arpi was legendarily established by Diomedes, King of Argos, one of the heroes of the Trojan War (or, according to another account, by his son).

The Greek basis of southern Italian culture was not eradicated by the many waves of foreign peoples who washed over this country after the Romans, perhaps precisely because they were so numerous—none of them lasted long enough to substitute their own customs and traditions for those the Greeks had been able to instill during a period of dominance which lasted for some six to ten centuries. The Greeks themselves probably found no civilization when they arrived sufficiently developed to offer them much competition. There remain from those early times only a few mysterious and unexplained constructions —menhirs and dolmens around Lecce, and the conical *trulli* of Alberobello, still lived in—relics respectively, it may be, of the Stone and Bronze Ages. Illyrians preceded the Greeks, but were no match for them culturally.

XV · *Apulia*

After the collapse of the Roman Empire, various regions of Apulia experienced successively, some briefly, some lengthily, the rule of Goths, Longobards, Saracens, Byzantines (renewing the Greek influence), Normans, Hohenstaufens, Angevins, Venetians, Spaniards, and, reaching all the way down from Milan, the Sforzas. Different cities were subjected to different sets of invading influences, for different periods, and absorbed them to different degrees. It is even truer here than in the North that every town belongs to a separate species, that each has its own peculiar individuality, shaped by its own unduplicated history. In Apulia, isolation has accentuated and maintained localism. Even peasants tilling the soil tend there to congregate into fairly large towns, leaving the spaces between them almost empty of villages, hamlets or farmhouses—in short, of an interurban population which if it had existed might have acted as a transmitter of customs from one locality to another and thus diminished the differences among them. As it is, each Apulian community lives in its own atmosphere, surrounded by a vacuum. The chief unifying element is the Greek background.

From the high plateaux of the Abruzzi, great trails, sometimes 350 feet wide, lead downward to the plains of Apulia. They were trodden by the vast herds of sheep which since ancient Roman times at least have sought winter pasturage on the plains of Apulia, once able to provide grazing for 1,000,000 head, but now for only half as many; crops have taken over some of the land once used for pasturage. If proof were needed that the Abruzzi, despite its latitude, belongs to the South, this umbilical cord with undisputedly Greek Apulia would provide it; and there is, defying ordinary anatomy, a second umbilical cord as well, the great Apulian aqueduct which brings to this parched country, across the region of Abruzzi e Molise, the waters of the Sele, an important river of Campania, thus linking the two Greek regions of peninsular Italy, the Bay of Naples and Magna Graecia.

Apulia, which takes its name from the Samnite tribe of the Apuli, is La Puglia in Italian, or sometimes Le Puglie, the plural because the present region includes parts of three different ancient political units. It is the richest of the three southernmost provinces, which is not saying much since the other two are poverty-stricken. It produces abundantly the three dominant crops of the Mediterranean, wheat (and other cereals), olive oil, and wine, plus grapes for the table, almonds, figs, melons (from Apricena, Brindisi and Ostuni), citrus fruits (the Gargano peninsula and the Ionian coast, especially in the neighborhood of Palagiano) and vegetables (Foggia and Taranto), including especially potatoes, eggplant, artichokes, celery, fennel, peppers, broad beans and asparagus. The soil is productive, less because of original fertility than by dint of much hard work over the centuries. Apulia produces more dessert grapes, wine, olives and olive oil, almonds, figs and tobacco than any other single region of Italy, despite certain special difficulties, natural and artificial. Among the first are the not infrequent invasions of army caterpillars, locusts and moles, and the circumstance that much of the region is swept by high winds from time to time and is often torrid in summer. Among the second is the strain on the economy constituted by the existence of large unexploited estates on a territory which cannot afford to leave any arable land uncultivated.

The region is amply supplied with seafood, as one might expect simply from glancing at the map. Long and narrow, it has the longest coast of any Italian region, 426 miles, for an area of only 7,470 square miles, less than that of the state of New Jersey, whose coastline is 130 miles long. Of its five regional capitals, three—Bari, Brindisi and Taranto

—are on the sea, and the other two not far from it. Apulia's five provinces, from northwest to southeast, are Foggia, Bari, Taranto, Brindisi and Lecce. The geography of Foggia is peculiar. Its most striking feature is the Gargano peninsula, the spur of the Italian boot, which is both a peninsula and a mountain. Mount Gargano is not part of the Apennines, but a separate formation, and between it and the Apennines lies a low fertile plain, the Tavoliere ("checkerboard"), with Foggia in its center. This is one of the rare examples in Italy of monoculture. Virtually all the arable soil is devoted to the production of grain, developed by dry farming because of the regional water shortage. Foggia is generally referred to as wheat country, a convenient generic term for grain in general, but it is also an especially large producer of barley. Cereal production here goes as far back as history. The area was largely responsible for the description of Apulia in the 14th century as "the granary of Venice," but this was already late in Foggia's grain-producing career. Its very name is believed to have been derived from a great underground silo, the *fovea*, constructed in ancient times as a temporary storage place for grain under the pavement that covered its central square.

Alfonso I of Aragon gave Foggia another specialty in 1445 when he made it the official market (and tax-control center) for the wool and mutton provided by the sheep wintered in the province or raised there. It was, of course, already an important grain market, and still is today, with many flour mills and pasta factories. The area also produces, outside the Tavoliere, small vegetables and fruit, plus the produce of the Gargano peninsula, which is a special case.

The Gargano includes arable land in its high valleys; meager pasturage on its plateaux, where sheep, goats, and black pigs are raised; a coastal plain on its southern shore planted with olives, in whose center lies Manfredonia, founded by Manfred (not far from Monte Sant'Angelo, which displays a Norman castle and a mysterious monument known as the Tomb of the Longobard Kings); the salt flats of Margherita di Savoia at its southern extremity, an important element in the provincial economy; and on the north coast, the large fish-filled lakes of Lesina and Varano. Off this coast line are the Tremiti Islands, famous for the quality of their lobster, and also for the extraordinary variety of fish found there, which makes the islands a happy hunting ground for underwater fish spearers, who can cope, in a not overcrowded area, with the royal and the common ray, the sea bass, the sea perch, the moray, the sar, the meagre, the dentex, the chrysophrys, the gray mullet, the red mullet, the hogfish, the sole, the cod-like *mormora*, the squid, the octopus, and many others. The most striking feature of the peninsula is Italy's Black Forest —the Bosco d'Umbra, a thick growth of beeches, pines and other trees, one of the richest game regions in Italy. It is also noted for its citrus fruits and its prickly pears, eaten all over the South, known in Italy as Indian figs—*fichi d'India*.

The richest province of Apulia is Bari, which spreads across a highly fertile plain. More than three-fifths of all the region's produce comes from here, leaving only one-tenth apiece for the other four provinces. Bari leads the region in its production of olive oil and wine, and also raises important quantities of almonds, fruit, vegetables, cereals and seeds. The table grapes—*baresana, refina, prunesta*, etc.— are renowned. Its figs are sold all over Italy fresh, stuffed or dried. Of the last, the best in Italy, perhaps the best anywhere, are the *fichi mandorlati*, which have been not quite cooked, but heated, and flavored with almonds, fennel seeds and bay leaves. Unlike other dried figs, they somehow remain moist and juicy. Many towns of the province have their own specialties. Barletta, on the northernmost coast of Bari, cheek by jowl with Foggia's salt-producing Margherita di Savoia, lives on salt and wine, and is also known for its outsize onions. Bitonto is a center for the production and marketing of cereals, fruit and one of the finest olive oils in Italy. *Scamorza* cheese comes from a town picturesquely named Joy of the Hill, Gioia del Colle, and mozzarella is made not only in the province of Bari, but in many other parts of Apulia.

The province's products give rise to important food industries. There are 40 flour mills and 50 pasta factories in the province of Bari; 1,000 small old-fashioned refineries for olive oil and 20 big modern ones; canneries for jam, vegetables and fish; and distilleries which convert the local wines into liqueurs.

The city of Bari, which presides over all this, does not regard its achievements with modesty. "If Paris had the sea, it would be a little Bari," they say. It is true that in comparison with Bari, Paris is a Johnny-come-lately. Its site has been inhabited since 1500 B.C.; the city is believed to have been founded by Illyrians from across the Adriatic. Possibly colonized by the Greeks or at least in close trading relations with them, Bari has been the chief city of Apulia since the 2nd century B.C.; whoever was ruling the area usually did so from Bari. Bari's Fiera del Levante was in the Middle Ages one of the seven great trade fairs of the kingdom, and to this day, when it takes place annually in September, it is one of the two great commercial fairs of Italy, the other being the fair of Milan. It was very probably at this time that the saying was born, "*La gente di Bari o vende o muore*"—"the people of Bari must sell or die." They did not die, though the city suffered a decline under the Spanish in the 15th century, which continued under the Sforzas until, in 1557, it reverted to the Kingdom of Naples. Today a prosperous city with half a million population, Bari still dominates southernmost Italy.

As you move southward in the province of Bari, you encounter the region of the *trulli*, among the most curious and mysterious manifestations of the regional civilization, which are particularly plentiful in and around Alberobello and extend across the provincial border to Selva di Fesano in the province of Brindisi. They are beehive-shaped houses, made by piling up mortarless stones in layers of ever-decreasing diameter, completed by conical roofs of flat slabs of slate; the summits are often decorated with crosses, statues or other finishing touches. This mode of construction allows for only one room, with attic, under each high dome, but larger habitations can be achieved by connecting a number of *trulli* together. Usually whitewashed, they can be seen gleaming in groups of two or three among the vines and orchards of the countryside, but in Alberobello (where the traditional local costume is still worn) something like a thousand of them are inhabited.

Brundisium, not Bari, was the favored city of the ancient Romans, who made it the terminus of the Appian Way, which did not pass through Bari. Of the two columns which marked the end of the Appian Way, one, a 65-foot pillar of marble with a capital embellished with figures, is still standing, but only the base of the other remains. The rest of it stands today in Lecce's Piazza Sant'Oronzo; the story is that Brindisi swapped it for a mess of *sanguinaccio*, a much prized Lecce sausage made of pig's brains and blood, boiled before serving. The truth is less picturesque. The column fell in a 16th-century earthquake, and for two centuries the citizens of Brindisi never got around to picking it up. When Lecce asked for it in 1735, Brindisi, tired of stumbling over it for 200 years, was happy to have it carted away for nothing—not even sausages.

Brindisi and its province were already well developed before the Romans got there. The Italian word *brindisi* means a toast, but the city was not named for this pleasant custom, though, since it is in wine country, it could be argued that toasts were called for the city. The name is believed to have come from the Messapic language spoken in Apulia from 1,000 B.C., when it was brought into the region by the Illyrians, and to mean "stag's head," describing the shape of the harbor.

The agricultural products of Brindisi which are the most noted are, for the capital city itself, cauliflower and *poponi*, the strongly perfumed melons of the region, which are eaten ice cold. These melons are also raised at Apricena and Ostuni, the latter also noted for the fine quality of the olives raised about its whitewashed houses, gleaming in the strong southern sun, which has given Ostuni the nickname of "the white queen of olives."

Olives were also the earliest source of the wealth of Taranto (in ancient times Tarentum), along with the priceless purple dye that was used among other things to color the togas of Roman Emperors. As it was derived from shellfish, it appears that Taranto from the very beginning of its history was already practicing what is still its specialty; and since the nearest known dye-works to Italy were in Athens, the presence of this industry there might provide an indication of the Greek origin of Taranto (the other producer of purple dye in Italy was Pompeii, also once Greek) even if we did not already know that Taranto was Greek. Following the Cretans, the first mainland Greeks arrived at the end of the 8th century B.C. Taranto enjoyed a period of splendor in its early days as the leading commercial center of Magna Graecia, and also of Greek civilization and culture; it retains a Doric temple from those days, an exceptional monument, for Greek remains are curiously rare in the foot of Italy. The city remained profoundly Greek even after it had become politically Roman. To this day its fishermen speak a dialect marked by traces of Greek.

The great specialty of Taranto, in ancient times and today, is the raising of oysters. The oyster beds of Lake Lucrino in Campania may have been the first big commercial venture of the kind, but it seems probable that oysters were already being bred less conspicuously at Taranto when Sergius Orata started his Campanian enterprise; some accounts say he began by seeding Lucrino with oysters obtained from the Apulian coast. Whichever was first, Taranto is last. It is still producing them today, by methods very much like those used in the days of ancient Rome, some 3,000,000 a year, which makes Taranto by far Italy's greatest supplier of oysters. It is ideally located for the purpose, lying as it does between the Mar Piccolo (Little Sea) and the Mar Grande (Great Sea). The former is a coastal lagoon fed both by fresh water and salt water flowing in from the sea through the two channels on either side of the center of Taranto which make it an island, thus providing the varying salinity which everywhere in the world produces the finest oysters. The Mar Grande is part of the salt-water Gulf of Taranto, a body of the Ionian Sea, sheltered by a curve of the coast, by islands and by breakwaters. This is one of the few places in the Mediterranean, excepting the Adriatic, where the tide is perceptible, serving to carry food to the oysters and to mingle the water of the outer and the inner seas.

The baby oysters are started in the Mar Piccolo, moved to the Mar Grande for fattening, and then taken back to the Mar Piccolo for finishing. This is usually done in spring and summer, and the growing oysters are placed in what are locally called *sciaie*. These are rectangular frames of horizontal wooden bars just above water level, supported by piles driven into the bed of the lagoon. Ropes of some vegetable material hang from these frames, and every fifteen feet or so under water spreading branches are attached to the ropes, on which the oysters cluster—which is the way the ancients raised them. It takes at least two more months for the oyster to reach eatable size, the whole process taking between 18 months and two years—longer than for northern oysters, for shellfish grow faster in cold water.

Taranto raises other mollusks too—sea urchins, various types of clams, and mussels of all sorts, especially the black *cozze*, which are packaged in kegs with a special sauce for shipment elsewhere. This is also a rich fishing center—83 species of edible fish are known in the Mar Piccolo alone. The province of Taranto also produces considerable quantities of dessert grapes, for which Martina Franca is the most important center in Apulia, particularly juicy figs, olives, vegetables and wheat.

Lecce, occupying the very end of the Italian heel, lying between the Ionian and Adriatic Seas, is three-quarters surrounded by water. The region has been inhabited since prehistoric times; it is here that dolmens and menhirs, locally called *pietrefitte*, are found. Strong Eastern influences are evident; Otranto, on the Adriatic coast, the ancient Greek-founded Hydrus, or Hydruntum, with its Byzantine mosaics, has been called the most Oriental city in Italy; Gallipoli, on the Ionian coast, whose very name shouts its Greek origin (it was Kallipolis, "beautiful city," to the Greeks, though Anxa for the Romans), also looks very Oriental today with its white buildings reflecting blindingly the brilliant sun. As for the capital, Lecce itself knew its most prosperous moments under the Normans and the Angevins, before becoming submerged in the Kingdom of Naples in 1463. Lying in the center of a fertile agricultural district, Lecce leads all the other provinces of Italy in the production of oil, and also in the production of tobacco, its most important crop. The province grows a great deal of wine, and the cauliflowers of Otranto and the potatoes of Salento enjoy a widespread reputation.

* * *

The patchwork history of the provinces and cities of Apulia, of which Bari, with its long succession of different masters and influences is a perfect example, has created a diversity of cuisines, despite the presence of identical raw materials throughout the area. This makes it difficult to make any statements about Apulian cooking in general which will be valid everywhere in the region. However, it is possible to describe it as resolutely peasant in spirit, especially in the interior, though the ubiquity of fish has produced some of the sophisticated refinements which this type of food seems to generate spontaneously. Secondly, one may note a particular tastiness of seasoning, but not of violent seasoning. The South is usually thought of as garlic country, but Apulia is cool toward garlic. "In this cuisine," writes Italian food expert Felice Cunsolo, "garlic does not play a leading, but only a secondary, role; it should not call attention to its odor or its presence. Precisely for this reason, many specialties are characterized by a pleasing sweet undercurrent which comes from onions, substituted totally or partly for garlic." Every rule has its exceptions, and this one is contradicted by a pasta dish of the Tavoliere area which reeks of chopped garlic and is fiery from its rich dosage of hot little red pimentos. It is food for strong men, which explains its name, *spaghetti alla zappatora*, ditchdiggers' spaghetti. Do not let the first mouthful frighten you off. After half a dozen swallows, you get your breath back, and lips, palate and throat are sufficiently numbed so that you can pierce beneath the surface heat and appreciate a basic rich tastiness. One of the advantages of this dish is that it can be made very quickly, a characteristic of foods invented by famished peoples.

Since this is country of a very old civilization, it is normal that many of its most characteristic dishes should be very old too. The dean of them all is probably not the

3,000-year-old fish soup of Gallipoli, made today as the ancient Greeks made it, but *caldariello*, a specialty of the town of Gravina, which is said to go back three or four thousand years. It should be pre-Mosaic if it is true that this is the very dish condemned in Exodus 23:19, "Thou shalt not seethe a kid in his mother's milk," the basis for the kosher prohibition against eating milk and meat at the same meal. *Caldariello* is lamb (or kid) cut into pieces and cooked in a specially shaped fat-bellied cauldron (hence the name of the dish, from *caldaro*, cauldron), along with olive oil, onion, parsley, wild fennel and sheep's or goat's milk.

It may well be that the second oldest dish of the region is the *zuppa di pesce alla gallipolina*, a fish chowder containing hogfish, *cernia* (a white-fleshed fish which seems to be a sort of sea bass), sar, cuttlefish and giant prawns, flavored with onions, herbs and pungent spices. (Crustaceans often go into *brodetto* in Apulia, though less often farther north.) The Taranto idea of *zuppa di pesce* is very different from that of Gallipoli; it involves different kinds of fish, mussels and oysters, stewed together very slowly. Brindisi comes closer to the Gallipoli chowder, though it replaces the onions with garlic, uses eel, chrysophrys and dentex instead of hogfish and sar, and adds much tomato and parsley. Brindisi may be trying to vie with Gallipoli for antiquity with its *zuppa alla greca* (this could, of course, refer to modern Greeks), which uses only the red hogfish along with celery, potatoes, onion and grated cheese.

Another very ancient dish is eel cooked only by the heat of the sun. The newly hatched tiny blind eels of the Lake of Lesina are placed in a wide shallow pan of sea water and left in the sun until all the water has evaporated. The eels are then ready to eat, with a touch of vinegar.

Common everywhere in southern Italy is *capriata*, a

dish of Magna Graecia. This is simply dried beans, first boiled, then mashed into a purée with olive oil, and served accompanied by some form of greens—endive, for instance —to provide a contrast in tastes. Sometimes pimentos fried with onion and tomato are substituted for the greens.

Today the greater part of the diet of the Apulian workingman is composed of doughy dishes. Between 1.75 and 2.2 pounds of flour are consumed per person per day, varying with the locality. Despite the multiplicity of varieties of pasta, characteristic of the South, much of this flour is eaten in the competing form of bread. Bread is still in Apulia the veritable staff of life; bread, oil and wine are the three pillars of the Apulian diet. Bread is made in large round loaves at home (and in small bakeries) not with purchased yeast, which the really conscientious Apulian housewife regards with suspicion, but with each household's, or each bakery's, home-produced leaven, handed down from generation to generation—for thousands of years, some families claim. The bread made from it is said to preserve the unmatchable taste of the ancient product, which is difficult to prove, since no one alive has ever tasted the bread of 2,000 years ago, but in any case, it is highly superior to what is bought from the large industrialized bread makers. Sadly, as everywhere else in the world, the homemade loaf is losing out to the commercial product, whose availability does take a load off the housewife, in Apulia for an additional particular reason—the nature of homemade yeast. It is slow to rise and requires considerable kneading, which means, if fresh bread is to be available for breakfast, night work. Yet the traditional bread of Apulia is still to be found in small villages, and also in some larger places, especially in the two provinces which are the biggest wheat producers—San Severo, Rodi Garganico and San Marco in Lamis in Foggia; Sannicandro, Altamura and Gravina in Bari. It is worth taking the trouble to track it down.

One form in which bread is commonly eaten is *frisa*, which starts with a round whole-wheat bun deeply scored horizontally on its circumference so that it can be broken into two circular pieces. It is dipped for a few seconds into cold water to soften it, soaked abundantly with oil, spread with chopped onion, covered with a slice of fresh salted and peppered tomato, and that is all. The buns are available in all Apulian bakeries, and a *frisa* or two, helped down with a bit of wine, is considered a plentiful repast by an Apulian shepherd or farmhand. It is a descendant, like the Neapolitan pizza, of the ancient Roman snack, bread with a relish—which was an ancient Greek snack too.

A similar humble dish is the *tarollo*, an unsweetened biscuit designed to be dunked in or munched with wine. It requires a complicated cooking process, boiling first and baking afterward; in other words, it is a true biscuit, for that, of course, is what this word means, in French *bis cuit*, twice cooked. The flavoring of *tarolli* tells you where they come from—in Bari, they are left plain; in Taranto they taste of fennel; and in Brindisi and Lecce they are well peppered. Brindisi also has a specialty of *puddica*, a sort of bun containing greens, black olives and anchovies.

Of the many varieties of pasta, some of the most popular in Apulia are: *recchietelle*, which elsewhere in Italy would be called *orecchiette*, little ears, from the shape given them by a simple pressure of the thumb, whose hollow traps whatever sauce is used with them, often served with sautéed green vegetables or fresh ricotta cheese; *panzerotti*, like ravioli, with a filling of buffalo cheese, anchovies, eggs and butter, first fried and then browned in the oven; *turcinielli*, little spirals of pasta served with meat or tomato sauce and grated cheese; *stacchiotte*, shaped like seashells with the aid of the point of the pasta maker's knife; *lagane*, the local name for lasagna; *strascenate* (*cagghiubbi* in Brindisi), strips of pasta rolled around a metal spit to leave a little hole in the center; *fusilli*, wire-thin pasta, similarly rolled into a spiral with the aid of a spit; and *mignuice*, small semolina dumplings.

These are all homemade dishes, but for holidays and other festive occasions the family may resort to store-bought macaroni, the nearest baker's oven and perhaps even to a professional cook for a mess of *maccheroni al forno*, oven-baked macaroni, for which the pasta is combined with buffalo cheese, sausage and meat balls into a sort of pie. This is a festive dish in all three of the southernmost provinces, sometimes under the alternative name of *timballo di maccheroni*.

The various sauces served with these many forms of pasta usually have one characteristic in common: they are made by adding vegetables to a meat sauce base—the only form in which many families get meat at all regularly. The vegetable is likely to be artichokes for *maccheroni al forno;* the town of Andria uses bitter rue in both the white and red sauces it applies to all kinds of pasta; cabbage and turnip sprouts often go into the sauce for *recchietelle;* and, of course, hot red pimentos fit ditchdiggers' spaghetti.

All Apulia is appreciative of pasta, but Bari appears to be the only place that has ever staged a revolt in defense of it. This happened in 1647, when the Spaniards were governing the city. Though they were ingenious in matters of taxation, they had pretty much run out of ideas when it occurred to them to clap a levy on flour. The citizens of Bari accepted this passively enough until Spanish soldiers began entering their kitchens to check on the amount of flour in their possession. This was too much, and they revolted. Street fighting lasted for a week and then the Spanish gave up. Bari was able to return to eating bread and pasta made with untaxed flour. It has been suggested plausibly that the men of Bari were defending not only their pasta but also their women. Spanish soldiers had a reputation for gallantry, and when they invaded the family kitchens, it appears the flour was not always the only thing they inspected.

In recompense, the Spanish left to Bari one of the few Spanish dishes which have been taken into the Italian repertory, *tiella*, distantly related to *paella*. It is a dish built up of layers of different ingredients, baked in the oven. *Tiella* is versatile; it is not likely to be quite the same in any two places. One version of *tiella di cozze* starts with a layer of rice, followed by another of thickly sliced potatoes, above that a mixture of onions and parsley, and on top the black mussels (*cozze*) which give the dish its name. This is doused with olive oil, sprinkled with grated cheese, and topped with bread crumbs before it goes into the oven. You can put a *tiella* together from any combination of ingredients which strikes your fancy, but purists insist on one point—you mustn't leave out the potatoes. In a Spanish *paella* it would be the rice (flavored with saffron) that you couldn't leave out; but Apulia is not rice country. It *is* potato country, which seems out of step with a hot climate (mitigated, however, by breezes from the sea), especially as Italy in general is not much enamored of the potato, preferring lighter vegetables. These stand out less in Apulia, where the chief vegetable dishes meriting mention are endive with a purée of broad beans and oil, favored in Brindisi and Lecce, and the ubiquitous eggplant of the South—*melanzane ripiene*, stuffed with anchovies, capers, olives and garlic, or Foggia style, when the stuffing is made of the eggplant pulp mixed with tomatoes, chopped parsley and basil, garlic, olive oil and bread crumbs, the whole served with a tomato-and-olive oil sauce. Apart from this, the chief vegetable dish is Taranto tart, which brings us back to the potato again, for its base is mashed potatoes, placed in the bottom of an earthenware baking dish, sprinkled with olive oil, and covered with a layer of tomatoes, mozzarella cheese, freshly ground pepper and oregano.

The potato is in tune with the rustic rather coarse cooking of the interior, with its heavy proportion of doughy foods, and also with the dishes Apulia owes to its shepherds. One of these is *gnumeredd*, chunks of lamb or kid, enveloped in casings of intestines from the same animal, which may be cooked in a saucepan with a little water, onions, tomato and parsley, or, as they do it in Brindisi, where it is called *gnummarieddi*, spitted. Another is *quagghiaridd*, sheep tripe stuffed with lamb's liver, salami, cheese and parsley, chopped fine and bound with raw egg, after which it is cooked in an earthenware dish in the oven and eaten with boiled rue. *Capretto ripieno* has risen a little in the social scale and acquired a non-dialect name; it is kid stuffed with aromatic herbs and spices, cooked lightly with olive oil in the oven.

Apart from this, not much meat is eaten in Apulia. Beef is practically nonexistent. You may encounter veal rolls (not to mention *involtini* of horse meat) and pork, mutton, lamb, kid and poultry are available, but the country works up no passion for them, and, consequently, has few special local methods of dealing with meat. A minor exception is sausage; besides the Lecce *sanguinaccio* which was not exchanged for a pillar of the Appian Way, there is a strongly flavored Apulian sausage called *capocello*. The major exception is game, especially in Foggia, which is a hunter's paradise; but there are also game specialties in cities well removed from the forests of Foggia's Gargano peninsula. Bari treats hare with a sweet-and-sour sauce, *lepre all'agrodolce alla barese;* Brindisi cooks thrushes in a "secret" local sauce; Martina Franca, in Taranto, preserves them in white wine. Elsewhere these birds are prepared in many different fashions, one favorite way being to cook them with bay leaves and fennel seeds.

The chief reason why Apulia eats so little meat, of course, is that it eats so much fish (others are the climate and expense). The bourgeois diets of Lecce, Taranto and Brindisi are oriented almost exclusively around fish. At Taranto, not only the Mar Piccolo but also the Mar Grande is extraordinarily rich in fish. Red mullet, *orata*, fresh sardines and eels are particularly popular. Specialties include *calamaretti in casseruola*, a stew of squid, shrimps, tomato, celery, olive oil, oregano and rosemary; and *alici recanate*, a sort of tart of anchovies, olive oil, parsley and bread crumbs. *Cozze* (mussels) *alla tarantina* and the Taranto seafood spaghetti, which includes these same black mussels, are renowned throughout Italy. Taranto itself calls mussels *mitili* rather than *cozze*, and has dozens of ways of preparing them—*zuppa di mitili*, cooked in oil, parsley, garlic and white wine, and poured over slices of bread on serving; *risotto di mitili*, mussels cooked first in oil, parsley and garlic, with tomato optional, and finished with rice and white wine; *mitili all'agro*, boiled, and eaten cold with a dressing of lemon juice, olive oil and chopped parsley; *frittura di mitili*, dipped in beaten egg yolk and bread crumbs or flour, and fried in olive oil; *mitili arracanate*, in their shells, the top one lifted open, cooked in a slow oven with heat above and below, with chopped parsley, crumbled bread (minus the crust), olive oil, a little tomato, and dry white wine, added last; *mitili ripieni*, stuffed with hashed veal, brains, egg, bread crumbs and nutmeg, cooked in oil, garlic, parsley and tomato; *zuppa di mitili alla marinara*, cooked in olive oil, chopped onion and tomato and served on slices of toast; *polenta al sugo di mitili*, mussel sauce poured over polenta (it also serves as a sauce for pasta); *mitili con zucchini*, diced zucchini cooked in olive oil with a little onion, to which are added first the mussels and then beaten eggs and a touch of lemon peel;

and I will let you off on *pasticcio di mitili, mitili ripieni al sugo, mitili ripieni alla salsa, costolette di mitili, mitili in umido, mitili al tegame, mitili in graticola, insalata di mitili, mitili marinati,* and several other kinds of mussel soup, fried mussels and risotti with mussels. As for oysters, Taranto holds they should be eaten raw, but grudgingly admits roasting them lightly on a griddle, seasoned with pepper and lemon juice, or coating them with beaten egg and bread crumbs and deep-frying them.

Brindisi bakes fresh anchovies in the oven, covered with chopped parsley and bread crumbs (Taranto's anchovy tart without the tart), and also bakes the black mussels with potatoes. The rocky coast of the Bari region provides clean feeding bottoms for fish, and contributes to their tastiness; it seems particularly propitious to red mullet and spiny lobster. The former are often cooked on a grill over an open flame and served with lemon juice. In the San Nicola quarter of Bari, *orata* is washed in sea water marinated in oil and aromatic herbs, and grilled. Dentex are cooked in the oven in oil and vinegar, with pitted black olives, added toward the end of the cooking. Bari is also the inventor of *ciambotto* (a local word which means "mixture"), a fish sauce for spaghetti which is for Apulia what the *ragù* meat sauce of Bologna is for Emilia-Romagna.

When you fry fish, Apulians say, you should use only olive oil, never fat or butter; and, they insist, the best oil for this purpose is Apulian. They admit that the olive oil of Lucca, generally described as the finest in Italy, is superior for salad dressings or making mayonnaise; but to fry Apulian fish under the Apulian sun you must use Apulian oil. So be it.

The normal dessert in Apulia is fresh fruit; but if you prefer pastry, there is enough to choose from—*scatagghiett*, ribbons of sweetened dough soaked in honey *castagnedi*, little balls of sweetened dough and almond paste with chocolate frosting; *bocche di dama*, "ladies' mouths," cream puffs with white frosting; *pettole*, sugared fritters; *pan pepato*, a dry cake of almond paste, raisins and candied fruit; and the cookies of Alberobello, the *trulli* town. Lecce has several dessert specialties of its own (aside from pistachio sherbet), including the cookies called *sfogliate leccesi* and *cartellate*, a fritter juicy with honey and Marsala-type wine, which is eaten especially for Christmas. Some of these pastries are probably ancient too—the widespread use of honey would suggest either Greek origin or the influence of the Saracens.

Apulia produces more wine than any other region in Italy, some 200,000,000 gallons a year, but very few persons who have never been there could name a single Apulian vintage. Apulian wine is not subtle, but it is strong. The nature of the soil; the manner in which the grapes are grown, trained just above the ground over intricate low trellises, so that the heat reflected from the earth almost bakes the grapes; and of course the method of treating it, give it a very high alcoholic content. Most of it is therefore used anonymously to cut Northern wines of more distinguished flavor, which are low in alcohol. Of the wine consumed for its own merits, usually where it is made, much is drunk directly from the cask; no one takes the trouble to bottle it.

A good deal of Apulian wine is deliberately "neutral"— that is, it has no particular flavor of its own, and is not intended to have any, being designed simply to be drinkable alcohol. Its destination is, chiefly, Piedmont, where it serves as the basis for vermouth. Martina Franca is the most important market center for the neutral wines of Apulia, and Trani for such wine intended for direct consumption as gets out of the province. That is why in Milan, where Apulia wine is the ordinary low-priced beverage served to workmen at stand-up bars, the slang word for a drunkard is *tranatt*.

The high alcoholic content of Apulian wines makes strong dessert beverages typical of the region. The best known white dessert wine is probably Moscato di Trani, made from the same grape which in the North produces Asti Spumante, which sometimes gets up to 17 degrees of alcohol. The same phenomenon also appears in reds, for those who can tolerate sweet red wines, like Aleatico di Puglia, which varies between 14 and 17 degrees, and is a curious orange-red color. Also curious is the rare Manduria, from the Taranto area, which is a naturally sparkling red wine which sets something like a record for alcoholic content—20 degrees.

Another wine which may be called distinctive, though not distinguished, is Primitivo, the word in this sense meaning "early." It is indeed the first grape to ripen in Italy, or for that matter in Europe, making the timing perfect to get Primitivo to the North for its principal function of fortifying weaker wines. Only the outer bunches of grapes are picked for this first usage, before the shaded inner bunches are ready. From the second picking a full-bodied red wine is made which is well worth bottling and has the property of holding out for many years.

All five provinces of Apulia are wine producers, but Bari, which holds a National Wine Fair every year in the last week of May and the first in June, and Lecce are considered to make the best—within the regional limitations, of course. Bari also brews beer.

XVI

Basilicata

The Emperor Augustus did not succeed in fixing a Roman character on the instep of the Italian foot, even in name. He called it Lucania, after the Lucani, who had conquered it about the middle of the 5th century B.C., but even its Latin name, much less a Latin character, did not last. Though it is still sometimes called Lucania, it has reverted more generally to its Greek name of the Basilicata, which is only second-hand Greek. It gained that name nine centuries ago when its Byzantine rulers dubbed it with the title of the reigning governor, Basilikos.

If the Basilicata was never Roman in spirit, it cannot be said that it was profoundly Greek either, having been

561

touched only lightly by the Achaeans who reached its coast, but were not tempted to push into the almost impenetrable mountainous interior; and the coast did not offer them much room for settlement. Basilicata touches two seas, but it would be difficult for a country with two coastlines to have less—a foothold of 24 miles of frontage on the Ionian, a toehold of 12½ on the Tyrrhenian. This allowed the Greeks room for just one settlement, on the Ionian, Metapontion (Metapontum for the Romans), founded by Achaeans from Sybaris and Croton about 700 B.C. It still exists under the name of Metaponto, and has preserved two Doric temples from its Greek epoch.

The spirit of the interior, which bequeathed to the Basilicata its spirit of today, came neither from Greeks nor Romans, but from the Oscan-Samnite tribes of the mountain regions of central Italy who moved into this area before them. Many of the present place names are derived from their forgotten language, whose inscriptions run in alternate lines from left to right and then right to left—boustrophedon writing, named from the Greek word which describes the movement of an ox turning at the end of one furrow to start plowing the next in the opposite direction. There are still traces of Oscan in the local dialect.

In post-classical times, the region was subjected by the usual set of masters—Goths, Longobards, Byzantines, Saracens, Normans, and a few others. Their foreign power was exercised in a few of the accessible cities of the region, but its yoke rested lightly on Basilicata as a whole. The interior was too difficult to penetrate. It is still well off the beaten path today.

The Samnites introduced agriculture into Basilicata. It was not easy. The region is so mountainous that it has been claimed that there is not a square yard of plain in the whole area. The territory is segmented by good-sized rivers which flow into the Ionian Sea, the Bradano, the Basento, the Agri, the Sinni. Politically the region is split into only two provinces, Potenza on the Tyrrhenian side, Matera on the Ionian. Potenza, an almost vertical city, provides a striking indication of the mountainous character of the country; despite its southerly position, which would lead anyone looking at the map to deduce that it is hot, it is actually one of the coldest cities in Italy. It is 2,700 feet up.

The nature of the terrain has made Basilicata a prime example of a general Italian phenomenon—to reach regions of a different flora, you don't need to move north or south, you can move up or down. Vertical stratification is so marked in the Basilicata that its vegetation has been classed into three categories, which have been given the Latin names of *lauretum*, *castanetum* and *fagetum*, after typical plants which flourish best in each of three altitude zones. *Lauretum*, from the laurel, is the lowest level, an area of intensive cultivation, characterized by vines, olives and citrus fruits. *Castanetum*, chestnut tree country, is the next stage up. Agriculture is still important here, but much of the land has been taken over for grazing by goats and sheep. The summit, *fagetum*, is the realm of the beech. Both tilling and pasturage disappear here, but thick underbrush makes it excellent country for game, including wild boar. This is one of the rare regions of Western Europe where wolves still roam.

Except for small patches along the coast—around Metaponto for example—the soil here is generally poor, and even where crops can be grown, the results are hardly lush. Olive oil is the most important product of the region —Barile, in Potenza, produces some of excellent quality; Ferrandina, in Matera, makes oven-dried olives; Montalbano and Tursi (still in the Matera province), grow citrus fruits which can hold their own in competition against those of other regions.

Probably the food products for which Basilicata is best known outside its own area are its preserved meats. The local sausages are so highly esteemed in the North that they are not only imported but imitated. Sausages made in the North are described as *lucanica* (or *luganiga*) to indicate that they have the same flavor and quality as the Basilicata products, for instance in Milan, whose consciousness both of these sausages and of the Apulian wines of which she is almost the sole northern consumer, aside from those which go into vermouth, probably dates from the time when the Sforzas ruled in Bari. Basilicata sausages usually reach other parts of Italy seasoned and dried for export and long keeping, but on the spot they are often eaten fresh, fried. Once they have been dried, usually by smoking, and sufficiently aged (the state called *stagionatura*), they are no longer cooked before eating in their home territory, but are consumed raw. The most celebrated Basilicata sausage is *soppressato*, large, flattened and oval, flavored with ginger, and then preserved in oil, a favorite type in Matera, though Potenza makes it too, and adds the fine smoked ham of the towns of Picerno, Vaglio and Cancellara.

The *provolone* cheese of this region is sharp in taste. Milder is *caciocavallo*, the small hard *casiddi* and cottage and cream cheeses. Potenza makes a special cottage cheese which is packed in little wicker baskets to let it breathe and remain soft and fragrant. Ricotta is made of sheep's milk and appears in various forms, salted or unsalted, fresh or dried. *Manteca* is semi-soft.

Basilicata has always been very poor country, and its cuisine shows it. True, there has been some improvement in recent years. Land reclamation has increased agricultural production in the Agri and Sinni valleys. Potenza is becoming modernized and is acquiring some industry, in a region which had never had any. Matera may develop through the discovery of oil, though in what quantity has not yet been established. So far, however, this has had little effect on the local economy. It is not a place to expect sumptuous food.

In the confection of its simple hearty peasant dishes, Basilicata starts out with one advantage common to areas where the raw materials for the kitchen are produced, if not by the cook's family itself, at no more than one remove away. The original ingredients which go into almost any dish are entirely local, pure and undoctored. You may have to get your palate tuned to the regional taste scale before you can pierce its trumpet tones and perceive the underlying purity; Basilicata likes its food hot. Although many of its most common dishes are also found in Apulia, the discretion of Apulian seasoning is rarely met here. The former presence of Saracens in this region may account for these explosive tastes, like the abundant use of ginger, which we have already encountered in the *soppressata* sausage. It is so common in Basilicata cooking, that its presence is not even announced by the use of its name. Ginger is referred to here simply by a word meaning "strong." Then there are the tiniest hottest red pimentos, which submerge the flavor of many dishes in their own —you will run into them even with fried eggs. They change also the character of the *cacciatora* sauce, made without them elsewhere in Italy. Basilicata likes its sauces highly seasoned (particularly the rich ones used on game), its sausages and treated meats highly spiced, its cheeses sharp.

This taste for the dramatic enables Basilicata to claim a distinctive cuisine, which it could hardly do otherwise since almost all its dishes are borrowed, chiefly from Apulia, but occasionally from farther afield. Most of them are of inland or mountain type. The shortness of the two coastlines and the abruptness with which the mountains rise from them at the edge of the sea means that there is very little fish on the Basilicata menu, and what there is is either preserved (*baccalà ai peperoni*, salt cod with the ubiquitous hot peppers) or fresh-water fish—the trout of Lake Sirino, which are either baked in the oven with olive oil and parsley or cooked in a court-bouillon and served sprinkled with oil and lemon juice, and the eels of Lake Monticchio, roasted over hot embers, or fried and then marinated in vinegar flavored with sage, garlic and rosemary.

The favorite forms of pasta are about the same as in Apulia. The ear-shaped noodles so popular there are also found in the Basilicata, called *orecchiette* in Matera and *ricch'tell* in Potenza. The Basilicata, like Apulia, likes *fusilli* (*macc'roni a firrett* in Potenza) and serves it with exceptional mildness, under a meat sauce and grated cheese. Usually homemade, this is a favorite for daily use in Matera, but on Sundays the family often switches to *panzerotti*, the ricotta-stuffed ravioli also encountered across the Apulian frontier; but in Basilicata the cheese is more highly spiced. Potenza makes all these with the simplest possible dough, of hard wheat and water, also used for *strascinari* (*strascenate* in Apulia) and *laàn*, which is simply *tagliatelle*, but does acquire a local accent by being mixed with a purée of chick peas, or peas, or lentils (preferably the very small tender tasty ones of Vaglio), instead of being served with *ragù*. Basilicata does appear to have a special dish of pasta from the name, unknown elsewhere, of *maccheroni alla trainiera*, but it is in essence what is known elsewhere in Italy as teamsters' maccaroni, *alla carrettiera*, except that it inserts the inevitable ginger among the capers, olive oil, garlic and strong spices which characterize this sauce elsewhere. Quite original in the category of doughy dishes are the *biscotti aviglianesi* (from the town of Avigliano), unleavened bread made of mixed flours, including potato, which has the advantage of remaining fresh over a long period.

Many of the meat dishes of Basilicata we know already from Apulia. *Gnumeredd* is called *gliumariedd* in Potenza and *gli gnummerelli* in Matera and in both places is cooked on spits, whereas in Apulia it may be either spitted or oven-cooked. In general, lamb is the favorite meat of Matera, but Potenza also appreciates kid, which is cooked in a variety of fashions, all of which involve aromatic herbs. Either lamb or kid may be used for *capuzzedde*, which is the head of the animal cooked on a spit. In Potenza chops are cooked with olives, chicken livers go into fricasées. Game is frequent—salmis of woodcock; wild boar in a highly seasoned sauce; *lepre alla cacciatora*, which in the Basilicata means that the hare is cooked in a hunters' sauce which contains not only the classic oil, garlic, sage and rosemary, but also tomatoes and ginger.

The *capriata* of Apulia is echoed by the *cicorie e favetta* of Matera, a purée of white beans and endive served on slices of bread moistened with olive oil. Artichokes are a favorite vegetable. Cabbage is cooked with bacon and those little hot peppers.

Basilicata does not go in heavily for desserts, and one which is often cited there is borrowed from Bari—figs, lightly roasted, stuffed with almonds and fennel seeds, and then roasted a little more. *Mostaccioli* are very hard little cakes of flour and honey, sometimes containing raisins. One whose ingredients sound rather curious for a sweet is *pizza rustica*, which is puff paste stuffed with grapes, sweet *ricotta* cheese and sweetened salami (!) eaten hot from the oven.

* * *

The spicy seasoning of the Basilicata cuisine promotes thirst, but unfortunately the province does not provide much to satisfy it. Not a great deal of wine is produced, for the amount of soil suited to vines is limited. What there is is apt to be fiery and potent, not exactly on the refreshing side. Many of the wines tend to be naturally sparkling, and there is a considerable proportion of heavy dessert beverages, as in Apulia.

It would be possible to dismiss the vintages of the region with a single name—Vulture; but if there is only one really worth mentioning, it happens that this sole representative is quite good. Aglianico del Vulture is one of the best wines of southern Italy, though admittedly there is not a great deal of competition here.

The Vulture is a formerly volcanic height in the north of Potenza, near Melfi. Volcanic soil often produces distinctive wine, and it does here. It also often imparts a sharp taste to wine, and that also it does here, to such an extent that some persons trying it for the first time find it disagreeable. This is because of high acidity, but as it is a full-bodied wine it can stand aging, and after three or four years in the bottle it becomes more suave, while its particular flavor develops richly. Young, it is of a ruby color; as it ages, it turns toward pomegranate. It runs from 12 to 14 degrees, and is reputed to have tonic qualities. There is also a sparkling Aglianico Mussante.

The Vulture vines grow up to 2,600 feet. The best is produced around Barile, Rionero, Melfi, Meschito, Venosa and first of all Rapolla. It is made of course from the Greek grape whose acquaintance we have already made—*aglianico*, *ellenico*, Hellenic. There is also an Aglianico di Matera, 12 to 14 degrees, but it can't touch the Vulture wine.

Other grapes much grown here are the Muscat and

Malvasia varieties which as in Apulia produce heavy sweet dessert wines, often made by the *passito* method, which lets the grapes dry before fermentation. These come in both reds and whites, reaching an alcoholic content of about 15 degrees. They are much inferior to the Aglianico del Vulture, and indeed the best wines made from these grapes are also those of the Vulture region, Moscato del Vulture and Malvasia del Vulture, the latter a naturally sparkling sweet wine, golden in color, lighter than many of the others, 10 to 12 degrees; here again the best comes from Rapolla. The Moscato is much like it, a cut below.

We might mention two more for the record. Metaponto has Amaro Lucano, which from its name (*amaro* means bitter) ought not to be sweet, but actually it is a dessert wine. Possibly the name refers to bitter almonds, since some drinkers profess to detect an almond flavor in the wine. The other is Aspringo or Asprino, which seems to be the only wine except Vulture that travels outside the region. It does not get very far, only to Naples, where it is usually drunk as a refresher, for an apéritif, or between meals. A light dry white, slightly sparkling, it serves well enough for this purpose, but it hardly has enough authority to accompany food—at least not the sort of husky, fiery food offered by Basilicata.

Calabria

Today the second poorest region in Italy after Basilicata, Calabria 2,500 years ago was the richest. Its chief city then has given to many languages a word which signifies sometimes luxury and wealth, sometimes the effeminacy and degeneracy that excessive luxury provokes —sybaritism. Sybaris was on the Ionian coast of Calabria. No trace of it remains.

Calabria is the toe of the Italian boot; and Sybaris very possibly was the first of many colonies which the Greeks established there. It was founded by Achaeans about 720 B.C., on what was then fertile land, which became exhausted later. It was productive enough then to make

Sybaris a flourishing city. By the 6th century B.C., it was so resplendent, its wealth was so great, its luxury so unexampled, its power so unquestioned, that no city in the home country, even Athens itself, could be compared with it. A sybarite meant in Greece then, as it means today, a dweller in magnificence, the pampered pet of pleasure. The Sybarites abandoned themselves to the pleasures (among others) of the table. They crowned cooks for creating new dishes.

Calabria was probably the most thoroughly Greek area of Italy, with more colonies thickly planted along the coast, and more penetration into the interior. Elsewhere, except in Sicily, the colonies were all on the sea. But in Calabria, inland from Crotone, the town now called Santa Severina was Greek; Filottete, near the high-perched town of Tiriolo, was Greek; Vibo Valentia, inland from the Tyrrhenian coast, was Greek—the ancient city of Hipponium. There are others about which history may be silent, but which seem to claim a Greek origin by their very names—for instance, Filadelfia. The Greeks had to go well inland when they built ships from wood cut on the Sila plateau (the Romans did the same; the present name of this area is derived from the Latin *silva*, forest). Greek ruins are more widespread in Calabria than elsewhere in Italy (Sicily excepted), though there are no large relatively intact groups, as at Paestum (originally a colony of Sybaris called Poseidonia). Reggio Calabria was still speaking Greek under Augustus, and today the raisers of citrus fruit of that province call orange and lemon blossoms *zágara*, the Greek word for flower. The fishermen of Bagnara harpoon swordfish, using the tackle and the technique of the ancient Greeks.

The most striking feature of the modern town of Scilla is an enormous rock, rising at the head of a short promontory. This was the lair where Homer placed Scylla, on the

Strait of Messina, guarded on the Sicilian side by Charybdis. The roaring monster which Homer described as a six-headed woman, each of whose heads snatched a sailor from the decks of every passing ship certainly did not exist, but the roar did. It was produced by a hole in the wall of a cave through which the wind rushed, producing the sound Homer described. Part of the rock has since fallen, taking the hole with it, so Scylla has been silenced.

The Byzantines gave Calabria its name. In ancient times, the southern part of Apulia was called Calabria, and still was when the Byzantine Empire held it. When the Normans took Apulia, the Byzantines, using a device worthy of modern public relations men, disguised their loss of Calabria by transferring the name to the area they still held, the toe of Italy, where it came into general use during the 8th century A.D. The Byzantines founded Catanzaro in the 10th century, and this link with the East made Catanzaro prosperous in the 11th from the manufacture of silks and velvets, whose secrets were transferred there from the Orient.

The Saracens were intermittently present in Calabria. They left architectural traces in Cosenza, and held Reggio Calabria, with interruptions, for most of the 10th century and the beginning of the 11th, and even after the Normans had taken over in 1060, raided and pillaged the city from time to time, continuing through the sovereignties of the Normans' successors as late as the 16th century. Following the Hohenstaufens, the Aragonese, the Angevins, the Orsini, the Sforzas, and the most improbable overlords of all, the Poles, the last foreign rulers of Calabria were the Spanish Bourbons, whose capital was Naples. Their memory is preserved, faintly, in the name of the Piani della Corona, the Plains of the Crown, near Palmi, for the crown which is meant is that of the Bourbons.

XVII · *Calabria*

Besides the foreigners who came to conquer, there were the foreigners who came to hide. A peculiarity of the province of Cosenza is an Albanian population which inhabits 79 towns and villages of the region, speaking their own language and preserving unaltered the habits and customs, rites and dialects, of the regions from which they came. Many of them are blond, in striking contrast to the ordinarily dark Calabrians. They fled here during the Turkish invasion of Albania in the middle of the 15th century, and have remained together ever since, without becoming assimiliated into the surrounding Italian population. This is the most important Albanian colony in Italy, though there are others—in other provinces of Calabria, in Abruzzi e Molise, in Apulia, in Basilicata and in Sicily, a quarter of a million in all.

Another curious ethnic enclave is at Guardia Piemontese, also in the province of Cosenza, which dates from about a century later. It might better have been called Guardia d' Aosta, for the French-speaking enclave in Piedmont, for the language and the costumes here are French. The inhabitants of Guardia Piemontese are descendants of Protestant Waldensian heretics, who fled here to escape persecution in the north. Persecution followed them to Calabria anyway, where the Inquisition worked diligently against them, but they stayed on all the same, and are still here, quite unassimilated, like the Albanians.

Calabria hardly needed to import picturesqueness, for it possessed plenty of it already, and plenty of variety too, for in its mountains each isolated community preserved its local customs, untouched by the waves of invasion which swept over the coasts. Colorful traditional costumes going back for centuries are still worn regularly in many villages. The late Robert Sage described Calabria as "a mountainous country of magnificent wild beauty, strange customs and a life that differs from all else in Europe." Among

573

the strange customs are those pertaining to marriages. The ceremony is sometimes held up while the parish priest tries to track down the keys to the church; they are frequently stolen, for they cure toothache. On the wedding night, a witness for the bride and another for the groom post themselves before the door of the nuptial chamber to keep out the *monachello*, or little monk, a mischievous spirit who might bring them bad luck. Meanwhile, newspapers have been spread before all the openings to the house because the *malocchio*, the evil eye, is illiterate, and if he attempts to enter the house will be delayed by the necessity of counting one by one all the characters printed on the pages, being unable simply to read them. A plowshare is placed under the bed, point upward; this insures fertility. The following day the bride must be careful to pass under neither a harness nor an arch; and if she meets an old woman, she must bow to her three times. These precautions should protect the young couple, unless, of course, someone bewitches them by inducing them to drink coffee with a little blood in it.

The terrain of Calabria is spectacular. Three-quarters of its area is mountainous. The northern frontier is marked by the Pollino mountains which block off the end of the Apennines like the crossing of a T and erect a wall between Calabria and the rest of Italy. A spur of different geological formation strikes southward, cutting through the middle of the three provinces, north to south, Cosenza, Catanzaro and Reggio Calabria, each of which has a coast on both seas, the Ionian and the Tyrrhenian, of quite different characters—low and marshy on the Ionian, rocky and indented, broken by sandy beaches, on the Tyrrhenian.

In the north, the most prominent geographical feature is the vast Sila plateau at an altitude of 1,500 feet, covered with a dense forest of laurel, beeches, pines and other firs. Sometimes called the Italian Little Switzerland, it is a world apart, where the women wear an austere black costume with a heavy pleated skirt of wool or velvet, and where customs have remained unchanged for centuries. The snow stays on the ground until May or June, despite the southerly position of Calabria; and throughout the region, because of its mountainous nature, the climate is hardly what you would expect from southern territory so closely surrounded by the sea. It resembles a continental climate, marked by great extremes of temperature, very hot in summer, very cold in winter, with the heights under snow at least six months during the year. As in Basilicata, the high forests are refuges for wolves.

Moving south, in Catanzaro you reach the region where the Italian toe is at its narrowest; from the central mountains you can see both the Tyrrhenian and the Ionian Seas.

Passing into Reggio Calabria, along the western coast, you encounter some of the finest scenery of the region. Palmi must be one of the few places in the world where you can see two active volcanoes at once, neither of them too near—Stromboli on its island to the northwest, Etna, in Sicily, to the south. Palmi lies on the Calabrian Riviera, where a scenic cornice road runs along the coast from Gioia Tauro, almost lost in the thick olive woods which surround it, to the capital city. Reggio Calabria is one of the dozen or so places in the world with a legend of a submerged city; indeed you can see it yourself if you happen to be there when the conditions are right—at dawn, in calm weather. What looks like an underwater city is actually the reflection of Messina on the other side of the strait, which becomes visible here by some strange effect of light called locally "the mirage of the Fairy Morgana." Behind Reggio Calabria rise the heights of Aspromonte, whose summits rise in the form of towers, as though they had been made by the hand of man. As you round the corner of the coast at the very tip of Italy, you encounter an even more spectacular formation, a mountain range which thrusts five probing peaks into the sky, like an opened hand with its fingers pointing upward; this is the Pentedattilo, which means "five fingers" in Greek. The Ionian coast is forbidding as soon as you leave the sea, arid and parched behind the beaches, an area of badlands and parched earth.

It is obvious that such terrain is not going to provide much arable land, yet agriculture is the chief occupation of the Calabrians, whose problems in drawing sufficient sustenance from soil which is none too fertile even where there is some are increased by addiction to large families. The Ionian coast has a clay base and about everything else has eroded away from it. The Tyrrhenian coast is more promising, and there are a few areas of rich plain around Sibari, Santa Eufemia and Rosarno. A problem on the Ionian side has been the latifundia, but of late years the big properties have been broken up, smaller landholders have taken over, and the result has been more varied crops —wheat, forage and fruit trees. On the Tyrrhenian side, small properties have always been the rule.

The neighborhood of Cosenza is intensively cultivated, although the methods used are sometimes primitive. They must have been primitive in ancient times too, yet Varro reports that Cosenza in those days used to get two crops a year from its apple trees, and Pliny praised the region's wine. To the south, on the Tyrrhenian coast, there is a region of high fertility around Gioia Tauro, which enjoys a fortunate situation, shielded from cold winds by mountains behind it, while sea breezes carry moisture to the soil. This makes it first-rate ground for olives, and helps Reggio Calabria to hold second place for olive oil production in Italy. The olives are harvested in December and

January, and the general rule is that they are pressed in small local establishments, often by the grower himself. The oil thus handmade, so to speak, is more expensive than the product offered by the big processors, but it is also better.

It is when you reach the immediate neighborhood of the city of Reggio Calabria itself that you come upon the richest agricultural country. Some fine figs are grown here, but the great specialty of the area is citrus fruits. Some 40,000 acres around Reggio Calabria are planted with citrus trees, 6,500,000 of them, which produce up to 135,000 tons of fruit annually. Every citrus fruit you ever heard of is grown here, and probably one or two of which you have not, like the *megalolo* and the *verdello*. The *megalolo* is a lemon grafted onto a bitter-orange tree, which enhances its flavor. The *verdello* is an ordinary orange, but one which is produced by a process of forced growth. The roots are uncovered and left bare under the hot sun "to make the tree thirsty." They are then covered up again, watered abundantly, and heavily manured. The sap rises rapidly and the tree flowers overnight. This gives extremely highly flavored very soft oranges—indeed, a little too soft for eating, but they are not designed for that. They are used for making perfume.

Perfume is also the destination for one citrus fruit raised here, and only here, which is never eaten. No one could afford to. The bergamot is worth too much as an essential element in eau de Cologne, which, though it bears the name of a German city, was first made there by Italians. The recipe is supposed to have been brought to Cologne by Paul de Feminis, from Milan (a city which still buys a great deal of bergamot essence from Reggio Calabria for the making of perfume), who passed it on to his nephew, Giovanni Farina. Eau de Cologne is still made under the Farina label.

The bergamot, which looks like a large lemon, is something of a mystery, beginning with its name. The theory that it is derived from the city of Bergamo, in Lombardy, seems curious, since the bergamot cannot be grown there; perhaps the Lombards were alert enough to import the fruit first and take the credit for the perfumes made from its oil. (Paul de Feminis was a Lombard, and this would explain why Milan is still an important producer of bergamot perfumes.)

The history of the other citrus fruits in Italy is without mystery. The first to be introduced was the citron, in the 3rd century. The lemon appeared in the 7th, the bitter orange in the 10th. (The ancient Romans knew the lemon, and the bitter, or bigarade, orange, but they imported them.) The true orange was first grown in Italy in the 14th century, when it came from the Saracens. But there is no record of any introduction of the bergamot. Apparently about the middle of the 17th century (that is to say, about 40 years before Paul de Feminis turned up in Cologne), the citizens of Reggio Calabria discovered that they had growing in their gardens here and there a type of citrus tree which was different from any they had previously known. Perhaps it was a lucky cross which had produced a stable hybrid, perhaps it was a mutation. In any case, there it was and there it has been ever since. Reggio Calabria has a world monopoly on bergamot oil; the entire supply comes from there. Attempts to grow it elsewhere, for instance by the Japanese on Formosa, in the days when they still held that island, have failed. The Calabrians explain it by the even temperature, the prevailing winds, and the climate, which, owing to special local conditions, produces springtime all year round.

This monopoly looms large in the economy of Calabria, since the sale of bergamot oil brings in some tens of mil-

lions of dollars every year, a tremendous item for an otherwise poor country. Bergamot plantings have increased regularly for the past century. There are some 8,000 acres devoted to bergamot trees now. To see them in flower, visit
the area between May and July; the fruit is picked from
December to March. One perfume has led to others; Reggio Calabria produces essences from a considerable number
of crops, some edible, some not—acacia, tuberose, rose,
geranium, lavender, mint, basil, sage—and also flavoring
extracts for candy (mint, lemon, orange).

For the rest, farming consists chiefly of growing vegetables. Little meat is produced. Pork is the most important,
followed by kid, lamb, and very little veal.

Fish is of course an appreciable addition to an otherwise
rather restricted diet. The Strait of Messina is the best
spot for coastal fishing for a wide variety of small and
medium-sized species, but the great prizes are two large
fish. Tuna are taken around a number of ports; Bagnara
specializes in swordfish. The latter are present in these waters between April and July, migrating from Arctic waters
to spawn here. Some of them run to a length of 15 or 16
feet.

Calabrian sausages resemble those of Basilicata—the preserved pressed pork *soppressata*, and the highly seasoned
smoked sausage called "end of the neck"—*capocollo*.
There are a few cheeses—mozzarella; Crotonese, from, of
course, the Crotone area, which is like pecorino, but of
mixed sheep's and goat's milk, instead of sheep's milk alone,
and peppered; and, the most local of the lot, and therefore
known by a local word, *butirro*, a ball of *caciocavallo*,
which encloses a kernel of butter, reversing the Campanian
trick of enclosing a center of hard cheese in a casing of
mozzarella by putting the softer element inside. Confusingly, *butirro* is sometimes used to mean the same bland

cheese called *manteca* in Basilicata.

These are the principal items in the Calabrian larder, a meager one. I have read that it has been enriched on occasion by storks and eagles, but this I fear I am unable to confirm.

Given the available resources, Calabrian cooking is based almost entirely on pasta and vegetables. Few of the inhabitants can afford very much beyond what they can raise or fish or shoot themselves. Reggio Calabria eats better than the rest, being richer, largely because of its production of perfume essences; nearer to the best fishing grounds; and, when it comes to the art of preparing food, influenced by Messina, just across the Strait, gastronomically better developed. This is olive country, so the chief cooking fat is olive oil, but lard is used for some dishes, a result of dependence on the pig for what meat there is. Almost everything is hotly peppered. This is no country in which to seek refinement, either in the materials or the fashion of treating them; simple peasant food is the rule, but simple peasant food can be very good if you make it as the peasants do, without attempting to add to it a sophistication hostile to its nature. Peasants everywhere tend to prepare their food in the simplest manner possible, by putting everything together in the same pot—in a word, soup. Since the Calabrian diet is composed mainly of pasta and vegetables, the most common general-purpose dish is a soup of whatever appropriate vegetables are at hand, combined with generous additions of pasta. This makes a very thick soup, described in a bit of doggerel which recalls the similar saying extolling the virtues of Piedmont *tome* cheese. Calabrian soup goes Piedmont cheese one better, or more exactly four better, for to the three merits claimed for Piedmont cheese, the Calabrians add four more for their soup, as follows:

Sette cose fa la zuppa:
Cura fame e sete attuta,
Empie il ventre,
Netta il dente,
Fa dormire,
Fa smaltire
E la guancia colorire.

That is to say: "Soup does seven things: it appeases your hunger, slakes your thirst, fills your stomach, cleans your teeth, makes you sleep, helps you digest, and puts color in your cheeks."

When this thick soup is served in the peasant family, it is the main dish of the meal, and in general the only dish, unless it is followed by a bit of cheese or home-grown fruit. In the absence of soup, the main dish is usually pasta, which appears in infinite variety. *Pasta asciutta alla calabrese* is spaghetti or macaroni with a thick tomato sauce and a fiery addition of ginger, recalling the *maccheroni alla carrettiera* of Basilicata; but when Calabria makes *maccheroni alla carrettiera* it does not use ginger. *Maccheroni alla pastora*, shepherd's macaroni, is indeed a dish eaten by the shepherds of the mountain pastures, and is simplicity itself; into a soup plate containing some melted fresh ricotta cheese, plus a little butter if there is any handy, some of the salted water in which macaroni has been boiled is poured, mixed with the cheese, peppered, and used as a sauce for the macaroni. For *maccheroni con i carciofi*, the sauce is made of bits of artichoke browned in lard with garlic, onion and parsley, well salted and peppered; sharp grated pecorino cheese is sprinkled thickly over the macaroni and its blanket of sauce. *Maccheroni con l'arrosto*, macaroni with roast, appears only on festive occasions, since it calls for meat, but it can be leftovers, for what is here meant by roast is a mixture of meats, for instance a piece of pork, a little turkey, and a quail or any other small bird the family hunter may have bagged. These are roasted well, doused with a heavy red wine, thickly peppered, of course, cut into small pieces, and mixed with the macaroni. Housewives proud of their culinary reputations take the macaroni out of the water half-cooked, drain it, and let it finish its cooking in the same pan as the meat, to absorb its flavors.

Spaghetti con lumache, a specialty of Cosenza, has a sauce made from snails—thickly peppered—first scalded in water, then cooked in olive oil with onion, tomato and parsley. *Sagne chinne* is dialect for what would be called elsewhere *lasagne imbottite*, stuffed lasagne. The lasagna is usually homemade, from hard wheat and without egg. It is boiled in salted water until it is *al dente*, then removed, strained, and placed in an earthenware oven dish in alternate layers with sliced hard-boiled eggs, slices of soft cheese, and little chopped meat croquettes (*polpettine*) previously cooked in their own juice with lard, onions, mushrooms, peas, artichokes, and a bay leaf or two. The *polpettine* cooking juices are poured over the stuffed lasagne, and a thick coating of grated pecorino is spread on top, to give it a good crust when it is finished in the oven. *Soffritto* is elsewhere a term which usually designates the basic flavoring liquid which is the very first step in the process of cooking something else—for instance chopped onions and/or garlic browned in olive oil or lard, in which other ingredients will ultimately be cooked. In Calabria, alone on a bill of fare, *soffritto* means pasta for which an enriched *soffritto* serves as the sauce. It is made of finely chopped pig's liver, lungs, heart and, optionally, a bit of tripe, cooked with garlic, tomato extract and pimentos until it has become quite thick. *Schiaffettoni*, a word which means simply "stuffed," demand careful work from the cook. A stuffing is prepared first, of chopped meat and sausage, bound with egg, and separately cooked. Then large-caliber macaroni, cannelloni size, say, are cooked in well salted water and drained. The finicky part of the process begins now, for each tube must be closed at one end to keep the stuffing in, and filled individually. The stuffed pasta then goes into an oven baking dish, the gravy from the cooking of the stuffing is poured over it, it is thickly sprinkled with grated pecorino, and finished in the oven.

The principal vegetables of Calabria are peppers, tomatoes and eggplant, of which the last is subjected to the most diverse manipulations. *Melanzane alla finitese* is so called because it is a specialty of San Martino di Finita; the eggplant is cut in two, lengthwise, scalded in boiling water, coated with heavily peppered grated pecorino, flavored with basil, floured, dipped in beaten egg, either floured a second time or coated with bread crumbs, and fried in oil. *Melanzane all'agrodolce* is decidedly Oriental in character; after being browned in olive oil, it is cooked in a thick sauce of vinegar, chocolate, sugar, cinnamon, pine nuts, walnuts, finely chopped candied citron, raisins and a touch of Marsala-type wine. A simpler version uses only sugar and vinegar. *Melanzane al funghetto* is not, as you might think, eggplant with mushrooms, but eggplant treated as if it *were* mushrooms—chopped small, and seasoned with garlic, oil, parsley, and, as usual, much pepper. *Melanzane ripiene*, stuffed eggplant, is very much like the same dish in Apulia, using tomato, anchovies, garlic, olive oil and parsley. For *melanzane sott'olio* you cut the unpeeled eggplant into slices, and put it in pickle for 24 hours with a heavy weight on top of it. Remove it, let it rest for two or three hours, put it into a glass or earthenware pot with bits of garlic, pimentos and basil, and press it again. Remove the weight, and fill the receptacle with fine olive oil. It will keep until you are in a mood to eat it; if in the meantime it absorbs all the oil, add more.

Stuffed tomatoes (*pomodori ripieni*) are filled with

chopped meat and fried, a formula hardly peculiar to Calabria, but a more localized version appears with *rigatoncelli con pomodori*. For this, firm but ripe tomatoes are used. The top is sliced off, like a cover, the seeds and watery part of the pulp removed, and the hollow filled with the kind of pasta called *ditalini rigati*, previously cooked *al dente*, along with parsley, mint, chopped garlic, pepper and a little olive oil. The top is then put back on and the tomatoes cooked in a moderate oven. *Peperoni ripieni*, stuffed peppers, are very simple; the seeds are removed and the peppers stuffed with a paste made only of bread crumbs, grated cheese, ground garlic and vinegar, and fried. For *peperoni alla calabrese*, you use red, green and yellow peppers, which you seed, cut into strips, and fry in oil; toward the end of the cooking, you add bits of fresh tomato and a liberal dollop of tomato extract. For a relish, Calabria offers *olive schiacciate*, hard green olives crushed into a paste with a pestle. It is then left in brine for several days, with a weight compressing it. Taken out, it is then spiked with bits of garlic and pimento, and preserved in vinegar.

On the coast, sample the fish of the province, but try to get it prepared as the Calabrians make it for themselves, and not as they may try to improve it to do honor to an outsider. The fish is of high quality, and the less the cook does to it the better. Tuna is served boiled, cut into large chunks, flavored with olive oil, parsley, garlic and much pepper, plus, sometimes, vinegar; or, also cut into large pieces, spitted and grilled over a wood fire, sprinkled during the cooking with a mixture of lemon juice, salt, pepper and olive oil by means of a sprig of oregano, and served in a platter containing what remains of the basting liquid. Calabria offers a rather special fish not eaten much elsewhere, a species of lamprey different from that so much appreciated by the ancient Romans, which is often served fried but is better grilled or baked. Red mullet is cooked in an oiled frying pan over a high flame, sprinkled with lemon juice and more oil, flavored with orégano. Herring are cut into small pieces and fried in oil with garlic and pepper until they are reduced to the consistency of a paste, which is served spread on thick slices of bread.

The interior is not entirely devoid of fish. The trout of the Sila plateau are particularly flavorful. They are cooked either as *trote arrostite*, roasted in the oven or over embers, well spiced; or *in bianco*, cooked in a court-bouillon and seasoned with oil and lemon juice.

The most typical of Calabrian meat dishes is the one which contains the least meat. It is particularly characteristic of Catanzaro, where it is called *u murzeddu*, while in other parts of the region it is *morseddu*, both dialect words from *morso*, bite. This is because it is held in the hand and bitten into. It is a hash or paste of pig or calf giblets, seasoned with tomato sauce and much pepper, with perhaps other spices as well, which in Catanzaro is spread between two slices of bread, and elsewhere often fills a crusty base which would be called a pizza in Naples, and is a *pitta* here. *Frittole* provide likewise a minimum meat dish, pieces of pork crackling with some of the meat adhering to it, cooked slowly for two or three hours in melted fat pork.

More orthodox meats begin with roast kid. This you are most likely to encounter in the mountains. *Capretto ripieno al forno*, as made there, begins by cooking the internal organs of the animal in order to make gravy from them. This is used to flavor spaghetti cooked *al dente*, which goes into the animal as stuffing. It is then heavily peppered, barded with pork fat and roasted in the oven. It is usually served with sliced boiled potatoes and leek stalks cut up into little cylinders. Lamb chops are floured, fried in lard, and placed on a straw mat to absorb excess fat, after which they are served with anchovy fillets, capers, and mushrooms and artichokes in oil. Pork is roasted, heavily peppered, with a seasoning of bay leaves.

Calabrians do not go in for rich desserts. They do have, however, some local pastries—*turiddu*, biscuits of flour, eggs and almonds, powdered with sugar; the similar *mustazzoli*, shaped in conventional designs—hearts, fish, colts, etc.; and *cannariculi*, fritters whose dough has been moistened with Marsala-type wine, which, after being deep-fried in oil, are soaked in honey. For a non-pastry dessert there are *crocette*, figs half roasted in the oven, stuffed with almonds and fennel seeds and then roasted again, the cousins of the famous preserved figs of Bari.

Only a small proportion of the scanty arable land of Calabria is devoted to wine grapes, which are grown in widely scattered small patches in various parts of the region. It is possible that more wine was produced here in ancient times than today, for the history of Calabrian wines is very old. The Balbino and Aminci of Sybaris were renowned, which takes us back at least to the 6th century B.C. A few centuries later, Pliny praised the wines of Consentia, Rhegium and Tempsa. Many presently existing wines trace their ancestry to Greek and Roman times. Calabria may indeed provide the only opportunity still existing of discovering what ancient Roman wine really tasted like, if you can find one called Trasfigurato di Seminara. It is on record, but I know no one who has ever tasted it. It is described as a wine put in jars and smoked. This is exactly what the Romans did—their wine was kept in amphorae and stored, not in a cool cellar, as ours is, but in the garret through which the smoke of the kitchen and heating systems passed.

One could understand a smoked wine persisting in Calabria longer than elsewhere, not only because of the antiquity of the country and the longevity of its ancient customs, but also because even modern Calabrian wine is heavy and often coarse. This is partly the result of the method, already witnessed in Apulia, of training vines close to the ground, so that they bake in the heat reflected from the earth. Calabria is without wines of distinction, capable of competing off their home grounds with others. You will have to sample them here or nowhere. They do not get outside their own region, except for blending with lighter northern wines. There used to be one exception to this rule, Savuto, which was exported to the United States, where it was consumed by emigrants from Calabria, who provided a market for it out of habit or homesickness.

Savuto is not the Calabrian wine likeliest to be chosen for export on the grounds of merit, if any were. Savuto di Rogliano, the best, is a harsh, bright ruby wine, with garnet-orange highlights when it ages, 13 degrees of alcohol, sometimes slightly sparkling naturally. It should be drunk with discretion unless you enjoy morning-after headaches. It is not unlike the heavy Pollino wines, of which the best is probably Lacrima di Castrovillari, dry and light for this area, 12 to 13 degrees, which ages better than most Calabrian non-fortified wines. If it were necessary to pick any red as the best in the region, it might perhaps be Cirò of Catanzaro which since the time of the ancient Greeks, who grew it near Crotone, has maintained a degree of quality well above par for the course. It is dry, ruby-red, 14 degrees, tonic, and though it suggests Marsala in taste (the savor becomes more subtle as it ages), it goes well enough with red meat. There is also a sweet variety, 15 degrees, and a rosé. The only other reds necessary to mention are the strong demi-sec Pellaro (it gets up to 16 degrees), which treacherously doesn't betray its power, for it is a disarming innocent pinkish color, almost a *rosato;* and Magliocco, grown near Nicastro (Catanzaro), dark red, 14 degrees.

Rosé wines are usually popular in hot countries, and they slip down easily, without betraying an alcoholic content which can be quite high without revealing itself as it would in reds. Beware of the one served currently in Reggio Calabria, Archilla Rosato. Sharp in taste, it can get up to 17 degrees.

In whites, Calabria runs to sweet dessert wines. The best by far is Greco di Gerace, whose name might suggest an ancient origin, but it means only that it comes from the *greco nero* and *greco bianco* grapes, which do not necessarily hark back to antiquity, though they may. The Greco di Gerace territory is old enough, though, in the mountains back of the once-Greek colony of Locri. It is a velvety deep amber wine, with a bouquet suggesting orange blossoms, 16 to 17 degrees of alcohol. Unfortunately not much of it is made. Production of lesser white dessert wines is falling off too; perhaps even in Calabria the modern tendency to abandon very sweet wines is making itself felt. However, there is still much more of it around than there is of the Greco di Gerace, probably the best Calabrian wine of all categories.

THE
DOMAIN

OF THE
SARACENS

XVIII

Sicily

Nowhere in Italy did the Greeks pervade the country so completely as in Sicily. Greek colonies were implanted side by side along the eastern and southern coasts. They appeared more timidly in the north, did not in most areas probe deeply into the interior, and never succeeded in taking the extreme western tip from the Phoenicians and their heirs, the Carthaginians, until a defeated Carthage ceded it to Rome. But except for this minor territorial gap, Greeks impregnated Sicily; and from the 5th century B.C., Syracuse, the brilliant city which gave birth to Theocritus and Archimedes, and attracted Plato and Aeschylus, dominated the Sicilian Greeks. It was the fleet of Syracuse which defeated the Etruscans in the naval battle of Cumae in 474 B.C. When Athens, jealous of the growing power of Syracuse, sent a fleet of 134 triremes carrying an expeditionary force of 30,000 soldiers against Syracuse in 415, the Sicilian city defeated it ignominiously in what Thucydides called the greatest action in Hellenic history, and ended forever the power of Athens in the western sector of the Greek world. Syracuse imposed her power on the mainland colonies of Magna Graecia along the sole of the Italian boot, and Syracusans even pushed deep into the Adriatic to found Ancona. In the 4th century B.C. Dionysius of Syracuse ruled broader dominions than were controlled by anyone else in the Occident until the time of Alexander the Great. Sicily was still speaking Greek under the Emperor Augustus; and the Hellenization of the island actually increased under the Romans and their successors until the Saracens moved in, early in the 9th century. Even under Arab rule, the Greek language did not disappear. It took some centuries to fade away, leaving its mark on Sicilian dialects and contributing some Greek words to the island's vocabulary.

Yet in spite of this ancient and obstinate Greek influence, in the end it was the Saracens who left their impress most obviously on Sicily. The shift of cultures was symbolized by the shift of capitals. The Saracens made Palermo, instead of Syracuse, the capital of Sicily in 831, and it still is. Old Greek names remained throughout the island, but new Arab names were added to them. Marsala means either "the port of God" (Marsah el Allah) or, more prosaically, "the port of Ali" (Marsah Ali). Sometimes ancient names were Saracenized as well. Caltagirone, the Kakgron of the Greeks, takes its present name from the Arabic *qualet*, castle, plus *algerun*, grotto. Until 1927, when Sicily became conscious and proud of its past and returned their ancient names to a number of cities which

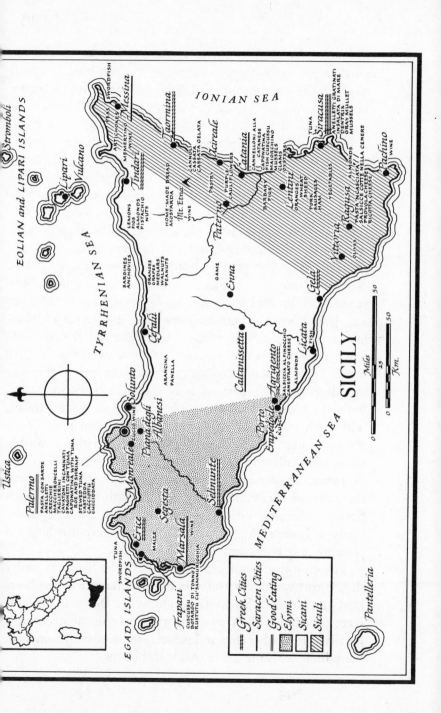

had been deprived of them, Enna was known as Castro-giovanni; it looks like good enough modern Italian, which might mean "the camp of John," but actually the name resulted from an Arabic corruption of Latin—from Castrum Ennae through the Arabic Kasr-Yani.

During the two centuries of Saracen rule, Arab immigration from North Africa was so heavy that when the Normans became political masters of the island, they had little choice but to share cultural and administrative condominium with the Saracens who outnumbered them. Besides, the Normans, after all a rather rude people, were dazzled by the sophisticated and luxurious habits of the Saracens. The conquered absorbed the conquerors. "The Norman conquest of Sicily turned into something of a scandal," John McPhee wrote in *The New Yorker* of May 14, 1966. "Norman minds dissolved in the vapors of Muslim culture. Austere knights of Honfleur and Bayeux suddenly appeared in the streets of Palermo wearing flowing desert robes, and attracted to themselves harems of staggering diversity, while the Church raged. Norman pashas built their own alhambras. The Normans went Muslim with such remarkable style that even Muslim poets were soon praising the new Norman Xanadus." Saracen institutions, especially the harem, intrigued later comers than the Normans. Frederick II of Hohenstaufen, after he became the ruler of Sicily, not only fell in enthusiastically with Saracen customs, but even settled 20,000 Saracens from Sicily in Lucera, Apulia, and established there, for his own pleasure, a harem complete with eunuchs.

The continuing cultural influence of the Saracens under the Normans is visible today in the architecture of the Norman (or Norman-Saracen) period, when Norman builders were obsessed with Arab art, particularly in the decorative details of their churches and palaces, some of which, indeed, were built with the aid of Arab architects.

For those Sicilians who were neither Arab nor Norman, there may have been little discernible difference when the latter took over from the former. The Saracen officials often continued in the same functions under the Norman reign. In particular, financial posts continued to be held by Saracens, good mathematicians ever since the Arabs invented the numerals we still use today and the science of *al gebra*. The treasury was known as the Divan, as it was in the Ottoman Empire, which is why customs services are called in Italian today *dogana*, in French *douane*, and in Spanish *aduana*. Arabs also remained in the armed services. After the Normans took Sicily, Saracens furnished almost all the foot soldiers for the island's army, under command of mounted Norman knights. Roger II built up a strong fleet some of whose officers had already served under the Saracens. They were therefore known by the title of Emir (Arabic, *amar*), hence our word "admiral."

The Arab majority was not long maintained, at least in official statistics. Mainlanders poured in, described indiscriminately as "Lombards," wherever they came from. "Lombards" included some French-speaking groups, probably heretics from the Valle d'Aosta, like those who settled in Calabria, and also Albanians, again as in Calabria, fleeing from the Turks, who established at Piana degli Albanesi a community which still speaks Albanian, maintains its old customs and wears its old costumes, and follows the Orthodox rites. The Greek and Arab populations became unimportant minorities, or so it seemed. Probably what happened was not a diminution of these ethnic components of the Sicilian population, but simply a new description of them in official classifications, especially of the Saracens. Many Arabs found it advantageous to be converted to Christianity, and thus, in the view of census takers, disappeared from the Moslem category. They were still there, however, and as late as 1958 a French writer was able to describe Sicilians as "changeable and diverse, maintaining the Arab type and mentality, sometimes with reminders of the Normans, found in certain women who are blonde and blue-eyed." The inhabitants of the Lipari Islands have been described as of Spanish-Arab type. It is possible that the Saracens are still with us.

They are at any rate still with us in the kitchen. Almost everything which strikes us today as typically Sicilian is typically Saracen. Nevertheless, the most renowned gourmet of the ancient Greek world, Archestratus, was a Sicilian, born in Gela early in the 4th century B.C. He has been called the Brillat-Savarin of ancient times, though Brillat-Savarin was deadly serious about a subject which Archestratus treated lightly in his mock heroic poem, *Gastronomie* (or *Houpatheia*), of which only some 300 lines have been preserved. In typically Sicilian fashion, he interested himself particularly in fish. Yet little trace of Greek cooking (perhaps fish chowder) remains in Sicily. It may be that what was Greek has been merged into what was Saracen because the last comer from the East absorbed without resistance preceding similar cuisines which had originated in the same part of the world—Greek, Carthaginian, Phoenician. The Normans contributed one item, which they left all around the Mediterranean, salt cod, though under a mysterious name. Air-dried cod, also a gift from Scandinavia, is known in Italy as *stoccafisso*, which comes naturally enough from the Norwegian *stokfisk*. But why is the salted variety known by a Dutch word? *Baccalà* is apparently derived, with an inversion of consonants, from *kabeljauw*. Nobody else since the Saracens has added anything at all.

Before the Saracens—and before the Greeks, the Carthaginians and the Phoenicians—the picture is different. In Syracuse I put to Dr. Guido Carnera, the representative for Sicily of the Italian Accademia della Cucina, the question: "What is the essential difference between Sicilian cooking and mainland cooking?" I received an unexpected reply. "That is hard to answer," he said, "because there is no such thing as a Sicilian cuisine. There are at least three distinct schools of cooking in Sicily, eastern, central and western. . . . Sicilian cooking is more indigenous than is generally realized."

Eastern, central and western: these are, respectively, the regions held by the three older races the Greeks found when they arrived in Sicily—the Siculi, the Sicani, the Elymi. Through all the changes that have occurred since, the spirit of these three peoples, all established in Sicily at least a thousand years before our era, and probably longer, has subsisted. The distant echoes of these archaic cultures have come down to us so attenuated, so refined, so impalpable, that it is impossible to discern why the same materials and the same dishes, treated apparently in much the same fashion, produce different effects depending on whether you sample them in the east, the center or the west: but they do. The intangible soul of these forgotten civilizations seeps through the later overlays. States of mind which have persisted for 3,000 years in the spirit of cooks who know nothing of their most distant ancestors except that which is so deeply buried in their natures that they cannot possibly be conscious of it, are still shaping their cooking.

Yet however it may have been affected by its foundations in the distant past, or modified by the changes of later centuries, the cooking of Sicily is marked most clearly by the imprint of the Saracens.

Very little is known about the three ancient races whose existence accounts for the three schools of Sicilian cooking. The Sicani, who were occupying the center of Sicily when the Greeks arrived, were perhaps the firstcomers. The Greeks, who had originally called Sicily Trinacria, for its triangular shape, shifted to Sikania when they became aware of these inhabitants, before finally settling on Sicily, for the Siculi.

The Elymi occupied the extreme western tip of Sicily and thus fell under the thrall of the Phoenicians and Carthaginians, who established themselves there. There is a theory that they were of Trojan origin, which seems to have been held also by the ancient Romans, since Virgil represented the death of Anchises, the father of Aeneas, as having occurred on Elymian territory in what is today Trapani.

The Siculi, who were to give their name to the island and also to several places within it (Siculiana, near Agrigento; Scicli, in Ragusa province) are believed to have come from the mainland, for they spoke an Italic dialect, probably from the area east of what would later become Rome, to occupy first the eastern part of Sicily. Not only did they spread over a considerable part of Sicily, but also had settlements in the Lipari Islands and even reached the remote island of Ustica. When the Greeks arrived in Ortygia, which was to become Syracuse, they found the Siculi installed there. Many of the Siculi became serfs of the Greeks and others voluntary captives of Greek culture; but they continued to maintain an independent existence as an unassimilated race until 450 B.C., when the remaining independent Sicilian towns imprudently formed a league against the Greeks. The Greeks promptly defeated them and the Siculi disappeared from history. The Sicani and the Elymi had preceded them.

The first Greek colony in Sicily, according to ancient chroniclers, was Naxos, on Cape Schisò, near Taormina, founded in 734 by Chalcidians. It no longer exists, having been destroyed in 403 by Syracuse, the second Greek colony, established by Corinthians the year after Naxos. Syracuse very definitely does still exist, a spectacular city crammed with the magnificent ruins of the past during which it was the first city of Sicily for 1,500 years. Today it is the fourth—behind Palermo (to which the Saracens moved the capital); Catania, the third Greek colony (728 B.C.); and Messina, the fourth (721 B.C.).

The Romans learned more from Sicily than Sicily learned from them. They took Catania in 263 B.C. and carried away as part of the spoils of war that city's solar quadrant, which became the Romans' first clock, from which they learned how to calculate time accurately. When they captured Syracuse and saw the operation there of the laws on agricultural tithes which had been put into effect by Hiero II, an expert on farm property and management, they adopted them to a considerable extent. Their own innovations in Sicilian agriculture were not happy. They replaced small farms by vast properties worked by imported slave labor as in Italy, with the same result—economic decline and the fixing upon the island for 2,000 years of the deadening weight of the latifundia. A Roman *praetor* (governor) was installed at Syracuse, but the Romans left the Greek-speaking Sicilians pretty much to their own devices. They were interested in the island, aside from its strategic usefulness, only as a source of grain and a place to spend vacations.

In Sicily, as everywhere else in Italy, the collapse of the Roman Empire initiated a long succession of raids, invasions, conquests and transfers of power from one foreign sovereignty to another, aggravated by the circumstance that from her earliest beginnings, Sicily had always been in the main current of Western history. She knew therefore a longer list of alien rulers than any other region of Italy.

Among the more spectacular rulers of Sicily was the Hohenstaufen Emperor Frederick II (Frederick I for Sicilians), whose qualities earned him the sobriquet of *stupor mundi*. Though he was Swabian by his family, and King of Germany by election at Frankfort, as well as Holy Roman Emperor, he was born in Italy, at Jesi, in the province of Ancona. Bald, short-sighted and with a bloodshot complexion, he was not personally prepossessing, but he made up for it by his diverse and dynamic intellectual qualities, which included the ability to speak six languages, a curiosity which led him to maintain an exotic menagerie and to write a treatise on falconry, and an acquaintance with mathematics, philosophy, natural history, medicine and architecture. His brilliant court attracted Arab, Jewish and Christian luminaries, including Michael Scot, who introduced Arabic numerals to the West.

After Hohenstaufens, the brief Angevin rule was a disaster from the outset. The Sicilians called it the *malasignoria*, the bad overlordship. They despised the French, whom they referred to as the *tartaglioni*, the stammers, because they spoke Italian so badly. The kingdom was in a constant state of incipient revolt, against which the French tried to defend themselves by frequently searching Sicilians for arms. The traditional story is that a French soldier decided on Easter Tuesday 1282, when vespers were being celebrated in the church of Santo Spirito, that it would be interesting to search a comely young girl of Palermo, which enraged her fellow countrymen to such an extent that they rebelled, in the bloody Sicilian Vespers, murdering every Frenchman they could identify by inability to pronounce correctly the word *cicero*, chick pea.

The Aragonese followed, contributing little, and passing on the crown to the Spanish Bourbons, who came in after a 25-year period of confusion, during which various other largely unheralded foreigners appeared briefly. Savoyards installed themselves on the island for five years and Austrians for 16. But the Bourbons held on, by their fingertips, for more than a century, until Garibaldi landed at Marsala on May 11, 1860, and Sicily became part of united Italy.

The triangular island of Sicily, largest in the Mediterranean (9,925 square miles), is bathed by three seas—the Tyrrhenian to the north, the Ionian to the east, the Mediterranean to the south. It is a land spectacularly colorful on its coasts and magnificently savage in its interior—endless expanses of bare sun-parched earth and burned plateaux, with less than 25 inhabitants per square mile, mountains covering more than one-fourth of the island's area. Two-thirds of Sicily lies at an altitude of more than 900 feet; only 15 percent is under 330. The sirocco, carrying on its burning breeze great clouds of dust, frequently sweeps over the island in the summer. There is a perpetual shortage of water; rainfall is slight and unfavorably distributed, falling mostly in the late autumn and winter. Much of this runs off quickly in the almost treeless interior; only 3½ percent of the territory is covered by forest, though when the Greeks arrived, the island was much more thickly wooded. Despite these unpromising circumstances, more than one-half of the population is engaged in agriculture, and is surprisingly successful at it. Aided by a climate which is Mediterranean in the north and subtropical in the center and the south, Sicily manages to use 95 percent of her land for agriculture (including the scanty forest), much of which would be considered uncultivatable in other countries. A figure that reveals how closely the land is worked is that of the average size of farms in the fertile area—less than seven acres. In the interior, however, Sicily has been plagued with the problem, so often felt also in many regions of the mainland, of the latifundia. Before the war, one percent of the number of farms accounted for 36 percent of the land. This was one of the reasons for the poverty of Sicily, plus the added weight on the economy of supporting the Mafia (a name which may come from the Arabic *manfa*, "place of exile," referring to the Saracens who, after they lost control of the island, became "exiles" on their own former territory, taking refuge in an occult government parallel to the official one).

The most spectacular physical feature of Sicily is Etna, Europe's largest active volcano, whose height of 10,749 feet means that its top is covered with snow six months of the year. Its name comes from the Greek *aitho*, "burn." The Greeks had every reason to be conscious of Etna's fiery character, for in ancient times, 135 eruptions were recorded. During the period covered by history, Etna has averaged one eruption every six years, some of them disastrous, as in 1329, 1381 and 1669, which was one of the worst; the flow of molten lava passed over a large part of the important city of Catania. In recent years, there have been relatively spectacular outbursts in 1910, 1917, 1923, 1947, 1949, and 1950–51. One might wonder why, under the circumstances, one of the most thickly settled regions in Sicily clusters around Mount Etna; but Etna is not an unmixed evil. The volcanic soil which it has laid down around its base is extremely fertile, producing good crops of oranges, lemons, tangerines, figs, prickly pears, olives and vines, for some of them five harvests a year, in the lower *regione coltivata*. This gives way at about 4,000 feet to the *regione boscosa*, the wooded zone, which produces chestnuts. Above 6,000 feet is the *regione deserta*, which produces nothing.

The only Sicilian plain of any importance lies in the fertile Etna district, that of Catania, where the cauliflowers are purple and the prickly pears ubiquitous. Palermo and Monreale lie in a great hollow called the Conca d'Oro, the Golden Shell, from the color of the oranges which grow there so thickly, on soil rich enough so that ground crops are raised between the rows of citrus trees, while palms provide a decorative background. The hinterland of Syracuse is productive enough, making the city an important market for the foods produced in the interior—the varied agricultural products of Floridia, in the rich delta of the Anapo River; the almonds of Avola; the oranges of Lentini and Francofonte, whose own special variety of blood orange, the *tarocco di Francofonte*, is particularly prized; and the wheat and lamb from the higher altitudes. The province of Messina is relatively fertile for Sicily. Trapani, turned though it is to the sea, has an agricultural economy, growing a good deal of corn, and a non-edible crop in cotton. The asset which made Agrigento in ancient Greek times second only to Syracuse was that the country it dominated was favorable to cultivation. In the interior, the great crop was wheat.

Wheat, along with some other grains, has been the mainstay of Sicilian agriculture for 2,000 years. In what we would call today the colonial economy of Greek Sicily, which exported food and imported manufactured objects, wheat was the leading product, followed by fish, sheep and cattle. Sicily always had a surplus of grain. In the times of the Siculi, inland Enna, which was considered the omphalos of Sicily, was the center of the cult of Demeter, the goddess of grain, one of the most important deities of the Siculi, who also worshipped demigods known as the Palici, protectors of agriculture and of sailors—the principal sources still of the food of Sicily, which lives on cereals, vegetables and fish. Sicily was selling wheat to Rome as early as the 5th century B.C. When the Romans took power in Sicily, it became the granary of Italy; and today wheat is still the most important crop, with Sicily producing 10 percent of the total Italian production, despite a falling off of the yield, ascribed to neglect of the soil and the abuses of the latifundia.

Sicily's second most important crop is citrus fruits, for which she holds first place in Italy, especially lemons, of which she grows 90 percent of the Italian total. Citrus trees are distributed so widely throughout the island that their perfume seems to hang over it wherever you go, particularly in the north, around Palermo; but it is Paterno, in the province of Catania, which is reputed to produce the very best oranges of Italy (and also superior honey, no doubt from bees feasting on orange blossoms). Every variety of edible citrus fruit is grown in Sicily—the ordinary orange, the bitter orange, the blood orange, the double blood orange, the tangerine, the ordinary lemon, the sweet lemon, the citron, the lime, the grapefruit, and the artificial creations we have already encountered in Calabria, the *megalolo* and the *verdello*. There is a story which attributes the Norman conquest of southern Italy and Sicily in part to a present of oranges sent to the Duke of Normandy in the 11th century by a prince of Salerno, which tempted the Normans to acquire the land producing such treasures—the same story told about the Longobards five centuries earlier.

Sicily is the second region of Italy for the production of almonds and olives, and from the second makes 90 percent of the country's olive oil. Sicily also supplies the mainland with loquats, Japanese medlars, pomegranates, prickly pears, and two fruits you are likely to meet puzzlingly under their dialect names—*zibibbo* (the Arab word for raisin) and *bastarduna;* the first is the Smyrna grape, an early-summer table variety, and the second the best type of Smyrna fig. There is also a large production of walnuts, pistachio nuts and peanuts.

The coming of spring is announced everywhere in Europe by the appearance of the vegetables of Sicily, whose savory artichokes and tender peas are flown to the north often when this part of the continent is still under snow and ice. Sicilian tomatoes and beans also deserve special mention.

Seafood is available everywhere in Italy, but the west (Trapani) and the Ionian coast are particularly favored. One-quarter of the Italian fishing fleet is registered in Sicily, and takes one-third of the country's total catch of fish, including one-half of its most valuable fish, the tuna. Messina is a center for swordfish, taken by the same methods used in Homer's time. Sardines and anchovies are found everywhere. Mussels, clams and oysters are cultivated along the Catanian coast.

Sicilians do not go in much for meat, partly because they do not raise much. Though there are enormous numbers of donkeys and mules, the chief working animals of Sicily, there are not many other domestic animals, for there are few permanent meadows, the supply of fodder is short, and what pasturage there is is suitable only for rough grazing, which is all right for donkeys, permits the raising of goats and some sheep, but is not much good for cows and steers. The production of pork is a local phenomenon, since pigs are choosy about their environment, and Sicily is a much compartmented country, whose patches of differing cultures are shut off from each other not only by the wall of its mountains, but also by changes in altitude. Thus at Gulfi, near Chiaramonte (Ragusa), well inland, with difficult access to the sea, the diet is composed almost exclusively of pork, fresh or in the form of sausage or ham; that is what they have. Move on to the next villages, a little higher, and pork disappears from the menu; the altitude is too great for the successful raising of pigs.

Since Sicily is less well supplied with pork than most parts of Italy, it is not particularly rich in native sausages. Nevertheless attention should be called to the *salsiccia al finocchio*, flavored with fennel, of Agrigento, and Ragusa's *salsicce cotte nella cenere*, which is cooked in the ashes of the hearth. It does better on that other rustic staple, cheese, mostly made from goat's or sheep's milk. I once counted more than a score of different kinds of cheese displayed in a small country grocery store.

Among Sicilian cheeses are *pecorino siciliano*, almost identical with Roman or Sardinian *pecorino*, hard and white, of cylindrical form, often shaped in a wicker basket which leaves its imprint on the surface of the cheese, then called, consequently, *canestrato*, from *canestro*, basket (the same name is also sometimes applied, for the same reason, to a cheese of mixed sheep's and goat's milk); the Agrigento *formaggio al pepe*, which puts pepper into cow's milk cheese, and it needs it, for it is bland, white, and almost tasteless; *pepato* or *Siciliano pepato*, also a spiced cheese, again of sheep's milk; *caciocavallo*, of cow's milk, usually made here in tremendous cartwheels; *maiorchino*, from Catania, sheep's milk; *Ragusano*, made from whole cow's milk (of exceptional quality in Ragusa, where there is better than ordinary pasturage), which comes in bars, pale yellow for the table, dark brown for grating cheese (it may also be smoked), and should be consumed for the first purpose within six months, after which it is used only for cooking; *casigiolo*, also called *panella* or *peradivacca*, a cow's milk cheese of firm but yielding flesh, made something like *caciocavallo;* and many cheeses which differ little from their homonyms in other parts of the country, like the *provola* and ricotta produced especially in Ragusa.

If you come from the mainland through "the Gate of Sicily"—Messina—you will have crossed a strait only two miles across at its narrowest point; but it is less significant that you are only two miles removed from mainland Europe than that you are only 90 from mainland Africa (Cape Bon, in Tunisia, the land Sicily's Saracens came from). Sicily is a different world. Sometimes it looks and feels more like North Africa than like Europe. One phenomenon common to North Africa and Sicily is the huddling together of the population. Drive through Tunisia, Algeria or Morocco, and you will traverse vast spaces of emptiness, dotted sparsely with teeming towns. Sicilians cluster too. The Tyrrhenian and Ionian coasts, and the fertile lower slopes of Mount Etna are densely populated; in the interior, you can ride for miles without seeing a house. The great majority of the population in the interior lives in towns with populations of at least 5,000 inhabitants; the majority of this majority lives in towns of at least 10,000.

Sicily is the largest region of Italy, and the largest province of Italy is Palermo, site of the island's capital. Sicily is divided into nine provinces; running clockwise around the coast: Palermo, Messina, Catania, Syracuse, Ragusa, Caltanissetta, Agrigento, and Trapani, with landlocked Enna nested in the middle.

Palermo, the Greek Panormos, the Latin Panhormus, the Saracen Khalesa, is the most colorful city of Sicily, indoors and out, with its glittering Byzantine-inspired mosaics and its Saracen arabesques; its enchanting market, the *vucciria*, astir with all the animation of the Orient; the magnificent park which is the oldest public garden in Europe, the Villa Giulia; and in the Garibaldi garden, what is claimed to be the oldest fig tree in the world. Palermo itself is old, of Phoenician origin, and the site of a Carthaginian military base, but no traces remain of this earliest era; however, in nearby Solunto—the Greek Soloeis or Solous, the Roman Soluntim, which was one of the three chief Phoenician settlements on the island—you can still see traces of their passage, and of the Roman period too. As far as the capital city itself is concerned, life began with the Saracens.

Eastward from Palermo is the province of Messina, with both a Tyrrhenian coast and, turning the corner, an outlook on the Ionian Sea. Its capital was first called Zancle, meaning a sickle, from the shape of the promontory curling around its harbor, and the narrow stretch of water which separated it from the mainland was the Fretum Siculum. Messina was a refuge of pirates until Greeks crossed from the mainland to restore order, and acquired its present name in 494 B.C., when the Messini arrived, fleeing from Greece after defeat by the Spartans. In spite of its early beginnings, it is a modern city today; 90 percent destroyed by the earthquake of 1908, which killed 84,000 people, it had to be completely rebuilt. The chief cities of the province besides Messina itself are, on the north coast, Tindari, the ancient Tindaris, certainly once Roman and probably also Greek, where today citrus fruits and wine are produced, and Taormina on the east coast, which was both Greek and Roman.

Proceeding southward down the Ionian coast, the next province is Catania, along whose coast twisted tormented boulder-islands lift from the water, interspersed with what look like fragments of broken walls extending into the sea, both reminders of lava flows from Etna, which account also for the gaping grottoes along the shore. According to Thucydides, Catania was founded by Greeks in 728 B.C., but the Siculi must already have been there, since the ancient name, Catane, is of Siculian origin. It seems to have been a brilliant city from the beginning. Charondas, a native of the city, gave it its early laws, based largely on family rights; a family was defined as composed of *homosipyoi*, which is to say those who eat from the same dishes. Later Catania was to be the first city in Italy to have a *studium generale*, an educational institution open to studies of all kinds, with the right to confer degrees, which in those days meant licences to teach. Catania's emblem is the elephant, the symbol of Minerva, goddess of wisdom. The most fertile province of Sicily, Catania is the only place in Italy, except for the island of Ustica, where bananas ripen; it also grows *glycyrrhiza glabra*, from whose roots licorice is made.

South of Catania, the rest of the Ionian coast is occupied by the province of Syracuse. The oldest gastronomic note in its history dates from 344 B.C., when Syracusan and Carthaginian soldiers renounced fighting for fraternizing, fishing together for eels in the marshy rivers around Syracuse (named for the neighboring Syraco swamp); in the end the Carthaginians departed without giving battle. Another bellico-gastronomic item, dated more than 1,200 years later, is grimmer. When the Saracens ended their conquest of Sicily by taking Syracuse in 878 A.D., after a siege which lasted several months, food became so short that the Syracusans ate "human flesh and grass, leather and the skins of oxen."

The wealth of Syracuse was derived originally from its soil, and though it was probably more fertile in ancient times than it is now, the province is still comparatively productive for Sicily. The capital is the chief distributing center for the meat and crops of the province, but turns its back upon them, preferring a diet based chiefly on fish, including tuna from its own fisheries at Marzamemi, one of the most important of Sicily.

The easternmost province on the southern part of the island is Ragusa; the lower part of its capital city is believed to cover the site of Hyblea Heracea, a stronghold of the Siculi. The province is primarily agricultural. Vittoria is a center for the local wine industry, but the most important product of Ragusa is olives, whose oil dominates Ragusa cooking, characterized by simple dishes displaying the homemade touch.

Proceeding westward along the southern coast, the next province is Caltanissetta, which contains the ancient Gela, founded by Cretans or Rhodians or both in 689 B.C. Greek also is the next province westward, Agrigento, whose capital city, once Akragas, is the site of the famous Valley of the Temples. The patron of Agrigento is Saint Calogero, a hermit who contributed a grace note to gastronomic history by living on a diet consisting exclusively of the milk of the wild deer of Monte Cronio, where he inhabited a cave.

Agrigento is almond country, where an Almond Blossom Festival is held every February, at the time when the thickly planted trees burst into snowy bloom.

Trapani, at the western extremity of the island, a stronghold of the Phoenicians before the Greeks reached Sicily and of the Carthaginians thereafter, has often been more conscious of Africa than of Europe. Its gleaming white capital even looks African; and the geography of the area has fallen in so appropriately with its history that when atmospheric conditions are right, the distant island of Pantelleria and on occasion even Africa itself can be seen from nearby Erice (Eryx for the Phoenicians and the Greeks).

The provincial capital, Trapani, shows no visible signs of its Phoenician-Carthaginian past. Its very name dates only from the Greek period, when it was called Drepanum, which, like the original name of Messina, means "sickle," and was given to Trapani for the same reason, the shape of the curving peninsula on which it stands. Its historical record does not really begin until the 12th century, with the arrival of the Normans, though it must have been important in the time of the Saracens, since they fixed their stamp upon it, making it, among other things, the capital of Saracen cooking. More is known about Marsala, the Lilibeo of the Carthaginians, who founded it in 397 B.C. and made it their principal stronghold in Sicily; as we have already seen, its present name is Arabic. The ruins of Segesta, chiefly a theatre and excellently preserved Doric temples, give the impression that it was a Greek city; but though it derived its architectural inspiration from the Greeks, it was politically first Phoenician and then Carthaginian. Its rival, Selinunte, was an out-and-out Greek colony, established in 628 B.C., one of the most progressive of its times. It owed its name to the Selinus river (ancient form, Selinos), from *selinum*, "parsley" (sometimes translated "celery"); it grew wild on the river's banks (and still does), and was depicted on almost all the coins of ancient Selinunte.

Trapani is agricultural country, but a large part of its

farming is farming of the sea—beginning with the beaches, for an important export is salt, from the salt flats which lie along a 15-mile stretch of coast south of the capital, threaded with grassy paths and studded with old windmills. A wide variety of fish are taken here, supporting a considerable canning industry, but the most important is tuna. Much of it is taken from Mazara del Vallo, the most productive fishing port of all Italy, which also serves as the market for the farm products of its hinterland, holding every two years the biggest agricultural, commercial and industrial fair of the province. Tuna fishing rises to the excitement of a festival, called the *mattanza del tonno*, which takes place in May or June, depending on the weather and other local conditions that determine when the largest catch is likely to be achieved. Not only Mazara, which is a new port, but also old ones—San Giuliano, Bonagia, Castellammare, and the islands of Favignana and Formica—catch tuna according to a carefully organized ritual which is said to go back to the Phoenicians; in any case, Aristotle in the 4th century B.C. had already recorded the migration of the tuna, which spawn off the Sicilian coast in May or June, especially off Trapani, where ideal conditions of salinity and water temperature prevail. The Sicilian *mattanza* is placed under the absolute dictatorship of *il rais* (Arabic for "chief"), who determines where and when the *isole* (islands) shall be placed, and how they shall be disposed. The *isole* are great complexes of many-chambered nets, half a mile to three miles long, anchored parallel to the coast, in positions determined by such considerations as the direction of currents, to entice the tuna to the entrance and then induce them to sort themselves out conveniently in the different partitions of the net. Tuna are economically the most important fish for Trapani, which catches 10,000 of them a year, and makes a second income from the tourists who come to watch the tumultuous spectacle of the great fish thrashing about in the nets as they are hauled into the fishing boats. Some of them run 10 feet long and weigh well over 1,000 pounds, though the average weight is only 330.

Tuna fishing is far from the thoughts of inland Enna, where boats are used not for fishing, but for hunting. This phenomenon occurs on Lake Pergusa, whose water is somewhat saline; the rolling hills surrounding it are nevertheless covered with a thick mantle of vegetation which caused Ovid to note that the countryside is always green: *perpetuum ver est*. There is so much game here that potshots can be taken at it from the lake, especially, of course, at the waterfowl which fly above it; the open season runs from November to March. Otherwise, Enna leads a quiet retired life, devoting itself to what has been its main business for something like 3,000 years now, the growing of wheat.

No less fascinating than Sicily itself are its satellite islands —the Aeolian or Lipari Islands, off the eastern half of the north coast; the solitary Ustica, off the western side; the Aegadians, off the west coast; another loner, Pantelleria, off the southwest coast, two-thirds of the way to Africa (to Sicily 62 miles, to Africa 44); and the Pelagian Islands, 112 miles south of Sicily, which are not, however, nearer to Africa than is Pantelleria, since at this point the cost of Africa pulls away.

The Lipari Islands (or the Aeolians, as the authorities prefer to call them, since the name Lipari acquired unpleasant connotations when Mussolini used the islands as a place of exile for political prisoners) are phantasmagoric. They are spectacularly volcanic. Stromboli and Vulcano still have active volcanoes, and all the others sprout dead craters. There are hot springs everywhere, marshes of boiling bubbling mud, beaches of black volcanic sand, and encircling rocks of nightmarish forms rising from the sea— the *faraglioni*, great towers of lava which were cooled and frozen abruptly into their twisted shapes when the volcanoes flung them hissing into the sea. Stromboli, anciently Strongyle ("spinning top"), is probably the best place in the world to view an erupting volcano without danger. Eruptions occur regularly, about every two hours, and the nature of the terrain is such that all the molten lava flows safely to the sea down the same 2,000-foot channel, the Sciara del Fuoco, which can be viewed safely from the water, a brilliant spectacle at night. Vulcano, whose peninsula of Vulcanello rose from the sea within historic times —in 183 B.C., according to Pliny—has calmed somewhat since. Its three active volcanoes have now been reduced to one mildly smoking cone, but there are still boiling streams of water.

Vulcano was known in ancient times successively as Thermessa, Terasia and Hiera; the last means "sacred"— sacred, not surprisingly, to Hephaestos (Vulcan), so the island was also sometimes called Efesto. For the islanders, this was his abode, though main-island Sicilians located it at Etna. It was also held to be the residence of Aeolus, king of the winds; but all the islands are windy, and it is on Lipari, not Vulcano, on the Piano dei Greci, the Plain of the Greeks, that you can see what ought to be the palace of Aeolus—the ruins of an ancient building one of whose walls is honeycombed with terracotta pipes which produce plaintive musical sounds when the wind blows through them.

Animal and vegetable life had difficulty in surviving the fiery past and windy present of these islands, and is sparse today. The only wild animals are rabbits, and they are few. Plants have done somewhat better. The hardy heather is widespread, and there are many ferns. As for food, the islands produce capers, olives, figs, prickly pears, almonds and the strange carob tree, a locust with edible pods used chiefly for fodder, but also edible by man. Fruit is not abundant, but what there is is of high quality. The islands reach luxury markets with their dried seedless grapes, and they also produce Malmsey (Malvasia) wine. Salina is the most fertile of the seven inhabited islands, growing especially capers, grapes (from which it makes raisins) and, on the non-edible plane, plants which produce coloring matter for dyeing. The salt flats on its south coast give it another food product and its present name; in ancient times it was called Didyme, "the twins," from the two now spent volcanoes rising from either end of its flat center. Stromboli grows olives and grapes. Tiny Panarea (two square miles), the ancient Euonimo or Hicesia, manages in spite of its minute dimensions, further reduced for growing purposes by patches of hot ground, to raise olives, grapes, capers and even grain. The largest island, Lipari, 23 square miles, pays little attention to agriculture, preferring to gain its living from volcanic by-products. As the ancient Meligunis or Meligunte, the island exported *ossidiana* (obsidian), volcanic glass, and still does; but its biggest business now is in pumice stone, another volcanic creation.

The sea here teems with fish, some of curious kinds. The decorative sea horse abounds, and you cannot stay long in the islands without glimpsing flying fish. Sea urchins lie in wait to prick the soles of unwary bathers, and the hammerhead shark appears occasionally, as do sea turtles. Professional fishermen, operating mostly from Lipari and Stromboli, concentrate on swordfish, tuna, and the tuna's smaller cousin, bonito. Underwater fishermen pursue morays, cuttlefish, soles and many others; the islands are a paradise for this sport, which is why the Sicilian Underwater Fishermen's Club has established its headquarters at Rinella, on the island of Salina. There is particularly good fishing around Vulcano for mullet and *cernia*, the latter much appreciated by underwater fishermen, since its fat bulky shape and comparatively sluggish movements make it an easy target. Both these fish, with grayling to boot, are plentiful around Filicudi, in ancient times Phoenicusa, because it is abundantly covered with ferns; its old windmills are still in use. The best place for sea urchins is Strombolicchio, Stromboli's satellite islet, a stone cylinder whose stark rock rises perpendicularly from the sea.

The lonely island of Ustica is a tiny spot on the map less than two miles across at its widest point, which has the inconvenience of being without water. This circumstance accounts for one of the two theories put forward to explain its name, which derives it from *osteodos*, ossuary, because of the bones left by 6,000 mutinous Carthaginian soldiers, who were marooned there as punishment and died of thirst. The other theory is that Ustica comes from *ustumbruciato*, "burned," for it also is of volcanic origin. Lack of water has not prevented settlement, however; men have lived, or at any rate died, on Ustica from the earliest times. The present population dates from 1763, when 85 valiant volunteer families from Lipari officially colonized the island, which still speaks the Lipari dialect. Water provided by a cistern which holds 5,000 tons (plus additional supplies ferried to the island in casks from Palermo) enables Ustica to maintain an all-year-round population of 12,000, 1,300 in the capital town of Ustica, who live on farming and fishing, especially the latter; the patron of the island is Saint Bartholomew, the patron of fishermen. Hunters find targets in hares, rabbits and especially birds; otherwise the fauna of Ustica is confined to domestic animals. Every peasant has a few—chickens, probably a few pigs, if he is well-to-do, cows or steers, sheep or goats, and necessarily the work animal which takes priority here over all others, the ass or the donkey. He raises a variety of vegetables, especially tomatoes, and in addition maize, wheat, figs, watermelons and even bananas, for the soil is fertile. Flying fish are common and intrigue the visitor, but the islander is more interested in the wealth of food fish which surrounds him: a wide variety of shellfish; spiny lobsters, the long-legged crabs known as sea spiders, shrimps, squill, sea urchins; octopus, rays, sword-fish, tuna, wrasse, red mullets, hogfish, conger eels, morays, dolphins; and sea turtles.

Off Trapani are the Aegadian Islands: Favignana, the ancient Aegusa, whose tuna fishery is the largest in Italy (Mazara exceeds it only if all sorts of fish are taken into account), good hunting territory for migratory birds between May and September; Marettimo, the ancient Hiera or Hieromesus; and Levanzo, the ancient Phorbantia, given over to vineyards and cereals.

Far south of Sicily lies Pantelleria, the Cossyra of the Greeks, a volcanic island inhabited in Neolithic times, and later held by the Carthaginians, despite the fact that, like Ustica, it has no source of fresh water; but for the Carthaginians it was an important strategic base between Africa and Europe, a role it was still playing in World War II. It is noted for the high quality of its table grapes.

Still farther to the south is Sicily's most distant outpost, the Pelagian Islands, as near to Tunisia as to Sicily. Phoenicians, Greeks, Romans and Arabs all left traces here. Of its three islands, Lampedusa was the ancient Lopadusa. The olive grows wild here, and other crops include cereals, figs, prickly pears, and carob trees. The island's fauna is limited to 22 species of birds. Linosa, like Favignana, was once known as Aegusa; possibly settlers from Favignana imported the name with them. Lampione is unhabited.

Where else but in Sicily would it seem defensible to start a study of the local cuisine with its most superfluous and dispensable department—desserts? In Sicily, sweets demand first attention not solely because Sicily inherited the sweet tooth the Saracens developed, partly, no doubt, because of the ease with which they could satisfy it through their early possession of sugar cane; and not only because sweets provide the most characteristic, the most striking and the most excessive category of Sicilian food; but for the profounder reason that in Sicily, where mystical currents run deep and the past lives in the present, the sweets embody most clearly the ritual role of food, forgotten elsewhere, which through the ages has bound it to magic, superstition and religion.

In other parts of Italy, the appearance of certain sweets at certain times, like fritters on St. Joseph's Day, hints at ancient ritual meanings as thoroughly forgotten today as is the significance of the appearance of hot cross buns at Easter. In Sicily memory of the magical meanings of certain foods is much nearer to the surface, barely beneath the threshold of consciousness, and in some cases perhaps not yet entirely beneath it. Sicily is a land of magic and superstition, and the occult significance once attached to the eating of certain foods is still sensed there, even though it has become imprecise and ill-defined. Legendary eating habits, embodied most often in the hidden significances of sweets, persist most strongly in Sicily, which is also a land of legend.

Homer used the Sicilian background freely in the *Odyssey*. We have already seen that Vulcano is identified with Aeolus, who gave Ulysses the sack in which contrary winds were imprisoned. The whole Lipari archipelago inspired the account of the Wandering Islands; surrounded by great blocks of pumice stone floating in the water, easily nudged aside by passing boats, they may well have given rise to the illusion that the fixed rocks, islets and islands were mobile too. The very strong currents at Messina, which reverse direction every six hours, were represented by Homer as a monster who periodically sucked in and spewed forth the waters of the Strait of Messina; their force must have been more redoubtable for the ships of his time than of ours, but it also appears that erosion of the coast has reduced it since his day, when it may have been something of a southern maelstrom. Sicily was called in ancient times the Island of the Sun, so it is supposed that it was there that Homer imagined the slaughter by Ulysses' sailors of the Oxen of the Sun, especially as Sicily was known in those days for its cattle, and there are many place names derived from *taurus*, bull, for instance, Taormina, once Tauromenium (but there are also several on the other side of the strait, in Calabria— Gioia Tauro, Taurianova).

Some Sicilians have appropriated by error a Homeric story which Homer set in the region of Naples, and have therefore named a cove on the Riviera of the Cyclops, north of Catania, Porto Ulisse, the Port of Ulysses. Sicily's Cyclops, however, though also named Polyphemus, is not the one who appears in the Homeric story. The Polyphemus of Sicily was the Cyclops in love with the nymph Galatea, who preferred the shepherd Acis, son of Pan. Surprising Acis with Galatea, Polyphemus crushed him under a great rock. The blood which flowed from his body became a river, the Fiume di Jaci of today, and his memory is preserved in the names of the high-perched Aci Castello, from which Polyphemus is supposed to have hurled his rock; Aci Trezza; Aci Catena; and the important city of Acireale.

The loves of nymphs seem to have fascinated the Sicilian Greeks. The Fountain of Arethusa at Syracuse, a spring so large that Nelson was able to water his ships there in 1798 on his way to win the Battle of the Nile, is the witness to one such story, whose various versions go back to the 6th century B.C. That ferocious virgin, the goddess Artemis, always ready to frustrate a love affair, intervened when Arethusa fled her lover Alpheus, turning Arethusa into a spring and Alpheus into a river. Even as a river he was a persistent suitor. Though Artemis had placed the spring in Sicily while the River Alpheus rose in the Greek Peloponnesus, the Alpheus flowed underground, and undersea too, to mingle its waters with those of the fountain. This feat was proved, ancient stories had it, because when oxen were sacrificed at Olympia, the fountain of Syracuse was reddened by their blood; and a cup thrown into the Alpheus at Olympia emerged in the Fountain of Arethusa. The fountain is mentioned, among others, by Strabo, Pausanias, Pindar, Virgil and especially Cicero, who visited it and described it as "an incredibly large spring, teeming with fish, and so placed that it would be swamped by the waves of the sea were it not for the protection of a massive stone wall." The pool is still teeming with fish today, principally gray mullet, which should be in salt water, not fresh; but the wall was once broken down by an earthquake, letting in the sea and the mullet as well; and though it has since been rebuilt, the mullet have apparently accommodated themselves to their changed environment.

The legend of Persephone was born, not in Greece, but in Sicily, and originated not with the Greeks, but with the Siculi. It is a food legend, which affects traditional observances of the present day, and it was engendered quite naturally from the two sets of divinities most important to the Siculi—those of the underworld, because of the presence of Etna, and those of fertility, because of the Siculian cult of grain, which they claimed they were the first to receive as a gift from the goddess Demeter. Hence the myth of the kidnapping of Persephone by Dis (Pluto), who carried her away to the underworld through a rift struck in the ground, now filled by Lake Pergusa.

Pluto performed this feat a second time when Persephone, finding herself lonely in the underworld, desired the company of her servitor, the nymph Ciane. Bursting from a bottomless cavern, Pluto caught the nymph up into his chariot and struck the ground with his trident, opening another passage to the underworld. The opening, filled by her tears, is now the spring from which the Ciane River flows. Spring and river are bordered by papyrus, the only place in Europe where it grows wild.

The descent of Persephone into the underworld in the

fall and her return in the spring is an obvious allegory of the growing cycle. In ancient times, the March feast of Demeter celebrated the arrival of Sicily's early spring, and today St. Joseph's Day, March 19, has replaced it. It is one of the most important festivals of Sicily. Bonfires burn all night throughout the island, while celebrants dance and sing around them. Persephone's annual descent to the underworld corresponds with the festival of Santa Lucia, celebrated in Syracuse in December. Legends about this saint differ, but all of them have to do with her intervention to save the city from the famine that afflicted it on her death. One story says that starvation was averted by mysterious ships, which heaped up cargoes of wheat on the shore and then disappeared as inexplicably as they had arrived. Another version credits her with having sent flocks of quail, which fell on the shore to be easily captured. The first story explains why the Syracusans eat only wheat, cooked in one form or another, during her December holiday, and the second why, on her secondary feast day in May, quails, turtledoves and other birds are loosed from the cathedral.

Sicilian religious festivals are characterized by color, vehemence, sometimes fanaticism, and there is a heavy mixture of superstition with religion. The brilliance, the passion and the excess of the Sicilian celebration is paralleled by the high exuberance, the color, and the exotic flavorings of Sicilian sweets. Sicilian festivals and Sicilian desserts are two consistent facets of a basically Oriental culture, but the correspondence between the two is more precise than this. In Sicily the eating of certain sweets on certain occasions becomes a rite, a devout observance, or the casting of a magic spell. "Every sweet represents a fact," a Sicilian writer has put it. "Every dessert is an episode."

Take, for instance, what gastronome Renato Giani has called "the two unshakable rocks" of Sicilian dessert making, *cannoli* and *cassata*. (Neither of them is the least rock-like between the teeth; on the contrary, both are lusciously melting.) *Cannoli* means "pipes," an accurate enough description of their shape, for they are cylinders of sweet pastry, whose filling varies from place to place, or for that matter, from cook to cook. A common combination is cream cheese, honey and almond paste; often bits of candied fruit are added; sometimes the cream is of the type used in cream puffs or éclairs; sometimes it is buttermilk cream; sometimes it is chocolate-flavored. *Cannoli* were also once called *cappelli di turchi*, Turkish hats, indicating a Sicilian belief that they were of Saracen origin; but while the various fillings no doubt are, *cannoli* are thought to antedate Saracen times and even Christian times. According to this theory, the shape of *cannoli* reproduces that of those mysterious prehistoric stone steles of magical or religious import called menhirs, which were probably fertility symbols. In any case, *cannoli* seem to have been served originally at weddings; the guests who ate them were participating in a ceremony designed to insure fruitfulness to the new family. Later, *cannoli* became associated also with Easter—a feast of rebirth—but nowadays, though the Easter association has not wholly disappeared, they are eaten all year round by persons most of whom are quite unconscious of the mystical past of this sweet.

Cassata is an Easter specialty too, but though I have seen it described as a "sacrificial dish," I have not been able to discover what precise significance is attached to its appearance at this season, if any, except perhaps that its rich deliciousness makes it appropriate for a festival of rejoicing. It appears in multiple forms, but I imagine the one I sampled at Acireale was more or less classic. Its base was of spongecake, combined with a rich cream of ricotta cheese, liqueur-flavored, spotted with bits of candied fruit and chocolate, combined with vanilla ice cream, the whole melting away together in the mouth. Ice cream is sometimes omitted; or the cream may be a sort of custard made without cheese; or lady fingers or almond cake may be substituted for the sponge cake. One thing that never seems to be left out is the candied fruit.

Frutta dei Morti, fruit of the dead, made from "royal dough," *pasta reale*, flavored with almonds, is very definitely a dessert whose magical and superstitious connotations have not yet receded entirely into unconsciousness. They are eaten on All Souls' Day, the Day of the Dead, and in ancient times they may have been placed before tombs, for the dead to eat. Later they were eaten on that day by the living, either as a protective charm against the spirits of the dead or as a form of communion with them. Nowadays they are for most persons no more than exquisitely decorated delicious pastries, but they remain attached to this particular holiday, and in the rural districts have not lost all of their mystic meaning.

The sugar-coated almonds thrown at the bride and groom at weddings are a memento of an ancient practice which has not yet entirely died out in Sicily—marriage by capture. There are still some districts where a mock kidnapping of the bride is staged, with the groom's men helping to carry her away, while the opposition, representing perhaps the bride's family, perhaps other potential suitors protecting their future chances, feign opposition. The missiles of this ritual battle are the almonds, originally thrown at the contending warriors; but now the target is the newlyweds, and the almonds are often replaced by confetti.

There are some Sicilian pastries whose names, and shapes, may strike the Anglo-Saxon mind as irreverent—for instance, nipples of the Virgin and St. Agatha's breasts. The Sicilian mind seems to react differently. The first originated in a monastery and the second (which appears both as pastry or as nougat, indifferently; it is the form that matters) seems still to be eaten with a conscious sense of ritual.

St. Agatha, the martyr whose breasts were cut off, is the patron saint of Catania, and it is on St. Agatha's Day that this sweet appears in the pastry shops of that city.

The number of other sweets which mark specific saints' days is numberless, and it is to be assumed that most of them are consumed, as in other parts of Italy, without ritualistic intention. *Pietrafendola*, rocksplitter, a cylindrical cookie so hard as to threaten the teeth, is associated with the feast of the Immaculate Conception. St. Joseph's Day sees the appearance of the *sfinci di San Giuseppe*, flavored with orange peel. Of the many sweets created in convents or monasteries, some are produced for specified religious festivals, though more are destined for all-year-round eating, with the object of producing revenue for the institution from the sale of pastries of which it has a monopoly because the recipe has been kept carefully secret. Such are the *fette del Cancelliere*, made in the Palermo monastery of that name; the *trionfo di gola*, the triumph of the palate; and the *pantofole* (slippers). *Frutti alla Martorana*, the pastries whose shape and colored frosting makes them resemble natural fruit deceptively, are so called because they were originally a specialty of the Martorana monastery.

Other common Sicilian sweets may be made in monasteries, convents, or ordinary bakeries: the pine-nut *pinoccate*; the hard *mostaccioli*; the *pizzicati*, close relatives of the Neapolitan honey cakes called *strufoli*, made preferably with the exceptionally fine honey of Mellili or Floridia; the *biscotti di San Marco*, of fine wheat flour, lard and sugar; biscuits whose dough has been mixed with honey and Marsala wine, flavored with anise seeds; pistachio-flavored cookies; *taralli*, rings of puff pastry frosted with confectioner's sugar. One Sicilian dessert, *zuppa angelica*, angel's soup, may throw some light on the mysterious name of the custard-filled liqueur-drenched cake called *zuppa inglese*, English soup. It is not soup, but here *zuppa* is equivalent to "sop," a moistened bread or cake; is *"inglese"* a distortion of *angelica*, which makes more sense than *inglese*? *Zuppa angelica* is a sort of sponge cake swimming in an egg-and-chocolate cream; eliminate the chocolate and transfer a thickened cream to the inside of the cake instead of the outside, and you have a reasonable facsimile of *zuppa inglese*.

All these rich, colorful, highly-flavored and almost cloyingly sugared desserts suggest the Orient, and for many of them Saracen origin has been established. A great deal of marzipan appears in Sicilian confections; the very word, *marzapane* in Italian, comes from the Arabic *martabān*. *Torrone* (nougat) is believed to be of Saracen origin also, and though it is made in various forms in many parts of Italy today, it is probable that it started its Italian career from Sicily. In any case, no other place, even France's Montelimar, makes it better; a piece of Sicilian *torrone* often has the gloss of fine porcelain (it is better eating). Candied fruit, *frutta candita*, are probably of Saracen origin also. Almost any fruit can be so treated—oranges, lemons, figs, pears, cherries and even squash—and Sicily claims to have mastered the technique of making them so that the flavor of the fresh fruit remains unaltered in the candied form. The fruits are candied whole, and eaten for their own sake, or cut into tiny bits to enrich other desserts —nougat, marzipan, pastries, creams, ice cream.

Ice cream may not have been a direct invention of the Saracens, but it was in any case a development of one of their gifts to Italy, sherbet—which they themselves are supposed to have learned to make from the Chinese. It very probably got its start in Sicily, which still, at its best, outdoes even Naples, and is often credited with making the best ice cream in the world. Italy introduced sherbet and ice cream of all flavors—one made of the same cream used one celebrated case, the Italian who did so was a Sicilian.

This was Francesco Procopio, who popularized ice cream in Paris when he opened there, in 1670, the first ice-cream parlor, the Café Procope; it still exists, though it is a restaurant now.

A Sicilian ice-cream parlor would strike no visiting American as foreign. Here are rows of great canisters of ice cream of all flavors—one made of the same cream used in a zabaglione is particularly tasty—and here are fancifully named mixtures like American sundaes: the Cardinal's Cup, the *semifreddo* Misto Umberto (a variant of *cassata*), and dozens of others, crowned with whipped cream, chopped nuts, fruit and fruit syrups, maraschino cherries. Instead of soda, you have *granita*, a frozen drink, of which lemon and coffee seem to be the most popular flavors, which looks in the glass like chopped ice. Chocolate ice cream is frozen into the shape of truffles, apples or other decorative forms; orange sherbet is served in chilled hollowed-out oranges; different-colored ice creams are used to produce elaborate pyramids, erupting volcanos, imitation bouquets, or foliage. These elaborate confections are on tap in shiningly modern ice-cream shops, while the humbler kinds are sold at street corners from brilliantly painted venders' carts—not so very humble, for even the simplest of Sicilian ice creams are likely to contain morsels of fresh fruit, or of candied fruit, like the *cassata gelata*, sold from the carts as brick ice cream, with a light-colored (perhaps vanilla or hazelnut) center studded with fruit and perhaps flavored with liqueurs, and a surrounding border of sherbet (currant or strawberry).

Because it seems to belong in the same gamut, I suspect Saracen origin also in a mysterious homemade dessert I tasted at an isolated farm in a place so obscure that if it has a name, I never learned it; but I could find it again by driving from Francavilla di Sicilia (Messina) into the savage interior. I have never encountered it anywhere else, nor seen it mentioned in tourist guides or articles on Sicilian gastronomy. As offered to me by the farmer's wife, it was an almost forbiddingly dark jelly, which had hardened in attractive light earthenware molds, also homemade, with traditional designs cut into their bottoms—heads, acanthus leaves, cuttlefish, dogs, hearts, escutcheons and many others —which of course embossed the jelly when it was turned out on a dish. Its maker called it *mostarda*, but it bore no relationship to the chutney-like condiment of Cremona of the same name. The ingredients, I was told, were sugar, grape juice, mustard and the ashes of grapevine twigs, which reminded me a little of the concoctions medieval doctors used to prescribe for their hapless patients. I tasted it gingerly. The flavor, rich and complicated, defied analysis, yet it was strangely familiar. The cook insisted stoutly that there was nothing in it except the four ingredients she had named. Suddenly I realized what it reminded me of— pumpkin pie. "Are you sure there's nothing else in this?" I asked. "For instance, spices?" "Oh, spices, of course," she said. "Especially cinnamon." The mystery was solved.

Even more so than in the rest of Italy, desserts, especially pastries, tend in Sicily to become localized. Each town has its own special cakes or cookies, which differ from those of the next place. It is a safe bet that if you have never been in Palermo you have never tasted *cucciddata*, made of almond cream, dried figs, candied squash, sultana raisins, toasted hazelnuts and bits of chocolate. Palermo is particularly rich in sweets, which her citizens tuck in while seated agreeably under the trees of the Piazza Castelnuovo; bun-like cakes filled with chilled cream; fritters; ring-shaped cookies which may be normally sugared or may surprise you, when you bite into them expecting a sweet taste, by being sharp with anchovy; the local version of *cassata*, of course; *fruttate*, which here means sherbets; scooped-out melon containing ice cream; and all the standard pastries of Sicily. Catania is known for its *schiumoni*, of egg whites, sugar and almonds, as well as its St. Agatha nougat, its *moscardini*, its *ossa di morto*, dead man's bone (which plays the same role as the *frutta dei morti* elsewhere), and its fine ice cream, whose rich fruitiness has caused it to be dubbed "country ice cream," *gelato di campagna*. Ragusa has *schiumoni* too, but calls it *schiumette*, and also *giuggiulena di miele* and *pagnuccata, torrone gelato* (frozen nougat) and *torrone cedrato* (citron-flavored nougat). Whatever else goes into it, nougat must include nuts (its very name in English and French comes from the Latin *nux*, via popular Latin *nucatus*) and the nuts must be roasted, in Italy, at least, since *torrone* comes from the Latin *torrere*, to roast, even though Cremona tries to derive the name of its variety of nougat from *torre*, tower. The province of Caltanissetta has a couple of other famous sweets to its credit, the ring-shaped *ciambelle* of San Cataldo and the almond pastry of Mussomeli.

Among Sicilian desserts, *crostata alla Siciliana* is also worth noting. It is a sort of open-faced pie, whose crust is filled with a compound of heavy cream, a little potato flour to thicken it, vanilla, orange and lemon peel, and chopped pistachio nuts. *Zabaglione, sbaglione,* or *zabaione,* however you feel like spelling it, of egg yolks, Marsala wine and sugar (heavy cream can be added), is known all over the world. A variant is what Syracuse calls wine sauce—egg yolks, Moscato wine, raisins, cloves and cinnamon, cooked in a double boiler until it thickens slightly; you can eat it that way if you want, but it may also be poured over a variety of other desserts to add lusciousness.

The tendency of every Sicilian town to devise its own particular sweets persists for other categories of food as well. "The island's cooking," one gastronomic expert wrote, "may have common bases, but it varies from town to town, from region to region, one might even say from family to family." It is therefore somewhat rash to attempt to find a common denominator for the Sicilian cuisine, though some specialists have tried. One of them wrote that "Sicilian cooking tends to be rather strong, and in its choice of ingredients reflects the optimistic and rugged character of the Sicilians themselves." I do not think the description "optimistic" would have occurred to me. Perhaps he was thinking of those brilliant desserts, gay in color and spicy in taste, which are flamboyant and exuberant, surely; but exuberance is the lighter side of explosiveness, of violence, which does seem to be a part of Sicilian character insofar as one dares apply any generalization to Sicilians as a whole. The people of Catania, of Syracuse, of Enna, of Palermo, of Trapani, are all products of different mixtures; but one thing they have in common at least is that all of them *are* mixtures; and the same thing is true of the cuisines they have developed. "As for the blended savors which are the major characteristic of Sicilian cooking," wrote Gaetano Falzone in *Itinerari Palermitani*, "the field in which it beats all other cuisines, it derives from the mixing not only of the different races which have come onto Sicilian soil, of the different civilizations, of the different cultures, but also of the different cuisines." Every Sicilian dish is a medley. What they have in common is that they are blends. There are very few straightforward creations in the Sicilian repertory, based on single ingredients treated with simplicity, exception made for such oddities as chick peas cooked by being stirred violently in a kettle with heated pebbles, which Trapani took over from the Arabs a thousand years ago and has preserved unaltered. Even in Ragusa and Enna, the two provinces whose cooking is the simplest, most dishes are compounded of mixed flavors, and many of them are heavily spiced, often with such exotic seasonings as sesame seeds, squash seeds or the edible pods of the carob tree, the Saracen touch again.

The Sicilian habit of mixing different culinary influences in a single dish accounts, Falzone maintains, for one of the island's most characteristic dishes, *caponata* or *caponatina*, which, whether it is a mixture of different cuisines or not, is indisputably a mixture of ingredients. He waxes dithyrambic about it. "He who has not eaten a *caponatina* of eggplant has never reached the antechamber of the terrestrial paradise," he wrote, "a mixture of vegetables, greenery and the essences of the sea in which figures as the base eggplant cut into cubes and fried, with an addition, in a fantastic sauce, of tomatoes sweet and sour, celery, capers, olives, tuna roe, crayfish tails or lobster claws, a composite flavor comparable to no other, but which recalls nostalgically exotic lands and seas, whose mingled aromas evoke the chief characteristic of Sicilian cuisine, the field on which all the other cuisines give battle to one another." He was writing of Palermo, where the seafood component of this dish is important, but its capital is Catania, where it is strictly a vegetable dish, unless you count a dash of anchovy juice.

Whether or not Catania originally mothered *caponata*, it refers to it with maternal affection by the tender diminutive form, *caponatina*. So far as I have been able to find out, there is no difference between *caponata* and *caponatina;* some places call it one, some the other. You should be warned, parenthetically, that if you see *caponata alla marinara* on a menu, it is a sarcastic name given to ship's biscuit (or stale bread), soaked in water to soften it, impregnated with garlic, and eaten with a flavoring of basil or orégano, spread with pitted black olives and anchovy fillets; the ambitious strive to make it approach real *caponata* by adding one or all of such relishes as pimentos preserved in oil, pickled eggplant, capers or onions.

It may have been confusion with the enriched *caponata alla marinara* which caused the author of one Italian cookbook more honored in the United States than in her native Italy to define *caponata* as "a Sicilian combination of pickled vegetables." True, *caponata* is often served cold, as a side dish, as well as hot, but it is decidedly not pickled. A tourist publication designed to introduce foreigners to Italian cooking defines it as "chopped eggplant cooked in an open pan with a sauce of tomatoes, onions and mixed herbs." This is all right as far as it goes, but it is incomplete. It suggests a pleasant but not necessarily subtle dish something like the French *ratatouille niçoise* (eggplant, zucchini, tomatoes and sometimes peppers, stewed together), also served either hot or cold, and, I am inclined to think, better cold than hot. *Ratatouille*, lackadaisically cooked, as, alas, it usually is, can be a limp lifeless unarresting concoction (indeed, *ratatouille* not described as *niçoise* means simply a mediocre stew, from the contemptuous Provençal word *ratatoulho*, which has also given the French their slang word for Army food, *rata*), and the same is true for *caponata*. I had eaten *caponata* on the mainland and wondered why Sicilians made such a to-do about what seemed a characterless uninspiring mess of pottage. Then I met it in Catania.

The Catania *caponatina* was a marvel, but a marvel whose secret was easy to understand. It consisted simply in cooking each of its chief ingredients—eggplant, peppers, tomatoes, onions and celery—separately. Thus each could be sautéed in the *soffritto* most appropriate to it, with the dosage of cooking fats (chiefly olive oil) which it could most advantageously absorb. Each could be seasoned by its own selection of herbs and spices. And, perhaps most important of all, each could be allotted its optimum cooking time. The different components of my Catania *caponatina* had been started on their way at different times, so that all of them reached simultaneously the perfect state for being combined to finish their cooking in an enormous iron skillet with vinegar, capers, olives, a little tomato sauce and a hint of anchovy juice; it was served still sizzling in the skillet.

With the first taste, I saw Signor Falzone's point. The dish was a blend, true, but a blend in which each ingredient asserted its own flavor at the same time as the others. The dish did not give the impression of having a single taste, a synthesis produced by its several components. It had as many different flavors as it had ingredients, which were all perceived at the same time without losing their separate personalities; and it melted away in the mouth almost as literally as ice cream. I would have arranged to come back the next day to sample the cold leftovers, but there were no leftovers. For a *caponatina* like that there shouldn't be.

It is no doubt because of its nature as a supreme mixture that *caponata* has spread everywhere over an island where all of the eaters are mixtures too, particularly since it is capable of infinite transformations and is therefore readily adaptable to any taste. Every city, town, village and hamlet in Sicily seems to have its own sacrosanct recipe for *caponata*, the basic element which links them all together being the eggplant. To this each locality brings its own additions. Some of them, besides those of Palermo, noted above, are octopus, hard-boiled eggs, artichokes, asparagus and, a curious variant, the omission of tomato and the addition of grated chocolate. This appears in Syracuse, the city the Saracens slighted, which seems strange since the rich unctuous flavor of chocolate might seem more in tune with palates shaped by Arab tastes than with those of a city antithetical to the Saracens. (But chocolate, of course, though it may seem to have a natural affinity for Oriental aromas, was unknown in Sicily in Saracen times, being a New World product.)

The converse to the wide circulation of *caponatina*, a protean confection acceptable to all of the many elements which make up the Sicilian population, is the restricted range of the dish which has been transferred most directly from the Arab to the Sicilian cuisine, *couscous*. If any import of distinctly foreign nature were to become universal in Sicily, one might have expected a Saracen dish to make it. Nevertheless, *couscous* has remained peculiar to the region of Trapani, the area which to this day shows most distinctly the imprints of its Saracen past; and even there it is seldom found on restaurant menus, which might get it into more general circulation, but is eaten generally in private homes.

Couscous as found in all Arab countries is made from coarsely ground semolina flour (others are sometimes used, for instance, millet) steamed over bouillon, and served with mutton or chicken and vegetables, usually cooked in the same bouillon which is simultaneously steaming the semolina. This can be done in a double-boiler, but the utensil originally used seems to have been a large, round, almost flat perforated spoon, through whose holes the steam could rise into the semolina, heaped up on it, and laid simply over the pot containing the bouillon. This utensil is called a *couscous*, hence the name of the dish. (A second theory holds that the word is onomatopoeic, representing the hissing of the steam, which might very well be the case whether *couscous* referred originally to the food or the utensil with which it is made.) In Trapani, the word is spelled *cuscussu*, which is obviously the same.

If you are familiar with North African *couscous*, you may be surprised when you meet the Trapani variety. Instead of mutton or chicken you will get fish, which is cooked in the liquid under the semolina before being heaped on it when served, and the chances are that in North Africa itself or in North African restaurants abroad, you have found that *couscous* has almost invariably meant mutton, though sometimes chicken. This is indeed the general rule. The dish apparently developed among nomadic tribes in the interior, and they made it with what they had, the sort of animals that could travel with them. But though it is comparatively rare, fish *couscous* does exist on the North African coast. Trapani is thus violating no Saracen traditions in making *cuscussu* with fish, and, since this province has practically no meat but plenty of fish, it is conforming to the Arab example by making it with what it has. Trapani *cuscussu* is made in an earthenware double boiler called a *mafarhada*—the Arabic name for this utensil. At a little distance from Trapani, I have heard *cuscussu* defined as "fish stew with semolina," not too far off, for in North Africa also the semolina or other grain is occasionally cooked in the bouillon instead of being steamed over it, though this is not quite simon-pure *couscous*. Another description heard in the region was "fish soup with macaroni," but at this point I fear *couscous* has been left definitely behind. If at Porto Empedocle you see *kuscus* on a menu, don't order it in the expectation of getting Trapani *cuscussu*, or you will be in for a surprise; *kuscus* there is a sweet cake of semolina flour, sugar and pistachio nuts.

As *cuscussu* is restricted exclusively to Trapani, so *pasta con sarde* (pasta with sardines) is restricted exclusively to Palermo. The gastronomic guidebooks will not tell you this; they list it as a "Sicilian" specialty, which I had always supposed was common to the whole island. But when I asked for it in a restaurant in Catania, I was met with a blank stare. Not only did they not have *pasta con sarde*, they evidently had never even heard of it. It was on the third or fourth try that I got the right answer: "If you want *pasta con sarde*, you will have to go to Palermo. Nobody makes it here."

Perhaps other localities have renounced trying to reproduce this dish, knowing that they would be incapable of holding a candle to Palermo, which makes almost a cult of it. The recipe that comes as close to being the standard version as any starts with the rich tasty *'ncasciata* pasta, which looks like overgrown spaghetti, and smothers it with a mixture of sardines, onions, toasted almonds, sultana raisins, wild fennel and tomato extract. There are innumerable variations on this. One I encountered compounded the sauce with chopped sardines, olive oil, pine nuts, fennel and assorted spices. Another used beaten egg, wild fennel, almonds, onions, crushed sardines and the sardine cooking juices. Sometimes the dish appears garnished with slices of hard-boiled egg.

A well known Sicilian dish which has gotten around more than the others, and which is not very different from similar dishes on the mainland, except for higher seasoning and its intriguing name, is *farsumagru*, which means "false lean." The exact meaning of the name escapes me; in Italian it is *falso magro*, of which the second word often refers to Lenten fare, but that does not appear to be the idea here, since it is a meat dish. It might refer to the fact that the meat may be adulterated by a plentiful addition of bread, but not all *farsumagru* recipes contain bread. The simplest way to describe *farsumagru* is to say that it is a braised beef or veal roll, whose stuffing may contain a great variety of ingredients, but necessarily chopped hard-boiled eggs, and, among the various possible seasonings, nutmeg.

Another dish that has managed to spread pretty much over the whole island is *arancine*. These are balls of fried rice containing chopped meat sprinkled with grated *caciocavallo* cheese, which can become rather complicated when in addition to its customary beef it is adorned with chicken livers, mushrooms and egg. This is another joking name. *Arancine* ought to mean "little oranges," but there is no hint of oranges in this dish, except that the shape of the balls of rice suggests them. Playful names are not rare in Sicily; for instance, when you see *quaglie*, quail, offered in a Sicilian *friggitore*, that is to say a sort of snack bar specializing in deep-fried tidbits, don't expect it to mean a game bird. What you get is a chunk of eggplant, crisply fried, which you fit into a bun, salt lightly, and eat from your fingers, standing up before the counter.

The cousin of the *friggitore* is the *rosticceria* ("roastery"), a feature of Sicilian life, which, like the *pizzeria* of Naples, is prepared to offer stand-up snacks at all hours of the day or night (within reason), based on some of the more complicated manipulations of bread. Palermo is especially given to the *rosticceria;* instead of sitting down to a formal lunch, Palermitans often prefer a quick bite at the counter of the *rosticceria* or at one of the tiny tables provided wherever there is room. The choice is ample. The simplest is *sfincione*, a sort of scone covered with grated cheese. For those who are hungrier there is St. Vitus's *sfincione* (*sfincione di San Vito*), for which the scone is converted into a sandwich of cheese, salame and meat sauce. At the Christmas–New Year's season, the *sfincione di Natale e Capodanno* is made of finer kneaded dough, with a filling of béchamel sauce and a purée of chicken and peas. *Cacciottu* is a lozenge-shaped bun split open along one side, filled with thin strips of cheese and salame, its slit sealed with soft creamy cheese, dipped in melted lard, and heated briefly in the oven. *Guastella, focaccia* or *vestedda* (the name varies from place to place) is a very soft round bun sprinkled with sesame seeds, with a filling of a thick slice of ricotta cheese, thinner slices of a harder cheese, cubes of bacon, and calf's spleen (*meusa* in the Palermo dialect, *milza* in Italian), dipped in hot lard before eating. This is *vastedda schietta*, unmarried *vastedda; vastedda maritata* (married *vastedda*) adds strips of pork and pork spleen. Pizza in Palermo has a crust of unleavened bread, moistened with olive oil and filled with salt fish (in Catania the filling would be cheese and anchovy). Either the *rosticceria* or the *friggitore* usually makes *panelle*, little balls of chick pea flour, deep fried, and although this ought to be rather the prerogative of the *friggitore*, the *rosticceria* also may offer deep-fried pieces of vegetables—potatoes or cauliflower especially.

The penchant for lunching on the Sicilian equivalent of the sandwich is one manifestation of the importance bread has in the Sicilian diet—one of the few statements which can be made about Sicilian eating habits which applies generally everywhere in the island. Bread is the basic food of Sicily's hard-working frugal population, so it is natural that considerable attention is given to it and that it comes in a great variety of forms. The sort of bread the Sicilian eats most often is *casareccio* (homemade), of unkneaded dough. It is somewhat heavy, but lighter breads of every kind abound. This homemade loaf is usually large, round and coarse in texture; the more subtle varieties are provided by professional bakers. Sicilians are much given to the offshoot of the bread family called *frittelle*, fritters. They have a knack for producing tasty fritters with a minimum of means—the dough contains no egg, it is simply flour, water and salt, though sometimes fritter dough is enriched with the addition of mashed potatoes or rice. Plain fritters may be served as a hot bread accompaniment for the meal, but usually the fritter dough is only the envelope for something else—anything else, almost, for the variety of fritters is endless. They may contain anchovies, tomato or other vegetables, chopped meat or fragments of meat, or chopped jet black Sicilian olives, with their agreeably bitter tang, sometimes surprisingly countered by the addition of a sultana raisin or two. In Catania, very simple fritters enclose either ricotta cheese or anchovies, and are called *crispeddi*.

The importance of bread does not reduce the appeal of pasta. "No region," writes Falzone, "can boast of the variety of *pasta asciutta* which Sicily offers: among types of pasta made by hand, are *anelletti; orecchie* Jewish style; *maccheroncelli* breaded or twisted; *taglierini* made of semolina flour; *cavatoni incannati*, prepared with a rich sauce of tuna or of meat, or with tomato sauce, accompanied by zucchini or slices of fried eggplant or peas. Other dishes are cooked with machine-made pasta, for instance, spaghetti with *tuma*, a very fresh cheese laid in thin slices between two layers of pasta well soaked with sauce, so that when you lift it on your fork it is a pleasure to see its filaments spin out as from an old-fashioned spinning wheel; or the lasagne of New Year's and Carnival time, three fingers wide, put into the oven with a sauce of pork, chicken giblets and generous pieces of cheese." Catania has its own lasagne, *lasagne alla catanese*, with a sauce of eggplant, yellow peppers, anchovy, olives, capers, tomato pulp, garlic and chopped parsley. From Catania also are spaghetti with eggplant, and, this being a city of ingenious cookery, there are a number of other local pasta dishes. One so indigenous that its name is in local dialect, *chiama vinu*, "the wine call," is a coarse country dish made with short pasta boiled, then coated with bread crumbs, and finished in a covered frying pan, with the addition of chopped anchovy fillets. Dry and thirst-provoking, it is usually accompanied by a flood of Etna wine, hence its name. Then there is *cannelloni alla catanese*, egg pasta stuffed with chopped meat, smothered in a thick tomato sauce, covered with a layer of pecorino cheese and baked in a very hot oven so that the cheese covers it with a crunchy golden-brown crust. Ragusa has its *pasta 'ncasciata*, with a sauce containing cottage cheese, chopped meat and hard-boiled eggs, baked in the oven; *anchellini*, a sort of ravioli stuffed with chopped meat and fried; ravioli under its own name, stuffed with ricotta cheese and served with tomato sauce and grated *caciocavallo* cheese; *lasagne in foglie*, alternate layers of the pasta and of chopped meat, meat gravy and grated cheese; *la scaccia*, oven-cooked pasta pie filled with cut-up tomatoes and broccoli or cheese; *la sfoglia*, also a pasta pie, in this case with a filling of sausage and ricotta; and *i gnucchitti*, homemade macaroni seasoned with pork gravy. Besides the Palermo pasta specialties already mentioned above, the capital has other specialties, like spaghetti, with tomato sauce and slices of fried eggplant, seasoned abundantly with basil, and thickly powdered with cheese; and with macaroni, prepared *alla paolina* with cabbage, pine nuts and raisins. Enna makes *lasagne ricce*, of egg pasta with a chopped meat sauce, which is orthodox enough, but then gives it a special and surprising flavor by a light powdering of sugar and cinnamon; and *maccheroni a treddita*, the thick macaroni here seasoned with a sauce containing eggplant and cheese. Spaghetti in Syracuse comes with a dressing containing tomatoes, green peppers, eggplant, olives, anchovy fillets, capers, basil, garlic and olive oil. Trapani combines lobster with pasta. Add to these local forms of pasta the Sicilian marriages of pasta with fish, either as *pasta in brodo* (*brodo di pesce con gli attuppateddi*, tiny elbow-shaped noodles in fish chowder), or *pasta asciutta* (spaghetti with inkfish in its own dark juice), and you may find yourself obliged to accept the Sicilian claim that it outdoes Naples in the realm of Southern pasta, as Bologna outdoes all other localities in the realm of Northern pasta.

The cereal dishes, bread and pasta, constitute with fish and vegetables the trinity of the Sicilian diet. Here the king of fish is the tuna. It provides many of the favorite fish dishes of Sicily, and especially of Palermo, which makes a tuna stew: the fish is baked in the oven with onions and a rich but subtly seasoned sauce; and has a specialty made with *lattume*, soft tuna roe, browned and fried; elsewhere *bottarga di tonno*, the hard roe, is either grilled or boiled, and served with olive oil or lemon juice. Cold preserved tuna may go into a sandwich with hard-boiled egg, sausage and cheese. Swordfish, particularly prized in Messina, may appear as *rustutu cu'sammurigghiu*, fried in oil and seasoned with salt, pepper and marjoram; or with a crusty coating of cheese or bread crumbs; or more sophisticatedly with its slices sautéed in oil along with tomato, onion, celery and capers. If you see *anelletti gratinati* on the menu you may expect ring-shaped pasta, but it may also mean rings of cuttlefish dipped in oil, bread crumbs, chopped parsley, salted and peppered, and baked in the oven. The adventurous may be tempted by boiled octopus, which weigh eight to ten pounds and have tentacles as thick and fleshy as a baby's leg.

All the smaller fish of the Mediterranean are prepared in Sicily in every conceivable manner, with every city boasting its own specialties. Licata (Agrigento) is reputed to do the most skillful job of cooking fish in general. Porto Empedocle is ranked first for frying sole. The best eels are those of Lake Lentini, though eels abound everywhere in the coastal lagoons. Ragusa is rated high for its treatment of fish, fried; stewed; *in brodetto;* accompanied by shellfish or custaceans; or baked with olive oil, onion, tomatoes, celery, olives and capers. Messina is reputed for *sciabaccheddu*, tiny fish deep-fried; for its two chief fashions of cooking dried cod, called *stoccafisso* in most parts of Italy, but *pesce stocco* here—*in bianco*, which means boiled and served with oil or lemon, and *alla messinese*, with tomato sauce, onion, celery, olives and capers; and for the mussels and *vongole* clams it raises in the lagoons of Ganzirri and Il Faro, of which the latter often go into sauce for spaghetti while the former can be cooked in any number of ways. Syracuse might perhaps be rated ahead of Messina for its treatment of mussels; I recall from there breaded mussels cooked in their shells, with a bit of cheese, olive oil and a delicate dosing of herbs, and an *insalata di mare*, in which the mussels were combined with prawns and squid. The white-fleshed Syracuse *dentice* (dentex) with artichoke hearts is worth mentioning too. Syracuse also raises shell-fish, including oysters, and is noted for its large and luscious *gamberoni rossi*, marine crayfish or shrimp which I cannot identify more precisely among the several hundred species of these animals. Palermo is noted for a number of fish dishes, for instance its *capone*, a box-headed fish of delicate flavor, cooked here with celery, olives and capers; its red mullet, carefully sorted out into *triglie d'alga* and *triglie di scoglio* (seaweed mullet and rock mullet—the latter are better), which are fried in olive oil and served with lemon juice and chopped parsley; and above all the sardines. A curious Palermo treatment of this fish involves, along with the expectable olive oil, herbs and lemon juice, the curious combination of anchovies, pine nuts, raisins, a little sugar and a dash of nutmeg. This does not exhaust Palermitan ingenuity in dealing with the sardine, which it also treats in fashions described as "like sausage," "like cuttlefish," "like cutlets" or "like thrushes." Catania produces a *brodetto* of octopus, rockfish, mussels and a trifle too generous a proportion of the often rubbery squid for my taste. The maigre is often stewed with wine, onion and herbs. Fresh-water fish attract minor attention in an island so rich in the salt-water varieties; it is usually treated very simply, fried in olive oil and served with lemon juice.

At a time when most of the rest of Europe is under snow and ice, the peas and artichokes of Sicily begin to appear. The mean Sicilian temperature for January is 51 degrees, seven above that of Rome, 18 above Milan. Hardly have the last vegetables of early winter passed than the first of spring arrive. Sicilians take ample advantage of this practically year-round procession of vegetables, preparing them in a limitless variety of ways, but so regularly using one flavoring agent that it might be possible to say that while mint is a mark of Roman cooking and nutmeg of that of

Modena, the Sicilian cuisine is characterized by a fondness for the sharp tang of anchovy.

As in southern mainland Italy, the eggplant is in high favor in Sicily. The simplest way to cook it is to make slits in the lower half of a whole unpeeled eggplant to let the heat reach the inside without burning the outside, and fry it in pre-heated oil with no seasoning except salt and pepper. Almost as easy is to cut the unpeeled eggplant in half, stuff it with its own scooped-out pulp mixed with chopped black olives, chopped anchovy fillets, cut-up bits of tomato and capers, season it with black pepper but no salt, moisten it with olive oil, and bake it in the oven in an oiled dish, producing *melanzane alla Siciliana*. Another oven dish consists of skinned sliced eggplant placed in the cooking dish in alternate layers with a filling of chopped meat, tomato sauce and grated cheese; egg beaten together with more grated cheese is poured over the top, and the whole baked in a pre-heated hot oven. Stuffed tomatoes may be an economical dish in Sicily, where instead of the chopped meat commonly used elsewhere, the main ingredient of the stuffing is often bread crumbs. This is made tasty with the addition of onion, anchovy, capers, parsley and nutmeg; a layer of bread crumbs moistened in olive oil is spread on top to make a crust, the whole is sprinkled with olive oil, and baked in a moderate oven. Broccoli is bedded on thinly sliced onions, moistened with olive oil, pointed up with bits of anchovy fillets, and sprinkled with grated cheese; red wine is then poured over it and it is cooked in the oven. Broccoli, squash and eggplant are all frequently cut into small chunks, coated with batter, and deep fried. Palermo *frittelle* is a mixture of artichokes, fava beans and peas, cooked in an *agrodolce* sauce with onions. Artichokes alone are often given the *agrodolce* treatment also. Squash, sliced thin, and cooked in a frying pan with oil and garlic, to which vinegar and sugar are added for the last two minutes of the cooking, is of course an *agrodolce* dish too. Caltanissetta is noted for the variety of its mushrooms and its many ways of preparing them.

Sicilian salads are usually gay mixtures of a variety of vegetables, devoid of lettuce, a plant which grows better in cooler soils. *Insalata siciliana* is extremely simple, just quartered tomatoes, with basil and chopped garlic, and the standard salad dressing of olive oil, wine vinegar, salt and pepper. *Olive schiacciate* (crushed olives) has a good deal more than olives in it. Green olives are crushed sufficiently so that the pits start from the pulp but are not removed; they give added flavor to the dish, during the time it is allowed to stand (it is usually made a day in advance) to exchange perfumes with the other ingredients—diced celery, sliced onion, cut-up preserved red peppers, chopped garlic, capers, and, if you want an added tang, chopped anchovy fillets—of course.

Sicilian tomato sauce differs from similar confections made elsewhere by the addition of diced eggplant and sweet red peppers to the extra-ripe tomatoes from which it is made; basil and anchovy provide flavoring highlights, along with olive oil and garlic.

Sicilians do not eat much meat, partly because it does not accord with the climate, partly because it is the most expensive category of food, and this is today a poor country. But of what they do eat, a larger proportion than in most other countries is what is considered a luxury in the United States —game. It is not a luxury in Sicily, being at the end of everybody's rifle; but since there is little forest, it is small game. Agrigento cooks wild rabbit in an *agrodolce* sauce, of which the sweet element is composed of a mixture of honey and sugar, and the sour of a blending of vinegar and lemon juice; it is served surrounded by eggplant, celery, olives, capers and toasted almonds. Trapani also cooks it in an *agrodolce* sauce, but there the accent is on the rich mixture of herbs that goes into it. Caltanissetta, as an inland city, is noted for its game dishes, especially partridge. Enna is also inland and also good for game. The bridge from wild to domestic meat is provided by rabbit, cooked according to one fashion in vinegar with fava beans, and served with any handy vegetables. Ragusa produces it "Portuguese style," *coniglio alla portoghese*, stewed with mixed vegetables, Palermo in *agrodolce* sauce with capers, olives and celery.

Sicilians are experts at grilling meat, on those comparatively rare occasions when they eat it. Palermo is as good a place as any for beef, rare and not usually of particularly good quality in Sicily, but the capital has a specialty of *braciolone* or *braciolettine avvolte*, meat roasted in a crust. *Braciola*, however, is roast pork stuffed with pine nuts, raisins and almond paste, which may sound like a rather sweetish combination for meat, even pork, but Ragusa goes even farther in this direction with its so-called meat "cake" (*grattò*), in which meat swimming in its gravy is combined with sugar, almonds and walnuts. Ragusa is pork-eating, known for its stuffed pork chops (*costate di maiale ripiene*) and its cold jellied pork (*gelatina di maiale*). Its most famous meat specialty, however, is a meat pie made of lamb or kid, hotly peppered and sprinkled with chopped parsley (*pasticcio di agnello o di capretto*). Palermo prefers baking kid in the oven (*caprettu o forno*, in the local dialect). Palermo also eats a good deal of veal—*cuscinetti alla siciliana*, veal roast with mushroom sauce, or *involtini*, veal rolls, popular throughout the island with various kinds of stuffing; Palermo is apt to put in bread crumbs, chopped prosciutto, grated cheese and parsley, and grill it on a spit. Finally a stand-up dish in Agrigento, since you eat it at stalls in the market, but are not likely to find it in restaurants, is *gli stigghioli*, kidneys, liver, and more exotic inner morsels grilled or deep-fried before you as you wait.

Poultry dishes are curiously rare in Sicily; like the ancient Romans, the Sicilians seem to raise hens chiefly for their eggs. By the time they have ceased to give eggs, they are rather tough and stringy for the table. Nevertheless Ragusa has a notable specialty in this category, *pollo sultano,* the sultana hen, which, like guinea hen, has a taste halfway between domestic fowl and game; and whether it should be classified as poultry or game, I frankly do not know. Wild, it lives in marshes, being almost an aquatic bird (not one with webbed feet), but whether Ragusa catches the wild fowl or domesticates it I have not discovered. It is easy to domesticate; the ancients raised it as a decorative bird which, like the peacock, strutted about temples and palaces, displaying its purplish and dark green plumage, pointed up by its red beak and feet. Wild or tame, its flavor is superb. The only other poultry dish it seems necessary to cite here is also a specialty of Ragusa, turkey stuffed with bread, pasta and chopped meat.

Two other Sicilian dishes might be mentioned also. On Mardi Gras, Christmas and New Year's, Ragusa makes a turkey or chicken soup thickened with pasta. Snails are cooked in a garlic sauce, and turn up especially on festivals, since they provoke a thirst which leads to much consumption of wine.

The ancient Romans esteemed the wines of Sicily, first of all Mamertino, a favorite of Julius Caesar, followed by Tauromenitanium, from what is today Taormina, Potulasum and Biblinum. Caesar had Mamertino served at a banquet to celebrate his third consulship. Martial and Pliny are among the Roman authors who mention it. "If in your green old age, like that of Nestor," one Roman wrote, "they give you an amphora of Mamertino, you can put what name you will to it, even that of the most famous vintage." Modern experts might not go quite so far, though the dry, golden-yellow, fruity, strong (15 to 17 degrees) Mamertino, which goes well with fish, is still recommendable enough, but the sweet variety, usually drunk with dessert, may better be left to the people who produce it, who consume almost all of it anyway. Its production is very limited.

The ancient Greeks, whose wines were then considered better than those of Italy, may have been closer to the modern estimate of Sicilian wines—Sicilian Greeks are believed to have invented a game called *kottabos*, of which the object was to throw wine from a glass into a vessel on the other side of the room without spilling any, an amusement which would hardly occur to anyone in possession of a glass of really fine wine. Today, Sicily's rank of third in Italy for wine production is for quantity (some 160,000,000 to 185,000,000 gallons a year), not for quality. Most Sicilian wines are coarse and heavy, and are used chiefly for blending. They are made almost entirely from local grape varieties (two of which, Grecanico and Greco, hint at a Greek origin by their names) and perhaps the island could produce finer varieties if it imported different vines. Val di Lupo, which exceptionally uses mainland grapes, is much more delicate than most Sicilian wines. The high sugar and alcohol content of the others is no doubt encouraged by the common method of pruning and training the vines close to the ground, so that they are half-cooked by reflected heat from the soil. As a result, no Sicilian wines are really dry, though some are so called because they are relatively less sweet than the others, which is the sense in which that description should be understood in this chapter. Another impediment to any desire, if it exists, to develop fine wines in Sicily, is that the island's vineyards are often divided into very small parcels, making it difficult to produce wines of uniform quality in commercially profitable quantities. The most notable wines of Sicily therefore fall into the category of heavy sweet liqueurish dessert or apéritif wines. The greatest of these is the only Sicilian wine with an international reputation—Marsala.

Marsala is a thoroughly artificial product, though it started out naturally. Its development was more or less accidental. In the 17th century, a period when drinkers liked their beverages heavy, a great deal of Sicilian wine was shipped to England. To fortify it for the journey, alcohol was added, in the proportion of one part to 50 parts of wine. The strengthened wine sloshed around in its barrels on the often storm-shaken windjammers on which it traveled, acquiring an agreeable richness and smoothness in the process. It took about 100 years, however, before it occurred to anyone to produce this result purposely. It was normal that an Englishman should interest himself in a fortified wine, since the English have always shown a particular fondness for this sort of drink, which accounts for their strangleholds on port, sherry, and Madeira. The Englishman who became in 1773 the impresario of Marsala was John Woodhouse, who realized that these west Sicilian wines showed a certain natural similarity to the other three and could perhaps be developed to compete with port, which somebody else was handling. He proceeded to improve both the primitive methods of cultivation which had previously existed and the treatment of the wine thus produced. Marsala became a favorite wine in England, and spread throughout northwestern Europe. It seems only just, under the circumstances, that Marsala's cathedral is dedicated to St. Thomas of Canterbury.

The mixture of grapes from which Marsala is made today produces a wine high in alcoholic content (17 to 20 degrees), rich in sugar (between 5 and 10 percent) and low in acidity (five or six parts per 1,000). To this is added a *passito* wine of the region (that is, one made from partly dried grapes, which is consequently very sweet, further fortified by the addition of brandy), and finally a must of unfermented grape juice which has been "cooked" (actually it is only heated to convert it into a thick sweet syrup). This is aged in red oak casks, in which it should be left at least two years, but five is better. The result is a dark-colored wine, sometimes described as orange or amber, but brown would not be far off, with a very sweet caramelish taste, meant for a dessert wine or an apéritif. To get the best, there are several traps to avoid. For one thing, Marsala needs age, but if a year is indicated on the bottle, all it means is that this is the year of the *oldest* wine it contains. Marsala is usually a blend of the wines of several years, and there is no way of knowing what their proportions are; the only protection against disappointment is to buy the product of a reputable house. Also important is the place where the wine is grown. In principle it comes, of course, from Marsala, but as a matter of fact from anywhere in the province of Trapani, and it also overflows into the provinces of Palermo and Agrigento. To make sure that the Marsala you buy is really Marsala, look for the neck label with the silhouette of Sicily on it. Within the category of genuine Marsalas, there are various qualities. S.O.M. (Superior Old Marsala) should be reliable, and may reach 18 degrees of alcoholic content. If what you want is the dessert wine, do not be led astray by the name Ribollito di Marsala. This is a table wine, dry as Sicilian wines go, and rather rich, a result of leaving the stems in the must during fermentation; it is rather heavy, 12 to 14 degrees.

The taste for very sweet wines has declined of recent years, and Marsala does not enjoy the demand it once did. However, it has a few other strings to its bow. It is the ideal wine to combine with egg yolks to produce *zabaglione*. Bottles labeled Marsala all'uovo are an approximation of this—Marsala wine, spirits and egg—but this is to my mind a rather sickly concoction. There remains its utilization in a rich sauce to embellish ham, preferably the boiled variety, or veal.

Every province of Sicily has its own wines, but most of them are found only on the spot. If they leave the island, it is for blending. An exception is Faro, a dry red which is exported to several countries, including the United States, probably because emigrant Sicilians have created a demand for it there. Faro is not a bad choice, as Sicilian wines go. An attractive ruby in color, it is harmonious and generous in taste, and with a couple of years' aging can work up to as much as 14 degrees, and accompany red meat successfully. It comes from Messina, which also produces Capo Bianco and Capo Rosso; of these the white is dry and light for a Sicilian wine, only 12 to 12.5 degrees, not bad with crustaceans, or any fish for that matter, the red, though very light in color, more authoritative, 13 to 15 degrees; Taormina Scelto, an agreeable though rather thin not quite dry white, which I drank on the spot and found passable enough, though the Taormina label covers a multitude of sins; and the descendant of Julius Caesar's favorite, Mamertino.

The Etna region straddles the provinces of Messina and Catania; the volcano's famous name probably causes more attention to be paid to Etna wines than they would be given if they grew on less eventful soil. Vines are cultivated on the slopes of Etna up to 3,900 feet, and Sicilians of the region have told me that the higher the vineyard, the stronger the wine. If true, the labels ought to identify the wine by altitude rather than by place names, and as a matter of fact, one of them does, Etnei di Mezza Montagna (Halfway-Up Etna); this is the height at which the best Etna wines are supposed to grow. Most of the Etna wines you meet will be white; more whites are produced to begin with, and what reds are made are usually exported for blending. The Etna whites are dry, run from 12 to 13.5 degrees, and are sometimes slightly sparkling naturally, good enough with fish without breaking any records. The inferior reds are apt to be tart, and the 12 to 14 degrees they reach ordinarily is not enough to take the curse off this. If you want to sample a red Etna, one of the Catania wines, Biancavilla, is full and strong, 12 to 14 degrees, but sharp, though with age its bitterness tends to soften. One wine I drank myself at Catania, which I suppose was local, I do not find listed in any reference book; called Rimasole, it was a quite recommendable table wine, white, dry and rather full-bodied.

Syracuse offers a lengthy list of better than ordinary wines. Albanello di Siracusa is a white which comes in dry and sweet varieties. The first is a straw-yellow, with a pronounced flavor which may be a result of the unusually long aging period it spends in the wood (eight to ten years), high alcoholic content for a dry (17 to 18 degrees), and a certain bitterness; though it is recommended for fish, its overpowering qualities make it a better apéritif than an accompaniment for food. The sweet variety is a dessert wine, made from grapes allowed to wither on the vine, like French Sauternes. The Eloro wines, white and red, have retained their ancient name, though the river they took it from has now changed its own to Tellaro. Italians esteem them, considering them superior to most other Sicilian wines, though less flattering opinions have been expressed by foreign experts. Perhaps one reason why the islanders attribute finesse to the white is its unusual lightness for Sicily, only 10 to 11 degrees. It is golden yellow in color, dry, agreeable and refreshing, excellent with fish, and, somewhat surprisingly, can stand aging. The red, a brilliant pomegranate, is full-bodied (14 to 15 degrees) with a rich taste, and, if sufficiently aged, can accompany a roast with considerable distinction. There is also a rather heady *rosato*. Val d'Anapo comes in either white or red, and with a year or so in the bottle, is one of the island's better productions.

The white is exceptionally dry, 12 to 13 degrees, and of a deep golden color; the red, also dry, is light in color and body (also 12 to 13 degrees). Pachino Rosso, on the contrary, is a very heavy powerful wine (14 to 17 degrees), of a rich ruby color, most of which is exported for blending; when it reaches the table, it is usually a mixture of the vintages of several years. Syracuse dessert wines are among the best on the island, either Moscato di Siracusa, 14 to 17 degrees, which though velvety manages somehow to give the illusion of being relatively dry, or Naccarella, 18 degrees, whose sweetness goes undisguised. The coarse red Francofonte of Syracuse is mentioned in *Rigoletto*, presumably because its name is singable; there is no other evident reason for distinguishing it.

Ragusa has Cerasuolo or Frappato di Vittoria; the first name means cherry-colored, as the wine is, and the second is the name of one of the grapes which go into it, but whichever label you meet, it is the same wine—fruity, heavy in alcohol (15 to 17 degrees), ranging from semi-sweet to very sweet. A dry white from the same province, Ambrato di Comiso, deep amber in color, is also heavy, 18 degrees at its top.

Caltanissetta has no wine we are obliged to list, but its neighbor Agrigento offers one under its ancient name, Akragas Bianco, a dry white running 12 to 15 degrees, which doesn't get outside the province except for blending. Agrigento also produces an apéritif wine, Aragona-Canicattì, whose name suggests Spanish inspiration, and whose strength (13 degrees) is the result of adding concentrated sweet must to its own, from which the skins are removed early, as if it had been intended to make a rosé; it still reaches only a cherry red color, and despite the sweet must is dry. Trapani, besides Marsala, has Alcamo, also a dry white, 12 to 15 degrees, rather neutral in character.

Palermo vies with Syracuse in offering a large gamut of

better-than-average wines. One of the best is the red Corvo, which means "crow"; there is a legend that the first Corvo vine sprouted from a stick which was being used to drive away an annoying crow. The best are the Corvo di Casteldaccia and the Corvo di Salaparuta. Light colored, it has a pronounced perfume and a high alcoholic content, 13 to 14.5 degrees. After three years in the bottle, it is a worthy accompaniment for meat. There is also a white Corvo, bland and unexciting, 12 to 14 degrees, pale, and not quite dry enough to reach distinction. Valledolmo as a white is golden, dry and rather rich, 12 to 13 degrees, and the also dry red, with the same alcoholic content, is pleasingly light for a Sicilian wine. But the best Palermo wine is perhaps Zucco, which I cite last because you will be very lucky to find a bottle of it; it has almost disappeared. Most of the domain from which it came once belonged to the royal House of Orleans. It is a brilliant yellow-to-amber wine, with a rich flavor and a high alcoholic content for a dry white, 15 to 15.5 degrees, wonderful with fish. What you can find easily enough is a Zucco dessert wine, but this is not the same thing at all. It is like any number of similar wines, which you can take or leave alone. But if you come upon the dry Zucco, seize it.

Enna, the inland province, is the country of the Val di Lupo, made of off-island grapes. It comes in white, red and rosé, runs about 11.5 to 12 degrees, and is suave, a quality not noticeably Sicilian.

The satellite islands remain. Their most notable wine is Malvasia di Lipari, produced chiefly on Salina and Stromboli; the grapes are allowed to dry on the vine for a week after ripening to obtain an alcoholic content of 15 to 16 degrees. It is thus a sweet dessert wine, of a rich golden color, one of the best of this type in Sicily, which does not lack such wines. Pantelleria uses the *Zibbibo* or Alexandria muscat grape, to make the amber sometimes cloudy Moscato di Pantelleria, spicy, velvety and heavy (15 to 16 degrees). Finally Ustica produces a beverage which, if you are willing to take the word of an enthusiast for the island, is "an agreeable white wine, with bronze highlights, dense, perfumed and highly agreeable, which carries in itself the caress of the sun and the force of volcanoes."

Sicilians seem more given to soaking pastry than themselves in liqueurs, but let me call attention to just two drinks which fall into this category: Caltanissetta makes a digestive called Amaro Siciliano, and throughout the island you may find A.L.A., otherwise Antico Liquor Amarascato. This is said to go all the way back to the days of Greek Sicily. Partly dried grapes, like those used for making *passito* wines, are fermented in cherry-wood casks (a refutation of the story that it was the Roman Lucullus who introduced the cherry into Italy), and take on a mingled flavor of grape and cherry. The result is technically a wine, heavy (19 degrees) and sweet, but it tastes more like a liqueur, and is drunk either after the meal, as a digestive, or before it, to prepare the spirit for the good cheer to come.

THE
DOMAIN

OF THE
STONE AGE

XIX

Sardinia

When God had finished making the world, some un-promising material, bare rock and thin soil, was left over. He disposed of it by tossing it into the Mediterranean and pressing it down with his foot. It was named Ichnusa, from the Greek *ikhnos*, footprint, which was its shape, as you can see by looking at the map, if you exercise a little imagination and remember that mapmaking at the time this legend was born was only approximate. Ichnusa is today, of course, Sardinia (Sardegna in Italian), and modern geologists are not in agreement with the legend. Far from being made last, Sardinia, in its region, came close to being made first. It is rich in primary rocks, geologically older than either Sicily or the Italian mainland itself.

Sardinia has stayed older. On its ancient soil, the Stone Age still exists. Its monuments remain, the *nuraghi*, stone structures built before historic times of heavy blocks of stone laid in courses, one upon the other, without mortar. There are 7,000 of them today; it is estimated that there were once at least three times as many. Some of them are extremely elaborate. The Nuraghe Losa at Abbasanta is three stories high, and contains built-in closets. The *reggia nuragica* of Sant'Antine at Torralba (the "palace *nuraghe*") is in reality not a palace but a defensive work, consisting of one large *nuraghe* in the center and three small ones arranged in a triangle with protecting walls around it. Serra Orios is a village of 70 *nuraghi*, arranged in blocks with a system of streets, some of them paved, with squares dominated by temples. At Barumini is one of the most stupendous examples of megalithic architecture ever discovered in the western Mediterranean area, the Nuraxi, a city of *nuraghi* dominated by a great fortress, dated at about the 13th century B.C. At least contemporaneous with the *nuraghi*, and perhaps earlier, are the *domus de janas*, called sometimes "tombs of the giants" and sometimes "witches' houses," artificial caves used for burials. Definitely earlier than the *nuraghi* are the megalithic constructions on Monte d'Accoli; the dolmens and megalithic buildings at Arzachena; the Neolithic necropolis at Anghelu Ruiu; and, on the deserted plateau of Ortu Abis ("garden of the bees"), the unexplained beehive-shaped stones found there. At Macomer vestiges have been discovered of a Stone Age culture which knew no metal, and the "Mediterranean Venus," a female figure of black basalt classified as Neolithic.

Man-made structures are not all that remain in Sardinia of the Stone Age. Man himself reached the island in the Stone Age, and it is arguable that he has never emerged from it.

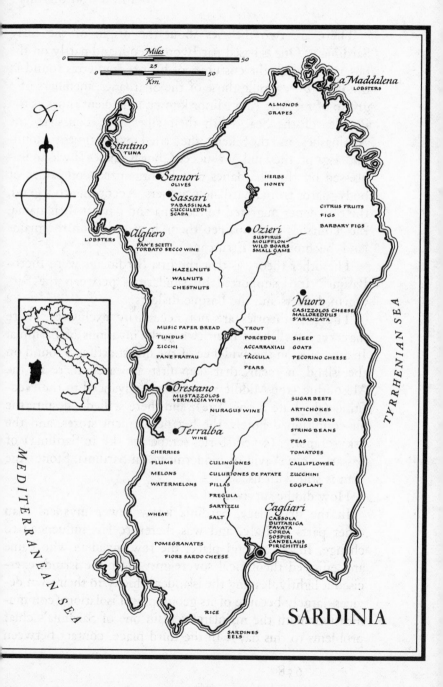

Miles
0   25   50
Km.
0   50

N

La Maddalena
LOBSTERS

ALMONDS
GRAPES

Stintino
TUNA

Sennori
OLIVES

HERBS
HONEY

Sassari
PABASSINAS
CUCCILEDDI
SCADA

CITRUS FRUITS
FIGS
BARBARY FIGS

Alghero
PAN'E SCETI
TORBATO SECCO WINE

LOBSTERS

Ozieri
SUSPIRUS
MOUFFLON
WILD BOARS
SMALL GAME

HAZELNUTS
WALNUTS
CHESTNUTS

Nuoro
CASIZZOLOS CHEESE
MALLOREDDUS
S'ARANZATA

MUSIC PAPER BREAD
TUNDUS
ZICCHI
PANE FRATTAU

TROUT
PORCEDDU
ACCARRAXIAU
TÀCCULA
PEARS

SHEEP
GOATS
PECORINO CHEESE

Orestano
MUSTAZZOLOS
VERNACCIA WINE

NURAGUS WINE

SUGAR BEETS
ARTICHOKES
BROAD BEANS
STRING BEANS
PEAS
TOMATOES
CAULIFLOWER
ZUCCHINI
EGGPLANT

Terralba
WINE

CHERRIES
PLUMS
MELONS
WATERMELONS

CULINJONES
CULURJONES DE PATATE
PILLAS
FREGULA
SARTIZZU
SALT

WHEAT

Cagliari
CASSOLA
BUTTARIGA
FAVATA
CORDA
SOSPIRI
CANDELAUS
PIRICHITTUS

POMEGRANATES

FIORE SARDO CHEESE

RICE

SARDINES
EELS

TYRRHENIAN SEA

MEDITERRANEAN SEA

SARDINIA

There are two theories about the origin of the early Sardinians. One is based partly on legend, and partly on the observation that the costumes of bronze statuettes found in the *nuraghi* resemble those of the Shardanes, members of a group of races of Asia Minor known in ancient times as the Peoples of the Sea. With their allies, the Tourshas, the Akaiuashes, and the Sikeles, they tried several times to dominate Egypt; they did not succeed, but Rameses II was so impressed by the Shardanes that he organized companies of bodyguards from Shardane prisoners. According to legend, the Shardanes migrated to Sardinia and gave it their name; the Tourshas accompanied them, but settled on the mainland, becoming the Etruscans.

The other theory is that the first Sardinians were Ibero-Basques. It is supported by similarities between the Sardinian dialects and the Basque dialects.

The two theories are not necessarily exclusive. There may very well have been two early invasions of Sardinia. In any case, on the evidence of the oldest artifacts found on the island, it seems that man first appeared there in the Mesolithic (the Middle Stone Age), advanced to the Neolithic (the Late Stone Age), and there stalled—despite the air-conditioned hotels, the big department stores, and the "skyscrapers" (seven stories scrape the sky in Sardinia) of Sassari, a city "avid of modernity." In Sardinia, Stone Age man is still with us.

How did he survive?

In the first place, Sardinia knew fewer invaders than other parts of Italy, and was therefore less influenced to change. In the second place, the few invaders who came and enjoyed theoretical sovereignty over the island, exercised it lightly, leaving the islanders chiefly to their own devices, largely because of its geographical isolation (communications with the mainland remain one of Sardinia's chief problems to this day). In the third place, contact between new arrivals and the original population were minimal. Not only was Sardinia isolated; its population was isolated from external influences also, both collectively and individually.

Collectively, the original population withdrew almost entirely from the purview of the invaders. Invasion of an island, in pre-aviation days, meant necessarily establishment on the coast. Various occupiers set up beachheads there, but this afforded them only slight leverage on a population which preferred to inhabit the interior. The Sardinians present the anomaly of a people of islanders who abhor the shoreline and the sea. Of the three provincial capitals of the island, only one, Cagliari, is on the water, and Cagliari was founded by Phoenicians, not Sardinians. It has been suggested that Sardinians fled the coast to avoid the attacks of pirates and other raiders. The real reason seems to have been different. Until a quarter of a century ago, the coasts were miasmas of malaria. The Sardinians considered them fit only for animals.

How could foreign influences penetrate a people which, though it inhabited the same island as its invaders, lived in a different part of it? How could they propagate their innovations through a discontinuous population many of whose individuals lived the lives of hermits, maintaining only intermittent contact even with their own fellows? John Donne to the contrary notwithstanding, many a Sardinian was an island—the mountaineer alone in his cabin, the shepherd alone with his sheep, the peasant alone on his land, the bandit alone in his lair, the fisherman (where there were fishermen) alone in his cockleshell of a boat.

In any case, no invader ever came in force or attempted genuinely to colonize the island. The first—Phoenicians from Tyre and Sidon, who turned up about the 9th century B.C., attracted by Sardinian minerals—were interested only in trade, not in conquest. It was to have a port and a trading counter that they founded Karalis (Latin Carialis,

Italian Cagliari) in 814 B.C., making it older than Rome and possibly than Carthage also. The Carthaginians, who appear in the 6th century, *were* interested in conquest, and held the coast, while the Sardinians remained non-cooperatively in the interior, until the Romans dislodged the Carthaginians after the First Punic War in 238 B.C. Meanwhile the Carthaginians had kept the Greeks out; the only Greek survival on the island is a name, that of the city of Olbia (which means "white"), where Phocaean Greeks from Marseilles had attempted unsuccessfully to set up a beachhead of their own. The Romans held Sardinia at arm's length, supplying administrators and soldiers to police the population, but making no effort to colonize it. After the collapse of the Empire, the Vandals, the Byzantines, and for a single year the Goths, held nominal sovereignty over the island, but none of them attempted really to exercise it. The Saracens, so successful in Sicily, occupied only temporary toeholds in Sardinia. A probable Arab settlement was Dorgali, supposed to have been named for a Saracen pirate who founded it. The guttural accent of the dialect spoken in Dorgali is sometimes held to be an echo of Arabic, while the former presence of Saracens may account for the soft black eyes and feline grace of the city's women. Some other possible traces of Saracen influence may have resulted simply from trade—for instance, some of the geometrical designs worked into the handwoven carpets which are one of the island's specialties, or into the lace of Bosa. This also could account for the fact that Sardinians today ride pure-blooded Arab horses, not the sleek racing animals into which they have been bred elsewhere today, but the kind the Arabs themselves rode in the 9th century, small, strong, wiry, swift and agile. Or they may be simply descendants of horses that escaped the few Saracens who were there and went wild; there are still herds of wild horses in the Giara di Gesturi, on the border between the provinces

of Cagliari and Nuoro. Saracen influence has also been in-
voked to explain the *vassoni*, boats of tressed reeds of a type
still operating in the Persian Gulf; but after all craft of this
sort exist also in Wales and on Lake Titicaca in the Andes,
where no one suspects Saracen inspiration.

Neither the Genoese nor the Pisans, who jockeyed for
control of the island from the early 11th to the early 14th
century, made any important impression on it—the Genoese left one or two small seaside settlements, the Pisans a
few Romanesque buildings. What could have been the most
important Genoese memento, the city of Alghero, founded
by the resplendent Doria family about 1100, was erased in
the 13th century when the Aragonese expelled its population and established a colony of Catalans in what Charles V
called "*Alghero bonita y bien asentada*"—"Alghero, lovely
and well situated." Alghero remains to this day a Spanish
city, whose inhabitants speak 13th-century Catalan, and
whose customs and appearance have given it the nickname
of Little Barcelona. No visible marks were left on Sardinian
life when Vittorio Amedeo II of Savoy became King of
Sardinia, and after the House of Savoy succeeded to the
rule of Italy and the island thus slid smoothly and automatically into the Italy which was unified under him, a century
of modern Italian government hardly touched the island
either.

During the three millennia of Sardinian history, only two
foreign contributions—one Roman and the other Spanish
—got under the Sardinian skin at all, and neither of them
penetrated deeply. The Romans found Sardinians speaking
a non-Indo-European language and left them speaking
Latin. Sardinian, the oldest of the neo-Latin languages, con-
serves in its vocabulary more Latin words than any other.

Sardinia was "strongly Hispanized" by the Aragonese,
according to one historian, but aside from the existence of
Alghero the traces today seem superficial—the 80 watch-

towers Philip II built along the coast to signal the approach of Moslem raiders; the Spanish-looking town of Teulada, well to the south of the Alghero area; and the local habit of calling the town of San Leonardo in Spanish Siete Fuentes, for the seven fountains which are its chief pride. There is no evident Spanish imprint on the population.

Otherwise, foreign influences seem to be confined to details of costume borrowed now and again from outsiders, and also perhaps to details of religious rites. Sassari's Festival of the Candles on August 14, when enormous tapers are offered to the Virgin, may be derived from a medieval Pisan custom, but the mantillas worn for it seem Spanish, and there are Spanish courtship dances in the Sicilian repertory, along with others which recall medieval and Renaissance steps of the mainland. The waist-constricting corsets and the ornaments of some Sardinian women's costumes are ascribed to very ancient Minoan and Mycenean examples. Gold ornaments, especially earrings, sometimes show Punic designs. In some localities, the women wear a high conical headdress which seems to be derived from the medieval *hennin* of the peninsula. The men sometimes wear what looks like a short skirt, occasionally referred to as a kilt, but if the jacket covering it is removed, its real nature is disclosed; it is a tunic, imitating the garment Roman soldiers wore under their breastplates.

The Sardinian shepherd today still dresses in sheepskins. On his head is the island's characteristic bonnet, the same which appears on the bronze statuettes found in the *nuraghi*, something like a stocking cap, but instead of ending in a point or a tassel, it has a broad flap, which may be thrown over the neck, to one side, or, most often, over the forehead, which it protects from the sun. He lives today much as his protohistoric ancestor must have lived. He spends his time with his roving flocks (and the swineherd with his horde of black pigs), moving when the grass is exhausted from one pasturage to another, taking his house with him —a portable shelter which he has tressed together from straw or weeds. Alone among his long-haired sheep, he makes cheese from their milk himself, and it is he who shears them. When he brings the wool down to the villages, the girls get together, and, sitting in a circle, prepare the wool for home spinning. It is a festive occasion, like a corn husking bee, at which cakes flavored with honey and orange, or *torrone* are passed around. It is called the *graminatorgiu,* and nobody knows for how many centuries it has been going on. Among the other traditional chores of Sardinian women are weaving carpets; producing home-spun cloth; making baskets of reeds, dwarf palms or asphodel— nothing is done here that could not have been done quite as easily and by the same methods in the Stone Age. Even the furniture in the house is homemade, from the beds, tables and chairs to the chestnut-wood kneading trough. The hearth is in the middle of the room, as it was in the *nuraghi.*

. The Neolithic Sardinian who was not a shepherd was probably either a hunter, a fisherman or a farmer. This is still true today. The hunters have abandoned the spear for firearms, but the others make do often with the pre-metallic implements of their ancestors. In the lagoon of Oristano, modern fishermen use wooden hooks; tuna are harpooned with the ancient trident. Farmers in the Stone Age were sometimes mere collectors rather than cultivators; in Sardinia today more than 730,000 acres, about 3.5 percent of the agricultural land, a trifle more than is devoted to utilizable forest, is given over to collecting wild or half-wild foods —from olive groves, for instance, which are allowed to grow as they will without attention and consequently give scanty yields. In the province of Cagliari you may come across a waterwheel of brushwood with pots tied to it, turned laboriously by a blindfolded donkey. A common sight is a yoke of oxen pulling a wooden plow. The bullocks of Busachi are hitched to primitive carts with solid wheels, probably already centuries old when Virgil described them 2,000 years ago. They have not changed since.

Indeed, nothing changes very fast in Sardinia. When the Romans came in the 3rd century B.C., some of the *nuraghi*, then 1,500 years old or so, were used as fortresses against them. The ancient worship of the island's most important god, Sardus Peter, persisted long after the coming of Christianity. Pope Gregory the Great tried to suppress the pagan rites being practiced in the Barbagia area in the 6th century B.C., but their remnants are still with us. The ancient agrarian cult is honored at Mamoiada by the masked *mammuthones* and *issokadores* dancers. Another ceremony of the agricultural cult is still performed today, the *penniris*, a purification rite of the summer solstice, though it has adopted a Christian garb. Petrarch saw it and described it as a harking back to the cult of Adonis, using a familiar Greek name to explain the nature of the equivalent Sardinian deity. Ritual dances may be accompanied in Sardinia today by the music of the *launeddas*, or *launus*, vertical triple flutes, with a long central pipe and two shorter ones at either side. Sardinia is the only place in Europe where it survives.

The Sardinian, as we shall see, also eats like Stone Age man.

Sardinia is the second largest island in the Mediterranean, Sicily being the largest. The two are separated by a considerable stretch of open water (14 hours by steamer) and have more dissimilarities than similarities. Sicily is closer to the toe of the Italian mainland (which it resembles in some respects, but not very much) than it is to Sardinia. Sardinia is closer to France's island of Corsica (which it resembles in some respects, but not very much) than it is to Sicily—or, for that matter, to the Italian mainland (13 hours by steamer to Genoa). It takes only about an hour to make the crossing to Corsica, 7½ miles away, visible to the naked eye.

Sardinia and Sicily are both mountainous, with only one plain of any importance in each—Campidano in Sardinia, Catania in Sicily. But Sardinia's highest point, the Punta la Marmora, on the Gennargentu plateau, reaches only 5,960 feet; Sicily's Mount Etna is 10,749 feet high. Sicilian heights rise to peaks, Sardinian heights to plateaux.

Both islands have a water problem, more acute in Sicily than in Sardinia. Cagliari, where the Campidano plain begins, gets only 19 inches of precipitation a year and throughout the island, practically all the rain falls in the late autumn and spring, quickly running off the bare rocks of the heights and land now depleted of its ancient forests and thus unable to retain moisture. This is largely the fault of man. The Carthaginians, when they held Sardinia, forbade the planting of trees, so that all available land might be devoted to raising grain. The Piedmontese, 2,000 years later, systematically cut down the woods with the illusory object of denying cover to the bandits who hid in them. The huge herds of sheep and goats which the island supported also played an important part in the destruction of the forests. Man, however, was hardly to blame for the vast fire which over a century ago destroyed the forests in the area of Nurra, in the province of Sassari, converting it into a wasteland.

Despite the paucity of woods, Sardinia enjoys a more uniform cover of vegetation than Sicily, which includes extensive areas of almost bare, sun-parched earth. Sardinia does display an alternation of fertile zones with near desert, but there is much less bare earth than in Sicily. The heights are covered by the *macchia*, the brush, which has replaced the ancient forests—spurge, asphoded, lentisk, cactus, wild roses, arbutus, eucalyptus, myrtle, fig trees, medlars. This is a flora much more like that of Corsica than of Sicily; and this is true of the fauna also. It is only in Sardinia and Corsica that the genus of wild sheep called *ovis musinon* is still found. Sardinia has one animal that even Corsica does not know. In certain grottoes hollowed out by the sea live the last survivors of the otherwise extinct Mediterranean seal (*monacus albiventer*), supposed to have found shelter there during the ice ages. The most important of the seal caves is the Bue Marino grotto, meaning "sea ox," which suggests that the seals may once have been considered as food. Any appetites they may provoke nowadays are bound to be frustrated; the seals are stringently protected by law.

Of the natural features of Sardinia, besides the Campidano plain, that which has perhaps determined most sharply the life of the island is the savage Gennargentu plateau, robed in chestnuts and cork oaks, which runs across the center of the island. This, with its accompanying Barbagia region, is the Sardinian heartland, the cradle of early Sardinian culture.

Just north of this central area the zone around Pozzomaggiore, in the province of Sassari, is the best natural pasturage in the island, and consequently an important dairy and breeding center, renowned especially for its horses. Another important breeding and agricultural center is Ozieri in the center of the province, noted for its cheeses, and delicate almond-flavored sweets called *sospiri*, sighs. It is in the Loguduru, the land of "golden speech": "melodious" might be a more apt translation, for this is where the Sardinian dialect is supposed to be spoken in its most harmonious form.

The most marked natural region of Sassari is the Gallura, which comprises the whole northeast corner of Sardinia, starting on the east coast at Olbia and running on the bias to the middle of the northern coast, with the Aggius mountains, a stamping ground for wild boar, as its western boundary. It is a land rich in cork forests, which have endowed Tempio Pausania, the chief town of the district, with a cork-working industry unique in the world. Here is the Costa Smeralda, geographically in Sardinia, but culturally centuries away ever since the Aga Khan made of it a refuge for millionaires, a sort of international enclave for excessive fortunes.

The political divisions of Sardinia lie across its natural divisions in three bands, south to north the provinces of Cagliari, Nuoro and Sassari. All three cut clear across the island, with coasts on both Mediterranean and Tyrrhenian sides, dividing it into three slices, though pretty irregular ones.

The three provinces do not differ very much in climate, and therefore not in food resources either. The greatest deviation is displayed by Cagliari, which because of its comparatively low altitude and exposure to the sirocco is subjected in summer to an almost African climate. It is in Nuoro that the wearing of local costumes is most general and here also that the prehistoric agricultural cult is still celebrated. Nuoro is much given to festivals. On January 17, the feast day of St. Anthony, large bonfires blaze to celebrate the holiday, and visitors are offered *su pupasinu,* sweet bread, in honor of it. The festival of St. Cosimo lasts for a whole week, and the rustic gastronomic specialties of the region are served from stalls set up in the open air. Sassari is the most modern of the three provinces, or at least its capital city is. It was apparently founded in the 12th century, when it was called Thatari, by coastal inhabitants, from Porto Torres especially, fleeing pirate raids. Its chief industry is food processing, for it is the market for a hinterland which produces wheat, vegetables, olive oil, dairy products, meat, game and tobacco.

Attached administratively to Sassari are some islands of more than ordinary interest.

Off the coast from Olbia is the island of Tavolara, whose

peculiarity is that it is populated by goats with golden teeth; they were originally deposited there by pirates, to assure them of a supply of meat and milk during their raids, and developed their peculiar tooth color by an equally peculiar diet—lichens and seaweed. On the far side of Sassari, prolonging the northwestern extremity of Sardinia, is another island with zoological overtones—Asinara, which the Romans called Herculis Insula, and changed it to Insula Asinuaria when they became aware of its peculiarity, a breed of white asses. (There is also a theory that the island's name was Insula Sinuaria, or sinuous island, because of its irregular shape.) There is no dispute about the meaning of its Punta Scomunica, Excommunication Point. This comes from a distant and undated epoch when a swarm of locusts was spotted heading for the island, threatening to eat it bare of vegetation. A holy hermit promptly excommunicated them, whereupon they quite properly fell into the sea and were drowned.

The most visited islands of Sassari province are those of the Maddalena archipelago, which has the rare distinction of having routed Napoleon. He once tried to occupy it, but was beaten off by local forces; it is possible that he did not care enough about Maddalena to try again. What attracts tourists is the tomb and house of Garibaldi on the second largest island of the archipelago, Caprera, now attached to the mainland by an isthmus. After his work of uniting Italy was finished, Garibaldi retired to this island, and ended his life there 26 years later. On his arrival, he assured his future livelihood by thoughtfully bringing with him a large package of seeds.

Sardinia is sparsely populated. On an area slightly larger than that of Lombardy (Sardinia 9,301 square miles, Lombardy 9,191), live, in contrast to the more than 7,000,000 people of Lombardy, only 1,500,000 Sardinians, of whom

450,000 are active—which means that on Sardinia's meager soil every earner is supporting three other persons. Compared to a density of 767 inhabitants per square mile in Lombardy, Sardinia has 136.2, but this overall figure drops sharply over considerable areas. You can drive for miles in some parts of Sardinia without being aware of a human presence. There is nothing but hallucinatory empty space, a limitless expanse of open sky and blazing sun above, vast empty treeless burned plateaux below, roofing heights of bare rock. When you do come on a settlement, it is probably a village of 1,000 to 2,000 persons. Almost all the population lives in places which are not much larger. The only city with more than 100,000 population is Cagliari. Sassari falls a little short of this, and the third provincial capital, Nuoro, has only about 25,000.

More than half of the population lives on agriculture, with little help from nature.

Sardinia enjoys the typical climate of Mediterranean islands, with mild winters and torrid summers, and only slight variations of temperature, or even of humidity, between the coast and the interior. This is agreeable enough for the transient, but the farmer who makes his living from the soil is plagued by violent winds, the *maestrale* (the mistral of France) from the northwest, and the hot moist sirocco from the south; however his greatest problem is drought. Lack of water at useful times, in useful places, and in useful amounts, has been a flail of Sardinia from ancient times, when in Barbagia water was worshiped. The extreme dry season lasts from four to five months; the fields are burned by the sun from May to October. By the end of the summer, the only two Sardinian rivers of any size, the Tirso and the Coghinas, are almost dry, not to speak of the Flumendosa, another of the island's principal water courses, and the Temo, its only navigable river. Then winter comes, and the countryside is flooded with torrential rains, which wash away the topsoil.

These conditions are discouraging for a predominantly agricultural population, and as a result one of Sardinia's difficulties is lack of manpower—an apparent paradox, since there is heavy emigration from the island, 150,000, 10 percent of the population, in the past few years, not, as in southern Italy or Sicily, because there is no work, but because the work available is so unremunerative. Yields are small, partly because methods are archaic, partly because much of the soil is naturally infertile, partly because that which might be fertile lacks water. Irrigation would cure this, and a number of dams have been constructed for this purpose, but for various complicated local reasons, the water held in the reservoirs often remains undistributed to the farms. One of the factors making irrigation and the use of modern machinery impracticable is the small size of farms; more than half do not exceed 7½ acres, a quarter are under 1½. Even these small holdings may be broken up into several plots separated from each other, adding the loss of time involved in getting from one patch to another to the loss of time already incurred in many cases in reaching in the first place the cultivated land from the towns in which 92 percent of the population lives. Most town-dwelling farmers walk to their land, consuming two or three hours daily in this unprofitable fashion; and almost all farmers are town dwellers. Isolated farmhouses (in which it would have been imprudent to live in the not so distant bandit-infested days) are so rare in some parts of the island that it has appeared necessary to coin special words to describe dwellings so daringly located. In the mining area of Sulcis, Cagliari, where some of them do exceptionally exist, they are called *furria-droxius;* in the Gallura (Sassari) region, *stazzi.*

In Sardinia, agriculture means first of all grazing. Only 27.8 percent of the land is arable, as compared to 47.3 percent for all Italy, but there is a staggering 48 percent of rough permanent pasture (the all-over Italian figure is 14.1 percent). Raising livestock is therefore the backbone of the island's economy. First in importance are sheep, of which there are 2½ million head, about a quarter of all the sheep in Italy, more than any other single region can boast. Their chief contribution to the island's revenue is provided by their milk, from which a great deal of cheese is made for export, of which much reaches the United States. The wool is coarse, but since it produces a strong, almost waterproof cloth, it is exportable also. Not much meat goes off the island. Sardinian lamb is tasty, and is sufficiently prized by mainlanders so that they are willing to pay the considerable premium of its costly transport to the peninsula. Mutton does not enjoy this preference and therefore is not an important export item.

Goats come second. Once again, Sardinia has more of these animals than any other region, about 420,000, and once again they account for a quarter of the entire Italian goat population. Like the sheep, goats provide not only milk and meat, but also clothing. The women of Ollolai (Nuoro) dress in vividly colored goat-hair costumes, the men of Osilo (Sassari) wear clothing of handwoven goat-hair cloth; and the same material can be found in many other parts of the island.

Cattle are reasonably plentiful, about 210,000 head, but their importance as a food source is not in proportion to their number, since they are bred chiefly as draught animals. The telltale word *vitella* on Sardinian menus gives this away, the feminine form of the word for veal indicating that it is the heifers, not the calves, which are slaughtered for the table. The hard-worked oxen are apt to be tough and stringy by the time they reach the table; the scrawny cows are poor producers of milk. What milk there is goes into cheese, the cash crop of impoverished subsistence farmers.

There are over 100,000 pigs on the island, whose flesh is tasty from the acorns on which they graze. Oaks are among the most common trees on Sardinia; they are encouraged to grow tall, in order to drop as many acorns as possible.

The chief food product Sardinia derives from its livestock is cheese, above all sheep cheese, the hard type known as pecorino. Pecorino is one of the most popular of all Italian cheeses, accounting for one-seventh of the national output, despite the competitive existence of such other widespread favorites as Parmesan, Gorgonzola and Bel Paese; and although many regions produce it, notably Abruzzi, Tuscany, Apulia and Sicily, Lazio and Sardinia between them account for nearly half of the whole. *Pecorino sardo* does not differ very much from Lazio's *pecorino romano* when made by cheese factories; but some individual touches may creep into the cheeses produced by the shepherds among their flocks, a process often followed because the shepherd, alone on the plateau with his sheep, has neither storage facilities for keeping his milk fresh nor transport to carry it to town regularly. The only way not to lose it is to turn it into cheese on the spot. The piquant *fiore sardo*, "Flower of Sardinia," is in principle always the product of shepherds, and the Sardinians prefer it to all others as a grating cheese for pasta. It is ready for this use after six months' aging, but is also eaten as a table cheese for the first two months of its life. It comes in wheel-shaped form, the individual cheeses weighing anywhere from 3½ to 9 pounds each; the crust is dark yellow, the firm interior varies from straw-yellow to white. *Dolce sardo* is a soft cheese. Usually made from sheep's milk, but sometimes also from that of goats, *fetta* is salty and white, which the ancient Sardinians may have learned to make from the Greeks; at least it is practically identical with the Greek *feta*. *Fresa*, from cow's milk, is best in autumn; so are *preddas* and *taeddas*, pear-shaped varieties of *caciocavallo*. *Su caseggioni*, also of cow's milk, with a taste of the herbs on which the animals feed, is a mountain product. There are also cheeses of mixed cow's and goat's milk. The Gallura region produces a smelly confection referred to unflatteringly in the local dialect as *o casu marzu*, "rotten cheese," or *casu becciu*, but connoisseurs pronounce it delicious. The Barbagia and Gallura regions like *su casu cotto*, fresh cheese grilled to a golden color. The *casizzolos* of Nuoro comes in the shape of a large pear. *Gioddu* you might not recognize under this Sardinian name, but you should when it is called *junchetta*—junket. Somewhat similar is *cazzau*, curds eaten with sugar.

The pigs of Sardinia naturally give rise to preserved pork, and Sardinia is well prepared to produce salted meat— nearly one-half of the total Italian salt supply comes from the coastal flats which run from Cagliari all the way to the also salt-collecting southwestern islands of San Pietro and Sant'Antioco. Salt has been exploited commercially here since 150 B.C., and today the salt works of Cagliari are the largest in Europe. With the aid of this salt, Sardinia produces excellent ham and sausage. The highly flavored mountain ham of Ogliastra is particularly prized. The province of Nuoro produces *prosciutto alla toscana*, ham cured in the Tuscan fashion. The central Barbagia area makes smoked ham. The Gallura district is known for a sausage of the cervelat type, while *sartizzu* is a smoked sausage of pork, highly spiced with pepper, cinnamon and fennel, in a beef intestine casing. Sardinia's leading specialty in the cured meat category is none of these, but *prosciutto di cinghiale*, wild boar ham, which is unfortunately becoming rare though Sardinia is rich in game—richer, probably, than any other region of Italy.

The *macchia*, underbrush, which covers so much of the island, provides ideal shelter for game. The wild animals lurking in the *macchia* are not always the same as those of the mainland. There are distinct Sardinian varieties of red deer and of hare. The Sardinian partridge is found nowhere else in Europe, but does exist in Tunisia, Algeria and Morocco. "The wild boar," writes Remo Borzini, "is related only to that of the Maremma. Bristling and ferocious, courageous and aggressive, living in the great silence of the *macchia*, he is as antique as the man who hunts him." The comparison with the boar of the Maremma, on the Tuscan coast, is with the most esteemed animal of the mainland, but perhaps the Sardinian wild boar differs even from the Maremma variety. He is a tougher, more bristly, more ferocious, blacker character than his counterpart on the mainland, and at the time of writing he was the only big game animal which could be legally hunted on the island, the favorite target both for visiting sportsmen and islanders hunting for the pot.

Time was, and not so very long ago, when the Sardinian peasant could take his rifle and knock down whatever budged in front of it, no matter when. But the hunters were too successful. In 1956, the government took a count, and discovered that there remained only 2,000 moufflon (*mufflone* in Italian), a species threatening to become extinct; only 300 of the small stags peculiar to the island; and only 100 bucks of the Sardinian deer called locally *cabriolu*. All these animals are now protected by an all-year-round closed season, but restocking is being pursued for the deer, which may have become fair game again by the time this book reaches your hands; intending hunters should inquire.

Plenty of small game remains: only the Sardinian partridge was fully protected at the time of writing. There remain hare and wild rabbits, and among birds, which acquire a particularly savory gamy taste from the berries and wild herbs of the *macchia* or heather-covered plateaus where they live, are other varieties of partridge, woodcock, snipe, thrushes, blackbirds, larks, whitethroats, wild doves, and wild pigeons. In the ponds and lagoons there are ducks, coots and wading birds. I do not know if there is a season for flamingos, which are not uncommon on the island, where they are referred to affectionately as "the rosy folk," *gente rubia*, but I have been told that they are sometimes eaten here, though I have never been offered any. They are not rated high for gourmet consumption.

The chief crop of Sardinia is, and always has been, wheat. The Carthaginians exploited Sardinian wheat and so did the Romans. It was a form of tribute, so that the growing of grain became more or less synonymous with forced labor. In the Sardinian tongue today, wheat is called *laore*, labor. More than half of the cultivated land of the island is devoted to cereals, chiefly wheat; but Sardinia has fallen far behind in grain production since the days when it could export great quantities to Carthage or to Rome. Today the island raises only enough for its own consumption. Yields are low, partly because of primitive agricultural methods; and perhaps the soil produced more abundantly also in the days when there was more tree cover to hold humidity in the earth and prevent erosion. Almost all the wheat grown is of the hard (durum) species, which originated in the Mediterranean area and is resistant to the long dry summers of Sardinia. Some barley is grown, but it gives a low yield too and is used mostly for fodder. There is also a little upland rice.

The climate of Sardinia, with its too dry, too hot and too long summers is not particularly propitious to vegetables. The chief exception is the artichoke, of superbly fine flavor, which makes it important to the island's economy, for it is extensively exported. Tomatoes do not do too badly, and you will see them spread out on roofs or hanging from the eaves to dry in the sun. They keep for a long time, and are used in cooking to replace the tomato extract used elsewhere, a manufactured product too expensive for poor

Sardinia. Apart from these, the most common vegetables are eggplant, zucchini, cauliflower, peas, string beans and fava beans. Sugar beets are also raised. Olives grow up to 2,300 feet in Sardinia, and come in curious colors, purple, brown and yellow; many of them produce good oil, for which Sorso and Sennori (Sassari) are especially noted. Grapevines grow even higher, to 3,000 feet, but most of them prefer less lofty slopes, rising on the edge of the lowlands, and wherever they grow their output is small, whether for table grapes or for wine. Citrus fruits exceed the demand for consumption fresh, and go into sweets of various kinds. Other common fruits are figs and prickly pears, melons and watermelons, pomegranates, cherries (including the famous ones of Galani in the province of Nuoro), plums, pears and occasionally apples. Chestnuts, walnuts, almonds and hazelnuts are plentiful. The aromatic herbs that grow everywhere give special flavor to Sardinian honey.

The curious distaste of Sardinians for the sea results in a gastronomic anomaly; inhabiting an island set in waters teeming with fish, one of them (the sardine of course) named for it, Sardinians show little interest in seafood. This phenomenon goes back as far as the records. Until fairly recently, the only communities of fishermen on Sardinia were at Carloforte, after the Genoese took it over, and Alghero, after its settlement by Spaniards. Even today, the principal fishing ports of the island are, in a sense, foreign. They still include Alghero (which also derives income from non-edible products of the sea, coral and sponges) and Carloforte, to which Porto Torres-Stintino and Cagliari have now been added. Stintino is the capital of tuna fishing, but for the main it is not carried on by Sardinians, but by Sicilians, who have established themselves there and have brought with them the *mattanza* celebration, which takes place in May or June, as in Sicily.

This leaves Cagliari as the sole exception to the rule that Sardinia's fishing is done by immigrants, possibly because, as the island's largest city and most important port, it necessarily does a little of everything; and even if the proportion of fishermen in its population is low, the population is large enough so that they still add up to a fleet of respectable size, able to supply the capital with one of Italy's most picturesque fish markets. It would seem that a stroll through it, with its tempting wealth of fish of every conceivable shape, size and color, heaped up in enormous round flat baskets, would convert the most obstinate meat eater to the delights of seafood. But the official statistics are there to prove the contrary: Sardinia is one of the least active regions in all coastal Italy for fishing. The Sardinian simply does not like fish. A possible exception is visible in the small tasty lobsters for which Alghero, Bosa Marina and the Maddalena archipelago are known. These are all in the northern half of the island, which must be especially propitious to this section of the fish family. The northernmost town in Sardinia, Santa Teresa, has a reputation for crustaceans of all kinds, crabs as well as lobsters, and also for shellfish. The clams called *vongole* in Rome or Naples are *arselle* here, the word also used for them in Genoa, which once held the northern coast.

The most important food fish for Sardinia, but for export more than for home consumption, is the tuna, of which some 9,000 tons are taken annually. Next in importance come the lobsters, and then the eels. The inland-oriented Sardinians are perhaps more attracted by fresh-water fish than by fish from the sea. Sardinian streams abound in native trout of kinds not common on the mainland, but which are duplicated in Algeria, Asia Minor and, mysteriously, Iran. The rivers are restocked regularly.

677

* * *

"In Sardinia," writes Remo Borzini, "the cuisine is archaic and unspoiled: archaic because, like everything Sardinian, it is linked to tradition and conditioned by the simplicity or the ingenuity of its own original peasants; unspoiled because incursions, invasions, dominations have alike left only superficial traces. Sardinia has a tough hide. . . . No cuisine is more typically *typical* than that of Sardinia. Born from the simple but exigent tastes of farmers and shepherds, it shows a plebeian refinement which does not exclude sensuality."

It is also a poor country's cuisine. The diet of poor countries is determined by which raw materials are available for the expenditure of the least cash. Thus in the Basilicata, as poor as Sardinia, the basic diet is of fish, vegetables and pasta. Anyone with a fishhook can take the first; in this predominantly rural area, everyone raises his own vegetables. The only thing for which it is necessary to have money, except for the farmer who raises his own grain, is the flour to make pasta—probably the most economical form in which to buy a given amount of nourishment.

The Sardinian has his trio of basic foods too, also determined by the principle of minimum expenditure; but it happens to be his good luck that the cheapest foods for him offer a menu which would be expensive elsewhere. His trio is game, meat and bread. Game, a luxury in (shall we say?) overdeveloped countries, replaces fish, which he doesn't much like anyway, for it is available to anyone who has a few cartridges. Bread replaces pasta, a more sophisticated fashion in which to eat cereals, because the Sardinian prefers bread. Meat replaces vegetables, which do not grow too readily in the Sardinian climate, because though it is rich man's food in the Basilicata, it is poor man's food in Sardinia. Sardinia raises great numbers of meat animals, but has little external market for them. The mainland is too far away and the cost of transport too great for Sardinian meat (except lambs) to be competitive in Italy; so the Sardinian eats it himself.

Game, meat and bread—but these are the basic foods of Neolithic Man!—of inland Neolithic Man at least, and the Sardinian has chosen to be a man of the interior in defiance of geography. Game probably still took precedence over meat in the Late Stone Age, but domestic animals already existed. Agriculture dates from Neolithic times, and one of the earliest crops was wheat. Stone Age Man, like the Sardinian, would not have eaten many vegetables, for he had not yet gotten around to cultivating them, so he was limited to collecting what grew wild. But he was undoubtedly capable of making bread from his wheat, for he knew how to grind flour. Even before the rotary millstone had been devised, men were grinding grain between two stones with great efficiency. The lower stone was flat, the other one shaped to fit the hand, but with a flat bottom surface incised with deep cuts to break up the grain when the upper stone was planed back and forth over it. The cuts were slanted inward, to produce the greatest bite during the forward pushing movement, which was when the maximum force could be applied. The closer together the cuts, the finer the flour.

Not only does the modern Sardinian eat the same foods as Stone Age Man, he cooks them the same way. Neolithic man did possess pottery, but at first it was probably not sufficiently resistant to flame to be used for cooking utensils, and perhaps too porous to hold water for boiling; but in any case, cooking habits die hard, and Stone Age Man was used to cooking his meat outdoors over an open fire on a spit, or perhaps in a pit in the ground lined with heated stones, as Sardinians cook meat today. Another characteristic of Sardinian cooking is lavish use of the aromatic herbs which grow wild on the Sardinian plateaux. They were there in Stone Age times too, and Stone Age Man could have collected them and used them to enhance the taste of his food, and probably did, for he invented seasoning. It was Neolithic times that saw the second great culinary invention (the first was cooking food instead of eating it raw), when Neolithic Man for the first time deliberately added salt to his meat to bring out its flavor. Sardinia's favorite flavoring is myrtle, a preference which may well go back to the Stone Age, for there was plenty of myrtle about then on this island where it grows so abundantly that in Nuoro (where man first appeared on Sardinia during the Stone Age) there is a whole plain known as the *Planu de Murtas* carpeted with myrtle bushes.

Sardinia's most typical cooking technique is, then, the open-air roasting of whole animals, wild boar, calves, kids, lambs or pigs. The least complicated method is to spit it aboveground, turning the spit by hand as the cooking progresses, a lengthy process when it is done in the ancient fashion. The fire is made of bundles of arbutus, lentisk and myrtle twigs, which are allowed to die down to mere embers, and the animal to be roasted is turned very slowly over them, the art of the cook consisting in maintaining a fire so low that sometimes it looks as if it had gone out. Cooked this way, the meat is usually not seasoned; the smoke from the smoldering twigs suffices to perfume it, and also drive the expectant diners to near madness from its appetite-rousing odors during the slow cooking of the meat. Another system, used especially for *porceddu*, suckling pig, is *carne a càrrarglu* ("meat in a hole"). It consists in digging a pit in the ground, cleaning the inside, lining it with branches and leaves, especially of myrtle, placing heated stones on the bottom, laying the animal or meat to be cooked on them, placing another layer of heated stones on top, and then filling the hole with earth again so that the meat roasts slowly and evenly underground. The exquisitely delicate flavor cannot be duplicated in oven cooking. When a whole animal is cooked this way, it is often stuffed and seasoned with herbs, but it may be cooked whole, unemptied, in which case, once more, seasoning may be omitted, except for that which the meat absorbs from the leaves and branches lining the pit. In a variant of this method, instead of putting hot stones in the pit, the hole is filled in and a hot fire built on top of the ground. This method is said to have been invented by bandits or thieves, whose problem was to hide the animal while cooking it. Many a shepherd or swineherd has probably sat down around a bonfire with strangers he has happened upon, sharing a bottle of wine with them, quite unaware that one of his own animals was cooking underground. In such cases, of course, the animal was never gutted, for the leftover offal would have been a giveaway.

Nowadays, the Sardinian is often reluctantly obliged to do his cooking indoors; but even indoors he prefers to spit-roast his meat over an open fire whenever it is possible. He has been cooking it this way for four or five thousand years, and he sees no reason to change.

It is obvious that the visitor to Sardinia obliged to do his eating at hotels and restaurants is not going to have much chance to sample *carne a càrrarglu*, and for that matter he will not find it easy to sample any genuinely Sardinian dishes at all. The Sardinian cuisine is almost exclusively home cooking, confined entirely to private families. Hotels and restaurants which cater to tourists offer them what they think tourists want—and in most cases I fear they are right: the standardized international hotel menu, often in humdrum form. You are not likely to find the islanders' own dishes even if you sniff out restaurants patronized by Sardinians themselves, of which there are not many, for almost all Sardinians manage to eat most of the time at home. When exceptionally they do eat out, they want a change, so their own restaurants give it to them by attempting to reproduce the cooking of Bologna. Gastronomically alert visitors to Sardinia would no doubt like a change too, though in the opposite direction, but it is no simple matter to manage it. The best solution might seem to be to make a few Sardinian friends, but for the outlander from another world and another age, Sardinians are not the most approachable people on earth. Among themselves, Sardinians exercise the virtues of the shepherd and the mountaineer—hospitality and an acute sense of honor, of which the latter made Sardinia until very recent times a land of vendetta; but outsiders find it very difficult to get under their skins. "The people," Alan Ross wrote of them, "display none of the superficial gaiety of the Italians, none of their malleability or lightness of heart. They are courteous, generous, but essentially reserved." The Scots of Italy!

However, if you do succeed in being invited into a Sardinian home, your welcome will be assured if you happen to arrive while bread is being baked. "*Deus vos vardet*," your hostess will exclaim, for your arrival at so propitious a moment is a good omen, a sign that God is watching over both of you. Making bread is almost a religious rite in Sardinia. The link between bread and religion is deeply rooted in many countries. Deities responsible for grain were worshiped in many early societies, while more developed ones say grace for their daily bread. The connection is explicitly recognized at Quartu Sant'Elena, near Cagliari, on May 21, when eight large loaves of bread, whose dough includes wine and honey, sweetened with jam, are carried as thanks offerings to St. Elena, in a procession for which the population dresses in its traditional costumes. (Similarly at Stilo, Calabria, ring-shaped loaves are carried in the Holy Saturday procession.)

The most distinctive and most unusual type of bread made in Sardinia is *o pane carasau*, also called *fogli di musica*, "music-paper bread," because its unleavened sheets are so thin, and also because it tends to develop long cracks on its surface which suggest the lines of the staff. It comes out of the oven in crisp round leaves, which are piled up on one another, like Mexican *tortillas*, in a snowy white heap, the color of the fine white flour made from Sardinian hard wheat. This is the sort of bread Sardinian shepherds have been eating for centuries, since it keeps amazingly well and may be carried up into the high pastures to feed them over long periods. The women of Ollalai cater to *carasau* bread by weaving flat round baskets called *corbule* from asphodel stalks, especially to hold it.

Almost all Sardinian bread is made from the same flour— the ring-shaped loaves of Planargia, called *lotture;* the Campidano *coccoi,* also ring-shaped, and *muddizzosu;* Alghero's *pan'e scetti* and *cocca; pan'e simbula;* the crunchy biscuits called *zicchi;* and best of all, in some opinions, *tundus,* which is simply the everyday run-of-the-mill homemade bread every Sardinian housewife knows how to bake.

Though bread takes in Sardinia the place reserved in most other regions for pasta—curiously, for the durum wheat Sardinia grows is especially esteemed for pasta elsewhere— it has not eliminated pasta entirely. Indeed in some cases bread *becomes* pasta. For instance *pane frattau,* particularly popular in the province of Nuoro, starts with music-paper bread, softened in warm water and served with a sauce of tomato, cheese and eggs. *Zuppa sarda* is stale bread with mozzarella cheese, egg, parsley and pepper in consommé. Among Sardinian forms of pasta proper is *cu'irgionis,* a sort of ravioli stuffed with cottage cheese, spinach, eggs and saffron, served with meat or tomato sauce and grated cheese; in some parts of the island it is called *pulilgionis.* *Culurjones de patate* is also ravioli, but the dough is made with mashed potatoes, plus butter, eggs, pecorino cheese, a touch of onion and another of peppermint; it is served with *ragù* sauce, and is a favorite of Nuoro. *Pillas* is alternate layers of pasta and hashed meat, ham, bland cheese and egg, moistened with white wine, covered with tomato sauce, baked in the oven, and served in the cooking dish. *Ferittus*, also called *maccarones*, means pasta with a sauce of chopped pork or lamb, tomato, oil and garlic. *Su farru* is dough of semolina flour and milk in consommé, with the addition of sour milk. *Farro*, another form of the same word and the same dish, is a gruel of barley flour boiled for half an hour in beef consommé, and fresh cheese cut into cubes at the end; when the cheese has melted into leaf-like thinness, powdered mint is sprinkled over the whole and it is ready to eat. *Succu tundu*, also called *frègula*, means a tiny saffron-flavored ball of pasta dough cooked in consommé and served with salted ricotta cheese or, better still, with *merca*, curds. The recurrent use of saffron in pasta suggests Spanish influence; it turns up again in one of the best known of Sardinian dishes, *malloreddus*, little cornmeal or hard wheat dumplings flavored with saffron and served with a highly seasoned tomato sauce and grated pecorino cheese. *Ciciones* is a variant you will meet in the province of Sassari. Polenta is also encountered here, sometimes combined with pork and fresh cheese, cooked in the oven, sometimes fried along with bacon, sausage and cheese, and eaten either hot or cold.

Other openings for the meal which may take the place of pasta include the local minestrone, a thick mixture of string beans, dried beans, chick peas, cabbage, potato, fennel, pasta and pig's ears; Sassari's *la cauledda*, cauliflower soup; *favata*, otherwise known as *fava e lardu*, dried beans, previously soaked, stewed with salt pork, crackling, sometimes a pig's foot, green cabbage, wild onion, wild fennel, tomato paste and borage, eaten particularly in the Barbagia region on Shrove Thursday; *cavolata*, cabbage with crackling, often served with a pig's foot and potatoes; the delicate *sospiri* ("sighs"), flakes of egg white cooked with myrtle leaves, not to be confused with the sweets of the same name; *zuppa di finocchi selvatici*, which is not soup, but wild fennel boiled in salted water, after which fried croutons (*crostini*) are spread with fresh cheese, covered with a layer of the boiled fennel, moistened with the fennel cooking water, finished in the oven, and served with pats of butter on top; *monzette*, stuffed snails, otherwise *cocoidu a pienu*, which in Sassari, where they are simply boiled, are called *gio ga' minuda*; or simply a Sardinian omelet, which adds to lightly beaten eggs a mixture of zucchini, bread crumbs previously soaked in milk, and grated *fiore sardo* cheese, with the merest touch of grated lemon peel and sugar, and is cooked not on top of the stove, but in a baking dish greased with olive oil, in the oven.

These dishes lead us to the *pièce de résistance*, which is, of course, meat or game. One of the most spectacular items in this category is *accarrexiau*, a rich dish for a poor country—and it is indeed reserved for festive occasions among the shepherds who invented it. It is a whole sheep stuffed with a suckling pig, cooked in the open, over a pit of glowing embers, or buried in the earth, in one of the fashions described previously. After this, dishes involving only one animal, even a whole one, sound as if they were designed for the underprivileged. We have already met *porceddu*, suckling pig (in Italian, *porchetta alla sarda*), as cooked outdoors, but an effect almost as tempting can be produced indoors, given the necessary set-up. The method is to split an animal of between 6½ and 11 pounds lengthwise, spit each half, and cook them on the turning spits over a wood fire, basting constantly with the drippings. When the skin crackles, the pig is done. It is bedded on myrtle leaves on an enormous platter, more myrtle leaves are spread on top, and it is allowed to stand for a while (the myrtle leaves keep it from cooling too fast), until it imbibes their flavor. Those who can't spit-roast their pigs cook them uneventfully in the oven. Kid and lamb are often spit-roasted also, or failing the equipment for that, roasted in the oven with an egg-and-lemon-juice sauce, or fricasséed, for instance with fennel, plus a little onion and the famous Sardinian dried tomatoes. *Vitella a s'ispìdu* is milk-fed veal, roasted over wood or charcoal.

By the time an ox has ended his useful working life, he is likely to be too tough to provide recommendable steaks or roasts, so beef turns up as *grisau* or *stufau* (stewed) or *filetto di manzo marinato alla sarda*, a slice of beef first soaked in a bath of white wine with chopped mushrooms and parsley, then cooked over a low flame in white wine and consommé, and served on a slice of bread soaked in the cooking juices and enlivened with a touch of anchovy. *Padedda*, also called *pingiada*, is beef boiled together with chicken and pigeon, with tomatoes. *Impanadas* is a meat pie of chopped pork and veal, egg, onion and herbs in a crust of semolina flour shortened with olive oil or lard; another formula omits onion and egg, but adds dried tomatoes, garlic, parsley and saffron. *Zurrette* starts out with sheep blood pudding, seasoned with a mixture of *carasau* bread crumbs, the chopped lining of the body cavity (for which the anatomical word is *omento;* I know of no culinary word for it in English, possibly because it has never occurred to Anglo-Saxons to eat it), pecorino cheese, and round-leaved mint; it is either boiled or grilled.

Poverty dictates wasting no edible part of the animal, which accounts for *ventrelle d'agnello di latte*. When shepherds kill suckling lambs for the mainland market, they retain a commission for themselves by carefully removing the stomach, stuffing it with blood from the slaughtered animal, small pieces of soft bread, bacon, onion, curds and seasoning, sewing it up and boiling it in clear water taken from a mountain stream. It needs only a few minutes to cook, providing a quick snack to invigorate the shepherd in the midst of his work, and leaving him with a complete carcass to sell.

Sanguinacci di maiale is pig blood pudding stuffed with a curious mixture of the pig's blood, fennel, raisins, chopped walnuts and pine nuts, and *saba* (cooked wine must). It is boiled, allowed to rest a day or two, and then grilled or cooked on the embers of the hearth. *Corda* (or *sa colda*) or *cordula* (they all mean "rope") is lamb or kid tripe, cut into strips which are twisted together into a long plait some three feet long, with different kinds of tripe alternating so as to get as varied a selection as possible in each individual portion; it is cooked on the spit, grilled, or stewed in olive oil together with peas and/or small flat beans, in which last case it is cooked over a very low flame for about two hours. *Su tataliu* (or *trattaliu*) is made by skewering bits of liver, lungs, heart, and fatty pieces of lamb alternately with morsels of bacon or ham and a bay leaf, the whole held together by barding them and then wrapping sausage casing from the lamb's stomach around the whole, and cooking on the spit (preferably) or in the oven. *Granelli di ovini* are various sheeep innards, breaded and deep-fried; the same ingredients fricasséed produce *fricassata*.

The great game dish of Sardinia is of course wild boar, which is almost always skinned, cooked and eaten on the spot where the boar was taken according to one of the methods of outdoor cooking already described. Cooked indoors, it is also spitted, if the hearth is large enough. Otherwise, it is stuffed with myrtle flavoring, and roasted in the oven, again if the oven is large enough, failing which it has to be cut into pieces, and treated like domestic pork. There is nothing special to report on the Sardinian fashion of dealing with hare or wild rabbit, usually cooked *alla cacciatora*, with tomato, garlic and parsley. But the Sardinians have developed some special ways of handling the small game birds of which they are so fond. *Tàccule* (locally called *is tacculas*), small birds resembling thrushes, are treated with special delicacy. The Sardinians like their favorite flavoring of myrtle with them, but if they were cooked with myrtle leaves, the aroma of the myrtle would overpower such tiny morsels of meat; so they are first boiled (or roasted) and then popped piping hot into small bags lined with myrtle leaves, and allowed to absorb their fragrance by osmosis. Partridge are boiled and served with salad or green sauce. Small birds—*tordi, merli, beccacce, quaglie* (thrushes, blackbirds, woodcock, quail)—are preferred spitted, or failing that, cooked in a frying pan. Otherwise, they are prepared to be eaten cold later. Thrushes and blackbirds are barded, because they lose their natural fat in the cooking, and boiled in salted water, to which a myrtle leaf is added at the end. They are then allowed to cool, and are wrapped in myrtle leaves, to be eaten in the days that follow. They will not keep long, so game birds are sometimes pickled for preservation. For *pernice sott'olio*, partridge is boiled in salted water, half an hour if it is tender, an hour if it is tough, then drained and the drumsticks and breast fillets are cut away from the carcass. These are allowed to dry well in the air, and then are submerged in vinegar for two hours. Taken out and dried with an absorbent cloth, they are then packed into a glass jar and covered with olive oil for future reference. When thrushes are preserved in this fashion, olives usually go into the jar also.

Sardinians prefer game birds to domesticated poultry, but they will accept the latter when game is lacking. *Gallina col mirto* is chicken boiled with celery, carrots, onion and parsley, bedded still warm on myrtle leaves, and covered by them, with a plate on top pressing the leaves tightly against the flesh so that it will absorb their flavor; it is eaten cold the next day. *Puddighinius* (or *puddichinos*) *a pienu* is roast chicken stuffed with its own chopped internal organs, mixed with bread crumbs, tomatoes, egg and milk.

Though Sardinians show little enthusiasm for fish, when they do serve it, it is in the tastiest of fashions. Fish reach the cook in a state of freshness which most city or inland dwellers have never experienced, and therefore require no elaborate accompaniments or disguising sauces; they are cooked, quite properly, in the simplest of fashions, fried or grilled, to preserve the natural unspoiled flavor of the fish. This appeals to the foreigner, when individual fish are served alone, but the Sardinians seem to like it most, or dislike it least, when different fish are mixed together in a chowder. Every Italian region with a seacoast will tell you that its fish soup is the best in the world, and Sardinia is no exception. Here it is *sa cassola*, and in what specific aspects it differs from the many other *brodetti* of Italy, I am afraid I have not been able to make out. I suppose there is also a distinction between *cassola* and *zimino*, which is obviously the Sicilian *ziminu*, which contains gray mullet, eel, *capone*, cuttlefish, *orata*, goatfish, shellfish, and apparently any other fish that happen to be handy, but what this difference is I am not sure, except perhaps that *cassola* eschews shellfish; or it could be that different parts of the island use different names for the same dish. *Zuppa di frutti di mare*, include *only* shellfish, mostly mussels and different sorts of clams, in various combinations. The gray mullet is relatively popular, preferably cooked on the spit and flavored with a bay leaf or two; when it is smoked, it becomes *mugheddu*, while Oristano, which enjoys one of the best and most varied cuisines in the island, makes a specialty of it called *merca*, for which it is boiled in sea water and then preserved in seaweed. Tuna, economically the most important fish of the island, it not much eaten by the Sardinians themselves; when they do indulge in fresh tuna, it is simply grilled or boiled, and eaten either hot or cold. A refinement is *surra*, the grilled belly meat of tuna. An undoubtedly Sardinian specialty derived from tuna (or from gray mullet, which the Sardinians seem to prefer) is the roe, pressed, salted and dried, a sort of local caviar, eaten, of course, as an hors d'oeuvre. Sole is cooked simply, grilled, baked, or fried with butter and grated cheese. Eels may be spitted, grilled or baked, and in the higher parts of Nuoro, stewed. *Calamari ripieni* are stuffed with themselves: that is to say, the tentacles are cut off and chopped together with bread crumbs, anchovies, garlic and parsley, with an egg or two for a binder, to fill the pocket of the squid, which is then moistened with olive oil and baked in the oven. *Buridda* is spotted dogfish stewed with olive oil, bread crumbs, pine nuts and walnuts.

Buconis, shellfish, are not only eaten raw, but also boiled in heavily salted water, while *frègula cun còcciule* is the *succu tundu* pasta we have already met with the type of clams known here as *arselle*, or, if you want to be really Sardinian, *còcciule*. Whatever you call them, the clams, shells and all, go into a *soffritto* of olive oil, garlic, parsley and tomatoes. When all the shells have opened, enough water for cooking the pasta is added, and after the clams have finished cooking, the pasta is boiled in the same water. Mussels (*cozze*) are often breaded, moistened with oil, flavored with herbs, and fried. Lobster is grilled and eaten hot, or boiled and served cold with salad. The crabs known elsewhere as *granseole* are called here *longobardi* or *capre di mare*. Trout, whose most prized varieties come from the Tirso, Mannu, Flumendosa, Coghinas, Cedrino and Gologone rivers, are cooked in a variety of ways: fried, baked, in sauce, or lapped in the island's very individual Vernaccio wine.

The usual accompaniment for the *pièce de résistance* is bread. Sardinians do not go in much for vegetable side dishes; when they use vegetables, they become component parts of the main dish, but there are of course exceptions. The island's leading vegetable, the artichoke, whether eaten raw or fried in olive oil, may serve as an hors d'oeuvre. Asparagus turns up by itself, boiled, or, after having cooled off, as one of the components of a salad; many persons prefer wild asparagus, which they claim is tastier than the cultivated variety. *Fagioli e cavoli alla gallurese*, a dish of the northeastern corner of the island, is a stewing together of dry red beans, green cabbage, fennel (preferably wild), onions, bacon and garlic. *Turta de faiscedda*, which sounds as though it ought to be a vegetable tart, is actually an omelet with fresh broad beans. Mushrooms are served with green sauce.

If the list of vegetable dishes is scanty, the sweets make up for it. Perhaps not even in Sicily is there such a variety of cakes, pastries, cookies and other sweets. One particularly Sardinian dessert is *sebadas*. You start with a batter of two heaping tablespoons of flour, one tablespoon of melted butter, an egg yolk and a cup of milk, all whipped together lightly and allowed to stand, preferably overnight, but at least for a few hours. Thin slices of cheese are dipped into this batter (the Sardinians use mild goat cheese), are fried quickly on both sides on a very hot lightly greased griddle, and honey is poured over them. Sardinian honey, made by bees that roam the wild heath of the plateaux, is often sharp, in which case sugar is added. *Tumbada* is a pudding of macaroons, milk, eggs and lemon juice.

In Sardinia, as elsewhere in Italy, every locality is likely to have its own specialties in the way of cakes, cookies and pastry; many of them are linked to holidays. Quartu Sant'-Elena, near Cagliari, must come close to holding the championship for original sweets. It is the home of *pirichittus*, spherical goodies flavored with orange or lemon extract; of *candelaus*, molded into traditional shapes, and flavored with almonds and orange blossoms; of *gesmini*, little cakes of egg dough with lemon juice and crushed almonds; and *guelfus*, which make do with almond flavoring alone. Oristano lays claim to *mustazzolos*, lozenge-shaped cakes of raised dough, crushed almonds and sugar, and also to especially fine macaroons. Sassari makes *pabassinas* (or *papassinos*), whose egg dough, dampened with the juice of green grapes or Barbary figs, and studded with raisins, pine nuts, bits of walnut, etc., comes in different sizes of cones or lozenges, and also *seada*, a sort of cheese cake. The Gallura district is known for its *neuleddi*, little buns made of biscuit dough, mixed with honey, and hardened. Ozieri is famous for its *suspirus* ("sighs"), of crushed almonds, white of egg and sugar. Terralba, Oliena and Castelsardo make the best sweet biscuits on the island. Tonara and Villaputza have a reputation for fine *torrone* (nougat), and the latter also claims *ziddinis*, of almonds, honey, *sapa* (another form of the word denoting cooked grape must), bran and cinnamon, which recalls Siena's *panforte*, as does the similar *pani de saba*. Nuoro boasts a special sweet called *zerminos*, but exactly what it is remains a mystery for me; I have never been able to track it down. The same city's honey-almond-candied-orange-peel *s'aranzata* is far too famous to be a mystery, however. The reason why Nuoro does so well by these delicious cookies that *aranciata di Nuoro* is known all over Italy appears to be that here infinite pains are applied—for instance, to give only two details out of many, the orange peel used, after all its white lining has been carefully scraped away, is soaked in clear water for five days, changing it every day to get rid of any bitterness; and when honey is added to the mixture, it is dripped in slowly during constant stirring with two small forks.

Pabassinos are associated especially with Christmas, and *angulis*, ring-shaped confections of sweet dough made gay with coloring matter, with Easter. Carnival is the season for the sweet fritters called *zippulas* or *cattas*, raised dough moistened with liqueurs. *Zippulas* is the same word as *zeppole*, often associated on the mainland with holidays, especially St. Joseph's Day, but Sardinians maintain that their product is superior because they make it more carefully. *Fruttulus* is not exactly a holiday dish, but it is made expressly for a special purpose, of the finest flour and sugar alone; it is the first sweet given babies at weaning.

Many other typical Sardinian sweets are not especially attached to any one place or time. *Abufaus* is a sort of gingerbread, flavored, among other things, with honey, cinnamon, pepper, pine nuts, walnuts and currants. A biscuit of fine flour and eggs, powdered with vanilla flavored sugar, is called *pistocheddus*. *Trincas* are buns with a filling of *sapa*, the cooked must that appears in many Sardinian sweets. *Caschettas* are pastries in a variety of shapes, whose outer covering conceals an interior of crushed almonds and sugar. *Pardulas* or *casadinas*, made of hard brittle dough, in the shape of rosettes or little pots, have cream cheese in them. To put an end to this list, which could continue indefinitely, let us note finally *pompie*, candied bitter orange or grapefruit, which succeed in being both tart and sweet at the same time.

The only Sardinian wine which has ever inspired a nationally known tribute is Oliena, from a city in the province of Nuoro noted for the beauty of its women and the colorfulness of their costumes. "The perfume of the wine alone is enough to make you drunk," d'Annunzio said of it. D'Annunzio's enthusiasms were easily aroused, especially in the presence of beautiful women, but it is true that Oliena is a robust lusty red wine, well adapted to the game in which Nuoro abounds. The perfume which d'Annunzio admired is of roses; the aftertaste, disconcertingly, recalls chocolate. Oliena manages simultaneously to be dry, warm, full-flavored and a little bitter.

But though Sardinia has no great wines, she has distinctive ones. Sardinian wines are as individual as Sardinia itself; and Sardinians, by mainland standards, are idiosyncratic in their drinking habits. A sweet dessert wine—or what would be considered a dessert wine anywhere else—may be drunk as an *aperitivo;* a dry wine may be drunk with the dessert. Wine of an alcoholic content too high to be considered in Italy proper as a reasonable accompaniment for food is consumed throughout the meal; this is likely to make for drowsiness afterward, but Sardinia has a siesta climate anyway.

One characteristic shared by most Sardinian wines is heaviness. They carry a powerful impact. This comes partly from the fashion of growing the wines, *ad alberello*, close to the ground, which reflects the strong Sardinian sun against the clusters of grapes, increasing their alcoholic content and giving them a coarse quality—which, after all, does not go badly with a typical Sardinian meal of game and bread, preferably cooked and eaten outdoors. The wines signal their strength by their color. Whites are amber or almost undistinguishable by the eye from rosés; rosés look like reds; and reds are often so dark as to seem almost black, which, indeed, is what they are called, *vini neri*.

In most parts of the country, when you reach 12 or 13 degrees of alcohol, you feel you are drinking rather heavy wine. But Sardinian wines easily reach 14 degrees in alcoholic content, and often get up much higher. Even *rosato* is likely to run to 14 degrees; rosés can be heady on much less alcohol than that. You reach 18 or 19 degrees with the heavy sweet dessert wines, of which Sardinia makes a great many, including red ones; this seems to be a taste peculiar to hot-weather areas.

Sardinians drink wine rather than vermouth or similar apéritifs. Intricately made vermouths are more expensive than wine, so Sardinia, as a poor country, should naturally tend to prefer wine; but it does not eschew vermouth solely for reasons of economy; many Sardinian wines are natural apéritifs. They are not especially treated to produce this effect, they just turn out that way. It has often been noted that many Sardinian wines recall sherry (without tasting like it), while others are compared to Port, Madeira or Malaga; but this character in Sardinian wines is attained by letting nature takes its course, without going through the elaborate (and costly) process which results in Spanish sherry.

Most Sardinian wines are made from local grape varieties —*cannonau, nasco, girò* and *monica*, of which the last two are believed to have been developed from Spanish roots. Monica produces in Cagliari (probably the best province for it) a ruby-red dessert wine which has been compared with Malaga, both as to smell and taste, of which the latter is strongly pronounced, with a hint of acidity beneath its velvet smoothness. Sardinians sip it with sweet pastry. Girò makes a dessert wine of much the same type, but instead of being compared to Malaga, it is generally described as being like Port, but lighter and sweeter.

Cannonau is widely grown throughout the island, and you find Cannonaus everywhere, varying greatly in nature and quality. The ideal Cannonau, which should be served at room temperature, is a clear garnet red in color, 15 to 16 degrees, robust, strongly flavored and a little sweet; consequently it is often drunk as a dessert wine, though it is not as sugary or liqueur-like as dessert wines are prone to be. But you will meet Cannonaus in dry (not to my taste really dry), semi-sweet and sweet reds, in rosés, and in so-called whites, hardly distinguishable from rosés. One of the most trustworthy is the Cannonau del Campidano, or Cannonau di Cagliari, as dry as Cannonau comes.

Nasco is probably an entirely local grape, which seems to have originated in the province of Cagliari, still the best place to drink the wine it produces; at its best it rates high among Italian white liqueur-like dessert wines (it is also drunk alone between meals). A golden yellow, more or less intense, but always brilliant, its perfume suggests the mingled scents of orange blossoms and the flowers of the field, and it has a slightly bitter undertaste.

Vernaccia is a grape name too, and this is perhaps the most widely known of Sardinian wines, the most characteristic, and the most different from the norm of the mainland. This is one of those wines which make you think of sherry, at least when it is young, but it changes character with age, and apparently can age indefinitely. During its first year it is drunk as an apéritif, and, by Sardinians, also with hors d'oeuvres and fish. By its third year, the color has deepened to a warm golden amber, and it has lost the cooked wine quality, but its alcoholic content has lifted well above average, which seems also to accentuate its perfume and flavor—dry, strong, warm, a trifle bitter, and persistent; its almost almond-flower taste remains in the mouth long after you have finished it. Blessed with a sherry-like wine perfectly adapted for apéritif drinking, the Sardinians perversely drink Vernaccia as a table wine. It is difficult to imagine drinking sherry straight through a meal (*manzanilla* perhaps at a pinch, if it is not a very good meal nor a very good *manzanilla*) but the Sardinian treats Vernaccia that way. You will find Vernaccia all over the island, but the consensus seems to be that only in the Tirso valley do the Vernaccia vines produce really high quality grapes, so the Vernaccia di Oristano is the most prized—and within this category the best sub-varieties are those from the villages of Tramatza, Zeddiani, Baratili and Solarussa. The producers of the best Oristano Vernaccias have banded together to protect the labeling of their wine, which is marketed as Oro di Sardegna, Sardinian Gold; you can buy bottles thus marked with confidence.

Nuragus, a native Sardinian grape, is economically the

most important on the island, but you are unlikely to encounter it. This is because it is chiefly exported for blending and for making vermouth, being a neutral wine whose alcohol content is often as low as 11 degrees, unusual in Sardinia. However the better varieties, produced especially in Cagliari, do sometimes appear as table wines; dry, heady, pale-yellow, only lightly perfumed, but refreshing, they are drunk as pasta wines during the first year of their lives, and promoted to fish wines the year after. They are generally reported not to gain with much aging, but Giovanni Dalmasso, President of the Italian Wine Academy, a knowledgeable authority, maintains that if left to age in oak casks, Nuragus develops its qualities, taking on an amber color, increasing its alcohol content to 16 degrees or more, and developing its subtle flavor, which still remains delicate, and gives it a slightly bitter aftertaste. It is believed to be the oldest vintage in Sardinia, going back to prehistoric times. If this is so, it was the beverage of Stone Age man.

Vintners concerned with producing somewhat subtler wines than native Sardinian grapes are likely to provide have lately experimented with importing vines from other parts of Italy. Thus Arborea, produced near the town of that name in Cagliari province, is a new vintage made from the Sangiovese grape which is the mainstay of Chianti, and it carries a suggestion of the Chianti flavor, but is a trifle rougher and heavier, with an alcoholic content of 13 to 14 degrees. Trebbiano grapes from Emilia-Romagna, and Barbera from Piedmont have also been introduced to produce the dry white Trebbiano Sardo and the dry red Barbera Sardo, both of which seem to be developing well, with a somewhat higher alcoholic content than on their home grounds. An experiment not with new grapes but with new methods has produced Capo Ferrato, made from the local Cannonau grape, a wine which is dry but suave, gains subtlety with age, goes well with roasts and game, but remains typically Sardinian in its high alcoholic content, 16 to 17 degrees.

There are too many wines in Sardinia to permit anything like a complete listing, but here are some of the more important:

TYPICALLY HEAVY TABLE WINES. Dorgali, reputedly the strongest table wine in Italy, is a dry red which gets as high as 19 degrees, though 15 or 16 is more common. Rosso Extra di Dorgali is aged at least three years and starts at 16 degrees; the *rosato*, dry and smooth, is 15 to 16 degrees. Sardus Pater, named for the island's ancient god, an authoritative red, 16 degrees, strong in flavor, comes from the southeastern island of Sant'Antioco; the Sardus Pater Rosato, which unlike many rosés can stand aging, is lighter and occasionally naturally *frizzante*.

SOMEWHAT LIGHTER TABLE WINES, which appeal to outsiders who do not share the Sardinian taste for heaviness include: Gallura, a dry red with a touch of tartness; Arbaia is a superior Gallura. Rosso del Logudoro, though like Gallura it has an alcoholic content of 11 to 13 degrees, seems lighter. Nuraghe Majore, which takes its name from the imposing *nuraghi* near Sassari, where it is grown, not from the Nuragus grape, is one of the better Nurra region wines, which come in both reds and whites, though in general the whites are superior.

DESSERT WINES. One of the best known is Sassari's Anghelu Ruju, of which not very much is made, an attempt to duplicate Port by letting the grapes dry in the sun for a week after picking before fermentation starts; it does achieve a slight family resemblance. Rosso di Sorso, or Cannonau di Sorso, is also frequently compared to Port, but misses the mark more widely; the white, Dorato di Sorso, aged in red oak casks imported from Yugoslavia, 16.5 degrees, is not a sweet wine, having, indeed, a rather bitter tang. Sardinians drink Vermentino di Gallura as a dessert wine, but outsiders are more likely to prefer it as an apéritif; it is one of the sherry-like vintages, and very dry.

Though Sardinia has no need to manufacture apéritifs or liqueurs, since its natural wines suffice to replace them, it does make a small quantity of *vin cotto* (cooked wine), produced by reducing the volume of natural wine by a gentle application of heat to about two-fifths of the original, and then replenishing the volume with must, after which the whole is fermented and aged. It produces a sweet rich strong (20 degrees) beverage similar to Malaga. The only liqueur that need be mentioned is Villacidru, from the village of the same name. Stone Age man did not drink brandies, for the art of distillation was yet to be invented, but Sardinian *grappa* is, nevertheless, a drink for men of stone.

GENERAL INDEX

This is not a guidebook; but with the help of this index it can serve as one. Remember these points: to save time, first consult references given in boldface type; these are the most important. Cross references may refer to either of the two indexes. Names of members of the great Italian families (Catherine dei Medici, Beatrice d'Este) are grouped under the family name (Medici, Este). The following abbreviations are used: ap. = apéritif; ch. = cheese; dig. = digestive; edv., = eau-de-vie; gr. = grape; is. = island; liq. = liqueur; mt. (mts.) = mountain(s); p. = pasta; prov. = province; R. = restaurant; riv. = river; saus. = sausage; val. = valley; w. = wine.

General Index

General Index

General Index

dessert wines, 65–66, 462, 650, 651, 698
dialects, viii, 7–8, 268, 462, 661
dictionary, first modern, 30
Diderot, 229
Diogenes, 165
Dionysius of Halicarnassus, 17
Dionysius of Syracuse, 592
Diomedes, 496, 540
Diosconides, 80
distillation, 5
Doge's Palace, Venice, 391
dogs, truffle, 318
Dolceacqua, w., 383
dolce stil nuovo, 29
Dolcetto, gr., w., 330
dolmens, 540, 549, 656
Dolo, riv., 227
Dolomites, mts., 438, 473
domus de janas, 656
Don Giovanni, 474
Donnaz, 342; w., 346
Dorato di Sorso, w., 698
Dorgali, 660; w., 548
Doria family, 661
Doss Trento, 461, 462
double boiler, 36–37
Dover sole, 159
Dumas, Alexandre, 229, 399–400
Dunand, Napoleon's cook, 321
Duse, Eleonora, 175
dye, imperial purple, 547

earthquakes: Messina, 608; Modena, 204
Easter: eggs, 196; foods, 84, 103, 157, 288, 365, 378, 379, 419, 432, 437, 526, 534, 621; Pope's dinner, 115–16
Easter Monday food, 184
eau de Cologne, 577
eaux de vie, 249–50, 487
eglantine, edv., 460
Egypt, 393, 658
Eisenhower, Dwight D., 157
Elba, 50, 51, 54–55, 68, 133; w., 69
Elefante, R., 464
Elena, Queen, 331
elephant, 463–64

Elephant Platter, 464, 469
Elisir China, ap., 336
Elisir d'Oropa, ap., 336
Elixir of the Popes, liq., 41
Eloro, w., 649
Elymi, 597–98
emigration, 670
Emilia, 145
Emilia, Via, 140, 141, 238
Emilia-Romagna, 140–250; character, 146; cooking, 146–47; w., 242–247
Encyclopedia of Wines and Spirits, 244
Enna: city, 594, 603, 638; prov., 612, 628, 638, 643, 651
Enoch d'Asoli, 129
Enza, riv., 228; val., 228
Epomeo, mt., 496
Erba Luce, gr., 332
Erice, 610
ermine, 339
Est! Est!! Est!!!, w., 99, 105
Este, 390, 432
Este: family, 148; Alfonso I d', 148, 155, 197; Beatrice d', 148; Borso d', 155, 157; Cesare d', 179; Dukes of, 211, 218, 220; Ercole II d', 156; Hercules I, 149; Hippolito, Cardinal, 218; Ippolito II d', 156; Isabella d', 148; Lucrezia d', 189; Luigi d', Cardinal, 148
Este, Villa d', 218
Etna, mt., 575, 602, 607, 608, 613, 665; w., 648–49
Etruria, 28, 30, 113
Etruscans, 3, 4, 8, 32, 55, 144, 428; cities, 31, 52, 114, 181, 185, 204, 232, 253–54, 303; food, 3–4, 16, 78, 98, 369; history, 7, 9, 113–14, 253–54, 421, 658; language, 7, 9, 16–17
Euganean Hills, 390, 428, 431; w., 457
Euganei, 390–91, 461–62
Exarchate of Ravenna, 126, 144, 147

709

General Index

General Index

Macerata, city, 127, 128; prov., 126, 133
Macomer, 656
Maddalena Islands, 618, 677
Madeira, 646
Madonna dell'Acqua Selvatica, holiday food, 366
Maecenas, 40
maestrale, 53, 54, 669
Mafia, 601
Maglioceo, w., 587
Magna Graecia, 540
Maia, 205
maigre, 640
maiorchino, ch., 606
Majani, Augusto, 197
malaria, 51, 52, 100, 659
Malmsey, w., *see* Malvasia
Malvasia, gr., 63, 488, 569; w., 114, 216, 484
Malvasia di Lipari, w., 651
Malvasia di Nato, w., 457
Malvasia di Nus, w., 347
Mamertino, w., 644, 648
Mamoiada, 664
Manarola, w., 381
Manduria, w., 560
Manfred, 544
Manfredi family, 179
Manfredonia, 543
Mangiari di Romagna, 149, 169
manioc, 6
Mannu, riv., 690
manteca, ch., 564, 579
Mantegazza, Paola, 268
Mantua: city, 303; prov., 228, 287, 303, cooking, 303
Manutius, Aldus, 401
Manzanilla, w., 696
Manzoni, Alessandro, 280
marble, 31, 58
Marches, The, 50, 74, 124–39; cooking, 126–27; w., 138–39
Marciano, 122
Marco Polo, 78, 369, 393, 397, 398
Mardi Gras food, 644
Maremma, 51–52, 76, 674
Marengo, 321; chicken, 321–22; veal, 321

mare's milk cheese, 94
Marettimo, is., 616
Margherita di Savoia, 544
marina squash, 221, 277
Marina di Ravenna, 170
Marino, 106; w., 107
markets: Cagliari, 677; cattle, 181; Modena, 206, 207; mushroom, 445; Palermo, 607; Rome, 83, 92; Treviso, 445; Venice, 402, 417; Verona, 432–33
Marmora, Punta La, mt., 665
Marostega, Taverna di, R., 437
Marostica, R., 437
marriages, 184, 574, 621, 622
Mars, 135
Marsala, 592, 610; w., 556, 646–48; all'uovo, 647
Marshall Plan, 199
marshes, 51–52, 77, 100
Marta, riv., 99
Martial, 14, 509, 644
Martignacco, 482
Martin IV, Pope, 99
Martina Franca, 549, 556, 559
Martini, 338; Martini e Rossi, 332
Martorana monastery, 623
Marzabotto, 186
Marzememi, 609
Marzemino, gr., w., 474–75
mascarpone (mascherpone), ch., 261
Massa Carrara, 31, 58–59; w., 68
Massaciuccoli, Lake, 58
Massico, mt., 101, 492
Matera, 563, 565
mattanza, 611, 676–77
Mattiolo, Pierandrea, 80
Maultasch, Margaret, 472
Maximilian of Austria, 463
Mazara del Vallo, 611–12, 616
Mazzini, Giuseppe, 207
Mazzotti, Giuseppe, 404, 405, 406, 419, 436
McPhee, John, 265, 544
meagre, 163
mealtimes, Etruscan 33; Florentine, 33

715

General Index

General Index

Scaligers, 433
scamorza, ch., 503, 517, 531, 532, 545
Scanno, 515, 517
Scanzano, w., 68
Scappi, Bartolommeo, 403
Schedel, Giovanni, 187
schiave, gr., 473
Schiccetrà, w., 381, 382
Schisò, Cape, 598
Schoonmaker, Frank, 242
Schopenhauer, 370
Schott, Andrea, 187, 191
Scicli, 598
Scilla, 571
Scipio the African, 48
Scot, Michael, 600
scurvy, 356
Scylla, 571–72
sea bass, 162
seafaring, 356, 393, 497
sea heart, 167
sea horse, 614
seal, Mediterranean, 666
sea ox, 666
sea perch, 162
sea walnuts, 167
seaweed, 668
Secchia, riv., 205, 214, 227
Secondigliano, 507
Segesta, 40
Sele, riv., 542
Selinunte, 610
Selinus, riv., 610
Sella di Corno, 519
Selva di Fesano, 546
Senigallia, 126, 132
Sennori, 676
Senus, 47
Sepino, 518
Serano, Paolo, 131
Serbian influence, 465
Serchio, val., 58
serò, ch., 345
Serpina, gr., 457
Serra Orios, 656
Sesia, riv., 299
Sesta Godano, w., 382
Sestri Levante, 373

Setino, w., 106
Sezze, 106
Sforza, Francesco, 302
Sforza, Galeazzo, 257
Sforza family, 541, 545, 564
Sfurzat, w., 308
sgombero, 160
shagreen, 164
Shakespeare, 297
Shardanes, 658
sharks, 164; hammerhead, 614
Shelley, Percy Bysshe, 53, 428
Sherry, w., 646, 696
shrimp, 166
Shrove Thursday, food, 419, 684
Sibari, 576
Sibilline, mts., 125
Sicani, 597–98
Sicilian Vespers, 600
Sicily, 5, 12, 133, 591–652; character, 628, 664; cooking, 597, 628; w., 649–52
Siculi, 597–98, 603, 608, 609, 619
Siculiana, 598
Sidon, 659
Siena: city, 47; prov., 31, 47, 50, language, 29, meat cutting, 43; w., 60, 67
Siete Fuentes, 662
Signorelli, Luca, 29, 121
Sikeles, 658
Sila plateau, 571, 574–75, 585
silk worms, 125, 303
Silo, riv., 444
Simon, André, 113, 511
Sinni, riv., 563; val., 564
Sirino, Lake, 566
sirocco, 667, 669
Slambrot dialect, 462
Slavic influences, 6, 416, 482, 483
Slovenia, 483
Smile of Italy, w., 106
Smollett, Tobias, 53
Soare di Cittadella, 432
Soave, w., 309, 454–55
Solunto, 607
Sondrio, 259, 304, 305–07; w., 307–08
Sono-Custoza, w., 452

723

General Index

General Index

INDEX OF FOODS AND DISHES

This is not a cookbook; but a good natural cook may be able to reproduce some of the dishes here named, even though exact proportions and cooking techniques are not ordinarily given. The creations described in sufficient detail to make this possible are marked below with an asterisk.

Index of Food and Dishes

Index of Food and Dishes

Index of Food and Dishes

Index of Food and Dishes

Index of Food and Dishes

Index of Food and Dishes

Index of Food and Dishes

Index of Food and Dishes

About the Author

WAVERLEY ROOT has been eating in Europe and writing about it for over 40 years. A veteran foreign correspondent, he has represented the *Chicago Tribune, Washington Post,* United Press, *Time* and the Mutual Broadcasting System, and has been Paris correspondent for the Danish *Politiken.* He also contributes frequently to *The New York Times Magazine, The International Herald Tribune,* and *Gourmet.* Mr. Root is an officer in the French Legion of Honor and a leading authority on French and Italian restaurants. His published books include *The Food of France, Contemporary French Cooking, The Paris Dining Guide, The Best of Italian Cooking* and *Eating In America* (with Richard de Rochemont). He lives abroad.